The Horseman's Encyclopedia

Other Books by Margaret Cabell Self

Horsemastership
Horses, Their Selection, Care, and Handling

The Horseman's Encyclopedia

By Margaret Cabell Self

New and Revised Edition

New York: A. S. Barnes and Company, Inc.

London and Toronto: Thomas Yoseloff Ltd.

Library of Congress Catalog Card Number: 63–9365

A. S. Barnes and Company, Inc.

South Brunswick, New Jersey

Thomas Yoseloff Ltd.
18 Charing Cross Road
London W.C. 2, England

6039
Printed in the United States of America

Preface

The purpose of this volume is to put before the reader in encyclopedic form the facts pertaining to horses as established by recognized authorities. That it is manifestly impossible to cover any of the larger subjects, racing, hunting, polo, etc., in as great detail as they deserve is obvious. The best one can hope to do is to give a brief outline. Most books on horses take up only one breed, or one phase of riding such as jumping. But the person who is genuinely interested in horses and riding likes to find out all he can about every phase and so broaden his knowledge of the subject. The tyro who has just started his career as an equestrian is frequently puzzled by the terminology of this new horse world. Even the person who has spent all his life with one breed or in one locality may find himself completely ignorant when he is transported to another locale. The owner of a stable, whether it be a stable of two, ten or twenty head is constantly being faced with new problems. Many of these problems have been discussed in print but it is often difficult to look through a library to find the answers. And so I have tried to assemble and index many facts that would be of interest and service to all horse lovers. Most of these facts will be found in the main body of this volume. Statistics pertaining to the Quarter Horse, to racing (harness, flat, and hurdle), recognized hunts and shows, and steeplechase and hunt associations, will be found in the appendix.

I should like to thank the officials of the Steeplechasing Association, the Jockey Club, and the Thoroughbred Racing Association for their kindness in supplying me with material for racing statistics, as well as the editors of the *Middleburg Chronicle* for making available lists of hunt clubs and horse shows. I should also like to thank the various Breeders Associations for the literature and photographs which they have provided. And I should like to dedicate this volume to horse lovers of all ages.

MARGARET CABELL SELF

A

ACCIDENTS

In virtually every accident the blame may be laid fairly and squarely upon the shoulders of the rider. He has either been reckless, ignorant or is not a sufficiently good horseman for the quality horse which he is riding. By far the greater number of accidents are caused by the two latter conditions.

Common "horse sense" in the rider seems to be sadly lacking in this mechanical age. The French have a proverb, "There is no safe horse except a dead horse!" One might more accurately say, "There is no safe horse for the *ignorant, inexperienced or thoughtless horseman* except a dead horse." The experienced horseman knows that he must do the thinking and reasoning for his mount. He keeps himself alert and his horse under control at all times. He watches ahead of him, behind him and around him, knowing that the eyes of the horse are set on the side of his head and he can be frightened by the unexpected though he may already have passed it.

The careless horseman we will always have with us. It is he who forgets to check his girth before mounting, he who, in the hunt field, lets the gate swing back in the face of the timid, four-year-old filly just behind him. He does not see that his horse is properly shod and that his saddle and bridle are comfortable. Hand-in-hand with the careless rider goes the inconsiderate rider, the one who, being at the head of a line of less experienced people, leads them down a slippery incline at a walk but, on reaching the bottom himself, immediately trots out, forgetting that the other horses, not wishing to be left behind, will match their gaits to his, resulting perhaps in broken knees for the horses, broken

heads for the riders. Again it is the thoughtless rider who gallops past a line of slowly trotting beginners, at which the whole flock takes off and there is a mad melée of runaway horses and screaming, terrified riders.

Bad judgment is often the cause of accidents among men or women who might be classified as good riders but extremely poor horsemen. It is very common in the over-confident, active boy who has no real sympathy or understanding of his mount, thinking only of how fast he can go or how high he can jump. One would not mind seeing this type come a cropper but only too often it is the over-ridden horse that suffers.

Many horses suffer accidents due to carelessness and ignorance while in the stable or out at pasture. Prevention consists in making sure that there is nothing in the stall, around the paddock or in the field on which the horse might hurt himself. Particular care should be taken in leading a nervous horse through a narrow doorway (see also *LEADING*). Some riders are careless while mounting and dismounting. There is a period when the rider is neither in the saddle nor on the ground and at this time he has little control. If the horse is high strung it is best to have someone at his head when he is mounted.

To avoid accidents study your horse and yourself and think of the former first. Do not ask him to do anything for which he has not been trained or for which he has not been conditioned. Ride only an animal suited to your own experience and ability. Learn to know what your horse is going to do before he knows himself. Practice vaulting off a moving horse until you have mastered the knack of falling without hurting yourself. Suit your gait to the terrain, to your own ability as a rider or, if riding in company, to the ability of the least experienced rider in the group. Above all, keep alert! See also *RUNAWAYS; FALLS; CAST HORSE; BOLTING.*

ACROSS THE BOARD

When a horse is bet on to come in first, second or third (win, place or show) the bet is said to be "across the board" or to be bet on a "combination ticket."

AGE

Average age of horse

A year of a horse's life is equivalent to three of a man's, thus a seven-year-old horse is considered mature. A twenty-year-old horse may be compared to a sixty-year-old man. Most horses are not useful beyond the age of twenty-three or four for other than very light work. The usefulness of a horse's life depends somewhat on the work he has done. Horses raced as two-year-olds usually develop blemishes which prevent their remaining in service very long and, if stallions or mares of good blood lines, are usually retired to the breeding farm when still quite young. On the other hand, the three horses competing for America in one of the most recent Olympic trials were aged seventeen, seventeen and eighteen respectively. Horses have been known to live beyond the age of forty. There is a supposedly official record of an English horse that lived to be fifty-five, and an unofficial record of a horse living to the remarkable age of seventy-two!

How to tell the age of a horse

The accepted and most accurate way of telling a horse's age is by the appearance and condition of his teeth. (See *TEETH*) Figure 143, page 356, shows the ages at which the various teeth appear and the changes that they undergo due to wear. The incisors (biting teeth at the front of upper and lower jaw) first show black depressions or cavities in the center. As the outer walls wear down the cavities disappear. Of course this method of determining age cannot be absolutely accurate as the amount of wear in the individual horse will depend to some extent on how the horse has been fed.

As the horse grows older his teeth become longer and the angle of them becomes more oblique. At the age of nine a well defined groove appears in the upper corner incisors at the gum line. This is known as *Galvayne's Groove.* Year by year it advances down the tooth until at twenty it runs the length of it. Then gradually, beginning at the upper end, it fades out until at thirty it is entirely gone.

The molars of a very old horse are sometimes so worn away that nothing is left except a row of stumps and the horse must be fed soft foods entirely.

In addition to the teeth there are other and less accurate signs which indicate age. The withers become more and more knife-like and prominent, with a downward curve in front of them at the base of the neck. The temples deepen, the lower lip relaxes and hangs loose. Sometimes there is a clicking noise in the hocks and knees and the latter may show signs of buckling. All these signs tell the humane horseman that it is time for him to give his faithful servant and companion his well deserved rest. If he cannot afford to turn him out to pasture and let him end his days as he began them, running at will, then, by all means, send for the veterinarian and have him given a speedy, painless and dignified end. There are so called lovers of animals who, when their horses passed beyond the stage of usefulness, would send them to the auction block because they "could not bear to see them put out of the way!" Out of sight being out of mind it worried them not at all to think of the worse fate of ill-treatment that might befall the animal that had given his best years to their service.

AGED

A horse is said to be "aged" when he has reached the age of eight years. As one year of a horse's life corresponds to three of a man's it will be seen that at seven he "comes of age" or attains maturity. The term "aged" is invariably used in horse show programs and by dealers in describing mature horses. The purchaser may decide for himself whether the animal has just entered into the period of full maturity, or whether he is, in truth, aged, or about ready for the knackers. Inasmuch as the marks or cups disappear from the teeth at the age of eight, making the exact determination of the animal's age more difficult, if one tries to pin a dealer down as to a mature horse's age he will invariably say that it is "rising nine."

AGORAPHOBIA

Fear of the outside. Horses develop this fear after confinement for even a fairly short time in a stall. All horses should have daily exercise. Sometimes this is impossible in inclement weather, therefore the type of box stall with a double door opening out on a covered runway is very useful for rainy weather for then the upper half may be left open and the horse, being allowed to watch outdoor goings on, will not develop agoraphobia nor "stall courage" which is one of the symptoms.

AIDS (natural)

The "natural" aids are the rider's hands, legs, back and the way he distributes his weight. The rider's voice is also considered a "natural" aid but may not be used in certain competitions.

The aids are the language with which the horseman communicates with his mount. They work together and supplement or assist each other. The language of the aids is not an easy one to learn. Let us look at each one individually and then see how they are used together.

The portion of the horse that is behind the rider is called the hindquarters. Under the direction and control of the rider's legs, back and weight the hindquarters are the seat of impulsion. The horse cannot move in any direction unless his hindquarters provide the power. They may be likened to the pedals of a tricycle.

The portion of the horse in front of the rider is called the forehand. It is under the control of the rider's hands

through the reins. The reins indicate the direction of the movement to the horse. They also, when it is desirable, oppose the movement of the horse, causing him to slow his pace or to stop.

The rider, through means of his aids, strives to coordinate the forehand and hindquarters of his horse in such a manner that they move freely and smoothly in the direction and at the gait and speed that the rider wishes.

Generally speaking, the horse is trained to move his hindquarters *away* from the leg (when the rider applies his right leg the horse moves his hindquarters towards the left), whereas his forehand *follows* the direction demanded by the rein (when the rider increases the pressure on the right rein the horse turns to the right).

The use of the lower back is often ignored completely, yet it is one of the most valuable of the aids. It is used as one would use it to make a swing go higher. It assists the legs to put the horse into motion and also to collect the horse and push him up to the bit. Used with the legs in halting it brings the horse to a square halt with his hind legs under him and his head correctly held.

The distribution of the rider's weight is another aid which is often neglected. But the good horseman in demanding a change of direction or a slowing down of pace uses his weight first, before he uses either legs, back or hands. With a highly trained, sensitive horse this use of the weight is usually all that is necessary. In using the weight the rider puts his weight in the direction of the movement. If he wishes to turn to the right he steps lightly on his right stirrup. If he wishes to slow down he lets his shoulders come slightly back and sinks deeper in the saddle.

Now let us see how the aids are used to assist each other. One speaks of the "active" leg or hand and the "assisting" leg or hand. In performing a pivot on the forehand with the hindquarters moving to the left, the right leg is the "active" leg, for it pushes the quarters to the left. The left leg is the assisting leg, ready to be used should the horse move his quarters too suddenly or too far.

At the same time, in this same movement, we have an active and an assisting hand. The rider puts a little tension on the right rein, slightly bending the horse's head to the right; he also has some tension to the rear on the rein. If he did not do so, when the horse felt the rider's legs he might move forwards instead of keeping his forehand in place and swinging his hindquarters around it. The left hand is the assisting hand, ready to take over if the horse tries to turn his forehand to the right.

So you see that the rider must be able to use each aid individually; but he must also think of them as being part of a team, all members of which are needed if a smooth performance is to be attained.

It should also be kept in mind that the horse is taught on a system of reward and punishment. He has been trained to move away from the pressure of either leg, to move forward or backward on the pressure of both. Likewise he has been taught to obey the pressure of the bit upon his bars by decreasing the speed of his gait and to turn his forehand to the right or left either by direct pulling of the rein or by the indirect application of the opposite rein on his neck. The term "punishment" may seem a little confusing. It does not imply harshness or cruelty. In stopping the horse, for example, the pressure of the bit upon the bars is the "punishment," the relaxing of the reins when the horse has obeyed is the "reward." Never continue to apply pressure of reins or legs after the horse has obeyed the commands, by so doing you completely confuse him. Furthermore you take away his confidence in you by continuing to "punish" and failing to reward. See also *RIDING; COLLECTION; DRESSAGE; TRAINING THE HORSE; REINS, Use of.*

AIDS (artificial)

The artificial aids are the whip and spurs; also any type of martingale, side or overhead check or draw rein is considered an artificial aid.

ALBINO HORSES

Most of the so-called white horses are born nearly black and turn white as they grow older. The exception to these is the albino which has no coloring matter in either hair or eyes. The true albino is prone to weaknesses characteristic of albinos of all kinds. An effort is being made by Mr. and Mrs. C. R. Thompson of Nebraska to standardize a breed of white horse which, like the albino, is white from birth. These horses, bred on their ranch The White Horse Ranch, have brown or blue eyes and seem to be strong. They are gaited horses with the general characteristics of the saddle, Arabian and Western stock. The foundation sire was Silver King, a show horse. Perhaps the most famous of these horses are those which were owned by the Emperor of Japan the picture of one of which is shown. Colonel Harry Disston, who is shown mounted, was in Tokyo immediately after the Japanese surrender at which time this picture was taken. The Emperor had a stud of about six horses which came originally from the White Horse Ranch.

ALLOWANCE RACE

A race in which the horse is handicapped both as to weight for age (see Appendix) and according to prize money earned.

ALTER

To castrate or geld a male horse thus making him more easily disciplined. An altered horse is known as a gelding.

AMATEUR

One who rides or drives for love of the sport and not as a profession. He must not trade in horses as a vocation. He must not allow his picture to be used in advertising in connection with the sport. The wife or children of a professional are considered professional if they are

FIGURE 1. THE ALBINO STALLION OF HIROHITO.
COLONEL HARRY DISSTON UP.

over thirteen and assist in the husband's (father's) profession.

AMATEUR CLASSES

Many classes in horseshows require amateurs, as described above, to ride or drive.

AMBLE

The amble is a form of the stepping pace. At the ordinary pace the horse's lateral legs move together as opposed to the trot in which the diagonal legs are raised and planted simultaneously. In the amble there is a slight break so that the lateral legs do not move at exactly the same time but are planted one after the other with a pause between. The amble is an easy gait for the rider but not a speedy one. It was the favored gait for the ladies palfrey in medieval times and is the natural slow gait of the donkey.

AMERICAN BREEDS

See individual names of breeds as listed alphabetically in this volume.

AMERICAN HACKNEY HORSE SOCIETY.
The address of the Society is 527 Madison Ave., New York, N. Y.

Graham C. Woodruff, *President*
Mrs. Wiliam P. Roth, *Vice-President*
Dr. Elise S. L'Esperance, *Vice-President*
Jack B. Ward, *Vice-President*

Horses and Ponies registered in 1960 Stud Book total 590 stallions, 760 mares and 224 Geldings, making a total of 1,574 animals.

AMERICAN HORSE SHOWS ASSOCIATION

The American Horse Shows Association came into being in 1917. At the call of Mr. Reginald C. Vanderbilt fifty delegates, representing twenty-six shows, met in New York City to elect officers, to adopt a schedule of dates and to appoint a committee to formulate rules. At this time there was no rule book pertaining to the showing of horses; there were no recognized judges. Only four divisions of horses appeared in the show rings—Hunters, Jumpers, Harness Horses and Saddle Horses.

The succeeding years have wrought many changes, due to the hard work of the A. H. S. A. It has formulated rules governing the running of shows, the types of competitions and the judging. It lists qualified judges and stewards. It publishes an annual rule book, free to members of the Association which is revised each year to meet changing conditions.

Interest in showing has become so great that in certain parts of the country it is possible for the enthusiastic competitor to show his mount in one or more large shows every weekend from April to November. Were it not for this tremendous interest the horse would be in a sad way for he has lost his position as a cavalry mount, the tractor is replacing him on the farm, the automobile on the road, and but few countries are still open to fox hunting. Were it not for the shows the breeding of outstanding animals in the sixteen different divisions would be almost at a standstill.

The address of the Association is 40 East 54th St., New York City. All those interested should become annual members and so keep in touch with the latest rules.

AMERICAN QUARTER HORSE ASSOCIATION

The address of the Association is P. O. Box 271, Amarillo, Texas.

The Officers and Executive Committee are as follows:

S. M. Moore, *President;* Wayne Vickers, *1st Vice-President;* Jess Hankins, *2nd Vice-President;* Hugh Bennett; Bud Warren; Roy Parks; Howard K. Linger, *Executive Secretary and General Manager;* Ralph E. Morrison, *Assistant Secretary;* Tol Ware, *Treasurer.*

The American Quarter Horse Association was founded in 1940, its purpose being to collect, record and preserve pedigrees of the Quarter Horses in America; to publish a Stud Book and to stimulate interest in the history, breeding, exhibiting, publicity, sale and improvement of the breed. It has beautiful modern offices in Amarillo, where it employs about a hundred men and women.

The Association publishes the *Quarter Horse Journal,* a big, well-illustrated monthly devoted to the breed.

Among the interesting activities which have developed since its formation we find American Quarter Horse Clinics, which are held several times a year at various state universities. These clinics, staffed by officials of the organization and sponsored by those interested in the breed, are open to the public. Their purpose is to provide information on the Quarter Horse, his history, breeding and training. The Association also has 16mm. sound films in color, which are available to organizations for showing.

Working in cooperation with the National Cutting Horse Association the AQHA awards performance points to registered Quarter Horses winning in competitions sponsored by the National Cutting Horse Association. These include competitions in the following: Cutting, Reining, Roping, Barrel Racing, Western Pleasure, Western Riding and Western Cowhorse. There are about 700 shows annually which include these classes, and many of these are adding classes for Juniors with emphasis on 4-H Club members. The American Quarter Horse Association also makes and enforces rules for recognized Quarter Horse racing. At the latest tabulation such races are being held in twelve Western states.

One of the most progressive and important publications of the AQHA is its splendid booklet *Training Riding Horses.* Up until recently many horses that might have become reliable, useful mounts were hurt or ruined by rough methods of breaking. Colts were allowed to run on the range until the ages of two or three, and were then roped, choked down and encouraged to fight and buck until they learned that they could not win the battle against man. The American Quarter Horse Association, with the aid of Mr. Wayne Dinsmore, who for many years was secretary of the Horse and Mule Association and the National Polo Pony Society, provides in their clear, well-illustrated booklet the step-by-step training of the Western horse, with emphasis on patience, gentleness and the importance of teaching the colt to have confidence in rather than to fear man. This booklet is available to all, and anyone interested should write to the Association. See also *QUARTER HORSE; RECORDS AND STATISTICS—AMERICAN QUARTER HORSE* (Appendix).

AMERICAN RACING MANUAL

An annual publication compiled and published by *Racing Form,* founded in 1894. Present editor, J. Samuel Perlman; Statistical Editor, Avery E. Brown. Printed by Triangle Publications, Inc., 525 West 52nd St., New York, N. Y. This is a reference book on Thoroughbred Racing which contains statistical information of past and present performances on all American Tracks, as well as complete statistical records of Horses, Breeders, Owners, Trainers and Jockeys. See also *RECORDS AND STATISTICS—FLAT RACING* (Appendix).

AMERICAN SADDLE HORSE BREEDERS ASSOCIATION, INC.

Headquarters 929 South Fourth Ave., Louisville, Ky. See also *SADDLE HORSE.*

ANTHRAX

Anthrax is a fatal disease which must be reported to the State Department of Domestic Animals. It is caused by a bacillus. The symptoms are a very high temperature, abnormal swelling of the throat and neck, and great pain. The animal usually dies within a very few hours. There is no treatment.

ANTITOXIN

The horse has become, in the laboratory, a factory for the manufacture of antitoxins to be used for the prevention or amelioration of many human diseases. Such horses are kept on farms and are known as "bleeders." The horse that can no longer be useful in harness or under saddle because of some chronic lameness or permanent injury may still finish out his life span having the best of care and contributing immensely to the human race. How much better this is than selling off an unsound animal to drag out the remainder of his days working for an inhumane master who wishes only to wring the last ounce of strength from the poor beast with the least possible cost to himself. See also *SERUMS.*

APOCALYPSE

The Four Horsemen of Apocalypse were made famous by Durer's wood-cut from the Apocalypse series, 1498, which shows the four horsemen carrying the sword, bow and balances charging over the world and mankind with the angel flying above them as described in Rev. VI, 2 to 8, quoted below.

"And I saw, and beheld a white horse, and he that sat on him had a bow; and a crown was given unto him; and he went forth conquering, and to conquer.

"And when he had opened the second seal I heard the second beast say, 'Come and see.'

"And there went out another horse that was red; and power was given to him that sat thereon to take peace from the earth, and that they should kill one another; and there was given unto him a great sword.

"And when he had opened the third seal I heard the third beast say, 'Come and see.' And I beheld, and lo, a black horse, and he that sat on him had a pair of balances in his hand.

"And I heard a voice in the midst of the four beasts say, 'A measure of wheat for a penny, and three measures of barley for a penny, and see thou hurt not the oil and wine.'

"And when he had opened the fourth seal, I heard the voice of the fourth beast say, 'Come and see.'

"And I looked, and beheld a pale horse, and his name that sat on him was Death."

APOPLEXY

The rupture of a blood vessel in the brain, known as apoplexy, occurs occasionally in horses. Excitable horses are more liable to this than others and it may be brought on by any undue exertion. The horse that is cast and is struggling to raise himself often succumbs to apoplexy.

APPALOOSA

This is a horse whose coat is either a mottled blue roan on a grey background, or a white background with elliptical or round black spots. Sometimes the forehand is mottled while the hindquarters are white with the black, or occasionally dark brown, spots. Because of the peculiarity of the marking, these horses are sometimes called "raindrop" horses. Appaloosas have been common in Spain and Central Europe for many centuries. Old pictures of Lipizzaner mares often show animals of this marking. One or more of these horses must have been with those brought over by the Conquistadores of Spain, for the Appaloosa Mustang was much prized by the Indians who claimed that horses of this coloring are tougher than ordinary horses.

FIGURE 2. CHICO'S SNOWCAP, CHAMPION APPALOOSA STALLION OWNED BY CARL MILES OF THE CEE BAR RANCHES, CELINA AND STEPHENVILLE, TEXAS. THIS SHOWS THE "BLANKET-TYPE" OF APPALOOSA MARKING AS OPPOSED TO THE "RAINDROP" TYPE.

APPETITE

Horse's appetite.

The saying, "Eating like a horse" is rather a misleading expression, for a horse has a very small stomach and cannot eat a great deal at a time. He is, by nature, a grazing animal. Grass is not a concentrated food; in order to get enough nourishment to keep his thousand or more pounds of flesh in condition to flee from enemies he has to graze more or less continuously, digesting as he eats, it is this continuous eating which has given rise to the above expression. The horse that gets into the grain bag may eat himself sick for his stomach will hold only so much after which the half digested food is pushed on into his intestines causing gas, colic, and possibly death. For tables on feeding see *FEEDING.*

Loss of appetite.

Loss of appetite in a horse may be caused either by illness or bad condition of the teeth. The moment the horse does not clean up his regular ration of grain he should be thoroughly examined to determine the cause. If illness is present he will show other symptoms such as a staring coat, lowered head, discharge at eyes or nostrils, fever, scouring, etc. Examination of the teeth may show an ulcerated tooth or sharp points which are cutting into the horse's jaws so that mastication is painful. See *TEETH.*

APPLES

See *FEED: Fresh Forage.*

APPOINTMENTS

By "appointments" is meant the uniform or livery, equipment and tack required for horses and riders in certain "appointment classes" in a horse show. The hunting appointments described are also those usually required by custom and tradition in the hunt field. Appointment classes are so described in the horse show catalogue and include the following: Hunt teams; Corinthian; Lady's Single Harness Horse, Mare or Gelding to be shown to a Phaeton; Gig Class; Lady's Pair; Tandem and Four-in-Hands; Stock Classes.

HARNESS CLASSES

Four-in-Hand

Park Drag of solid color to be drawn by four matched horses with park harness, two servants in livery. To be judged on performance, quality, manners, uniformity and appointments. These include extra collar, traces, reins, brake shoe, quarter blankets and cooler, runner coats, lap robes, water pail, tool kit.

Lady's Phaeton

A George IV, Peter's Phaeton, or, in summer, a Brewster basket phaeton may be used. Appointments to include lash whip, wet weather gloves, card case, lap robe, cooler, two rain coats, wheel wrench, umbrella and cover for servant's hat. Dash clock is optional. Horse's mane not to be braided. Standing martingale, Buxton bit, breeching and bearing rein compulsory.

Gig Class

Following gigs may be used: Park Gate, Gig, Very Spicy, Stanhope and Tilbury. The latter requires a horse 15:3 to 16 hands of great presence and lofty action; mane not to be braided; harness; Kay collar, standing martingale and kicking strap; gig bit with plain bridoon and short bearing rein to be preferred, Buxton bit and full bearing rein are permissible.

Servant

May be footman or coachman, appointments for former as follows; single breasted coat with six buttons in front and six on coat tails, full striped waistcoat, silk hat, tan driving gloves, boots with tops of mahogany, tan or pink, coachman's collar and flat white ascot tie. He should be smart looking, active and not tall or heavy. The coat should be either black or should be the same color as the upholstery of gig. Breeches and coat should show that they were made for him. Boots should fit perfectly and the tops fit very close to the leg.

Coachman

He is similarly turned out but wears a

coachman's coat, six buttons in front and four on coat tails.

Pony Classes

Rules for harness horse classes apply to pony classes except that *Gig Classes* for ponies, *Lady's Pair of Harness Ponies* and *Lady's Single Harness Pony* are not appointment classes.

HUNTING APPOINTMENTS

Personal Appointments

Master

The coat is a square-cornered single-breasted frock coat, cut to suit the wishes of the owner. No flaps on waistline and no pockets on outside of coat except whistle pocket if desired. There should be not less than four nor more than five large "hunt buttons" in front, two behind, and two or three small "hunt buttons" on the cuff of each sleeve. The material should be of melton cloth or heavy twill. Scarlet is the orthodox color for hunting, but if the regular hunt uniform is of another color, there is no reason why this should not be used. The color and facing of hunt coats should be in conformity with the regular uniform of the hunt.

The breeches may be brown or white, of leather, of heavy cord or of any other heavy material. Lightweight breeches of silk or of cotton duck not permissible.

The neckwear is a white hunting stock tied neatly and held with safety pin.

Note: The safety pin should be placed *horizontally*. Vertically, it might cause injury to the chin in case of accident.

The cap is a regulation black velvet hunting cap; the ribbons on the hunt caps of the riders of a hunt team should be worn in accordance with the regulations of the hunt entering the team.

The boots are regulation hunting boots of black calf (not patent leather) with brown or colored tops, either polished or powdered, preferably the former, tabs sewn on, but not sewed down, to tops which should be sewn on boots. White or brown boot garters to match breeches must be worn.

The spurs are of heavy pattern with moderately long neck and sharp or dull rowels. (Light racing spurs are not permissible.)

The gloves are of heavy wash-leather or, if preferred, brown leather gloves. Rain-gloves of either white or colored string must be carried under the billet straps.

The whip is a regulation hunting whip.

The horn is regulation hunting horn, carried either stuck in front of coat or, if mounted, in leather case fastened on either side of front saddle.

Flask and sandwich-case are optional, but, if carried, should contain food and drink.

Honorary Huntsman

Same as for Master

Professional Huntsman

Same as Master except:

He carries no hunting horn. He should carry spare couples (one set), fastened to a D on one side of the saddle.

Wire cutters should be carried in a leather case on one side of the front of the saddle.

Spare stirrup leather is optional, but if carried it should be worn over the right shoulder under the left arm, buckled in front with the point of the strap down. A professional usually carries the leather outside his coat, an amateur under, though this, too, is optional.

Honorary Whipper-In

Same as Honorary Huntsman except that he carries no horn. He should carry one set of spare couples fastened to a D on either side of the saddle. Wire cutters should be carried in a leather case on the side or front of the saddle. The Honorary Whipper-In usually wears the spare stirrup leather under his coat but he may wear it outside if he chooses. The leather is worn over the right shoulder and under the left arm. It is buckled in front with the point of the leather down.

Professional Whipper-In

Same as Honorary Whipper-In, except that he carries no flask or sandwich case.

Ribbons on hunt caps should be worn

according to regulations of Hunt entering team.

Coats should have a large "hare-pocket" on inside of skirt.

Member

Same as Master, except that he carries no hunting horn.

Coat may be of pattern known as "Shad-Belly" or "Weasel-Belly" if preferred.

Top hat (silk hunting hat) to be worn with hat-guard instead of velvet cap.

Note: A black formal hunting coat may be worn. Buttons may be the regular buttons adopted by the Hunt but preferably a dark bone button with hunt initials or crest design in white.

Lady Member (side-saddle)

The habit is of dark melton or other dark cloth, with either regular hunt buttons or else the "ladies" hunt button of the Hunt.

The hat is a top hat (silk hunting hat), or bowler unless a shad-belly is worn. Veils are optional but usually worn with long hair. Hair if long should be worn in a "chignon" below brim of hat.

Boots, black, patent leather "tops."

Spurs are optional.

Gloves are heavy wash leather or, if preferred, brown leather gloves.

Rain gloves, either white or colored string gloves are carried under the billets.

Neckwear, a plain white hunting stock neatly tied and fastened with a safety pin.

The whip is a light hunting whip with thong.

Sandwich-case is optional, but if carried it should contain food and drink, preferably thin sliced chicken or ham sandwich and port wine. Gentlemen carry brandy in the flask.

Lady Member (astride)

The coat is a hunting coat of black or oxford gray with buttons and trimming adopted by the Hunt represented. The collar of the coat is usually of flannel in the hunt colors. Note: only a lady Master wears the scarlet coat and velvet cap.

Breeches are brown or buff, not white cord or leather.

Boots are hunting boots of black calf with patent leather tops. Tabs sewn on, but not sewn down, to tops which should be sewn on boots, and black patent leather garters.

The hat is a black bowler or top hat (silk hunting hat).

Veils are optional.

Spurs are regular hunting spurs.

Gloves, same as for side saddle.

Neckwear, same as for side saddle.

Hunting whip, same as for side saddle.

Flask and sandwich-case, see above.

Note: hunting caps are worn in show ring only by individuals privileged to wear them in hunt field, the exception being children and farmers. No horn is carried except by Master or Huntsman.

Tack Appointments

The hunting bridle may be either double or single, but, in either case, bits should be sewn in. A cavesson nose-band should be used. Plain fronts.

If simple snaffle bridle is used, reins may be braided.

Breastplate, optional.

Martingale, optional.

Saddle; a heavy, plain-skirted hunting saddle, either leather or cloth lined, the former preferred. Saddle cloths or Nummah of any sort are not permissible. Stirrups irons should be large and workmanlike.

Girth; either leather or web, preferably former. If white, web should be properly clean and whitened.

Stock horse

Stock-saddle, spade (also known as Spanish) bit, or half-breed bit or ring bit; a leather or rawhide bozal may be used if desired, sufficiently loose to enable judge to place three fingers between chin and bozal. No martingale or tie down of any sort may be used. No wire, chain or other metal device may be used alone or in conjunction with or as part of a leather chin strap, and the violation of this rule will cause the horse and rider to be barred from and not permitted to re-enter the ring.

APPUYER

This is a French term meaning to move in two directions at the same time, generally forwards and to the side. There are several translations; "travel on two paths" and "two-track" are two.

We have several dressage figures in which the horse performs an *appuyer*. One is the *traversal*. In this movement the horse crosses the arena from one corner to another on an oblique line. His body remains parallel to the long wall of the arena, as he moves forward both his front and hind feet cross, so that he steps sideways. See *DRESSAGE —TRAVERSAL OR TWO-TRACK; RIDING—THE ADVANCED RIDER.*

Another movement in which the horse is on an *appuyer* can be seen on page 300, *SCHOOLING MOVEMENTS— THE HALF-TURN.* In this, the rider having executed a half circle or *volte* is returning to the wall on a shoulder-in.

APTITUDES

Aptitudes natural in horses

As in dogs specified aptitudes in horses have been developed through the selection and breeding. The Saddle Horse takes naturally to the rack, the Thoroughbred jumps willingly and easily, the Hackney picks up his feet, etc. These aptitudes should be taken into consideration in making the selection, especially when purchasing a foal or an unbroken colt.

Aptitudes in riders

In a group of children of the same age, there will always be a certain percentage who learn more quickly than the average and a few who learn more slowly. The mental characteristics of the pupil are as important or perhaps more so than physical strength. The coordination between mind and body is of utmost importance. But just because a child learns slowly and seems awkward is no guarantee that, under good instruction and with a suitable mount he will not make a good rider. On the contrary some children who at first appeared impossibly awkward have become excellent horsemen.

Any normal person regardless of natural athletic aptitude can learn to ride. Not all will become Olympic riders but persistence, lack of fear and love of the sport are really the deciding factors.

ARAB AND HIS HORSE

It has long been contended that the Arabian horse is more intelligent and gentle than the other breeds. If this be so it is undoubtedly because for centuries the Arab has treated his prized War Mare more as a dog than as a horse. Animals which associate with man develop in intelligence. Notice the vast difference between the intelligence of a kennel-bred and trained puppy and one which has been raised "by hand."

For a very interesting picture of the Arab and his horse in their natural habitat read Carl Raswan's *Drinkers of the Wind.*

ARAB HORSE JOURNAL

Published monthly except January by the Cruse Publishing Co., 2750 Vine Drive, Fort Collins, Colorado. Contains interesting news and educational material about Arabian Horses.

ARABIAN HORSE

Just as there have been certain famous "foundation sires" whose prepotency has been such that they have continued to pass their outstanding characteristics down to their descendants for generation after generation, so the Arabian horse may be looked upon as the "foundation strain" for all light horses of the present day and at least one draft breed (the Percheron).

It is known to be a fact in breeding that inbreeding is advantageous if the blood used is absolutely pure with desirable characteristics. But if sire or dam have impure blood, instead of the progeny showing a preponderance of desirable traits the weaknesses of both sire and dam will be exaggerated and monstrosities will be produced. It is the claim of the exponents of the Arabian horse that since this breed of horse has

FIGURE 3. IKTUJARIN, AN ARABIAN HORSE OWNED BY MR. AND
MRS. JEROME NOOD, NILES, MICH.

been improved by selective breeding for
many centuries it has greater prepotency
than any other breed, which accounts for
its "leavening" quality—the production
of such widely divergent breeds as the
trotter, the Saddler, the Thoroughbred
and the Hackney.

The exact origin of the Arabian horse
is unknown though the general consensus of opinion is that he originated in
India. It is definitely established that
line breeding and inbreeding of Arabian
horses was being practiced at the time of
Mohammed. Among the Arabian traditions accounting for the origin of the
Arabian horse is the one which tells of
how Ishmael, in the year 2000 B.C. received the present of a mare from
heaven. The mare had a foal and the
foal was crippled by being carried in a
camel's saddle bag. But this foal, *Benat
el Ahwaj* (son of the crooked), became
the foundation sire of the breed. Another belief is that the five famous
strains of the Arabian horse are descended from the five favorite mares of
the prophet.

Mythology also credits the birth of the
horse to the West Wind. The legend of
Ishmael and the crooked foal is given
credence by the fact that this is supposed
to have occurred at about the time of
the influx into Arabia of the Shepherd
people from further East and that the
horse seems to have been unknown in
Egypt until that time. In a direct line
from Ishmael five generations later Sala-
man (sometimes confused with Solomon)
who was known as Faris (the horseman)
is said to have selected the five mares
from which came the five favorite breeds
in the following manner. The mares and
horses of Faris had been traveling for
many days over the desert without water
and were frantic with thirst. Finally they
came to a river but just as they reached
the brink the trumpet call sounded the
call to arms. Five of the mares left the
water without drinking and responded;
these five Faris selected to found the
breed.

The Arab classifies the horses of his
country as follows: the *attechi* or foreign
group, the *kadischi* or impure group,

and the *kochlani* which is *asil* or pure. There are very, very few Arabians of the later classification in Arabia today, and they are highly prized, none ever being sold.

The scarcity of the *asil* type is understandable when one remembers that the Arab believes that a mare that has ever been mated with a stallion of impure breeding is forever contaminated and will not consider a foal from a later and purebred mating as *asil*.

FIGURE 4. IBN HABU, 1961 NATIONAL GRAND CHAMPION, OWNED BY GILBERT E. CHAVEZ, ALBUQUERQUE, N. M. THIS HORSE IS A MODERN TYPE OF ARABIAN BREED FOR USE IN THE WESTERN TERRAIN. *COURTESY BRIG. GEN. WAYNE O. KESTER.*

Contrary to European and American custom the Arab traces the genealogy of his horses through the mare. Blood lines in both parents are infinitely preferable to the conformation or characteristics of any particular specimen. This accounts in main for the purity of the Arab strains, the Arab refusing to breed a purebred mare to one of the *kadischi* regardless of how perfect in conformation the stallion may be.

The five accepted strains are the Kuhaylan, Saqlawi, 'Ubayan, Hamdani, and Hadban. These in turn have many offshoots, each family being distinguished by a suffix denoting the strain.

The Arabian horse has many physical characteristics which set it apart from all other breeds. The head of the Arabian is entirely different from the head of any other breed of horse. When a horse of another breed shows Arabian characteristics it is merely the proof of the prepotency of the Arabian blood. The Arabian's head is short from poll to muzzle, broad between the eyes with the latter set much lower down than in other breeds. The profile is "dished" or *camuse*. This concave profile is due to the outstanding bulge of the forehead known as the *jibbah* and the hollowness at the joining of forehead and nasal bones. The Arabs prize the *jibbah* highly, contending that it is this which accounts for the greater intelligence of the Arabian horse over all other breeds, providing, as it does, a larger brain pan. The straight profile and high-set eyes of the Greek horses of the Parthenon prove definitely that they were not of Arabian strains.

The ears of the Arabian are very curved and pointed, being so set that they nearly touch at the tips. The head is set on at an angle, the curve of the crest being repeated in the angle of throttle and windpipe. This gives the horse freedom of movement without restricting his wind. Arabs encourage their horses to move their heads freely from side to side and look at distant objects.

The eye desired in the Arabian horse is large and protruding as well as being low-set, the setting of the eyes well to the side and the prominence of the eyeballs enabling the animal to see objects to the rear. The muzzle is very small and delicate, this, with the deep jaw and prominent forehead giving the head a wedge shape quite different from other breeds. The lower lip is slightly longer than the upper and both lips protrude beyond the nostril.

The Arabian horse is said to be unusually free of respiratory troubles. Heaves and such ailments are largely unknown. This is attributed to the fact that the windpipe is unusually large and free, to the angle at which it enters the jaw and to the depth and breadth of the chest. All these factors mean free oxidation of air in the lungs. This characteristic would also account for such qualities as the speed and endurance of the Arabian horse.

It is interesting to note that the widely flared nostrils as well as the large windpipe are characteristics of horses that developed in hot countries, where they needed to breathe in as much air as possible. These horses also hold their tails well away from the buttocks. Pony breeds which evolved in cold countries such as Mongolia and Iceland carry their tails close to the buttocks to help retain the body warmth. Their nostrils and air passages are narrow, for huge drafts of

cold air drawn in to the lungs in freezing temperatures would damage them.

The neck of the Arabian horse varies with the strain, some families having longer necks than others. But all Arabian horses have very flexible necks, well-muscled and running well back into the withers.

The depth of chest, well sprung ribs and large circumference of girth in relation to the size of the animal mean a free flow of blood, which, in turn, guarantees endurance of fatigue and a speedy comeback. The wither, chest and shoulder are well muscled. The back of the Arab is one of his most outstanding characteristics for it is unusually short. This is due to the fact that the Arab has twenty-three instead of twenty-four vertebrae. This lack of a vertebra is the prime distinguishing factor of the purebred Arab, the cross breed usually having the full number, though two Morgans and one Standard-bred horse as well as a Connemara pony of Ireland have been found to be lacking the twenty-fourth vertebra. This fact alone would prove the presence of Arabian blood in these strains.

The pelvis is long and level, the tail set very high. The quarters, in relation to the back, are unusually long and account for the great speed of the Arab. This propelling action also gives the jumping ability, for though the Arab is not thought of as a jumper it must be remembered that the Thoroughbred gets his jumping talents from his desert blood, not from the cold-blooded English mares which form the balance of the stock from which he sprang. The bony structure of the legs is unusually strong, the joints being large, the cannon bones short and very dense. Shortness and density of cannons is greatly to be desired in running horses for they mean much less fatigue. The tendons of the legs are very prominent and the Arab has little trouble with such diseases as ringbone.

In disposition the Arabian horse is known to be very gentle and intelligent. In his native land the War Mare is a member of the family, sharing the tent of her master, and will defend him from enemies.

It is astounding to realize that the Arabian horse has made his way to every part of the globe and that virtually every breed traces its descent back to him. The Javanese and Cuban ponies are of desert descent. The Thoroughbred was an artificial strain which was developed in England from desert stallions bred to English mares. From the Thoroughbred came the Hackney, Morgan, Hambletonian and Denmark (Kentucky Saddle). The Lipizzan, Mustang, Waler and Criollo all are derived from desert stock, the last three via the Spanish horses. The Russian Orloff, a trotting breed, contains a high percentage of Arabian blood and Arab stallions are constantly used to renew and strengthen the strain.

One of the interesting facts that has been found to be true is that, though the Arab is a small horse, introduction of his blood with other small breeds usually brings increase in size. His smallness in his native land is probably due to environment, scarcity of water and scantiness of feed. The nomad tribes which raise horses spend their lives moving from place to place trying to find enough grass to feed their stock. The horses are not kept up in condition and it takes a very practiced eye to appreciate them. But this life has developed certain characteristics which have given the Arab substance and not taken away from his quality. He is said to be able to go for a longer time without food and water than any other breed. His skin, being dark, resists sunburn. His endurance is outstanding and he is less liable to many ailments than other breeds. He is the "big little horse" of the equine race. He has passed his courage, speed and stamina on to his descendants. They, in turn, on the battlefield have greatly affected the history of civilization. (See *INTERNATIONAL ARABIAN HORSE ASSOCIATION*.)

ARABIAN HORSE NEWS

Edited and published monthly by Anna Best Joder. Box 28, Boulder, Colorado. It is the official publication of the clubs and associations listed below and contains many interesting feature articles as well as news regarding Arab classes and shows.

Montana Arabian Horse Association
Iowa Arabian Horse Association
Desert Arabian Horse Association
Intermountain Arabian Horse Association
The Arabian Horse Association of Washington
The Arabian Horse Association of Western Canada
The Arabian Horse Association of the East
Arabian Horse Association of Northern California
Arabian Horse Association of New England
Arabian Horse Association of New York
Arabian Horse Association of Texas
Arabian Horse Breeders' Society of Oregon
Arabian Horse Club of Utah
Arabian Horse Association of Michigan
Arabian Horse Association of Wisconsin
Arabian Horse Association of Florida
Arabian Horse Association of Nebraska
Arabian Horse Association of Arizona
Arabian Horse Association of Southern Nevada
Arabian Horse Association of Ohio
Arabian Horse Association of Illinois
Arabian Horse Association of North Dakota
Arabian Horse Association of Minnesota
Arabian Horse Association of Missouri
Arabian Horse Association of New Mexico
International Arabian Horse Association
Indiana Arabian Horse Club
Midwest Arabian Horse Association
Colorado Arabian Horse Club
Arabian Horse Association of Dhahran, Saudi Arabia
Arabian Horse Association of Southern California
Arabian Horse Association of Central California
Arabian Horse Association of Eastern Canada

Inland Empire Arabian Club

Caballo Rangers, Bozeman, Mont.

San Joaquin Valley Arabian Horse Association

Arabian Horse Association of Western Montana

Arabian Horse Association of Oklahoma

ARMS (of horse)

See Figure 51, *HORSE, Points of.*

ARROYO

A common Western term meaning a small, often dry water-course, channel, gully or ditch.

ARTHRITIS

Arthritis is a form of rheumatism which eats away the bone leaving a rough surface and causing great pain and incurable lameness. It occurs fairly often in old horses, coming on very slowly. There is no treatment which is effective.

A.S.P.C.A.

The American Society for the Prevention of Cruelty to Animals includes among its duties the inspection of stables and the investigation of cases of misuse or cruelty. Each state branch has its own procedures, some better organized than others. In Connecticut the A.S.P.C.A. issues a little booklet to horse owners with recommended stable procedures and information on proper care of the horse on the road. Rhode Island has a very broad horse program including a weekly inspection of all public riding stables, with emphasis on general condition of horses, stables and tack, and a check for injuries and saddle galls which would render the animal unserviceable.

The A.S.P.C.A. also sends inspectors to horse shows where such abuses as the use of the rapping pole for jumpers is often common. All lovers of horses should report any infringement of common humane methods to their state branch of the A.S.P.C.A. and should support it to the full extent of their ability even though horses are not as common as formerly nor their owners as knowledgeable and even though many forms of cruelty are practiced through ignorance and neglect.

ASTERISK (*)

On racing sheets or pedigrees, the asterisk (*) indicates an imported stallion or brood mare.

ASTHMA

True asthma is very rare in horses but it does occur. The animal's breathing is labored and the symptoms similar to those in humans. This may be caused by unsanitary conditions. It is advisable to give all food well dampened.

AUSTRALIAN HORSES

The horses of Australia are similar in type to the horses of our western plains and, like the latter, are descended from desert stock. The first Arabian stallion was brought into Australia in 1803 by Robert Campbell, another was imported in 1804. In 1826 the Australian Agricultural Company imported Arabian, Welsh and English breeds. As most of the horse breeding was carried on in New South Wales, Australian horses became known as "Walers." During the latter part of the nineteenth century many were exported to India for military purposes.

Australian ranches are fenced with wire as are our own in the west, but whereas the American cowboy would never think of trying to jump such a formidable barrier, the Australian schools his horses to fly barbed wire as readily as we would fly timber.

AUTOMOBILES

Few horses nowadays are afraid of automobiles. To insure that your colt becomes fearless of cars he should be pastured near a main highway if possible. Horses are never fearful of the accustomed and the sight of cars passing constantly will render them commonplace to the horse. Xenophon recognized this principle of training in his book on riding and recommended that the groom be instructed to lead the young horse through the marketplace so that he might grow used to strange sights. As a matter of fact, a horse is far more likely to shy at a boy pushing a bicycle (not because he is unused to bicycles but because he is unused to seeing one pushed rather than ridden) than he is to shy at the noisiest truck.

AZOTURIA (Monday Morning Disease)

The exact cause of this disease is unknown though it appears to be brought on by enforced idleness and overfeeding. The horse loses control of his hindquarters. There is excessive perspiration and the muscles quiver. If forced to work the animal may fall and be unable to rise. He will sometimes struggle violently. The temperature rises and the muscles of the loins become very hard and go into a condition of spasm. In severe cases death will follow. The horse suffering from azoturia should be gotten into a warm box stall, his loins should be covered with hot blankets, he should be given a hot enema and the veterinarian should be sent for. He should have a laxative diet.

B

BABBLER
See *HUNTING TERMS.*

BACK
See *IDEAL HORSE; CONFORMATION; BLEMISHES; HORSE, Points of.*

BACK
Double back. A back in which the muscles rise up higher than the spine on either side of it.

BACK (Hogback)
The back of a horse which is slightly bowed without prominent withers or croup. Jorrocks speaks of a hogback as being "wery stylish." He recommends to his audience his horse Star Gazer whose back had a hog bend and who was reputed to throw and arch over a jump like the "dome of St. Pauls!"

Seriously speaking there is no worse fault in a horse's conformation than a hogback, for the saddle will not stay in place and the rider has the constant feeling of being pitched forward over his horse's neck.

BACK
To try back. See *HUNTING TERMS.*

BACK
To back is often used to mean to mount a horse, i. e., get on the back of. For mounting see *RIDING.*

BACKING
To cause a horse to move backwards, see *RIDING.*

BACKING RACE
This is a good race for beginners. The horses are lined up with their tails to the finish line which should be at least fifty feet away. The winner must cross the line tail first, his two hind feet crossing before either front foot crosses.

BAGMAN
See *HUNTING TERMS.*

BALANCE
Horse's Balance

A horse running free has perfect natural balance. He continually shifts his center of gravity to fit his actions. The horse that is galloping at full speed stretches out his head and neck and puts his weight on his forehand. This frees his hindqarters, from which comes the power of propulsion.

Ordinarily the center of gravity is just behind the withers. However, if the horse at liberty decides to turn suddenly, pivoting on one hind leg, he puts his weight back, displacing the center of gravity to the rear, thus freeing his forehand.

In riding, the expert horseman adjusts his own balance to coincide with that of the horse, thus helping him to readjust himself and compensate for the added weight of a rider on his back.

In galloping fast the horseman raises his buttocks off the saddle, putting his weight over his stirrups and extending his arms as the horse extends his head and neck. For the ordinary trot and walk he sits in the center of the saddle, with his feet under him. For a movement demanding collection he pushes with his back and buttocks and flexes the horse's poll and jaw through his reins, which has the effect of shortening the horse longitudinally since it brings his hindquarters under him and causes him to raise his head and bring his nose to the vertical. In collection the horse is light under the rider's hand and in such perfect balance that he can move out freely at any gait and in any direction.

For turns and pivots on the hindquarters and for slowing the gaits the horseman lets his own weight come back and sits deeply in the saddle, putting the center of gravity back and enabling the horse to lift his forehand.

Before the colt has learned to adjust his own balance under the weight of a rider he is often clumsy and heavy on the forehand, hanging his head and leaning on the bit. The inexperienced rider tries to cure this by pulling his head up with the reins. Since this only makes it more difficult for the horse to balance himself the end result will be a toughmouthed, lug-headed animal. The experienced horseman makes no attempt to change the horse's balance through his reins. Instead he gives him a systematic course of exercises, with emphasis on circling, starting and stopping, increasing and decreasing the gaits, and changing from one gait to another. Working at the extended, ordinary and collected walk is particularly beneficial, as is going through the different phases of the trot; but the horseman should never demand the collected or even the ordinary phase of the gallop until the

horse has attained his balance. If he does so, the horse will develop stiffness and a bad way of moving at this gait which will be very difficult to correct later on. In all this early work the horse should be worked on a long rein with only light contact; the voice and the rider's weight should be the important aids. (It is assumed that the colt has already had a thorough course of work on the longe without the rider, and so knows the voice commands.)

Some colts find it difficult to balance themselves at the slower phases of the trot, as well as at the gallop. The rider can help here by riding "behind the motion." In posting he does not keep his body slightly ahead of the vertical but on the vertical. In sitting, the shoulders are slightly back.

Remember, however, that the rider who consistently sits back and pushes his feet out in front of him is handicapping his horse and making his own work harder.

Rider's Balance

The test of a rider's balance is whether or not he loses his position when the horse makes a sudden or unexpected movement. If the horseman is relaxed but in balance such movements will not disturb him, he will not appear awkward, his reins will retain the same tension on the bit, his heels will remain depressed and his whole body will swing easily to the motion of the horse with the grace of a ballet dancer. For exercises to improve balance see *RIDING*.

The Balance Seat

This is the accepted modern seat for jumping. Many horsemen also use it for ordinary riding and for hunting. It was developed by the United States Cavalry. Like the classical seat it places the rider in the center of the saddle with his knee and the point of his toe in line with each other. Like the Italian forward seat it allows the rider to balance in his stirrups and put his weight on the horse's forehand over jumps and at the extended gallop. By shortening the stirrups the rider is enabled to get completely out of

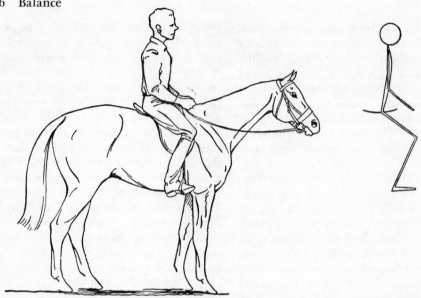

FIGURE 5. THE BALANCE SEAT AT THE HALT.

the saddle for high jumping. By lengthening the stirrups he can sit down in the center of the saddle as demanded by the classical seat, thus enabling him to use his back. Thus we see that the balance seat can be modified for any type of riding.

To take the balance seat sit in the center of the saddle or a little forward of the center, the legs hanging straight without the stirrups. There should be at least five inches between the back of the rider and the cantle of the saddle. The weight should be on the pelvic or "sitting" bones, never on the end of the spine, the rider's buttocks should not be tucked under him. Now, bending the knees but without disturbing the stirrup leathers which hang vertical put the feet into the stirrups from the *outside*. The foot should be inserted only as far as the ball. The ankles should be bent slightly in so that the flat of the stirrup slants up, the outside edge being higher than the side next the horse's body, the stirrup being squarely across the ball of the foot. The inside edge of the rider's foot rests against the inside edge of the stirrup. This throws the rider's legs and thighs against the horse without his having to

exert any pressure or tense the thigh muscles. It leaves the lower leg free to be used as an aid. It will be noticed that the rider's knees are well bent, the point of the knee coming well forward of the stirrup leather at least as far as the edge of the saddle flap. With some types of saddles it will extend in front of the flap.

To test the balance fold the arms and stand in the stirrups. If you can do so without effort when the horse is in motion then you are in balance, if you first have to hitch yourself forward your weight is too far back. It is extremely interesting to note how the modern conception of the seat and its benefits to the horse vary from that of fifty or more years ago. In former days the rider had all his weight on his buttocks and spine, the legs hung straight or were even thrust out in front of the rider, the heels might or might not be depressed, the rider depended on the strength of his muscles to retain his seat. This old-fashioned seat might be compared to the seat of a person in a rocking chair, if the chair be jerked out suddenly from under the sitter the latter will inevitably land on the ground. In the balance seat it is as though one stood on the floor, the knees well bent, the ankles bent in, and a horse were ridden between the legs. The weight remains over the feet and the rider has only to rise in his stirrups if the horse should buck or shy, thus avoiding the force of the shock, which is absorbed by the hip and knee points as a shock absorber on a car absorbs the bumps of a rough road.

BALKING
See *VICES*.

BALLASTING
Ballasting the horse

The rider's weight is the ballast of the horse. This ballast is movable and can be used to help balance the horse just as, with small cargo boats movable kegs were sometimes placed so that they might be shifted to balance the list of the ship caused by the wind. In such movements as the gallop change the ballasting of the horse is especially important, the rider shifting his weight from one side to the opposite as he changes from one lead to the other. When Major Tuttle used to give his dressage exhibitions at Madison Square Garden the only noticeable signal was this slight shifting of "ballast."

Correct ballasting aids in achieving a rhythmic accord between horse and rider.

BANDAGES
Bandages should be at least nine feet long. Three to four inches wide are the most practical. Bandages to be used for cold water applications are usually of flannel or canton flannel, they are sometimes made of a knitted jersey material. This last type is slightly elastic so great care must be taken that they are not wound too tightly. If wool bandages are used they should be kept wet and not allowed to dry on the horse as in drying they shrink and become tight. In applying the bandage to a horse's cannon bone or forearm it should first be wound up into a roll with the tapes inside. Start near the top, wind upwards three times around the animal's leg before beginning to descend, on reaching the bottom wind upwards again. If the bandage is long enough it may be then rewound, spiral fashion, to the top again. In bandaging a joint such as a knee or hock after the first few times around the leg above the joint the bandage may be applied in a figure eight, crossing behind the joint with a half twist to take up the slack.

For bandages where it is desirable to keep the injury cold and wet as in a sprain, or hot and wet as in treating infections plenty of cotton should be used under the bandage.

BANK
Irish Bank

The Irish bank is the most common obstacle encountered in certain parts of Ireland and also in England. It is rare in the United States but artificial banks are often introduced in stadium jumping contests.

The Irish bank, as found in Ireland, is the result of natural conditions. Ireland owes its famous emerald green to its heavy rainfall. When the native farmers attempted to cultivate their fields, or even to get them into condition as pastures, they found that they had first to drain them of the surplus water. To this end they dug ditches along all four sides of each field, piling the dirt into a bank on one side of the ditch. Through the years it became necessary to dig out the ditches afresh at regular intervals and the banks along the edges thus became higher. Sometimes another ditch was dug on the opposite side of a bank in order to drain an adjoining field.

These ditches and banks not only made the fields suitable for cultivation but acted as barriers to prevent cattle from straying. Often the farmer encouraged the growth of thorny underbrush or even small trees on his banks, to discourage further any ambitious animal that felt that the grass on the farther side of a fence is always greener.

Hunting is certainly the national

sport of Ireland. And a good hunter must be able to go across country and negotiate whatever type of obstacle he may encounter. The Irish hunter has learned his lesson well and to hunt safely over the Irish banks and ditches the horseman need only leave everything to his mount. However, contrary to what most horsemen suppose, the Irish horse does not fly these formidable obstacles, whose ditches often exceed twelve feet both in depth and in width and whose banks can be anything from six to ten feet in height. Far from it. Let us observe an experienced Irish hunter in the field. Hounds are running and Master, Huntsman and Whips are following close behind. Across an open field, still green though it is January, stream horses and riders of every description. There are gentlemen in top hats and pink or black coats. The village priest is present in formal, though often well worn, black hunting dress but wearing his clerical collar and black silk vest instead of the conventional white stock and yellow vest; grooms in soft flat caps and tweed coats are out on young horses; and a plowman, hearing hounds, has unhitched his horse, discarded all the harness except the bridle with its blinders and reins made of rope, and has joined the hunt. There are ladies riding "side," immaculately turned out in top hats, shadbelly coats and side-saddle safety skirts. There are others wearing ordinary formal cross-saddle attire but riding side-saddles. Some of these carry an extra stirrup and prefer to swing their legs across and ride astride while hacking from one covert to another, perching themselves once more in the side-saddle position when the hounds start to run.

There is a sprinkling of children, but not many unless it is the holiday season. The field itself is heavy, the horses often sinking well over the fetlocks, but this does not seem to bother them. The riders are balancing in their stirrups and the horses have their heads and necks well extended and are traveling at full gallop.

On the far side of the field is a wide ditch. The sides are straight and across the eight feet of muddy water rises a steep bank, probably ten feet high. It is of the "hairy" variety, with underbrush growing on it, but the top is about four feet wide and nicely rounded—not the sharp "razor-edged" type which requires that the horse teeter perilously as he changes leg.

As the horses approach this obstacle, of their own accord they begin to shorten stride. As our hunter arrives at the edge of the ditch he comes to a complete halt, pricks his ears, gathers himself and, at a growl from his rider, leaps from a standstill. Like a cat he lands half way up the bank and climbs on to the top. He again looks to see what is before him, and just as well, for there is an even deeper and wider ditch there, ending in a tremendous mud hole. But he springs far out, just makes the turf with his forelegs, scrambles safely out of the mudhole and is away. One of his fellows is not so lucky; he lands in the middle of the mudhole, sinking to his belly. An American hunter would simply quit at this point. But the Irish hunter, in some unknown manner, gathers his legs under him and scrambles up the sloping bank.

The ordinary ditch with its sheer sides presents no problem provided the horse clears it but, should he misjudge his leap and fall in, he will not be able to get himself out, for the ditch will be higher than he is. In this case the rider must lead him along until he comes to a place that can be negotiated.

In certain parts of Ireland there are very few banks or none at all, but many tremendous ditches. These have sloping sides and when they are very, very wide the horses have a special way of taking them. They slide carefully down the near bank for several feet, then launch themselves in the air and land on the opposite bank on a little shelf which has been formed by this practice, from which they scramble to the top. But be not deterred, you who are considering a trip to

Ireland for the hunting. Just trust your horse and you will have a glorious time.

BANK (v.)

To bank a jump is to jump on top of it and then down. In Ireland, except in the Galway country, where the stone walls are very narrow and flimsy, the ordinary Irish hunter wisely lands on top of all types of obstacles including the low walls, for he never knows when there is a ditch on the far side.

BARB

The Barb is the native horse of the Barbary States which include Algeria, Tunisia, Morocco, Tripoli and Fez. Some authorities believe that he was an offshoot of the Arabian horse, others that he developed at about the same time and from the same stock. He is a larger animal than the Arabian. His head is coarser without the typical "dished" appearance. His tail is set somewhat lower and there is some hair at the fetlocks. He has more knee action than the Arabian but less freedom of shoulder action. The *Godolphin Arabian,* one of the three foundation sires of the English Thoroughbred has since been thought to be a Barb. As one of the other two foundation desert sires was a Turk (Byerly Turk) which is also a related breed, only the *Darley Arabian* was a true Arabian. Perhaps the knee action of the Barb accounts for the trotting action of the modern standard bred horses which trace desert ancestry through Messenger though he goes back to the Darley Arabian not to the Barb.

BAREBACK RIDING

There is no more graceful nor secure seat than the real bareback seat. This must not be confused with the "plowboy" seat where the rider, elbows and

FIGURE 6. A GOOD SEAT BAREBACK.

legs flopping, depends upon his reins to maintain his balance. The true bareback seat as depicted in Greek sculptures and in the Remington pictures of the American Indian, show a completely different style. An expert rider is more than a horseman, he might almost be called a "man horse," a centaur. There seems to be perfect accord between himself and his mount, the two become a fluid unit. This unity is most completely attained when there is no saddle to come between the rider and his horse. It is most unfortunate that today, in most riding schools, so little emphasis is put on bareback riding. A few steps at a jog trot without stirrups is about the most experience that the average learner is given, and at many schools beginners do not have even this opportunity of developing their balance independently of reins. As in the balance seat, the good bareback rider does not use grip except when absolutely necessary, he rides on balance. The Indian needed both hands to manipulate his bow and arrow. The learner, wishing to attain a graceful seat, will do well to emulate him and tie up his reins. Any active boy or girl can become an expert bareback rider if he has a mount of a size suitable to his own; the exhilaration of galloping across a field, the muscles of the horse moving between the thighs is greatly to be prized and is far different from the feel of sitting in a saddle.

BAR BIT
See *BITS*.

BARN RAT
A horse that will not leave the stable yard willingly except in company. See *VICES*.

BARRANCA
This is a Spanish word meaning "ravine." It is important to the horseman for in Mexico the steep sides of these barrancas are used as slides to school the horse. They are usually sandy in composition, almost perpendicular, and from twenty to forty feet high, and the agile horses learn to go up and down them fearlessly. In negotiating a barranca one inclines the upper body forward, the head and eyes up, the hands following the position of the horse's head, maintaining a light contact but in no way attempting to act as a support, the legs pushed slightly forward so that the stirrup leathers may remain vertical to the ground. When they have slid down to within six feet of the ground many horses spring off from that point, so it is well to be prepared. In climbing the barrancas, which is best done at a strong canter with a run of twenty feet or so, the weight is kept entirely off the horse's back, the position being the same as that described above except that the legs need not be pushed forward. Most Mexican horses are flat shod, with no heels or toes on either front or back feet; yet they somehow manage to scramble up the steep, slippery sides of the barrancas with little difficulty. It used to be said that the criterion as to whether or not a horse could maneuver an incline with a rider on his back was that if a man could climb it without using his hands a horse could carry him up it. However, having personally ridden the barrancas of Mexico I know that no man could possibly climb them without the use of his hands, and would have great difficulty even with the use of them.

BARREL RACING
A race against time on course shown in diagram. One of the most popular of the events in shows sponsored by the National Cutting Horse Association; particularly suitable for women and girls.

BASKETBALL (mounted)
This game originated with the Cossacks and was played with a sheepskin. The Cossacks were very adept at "forward passing" the sheepskin, throwing it yards ahead while a member of the team raced and caught it at a gallop. The United States Cavalry uses a regulation basketball and the game is ex-

FIGURE 7. PAT DAWSON, 1961 AQHA HONOR ROLL BARREL RACING HORSE. *COURTESY JOHN E. SMITH.*

tremely rough with virtually no holds barred. See *PATO*.

BAY
See *COLORS OF HORSE*.

BELGIAN DRAFT HORSE CORPORATION OF AMERICA
Headquarters, Wabash, Indiana.

BELGIAN HORSE
The Belgian is one of the foremost draft breeds. He is the immediate descendant of the old Flemish Horse which existed in Belgium before the days of Caesar. Line breeding through inbreeding of this breed has been carried on in Belgium for a great many years. Blood of other strains has been introduced to give fineness. The original color was black but the predominant colors of the

modern Belgians are sorrel, chestnut, roan and bay.

The first importation of Belgian horses to the United States was made in 1866 by Dr. A. G. Van Hoorebeck of Monmouth, Illinois. More stallions were imported in 1885 and 1886. The American Association of Importers and Breeders of Belgian Draft Horses was organized at Wabash, Indiana in 1887. Belgian horses are now to be found in nearly every state in the union and a marked increase in their breeding both on the Pacific and Atlantic seaboards has occurred in the last decade.

BELLE BEACH
Belle Beach was a famous woman equestrian who published a book, *Riding and Driving for Women* in nineteen twelve. On her death in nineteen thirty-

FIGURE 8. A BELGIAN DRAFT STALLION. *COURTESY BELGIAN DRAFT HORSE CORP. OF AMERICA.*

three the newspapers had accounts of how she was said to go hunting, her reins consisting of strands of number fifty cotton thread. Miss Beach, as was natural, was a great advocate for the side saddle and predicted that riding astride would never become popular. This opinion was shared by Colonel Dodge, author of *Riders of Many Lands.* If all women could be as fine horsemen as Miss Beach one might have cause to regret the change in style for certainly there is a glamor to sidesaddle riding which is lacking in the cross saddle, but it takes a far better rider.

BENDING RACE

A row of jump standards placed about ten or twelve feet apart are the equipment needed for this game. Riders race against time weaving in and out between the standards. Anyone touching a standard is disqualified.

BETTING SYSTEMS

Before the days of organized betting side bets were made orally between friends. This was followed by the custom of appointing a "stake holder" who held the stakes when strangers wished to bet. The original stake holders got nothing out of it but when racing became more elaborate it was decided that stake holders should keep five percent of the stakes in return for their services. Later still when a number of horses were run instead of two or three a more exact system was required and bookmaking came into being. The bookmaker calculates his percentages in such fashion that he takes in a hundred and five percent and pays out a hundred. The odds he gives vary with the reputation of the horse. Thus he will pay even money on the favorite, two to one on a runner up and rate the balance of the field according to the number of horses running. A "round book" is one in which the book-maker has made an error and given such odds that there is no percentage left for him. A "dutch book" is one in which the bookmaker is bound to lose. Bookmaking has given way in most places to the pari-mutuel system of betting. In fact many states which permit pari-mutuels forbid bookmaking by law. The auction system of bidding is also extinct on running horse race courses though occasionally seen on trotting tracks. With this system the auctioneer published the names of the horses to run some time be-for the race. The persons assembled at the auction ring were asked to make their bids. Anyone could bid on any horse and his bid could be "upped" by anyone else. The person bidding the highest on a specific horse had that horse running for him for the day. Horses which were not well enough known to receive bids individually were classed together as "the field" and a bidder might bid in the field. The "owner" of the winning horse collected all bets made, less the five percent which went to the auctioneer.

FIGURE 9. CROWDS AROUND THE PARI MUTUEL WINDOWS AT BELMONT PARK. *BERT CLARK THAYER.*

Both the above systems have been superseded by the "pari-mutuel" method of betting. This latter is approved by the Jockey Club and is permitted legally on race tracks. It was invented by Pierre Oller, a Frenchman who ran a perfume shop in Paris. In 1865 Oller denounced the bookmakers as cheats and started his own system. This called for selling tickets on each horse in the race, all receipts going into a common pool. After the race Oller deducted five percent for his trouble and the balance went to the owners of the winning tickets. Thus if only one man had bet on the winner he won the whole pool. If two, it was split two ways. Some time later the actual machines which did the calculating were invented and, as racing became more complicated with different priced tickets being sold, they became more and more ingenious. Two men running a machine can handle countless bets and the bettors can be sure that the odds are right inasmuch as they are figured automatically.

BETWEEN THE RIDER'S HANDS AND LEGS.

This is an equitation expression. The rider that coordinates the movements of the horse's hindquarters and forehand through contact with the bit and on the horse's sides is said to have the horse "between his hands and legs." The aids are then used either together or individually. When used individually assisting aids may either help or oppose the active aids. For example, in asking the horse to move backwards the rider first applies his legs lightly to demand movement and light vibrations on the bit tell the horse to move backwards; the aids are now assisting each other. However, should the horse move backwards too rapidly the hands relax and the legs are used more strongly. Should he swing his hindquarters to the left in backing, the right leg opposes this action while the left hand, by bending the head slightly to the left, assists the leg by opposing the forehand to the hindquarters. See also *AIDS*.

BIKE

The modern racing sulky with bicycle type wheels is known as a "Bike."

BILLET STRAPS

See *SADDLE, Parts of.*

BINDER

See *HUNTING TERMS.*

BIRTH

See *COLTS, BROOD MARES.*

BIRTHDAY

All Thoroughbred foals are registered as of January first of the current year. This is done because of the racing classifications. Previous to this rule a colt born in May of one year could be raced as a two-year-old in April just before he became a three-year-old. Most colts are born between February and June. However, should a foal have the misfortune to be born in December he would be officially a year old on the following January first.

BITING

See *VICES.*

BITS

Driving bits. The most usual bit for driving is the Liverpool bit. This is a straight bar bit with rings at the cheek and long, straight shanks with slots in them for the reins so that the severity of the bit can be adjusted by the placement of the reins according to the need. The Buxton bit has a bent shank. The gag bit is similar to the Liverpool but has loops instead of slots on the shank and a bar across the bottom.

Riding bits. The most common type of bits used in riding are the *snaffle,* known when used in a full bridle as a *bridoon,* the *curb* and the *pelham.* The *snaffle* is a jointed bit with large rings. When used without a martingale it acts on the corners of the horse's mouth and tends to make him lift his head higher. It is the least severe of the bits. The *curb* bit brings pressure to bear on the horse's bars. With the addition of the curb chain which acts against the chin groove, very severe and painful pressure can be produced. This bit makes the horse bend at the poll and brings his head in towards the chest. The *pelham* is shaped like a curb bit but has an upper set of rings as well as a lower and is used with two pairs of reins. Some authorities believe that the pelham is an incorrectly designed bit and should not be used inasmuch as when the upper reins are applied the bit is raised in the horse's mouth to the position of a snaffle at which position it would be wrong to apply the curb rein

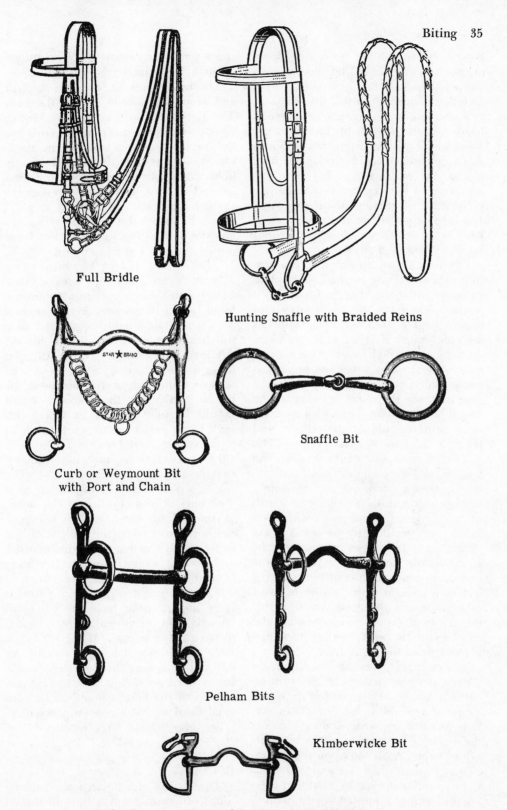

Full Bridle

Hunting Snaffle with Braided Reins

Curb or Weymount Bit
with Port and Chain

Snaffle Bit

Pelham Bits

Kimberwicke Bit

FIGURE 10. TYPES OF BITS AND BRIDLES.

for the bit would not be resting down on the bars as it should be. Nevertheless many horses go better in a pelham than in either a snaffle or a full bridle.

There is now on the market a modification of the pelham bit known as the *Kimberwick*. It was originated in South America and is used both for ordinary riding, for hunting and for jumping. As shown in the diagram it is actually a pelham cut off just below the top rings. It works very well on the horse that is fussy in an ordinary pelham and cannot be controlled in a snaffle.

For breaking and training colts a flexible rubber pelham is good, or a plain pelham with the bar covered with leather. There are many variations of these bits. The *Hanoverian pelham* has an exaggerated port in it. Some forms even have a rough wheel; these were used generally not when the horse was being ridden but as a training bit in the stall to teach the horse to relax at the jaw. The *gag snaffle* is one with an extra strap running along the cheek and through the ring to give leverage. The *double ring snaffle, wire snaffle* and *twisted snaffle* are all designed for horses that pull in a snaffle yet are apparently too nervous to take a pelham or a full bridle. However, a horseman with good hands can handle any except a horse that is an outlaw or so nervous that he is unsuitable for riding in one of the three conventional types of bits with the addition, perhaps, of a martingale. Lack of exercise and too good condition for the ability of the rider is more often the trouble with the puller or the jibber than is the type of bit being used.

The early rider used no bits. Raphael's "Attila at Rome" shows the Huns riding without bit or bridle, merely ropes or straps around the horses' necks. In certain pictures of early Roman chariots the horse is wearing a snaffle bit with but one rein. A bit found on the Acropolis, and whose date is about 500 B.C., is very similar in type to a modern driving bit, being a jointed snaffle with a roughened mouth piece and having

cheek pieces to prevent its being pulled through the animal's mouth.

The Indians used a loop run through and around the lower jaw at the bars. The horses of the West and of Mexico which are ridden in very severe curb bits are trained to turn readily on the application of the rein on the neck. The rider holds the reins in one hand and very loose. The horse, knowing the severity of the bit, stops instantly on the slightest pressure. Such a bit is entirely unsuitable for any riding in which the horse must be steadied as in jumping.

The choosing of bits. The bit used on a horse depends not only on the horse but also on the rider's hands. A mutton-fisted rider will not be able to manage a mettlesome, light-mouthed animal in a full bridle or a pelham. Better, for the day give him a snaffle; better still, put him on another horse. Some authorities feel that the lighter the bit used the better. Some feel that only a snaffle should be used. Usually a rider with light hands prefers either a full bridle or a pelham for every horse except the one who is nervous or has such a light mouth that he will go only in a snaffle. The snaffle is a very limited bit, acting as it does only against the lips of the horse. It raises the forehand but does not cause the horse to bend at the poll. With the full bridle or pelham one can demand and receive a much greater flexibility from the horse with much less effort.

The fitting and adjustment of bits. It is as important to have the bit small enough to fit the animal's mouth as it is to have it big enough. If the bit is too wide little disks of leather may be cut out and sewn on either side. The snaffle bit is fitted so that it just touches the corners of the horse's mouth. The curb is adjusted so that it rests on the bars. See also *BRIDLES; HACKAMORE BIT.*

BITTING

The bitting of a horse, i. e., teaching him to be supple and willing in the bit and to obey its commands is extremely

FIGURE 11. EARLY TYPES OF BITS. GERMAN, SIXTEENTH-CENTURY (*left*); BRONZE SNAFFLE, GALLO-ROMAN ORIGIN, SECOND CENTURY (*right*). *COURTESY OF N. TILLANDER.*

important in the training of every horse, and, being rather tedious, is too often neglected. For a practical training course in bitting see *COLTS, Breaking and Training.*

BITTING RIG

This is an arrangement used in teaching the horse to obey the commands of the reins. It consists of a harness pad fitted with special rings and two upright arms. The horse is bridled, the bridle reins are run back to the pad and adjusted to one set of rings. Long reins are also attached to the bit and run through another set of rings. In this way the position of the animal's head and its carriage can be accurately controlled.

See also *COLTS—breaking and training of.*

BLACK BEAUTY

See *FAMOUS HORSES OF FICTION.*

BLACK HAWK FAMILY

The Black Hawk line was an offshoot of the Morgan, Vermont Black Hawk, the foundation sire, being a grandson of Justin Morgan. The Black Hawks were longer legged, longer gaited, somewhat handsomer and faster than their cousins, the Morgans. The most noted specimen of the breed was Ethan Allen, a small bay stallion particularly noted for the smoothness of his movement.

BLACK POINTS

Bay horses are said to have black points, i. e., while the body of the horse is a bay or reddish brown, the mane, tail and generally lower legs are black.

Duns and buckskins also have black points.

BLANKETS

The horse that is clipped in winter needs a blanket when he is not working, to take the place of his natural coat.

There are a variety of designs and materials from which one may choose. The most common type has one or two breast straps and two surcingles, one of which encircles the horse at the girth line, the other just behind the swell of the belly. These surcingles are of webbing and are adjustable in length. A more satisfactory way of fastening the two surcingles is to cross them under the horse's belly, bringing the offside back surcingle forward to fasten on the near side front fastening, and vice versa. This helps materially in keeping the blanket in place when the horse lies down.

In fact there is a blanket on the market known as a *Baker* blanket, which has the surcingles sewed on diagonally so that they may be crossed under the belly.

The New Zealand Rug has only one surcingle at the girth line. At the back are leg straps, each of which encircles a hind leg at the gaskin.

The English Rug has no surcingles and is not shaped at the throat line. It is worn with a "roller." The latter is a very broad surcingle with padding on each side of the spine. The rug is put on so that it extends well forward over the neck; the surplus is then turned back and tucked under the roller. All of the above types are lined with coverings of different materials in plain colors, checks or plaids. Choose a blanket with a woven, not a jute, lining and of some tough outer fabric such as duck.

The cheapest type of blanket is the army blanket. These are khaki with a wool lining. However, they have canvas straps as breast straps, only one surcingle and a web tail strap. The throat is usually very big and it is extremely difficult to keep these blankets in place.

BLEEDER

A horse that is kept at a laboratory and used for the production of serum is known as a *bleeder*.

BLEMISHES

There are certain "blemishes" which are known as "honorable scars" or marks of service which do not count against a horse in a conformation class in a show if the class is so described. Such a mark is anything which does not interfere with his sight or wind or soundness. Wire cuts or scarred knees would be considered blemishes whereas any irregularity of gait would disqualify him. However, in a straight conformation class a blemish would be counted against the horse. Good horsemen who cannot afford to pay thousands for a first-class hunter or Saddler can sometimes pick one up for a fraction of his original value because he may have some slight blemish which would bar him from the show ring but will in no way affect his hunting soundness or his way of going.

BLIND STAGGERS
See *MEGRIMS*.

BLISTERING

When a horse develops a chronic lameness, or when he has an injury which is extremely painful which does not improve with ordinary treatment, his condition may be improved by the application of a "blister," namely, an ointment which has the effect of burning and blistering the skin. Most blisters have mercury in them and have to be procured from a veterinarian. It is best to have the vet apply the blister as he will know how severe a blister to apply and how long to rub it in. Its medicinal effect is to bring the blood down to the injured part and as it is through the blood that healing is accomplished, bacteria killed, and tissues renewed it is not hard to understand why the blister brings relief. When the horse is blistered his head must be kept tied up for twenty-four hours so that he cannot rub his nose in the blister and burn that as well. At the end of this time the blister is washed off. The part will swell and be hot. It will cool off after a few days but remain tender as the hair and skin will come off in scales. Do not consider the treatment ended or the cure to be tested until the new hair grows back. The horse meanwhile should be fed a light, laxative diet. He may be turned out to pasture if the weather is good and the flies not too bad. In event of the latter he may be kept in during the daytime and turned out at night. In severe chronic cases it is sometimes necessary to repeat the treatment.

BLOOD (blooded)
See *HUNTING TERMS.*

BLOOD HEAT
The normal temperature of a horse is 100° F.

BLOOD TESTS
Horses may be given blood tests to determine whether or not they are suffering from certain diseases. Some states require tests before allowing the animal to be imported.

BOG SPAVIN
An enlargement on the inside of the hock. See *INJURIES.*

BOLT (v.)
A horse that eats too rapidly is said to "bolt" his food. This is a bad habit as it means that the unchewed food will not be digested. A remedy is to put several stones or lumps of rock salt in his manger. A patented feed box may also be used. This is one with a number of partitions which divide the grain so that the horse cannot take too large a mouthful at a time.

BOLT A FOX
See *HUNTING TERMS.*

BOLTING
Running away or bolting is one of the most common accidents. It is nearly always caused by carelessness or ignorance. A colt that has been ridden only a little while will sometimes bolt at the sight of something strange but only a good horseman should ride an untrained animal and he will be able to handle the situation very easily. Bolting sometimes occurs as a vice in old horses. Such animals usually have tough, calloused bars from heavy hands, and thick necks. They are rarely animals of spirit, being rather on the stubborn side. Their practice is to bend the crest and tuck the chin into the chest, then plough forward. As they are not running from fright there is little danger; the horseman has only to retain his seat. If he can pull the horse's head around to one side he will be able to stop him quite readily for he will cause him to travel in a short circle. Pulling straight back does no good for the horse is much the stronger. Sawing on the bit will sometimes be effective or a sudden jerk followed by a complete release of the reins will often surprise the animal into letting go the bit and throwing his head up. The most important thing is for the rider not to get frightened but to continue trying to regain control.

The best cure for this vice is to head the horse for open, preferably hilly country and, by means of judicious use of a crop or spurs, ride him to a standstill.

The horse that bolts from fright is an entirely different problem. Here the danger is very great as he is as likely as not to run headlong into an approaching car or some other obstacle. The rider should try and ease him in slowly, talking to him and reassuring him as much as possible. He is easier to stop than the confirmed bolter as he has not learned the trick of bracing with his neck muscles.

Some horses bolt back to the stable. This can be prevented by riding with a severe bit, keeping on the alert and never letting the horse get off a walk once the stable has been sighted. See also *ACCIDENTS.*

BONE
When a horseman speaks of his horse as having "good bone" he is referring to the cannon bones, i.e., the metacarpal bones in the front legs and the metatarsal bones in the back legs. These run from the knees to the fetlock joints in

FIGURE 12. THE PULLEY REIN EFFECT.

the case of the metacarpal bones and from the hocks to the fetlocks in the metatarsal. In a well-formed horse, the cannon bones should be relatively short from joint to joint. They should be wide and flat when viewed from the side and thick when viewed from the front. The line from the knee should be straight and should not give the appearance of being "tied in" just below that joint. The tendons at the back should be well separated. The density of the bone is also very important.

The importance of good bone cannot be overemphasized in any animal that is required to gallop or jump. The horse whose cannons are too long will not be a good stayer as he will tire easily. The horse with thin, weak, tied in cannons will be much more subject to injury. Good bone is one of the first things for which a horseman looks when buying his horse.

BOOK
In reference to round book, dutch book. See *BETTING SYSTEMS*.

BOOKMAKER
See *BETTING SYSTEMS*.

BOOTS
Boots for the horse. Various types of boots may be used to protect the horse from injury in racing and jumping. Quarter boots for the trotter, for example, are used to protect his heels from being badly injured by overreaching. The horse that "brushes" may also be protected by special boots. The polo pony wears shin boots to guard the cannons from injury from the mallet.

Military organizations often use light canvas boots in exhibitions to give a uniformity of appearance. These are simply square-cut pieces of white or colored duck put on with tapes.

The shoe-boil boot is a doughnut

shaped leather boot put on around the ankle to prevent the horse from irritat-in the boil on his elbow. See *SHOE BOIL*.

Boots for the rider. A properly fitting boot not only looks well but it actually aids the rider, especially in jumping, and protects him from injury in cross-country riding and in polo. It is essential that the boot fit well, but this does not mean that it should be fitted as the shoe is fitted.

The well-fitting boot clings closely at the top, is broad enough at the toe to permit freedom of movement, and fits rather loosely at the heel. It should be of soft, flexible leather. Hunting boots should have thick soles. If you can pos-sibly manage it, have your boots made of the best leather obtainable by a good bootmaker. These may cost what to you seems a fortune but they will outwear the ready-mades by a good many years and will always be comfortable.

In buying new boots remember that they are often sold by shoe-salesmen who know nothing about riding. Don't be talked into buying too tight a boot or one that is too low in the leg. As the new boots are worn they wrinkle about the ankle and in so doing they shorten in length. They should not be so high as to bind at the knee but one should allow for at least a one to one and a half inch decrease in length.

People with high insteps frequently have great difficulty in getting into boots even with the aid of hooks. Field boots, those that have the laces at the instep, are easy to get into but they are not as correct for formal wear as the ordinary hunting boots.

Generally one wears black boots with a black or oxford gray coat and for all formal occasions such as hunting or formal horse shows; brown boots are worn with "rat-catcher" clothes for in-formal and country riding. Top boots, i. e., those with mahogany, tan or pink tops, are correct for hunting. Women wear black patent leather tops on their hunting boots.

Boot-trees are made to fit the boots and are essential if the boot is to hold its shape. Boot garters are worn with field and hunting boots but are not used in military organizations. They should run between the first and second button of the breeches' leg buttons. Men's garters match the color of the breeches, women wear black garters.

No matter how well made your boot may be it will require a certain amount of "breaking in." The wise horseman will do well to put a bandaid on the in-side and outside of each ankle bone and on the back of his heel at the line of the counter for the first half dozen times he sports his new boots.

BOTTOM
See *HUNTING TERMS*.

BOWED TENDON
When the tendons at the back of the cannon bones are severely strained or sprained they never entirely go back into line but heal in the shape of a bow. Sometimes a horse with badly bowed tendons wil be perfectly sound for light work including jumping but of course he will never be as strong as before the injury. See *INJURIES*.

BOWING
To teach a saddle horse or pony to bow is not a difficult trick and is a pretty one. The preliminary lessons are given on foot. The horse is ranged along a wall, the trainer standing on one side. The horse is first made to stretch or "camp" slightly, the trainer then, hold-ing the reins quite short, picks up the nearer front foot at the pastern and carries it back until the knee touches the ground. At the same time he pulls back on the reins until the horse's nose also touches the ground. He repeats this with a bit of sugar as reward for willingness until the horse is sure of what is wanted. The next step is to induce the horse to carry his foot back on signal, the trainer pulling back on the reins and, at the same time, tapping the front of the knee

with his whip. When the horse has mastered this the trainer then mounts and continues the training from there. He first makes the horse stretch by touching him on the backs of the leg at the knee. This step takes considerably longer than the first two steps as the pull back on the reins, coming from above, does not so readily suggest a lowering of the head and the horse also has the rider's weight to balance. In all probability the horse will simply "duck" a little and not bring the foot entirely back. An assistant standing on the ground can then carry the leg back completely as in the first lesson and eventually the horse will learn what is expected. He should be taught to bow with either leg and should always be rewarded for his willingness.

BOX STALL

The box stall, i. e., a big, rectangular space in which the horse is kept at liberty, not tied up as in a straight stall, is usually more satisfactory for the Saddler or hunter than is the straight stall as it gives him more freedom of movement and allows him to work off excess energy. However, some horses do better in a straight stall; they become excited in a box. Some few have stable vices which require that they be stabled in straight stalls and some have vices that demand a box. The horse that kicks at the man entering his stall must always be stabled in a stall where he is tied up and cannot swing his hind quarters around at will. The head-shy horse must also be kept in a straight stall. On the other hand the horse that, in a straight stall, kicks sideways against the stall partition when he is fed, will do better in a box.

The regulation size of a box stall for a hunter is twelve by twelve. A horse under sixteen hands will get along in a ten by ten; the pony needs eight by eight. Windows for ventilation and light should be above the animal's eyes. Box stalls may have dutch doors, that is those that are divided across the middle. If these doors open onto an aisle the horse will enjoy putting his head out and watching what is going on around him. If the doors open onto an overhung outdoor passageway as is common in the South the fact that the horse can see outside will prevent agoraphobia.

The flooring of a box stall should never be of wood, as this retains the odors and rots out. The usual method is to put a base of crushed rock with cinders on top for drainage. Over this clay is tamped down firmly. The only undesirable characteristic of this type of flooring for box stalls is that unless at least four inches of dry bedding is maintained the clay may become muddy.

Another method is to cover the crushed or loose rock with several inches of cinders, tamp it down and put the bedding directly on that, without the clay. Since cinders are hard to obtain in some parts of the country, six inches of "dead sand" may be used instead. Dead sand is sand which, owing to its formation, cannot be used in cement work and is therefore quite cheap. The side walls and partitions of the box stall *must* be of two-inch rough oak. The latter should be so constructed that the boards may be removed in case of emergency. This may be done by leaving channels where the side walls meet them or by using channel irons. The side walls go up eight feet, and should be covered with metal at the top. The partitions reach to the ground but extend upwards but five feet. Above them guard rails of iron rods or of very heavy gauge anchor fence reach up eight feet. This allows for better ventilation and also permits the horses to see their neighbors, yet prohibits their injuring each other.

A large square hole cut in the ceiling permits the hay being thrown down. Some people prefer to use hay racks which fit flat to the wall and gradually close as the horse eats the hay. Others feel that the horse should eat his hay off the ground, as this encourages the draining of his sinuses. Also, some horses are affected by dust or particles falling into their eyes when they eat hay from racks set above eye level.

The grain manger and the water bowl or pail should be in opposite corners. The former may have a two-inch pipe running down from the hay loft and the grain may be sent down that by means of a funnel; thus the horse may be both grained and fed without the attendant having to enter the stall.

BREAKING
See *COLTS, Breaking and Training.*

BREAKING CART or BREAK-IN CART
The ordinary type of breaking cart is characterized by low wheels, long shafts on which there are special metal attach-ments to hold the tugs so that breeching is unnecessary, and sometimes has an extension at the back to prevent the colt rearing and coming over backwards. Mr. Jack Widmer, author of *Practical Horse Breeding and Training* has an improved version of the breaking cart made from the rear axle of a car. This cart with a box body has regulation balloon tires and a brake on each wheel. The advantage of the brakes is obvious. The colt that tries to run can be controlled by the use of both brakes instead of simply through the bit, and in teaching him to turn, one of the more difficult lessons, he is helped by the application of one brake only.

FIGURE 13. A MODERN VERSION OF THE BREAKING (BREAK-IN) CART. *FROM PRACTICAL HORSE BREEDING BY JACK WIDMER, PUBLISHED BY CHARLES SCRIBNER'S SONS.*

BREAST HIGH
In reference to scent, see *HUNTING TERMS.*

BREASTPLATE
This is a leather strap going around the horse's neck just in front of the shoulder to which the two short straps are attached. These straps fasten to two small rings in front of the saddle. A

short leather loop attached at the bottom is provided through which the girth is run. The primary purpose of the breast-plate is to prevent the saddle from slid-ing back. It is especially useful on a horse with flat ribs. Where a martingale is used the latter may be attached to the breastplate.

BREECHES

For the uninitiated this word is usu-ally pronounced to rhyme with "itches" not "reaches." Breeches should be chosen according to the type of riding to be done and the climate. Formal hunting or showing breeches must conform in color and material to the tradition and requirements. See *APPOINTMENTS*. The polo player wears lightweight white breeches. Rust color breeches are very popular for hacking and perfectly per-missible but green breeches are an ab-horrence.

All good tailors have a saddle mounted on a rack which the prospec-tive buyer may straddle and it is of ut-most importance that he do so, for only in this way can he be sure that his breeches will not bind when he is mounted. Beware the breeches that are too long in the crotch; there should not be a band of material across the saddle which will be the case if the breeches do not fit close. The breeches that are too short in the crotch will bind most un-comfortably. Breeches should fit tight well above the knee, and the flare, or "peg" should not wrinkle in folds when the rider is standing. They should fit close to the calf of the leg and come well down, the lower buttons coming below the calf and so preventing the breeches from riding up out of the boot tops. Most people who are not accustomed to wearing breeches fit them much too loosely in the knee and lower leg. A character of Surtees tells his tailor that he wants his breeches made tight. "If I can get into them I won't wear them," he says. Perhaps we don't want to go this far but certainly the well cut breeches

are snug around the knee and leg rather than otherwise.

BREECHING
See *HARNESS, Parts of.*

BREEDING

Two major factors have influenced the development of the horse: environment and selective breeding. The former has given us such widely divergent types as the Welsh pony, the Arab and the west-ern mustang. To the latter we must credit many more modern breeds, includ-ing the Morgan, the trotting horse, the Kentucky Saddler and the Thorough-bred. In selecting brood stock one must first visualize the type of colt to be pro-duced. Are you breeding for a specialized market? For showing? For hunting? For polo? Are you to keep a number of brood-mares and a stallion to serve them? Will you keep a stallion and one or two brood-mares, depending on using the stallion on local mares? Or will you keep mares only, there being a desirable stallion in the vicinity?

It goes without saying that you must select your breeding stock from strains known to produce the type of colt de-sired. If your interest is in show Saddlers, then your mares should have good show records, your stallion should be as fine a show type as it is possible to get and have a good disposition. If you are breeding for racing, the track records of mares and stallions will be the important factor. Within each breed certain blood-lines are known as good "nicks," i. e., to always produce good results. These should be carefully studied before pur-chasing the breeding stock.

Polo ponies and hunters fall into the class of "working horses." They are bred for a certain purpose and although they may also win in the show ring it is their performance which is the outstanding factor here. The hunter is bred for his ability as a "stayer," and his ability to jump. Heavyweight hunters, i. e., those capable of carrying over a hundred and eighty-five pounds, bring higher prices than light or middleweight hunters. On the other hand a woman generally prefers the less heavy type and the latter is certainly apt to be a finer looking and more active going horse than the former. The type of country to be hunted must also be taken into consideration. Open country where there is much galloping will require a Thoroughbred type of mount, country which is sticky and the going heavy may call for a three-quarter bred. One customary method of breeding the heavyweight type of hunter is to use a mare that is three-quarters Thoroughbred, one quater Percheron and breed her to a fine type Thoroughbred stallion. The draft blood will ensure good bone and size while the predominance of Thoroughbred will give fineness, jumping ability and speed. In breeding by this method it must be remembered that occasionally one gets a throwback to the Percheron stock or, as in all crosses, the foal may inherit the weaknesses of both strains.

There is no established breed of polo pony but the most usual cross is Thoroughbred to western cowpony stock. The polo pony must have staying power, speed in spurting and handiness. He must not be too big but breeding to big mares and stallions and then stunting by underfeeding develops weaknesses of bone and muscle.

In selecting the brood-mare remember that she represents sixty percent of the foal. Examine her carefully for soundness, especially in the front legs. Ninety percent of the weaknesses in horses are in the legs and feet. Discard the mare whose pasterns are too sloping or too straight, whose cannon bones are too long or thin, whose frogs are not well developed or whose soles are flat. Look for well separated tendons, good knees, and, especially in the jumper, excellent hocks. Next make sure of the shoulders and quarters, the well sprung ribs and the "top-line." Remember that the longer the neck the smaller should be the head. The fencer knows that only a very small additional weight on the end

of his foil will seem like a ton, so too, a heavy head at the end of a long neck will make the horse low and awkward in the forehand.

Select your stallion for type, disposition and from the colts which he has sired. Though the mare may be sixty percent of the foal, she will produce a very few foals in comparison to the number for which the stallion will be responsible. In many parts of the country the government maintains stallions for whose service only a very small stud fee is charged. This practice has done much to improve the stock in country districts.

The mating of the mare and stallion next comes to the attention. The mare comes in season every fourteen to twenty-four days from February through the summer. Some continue to come in heat in the fall or begin earlier in the winter. The average mare comes in heat every twenty-one days and remains in heat for two or three. At this time they urinate frequently, the muscles of the external genitals are relaxed, and the mare shows excitement on seeing the stallion. Evidence of being in heat or in season is much easier to detect in some mares than in others, but as a general rule if the mare is suspected of being in heat and the stallion is led near her the mare will at once show interest, will raise her tail and spread her legs while the stallion too will become excited.

Before being mated the mare should have her tail bandaged to prevent injury, through stray hairs, to either herself or the stallion. Many breeders take the sanitary precautions of washing the external genitals of both mare and stallion to prevent the introduction of harmful bacteria. Most mares will submit to the mating without fighting but occasionally one runs across a nervous mare who will not permit the stallion to approach without kicking. In such case hobbles or a twitch may be used.

The stallion should be trained to mount the mare quietly from the side and only on command of the stud groom. Stallions are not the vicious creatures that many people believe them to be. If they are ridden or driven frequently in company and are handled from birth there is no reason why they should be any more difficult to work with than the mares or geldings. The man or woman handling the stallion must know him, and above all, must not be afraid of him. In France and Spain, male horses are seldom gelded, and the stallion is worked right along with the mare. I have raised and bred stallions of the Saddle, Thoroughbred and various pony types and I have never found that, given quiet handling, understanding, company and plenty of work they have been other than gentle and obedient both in the breeding corral and under the saddle. Our stallions are ridden by children in close order drill yet an occasional nicker is the only sign they ever give of their masculinity.

After breeding the stallion is returned to his stall, the mare should be walked for fifteen minutes. If she has a foal at heel the foal should have been in a pen where she could see him during the mating and may now be allowed to run with her. She is then turned out for two weeks after which time she is brought to the stallion every day for ten days to see if she is again in heat.

Normally, when a mare has once conceived she no longer comes in heat but once in a great while one runs across the mare that continues to come in regularly even when pregnant. I had such a mare and only realized that she was in foal six weeks before the foal was born when her bag became enlarged; veterinarians tell me this is not too uncommon but it certainly comes as a surprise!

BREEDING CLASSES

These classes, in which the entry is always shown in hand, i. e., led in by a groom or owner without tack other than a bridle, may be for stallions, mares, brood-mares (in which case the foal may be at foot) stallions with get, registered stallions of a given breed, Thoroughbred mares or mares other than Thorough-

bred, yearlings, two-year-olds, three-year-olds and four-year-olds suitable to become hunters. In the last four classes known as "suitable to become" classes the entries are generally for colts only or for fillies only.

Entries in breeding classes are judged on conformation, quality (fineness), substance (strength) and soundness. Separate classes for mares and stallions may also be judged on apparent ability to beget or produce hunters. In such classes transmissible unsoundness is only to be considered in the case of sires and dams of prospective sires and dams.

If there are breeding classes for both Thoroughbreds and other than Thoroughbreds in the hunter and the jumper division of a show catalogue, emphasis in the Thoroughbred classes will be placed on quality, in the other than Thoroughbreds it will be placed on substance. In all breeding classes each horse must be registered in the stud book of the breed and in addition to his name, age, sex, color, height (if over four years), his registered number and the names and numbers of sire and dam must be included in the catalogue.

BREEDS
Recognized

A recognized Breed is one which has an Association with a Stud Book and Breeding Record. Most Recognized Breeds have certain Foundation Sires, and all foals registered must trace their ancestry back to these stallions. For example, the three Foundation Stallions of the Thoroughbred are the Darley Arabian, the Byerly Turk and the Godolphin Arabian. Generally speaking, both the dam and the sire must be registered, in order for a foal to be registered. However there are certain breeds known as "color breeds," in which qualification is based on a specific color. Appaloosa, Palomino and Spotted Horse Associations are examples of these. In addition to the purebred Registrations, certain associations also have so-called "Half-Bred" books. These progeny may be registered if only one parent is purebred.

Below is a list of American Breeding Associations. See also each breed as listed alphabetically in this volume under the complete title shown in brackets.

Appaloosa

Arabian Horse (Arabian Horse Club of America, International Arabian Horse Association)

Barb (Arabian Horse Club)

Belgian (Belgian Draft Horse Corporation of America)

Cleveland Bay (Cleveland Bay Society of America)

Clydesdale (Clydesdale Breeders Association)

Hackney (The American Hackney Horse Society)

Morgan (Morgan Horse Club)

Palomino (Palomino Horse Breeders Association)

Percheron (Percheron Horse Association)

Quarter Horse (American Quarter Horse Association)

Saddle Horse (American Saddle Horse Breeders Association)

Shetland (American Shetland Pony Club)

Spotted Horse (Spotted Horse Association)

Standard Bred (United States Trotting Association)—see *HARNESS HORSES*

Suffolk Punch (American Suffolk Association)

Tennessee (Plantation) Walking Horse (Tennessee Walking Horse Breeders Association)

Thoroughbred (The Jockey Club)

Welsh Pony (Welsh Pony and Cob Society)

(Also the Miniature Mule Association)

BREEZE (*v.*)

To exercise at a brisk "breeze making" gait. Race horses are frequently "breezed under wraps" i. e., warmed up with a light blanket.

BREEZED UNDER WRAPS

This refers to a win in which the rider holds his horse in, so that he does not run as fast as he can.

BRIDLES

Adjustment of. The snaffle bridle is adjusted so that the bit just touches the corners of the horse's mouth. The pelham is adjusted so that it rests on the horse's bars. In adjusting the full bridle (bit and bridoon) the snaffle will be considerably higher in the horse's mouth than the curb. In every case care should be taken to see that the cheek-pieces are evenly attached to the crownpiece so that the bridle hangs straight, that the throat latch is loose enough to be comfortable (the usual test is the ability to insert three fingers under it) and that the bit is not too narrow for the horse's mouth. The adjustment of the curb chain, if one is worn, is extremely important. The chain should be unfastened on the near side when the bridle is put on. After the bridle is in place, the bit adjusted and the throat-latch fastened, the curb chain should be taken in the right hand and twisted until it lies flat, then hooked on the curb hook. Care should be taken to see that it is turned in such a manner that the upper edge does not cut the chin groove. The chain should lie loosely; one should be able to insert three fingers between it and the chin groove without disturbing the position of the bit, but it should not be so loose as to enable the horse to get it into his mouth. A slight pull on the curb reins brings the chain against the chin groove. Some horses have the habit of taking the arm of the bit in their mouths. The little loops on the arms and the extra ring in the center of the curb chain is for the lip strap, the proper adjustment and use of which will prevent such habits. The proper and comfortable fitting of the bridle and bit is all important. There used to be an old saying that there was a "key to every horse's mouth" meaning that if one tried a sufficient number of bits one would eventually find the one that worked best. But the horseman with light and sensitive hands can ride nearly every horse in nearly any type of bit with a maximum of comfort to both horse and rider. The school of thought that it shows good horsemanship to use only a snaffle bit is to be deplored. Rather, it shows far better horsemanship to be able to ride a nervous horse in a pelham or full bridle. The snaffle calls only for strength and the most mutton-fisted can get along in one. The more severe bridles require extreme dexterity and flexibility in the horseman, and, in turn, demand and get a much higher degree of flexibility in the horse.

Care of. A good bridle will last a long, long time but it must be well cared for. After each use the bridle should be well cleaned and with a good brand of saddle soap, working the soap into the leather both on the outside and on the flesh side. The bit should be kept shining. Steel wool is useful for this. A root of grass with soil clinging to it can be used very successfully. An old method is to put bits and other metal parts of the harness into a bag and shake them up with sand. The moment the bit is taken out of the horse's mouth the bit should be rinsed off. This will save work later on. The bridle may then be hung on the cleaning hook until the horse is taken care of. Every so often the leather will benefit by an application of Neatsfoot oil or other harness oil. When this is done the bridle should be completely taken apart, all hooks or buckles undone, so that the oil can penetrate everywhere. Use a small sponge in applying the oil and when the bridle is entirely dry wipe it with a clean cloth.

Bridles should be hung so that the reins can hang full length and are not looped back. There are specially made bridle hangers for this purpose; lacking them they can be improvised from saddle soap cans or half circles of wood. Do not hang a bridle on one hook or nail as it puts a crease in the crownpiece. It is a custom in the cavalry to change the adjustment of the cheek-straps on occasion when the bridle is hanging up in order that the strain does not always come in the same place. When the bridle is on

the rack the throat-latch may be brought around to the front, across and back again, the end run through the keeper of the buckle. This will keep brow-band and cavesson in place.

Types and parts of. The snaffle bridle consists of a bit, a brow-band, a crownpiece, two cheek-straps, a throat-latch and reins.

The pelham bridle adds a curb chain, and lip strap as well as an additional pair of reins.

The full bridle has a curb bit complete with strap, chain, cheek-straps, brow-band, throat-latch and reins. Under this goes an additional crownpiece and cheek-straps with the snaffle bit and reins. The snaffle reins are slightly broader than the curb and have a buckle at the center so that they can be used with a running martingale.

Any of these bridles may also be fitted with either a noseband or a cavesson. The former is a band with slots through which the cheek-straps run. The front is heavy and stitched. It is adjusted at the top of the bit. The cavesson is a noseband to which a head stall running behind the horse's ears and through both ends of the brow-band under the crownpiece of the bridle is stitched. Both cavesson and noseband have a buckle under the horse's jaw for adjustment. The purpose of the cavesson is to give more control. Some horses try to evade the bit when the reins are pulled by opening their mouths; the noseband or cavesson prevents this. Either one or the other is essential if a standing martingale is worn. Care should be taken in fitting the cavesson; if placed too high it will be useless, if too low it will press on the nostrils and restrict the breathing.

Another type of bridle with a buckle at the top of the crownpiece is often used for racing. The cheek-straps and crownpiece are in one. The throat-latch is entirely separate and passes through the brow-band to the rear of the main bridle. In order to keep this in place a bridle rosette is necessary. In putting this bridle together, first put the main part of the bridle through the brow-band.

Then slip the rosette over the loop of the brow-band, slide it as far to the front as possible and run the throat-latch through the rear of the brow-band loop.

A similar and very inexpensive type of bridle is one consisting of one very long strap with a buckle at one end, a shorter strap for a throat-latch, a brow-band and a bit, together with two rosettes to keep the brow-band and throat-latch in place and two keepers (little leather loops) to keep the bit snug. To put this bridle together hold the brow-band facing you, run the end of the long strap down from the top through the left loop of the brow-band and pull it through until the buckle is a few inches above the loop. Next slide on a keeper. Now run the strap through the left ring of the bit (the bit facing you, under the brow-band) from the outside, back through the keeper, back through the left loop of the brow-band, down through the right loop, through the other keeper, through the right ring of the bit from the *inside* this time, up through the last keeper, through the right loop of the brow-band and buckle on the top. Next put on the rosettes and throat-latch as described above. See *TACK, Parts of.*

BRIDLING

Bridling a horse is simple . . . to one who has had long experience. To the beginner it seems well nigh impossible. The latter will spend twenty minutes trying to get his bridle on while the horseman who has done it for years will have finished the job in as many seconds.

To bridle a horse take the crownpiece of the bridle in the left hand, the reins in the right. Approach the horse from the left side at about his shoulder. If you come at him directly from the front he will back away from you. With your right hand slip the reins over his head, allowing them to rest on the crest directly behind the ears. The reason for this position of the reins rather than sliding them back immediately on the withers is to give the horseman control should the horse, relieved of his halter, attempt to pull away suddenly. Should this occur the horseman grasps the reins together under the horse's throat and so retains his mastery.

If the horse is in a straight stall the

FIGURE 14. BRIDLING THE HORSE. THE LEFT HAND HOLDS THE BIT IN POSITION WHILE THE RIGHT HAND PULLS THE BRIDLE INTO PLACE AFTER THE HORSE HAS OPENED HIS MOUTH.

halter may now be removed. The horseman then places himself just behind the horse's head, facing front and takes the crownpiece of the bridle in his right hand. He slips the nose between the cheek-straps and through the cavesson or noseband if the bridle is so equipped. He raises the bridle, using the right hand, until the crownpiece is just in front of the ears, the bit dangling against the teeth. It is at this point that the tyro usually comes to grief for many otherwise amiable beasts are reluctant to open their mouths and accept the bit. But the solution is simple if one remembers that a horse has no teeth at the bars, and that the taste of human flesh on his tongue is extremely repugnant to him. With his left hand the horseman cups the horse's chin firmly, holding the bar of the bit across the palm and keeping it against the teeth with his thumb. Next he slips the ends of his fingers between the horse's lips on the far side and into the animal's mouth. The horse immediately opens his mouth and curls back his lips at which the horseman, with a quick pull on the crownpiece, brings the bridle up into position and slips it back over the ears. The whole thing can be done in a flash but takes dexterity. The important thing to remember is to use the right hand on the bridle crownpiece for pulling the bridle up. The left hand, cupping the chin and balancing the bit in correct position merely guides the latter and steadies the former.

A few horses, usually due to cruel

FIGURE 15.   PLACING THE BIT. FINGERS OF THE LEFT HAND ENTER THE MOUTH AT THE BARS TO CAUSE THE HORSE TO OPEN UP AND ALLOW THE BIT TO BE SLIPPED INTO PLACE.

handling, are exceptionally head shy when it comes to bridling them. In such cases a little different method may be tried. Instead of trying to slip the reins over the head from the front, unbuckle them, put them around the neck at the withers, and then slide them forward to just behind the poll. Now hold the bridle as shown in the accompanying cut. If the horse raises his head a steady pull down on the cheek-straps when in this position will bring it down again. Such horses are more easily controlled in a straight stall; it may be necessary to undo the halter, slip it off the nose and buckle it again behind the poll, leaving it attached to the tie rope and so prevent the animal from backing away and out of control during the act of bridling. With an animal that is head shy use coaxing and much patience rather than force.

FIGURE 16. BRIDLING THE HEAD-SHY HORSE. THE HANDS ARE HELD DOWN IN ORDER NOT TO FRIGHTEN THE ANIMAL. THE NEXT STEP IS TO PULL DOWN; THE CROWNPIECE WILL ACT ON THE HORSE'S NOSE TO LOWER THE HEAD, WHEREUPON THE BRIDLE MAY BE SLIPPED ON IN THE ORTHODOX MANNER.

BRIDOON
See *BITS*.

BRISKET
That part of a horse's body which is between his forelegs.

BROKEN AMBLE
One of the "slow" gaits with four irregularly cadenced beats.

BROKEN KNEES
When a horseman says a horse has "broken knees" he does not mean that the animal's leg is broken, he means that the skin is broken or has been broken and now shows a scar. In buying a hunter one looks for signs of broken knees as they indicate that the animal may not be very sure-footed over jumps. Some experts think that if a horse has one broken knee it means that he has received a good lesson, but if both knees are broken or if there are several scars it may mean that he has not learned it and will always be clumsy.

BROKEN LINES
A military equitation exercise. See *RIDING, Equitation Exercises*.

BRONC
In the West this means a mean, vicious horse that cannot be trained. In the East

it is frequently used to mean any western horse or cow-pony. The word "bronc" or "broncho" is from the Spanish meaning wild or untamed.

BROOD MARES

The period of gestation in mares is from eleven to twelve months. Some have been known to go as long as fourteen months. It is said that a mare carries a male foal twelve and a female foal eleven months though this is not always very accurate.

Several weeks before the mare is to foal the bag will fill with milk. In a mare bearing her first foal the bag may be full one day and perfectly slack the next. From twenty-four to forty-eight hours before parturition little white specks of milk known as "wax" appear on the ends of the nipples. Just before the foal is born these often disappear. Mares take only a very short time to bear their young, fifteen minutes to a half hour is the average. If a mare is straining for a longer period than that with no evidence of the foal appearing the veterinarian should be sent for at once. Some mares bear their foals standing, others lying down. Usually a mare will be very restless, bite at her flanks or get up and lie down again several times. When these symptoms begin she should be left alone in a very clean box stall but an attendant should stand outside the stall and watch carefully.

FIGURE 17. BROOD MARES IN PASTURE. *COURTESY OF R. C. WINMILL.*

Foals are born forefeet first, one fore-leg is extended, the other slightly bent with the head between the two. If any other part of the foal appears first the body will have to be pushed gently back into the mare and turned around before the foal can be born. Delay in doing this will result in the death of both mare and foal.

Generally the foal in its birth struggle breaks the transparent sac in which it is enveloped but if it does not do this immediately the sac should be broken by the attendant or the foal will suffocate. If the navel cord has not broken the attendant should cut it with sterile scissors and immediately paint the cord with iodine to prevent infection. If the foal's nostrils are filled with mucus they should be wiped clean.

The foal will lie quietly for a few minutes and then will attempt of its own accord to get up and nurse. The mare too will be on her feet a very few moments after parturition. The after-birth may follow immediately or she may not "clear herself" for several hours. It is best not to do anything about this for at least twelve hours after which if she has not taken care of it a veterinary should be called. After foaling, when the foal is sucking, the mare may be given a warm, very liquid bran mash. She should be fed lightly the first day or so and after that may go on a full diet. Many veterinarians now recommend the addition of vitamins to the diet of a nursing mare. For care of the colt after birth see *COLTS, Breaking and Training*.

BROOM POLO

This is a game suitable for intermediate riders. The rules are similar to indoor polo but a soft ball such as a basketball is used and brooms take the place of mallets. There is little danger and no head gear is necessary.

BROOMTAIL

A western expression meaning a small, stringy horse not worthy of breaking and training.

BROWN

See *COLORS OF THE HORSE*.

BRUSH

The fox's tail. See *HUNTING TERMS*.

BRUSH

A trial of speed between amateur drivers on a public highway. When racing was forbidden in New England and New York by the "Blue Laws," it became the sport to have a trial of speed with one's neighbor down the village street. These were called "brushes." For further details on how the trotting horse came to be through the popularity of these "brushes" see *HARNESS RACING*.

BRUSHES

Brushes needed in the stable

The dandy brush and the body brush are the ones most commonly used in grooming. For correct use of these brushes see *HORSE, General Care*.

BRUSHING

A horse that, while traveling, catches one ankle with the opposite shoe or ankle is said to have the habit of "brushing." This may be caused by bad shoeing, fatigue, or malformations of the legs. It can sometimes be corrected by correct shoeing but until all symptoms have disappeared the horse should wear ankle boots.

BUCEPHALUS

See *FAMOUS HORSES*.

BUCKEROO

Western term meaning a hard riding cowboy who usually spends most of his time breaking broncs. Sometimes applied to rodeo riders.

BUCKING

See *VICES*.

BUCKLING OVER

Buckling over at the knees

Old horses frequently buckle over, i. e., the knee appears slightly bent even when the leg is straightened. It is caused by a shortening of the tendon at the back of the cannon bone and is frequently the cause of stumbling. It may be partly corrected by fitting with shoes with raised heels but a horse that buckles over badly has passed his stage of usefulness and should be retired.

BUFFALO BILL

Known also as Wild Bill Cody. A famous scout, frontiersman and horseman whose real name was William Frederick Cody. He was born in Iowa in 1846. While still in his 'teens he became noted for his horsemanship. As the frontier moved west Cody moved with it. He became one of the Pony Express riders and thus had the opportunity of learning the trails and terrain of the West. During the Civil War he was an outstanding scout in the United States Army. He also took part in many forays against the Sioux and Cheyenne Indians, killing the Cheyenne Chief, Yellow Hand, in single combat. His name of Buffalo Bill was given him in 1867 when he contracted to supply the army with buffalo meat. He is said to have killed 4,800 buffaloes himself that year, sixty-nine in one day being his top score.

As the West became civilized, the Indians were conquered and the need for daring scouts grew less. William Cody conceived the idea of assembling a group of cowboys and Indians and touring the country putting on what came to be known as Wild West shows. Later he also toured all Europe with his shows.

He died in 1917 and was buried in a vault blasted out of solid rock on the peak of Lookout Mountain, twenty miles from Denver, Colorado.

BULLDOGGING

Steer wrestling. A competition common in rodeos in which the cowboy leaps off his horse, grasps the steer by the horns and endeavors to throw him in the shortest possible time by twisting his head to one side. He then ties his legs together with a short piece of rope, thus rendering him helpless.

The Mexican version of steer wrestling or bulldogging is very spectacular though practical only for exhibition or competition. In Mexican rodeos or *Charriadas* one sees an event in which the *Charro* (cowboy) gallops beside a steer, grasps the tail of the latter and pulls it under his own leg without slowing his gait. The forward momentum of the horse turns the steer around and pulls him off his feet. The *Charro* then lets go the tail and the steer promptly gets to his feet again. Another *Charro* with a lariat now ropes the steer around his horns or head, a second drops a loop over his hindquarters which is allowed to slip down over the hind legs, and both men then pull the steer off his feet and hold him.

BULLFINCH

A high thorn fence, unjumpable unless there is a hole through it as these are usually too high to be cleared. Common in England but occasionally seen here in hunter trials.

BUN EATING CONTEST

This game is most amusing for the onlookers. A rope or strip should be stretched the length of the hall or ring. From this are suspended a row of buns or rolls. Beginners play the game sitting in their saddles. They may not touch the buns with their hands. Experienced riders may play it standing in the saddle.

BURDEN *(of the horse)*

The addition of weight to the horse's back adds to his heaviness and consequently to the strain put upon his legs. One should differentiate between the live burden or weight and the dead weight. The dead weight is that used by the jockey in the form of lead inserted in pockets on his blanket to act as a handicap. This weight, carried to the rear of the center of gravity is indeed a handicap. On the other hand live weight which is shifted by the rider to conform with the gait of the horse is not nearly such a handicap to speed. The horse on the gallop moves somewhat like a seesaw, his forehand and hindquarters being lowered and raised alternately. If the weight is placed at the balance or center of the seesaw little effect is felt. See also *BALANCE.*

The amount of burden that a horse can carry will depend upon two things, his conformation and his breeding. The short-coupled, chunky little pony type will be able to carry much more weight than the rangy, sixteen or seventeen hand race-horse. Donkeys and burros often carry weights as heavy as themselves. In horse shows hunters are classified as to their ability or estimated ability to carry burdens, i.e., the lightweight hunter must be up to carrying one hundred and sixty-five pounds, middleweight up to a hundred and eighty-five pounds, and heavyweight over a hundred and eighty-five.

BURNS
Rope burns. See *INJURIES.*

BURST
See *HUNTING TERMS.*

BUSQUÉ
Roman nosed or having a bowed type of profile.

BUYING THE HORSE
The question of where to buy a horse is the first one that confronts every horseman desirous of graduating from the class of hirer-of-hacks or borrower-of-hunters to that of horse-owner. When horses were a part of every man's daily life a pride in ability to judge horseflesh became paramount, especially in the younger and more inexperienced rider. The professional dealer, knowing that the buyer would rarely admit to having been "stung" felt no qualms at all in improving his animal's appearance and performance by fair means or foul. Jor-

rocks' nightmare as told in *Handley Cross* tells how someone came to look at one of his horses and he, Jorrocks, could not find the ginger. This refers to the custom among dealers of inserting a stick of ginger under the tail of a dull beast to make him appear lively and spirited.

Many diseases which cause lameness can be temporarily obliterated if the dealer has warning of the coming of his buyer. Among them is founder in which the horse will walk tenderly until he is thoroughly warmed up when the lameness disappears. Vices, such as head shyness at bridling or fighting the girth may well be concealed by having the horse tacked up when the buyer arrives. For this reason if for no other the prospective buyer should never tell the dealer exactly when he expects to come and see the prospect.

The best place to buy a horse is at the breeding farm. Here the buyer will have a choice of animals all of the breed which he has chosen as the most suitable for his purpose. Breeders are very careful to be sure that the horses they sell are as represented, for their reputation and livelihood depend on how they please the buyers. One may pay a little more at the breeders but one is sure of getting a sound animal and if he does not turn out to be entirely suitable he can be returned after a reasonable time of trial and exchanged for another.

If it is not possible to go to a breeder go to as reputable a dealer as you can find. If you are not a thoroughly experienced horseman try and find such a man who will test the animal's gaits and manners and also get a veterinarian to pass on the physical fitness of your choice.

Many fine horses are sold at auctions and at the yearling sales but it takes a very experienced buyer to pick one of these for one has little opportunity to try them out and too often the fact that the animal is being offered at auction means that he is unsuitable for the work for which he was intended.

Beware of buying a horse from a

friend who has "just the thing." What may suit him perfectly may not suit you at all. But if a well known rider is giving up his string one may very readily find what one wants among them. In this case, a little inquiring ahead of time among riders who have been out with the horses to be sold may tell more than the short glance allowed as they stand on the auction block.

In buying a horse for yourself or for another think long upon the suitability of the mount to the rider. This is especially true of the children's pony. Too many parents, fine horsemen themselves, buy a young or inexperienced child a show pony. This usually results in a life-long distaste for riding on the part of the child and an immense disappointment for the parent. See also *MANNERS, tests for; VICES, tests for; SOUND-NESS, tests for; CONFORMATION; IDEAL HORSE; AGE, how to tell; and PONIES.*

BYE DAY

A hunting term meaning an unannounced meet.

BYERLY TURK

The Byerly Turk was imported into England in 1689 by Captain Byerly. He became one of the foundation sires of the English Thoroughbred, his most famous descendant being *Herod.*

C

CADENCE

Cadence is the rhythmic sound of a horse's gait. It is important to know and recognize the sound of an evenly cadenced gait as a variation in cadence means unsoundness. An instructor, riding in the lead of a group of beginners, can so accustom his ear to the cadence of the class behind that the slightest change in its rhythm indicating that a horse has shied, broken from a trot to a canter, halted, slowed down, etc., any of which might spell trouble, is instantly noted. Each gait has its own cadence or beat. The walk is a slow one-two-three-four. The trot is a brisk one-two, one-two. The pace is also a two-beat gait while the amble and rack are brisk four-beat gaits. The canter or ordinary gallop is a three-beat gait with emphasis on the first of the three beats. The very collected canter and the extended gallop become four-beat gaits. In using cadence as a test for unsoundness it is best to have the horse at a trot as this gait is the most evenly cadenced.

CALGARY STAMPEDE

This is the best known and largest rodeo held in Canada. Calgary is in Western Canada. The original Calgary Stampede originated before 1900. Today many thousands of people travel hundreds of miles to participate either as spectators or as competitors. The Stampede lasts several days and includes all of the ordinary rodeo events as well as special ones such as a chuck wagon race, exhibitions by the Royal Canadian Mounted Police, and Thoroughbred racing.

CAMP

To camp is to stretch the forelegs out in front while holding the back legs together in position. This was first developed in the ladies' harness horses. A horse, while camping, must first bring his legs under him before he can move forward. Coachmen taught their horses to camp so that they would not move forward while the lady was ascending or descending from the vehicle. This custom was later taken up by horse show people both for driving and Saddle horses. It is a trick very easily taught by tapping the back of each foreleg in turn until the horse places it in the desired position. If this is done each time the horse is halted he will soon come to take up the stretching or camping position without a signal from the master. If a horse, not trained to camp, stands so of his own accord it may indicate a weakness of the kidneys. Circus horses are taught to camp to such an extent that their bellies touch the ground.

CAMUSE

The opposite of *busqué; a cheval busqué* has a bowed profile or roman nose, the *cheval camuse* has a "dished" profile. The Arabians are noted for the *camuse* profile.

CANADIAN POX

This is a skin eruption which is highly contagious. Little clusters of pimples appear, most frequently behind the elbow and these turn into scabs which come off leaving bare patches. Treat with lysol solution.

CANNON BONE

See *HORSE, points of.* This bone, running from knee and hock to ankle is almost full length at birth. It is the bone referred to by the horseman when he says that a horse has "good bone." See also *BONE, LEGS (of horse).*

CANTER

A three-beat gait which, correctly speaking, is a collected gallop. The horse's feet touch the ground in the following order: on the "left lead" and beginning with the right hind leg the sequence is as follows, right hind, left hind and right fore almost simultaneously, left fore, followed by a period of suspension when all the feet are off the ground. One characteristic of the canter is the fact that either the left shoulder or the right shoulder leads, i. e., the leg on that side touches the ground somewhat in front of the other. In a true, balanced canter or gallop the hind leg on the same side should also "lead" its fellow. In a disunited canter the opposite hind leg will be in advance and the horse has a rough gait and may fall. See also *GALLOP DEPARTS.*

The canter or lope as it is also called

is the preferred gait of the West. It requires little effort on the part of the rider as does the trot. The lope, however, is not the collected gait of the show ring. In the canter, the horse, moving his legs in correct order, rocks back and forth with little movement. A horse with such a canter has been described as being able to "'canter all day under the shade of a tree." The Tennessee walking horse must canter absolutely straight with no diagonal movement as he has been bred to carry his plantation-owner at this easy, arm-chair gait, between the rows of crops. While these horses and the other Saddlers learn the canter with little trouble the trotting horse learns it with difficulty as his natural gait is to trot and he is loath to break it except to take the extended gallop. The plains ponies, on the other hand, have little of the trot in them and break readily into the canter or lope. The draft breeds canter very heavily, coming down with a jar at each step. The canter of the Thoroughbred is not generally as smooth as that of the Saddler for his breeding has been towards the speedier extended gallop, but many Thoroughbreds have very comfortable canters.

See also *LEADS; FLYING CHANGE; LOPE*

CANTLE

Back of saddle. See *SADDLE.*

CANYON PONY

In certain parts of Colorado there are deep canyons entirely enclosed by steep walls. In the past an occasional pair of wild horses has fallen by accident into some of these canyons. They may have misstepped in seeking forage or they may have been chased over the edges by mountain lions or Indians. In any event, once in they were powerless to climb out again. Thus imprisoned, they have propagated, and the resulting generations, growing in these confined areas where food is very sparse, have continued to shrink in size, becoming more and more stunted though retaining the physical characteristics of the true horse rather than those of the pony breeds.

CAPPED ELBOW (or shoe boil)

An injury caused by pressure of the horse's shoe when he is lying down. For treatment see *INJURIES*.

CAPPED HOCK

An enlargement of the covering of the hock due to injury is known as a "capped hock." See *INJURIES*.

CAPPING FEE

This is the fee paid by a non-member of a hunt when he goes out with the hounds at the invitation of a member. In the old days it was the custom of the hunt secretary, after the field had collected at the covert side, to go among them with his cap held out for donations from non-subscribers; hence the name.

CARRIAGE (of the head)

The carriage of the head depends largely on the build of the horse, his training and also on his breeding. The racing horse, both cold and hot-blooded, carries his head forward rather than up. The Saddler, on the other hand, has been bred for a lofty carriage of the head. Even the racer, however, should never be heavy of head giving the rider that unpleasant sensation of always having to be hauling up on the animal's head to keep him from dropping it between his knees. For this reason, in selecting an animal, the lightness of the forehand should be taken into consideration, remembering that the longer the neck the smaller should be the head. Horses which carry their heads low from habit may be helped by a thorough course in suppling exercises and by work in the bitting rig. In choosing a bit for this type of animal remember that the curb bit tends to depress the forehand while the snaffle tends to raise it.

CART (a two-wheeled vehicle)

In former times the types of carts were innumerable; now one sees very few. The dogcart was first developed for the purpose of carrying the hounds to the meet. It had high wheels and a box type of body in which the hounds traveled. The cocking cart, a still more lofty vehicle, was used for carrying fighting cocks to the mains. The governess or basket cart is often used with ponies and is considered safer than other types of carts because it is so low slung. It is characterized by a door in the middle of the back and two seats that face each other.

The Meadow Brook and Hempstead carts have a divided seat which folds back. Certain types of Irish carts have a double seat in which the four people may sit in pairs back to back, while the "side cart" has seats along the sides facing out. The cart, with the exception of the high cocking cart or certain types of tandem dogcarts, is certainly safer than a four-wheeled vehicle if one is driving a green horse; on the other hand it has a rough, bobbing motion. For types of breaking carts used in training young horses see *BREAKING CARTS, VEHICLES*.

CAST

To make a cast or to cast hounds. See *HUNTING TERMS*.

CAST HORSE

A horse that has fallen or lain down and, due to its position or the terrain, is unable to regain its feet is said to be cast. If the animal is excitable and cannot be controlled he may easily break a blood vessel and die in his struggles. Some horses will lie down in their box stalls and then roll over so that their legs are folded up and pressed against the wall of the box. It is fairly easy to extricate these as one has only to put loops of rope around the under ankles and then roll the animal back. If, in his struggles, the horse has crammed himself up against the end wall also and his head is bent back it may be necessary first to pull him away from that wall either by the tail or by a rope around his hind legs before rolling him over.

The most difficult problem is one in which the horse has become cast in a hollow so that his belly and legs are higher than his back and it is impossible to roll him onto his belly with his legs under him. A sling may be necessary but here again great care must be used as the horse may go into a frenzy of hysteria on feeling himself lifted.

If the horse gets himself wedged in a straight stall the best thing to do is to take down the partition between him and the next stall. Before helping him onto his belly, from which position he will be able to rise, make sure that his hind legs are under him but that his forelegs are stretched out in front. Try to keep the horse as calm as possible and do not let him use up his strength in unnecessary struggling; there is no more pitiful sight than a powerful horse struggling against his inability to regain his feet and many horses lose their lives in this manner. See also *FALLS, ACCIDENTS*.

CATCH WEIGHTS

This is a racing expression meaning that the horses running in the race which is advertised as being "catch weights" are not required to carry any specified weight.

CAVALLETTI

A series of jumps so spaced that they automatically place the horse in stride for a final obstacle are called a "cavalletti." Often a series of differently spaced bars set at different heights are permanently placed in the schooling area and horses are trotted or cantered over them as a part of their daily training. For work at the trot the bars are usually from six inches to eighteen inches in height and exactly four feet from the center of one to the center of the next.

For work at the canter they may run from eighteen inches to three and a half feet or higher. If it is desired that the horse take them in succession without an intervening stride then they are set at eight feet apart. If a stride between each is desired the bars may be set at from eleven to twelve feet apart, depending on the length of stride of the horse being schooled. For two strides apart one usually sets them at twenty-four feet apart. In using cavalletti as a means of calming the excitable horse which tends to avoid an ordinary obstacle a row of bars are laid on the ground exactly four feet apart and the horse is trotted back and forth over these until he takes them calmly. When this has been accomplished an obstacle eighteen inches high is set up eight feet beyond the final bar. The horse trots over the cavalletti and has space to take off without an intervening cantering stride. Some trainers keep this spacing until the final obstacle has been raised to two and a half feet; others take away the bar just before it and place it at the other end of the series each time they raise the final obstacle three or more inches. One thing should be remembered: in order to prevent the horse from anticipating a turn after taking the obstacle the rider should alternate the direction in which he turns each time he takes the course. See also *JUMPS, Types of.*

CAVALRY

The man, who, sitting on a horse could fight downwards, was at a tremendous advantage over his enemy on the ground. The early Persians and the Huns knew this. The ancient Gauls used a saddle tree which set them so high on their horse's back as to make one wonder how on earth they managed to balance there, much less fight as well. Alexander developed his Companion Cavalry with well disciplined drill and gave Darius a good chase with it. The Arab used the principles of selection in breeding his beloved War Mare who was destined to give fineness, speed and quality to every modern breed of light horse. The weight of the knight in armor required that those horses be bred for stamina and substance, and so on down to the present time when one finds the practice of the United States Cavalry of placing good stallions in the hands of farmers throughout the country that the general strain of horses may be improved. As long as horses played an important part in war it was to the great benefit of each country to see that the best possible animals were bred and raised. Now that horse-cavalry is retiring, for the most part, in favor of mechanized cavalry we will have to depend somewhat more on such sports as racing, hunting, horse-showing and polo to spur the interest in improving the stamina, quality and beauty of our horses.

FIGURE 18. AMERICAN CAVALRY OFFICER AND MOUNT. *COURTESY HARRY DISSTON.*

In addition to the benefits it has given us by improving the breeds of horses the cavalry of various countries has done much for the art of horsemanship. Fort Riley, the United States Cavalry School, Pinerolo and Tor di Quinto in Italy, Saumur in France, Hanover in Germany, Weedon in England and Vienna in Austria have been immeasurably responsible for the promotion of the equestrian's art in their respective countries.

The Olympic trials to which all the countries sent military teams for competition before World War II has also had its share in promoting interest. The careful study which the cavalry has made to determine the best methods of feeding and caring for its horses as well as the distance they can travel carrying a trooper with his equipment and still be in condition to fight on arriving at their destinations is of tremendous value to every horseman though he may never have thought of the cavalry as a specialized form of riding in which he has no interest.

Mounted close-order drill, designed primarily to enable a commander to move his troops across country, is one of the very best exercises in horsemanship that has ever been developed, demanding as it does, complete control of the horse at all gaits and in all formations. The general ability of the young riders of today would be greatly improved if all riding academies included practice in close-order drill for their students.

In the methods of training its horses the cavalry has many lessons to teach. Watch any open jumping class in a big horse show in which both military and civilian riders compete. The soldier will take his horse over the most formidable obstacles without using crop or sharp spur, with no excitement or rebellion on the part of the horse, while only too often one sees the professional civilian forcing his mount to take the jumps through fear of punishment rather than as a result of good schooling. I am told that at Tor di Quinto the horse is so schooled to jump at his rider's behest that for his final test he is asked to jump through an open window, from which he cannot see the landing. If this be true it would seem to be the highest possible means of testing not only the horse's obedience but also his faith in his master.

CAVESSON

A noseband attached to a headstall or strap running behind the horse's ears under the crownpiece of the bridle. The cavesson worn with a bitting rig has special rings for the longeing reins and a jaw strap to prevent the cheek pieces from getting in the animal's eyes. See *TACK, parts of saddle and bridle.*

In addition to the ordinary type of cavesson described above we have the *dropped noseband* as shown in the accompanying diagram. The dropped noseband works like the ordinary cavesson except that the strap runs around the horse's nostrils below the bit, and is therefore more severe. It is usually used with a simple snaffle bit.

CAYUSE

The Indian pony, descended from the Spanish horses imported into Mexico by Cortez. The cayuse is noted mainly for his stamina and ability to live off the land.

CENTAUR

The horse is the only animal in the world with which man may unite himself to such an extent that they move as one. The original conception of the Centaur, or "Man-Horse," must surely have been the result of man's wishful thinking and his visualized ideal of good horsemanship. Mexican and American Indians, when first confronted with the mounted Spaniards, took them to be Centaurs. Later, when they knew better and by gift or theft had acquired horses of their own they became themselves the nearest approach to the legendary Centaurs.

CENTER FIRE RIG

A single cinch encircling the horse midway between the pommel and the cantle of the saddle.

CERTIFICATION

When a purchaser asks a dealer if a horse is "certified" he wants to know whether or not the horse is guaranteed sound of wind and limb. Our friend Jorrocks mentions a horse-dealer who, when asked this embarrassing question, was wonted to say, "Warrant him sound? I wouldn't warrant he was a horse, much less sound!" The certification of a hunter means that he has been "qualified," i. e., has hunted for a season with a registered pack and may therefore compete in the "qualified hunter" classes. A certificate to this effect may be demanded by the secretary of the show before the horse is accepted for the class.

CESARESCO, COUNT MARTINENGO

Author of *The Psychology and Training of the Horse*. He is noted for being the first to put into words the fact that the "prime instinct of the horse is his excitability to motion."

CHALLENGE TROPHY

A cup or other trophy presented for a designated purpose, a duplicate of which is presented to the winner, the trophy remaining in possession of the club, donor or show. The following season it is again put up for competition under the same conditions. The name of each successive winner is engraved upon the original trophy. According to the conditions specified by the donor, the trophy may become the permanent property of the winner after having been won a designated number of times by the same contestant.

CHAMPING THE BIT

When a horse makes little snatches at the bit he is said to be champing it. Many well bred animals have this habit and some trainers consider it a very desirable one as in so doing the horse flexes the poll and relaxes the jaws. In a high-spirited, nervous horse it is also a way of expending his nervous energy when required to stand still. To induce champing of the bit, back the animal into a straight stall, put on his bridle with the bit hanging somewhat lower in his mouth than is normal, and fasten him in with side reins to the stall posts. Feeling the bit resting on the lower tongue the horse will begin snatching for it and playing with it. It is not wise to keep this exercise up for too long at a time, however, as it is somewhat of a strain on the nerves and also on the neck muscles.

CHAMPIONSHIP CLASSES

Those classes in which the winners of horses within a division compete on a score of points or on performance and conformation for the championship ribbons in that division. Championship, preliminary championship, final championship and grand championship classes must all be so announced in the catalogue. All horses eligible are required to compete, otherwise they lose the ribbons previously won. No entry fee is charged for the classes. In classes where the award is made on the record of the number of ribbons won in that show the scoring is folows:

Blue ribbon	5	points
Red ribbon	3	points
Yellow ribbon	2	points
White ribbon	1	point

In classes awarding more than four ribbons the lowest ribbon counts one point and each higher ribbon adds a point except for the highest ribbon which shall add two points. In classes in which the awarding of more than four ribbons has been announced but in which there are not enough competitors to give the number of ribbons announced the value of the ribbons is as just stated. Thus in a class where six ribbons were announced and only three given out the yellow would count one point, the red, two, and the blue, four. However, if it is stated in the catalogue that the management may reduce the number of ribbons due to insufficient entries as is sometimes done in stake classes, then the original scoring counts.

In computing the value of ribbons in the hunter and jumper divisions there are certain exceptions, namely, in CONFORMATION HUNTER CHAMPIONSHIPS ribbons count one half value if won in any of the following classes, Maiden, Novice, Limit, Suitable, Green, classes for Four-year-olds and under, and Handicap Classes in which a horse is required to jump three feet six inches. In HANDICAP HUNTER AND JUMPER CLASSES the scoring given above holds true but if the jumps are four feet the full value of the ribbon is awarded. In GREEN HUNTER CHAMPIONSHIPS the horse will receive full value for winning of ribbons in the classes named above but these scores will not qualify him to compete in the regular **HUNTER CONFORMATION CHAMPIONSHIP** classes; they do count and make him eligible for the **GRAND CHAMPIONSHIP**.

CHAMPIONSHIP—HUNTER PRELIMINARY

To qualify for this class a horse must have won a first or two seconds performing over a hunter course at four feet or higher except in the Maiden, Novice, Green, Suitable, Classes for Four-year-olds and under, Model, Hunter Hacks, Hunter under Saddle, Local and Fair Classes. If four horses do not qualify to compete then the next top ranking horses in total points regardless of firsts or seconds are considered eligible to compete. These horses are then shown at walk, trot, canter and gallop, they do not jump and are judged as independent hunters under the saddle with no consideration being given to the number of points won by each. If, as a result of score ties, more than four horses compete then the judges are to take soundness of wind and limb into consideration and excuse any horse that is unsound. Such horses are barred from competing for the Championship Final.

CHAMPIONSHIP—HUNTER FINAL

From the four or more horses competing as described above in the **HUNTER CHAMPIONSHIP PRELIMINARY** the management awards the Hunter Champion and Reserve Champion ribbons to the two horses having the highest *score* points. There is no judging in this class which always follows immediately after the **PRELIMINARY** Class. In case of a tie in score, however, the judges will then decide which is the winner on the basis of conformation, quality and substance.

CHAMPIONSHIP—GRAND

This may be awarded in the Hunter and Jumper division as follows:

a. Place winners
Winners of blues in classes designated in show catalogue as being eligible for championship to compete. Ribbon to be awarded to the horse which in the judges' opinion has shown the most consistent performance throughout the show and which has the best way of going and the best conformation, quality and substance.

b. Point winners
Grand Championship and Reserve Championship ribbons awarded on basis of points only.

CHAPARAJOS (or "Chaps")

Leather or fur "over-pants" which have no seat but which protect the cowboy from thorns and brush.

CHARGER (officer's)

The officer's charger must be a cavalry type horse with spirit and a good carriage. He is usually a little larger than the regulation cavalry mount.

CHARGER (officer's classes)

See *HORSE SHOW CLASSES*.

CHARGING

See *VICES*.

CHARRO

In Mexico there is an association called The Charro Association whose members, the *Charros,* are what might be termed "amateur cowboys" as opposed to *Vaquerros,* who are the "working cowboys." The *Charros* strive to perfect their horsemanship by continuous competition. Local *Charro* clubs are to be found in almost every small town; any man or woman or even youngster who is willing to work hard may join one of these clubs for a small sum and receive training in roping, riding, bulldogging, riding wild horses bareback, etc. At intervals the clubs send invitations to adjoining clubs to send teams to compete in a "charriada." Five teams of five members each generally compete in the vari-

FIGURE 19. A MEXICAN CHARRI-
ADA, ROPING THE WILD MARE.
COURTESY OF LOIS HOBART.

ous events. Handsome silver trophies are presented to the winning teams. In addition to the riding there is music provided by the *"Mariachi"* bands, and often dancing. *Charros* wear beautifully decorated costumes of brown, wine or black velvet trimmed with silver. Their felt sombreros are enormous, their horses well groomed and in good condition. In Mexico City, it is the custom for *Charros* of the local club to practice on Sundays in Chapultepec Park and to canter their gaily caparisoned horses up and down the bridle paths while the dark haired Senoritas watch admiringly.

'CHASER
Contraction of *STEEPLECHASER.*

CHECK, a
See *HUNTING TERMS.*

CHECKREINS (also called bearing reins)
A rein running from the bit back to the harness pad and whose purpose is to make the horse carry his head in a correct position. Checkreins improperly adjusted cause the horse great discomfort, but properly adjusted they do not worry the horse and do prevent vices such as kicking, boring, bolting, etc. Check reins may be either of the over-head type in which the strap runs between the ears, or the side type in which a strap on either side of the animal's head is run from the bit through Dees or metal loops that hang from the crownpiece, back to the terret of the harness pad. The overhead check is the more severe. A checkrein is also used with a bitting rig in teaching the young horse to hold his head properly. It may be used in teaching very young children to ride where, attached to a ring on the pommel of the saddle, it prevents the pony from grazing.

CHEEK PIECES
See *BRIDLES, Types and parts of.*

CHEEK STRAP
See *BRIDLES.*

CHEER (to cheer on the hounds)
See *HUNTING TERMS.*

CHEST
See Figure 51, page 150, *HORSE, Points of; CONFORMATION.*

CHICKEN COOP
A jump often used to panel country where the regular fences are unjumpable. The chicken coop is a good, safe jump and horses stand well away from it. For diagram see *JUMPS.*

CHINESE TAG
See *TAG.*

CHIN STRAP (LIP STRAP)
See *BITS, BRIDLES.*

CHRONICLE OF THE HORSE
A weekly publication was founded in 1937 under the name of *The Middleburg Chronicle.* At first a purely local paper it has grown in size and stature until it is recognized as the most important journal devoted to hunting, racing and showing. In its circulation of 10,000 are representatives from all fifty states and several foreign countries. It is the official publication of the Masters of Foxhounds

Association of America, the U. S. Equestrian Team, Inc., the United States Pony Clubs, Inc., the U. S. Combined Training Association, Riding Committee of the American Education Association, and the Roster of Packs of the National Beagle Club. It also has sections devoted to racing and showing. Each year it publishes special issues devoted to stallions, horse shows, ponies, polo, Keeneland and Saratoga Yearling sales, and the Roster of Hunts recognized and registered with the Masters of Foxhounds Association of America, Inc. The paper is printed in Berryville, Va., with editorial offices at Middleburg, Va. (Editor, Mr. Alexander Mackay-Smith; managing editor, Mr. Martin Resovsky.)

CHUCK WAGON

The wagon containing food, stove, etc., which goes out with the cowboys when they ride the range.

In the Calgary Stampede there is a "Chuck Wagon Race." The wagons are lined up and at a signal stove, food and equipment is put into them by the cook or a helper. The drivers then run a race around markers.

CHUTE

A narrow, box-like enclosure in the rodeo where horses are kept so that they may be saddled, bridled and mounted before entering the ring for competition. On the ranch the chute is used for branding, saddling green horses, etc.

CIRCLES

The horse must learn to execute a circle with his hind feet following in the track of his forefeet. To do this he must bend his spine from poll to dock. For diagram see *EQUITATION EXERCISES.*

FIGURE 20. CIRCUS DAY. THE PARADE FORMING TO MAKE THE OPENING MARCH AROUND THE TRACK. NOTE THE GAY TRAPPINGS AND GARLANDS, WHICH ARE TRADITIONAL. *CHARLES PHELPS CUSHING.*

CIRCUS HORSE

Who does not love the circus horse! He is so willing, so intelligent and so highly schooled. It is surprising that he has played so small a part in our literature. Horses used in the circus are of two varieties. The draft horse type which is used for the bareback riders, and the High School type. The former is always white and is chosen for his broad, flat back and the smoothness and evenness of his gait at a canter. The latter may be of any color. *Liberty Horses* in the circus are those which do their tricks and go through their routines without a rider. They are usually shown in groups where they wheel, bow, pirouette, find their places in the line according to number, etc. The straight High School work is done usually as a solo performance, the rider, generally feminine, dressed in a magnificent velvet habit with flowing plumes, putting her mount through various dressage steps and, more particularly, causing him to waltz, cake-walk or tango to the music. To the uninitiated it would seem that the horse kept time to the music of his own volition but as a matter of fact it is the rider who, with unobtrusive signals of reins, heels and whip, commands.

There is another and less dramatic member of the Circus Horse Family which deserves credit and that is the patient draft animal that in former days before the advent of the truck, played such a large part in the transportation of that great organization, the circus. Other animals might come before the spotlight to receive applause, human

FIGURE 21. THE EQUESTRIENNE AND HER MOUNT. *CHARLES PHELPS CUSHING.*

performers might risk their lives daily to please the audience, but had it not been for the draft horse and his assistant in time of need, the elephant, there would be no such thing as the circus.

The circus horse is greatly to be envied by other equines for he is given the very best care and treatment. He is never abused nor over-worked but is loved and admired from the time he enters his profession until he leaves it.

CLAIMING RACE

A claiming race is one in which the owner of an entry states its value before the race is run. The horse may then be claimed or bought after the race for the stated value. See also *RACING*.

CLASSES

See *HORSE SHOW CLASSES*.

CLAY FAMILY

The Clays were a family of trotters which most nearly equaled the Messengers for speed. The foundation sire was Andrew Jackson though the family took its name from his son Henry Clay. George H. Patchen was the most outstanding member of the tribe of Clay.

CLEANING

See *GROOM; HORSE, General Care.*

CLEAN LIMBS

When a horseman says that an animal has "clean limbs" he means that there are no blemishes such as splints, scars or puffs on them.

CLEANLINESS (importance of in feed and environment)

See *HORSE, General Care.*

FIGURE 22. THE CLEVELAND BAY STALLION, IMPORTED ORION. *COURTESY A. MACKAY SMITH.*

CLEVELAND BAY

This is the oldest known established breed of England and its origin is not entirely clear. For hundreds of years it was noted for its usefulness in agriculture, where it was said to have the strength and stamina of the draft breeds with more speed and willingness, and as a coach horse. Today the breed is imported and used chiefly, because of its qualities of stamina and substance, for crossing with Thoroughbred stock to produce hunters. As the name indicates, these horses are all bays, with only a small star being permissible and no more than a few grey hairs around the pastern and heel area. In height they run from 15:3 to 16 hands, legs are strong and muscular, and rather short, quarters powerful, long and oval, body not too long, head rather large but well carried on a somewhat long and lean neck.

CLEVELAND BAY SOCIETY OF AMERICA

Established in 1885. Headquarters, White Post, Va.

CLEVER

When a dealer tells you that a horse is "clever," he does not mean that the animal is intelligent. He means that it is quiet to handle, gentle, good-natured and free of vices, especially stable vices.

CLIPPING

See *HORSE, General Care.*

CLOSE A CAST

See *HUNTING TERMS.*

CLOSE ORDER DRILL

Close order mounted drill, or riding in formation, as developed by the cavalry is of the greatest use and importance in teaching control of the horse. For books giving exact formations of these drills consult the bibliography at the end of this volume.

CLOVER HAY

See *FEED.*

CLUCKING

A very bad habit practiced by some riders. When a horseman riding in company "clucks" to his horse to make him go faster he forgets that in so doing he may excite the mount of his neighbor. "Clucking" in a horsemanship class is justly penalized by the judges.

CLYDESDALE

The Clydesdale is one of the foremost draft breeds. It originated in the county of Lanark, Scotland, and received its name from the river Clyde. In 1715 a Flemish or Dutch stallion was brought into Clydesdale from England. He was exceptionally prepotent, passing his characteristics through both his sons and his daughters. The Clydesdale is not as large as the Percheron, Belgian and Shire breeds, his average height being from 16 to 16:2 and his weight about 1800 pounds. He is noted for his freedom of action, his color which is nearly always black or dark brown with a white blazed face and white stockings and for his enormous and flowing "feathers."

CLYDESDALE BREEDERS ASSOCIATION

Headquarters, Union Stock Yards, Chicago, Ill. Average annual registrations, 134.

COAT

The condition of the horse's coat is extremely indicative of the animal's general health. A dull, staring appearance, with hairs that refuse to lie in place, show that something is very definitely wrong and the animal should be carefully examined to find out the cause of this condition. The coat of a healthy animal, though it may be dusty from lack of grooming, will still have a smooth, silky appearance. Fineness of coat, thinness and shortness of hair in the unclipped horse also point to fineness of breeding.

COB

A small, chunky, short-legged, pony

FIGURE 23. CLYDESDALE STALLION, IMPORTED LINTON MARCEL-LUS. OWNED BY CRAIGIE BRAE FARM, JACKSON, MICH. *COURTESY CLYDESDALE BREEDERS ASSOCIATION.*

type of horse very common in England both as a light draft animal and a children's mount to hounds.

COFFIN BONE

A bone inside the horse's hoof. See Figure 33, page 114.

COLD BLOODED HORSE

Horses with predominantly Thoroughbred blood are said to be "hot-blooded," other breeds are said to be "cold-blooded."

COLDS

Horses catch cold more frequently when stabled in overheated quarters than from low temperatures. As colds go readily into pneumonia and other troubles a veterinarian should be called. Meanwhile the animal should be well blanketed and fed a laxative diet.

COLIC

Colic causes more deaths than any other illness. The death is due to failure of the heart from pressure of gases. Causes are bad feeding, overfeeding, poisonous weeds sometimes found in hay and feeding when the horse is in an overheated or excited condition. It may also be caused by a twisted gut. The symptoms are uneasiness, sweating, biting at the flanks and other signs of pain. The horse gets up and lies down again. It is advisable to keep a colic remedy prescribed by a veterinarian on hand at all times as the disease comes very suddenly and often at night. Hot blankets and rubbing with liniment, a hot enema as well as the medicine may relieve the pain.

COLLECTED GAITS

Every gait has its extended and its collected form, but the beginner must be careful not to confuse *slowness* of gait with collection. It is true that the collected gait proceeds forward more slowly than the extended gait, but it is more elevated in action, more showy and more animated than the extended gait. The so called "slow-gait" of the five-gaited horses and the Tennessee or Plantation Walker might be described either as an "animated walk" or a very collected rack. The collected trot of the Saddler is completely different from the extended racing gait of the trotter. The "show canter" is the collected form of the gallop. Horsemen desirous of improving their own skill and the flexibility and dexterity of their mounts would do well to change frequently from the collected to the extended forms of the various gaits, and back again.

COLLECTION

The horse must be visualized as being composed of two parts, forehand and hindquarters. It is up to the rider to unite these two parts (see *BALANCE*). The horseman must cause the horse to "collect" himself and thus be ready to move in any direction and at any gait demanded by the rider. To do this he must bring his legs under him. The rider induces collection by using his aids more strongly. In stride, as the horse becomes more and more collected, his motion will go into "elevation" rather than into forward movement. A "collected" horse is like an accordion which has been closed. The horse extended as in a racing gallop or trot, or over the hurdle, is like the same instrument stretched out. Certain members of the Italian school of thought do not believe that collection is either necessary or desirable, but to my mind it all depends on what kind of riding is being performed. Certainly the horseman going for a high obstacle will put on a better performance if he has his horse well collected, calm, and in hand as he approaches the jump than will the rider who lets his mount tear ahead at his own sweet will. There may be horses that have been so beautifully schooled that they are perfect judges as to rate of speed, etc., in hunting and jumping, as well as absolute masters of their own emotions. Such animals are certainly more rare than the intelligent horseman who, through the aids, demands and de-

cides the gait, speed and direction of the animal's progress. If one watches colts or high-spirited horses at play in a field one will see that not only do they put themselves through all the collected as well as the extended gaits, but they also do many of the very difficult High School and dressage movements, movements which a rider could not possibly demand without collection. See *AIDS, DRESSAGE; TRAINING; BETWEEN THE RIDER'S HANDS AND LEGS.*

COLORS OF THE HORSE

Beginning with the darkest the following are the basic colors of the horse. The abbreviation used in horse show catalogues, etc., to describe it is given after each.

Black, blk. . . . true black without any light areas.

Brown, br. . . . black with light areas at muzzle, eyes and inside of legs.

Bay, b. . . . reddish shades from reddish tan (bright bay) to dark mahogany brown, often miscalled brown. These shades may also be divided as follows though they are not so given in catalogues:

Brown and dark shades ...mahogany bay
Red shades .... Blood bay
Light shades .... Sandy bay

All bay horses have black manes and tails and usually black lower legs, these are known as *black points*. The black mane and tail is the deciding factor as to whether or not a horse is a chestnut or a bay, for in the mahogany colors of both classifications the body color is very similar.

Chestnut, ch. . . . shades from golden yellow to dark, reddish brown. Mane and tail are *not* black even in the dark shades but are about the color of the body hair or a little lighter. The chestnuts are divided as follows:

Liver chestnut . . . all dark shades, some have a red cast and some not.

Red and golden chestnut . . . the lighter shades, also called sorrel.

Palomino, p. . . . a color group having flax or silver manes and tails. The body color is anything from a very pale creamy yellow to a golden yellow. The Palomino usually has white legs and a white blazed face.

Dun, d. . . . a dead, gray-yellow with a black dorsal stripe, black mane and tail and sometimes zebra stripes on legs and a transverse stripe on withers. The body color may vary as follows:

Mouse dun ....dun imposed on any of the dark basic colors giving a smoky effect.

Buckskin dun ....dun imposed on light bay.

Claybank dun ....dun imposed on light chestnut.

Gray, gr. . . . with the exception of the Albino horse all so called white horses are born almost black. As they shed their baby fur the new coat comes in a dark iron gray which grows lighter and lighter with age. In some breeds the horse is very nearly pure white by the time he is a four-year-old, the Lipizzan being an example. In others, Arabian, Thoroughbred and certain draft breeds the horse may remain iron gray for many years.

COLOR PATTERNS

Roan, rn. . . . Any solid color with a mixture of white hairs throughout. Those with a roaned black coat are known as "black roans"; blue roans are the same with a few reddish hairs mixed in. Red roans are roaned bays, strawberry roans are roaned chestnuts. It is sometimes difficult to distinguish the gray roans from the grays, but there is a genetic difference in that the gray is born solid black whereas the roan is born with roan hairs mixed with the body color.

Spotted horses sometimes called "pinto" from the Spanish "paint," calico or paint ponies are correctly termed as follows:

a. Piebald, p.b. ....white and black

b. Skewbald, skbld. ....white and any color other than black.

An exhaustive study of coat colors has been made by Fred Gremmel at the Texas Experiment Station and his conclusions are that there is only one pigment which produces color in horses. This pigment is light amber. Whether the horse is dark or light, reddish, golden, brown, or black in hue depends upon the amount of pigment, the extent of clustering and the distribution of these pigment clusters in the hair-shaft. In a black horse the pigment is so thickly clustered that no light can penetrate, hence the horse is black. The variation in placement of the clusters in the hair-shaft account for the different shades in the lighter colors, those of the dun, for example, being all on one side of the shaft making the other more translucent and giving the characteristic watery appearance.

COLT

A male member of the equine race so designated from weaning to the age of four years. The female is called the "filly." Colts and fillies are also called foals (when still nursing), weanlings, (from time of weaning to age of one year), yearlings, two-year-olds, three-year-olds and four-year-olds. To understand the long-legged ungainliness of the colt as well as his amazing strength, speed and stamina from the time he is born one must go back to the prehistoric times and the *Hyracotherium,* the little, five-toed animal of over a million years ago. This little creature had no means of defense except running. In one of Rudyard Kipling's best loved "Just So Stories" one reads of how the kangaroo, chased by "Little Dog Dingo" hopped and hopped until his hind legs got longer and longer. In such manner the little *Hyracotherium* ran and ran and ran, through the centuries. With time he increased his height, for at first he was under twenty-four inches high. Gradually he lost four of his toes, one of the laws of evolution being that what is not used disappears; and of course the little creature could make better speed if he ran on the tips of his longest toes and not flat-footed. He passed through many stages of development, but for the first million years or so his weapon of defense was speed. The members of the bovine races have horns, the cats have claws and teeth, the wolves and dogs have tearing fangs; the kangaroo, another defenseless creature, has its long legs for speed but it also has a nice little pocket so that the baby kangaroo does not have to be on its own from birth. Even the hedgehog and the porcupine have their bristles, the skunk its smell and the snake race its venom or constricting muscles. But the poor little mother horse had no way to protect her young, her only defense was flight and, unlike the marsupials, she had no pocket in which to carry him. She could run with him and shield him to some extent, but he must be able to run too. And so he can. Within a few hours after birth the foal can keep up with the herd and within a few days he can outrun it. To accomplish this the foal must be born with long legs. The legs of a human baby are short in comparison to its body, but the legs of a foal are very nearly as long as those of its mother. In fact the cannon bone, the lower bone of the leg running from knee and hock to fetlock joint increases only slightly in length after birth.

The normal birth of a foal is only a matter of a few minutes. Within fifteen or twenty minutes of the time he is expelled, and sometimes within five minutes the little fellow is struggling to gain his feet. His grasshopper legs are totally unmanageable. Finally he succeeds in getting them all straightened out and in proper position. With a desperate heave he is up and stands swaying, but when he attempts to move, his legs buckle and he collapses panting for breath. Not for long, however. A second attempt is much more successful, he can not only stand but he can wobble over to the mare, nuzzling for her strength-giving milk. A draft of that is all he needs. Presently he can follow at a rather uneven gait to be sure, but at least he can follow. A short nap, another drink and our baby is able to trot. In a few short hours he will be frisking about, galloping in circles (and falling down frequently until he learns something about corners and at what speed they can be reasonably negotiated), an altogether independent little fellow. His cousin the calf, in this same period of time, has barely dried out and is just able to stand and move sluggishly. Why should he be stronger? His mother has a good pair of horns with which to protect him!

A few colts are born with two upper and two lower teeth. At all events these appear within the first week. At the end of that time the baby, watching his mother, is experimenting with grass as a substitute for milk, and not liking it. Usually he just chews and spits it out again, and as his legs are far too long for the length of his neck he must, perforce, in grazing bend them or eat off a bank. But it is not long before he is supplementing his good, rich milk diet with tender clover. His coat is thick and fuzzy and rain does not bother him. If the flies are bad he most sensibly stands under his mother's tail so that she may swish him, for his own little bush is too short at this stage to be of any use at all.

If he is allowed to run wild and is not handled he retains his inherited timidity and nothing will persuade him to let a human run a hand along the curly mane and down the toothpick legs, but if, as is proper, he is handled from the moment he is born, brushed regularly and halter-broken before the age of a month, he is as friendly as a playful kitten, as inquisitive and mischievous as a puppy and as demanding of attention as a two-year-old only child! The Frenchman, Baucher, in the middle of the eighteen hundreds, was the first man to realize this principle of handling colts gently and thus avoiding all resistance on the part of the colt when his formal lessons begin. Leland Stanford, in California, carried on this tradition and it is now the practice of every sensible breeding farm.

At a year old the well-grown yearling may receive his first lessons on the longe

FIGURE 24. THE COLT. FOALS SHOULD BE PLAYED WITH FROM BIRTH TO OVERCOME THEIR NATURAL TIMIDITY. THIS PONY FOAL IS TWO WEEKS OLD.

and in the breaking-cart. At two he may be trained under the saddle. At three his training begins to become specialized according to the career which has been chosen for him. But he should still be considered a colt and not given exhaustive work until he is at least five. The horse does not achieve his full size and weight until the age of seven, which corresponds in man to the year of official maturity, or twenty-one. Until that age the horse is growing in mental steadiness as well as in bulk. His actual height is attained several years before but not his weight.

So much for the general characteristics of the colt and how he grows and de-velops. Let us now take up in detail his education and health schedules.

Care and Feeding of Colts

Beginning at the birth of the foal it is essential that he nurse from his mother as soon as possible for the milk in the bag at time of foaling contains an essential laxative quality as well as being exceptionally high in vitamin content. Some foals have difficulty in finding the bag, they will try in every direction except the right one. Some mothers are nervous, especially with the first foal. Sometimes the bag is unusually hard and full, making it sensitive. In such cases the master must come to the assistance of the mare and foal. If it is just a question of the inability of the colt to find the bag the following is the procedure. Tie the mare in one corner of the stall or have an assistant hold her. Stand behind the foal, your body pressed against the little rump, one hand around the chest under the neck and the other hand under the jaw, the fingers encircling the chin. The colt may now be urged forward into the correct position by pressure of your body against the rump. He may be restrained, and if he struggles, controlled by the arm around the chest at the same time the hand under the jaw guides the small muzzle to the nipple, and, if necessary, milks a few drops into the outstretched mouth.

If it is the mare that is giving trouble it may be necessary to use a twitch and have an assistant hold up one leg while the colt is induced to nurse. As soon as the mare has had the pressure on the bag relieved by being well nursed out she will accept the colt and there will be no more trouble.

After the first day the mare and foal should be turned out in a grassy pasture where there is shade from the sun and shelter from storms. If the climate is warm they may be left out day and night. They should be brought in three times a day so that the mare may be fed and the colt handled. It is not wise to keep a halter on the mare at this time as there is the danger of the colt getting a leg hung up in it but the little foal should have a tiny halter that he may become accustomed to the feel of it.

As soon as the colt begins to steal bites from his mother's grain box he should have one of his own and receive as much crushed grain as he will eat readily. To this may be added cod-liver oil or a vitamin compound developed for horses. He should be thoroughly groomed every day for the brushing massages and strengthens the muscles as well as stimulates the circulation. Other than this handling and grooming the colt needs no other care until he is ready to be weaned.

Weaning

There is some disagreement as to the proper age at which to wean a foal. Some racing stables, desirous of getting quick growth on their foals in order to have them ready for the track at the age of two, wean them at six weeks, feed them four meals of grain a day, a total of sixteen quarts, as well as all the milk they will drink. That this puts growth on them is unquestionable but such horses are rarely the type that have a very long period of usefulness. All too often they develop weaknesses in leg or tendon when they should still, by rights be in the nursery.

Some breeders advocate leaving the foal with the mare until she weans him of her own accord. This will usually take place before he is a year old. But if the mare is in foal again it is a very severe strain on her to continue nursing a colt for so long and at the same time supply the nourishment to the foal she is carrying. Inevitably she will lose condition and both colts will suffer.

I have found that the average colt does very well if weaned at six to eight months. And what a time of woe is this weaning to mother and child! If possible the two should be in separate stables, out of sight and out of hearing of each other. For a few nights there will be a vast amount of nickering, especially on the part of the mare. They should not be allowed to come together again for from three to five weeks. By that time the mare's milk will have dried up and though she may still follow him about he will have lost interest in her. The colt will not resent his weaning nearly as much if he has a play-fellow, so if you have more than one foal to be weaned put them together in the same paddock and let them share a roomy box stall; misery loves company and they will console each other for the loss of their mothers. As for the care of the mare, as a general thing the milk will dry up with no help from outside. She should not be given any water for twenty-four hours and then watered sparingly for a week. She will do well with a bran mash to which some Epsom salts has been added. If the bag seems very swollen and hard it may be necessary to milk out a little, two or three times, and rub it with camphorated oil but never milk it dry and handle it as little as posible, for handling stimulates the flow of milk.

Feeding the Colt

From the time of weaning the colt should be given as large a feed of grain as he will readily clean up. He should be fed at least three times a day; four will not hurt him. He should have a good fork full of hay twice a day and the best pasture possible to find. Carrots are good for his coat and his eyesight. For general feeding schedules, value of different food, etc., see *FEEDING*.

Training the Colt

It has already been explained that the foal should be handled from birth and that he should be fitted with a halter before the age of a month. Let us now take up the individual steps of his training.

Halter-breaking

This, the first step of formal training, is the only time when the trainer may expect resistance on the part of the colt. After this step has been acomplished the training should go forward so gradually, each lesson leading to the next, that there should be no disobedience or resistance of any kind from the colt. But first the little fellow has to learn the lesson of the rope, what it means to feel the tug of the head-stall or the restraining pressure of the noseband.

A short rope or lead rein is first attached to the ring of the halter. The colt, being now about two weeks old, is allowed to follow his mother from box to paddock, but the trainer walks alongside him, holding the lead rope while an assistant walks beside the mother. The colt will follow his mother readily enough, he is not afraid of the trainer, but he may do so in short choppy little steps or small lunges. The trainer should talk quietly to him and steady him with very light pulls on the shank or lead rein. Once in the pasture the halter shank is unsnapped or, better still, a very short

six to ten-inch one replaces the long one so that the colt may become accustomed to the swinging end and so that he may be easily caught when it is time to come back again. When he is led back to the barn for his next feeding, the mother is again led ahead and the foal follows at heel, but this time the mother is stopped several times at the direction of the trainer who, as she is halted, brings pressure to bear on the leading rein in order that the foal may associate a slight pressure from the rear on his nose to mean that he must stop. Each time she is started up the trainer, not waiting for him to move of his own accord, tugs forward on the lead strap and the colt learns that a pressure behind the ears of the head-stall of the halter means go forward. So far there has been little or no resistance as the colt wants to follow his mother anyway.

The next step is a little more difficult. In this the colt is held stationary by the trainer while the mare is led away from him. He must be gently, but firmly, restrained from following her, the trainer putting his hand over the muzzle and keeping a strong hold on the halter shank. When she is perhaps twenty feet away the foal is led forward to join her but he must not be allowed to rush at her as he will try to do. During the same period that these lessons are being given the colt may learn further the discipline of the rope by being tied up in the stall for perhaps fifteen minutes each day, near his mother. The trainer should stand by, for if the colt struggles too hard to break away he may get his legs entangled in the shank and hurt himself. It goes without saying that in all these lessons the ropes and leather used must be absolutely sound and very strong. The colt that learns that by pulling he can break a strap or rope will have acquired a vice extremely difficult to break.

We now come to the third and most difficult step in halter breaking. The colt, at the behest of the trainer, must be made to go away from his mother. Two men can teach this better than one.

The trainer leads the colt as before, talking gently to him, while the assistant pushes him forward from behind. Undoubtedly the colt will struggle and rear and plunge. The trainer must be ready. He must not let the little fellow break away, nor must he pull sideways on the rope lest he injure the small neck or spine. With patience and tact and a strong hand the lesson is eventually learned and, once learned, never forgotten. From then on it is merely a question of enlarging the colt's experience by leading him frequently around the place. It is wise, too, to get him accustomed to stepping on strange floorings and going through narrow doorways. Some breeders and trainers teach their colts to climb in and out of trucks and trailers and to follow them up and down steps etc. Thus, when the time comes for the colt to be shipped he will have no fear of the van.

Leading him over logs and thresholds makes him both obedient and active.

The Hackamore

The hackamore, which is a bitless bridle, controls the horse by pressure of the noseband on the muzzle. Some trainers advocate the use of this bridle until the colt has become accustomed to obeying the reins. The simple hackamore is very like the head-stall of a bridle with a noseband to which two reins are fastened under the jaw. (See Figure 41, page 127). The regular hackamore with a hackamore bit adds two metal shanks to which the reins are fastened, giving great leverage. The colt may be driven in long reins, the trainer walking behind, an assistant at the animal's head until he learns the meaning of turning, starting and stopping. In driving in long reins the trainer should help the colt in demanding turns by stepping toward the center of the circle and allowing the outside rein to come along the animal's haunches at about the stifle or a little lower. This slight pressure on the outside helps the colt to learn to keep his hind-quarters on the track of his forehand instead of swinging them away. The trainer should use his voice to quiet

the colt and to tell him what to do. He should always use the same tone and the same words in commanding the colt to start, stop and turn. The assistant should first lead the colt and later walk beside him until the animal has thoroughly learned his lessons and responds immediately to the demands of the trainer. The trainer should not restrict his lessons to the paddock but should drive the colt down country roads well away from home so that he may get accustomed to strange sights. Thus he will not be afraid to leave the stable without the company of another horse.

The Longe

Along with the lessons in the long reins can go lessons in the longeing rein. Long rein driving, with the trainer afoot, is naturally at a walk or a very slow jog, but with the use of the longe the trainer can teach the colt to be steady at all the gaits and to take up each one on command. All that is needed is a

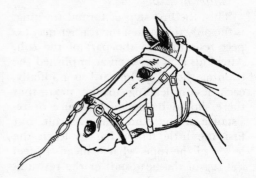

FIGURE 25. A LONGEING CAVESSON OR BRIDLE WITH LONGE ATTACHED.

thirty-foot rein, a trainer's whip such as one sees in the circus and an assistant.

The colt is now nearing or has passed his first birthday. He is thoroughly gentle to handle and has been driven or led a few times in the long reins. For longe lessons the trainer takes him to a small paddock or, preferably an indoor riding hall. The colt wears a cavesson. To the front of the noseband a ring is fitted. He also wears a harness pad or surcingle, fitted not too snugly. Bridle reins run from the hackamore loops to the harness pad. They are not attached to the regular driving terrets but to straps or loops low down on the surcingle at about the height of the animal's mouth when he carries his head in a normal position. The reins are left very loose. The end of the longe is now snapped into the ring on the front of the noseband. The trainer takes hold of the longe at about two feet from the end fastened to the cavesson. The rest of the longe is coiled in his left hand. The assistant walks on the other side of the colt. The trainer next walks in a big circle, the colt going with him and as he goes along he lets his hand slide down the longe so that he is now several feet away from the animal's head. By so doing the colt is forced to walk in a larger circle than the trainer. Gradually the distance is increased until finally the trainer is standing in the middle while the colt walks around him. The assistant, meanwhile, stays outside the circle ready to urge the colt on or start him up if he should stop. After walking for a while to the left the colt is asked to stop. With the aid of the assistant he is made to turn toward the trainer and go the other way, the trainer changing the longe to the other hand. The long training whip is useful in that, by holding it out as the circus trainer does, the colt is encouraged to keep out on the circle and not cut in; and by changing it from one hand to the other it acts as an additional means of telling the colt that he must

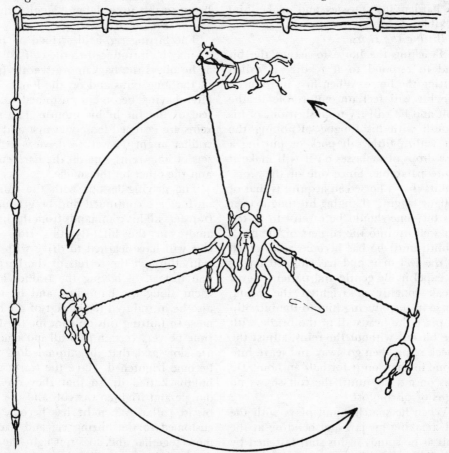

FIGURE 26. THE POSITION OF THE TRAINER IN LONGEING. NOTE THAT HE ALWAYS KEEPS THE HORSE BETWEEN HIS TWO HANDS.

turn and go the other way. A slight wave to the rear will show him that he is meant to start, and bringing it up in front of him will help him to stop on command. He should on no account be permitted to get excited.

When he has thoroughly learned the lessons of stopping, starting, turning and walking around the circle the length of the longe away from the trainer, the colt may be taught to trot slowly. How soon it will be advisable to teach him to canter on the longe will depend on how quickly he learns and on his excitability, but eventually he should be trained to take up any of the three natural gaits without restiveness and to continue them in either direction at the command of the trainer. If he is exercised for a half hour or so a day on the longe it will do much to harden his muscles and make him flexible.

Bitting the Horse

Teaching the horse to accept the bit and to respond to it readily is called bitting the horse. When first introduced the bit will feel uncomfortable to the colt and he will try to push it out of his mouth with his tongue.; Rubbing the bit with a little salt pork or putting a few drops of molasses on it will make it more palatable. Since one of the worst habits that a horse can acquire is that of tongue lagging (hanging his tongue over his bit) one should be careful to fit the bit well up into the corners of the colt's mouth until he has become accustomed to the feel of it and has stopped trying to expel it. Be gentle and patient, never speak roughly or frighten the young horse in introducing him to the bit. Slip in place the headstall of the bridle with the bit but without the reins, adjust the cheek reins, then go away and leave him alone to chew on it for half an hour. Do this once a day until the colt shows no signs of discomfort.

When he snatches and plays with the bit, relaxing his jaw and bending at the poll as he stands in his stall fastened by the side reins, the colt may begin his more advanced suppling lessons. Bridle reins are attached in the usual fashion. The colt, standing with the trainer at his head on the near side the latter takes the reins together about six inches and by little pulls induces the colt to relax at the poll and jaw and open his mouth. Immediately he is rewarded by having the tension on the reins relaxed and is given a pat and word of praise. The exercise is then repeated three or four times, the trainer being careful always to give the reward as soon as the colt obeys. Next the head may be gently raised and lowered by raising and lowering the reins, and it may be turned from one side to the other. The colt must not be allowed to move from his place while these exercises are being given and they must only go on for a few minutes at a time or the colt will get restless and begin to put up a defense against them.

The Bitting Rig

The bitting rig, as described on page 37 may be introduced to the colt as soon as he obeys the hackamore readily both in the long reins and on the longe, and after having become accustomed to the feel of the bit in his mouth. The side reins are fastened loosely at first and the trainer might do well to drive with two sets of long reins, one on the hackamore and the other on the snaffle.

The driving lessons with the trainer on foot are continued and he gradually transfers all his commands from the hackamore to the bit. By this time the colt will have learned to drive with the reins through the terrets of the harness pad instead of having the trainer hold them along the haunches, and he may also be introduced to the rest of the harness. In putting this on him for the first time be very certain that all movements are slow and that the animal does not become frightened. Have the traces and holdback tied up so that they do not dangle and frighten the colt and use the breast collar. When he has become accustomed to the bitting rig and hackamore together and does not fight the bit the hackamore may be done away with and the colt may be fitted with an ordi-

FIGURE 27. LONGEING IN THE BITTING RIG (DUMB JOCKEY).
FROM PRACTICAL HORSE BREEDING, *BY JACK WIDMER, PUBLISHED BY CHARLES SCRIBNER'S SONS. USED BY COURTESY OF THE AUTHOR AND PUBLISHER.*

nary hunting snaffle bridle. He may now take his longeing lessons in the bitting rig and if his head carriage is not good it may be corrected by the adjustment of the short reins to the arms of the bitting rig. He may also, at this time, be taught to follow on a lead from a mounted horse, still wearing his bitting rig, and may be exercised in this way along country roads, becoming more accustomed to traffic and other strange sights.

The Breaking Cart

For a description of the breaking cart see page 43. When the colt has thoroughly mastered the lessons previously described he may have his first lessons in the breaking cart. There are three new things which he must learn, one, to pull against the weight of the breast collar on his chest, secondly, to turn against the shafts, and thirdly, to hold back against the weight of the cart on the down grades.

He may be greatly helped in learning the first lesson if the assistant starts the cart rolling for him from behind the first few times. The trainer at this stage will still be walking along beside the cart driving with the long reins and there may well be another assistant ready to steady the colt at the head if he gets upset at the sound of the wheels. As soon as he has learned to start and stop quietly the trainer may get into the cart and drive from there but for a little while there should still be someone on foot in case of emergency. These lessons should be given in some quiet spot, preferably a training paddock out of sight of the stable or in the indoor hall.

Teaching the horse to turn against the shafts is greatly helped if the breaking cart is equipped with individual brakes for each wheel. Lacking these the assistant walking at the rear can help by holding back the cart on the turns and the assistant at the head should walk beside the colt's head while the command for the turn comes from the driver. The colt should be turned in large circles and figure eights until he is thoroughly accustomed to the feel of the pressure of the shaft against him.

Breaking carts are usually made with metal bars against which the tugs press and so do not require breeching. The horse soon learns to put his weight against the tugs and hold back but he may be frightened when he is first introduced to the breeching and feels the breeching strap pushing against his haunches. One method of getting him accustomed to this is to put him in a straight stall for a while and put a broad leather or webbing tape across behind him. He will soon learn the feel of this as he backs up in his stall and the breeching will not bother him so much, meanwhile the assistant who walks at the rear of the cart for the first lesson or so can help by holding back some of the weight on the hills.

Two or three lessons are generally all that are needed to teach the colt to go readily in harness and after that he should be driven regularly. Just be sure that the harness and cart are strong and

that the colt has had sufficient other training to be willing to obey the trainer without resistance and to have confidence in him. A carrot and a pat on the shoulder are simple rewards and the colt will work the better for them.

Introduction to the Saddle

There is much controversy among professional trainers as to when a young horse should first be ridden. Racing stables have their colts mounted and ridden before they become two years of age. Other trainers feel that no weight at all should be put on a young horse's back until he is at least three and a half. Certainly too much weight at an early age will bring later troubles in the form of a sway back or leg ailments. Probably the colt that carries no weight at all until the fall before he is three, and then no more than a hundred and twenty-five pounds until he is almost four, will suffer no serious damage to his soft bones.

Let us suppose that our colt is rising three. He has learned his lessons on the longe in both the hackamore and the simple snaffle bridle. He is accustomed to the feel of the bitting rig. Preparatory to mounting him for the first time the trainer must make him familiar with the saddle. He will show this new piece of equipment to the colt while he is in his stall, letting him smell it. Having taken off the stirrups and girth, and when the colt shows no signs of fear, he will place it lightly on his pupil's back. He will then attach the girth, but will not girth him up snugly, only drawing it tight enough to keep the saddle from turning. The colt may now be led and longed in the saddle.

The following day the stirrups, run up on the leathers, will be attached to the saddle. After the lesson the trainer will pull them down and let the colt become accustomed to seeing them swinging, but they should be run up again before removing the saddle.

Mounting

One assistant should be on the off side of the colt, a second should give the trainer a leg up and the latter should spring as lightly into the saddle as possible. If the colt has been properly schooled up to now, he will show no resentment. The trainer should sit quietly a moment, patting him and talking to him and then should quietly dismount. He may then reward the colt with a carrot, after which he mounts again. When the colt stands without fear one of the assistants may lead him a few steps, the rider having the reins in his hands and a light feel on the mouth. Only a few steps the first day. The next he may ride a little further and, if the colt is quiet he may dispense with the helper. If there is any sign of fear or resistance on the part of the colt at this stage of the training it is because the trainer has not done his job properly. Gradually the colt is asked to repeat the lessons he has learned in the breaking cart and on the longe at the behest of the man in the saddle. The latter must be sure that from the beginning he accustoms the colt to the aids and that he uses them all. He must never turn without applying his weight and legs correctly, etc. The colt must be taught to work in circles and figure eights at all the gaits, to start and stop readily, to back, and to be willing and flexible in everything he does. All this takes some time, but patience brings its own reward. By the end of his second year the colt should be well on the way to becoming a very satisfactory Saddler. See also *RIDING, THE AIDS, THE REINS, Use of; COLLECTION, JUMPING, EQUITATION FIGURES, DRESSAGE.*

COMBINATION HORSES

Horses that are trained and used both for riding and driving. See also *COMBINATION CLASSES under HORSE SHOW CLASSES.*

CONDITIONING

Making a horse fit. See *HORSE, General Care; FEEDING.*

CONESTOGA HORSES

A breed of horse descended from the Flanders horse which was shipped to Manhattan Island in 1629 by the Honorable Pieter Evertsen Hueft. These horses were justly prized on the farms of Pennsylvania and were used to pull the "Prairie Schooners."

CONFIDENCE (Of the horse in his rider and vice versa.)

The horse is a timid creature. He depends upon the steady hand and the judgment of his rider for confidence. The moment the rider, through indecision of application of the aids, or by his loose, insecure seat, conveys to the horse that he has not confidence in himself, the horse will know it and lose steadiness. The young horse will refuse to pass usual sights, he will shy and his gaits will be uneven. All this will tend to decrease the confidence in himself or the rider. The horse that has vices will take this opportunity to display them. He will kick at the nearest horse, buck and generally show off his bad manners. It will therefore be readily seen that only a sure, confident horseman should ride a young, partly trained animal, for the timid rider will quickly ruin the high-spirited, nervous colt.

But how is the beginner to gain confidence and also show the horse that he has confidence in his own ability? First by riding only horses which are specially schooled for beginners. Secondly, by making these horses obey absolutely. The rider who allows his horse to make up his own mind as to what gait should be assumed, who permits him to dawdle behind his fellows and then catch up at a canter or to travel so close to the rider in front that he almost steps on the other horse's heels; who, in a ring or indoor hall allows his horse to cut away from the wall and towards the center, is only telling his horse that he is merely a passenger and that the horse may do what he likes. Know your horse, anticipate his actions and make all the decisions yourself. Then your horse will know that he may depend on you when something terrifies him and he will be the better for your handling of him, not the worse.

CONFORMATION

The build of a horse. The ideal conformation of each type of horse is discussed under each breed.

CONGESTION OF THE LUNGS

This is due to the presence of abnormal quantities of blood in the lungs and may be caused by a variety of reasons, including bacteria, medicines, exposure to bad weather and a cardiac condition brought on by overwork.

The symptoms are dilated nostrils, very exaggerated respiration, suddenly increased temperature and cold sweat. The horse extends his neck and is in a staggering condition, unable to move. First Aid treatment consists of giving him air, covering him with warm blankets (coats will do if the horse gets the attack on the hunt field), removal of the saddle and drenching the animal with whisky or brandy well diluted. Bleeding from the jugular vein will also relieve the condition. The veterinarian should be sent for at once and the convalescence will be slow. Pneumonia often follows.

CONNEMARA

In the northwestern portion of "Southern" Ireland lies the district of Connemara. It is rocky, with sparse vegetation. Most of the natives there speak only Gaelic. In this area we find a distinct type of pony, the Connemara. It is, like the Shetland, Exmore and most other ponies, a direct descendent of the arctic wild ponies. The typical Connemara may run from thirteen and a half hands to fourteen one or two. It is built more along the lines of the Welsh than of the Shetland pony. Its most oustanding characteristic is its ability to jump. Bays and greys are common, also different shades of chestnut. Blacks and spotted Connemaras are rare. They are used for driving and riding, can both pull and carry heavy weights. They are bred extensively as hunting ponies also. In the United States the most famous Connemara emigrant was Little Squire, a thirteen-and-a-half-hand grey that in his heyday beat all the best jumpers (horses and ponies) of the United States and Canada. He cleared five feet easily and many times went much higher.

CONSTIPATION

Newborn foals are sometimes constipated and the condition should be immediately relieved by means of a warm enema. The first milk in the bag contains a laxative which works in normal conditions but sometimes this is not enough. Constipation in older horses should be treated with laxative foods such as bran mashes with a little Glauber salts or Epsom salts added. In severe cases an enema may be advisable.

CONTRACTED HEELS

A condition brought about by bad shoeing in which the foot narrows at the heels. This may cause severe lameness. See FEET.

CONTROLLING THE HORSE
See RIDING.

COOLERS

Light woolen covers extending from behind the ears to the dock and thrown over a horse after racing, polo or other strenuous work while he is being walked to cool him out are known as "coolers."

COOLING LOTIONS

Cooling lotions are useful to have around the stable for use on sprains and strains. Rubbing alcohol and the well known "white liniment" are usually favored. The latter can be purchased in the form of tablets. In applying a cooling lotion the bandage should be very heavy with plenty of absorbent cotton and should be kept wet.

COOLING OUT A HORSE
See HORSE, General Care.

COPPERBOTTOM
See *FAMOUS HORSES.*

CORINTHIAN
Classes which require that the riders appear with hunting appointments. See also *HORSE SHOW CLASSES; APPOINTMENTS, Hunting.*

CORN
See *FEED.*

CORONET
See Figure 51, page 150. *HORSE, Points of the.*

COUGHS
Certain types of coughs are symptoms of other diseases. The hard, dry cough accompanied by breaking wind is characteristic of "heaves." Coughs due to colds usually yield to a good cough mixture. Any horse with a cough should have both his grain and his hay well wetted down and he should not be ridden where there is much dust.

COUNTERCHANGE (of hands)
This is a dressage movement in which the horse, being on the traversal and moving laterally and forward in one direction, changes to a traversal in the other direction without interruption or change of cadence and gait. For diagram and exact explanation see *RIDING, The Advanced Rider.*

COUPLES
Two straps or collars fastened together and used on hounds. It is customary to keep young hounds coupled in pairs during their training periods when they are first taken out on the road.

COURTESY (when riding in company.)
There are certain little rules of courtesy which should be carefully adhered to when riding in company. Adjust the speed of your gait to the gait and ability of the slowest and poorest rider in the group.

Watch your horse for signs of his intention of nipping or kicking at his fel-

FIGURE 28. ARGENTINE GAUCHOS MOUNTED ON CRIOLLOS. NOTE THE SWINGING GAIT INHERITED FROM DESERT ANCESTRY AND THE BITLESS BRIDLES TYPICAL BOTH OF THE PAMPAS AND OF ARABIA. *COURTESY OF THORNTON CHARD.*

low. If he does the former, turn his head slightly away from your companion and rein back a step. If he tends to kick, swing his head *towards* the other horse and direct your companion to do likewise, at the same time give him a sharp rap with a riding crop. But remember that the punishment is only efficacious if it comes within five or ten seconds of the offense, thirty seconds is too late.

Do not "cluck" at your horse, it will tell your companion's horse also to increase his gait.

Never ride up from behind a group suddenly or rapidly, and never pass a group without first obtaining permission from its leader.

If someone wishes to pass you, turn your horse's head towards them and back off the trail to give them room.

In going through a gate, hold it until the person behind has caught it. In passing under low hanging trees, push through them and do not hold them, they will swing back into place before the person behind you reaches them.

If it is necessary for one rider to dismount, wait with him and hold his horse until he has mounted again and is firmly fixed in the saddle, then catch up to the group at a slow speed.

In leading a group down hill, make your horse take short steps at the bottom until all are down. Allowing him to take up an extended stride on the walk will cause the others to catch up at a trot while still on the hill.

Warn riders behind you of unsafe terrain.

Keep well to the side on public highways and do not cross until you are certain that it is safe. Where a long column of riders has to cross it is best to post "road guards" who will keep back the approaching cars until all have passed.

Do not wave your stick or hat around,

FIGURE 29. AN AMERICAN COWBOY WITH HIS PACK HORSE AND HIS COWPONY. NOTE THAT, LIKE MOST OTHERS OF HIS BREED AND TRAINING, THE COWPONY IS TRAINED TO STAND QUIETLY WHILE THE REINS ARE PULLED FORWARD OVER HIS HEAD. *CHARLES PHELPS CUSHING.*

nor catch at overhanging branches, you may frighten your own or your companion's horse.

COVERT

Sometimes spelled **COVER**. A copse or underbrush into which hounds are put to search out the fox.

FIGURE 30. FANCY TRAPPINGS FOR THE COWPONY. *COURTESY OF MADISON SQUARE GARDEN.*

COWBOYS

Men who make their living herding cattle on the Western Ranches. In the East the tyros who imitate the Western riding, or what they deem to be Western riding as learned at the moving picture theater, are sometimes call "Drugstore Cowboys" or "Garage Cowboys."

COWHOCKED

A horse whose hocks bend in too much behind and whose feet splay out is said to be "cowhocked."

COWPONY

The horse used by the cowboy. These horses are noted for their stamina, speed for distances and their dexterity in turning. They are not noted for their beauty although some are good looking horses due to the infusion of Arab or thoroughbred blood. See also *BREEDS.*

CRACKED HEELS

See *INJURIES, Cracked heels or scratches.*

CREST

See Figure 51, page 150. *HORSE, Points of.*

CRIBBING

A common vice the cause of which is unknown. The horse bites continually on any edge, preferably wood. As he does so he stiffens the muscle and tendon of the throttle and emits a characteristic grunt. Windsucking, a similar vice, is more serious as in this the horse actually sucks in wind which may cause colic. Some authorities think that cribbing is caused by too early weaning. Others classify it as a nervous habit. Some think it is from stomach troubles, the horse, having no vomiting muscles, tries to belch in this manner. Both windsucking and cribbing can be controlled by putting a tight, broad strap around the throat and neck just behind the ears. This will not interfere with eating or drinking but will prevent the animal from distending the tendon. Cribbing and windsucking constitute unsoundness.

CRIOLLO

The Criollo is the cowpony of South America. Like our own mustangs he is a descendant of imported Spanish horses. He is tough, wiry and fast, and though not beautiful is well suited to the work he is required to do. Mr. A. F. Tschiffely describes in his book, *Tschiffely's Ride,* how he rode ten thousand miles from Buenos Aires to Washington, D. C. on Gato and Mancho, two Criollo ponies.

CRITTER

Western term meaning calf, sometimes used to mean any cattle.

CROP

The stick carried for ordinary riding. It is usually of leather with whalebone or rawhide inside. Other varieties of crops are the *racing bat,* a crop with leather tags along each side, and the *hunting thong.* The latter is of hard wood, the bark left on and a natural crook forming the handle or hook. At the other end a leather loop is attached through which runs the long, braided leather huntsman's thong used in controlling the hounds. In horse show classes

calling for appointments the professional huntsman or whip carries his thong hanging down along the horse's shoulder when entering the ring, while the amateur carries his coiled in his hand.

CROP EARED

In the old days it was customary to crop a horse's ears to make them appear smaller. A horse with small ears may still be called "crop eared."

CROSSTAG

This is a game suitable for intermediate riders. The rules are similar to the same game when played on foot, i.e., if a player crosses between the person who is "it" and his quarry, the pursuer must leave his original victim and chase the new one.

CROUP

See Figure 51, page 150. *HORSE, Points of.*

CROWN PIECE

See *BRIDLES.*

CRUPPER, or crupper-strap

That part of the harness which runs from the harness pad under the dock. Although a crupper is not correct for riding one occasionally has to use one on a low-withered, round-backed pony to keep the saddle from riding forward on the shoulders. It may be attached to the saddle by means of a ring affixed at the cantle. Jorrocks, whose opinion is always contrary, advises buying a dun horse because the stripe down his back will make people think you are "riding with a crupper which is werry stylish!"

CRUSADER'S SADDLE

See *HORSE, Origin and Development of; SADDLE, History of.*

CUB HUNTING, CUBBING

Early in the fall, before the regular hunting season begins the huntsman takes his hounds to the coverts to steady the young ones and to teach the new litters of foxes that when they hear the baying pack it is better to break out of covert and run straight than to stay home and wait to be routed out. This opportunity is also taken by owners of young horses and parents of youthful riders to initiate them into the ways and traditions of the hunt field. In introducing these young riders and horses it should be remembered that the huntsman is there for a serious purpose and nothing should be done to obstruct him in his work. Children should not be allowed to chatter when hounds are thrown in, nor to get in the way. Young horses should not be "larked" over fences.

In cub hunting the formal uniform of the hunt is not worn, but field and hunt servants alike appear in what is known as "rat-catcher," i.e., informal, clothes.

CURB

This is a bony enlargement at the back of and just below the hock. See *INJURIES*.

CURB CHAIN

See *BITS, BRIDLES*.

CURBY HOCKS

The line from the point of the hock down to the fetlock joint should be straight. A curb is a slight enlargement on that line a little below the hock and horses with such blemishes are said to

FIGURE 31. CUTTING HORSES IN ACTION. *COURTESY OF CUTTIN' HOSS ASSOCIATION.*

have "curby hocks." For treatment see *INJURIES*.

CURRY COMB
See *GROOM*.

CUT AND COME AGAIN COUNTRIES
A favorite expression of our friend Jorrocks. He was not a good horseman though he loved to hunt. Hunts where the terrain and jumps were somewhat stiffer than he cared to negotiate he termed "cut and come again countries."

CUT AND LAID FENCE
See *HUNTING TERMS*.

CUTTING
A competition to show the training of the ranch horse. The horse must cut out animals from herd with no signal of any kind from his rider. The well-trained cutting horse is complete proof of the innate intelligence of the horse; he must think out and plan his own strategy. Competitions in cutting are a part of every Western Show. The judges are experienced and their obligation is to choose the horse which does the best and fastest job, with no help from his rider.

CUTTING OUT
Calves, steers, specified horses etc. from the herd. Very often it is necessary that one particular animal be separated from the rest. The cowboy, on a well-trained pony "cuts him out" from the herd by heading him off and cornering him or bringing him into the open where he can be roped.

CUTTING PONY
Western term meaning a cowpony that has been especially schooled in cutting out calves, etc., from the herd.

D

DAILY DOUBLE
A bet on two horses to win the first two races of a given day. If *both* horses selected do not win the bet is lost.

DAISY-CUTTER
Saddle-horse or hackney men's terms for the racing trotter or Thoroughbred. The saddle man is proud of the way his pet picks up his feet "until his knees knock his chin" as the expression goes. The same goes for the "fine harness" class of horse. But the race-horse puts all his energy in lengthening his stride and his feet are raised only a few inches off the ground, hence the term "daisy-cutter."

DAM
The mother of a horse. The mother or father's mother, in other words the grandmother, would be called the second dam, the great-grandmother the third dam, etc.

DANDY BRUSH
See *GROOM*.

DARLEY ARABIAN
One of the three Arab stallions which were imported into England about 1700, bred to English mares and so founded the breed known as the "Thoroughbred."

DEAD HEAT
When two or more horses cross the finish line at exactly the same instant the race is said to have ended in a dead heat. Before the days of the open shuttered moving picture camera now used, dead heats were often proclaimed as the human eye is not keen enough to judge split seconds. That there can be only a very few is easily understood when one realizes that two horses seldom travel at exactly the same rate. One is almost inevitably passing the other and it is only when the instant of their being exactly abreast coincides with the exact instant

FIGURE 32. A TRIPLE DEAD HEAT. *PHOTOCHART.*

of their reaching the finish line that there is a dead heat. The accompanying illustration shows what may easily be the only veritable triple dead heat ever to occur.

DEALERS
See *BUYING THE HORSE.*

DENMARK
Famous sire of the five-gaited American Saddle horse strain. He was introduced into Kentucky about 1850. Nearly every modern gaited horse traces his lineage back to Denmark.

DERBY
The Derby, which is a race for three-year-olds over a mile and a half course at Epsom Downs in England for the "Derby Stakes" was instituted by the 12th Earl of Derby in 1780. So famous has the race become that the word "derby" is now considered synonymous for any well known race. The race at Churchill Downs in Kentucky is known as the "Kentucky Derby." In England Derby is pronounced "dar'by." In America, "der'by."

DIAGONALS

When a horse trots his feet are moved forward alternately in diagonal pairs. If the rider posts, i.e., rises to the trot as the horse plants his right foreleg, he is said to be posting on the right diagonal and vice versa. The rider should make a practice whether riding indoors or on the trail of changing diagonals occasionally in order to rest the horse. In equitation classes in shows the rider is supposed to post on the outside diagonal and he may be asked to change diagonals at the desire of the judges. Learn to glance at the moving shoulder blades of the horse to know which diagonal you are riding.

DIRECTION (Changes of)

In riding in a ring or indoor hall, especially if the horse is being cantered or galloped for any length of time it is advisable to change direction frequently. In so doing the lead or diagonal is also changed and the horse is able to rest himself by shifting the bulk of his burden from one pair of legs to the other. The change of direction may be accomplished either by "changing hands" or by making a half turn. See *RIDING, equitation exercises*. In the show ring the judges always ask for at least one change of direction so that they may see the rider from both sides and so that they may see the horse on both leads. If the class is a horsemanship class the rider should make a half-turn towards the wall (half-turn in reverse). If the class is a Saddle horse or hunter class he should reverse towards the center. In either case the order from the ring-master will be "Reverse, please."

DISHING

Turning the hocks in and the feet out so that the feet do not travel straight is called dishing or paddling.

DISMOUNTING

There are several recognized methods of dismounting. That used in equitation classes is as follows. The rider prepares to dismount by taking the reins in the left hand together with a lock of the mane. The right hand is placed on the pommel of the saddle. Putting his weight on the left stirrup the rider disengages the right stirrup and carries the right leg over the horse's rump being careful not to touch the horse's croup. He next puts his weight on his hands, his legs being parallel, disengages the left stirrup and, pushing away from the horse, drops to the ground landing on the balls of both feet with the knees slightly bent.

The method used by the army differs in that the rider does not disengage the left stirrup until his right foot touches the ground. The purpose of this is that he may remount quickly if necessary but for ordinary riding it is undesirable, especially where the rider is short, for if the horse moves forward when the rider has one foot in the stirrup he will be thrown backward.

In dismounting from a moving horse the rider should disengage *both* stirrups before he begins his vault. The weight should all be placed on the hands and the rider should, after his right leg has cleared the croup, turn to the left so that he lands facing in the direction in which the horse is moving. Thus he is prepared to run forward a step or two if the animal does not stop at once.

Still another method of dismounting is to disengage the right stirrup and swing the right leg across in front of the saddle, then disengage the left stirrup and slide to the ground. This is a good equitation exercise but not to be recommended for ordinary use as the rider is off balance just before he slides off and, if the horse should shy or jump suddenly he may be thrown backwards off the right side. See *RIDING*.

DISTANCE

The interval between the nose of a horse and the tail of the horse preceding him is called distance. For ordinary trail and ring riding and for close-order mounted drill and music rides the normal distance is four feet. By maintaining this distance there is no danger of the leading horse kicking the horse behind nor of the latter stepping on the heels of the former. In the hunt field where jumps are being negotiated the rider is supposed to keep sufficient distance between himself and the horse ahead of him so that in the event of the latter pecking or falling he will not crash headlong into him. In jumping narrow panels it is always safest to hold your horse until the rider ahead of you has cleared the panel and gone on. In Hunt Team and Corinthian classes at shows the riders are supposed to keep three horselengths apart.

Long Distance Rides
See *ENDURANCE.*

Without Regard to Distance
This is an equitation command used in riding in a ring and means that the riders should spread out until they use the whole ring maintaining an equal distance between each. It is a most excellent exercise in equitation and should be frequently used in giving riding instruction to teach control of the horse. See also *RIDING, Equitation Exercises.*

DOCK
The bone in the horse's tail which is formed of the lowest vertebrae of the spine is the dock.

DOCKING
Docking is the practice of cutting the dock several inches from the tip. At the same time the tendons are also cut and the tail "set" to make the horse carry it high. This takes away the ability of the horse to brush off flies and is an extremely cruel practice unless the animal be always protected from flies. On the other hand a docked tail eliminates the possibility in driving horses of the animal getting a rein caught under his tail. Some horses will deliberately switch their tails over the reins, then clamping it close to the buttocks will take advantage of the helplessness of the driver to stage a runaway. If a green colt, just being broken to harness, gets a rein under his

tail it scares him and he is apt to start kicking. Just as the polo pony has his tail bandaged to prevent it getting in the way, so too the colt might well take his first lessons in the cart with his tail braided up and bandaged. Docking the tail of the hunting horse in England is also a common practice as it prevents the animal getting his tail entangled in the thorn hedges and bullfinch jumps so prevalent over there but one seldom sees American hunters so trimmed.

DOG
A dealer's term for a horse that has constantly to be urged along. A slow, unwilling beast only fit for the boneyard.

DOGCARTS
See *CARTS.*

DOORS IN THE STABLE
No stable doors should be so narrow that there is a danger of a horse knocking himself in passing through them. For leading through narrow doors and passageways see *LEADING.*

DOPING
Giving a horse dope in the form of drops or injections to make him run either faster or slower in a race. This is sometimes attempted by the unscrupulous owner, groom or rider who may have a fat sum placed one way or another on the outcome of the race. Race course officials, always on the lookout for such practices, have saliva tests, etc., which have done much to eliminate these practices. Any horse found doped is banned from the track for any time deemed proper by the race committee. The owner may also have his whole stable banned from racing. A jockey found guilty of doping a horse would, of course, lose his license.

DOUBLE
See *HUNTING TERMS.*

DOUBLE BACK
Horses of the saddle breeds often have

what is known as a "double back" i.e., the spine is depressed with the muscle rising above it on either side.

DOUBLE OXER
See *HUNTING TERMS.*

DRAG (*n.*)

This refers to a form of hunting in which a bag containing anise seed or litter from a fox's den is dragged by a runner over a chosen terrain. Later the hounds are put upon the line and follow the scent left by the drag. Drag hunting lacks the interest of fox hunting in which hounds must worry out a difficult scent and compete against the ingenuity of the fox, but a man with experience and imagination can lay a very interesting dragline. In many countries it is impossible to have fox hunting due to unsuitable terrain, lack of foxes or too much building. Drag hunting is the only answer unless one starts a pack of Bloodhounds.

DRAIN
See *HUNTING TERMS.*

DRAW A COVERT
See *HUNTING TERMS.*

DRAW REIN

A draw rein is used in training to teach the horse to lower his head and flex at the poll.   It attaches either at the girth or to a breastplate, runs through the rings of the snaffle bit and thence to the rider's hands. The *French* and *German Draw Reins* or *Martingales* are forms of draw reins which are more severe.

DRESS

The proper dress for riding will depend upon the type of riding being done, the climate and the customs of the country in which you are riding. For Western riding where the gait is the fox trot or the gallop and the Western saddle is used the Western dress of blue jeans (Levis), loose fitting shirt, broad-brimmed hat and neckerchief is correct and comfortable. With this are worn the low cowboy boots with high heels. The "dude" does not need the high heels but he wears them to be fashionable nevertheless. The cowboy needs them for he digs them into the ground to give himself purchase when handling an animal on the end of his lariat.

In the East, for warm weather hacking, jodhpurs worn with special jodhpur boots are comfortable. These were originated in India. They are specially cut long riding breeches with a flare above the knee. They fit close to the calf of the leg and have a suede or elastic strap which runs under the instep to keep them from riding up. Jodhpurs are fashionable for horsemanship classes and Saddle horse classes in the shows but they are not used in hunting or jumping classes and quite rightly, the high boot gives a firmer support for jumping. Riding coats are of various cuts, colors and materials. For summer riding and showing the so called "salt-sack" coat is both good-looking and cool. It is a creamy white coat made of a rather loosely woven very heavy material. This material keeps its shape much better than a linen or other light cloth and, being somewhat porous, is cool. For informal riding the tweed coat is good. It should be well cut, roomy enough for comfort but never so baggy that it looks sloppy. The cut of men's riding coats have not changed a great deal in the past fifty years but the women's have changed completely. In the nineteen-hundreds most women still rode sidesaddle and those who rode astride, wore awkward, clumsy coats coming down to their knees. All this has been changed and the new riding habits for women are both smart and practical.

Whip-cord is another good material both for breeches and coats. Melton cloth is used for more formal riding such as formal shows and hunting.

Yellow vests and those of tattersall plaids are permitted, but, generally speaking, the colors of riding clothes should be quiet. There is nothing more obnoxious than the park rider who appears in a bright green or red sleeveless flannel jacket, white, green or bright blue jodhpurs, a soft jockey cap and a flamboyant tie or neckerchief. Such an appearance marks the owner as one who knows absolutely nothing about horses or riding.

For habits and liveries for special purposes see *APPOINTMENTS—Hunting; BOOTS; BREECHES; RAT-CATCHER* (appendix).

DRESSAGE

This term is from the French and means "training." However it has come to have a special meaning in relation to the training of a horse. After the horse has learned to obey the simple directions of moving forward or backward, turning, changing gait, halting, etc., the horseman who wishes to develop his horse's strength, willingness and agility as far as possible continues his training by giving him special exercises to develop these traits. This training is called *dressage*. It may be compared to the vigorous training which an athlete of any kind goes through in order to perfect himself physically. The horseman's first aim is to strengthen the muscular system of the horse, particularly the muscles of the back and neck. When the weight of a man is put on the back of a horse the latter must develop a far stronger muscular structure than nature intended him to have in order to carry this weight easily. The good horseman does not try to develop these muscles too suddenly, for to do so risks ruining the horse by straining the back muscles. Rather he goes about the whole thing very gradually, working the horse on specially designed exercises every day, at first only for a few moments and later for longer and longer periods.

The first of such exercises is at the walk. If there are nearby trails or open fields which go up and down hills, the horseman rides at the walk every day up and down the inclines. Next, on the flat, he encourages his horse to extend his neck and head and push his hindquarters far under him, reaching forward with his back feet until their prints over-reach those of the front feet by many inches.

Gradually this same exercise is introduced at the trot. The strong trot in which the horse, at a rather slow cadence, takes long strides with his neck somewhat extended but his head almost vertical is of tremendous value in muscling up the horse, but it is very strenuous and must not be overdone.

The second purpose in the dressage training, that of making the horse agile and flexible, requires exercises which cause him to bend his spine. There are a number of these—the shoulder-in, the haunches-in and others. In all of these so called "lateral flexions" the horseman asks the horse to bend his spine from poll to dock in a smooth curve and, with it bent in this position, to proceed forwards at the different gaits.

The third purpose, that of making the horse willing and making him completely obedient, is accomplished by teaching him to move in any direction, at any gait, either laterally or on a diagonal, or with his forehand active while his hindquarters remain passive, and vice versa. He teaches this by means of the exercise known as the "leg-yield," in which the horse is first taught to step sideways and cross his legs; the pivots, in which he moves his forehand around his hindquarters or his hindquarters around his forehand; the traversal, or "half-pass," sometimes called the "two-track"; and by changing repeatedly from an extended form of gait to a "collected" form.

All of the exercises mentioned so far are requisite to the training of the horse to be ridden by an experienced rider and to be shown in competition in Olympic-type events which include dressage competitions, stadium jumping and cross-country work.

But in the days when knighthood was in flower a still more advanced stage of training was considered necessary. In this the horse was taught what we call "*haute école*" and "off the ground" movements. Let us take the case of a knight who in battle found himself surrounded by foot soldiers. He first put his horse into a *levade*, in which the horse sank back on his haunches and remained motionless, thus permitting the knight to use his spear to best advantage. From this position the horse then rose on his hind legs, rearing high over the enemies, and hopped forward a few steps (the *corbette*). Next he returned to the ground only to leave it again in a tremendous spring. At the height of his spring he suddenly kicked straight out behind him (the *capriole*). On returning once more to earth he performed a *pirouette*, pivoting in place on his hindquarters, his front legs off the ground, and carried his rider to safety through the path cleared by the *capriole*! (For pictures of these movements see *The Spanish Riding School*, by Mathilde Windisch-Graetz.)

Today, these movements are taught at only a few places in the world, as we no longer depend on this high degree of horsemanship to save our lives in battle.

All the movements described as *dressage* or training movements are based on natural movements of the horse while at liberty, and if you have the opportunity of watching a stallion and his mares and foals you will in time see all these movements and many others performed perfectly by the ordinary horse. Why then must he be trained to do them if he already knows how?

The training is necessary, first, because the horse must learn to balance himself under the weight of the rider, a feat which is far from natural and which requires tremendous development of muscle and agility; and second, he must learn to do them at the behest of the rider. In other words, the rider and horse must learn to communicate clearly and completely with each other.

Dressage training is usually divided into three stages: light or basic dressage, which does not include any collected work and which is considered complete when the horse is obedient at all gaits on straight lines and in circles; intermediate dressage which takes the horse through all the schooling figures mentioned, including the *passage* and the *flying change*; and heavy dressage, which includes the highly collected movements such as the *piaffe*, as well as the off-the-ground movements. Intermediate and Advanced Dressage Figures and Schooling Movements will be found listed alphabetically. See also *RIDING, The Advanced Rider*.

Do not confuse classic dressage training, all of which is based on the natural movements of the horse and the purpose of which is to develop the horse himself, with the "circus" dressage, which includes artificial movements designed to entertain.

See also *LIPIZZAN; RIDING, The Advanced Rider*.

DRIVING

Thirty years ago driving was the pastime of every man who could afford a good road hack. Because the roads in the North and East were better kept than those in the South there was much more interest in driving in these territories during the latter part of the nineteenth century than there was in riding. It has been said that in eighteen-seventy a horseman in Boston was considered a curious sight. However, riding again came into popularity as a sport in New England around eighteen-ninety and the interest in running-horse races, horse shows and equitation was revived. Driving, today, except for the professional or the breeder of fine harness horses is a lost art. One hates to see a skill which had been developed to so high a degree disappear but the drivers of yesterday have been replaced by the chauffeurs of today and these, in turn, must face competition with the pilots of tomorrow.

DRIVING WITH LONG REINS

See *COLTS, Breaking and Training of*.

DUDE

A Western term meaning a greenhorn. Applied specifically to the Easterner who comes out West to ride and take part in ranch life.

DUDE RANCH

A ranch which is run for the purpose of accommodating "dudes." There are many excellent dude ranches in the West. Here the newcomer is entertained, shown as much of real ranch life as it is practical for him to know and generally educated in cowboy life. There may be a hundred and fifty or more men and women staying at such a ranch. The cowboys employed for the purpose bring in horses for them to ride and saddle them up. They must try and assign a suitable mount to each and as far and away the greater number of the "dudes" are completely inexperienced it follows that the horses used are not of very high caliber.

Pack-trips are then arranged or all day rides. Rodeos and bucking contests are staged, etc. All in all, though the dude pays well he receives good value for his money. The real cowboy who works on a cattle ranch looks down on his fellow worker who earns his living catering to the whims of the "dudes" but perhaps the cattle are less of a nervous strain!

In recent years an attempt has been made to introduce this same type of ranch throughout the East. Inasmuch as there are no roving cattle to be herded in, no fence-riding to do, the Eastern imitation is but a travesty. Furthermore, all but one or two of these "ranches" provide only a very low grade of accommodations and equipment and consequently attract only a very low grade of customer.

DUMB JOCKEY

See *BITTING RIG, COLTS, training of.*

E

EARS

The ears of the horse are more important to the rider than might at first be apparent, for they are the semaphores which signal the intentions of the animal. Our friend Jorrocks also felt the ears were important though not for the above reason. He mentions that the ears should be as long as possible as it is by looking through them that the rider steers and that, if they are carried horizontally (lop-eared) the rain will not run in causing the horse to shake his head and perhaps bring on the blind staggers!

It was customary in the early days to crop a horse's ears as one would crop a terrier's and early paintings of horses frequently show the animal with tiny little ears, scarcely two inches long! The well bred horse has smaller, finer shaped ears than the common horse and the spirited horse carries his ears in an alert fashion. If your horse travels with one ear pricked forward while the other is turned back you may rest assured that he is too interested in the conversation going on behind him and the sights ahead to do any kicking or shying. If his ears are upright but relaxed he is not paying much attention to anything. If they suddenly shoot forward watch out for a sudden swerve and if they come back flat against his crest warn the rider behind you to stand by for a kick, meanwhile do something to prevent such a happening. Some horses habitually carry their ears laid back but it does not denote a good disposition and though the horse may not actually fight, one has the impression that it is not because he doesn't want to but because, from having been punished for just this offense, he is afraid to.

EARTH (*n.*)

See *HUNTING TERMS.*

EARTH STOPPER
See *HUNTING TERMS*.

EARTH STOPPING
See *HUNTING TERMS*.

EGG AND SPOON RACE

This is a gymkhana game suitable for beginners. Each rider is provided with a tablespoon and a hard boiled egg. He must balance the egg on the spoon without touching the egg with his fingers or thumb. The riders ride at a walk until told to trot. Anyone dropping his egg leaves the ring. If advanced riders are competing they may be asked to canter or take a low jump. An amusing stunt is to have the egg of one rider, unbeknownst to the others or to the audience, glued to the spoon. This rider passes all tests with flying colors, finally leaving the ring with the spoon held upside down in his mouth, the egg still suspended!

ELEUIN
See *HUNTING TERMS*.

ENCEPHALITIS (of the Horse)

This is a disease which attacks the brain and is generally fatal. It is carried by mosquitoes which become infected from wild birds. Previously it was thought that a mosquito, biting an infected horse, could transmit the disease to human beings, but tests by the U.S. health officials have determined that this is not so; an infected horse is not a source of danger to human beings.

There are two types of encephalitis, Western and Eastern. Almost no horses which have developed the type common on the eastern seaboard have recovered, but a number of horses suffering from the western type have survived.

The symptoms of this disease are high temperature, weakness and inability to control the hindquarters, and extreme sluggishness. A preventive serum is available, and it is advisable to have all horses inoculated annually in regions where the disease is prevalent.

ENDURANCE (of the horse)

It has been estimated that a horse can carry a full load and cover thirty-five miles a day as an average day's work. This work must be regulated as to speed with regular rests provided. The cavalry rider expects to march mostly at the walk and trot averaging about six miles an hour for six hours with ten minutes rest in each hour and a longer rest at noon. The man in the hunting field demands that his horse cover his thirty-five miles with a good part of it at the gallop. On the other hand there are long waits at the covert side while hounds are being cast as well as hacks at a jog trot from covert to covert. This amount of work is not too much for a horse in good condition four or five days a week.

The horse that is required to travel at his maximum speed will not be able to travel so far. In racing it is the harness horse which receives the greatest test of endurance. In a running race the horse to be raced may be galloped or "breezed" a few miles before the race, then he races and he is through for the day. Consider the harness horse. Before the actual race he may be brought out three times when he is "scored" the wrong way of the track for as many as twelve miles before the race begins. He then races in heats, three of them, at full speed. Small wonder that at the end of such a test it may take an hour and a half to two hours to "water him out."

Although the race horse of today, both the runner and the harness horse, travel at a greater speed than the horses of the nineteenth century and earlier, they are not required to cover the distance asked of their ancestors. Running races of twelve miles were not uncommon. These races were run in four mile heats, and the horse carried far more weight than does the modern race horse.

Trotting races, too, in the old days, under saddle, to sulky or to wagon were sometimes incredibly long. "Bishop's Mare" according to an old record, trotted sixteen miles on the Epsom road in sixty-eight minutes and thirty seconds. "Ogden's Mare" trotted thirty miles in two hours and ten minutes; while "Crocket's Mare" in 1793 trotted a hundred miles in eleven hours and fifty minutes!

Of course a group of riders cannot cover as much ground in a given time as a single rider. The cavalry records show that the longest peacetime distance covered by a troop of cavalry in which the men and horses arrived in fit condition is the Fort Riley hundred mile march which they did in the spring of 1931 and again in the spring of 1932. There are other records of marches made under war conditions. In 1873 Colonel Mackenzie rode his command into Mexico after the Kickapoo Indians, had a sharp fight and returned across the border making one hundred and forty-five miles in twenty-eight hours plus the fight. There have been several other such records, but the most outstanding and difficult to believe is that of the Pony Express rider who, according to Colonel Richard I. Dodge, carried the mail each week from El Paso to Chihuahua, a distance of three hundred miles. As the country was infested with Apache Indians his practice was to ride only after darkness. He rode a hundred miles a night for three successive nights, resting his horse all day, then rested for four days and nights and returned the following week on the same schedule. If true this is certainly a most outstanding performance when, according to Colonel Dodge, the man kept up his route for at least six months using the same pony and at the end of that time neither horse nor man were any the worse for it.

It is well known that certain breeds of horses have far more endurance, both as to ability to carry weight and ability to keep going, than others. The pony breeds can carry more weight in relation to themselves than can the draft breeds. The tough little Western horse can live off the land and outlast the Thoroughbred, the Saddler or the Arabian. Even within the breed the general conformation of the individual animal plays a large part. Although it is the fashion,

even among people who do not need a heavyweight hunter to carry them, to prefer the hunter of from sixteen:two to seventeen hands, it is seldom that these larger animals have the wind or the staying power of the hunter of fifteen:three or sixteen hands.

We have some interesting figures on the endurance and vitality of riders. In 1858, J. Powers rode a hundred and fifty miles in six hours and forty-three minutes; in 1868 N. H. Mowry rode, on the San Francisco race-track, three hundred miles in fourteen hours and nine minutes, and a man named Anderson in the same city rode one thousand three hundred and four miles in ninety hours! Of course these men changed mounts frequently but what an outstanding performance and what proof of the vitality of the American rider.

ENGLAND (the development of the horse in)

We have much for which to thank the English. Their interest in the sport of riding, i.e., hunting, polo and racing has been responsible for the Thoroughbred as we know him today. The British climate and terrain is extremely suitable to the development of bone and substance in horses. The Irish hunter is famed for his "lepping qualities" and his great frame. The Derby and the National have been the spur which speeded up the production of fast horses and then yet faster horses as well as keeping the interest in horses of the nation as a whole keyed at a high pitch. Furthermore, these races have provided the inspiration to poets and writers and they, by glorifying the horse, have prevented his falling into Limbo with the public at large. It is doubtful whether, without this great inheritance of the love of horses the American nation would ever have achieved the results it has in breeding top horses of every type. We can perhaps question the quality of the Englishman as a rider in comparison to equestrians of other nations, but his great interest in and love of sport has undoubtedly been the outstanding factor behind the development of the running horse.

ENGLISH HUNTING SEAT

Before criticizing the Englishman's seat one should take into consideration the type of jump which he is called upon to negotiate. Most of the jumps in America are walls, chicken-coops, post-and-rails, etc., they approximate the jumps that the show ring open jumper is called on to take. It has long been proven that a horse can jump higher and more freely if the weight of the rider is off his back, therefore in the hunt-field our riders come forward over the jumps wishing to help their animals as much as possible. If the horse hits the rail hard the rider may or may not be thrown ahead, depending on how good a horseman he is, but, because of the height of the jump the rider rightly feels that his best bet is to get his horse to clear it and so helps him by riding forward.

In a recent Olympic contest, after several days of grueling riding, the riders were called upon to take a formidable obstacle in the form of a wide brook which was unexpectedly deep. The man who made the best performance over this jump was a German who rode rather deep in the saddle and used his back muscles to urge his horse forward.

In the English country the most common obstacle is a double-oxer, i.e., a low thorn hedge with a ditch and low rail on both sides. There is no appreciable height to the jump but its width is formidable and the fact that the horse cannot see the ditch and rail on the far side when he takes off adds to the likelihood of his catching his hind legs in the latter and sprawling on his belly. In such a case the Englishman prefers to have the horse under him so he is rather prone to stay back in the saddle and have a "feet on the dashboard" position of the legs.

ENGLISH SADDLE
See *SADDLES*.

ENTER (to enter hounds)
See *HUNTING TERMS*.

ENTERING A STALL

Horses doze on their feet with their eyes half closed, this is made possible by the sling type of ligament which encloses the leg joints thus allowing the horse to relax and at the same time remain standing. But even in sleep the horse retains his prehistoric fears and if startled or awakened suddenly he may let fly with his heels before he realizes that you are a friend and not a foe. Even though he may not actually kick it is bad for his nervous system to be thus startled. Therefore, before entering any stall one should first warn its inmate. If the horse is in a straight stall, speak quietly calling the horse by name, then, putting your hand gently on the left side of his rump cause him to move over so that you can come past him. Go immediately up to his head and do not duck suddenly as though you feared for your life.

In entering a box stall first attract the horse's attention, then enter and again go at once to his head.

EQUESTRIAN
One who rides.

EQUESTRIAN CLASSES

Classes judged solely on the horsemanship of the rider. See *HORSE SHOW CLASSES*.

EQUIPMENT

See *APPOINTMENTS; BLANKETS; BRIDLES; DRESS; GROOM; STABLE EQUIPMENT; TACK; TACK ROOM APPOINTMENTS*.

EQUITATION (the art of riding)

See *RIDING; COLTS, Breaking and Training; DRESSAGE; JUMPING*.

EQUITATION CLASSES

Classes judged solely on the horsemanship of the rider. See *HORSE SHOW CLASSES*.

EQUITATION EXERCISES

See *RIDING, Equitation Exercises, The Advanced Rider;* also individual figures as listed alphabetically.

ERGOT

A small calliosity at the back of the fetlock joint. Some authorities believe that originally the horse's fetlock joint touched the ground as he ran and that the ergot is a protection provided by nature.

EWE-NECK

A neck which, instead of having a rising curve at the crest bends the other way, dipping down between withers and poll. A very bad fault of conformation.

EXERCISE (for the horse)

The horse should be ridden or otherwise exercised every day. If he is allowed to stand for any length of time he will develop "stall-courage" and become unmanageable. Furthermore he may well show signs of circulatory ailments. If the weather conditions are such that he cannot be ridden or driven out of doors he should at least be turned out for a short run in a sheltered paddock.

EXMOOR PONY

Across the moors of Devon and Somerset roams herds of wild ponies. These ponies are descendants of pure bred desert stock. They have retained more of the features of their ancestors than the Welsh, Shetland, Icelandic or Fiord ponies, having more slender builds and more delicate heads, but climate and environment have stunted them and the average is only about twelve hands.

Like all small breeds they make good draft animals as well as excellent children's Saddlers and hunters. Each October these ponies are rounded up and taken to the Bampton Fair where they are sold, "as is," to the highest bidder. Turned into a corral, covered with mud and burrs, the little wild creatures mill around while the crowd outside the fence sizes them up. They go for from twelve dollars for a six-months-old foal to about sixty dollars for a mature animal. The buyer must catch, halter, and lead out his purchase with no help from the herders.

These ponies are still used in the mines, where they put in a good day's work pulling the coal carts. The average size of the Exmoor pony is 12:2 for mares and 12:3 for stallions. They are identified by their mealy-colored nose and their sturdiness of build. The predominating body color is dark bay or brown, with some duns. All have black points. Though small, these ponies can easily carry a man all day. They are popular in England, both for driving and as children's hunters. Attempts have been made to improve and refine the breed by introduction of Arabian and other blood lines, but it has been found that in so doing the sturdiness and stamina of the ponies has suffered. Though formerly rarely to be seen in the United States there are now some breeders importing them. The name of the English Breeding Society is The Exmoor Pony Society.

EYE (of the horse)

The normal eye is a rich brown with the black pupil. In most horses no edging of white is shown and it is said that such an edging indicates meanness. There have been mean horses that showed the whites of their eyes. There have also been horses that showed the whites but were docile and gentle. Any bluish tinge to the eye should be looked on with askance as that is the first sign of ophthalmia. A milky appearance of the eye indicates cataract or some other form of ailment. This blueness and milkiness should not be confused with the so called "glass-eye." In these the eye-ball is perfectly clear and the sight is unimpaired but the pigment is a light blue instead of brown. Glass eyes are quite common in spotted horses and in Albinos. A "wall-eyed" horse is one that has one normal eye and whose other eye enlarges or who is near-sighted in one eye. Such a horse must be handled very carefully as he is apt to be easily frightened by objects on the side in which the size of the image is increased. If your horse is head-shy on one side only you may suspect that he is wall-eyed. For tests to determine the soundness of a horse's sight see *SOUNDNESS, Tests for.*

EYESIGHT (of the Horse)

A horse's eyesight differs from human eyesight in several ways which are important to the horseman. Let us first think of how the horse's eyes are placed and of their shape in comparison to those of a person. A human being has a very limited range of vision compared to that of a horse. A person's eyes, only slightly rounded and set in the front of his head, can see distinctly only those things directly in front of him. To be sure he can sense and see moderately well things on either side; but primarily his eyes are intended to see only those things upon which he is focussing. The eyes of the horse, placed on the sides (of his head), can not only see things which are directly in front of him but also those behind him, to either side and, to some extent, above and below him.

The eyes of the human being are further handicapped by being set deep in the skull. This gives good protection, to be sure, but the eyes of the horse, bulging out as they do, and set on his skull rather than imbedded deeply in it, have a much wider range.

How does the physical difference of location and shape, giving the horse the ability to see behind, around, above and below him, affect the way we treat him? For one thing, the good horseman never makes a sudden motion or one that might frighten a sensitive horse, even though he may be standing directly behind him or some distance away. Also, when riding, the experienced horseman is ever alert to objects so placed that though he himself would not normally notice them might easily frighten the horse, with his wider range of vision.

There is still another factor due to the placement of the horse's eyes that we must remember. A person's eyes are an inch or so apart; the horse's eyes somewhat more than six inches. Try this simple test. Extend one arm directly in front of you and hold up one finger. Now close one eye and look at the finger with the other, immediately open the eye that was closed and close the other, still looking at the extended finger. Repeat this several times and you will notice that your finger appears to jump rapidly an inch or so from one side to the other.

Let us now consider what happens when the horse, whose eyes are set so much further apart, approaches a small object such as a piece of paper lying on the ground. He first sees it, we will say, with his left eye; but as he draws nearer the right eye suddenly catches a glimpse of it. The paper, which he had supposed was inanimate, suddenly appears to jump sideways, not just an inch or so but a foot or more. No wonder the horse, whose ancestors learned through experience that only by running away could they escape predatory animals, shies suddenly at what to the rider is just an innocuous scrap of paper!

Horses are primarily far-sighted. Nature has made them thus in order that they may become aware of an approaching enemy while the latter is still some distance away. But because of this hyperopia they cannot see really clearly things that are close to them unless their noses are practically touching them. Our eyes change focus readily and, whether standing or sitting, we can look first at the horizon and then at a nearby object, and see both clearly. Not so the horse. With his head raised he can see and recognize objects a long way off, but, until he drops his head to the ground, the small log just in front of him is fuzzy rather than clearly defined.

A knowledge of how the horse sees is very valuable to the horseman who is training his horse to jump. Notice the green horse being put over a low fence for the first time. He comes galloping towards it readily enough; then suddenly, as he is almost on it, he stops, puts his nose down and then leaps into the air clearing it by several feet. This is because he has not seen it clearly; to him the obstacle is a fuzzy barrier of indeterminate height. Only after many hours of practice will he learn to judge accurately the height and width of the many obstacles he will be asked to jump.

F

FALLS
What to do in case of:
   a. *Horse falling.*

As a rule if a horse falls and does not injure himself seriously he will be able to get to his feet without help. Catch hold of the rein as he rises so that you may control him. When he is standing you can easily determine whether or not he needs First Aid treatment. If he moves out readily at a walk the chances are that he is all right, but do not start on a gallop until you are sure. Remember also that a fall is terrifying to a horse and that he may be jittery for some time afterwards.

Sometimes a horse, on falling, does not rise at once. This may be due to fear, to having a bridle rein caught under him so that he cannot raise his head, or to being in such a position or on such terrain that he cannot rise. First see that the reins are free, pull them over the animal's head. Next try to undo the saddle girth so that the saddle can be removed. If the front legs are doubled up under him it will be necessary to pull them out and straighten them as a horse cannot rise with his front legs under his belly. Make sure that there is no branch or large stone under him which would prevent his rising. If he is on his side and the ground is sloping it may be necessary to get three or four men to roll him over on his belly while his master,

whom he knows and in whom he has confidence, talks to him and helps him with the reins. Try not to let him get excited or struggle before he is in a position in which he can rise. A horse that is down and cannot get up is said to be *cast* and great care must be taken lest he rupture a blood vessel in his struggles. If, after getting him to his feet there are any signs of lameness or severe bleeding give him First Aid treatment or send for the veterinarian at once. See also *CAST HORSES; LAMENESS; INJURIES.*
   b. *Rider falling*

There are two kinds of falls; falls and bad falls. The former are very common, the latter, fortunately, very rare. In the past forty years, during which I have taught literally hundreds of children and adults to ride, when the time spent by these riders here in the ring and on nearby trails in games, jumping, bareback work, mounted gymnastics, breaking and training colts and hunting have amounted to hundreds of thousands of riding hours; in all this time with all these riders the number of accidents which have required a doctor's attention have been fewer than twenty. Curiously enough these have not occurred when the rider has been doing anything which might be considered dangerous, but rather they have been the results of slow falls when the rider has had time to put out an arm to save himself and so, instead of flopping over on his back, has received his full weight on his hand or wrist. One or two have occurred when the rider was in the act of mounting or dismounting, when something happened to frighten the horse before the rider was either firmly in the saddle or on the ground.

At a summer camp of a hundred and seventy-five boys and girls, a camp which provided all the usual summer sports including riding, statistics were kept of the various accidents reported. It was discovered than an average of twenty-five children reported each day for First Aid treatment of one kind or another. The cause might be anything from a splinter acquired at the waterfront, or a blister from a hiking trip, to a baseball finger; but only twice during the entire summer was anyone sent to the infirmary from the riding ring for treatment of any kind.

However, the occasional bad fall needs expert First Aid treatment and every rider should know how to ascertain the extent of the injury and what should be done.

If a rider makes no attempt to get up after a fall one should be very sure that there is no spinal injury before attempting to move him. Look for signs of shock, i.e., paleness of skin and lips, beads of moisture on forehead or upper lip, faint rapid pulse, chilling and sensation of coldness, particularly in the extremities . . . all these indicate a serious injury. The inability to move the lower limbs shows a lower spinal injury, the inability to move the fingers indicates a possible fracture of the neck. Unconsciousness, bleeding at the ears, nose, eyes, or mouth, pupils that are unevenly dilated, all point to a severe head injury. If any of the above symptoms are present the patient should, on no account, be moved. Cover him with blankets, give him a stimulant if he is conscious (never pour liquids down the throat of an unconscious person, it may go into his lungs instead of his stomach), keep him still, reassure him and send for the doctor at once.

If an arm or leg is broken or dislocated the patient will know it and tell you so. In the case of the former improvise a sling. The best way to avoid further injury to a broken leg is to apply a splint. The handiest splint is the other leg. Put padding between the two in the form of folded coats. Use stocks, handkerchiefs folded diagonally and tied together, or strips torn from shirts to make the bandages with which the limbs are tied together. Do not put a bandage directly over the fracture. Transport the patient on an improvised stretcher if possible. A broken collar bone is one of the most common types of fractures due to falls. The arm will be helpless and the shoulder will be lowered on the side of the fracture. Put padding under the arm, bind it to the body and provide a sling in which to rest the lower arm. In all fracture cases treat for shock with warmth, extra blankets or coats, and a stimulant. Falls rarely involve extensive bleeding from wounds but a rider might be kicked and so get a bad wound. The bleeding should be controlled either by pressure or a tourniquet but only a trained person should attempt the latter. If, in an emergency, it should be necessary for an untrained person to apply a tourniquet the following rules must be observed: Use only a bandage or strip of cloth not less than three inches wide, tighten only sufficiently to stop the bleeding, loosen every fifteen or twenty minutes. For arterial (spurting type) bleeding apply the tourniquet between the wound and the heart using a pressure point if possible. For venous bleeding, characterized by a steady flow of dark colored blood apply a bandage directly on the wound itself with pressure of the fingers. In using a tourniquet a little pad of gauze or bandage should be folded and put under the tourniquet directly over the pressure point; never use a stone or other hard object for this purpose.

Very frequently a fall that looks serious is nothing. One comon occurrence is for the rider to land on his stomach or back and have all the wind knocked out of him. For a moment he can neither talk nor move, then he catches his breath and all is well though he may feel a little dizzy for a while. In such cases, or where the rider suffers nothing worse than a few scratches and a deflated ego, he should be got back on the horse as quickly as possible and the ride continued. This is especially true with a rider who is very young or exceptionally timid. Failure to follow this rule may result in a permanent fear of horses. The attitude of the instructor towards common falls of this sort should be quite casual. Try to convey the impression that such occurrences are every day affairs and nothing to get excited about. Later, much later, when the young rider is calm and confident, explain to him just what caused the fall and how it could have been avoided.

FALSE CANTER
See *RIDING, The Advanced Rider.*

FALSE START

In changing from one gait to another a horse will often make a false start. This is especially true in taking up the gallop or, in the five-gaited horse, in taking the trot or rack. He should be given a step or two to take the desired gait and for which he has received the correct signal. If he does not do so he should be brought back to the walk again and started anew, this time with more definite signals. Do not continue to urge a horse that is trotting into a canter simply by renewed applications of the heels; by so doing you are not telling him to canter, you are teling him to trot faster. Instead, bring him down to a walk and give him the correct command for the gallop depart.

FAMOUS HORSES

In the list given below are horses who have made names for themselves either as Foundation Sires or heads of "horse families"; as the mounts of famous men or simply as outstanding personalities. The better known and loved equine characters in literature are listed under *FAMOUS HORSES OF FICTION.* Famous modern Thoroughbreds are not included in this list. Under *RECORDS AND STATISTICS* (Appendix) various racing records will be found.

Allen F-1. Foundation Sire for the TENNESSEE WALKING HORSE breed. He was foaled in 1886, bred by E. D. Herr of Lexington, Ky., and eventually became the property of J. R. Brantley of Manchester, Tenn. More than fifty per cent of all Walking Horses registered in the stud book of that breed show Allen blood.

Black Hawk. The Black Hawks were a famous family of trotters. The most famous stallion was Ethan Allen. They were in their prime in the 1850's and preceded the Hambletonians.

Bucephalus. Bucephalus was the favorite mount of Alexander the Great.

Byerly Turk. The Byerly Turk was the first of the three Arabian stallions imported into England to found the great race of horses known as the English Thoroughbreds. He was foaled about 1679. He is the great-great-grandfather of Herod. See also *Byerly Turk* (main heading).

Copenhagen. Copenhagen was the favorits mount of the Duke of Wellington.

Copperbottom. One of the most famous American Foundation Sires.

Darley Arabian. One of the three Arabian stallions which, imported into England, were the foundation of the English Thoroughbred line. He is the great-great-grandsire of the English Eclipse. See also *Darley Arabian* (main heading).

Denmark. This is the horse selected by the American Saddle Horse Breeders Association as the technical head of the American Saddle Horse Breed. His line is known as the "Denmarks." The other line of Saddlers, the "Chiefs," descended from Harrison Chief were rivals of the Denmarks and the two "familites" were found to "nick" well so that many of the most famous modern Saddlers bear the blood of both strains. Denmark sired three famous stallions, Gaines Denmark, Rob Roy and Muir's Denmark. The first is the best known. Denmark has *Pot-8-oes* blood on his father's side and his mother was a *Cockespur* mare, both these lines being Thoroughbreds but the dam of the mother was simply the "Stevenson Mare" and her pedigree is unknown.

Dictator. Dictator was the Foundation Sire of the Dictator line, family of pacers and son of Hambletonian.

Eclipse. There were two Eclipses. The English Eclipse and the American Eclipse. The English Eclipse, the great-

great-grandson of the Darley Arabian is the greatest of the Foundation Sires of the English Thoroughbreds. Practically all modern race horses trace back to this horse. He was foaled in 1764.

American Eclipse was foaled on Long Island in 1823. He was the grandson of Messenger and his pedigree goes back through the English Eclipse to the Darley Arabian. His most famous race was over the Union Course on Long Island on May 27th, 1823. Eclipse representing the North, his owner challenged the South to produce a horse that could beat him. The Virginians' entry was Sir Henry, a cousin of Eclipse. It was a twelve mile race in three heats, Eclipse winning the first and last. Both horses were cruelly used, coming in bleeding and cut from the beatings. Their time averaged about thirty miles an hour.

Ethan Allen. Ethan Allen, son of Black Hawk was one of the most famous stallions of that time.

Godolphin Barb. The Godolphin Barb, or Godolphin Arabian (there is some question as to exactly which he was) was one of the three Arabian stallions imported into England in the founding of the Thoroughbred line. He was foaled about 1724, stood about fifteen hands high and was the property of the Earl of Godolphin. He is the great-grandsire of Matchem, one of the three Foundation Sires of the Thoroughbred.

Iroquois. Iroquois was the only American bred horse ever to win the English Derby. He was foaled in 1878 and died in 1899.

Justin Morgan. The Foundation Sire of the Morgan breed of horse. He is the most prepotent of any Foundation Sire, his good disposition, tremendous endurance and strength being passed down to all his descendants. The Morgans preceded the Hambletonians as the favored trotting breed and from them came many other families such as the Black Hawks. See also *Justin Morgan* (main heading).

Mambrino. Mambrino is the sire of the famous *Messenger*. The latter is noted as being the Foundation Sire of the trotting and pacing lines. Mambrino's get also contributed to the founding of the gaited horse.

Marengo. Marengo was the favorite mount of Napolean.

Matchem. Matchem (1748), is the grandson of the Godolphin Barb and one of the three great Foundation Sires of the English Thoroughbred strain.

Nelson. Nelson was the favorite mount of George Washington.

Sleepy Tom. Sleepy Tom's outstanding feat is the fact that although stone blind he was for some years the outstanding pacer of the world. He raced at top speed in total darkness depending entirely on the voice and signals of his trainer. In one race his driver, Phillips was thrown from the sulky in a collision and Sleepy Tom stopped and stood until the man had recovered his seat.

Traveller. Traveller was the favorite mount of General Lee.

FAMOUS HORSES OF FICTION

Although the horse has been the subject of song and story from the beginnings of recorded literature it is amazing how few horses have been treated as personalities and come to us complete with name, etc. Most horse fiction has to do with the people rather than with the equine characters. In a few cases the horse plays an important part but is still nameless; in such cases I have listed the horse under the owner's name or under the title of the book.

Arterxerxes. Xerxes and Arterxerxes were the two horses of that famous huntsman, John Jorrocks. Jorocks liked to have his little joke. He drove his hunters tandem and as his lead horse was christened "Xerxes," he called his wheeler "Arterxerxes" because he came "arter" (after) Xerxes. Neither horse was noted either for beauty or amiability. Jorocks was always averse to jumping, especially when the jump had not been knocked down for him by another and more ambitious rider, but if he was unwilling, his horses were even more so. In the several volumes written by Mr. Surtees one never comes across a description of a properly negotiated jump on the part of John Jorrocks or either of his horses. And the commonest entry in Mr. Jorrocks' diary is "paid sixpense for the catching of my 'orse."

Black Beauty. Anna Sewell was about the first writer to produce a book in which the main character was a horse. The story of Black Beauty was primarily written to bring to the attention of the public the abuses which were common in the nineteenth century. She particularly emphasizes the misuse of the check rein, the overworking of the hack horse, the ignorance of grooms and the reckless riding of the thoughtless young "thrusters." The book is simply written; it is perhaps too sentimental from the modern standpoint but *Black Beauty* will remain a children's favorite for many years to come.

Corkran of Clamstretch. Corkran is not well known but he deserves to be. He is the hero of the story by John Biggs Jr. and is the only horse hero who loses his race and gains in prestige by so doing.

David Harum's balky horse. David Harum's horse had no name but he is well known nevertheless. He is introduced in the first chapter of *David Harum* by Edward Noyes Wescott, and serves to mark his owner as a shrewd trader in horseflesh. Briefly the incident tells of how David is sold a horse that is guaranteed "sound and gentle, to be as easily driven by a woman as a man and to stand without tying." On his way home with his purchase he discovers that the horse is a balker and has the habit of planting himself in the middle of the road and refusing to budge. David, by means of hobbles, breaks the horse of the habit for his own use and later palms him off on the "deakin" who has previously gypped Harum on a horse trade. The incident ends with David coming out very much to the good in the bargain.

Diamond. Diamond, or "Old" Diamond is the horse of "young" Diamond's father in that beautiful children's clasic *At the*

Back of the North Wind by George Mac-Donald. Anna Sewell, in *Black Beauty* brings out the hardships of a hack horse's life in the nineteenth century and Mac-Donald, while he does mention some mistreatment of Diamond after he has been sold, also tells of the humane treatment which was often accorded horses. When his father falls ill little Diamond mounts the box and with old Diamond's help is able to earn money as a cabby.

Emperor. Emperor, or "Hemperor" as he is called by the cockney characters in Thackeray's delightful *The Ravenswing* is the white circus horse, hired by Mr. Woolsey, the tailor, to acomplish the complete discomfiture of his rival, Mr. Eglantine, the perfumer and wig maker. Emperor's peculiar and outstanding characteristic was that he had been trained to lie down and die whenever the music to "God preserve the Emperor Francis" was played. Mr. Woolsey so arranged matters that Mr. Eglantine rode the horse while he himself accompanied the young lady of their mutual desires in a carriage. At an appropriate moment, while Eglantine was showing off his accomplishments in equitation a tally-ho appears with a bugler rendering the above mentioned melody. Emperor promptly lies down, depositing Mr. Eglantine in a mud puddle and ruining his new suit.

Flicka. My Friend Flicka by Mary O'Hara has already become a "must" in the libraries of all horseminded young people. It is the story of an army man's son, Rod, who is sensitive and dreamy in disposition. Rod is offered a colt and chooses a filly for he does not want his pet to go through the pain and danger of castration. He calls her "Flicka" meaning young girl and through her develops in character and health alike. Thunderhead who is the albino son of Flicka gives his name to the sequel of the first book and has proved equally popular.

Florian. Florian, the beautiful Lipizzan from the Imperial Spanish riding school in Vienna is the hero of the book which bears his name by Felix Salten. The Lipizzans are a unique breed which for centuries have been bred and trained for the use and amusement of royalty. The art of *"Haute Ecole"* reached its highest peak in this school. Men and horses devoted their entire lives to attaining perfection in its almost incredible gymnastic feats. Florian, one of these horses, lives through the last years before the First World War and sees his world of tradition and royal trappings fall to pieces around him.

The Lithuanian. Baron Munchausen tells of how he is presented with a magnificent horse from Lithuania which, though completely unbroken, he manages to mount and demonstrate dressage tricks on a tea table without disturbing the china. Later he rides the horse in battle and, being pursued by the enemy, gallops into a village just as the portcullis is lowered. He stops in the middle of the town to water his weary animal and wonders how the horse manages to contain so much water until, looking back he sees that the portcullis has chopped off the entire hindquarters of his mount. He hastily rides back to the town gates, attaches the still quivering rear end to the forehand by means of sewing with laurel sprigs and from then on is able to ride in the shade of his own and his horse's laurels! (From the *Travels of Baron Munchausen* by Rudolph Eric Raspe.)

The Maltese Cat. Kipling's endearing little polo pony who carried his master to victory in spite of the latter's broken collar bone is better known, perhaps than any other equine character of fiction. This is one of the best written of all horse stories and one of the very few in which the horse is really the main character and a distinct personality.

Pegasus. Pegasus, the winged horse needs no introduction. The best told description of him and his master Bellerophon is to be found in Nathaniel Hawthorne's *Wonder Book* and is part of the story, "The Chimaera."

The Pie. The piebald horse which wins the Grand National in Enid Bagnold's *National Velvet* is familiar to most readers. Unfortunately when the book appeared on the screen the equine actor chosen to play the part was a chestnut Thoroughbred which rather spoiled one of the main issues of the book, namely that the National could be won by a cold-blooded horse (no piebald could ever be a purebred Thoroughbred of course). *National Velvet* is a real contribution to horse literature even though the interest centers rather in the child "Velvet" than in the horse "the Pie."

The Red Pony. John Steinbeck's *Red Pony* is one of the most beautiful and harrowing books of which the main theme is the love of a child for a horse and the death of the latter. The pony's name is "Gabelan" meaning "the hawk." One loves and weeps with little "Jody" to whom his Red Pony is everything.

Roland. One of the most stirring narrative poems concerning riding and horses is the familiar *How They Brought the Good News from Ghent to Aix* by Robert Browning. Of the three messengers who start out only Roland, the horse of the teller of the story, survives.

Rosinante. The sorry looking steed of Cervantes' *Don Quixote* has almost become a synonym for undesirable horseflesh. Perhaps his only rivals for the place of ugliest animals are to be found in Surtees' *Handley Cross* who mounts many of his riders including "Captain Dismal" on equally unattractive beasts.

Thunderhead. See *Flicka.*

The Trojan Horse. The Trojan horse, though not of flesh and blood, surely deserves a place among famous horses of fiction. His complete description is to be found in Homer's Iliad.

Venus and Adonis. Though the stallion and jennet described by Shakespeare in his *Venus and Adonis* bear no names they are without peers in fiction. If one were to search through all of English literature for the best and truest description of the ideal horse one could but choose these magnificent lines which come early in the poem. Of the mare he says:

> Round hoof'd, short-jointed, fetlocks shag and long,
> Broad breast, full eye, small head and nostril wide,
> High crest, short ears, straight legs and passing strong,
> Thin mane, thick tail, broad buttock, tender hide:
> Look, what a horse should have, he did not lack,
> Save a proud rider on so proud a back.

And of the stallion:

> His ears up-prick'd; his braided hanging mane
> Upon his compass'd crest now stand on end;
> His nostrils drink the air, and forth again,
> As from a furnace, vapours doth he send:
>> His eye which scornfully glisters like fire,
>> Shows his hot courage and his high desire.

> Sometimes he trots, as if he told the steps,
> With gentle majesty and modest pride;
> Anon he rears upright, curvets and leaps,
> As who should say "Lo! thus my strength is tried;
>> And this I do to captivate the eye
>> Of the fair breeder standing by."

*   *   *   *   *   *

> Sometimes he scuds far off, and there he stares;
> Anon he starts at stirring of a feather;
> To bid the wind a base he now prepares,
> An whe'r he run or fly they know not whether;
>> For through his mane and tail the high wind sings,
>> Fanning the hairs, who wave like feather'd wings.

FARCY

This is a disease similar to glanders and often fatal. It is characterized by abscesses in the mucous membranes, in other glands of the head and occasionally of the legs. The abscesses are known as "farcy buds." The veterinarian should be sent for at once. Farcy is very contagious to other animals and occasionally to human beings.

FAULTS (in jumping)

When a horse touches a jump, knocks down a rail, shies out or refuses, it is called a *fault* and penalized according to Horse Show Scoring Rules. See *JUMPING FAULTS, Scoring of.*

FEAR (in horses)

Some horses are much more fearful than others, this is not so much due to inheritance as to upbringing. The colt that is handled from birth develops a confidence in man which will go far to allay his natural fears. A horse that is naturally timid should, under no circumstances, be handled roughly. The high-strung, sensitive colt or the Western pony that has never been handled until he is broken at the age of three or four, will be timid the first time he is clipped or shod, even though he may be gentle to ride. With sufficient men and strong ropes it is possible to subdue him forcibly so that the job can be done, but in so doing you have helped to build up a very serious habit; that of resistance to man. Rather one should strive with patience, tact and quiet handling, to show the colt that there is nothing to fear. If the colt is afraid of shoeing let him run barefoot for a few days, meanwhile pick his feet up two or three times a day, clean them out thoroughly and tap them lightly with a hammer. At first he will flinch but familiarity breeds contempt and before long he will submit quietly to the blacksmith. Never strike a horse suddenly or shout at him unless you intend to punish him for some deliberate offense such as kicking or biting another horse.

A green horse will be fearful of many strange sights along the roadside. If he is ridden in company he will have more confidence. Horses are particularly afraid of stepping on any strange footing such as a wooden or concrete bridge. If, while riding in company on a little-schooled colt you come to such an obstacle by all means let your companion precede you. The colt will follow peaceably enough. If you are alone you will just have to be patient and talk to him quietly, urging him with a firm application of the legs. Somtimes turning him around a few times, "rolling up" as the expression goes, will confuse him slightly and he will venture onto the bridge, or you may try to back him on it. Once he has planted a foot and found that nothing happens he will probably go along readily though somewhat unevenly. I remember trying to get a young colt across a bridge some years ago with little success. I had no one with me and the colt was determined he was not going to step on the wooden boards. Again and again I tried; he would go just to the edge, and then plunge away. As I was beginning to wonder what I could try next, for once having begun one must never let a horse win out in a contest of that sort, a car chanced to pass us. As soon as the colt saw that the car was willing to cross the bridge he lost his fear and followed placidly enough!

If your colt shows signs of shying at an obstacle ahead, talk to him and urge him firmly forward with your legs. If you can keep him in motion he will be less likely to whirl and bolt back along the way he has come. Remember he will be far more likely to be afraid of some little thing such as a blowing paper, a boy pushing instead of riding a bicycle, a baby carriage or a child on roller skates than of a steam roller or a concrete mixer.

Some horses and colts are very timid in the stall. These should be stabled in straight stalls for a while so that they cannot get away when the trainer enters. With handling they will usually get over this fear in a short time, meanwhile be especially careful not to make any sudden movements with either the groom-

ing tools or the stable implements. If you cannot trust your stableman to be gentle you had better take over entire charge of the colt yourself until he has gained confidence. The colt that is frightened, may develop habits of meanness which will never leave him.

Many horses are "head-shy," i.e., fearful of their heads. Starting from normal fear, the horse will develop this into such a vice that it may be impossible to bridle him. Frequent petting and offering of tidbits will help more than anything else. Some trainers rub the bit with salt pork to make it tasty. For bridling the head-shy horse see *BRIDLING*.

Many horses are not afraid of man but they are afraid to travel too near another horse. The rider must have a firm seat and know how to use his aids. The horse should be ridden beside another horse that is known to be good-tempered and the timid horse must be made to keep close to his companion. Bad eyesight is a common cause of fear in horses. Usually the horse that loses the sight of one eye will gradually adjust himself to the loss of it but the rider should forever be on the lookout for obstacles on the blind side.

Wall-eyed horses and ophthalmic horses suffer from headshyness.

A timid rider makes a timid horse. No beginner should ever attempt to ride an animal that is, by nature or training, nervous or high-strung. Both the man and his mount will only become more and more timid until the one loses all taste for riding and the other gains the reputation of being an outlaw. See also *TRAINING THE HORSE, Indian Method*.

FEAR (in the rider)

It is natural for all beginners to be fearful when they start their riding career. Fear of falling is one of the fundamental fears of mankind handed down to us from the days when our ancestors lived in trees. Fear of the unknown is an even stronger form of fear. The child, especially, finding himself high off the ground, riding a strange animal of whose habits and disposition he knows nothing, will often be nervous and tense. There is only one cure for these fears, *successful experience.*

There is a theory of certain riding instructors that the way to cure a child of timidity is to make them more fearful of the instructor than of the horse. Such an instructor will spend most of the riding lesson "bawling out" the children. Not only is this completely wrong from a psychological angle, for it gives the child two fears to overcome instead of one, but it is so silly from a practical angle! If all that is necessary is to give the child successful experience, why not mount him on an animal carefully chosen for his disposition, size in relationship to the child and easy gaits. In an enclosed ring, under the eyes of an intelligent teacher, the average child will get over his fear in just one lesson. He will leave the ring happy and wanting to ride again. He will have begun to substitute a feeling of superiority over the horse instead of inferiority.

Sometimes a child or an adult will make a good start, lose their preliminary fears and then, because of a fall or some such mishap, will become timid again. Preparation for such experiences is a preventive for such fears. The small child learns best on a small, gentle mount. From the very first lesson children should be taught to ride at a walk and a jog trot without stirrups and to dismount while the animal is in motion. After a few lessons he is taught to canter bareback on a specially schooled pony and to dismount at this gait also. As all riding masters know falls are common, bad falls rare. The child who slips off because his horse starts up suddenly, or shies, should be remounted with as little fuss as possible. If he is used to vaulting off a moving pony he may be a little crestfallen but that is all. The instructor must keep perfectly calm and act as though there was nothing to get excited about, taking for granted that the child will remount without objecting. On no account should the child be humiliated by laughter.

Occasionally one runs across the truly neurotic child or adult. These should be taken separately if possible and much more slowly than the average child. They will get over their fears but it may take a long time, meanwhile every precaution should be taken to insure that nothing happens to give them a "set back." See also *TEACHING RIDING.*

FEATHERED SHOES
See *FORGING; SHOES, Types of.*

FEATHERS
The long hairs running up the legs from the fetlock joint which occur in the draft breeds are known as "feathers."

FEED (types of)
Grains:
Oats
In the North and East oats or some mixture containing them usually comprise the horse's grain ration. These are muscle builders and providers of energy. They may be fed whole or crushed, sometimes called "crimped." Crushed oats are easily digested but care must be taken in purchasing them as the tendency on the part of unreliable dealers is to use only the poorer grade of oats for crushing as their quality cannot then be easily judged.

Many big stables have their own oat crushers. Good oats are plump, long, sweet and weigh forty to forty-five pounds to the bushel. They should not be dusty and never moldy, the latter condition is a frequent cause of colic and fodder poisoning. In measuring crushed oats remember that they are far more bulky than whole oats. The horse that has been getting three quarts of whole oats at a feeding will need four of crushed.

Bran
Bran is a laxative and has little nutritive value but most horses being fed on oats need bran as well. There are two methods of feeding bran. One is to give

one part bran to three parts oats, measured by bulk, not weight, at all feedings. In winter the formula can be two parts oats to one of bran. The other is to feed the oats separately and, once a week, preferably before a day of rest for the horse, give a good, hot bran mash. To make this put four quarts of bran in a stable pail, add a handful of salt, a handful of linseed meal if desired and enough boiling water to wet thoroughly. Cover with a feed bag and allow to steam until cool enough to eat.

Corn

Corn is a highly nutritious, highly heating form of food. Horses from corn producing regions which have been accustomed to corn as a ration thrive on it, but it can cause havoc with horses not accustomed to it and doing fast work, especially in hot weather. Corn may be fed either on or off the cob. In the latter case five to nine large ears is the usual ration. Corn may also be fed in combination with other grains which is an excellent method. The army, in winter, feeds a mixture of corn, oats and bran, one third of each, but they do not use this in hot weather nor when the horses are being used for polo, hunting or other very fast work.

Linseed Meal

Valuable as a conditioner and laxative it also makes the coat glisten but should not be fed too freely for fear of scouring. A handful three times a week is enough, or once a week in a bran mash.

Commercial Horsefeed

Sometimes called "molasses feed." This is a prepared feed containing oats, bran, corn, chopped alfalfa, linseed, salt and other minerals and vitamins. It is an excellent ration for horses doing average work. The proportion of foods used varies with the brand, if one with too high a content of molasses is chosen care must be taken in summer lest it become rancid. Feed about the same amount by bulk as oats. No other grain is necessary.

Fresh Forage

Apples are beloved by horses and fine as a tidbit or a reward. Do not feed them too freely; many a horse has died of colic from a stolen visit to the apple orchard.

Carrots are excellent for the coat and to stimulate the appetite. Break the carrots up small enough to overcome any danger of the horse swallowing them whole and choking.

Grass. This is the horse's natural food. It is a conditioner and tonic but if the horse has not been used to grass, such as one coming out of the stable after a winter without it, care must be taken. Let him graze only a short time each day for a week or two. Clover, especially when wet, can bring on flatulent colic. Never feed a horse grass that has been cut and allowed to lie on the ground for a few hours but has not been properly cured. This will cause a fermentation in the horse's stomach or intestines and may result in death. Horses may eat grass that has been freshly cut if it is fed to them within a few minutes of the cutting. In allowing a horse to graze along the road-side or near orchards be sure that the grass is not contaminated from the spraying of the trees to kill worms and other parasites. This spray is a deadly poison and it takes very little of it to kill a horse. Horses that have too much grass and too little grain develop a condition known as "grass" or "hay" belly. The abdomen swells due to the formation of gases and the horse's ribs stick out while his flanks and rump remain thin. To remedy this condition bring him in from the pasture, cut down on the hay, give more grain and plenty of grooming.

Hay. Hay forms the bulk of the horse's diet. It should be either timothy or timothy and clover with possibly a little alfalfa. Good hay is sweet to smell, crisp when crushed and of a greenish rather than a dead brown color. It should never be dusty nor should the stalks be either too fine or too coarse. See that there are no signs of discoloration in the hay which would indicate a presence of mold due to having been allowed to get and stay wet. Horses with respiratory troubles may have their hay wetted down with a sprinkling can just before they eat it. If, through inability to get anything else, a horse accustomed to timothy must be fed straight alfalfa give him only a very small forkful at a time and let him have oat straw to provide the necessary bulk. Alfalfa is too rich for horses unaccustomed to it and will surely cause trouble if fed freely.

Salt. All horses need salt, especially in hot weather. It may be fed in the form of a brick, in which case a special dispenser is necessary. Put this in the front of the stall where the horse can lick it at will. Or one may buy rock salt which looks like granite and comes in big chunks. Put a piece as big as your fist in the manger, it will provide the horse with the salt he needs and also act as a deterrent to the animal that likes to gobble down his oats. Do not put a big square of cattle salt on a spike in the pasture where horses can bite off large chunks, they will get so much that they may choke themselves as these squares are quite soft. The horse that is doing hard work or fast work and sweating in hot weather loses great quantities of salt through his pores, so special care must be taken to see that he has access to salt for replenishment or he will lose weight and condition.

FEED, SPECIAL TYPES OF

New Hope

One of the most common respiratory ailments in horses is that called "Heaves." There appear to be several types of heaves. Some are the result of overwork and bad feed, especially musty or dusty hay. Other types are after effects of pneumonia or of shipping fever. In this case the horse has a pocket of pus in his lungs which is not cleared up. A third type of heaves seems to be an allergy to certain grains, especially to oats.

In recent years a system of feeding using a combination of grains which does not include oats and which substitutes wet beet pulp instead of hay has been developed. This has proved very successful in arresting the symptoms of heaves where the lung damage is not too great and permitting a horse which would otherwise have to be destroyed to continue working.

Even more recently a pellet form of horse feed has come on the market. This is fed in larger quantity than the ordinary grain ration and, once the horses become accustomed to it, no supplementary feeding of either hay or beet pulp is necessary, though grass in season is recommended. Several commercial feed companies now have this type on the market, the best-known being sold under the name NEW HOPE.

Hydroponic Green Feeds

Grass is the natural food of horses as well as of all grazing animals. It contains more vitamins than any other known form of vegetation. Yet the grass season in many parts of the country is relatively short, and even good hay cannot be a complete substitute. There is now Hydroponic equipment on the market which permits the owner of a stable to grow his own grass the year round more cheaply than he can buy hay. This equipment includes an aluminum building inside of which are banks of metal trays. Through an ingeniously contrived irrigating system which works by gravity, water containing special chemicals water the grain placed in these trays. An air conditioner which contains a heat pump keeps the temperature of the building always at 68 degrees Fahrenheit. Fluorescent light ensures the light necessary to develop chlorophyll, and the oat grass grows to a height of from six to eight inches in seven days. Not only does this grass provide ample vitamins and trace minerals, the enzymes in its juices make the roughage in the other feeds more digestible. Thus the horse does not need as much of either oats or hay.

Since there is a large water content in the grass it cannot substitute entirely for the hay and grain ration, and it will depend on what type of work the horse is doing just how the rations are balanced.

The author has had one of these plants in operation for several years in a stable of thirty-five horses working from two to five hours every day in a riding school. The horses stay in hard condition on two-thirds of their normal grain and hay rations (the amount depending on the size and type of animal) plus about ten pounds of grass. There has been a noted improvement in the general health of the animals and the lustre of their coats, and a decided drop in incidents of lameness and of respiratory problems during this time. There has also been a saving of about a hundred dollars a month in feed bills. Since it is not possible to get local hay and since that imported from Canada varies in quality, we have now put the whole stable on the New Hope feed described above plus the Hydroponic grass.

FEEDING (principles of)

The stomach of a horse is very small in proportion to his body. Nature intended the horse to live on grass, grazing all day in order to sustain himself. He was a nomad, constantly traveling in search of greener pastures, his stomach never very full and seldom empty. Man changed that. He keeps his servant and companion standing hour after hour in a confined space, he feeds him highly concentrated foods, sometimes with discretion, more frequently without. The faults that he commits, often through ignorance, are manifold, the result, horses dead of colic or useless through being foundered or permanently lamed.

The teeth of a horse are flat and he uses them in a grinding, circular motion. His digestive juices are not strong, he has no vomiting muscles. What goes into his stomach can only get out again through the digestive tract. All these things must be borne in mind when feeding a horse. One must also consider the size, type and disposition of the animal and the amount and kind of work he is doing. A long rangy Thoroughbred, expected to gallop and jump will eat three or four times what a chunky,

heavy-set, close-coupled animal will require. An eighteen hundred pound draft horse will not require nearly the amount of grain that an eight hundred pound polo pony will need but he will need much more hay. A high-spirited colt, being given too little or irregular work, will look underweight but be unmanageable for a poor rider if given much grain while a phlegmatic beast will eat all you give him and still remain peaceful. But however much you give, certain principles remain the same.

Give the grain in three or even four feedings a day. This is because your horse eats it all up at once in a short time and it is a highly concentrated and rich food. Give hay night and morning, the bulk at night with an additional wisp at noon if desired. Put the hay in the racks before the grain. Many horses are greedy and will gulp down the first few mouthfuls of grain when very hungry, but a bite of hay takes off the first edge of appetite and they will chew their food more thoroughly as a result. Feed your horses regular amounts at regular hours. Decrease the amount of grain on days when the horse is not working. Omitting the noon feeding is one method of doing this. If a horse has had a hard day's hunting give him an additional feed at around ten o'clock. See also *FEED, Types of; FEEDING SCHEDULE; WATERING, Systems of.*

FEEDING (schedules and amounts of)

The United States Cavalry feeds its horses from nine to twelve quarts of grain and from twelve to twenty pounds of hay daily. The horses average a thousand to twelve hundred pounds in weight, fifteen to sixteen hands in height and are usually half or a quarter Thoroughbred, the balance being Morgan, Saddle, standard or western breeds. He is expected to work about six hours a day covering twenty-five to thirty-five miles carrying a fully equipped soldier. Most of the work is done at the walk and the trot, the rate being about six miles an hour with a ten minute rest in each hour. Forced marches may be as long as a hundred miles and the men and animals are expected to arrive at their destinations in fit condition to fight or carry out the work for which they have been sent. Using this as a basis the horseman should be able to work out a satisfactory feeding schedule remembering always to give the grain in three feeds at least, the bulk of the hay at night.

Plan the feeding schedule so that the horse has plenty of time to digest his food before being asked to work hard or fast, put hay in the mangers before grain and either keep water before the horse at all times or water him before he is fed. See *WATERING*.

FEED MANGERS

These should be of iron or of wood with a metal strip tacked on all edges to prevent the horse from cribbing. Iron mangers may be made in a triangular shape, designed to be fitted in to a corner, or of rectangular shape to be attached to a straight wall. Straight stalls often have the manger set into the corner of the hay rack. Never put your feed manger too near the water bowl and inspect it frequently to be sure that it is clean. For horses that bolt their food a special manger has been designed with sections which prevents the horse getting too large a mouthful at a time. For horses that scatter their food there is a type of manger with a broad, flat edge which will help somewhat.

FEEL

Necessity for the Rider to Feel

Before the rider can expect to learn to communicate with and so control his horse, he must learn to understand what the horse is doing. This is accomplished first by *feeling* what his mount does and then *interpreting* what he feels. The horseman feels through his contact with the horse, either directly with his body and legs or through his reins.

FEET (the horse's)

The feet of the horse are of utmost importance. Without a good foot a horse is worthless, therefore, in selecting a horse great attention must be paid to the foot, its conformation and build. The exterior of the horse's foot is horny and completely insensitive. It is composed of the wall, or outer shell extending from the bottom of the foot to the coronet, the sole and the frog. Within this horny case we have three bones, the pedal or coffin bone, the navicular or small sesamoid and the lower part of one of the pastern bones. See illustration. The healthy, strong foot is characterized by a wall which is not brittle or shelly and which has no longitudinal cracks in it; by a sole which is well cupped, not hard but slightly chalky in consistency and a frog which is tough, elastic, large and which should touch the ground even when the horse is shod. The necessity for the external parts of the horse's foot to be as described is self evident if one thinks of the basic design of the foot and why nature has built it in this design. The wall must not be shelly, else it will be impossible to keep the shoes on and the horse, the protective covering chipped, will constantly be going lame.

If the sole appears flat instead of cupped it may indicate that the bones inside have dropped. This may be caused by injury or by certain diseases such as founder. If the sole is too hard from being kept too dry the horse may go lame from that cause alone.

The frog is nature's shock absorber. Unless the frog is so well developed that it touches the ground all the shock received by the foot when the horse is traveling will be taken on the outside edges of the wall. A horse with poor frogs may last for a season or so, but he cannot be expected to stand up under very much hard going at the gallop, fast trotting or, above all, jumping.

In shape the bottom of a horse's front foot is almost round while the hind feet are slightly more elliptical. Some horses, through bad shoeing, develop contracted

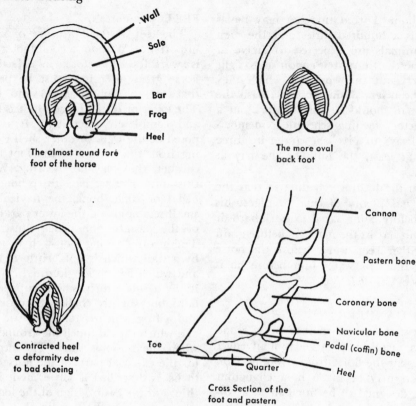

The almost round fore foot of the horse

The more oval back foot

Contracted heel a deformity due to bad shoeing

Cross Section of the foot and pastern

FIGURE 33. THE FEET OF THE HORSE.

heels. In this case the hoof narrows down at the heel and the frog becomes squeezed in. This condition always leads to trouble. It may be cured by turning the horse out to run barefoot or by corrective shoeing. For other diseases and injuries to the feet, see *INJURIES*.

FEET (position of rider's feet)
See *RIDING*.

FEET ON THE DASHBOARD
A term used to describe the old-fashioned seat in which the rider pushed his feet forward as though bracing them against the dashboard of a vehicle. One still sees this seat among riders of Saddlers and occasionally on riders to hounds of the English persuasion.

F.E.I. RULES
See *JUMPING, Scoring of.*

FENCING
The most common type of fencing and the most practical is the split-chestnut or post-and-rail fence. Four feet or four feet six inches in height, the average horse will not attempt to jump it. It may be left unpainted and will last for years especially if the post which is sunk in the ground be soaked in creosote and set in cement.

White board fences are very attractive and one sees them throughout the South. The upkeep is greater on these than on the post-and-rail due to the necessity for painting them, and they are more expensive to install. The ordinary wire fence is an abhorrence to the horseman as it may be the cause of serious injuries. Stone walls are the usual methods of enclosing the fields of New England, but these are not high enough to keep in a jumper and a rail must be added along the top. Sheep-hurdle fencing is more fragile than post-and-rail. The horse is much more apt to break it if he tries to jump it and fails; he can bend it by leaning against it and it is very difficult to install correctly. However it is an attractive looking type of fencing and may be painted or not as the owner chooses.

Electric fences have come to the fore very recently and, if you have horses or ponies that persistently get out, this is the best as well as the cheapest form of fencing. Anybody can put up an electric fence. One needs only some light posts, two inches in diameter, or some of the regulation metal posts used for wire fencing, a coil of wire, insulators and a transformer. If your animals are all about the same size only one strand of wire will be necessary. This should be strung at about the height of the animal's shoulder point. Directions that come with the transformer will show exactly how to string the wire. But the most important thing is to train the animals to respect the fence. This is done as follows. Fence off a corner of the paddock with the electric fence. Then place a little feed or a bundle of hay on the far side of the fence near enough so that the horse will be tempted to lean over and nibble at it. Lead your horse up to the fence and show him the feed. He will immediately lean over the fence. As soon as he feels the sting of the current he will jump back. Then he will try it once more, perhaps touching the wire deliberately with his nose to see if it was really that which caused him the shock. Finding that it was he will take great care never to touch the wire again. It really won't matter whether you have the current turned on or not. The horse will stay well away from the wire and your troubles, as far as chasing runaway ponies goes, will be over. Electric fences are practical but they are not pretty.

FEVER (in horses)

The normal temperature of a horse, taken rectally, is 100° F. Horses that run a temperature of a hundred and one or two should be watched carefully and those whose fever reaches a hundred and five must have drastic medication to bring down the temperature.

FIELD MASTER

A member of the hunt staff who is responsible for the conduct of the "field" or other riders is called the Field Master.

FIGHTING

See *VICES*.

FIGHTING THE BIT

If a horse fights the bit either by throwing his nose up and pulling, depressing his head and boring, shaking his head, or refusing to go against a light tension he should be given a complete course in bitting as described in *COLTS—breaking and training*.

FIGURE EIGHT

This is an equitation exercise designed to make the horse flexible and obedient. It may be executed at the sitting trot, at the posting trot with a change of diagonal on the change of direction, or at the canter. At the latter gait, horses that are in basic and intermediate stages of dressage training execute the figure eight at the canter with a simple or interrupted change of lead at the point where the change of direction is initiated. Horses in a more advanced stage of training may be asked to execute the first circle on the true lead, and make a flying change to the true lead for the opposite circle. The next stage is to have the horse execute the figure eight on the false canter, going from one lead to the other, first with an interrupted change, later with a flying change. For diagrams of the Figure Eight see *EQUITATION EXERCISES*.

FILLY

A female horse that has been weaned but has not reached four years of age. A male is called a colt. New born colts and fillies are known as foals. A mature female horse is a mare.

FIND
See *HUNTING TERMS*.

FINE HARNESS HORSE
Horses of the saddle breed which are driven are known as "fine harness horses." They wear a natural mane and tail and are asked to show good action but not speed. The "light harness horse" is a roadster, other types of harness horses are known as "heavy harness horses." For requirements in the different classes for these types of harness horses see *HORSE SHOW CLASSES, Harness Division*.

FINISH
The end of the race.

FIORD PONIES
These ponies are common in Norway and Denmark. They are stocky and of a chustnut or dun color with a black dorsal stripe. They are very hardy and of a quiet disposition but built more on the draft type than the saddle. The Fiord Pony, the Icelander and the Shetlander and the Moor ponies are supposed to be descendants of pure bred desert animals taken north from Constantinople by the returned Varangians in the eleventh century. The severe climate and lack of forage accounts for their degeneration in size and type from their Arabian ancestors.

FIRING (pin-firing)
If you notice little flecks of lighter hair giving the impression of pockmarks around your horse's knees, cannons, hocks or fetlock joints, you may take for granted that he has undergone the process of being "fired." Horses with severe injuries to ligaments and sinews or with bony excrescences such as splints are frequently given this severe treatment in hopes that nature, in repairing the new injury, will repair the old. Firing was formerly done with a hot iron. Now it is done with an electric needle. The injured part is jabbed a number of times after which the horse is rested until the hair has grown back. Horses that have been fired may go sound from then on but there is always the chance that the old injury will return.

In some racing stables it is customary to pin-fire the front legs of all young horses at the end of the first racing season, after which they are turned out for the summer. This practice is not so common abroad, and many veterinarians question the advisability of it.

FISTULA, FISTULOUS WITHER
This is an abscess on the withers. It is caused by a blow, an ill-fitting saddle or by the bite of another horse. It is an extremely serious condition which often calls for surgical treatment as not only the immediate tissues are involved but sometimes the ligaments above the vertebrae may be affected. The symptoms are extreme soreness and swelling. The abscess occasionally subsides but usually either bursts or has to be opened by the veterinarian. In severe cases poultices do no good but in milder forms antiphlogistene may be used to induce the abscess to come to a head. It may then be treated with B.F.I. powder or sulfa powder. The entire area around the fistula should be thickly covered with vaseline and the wound should be kept open and frequently washed with a lysol solution.

FIXTURES
See *HUNTING TERMS*.

FLAT RACING
A race for running horses in which there are no jumps. See *RACING*. Also *RECORDS AND STATISTICS—FLAT RACING* (appendix).

FLAT RIBS
The ribs of a Saddle horse should be well sprung, i.e., they should swell out from his sides. The draft breeds have ribs which come out almost horizontally giving them a very round barrel. A Saddler's back resembles a roof. The first three ribs should not spring out too far but as we move back along the barrel

the middle ribs should have a good bend. There are several reasons for choosing a horse with well sprung rather than flat ribs. In the first place such a horse has more room inside him for his lungs and larger storage space for food. Then, too, it will be found to be well-nigh impossible to keep a saddle in place on a really flat-ribbed hunter.

FLAX MANE

The cottony white mane and tail often found in chestnut horses and obligatory in Palominos are called "flax" manes and tails.

FLEXING EXERCISES (for the horse)
See *COLTS, Breaking and Training.*

FLEXING EXERCISES (for the rider)
See *RIDING; SUPPLING EXERCISES.*

FLEXING THE JAW
See *BITTING.*

FLOAT (teeth)
To float the horse's teeth is to file down the points. See *TEETH.*

FLOORING (for stalls)
See *BOX STALLS.*

FLY (to fly jumps)
A rider is said to fly his jumps when the horse, without changing his stride takes off well away from the obstacle and lands well beyond it with little appearance of having to exert effort in lifting himself.

FLYING CHANGE
When a horse is asked to change from one lead to the other at a gallop without coming to a half halt or reducing his gait he is said to be doing a "flying change." See also *DRESSAGE; EQUITATION EXERCISES.*

FOIL
See *HUNTING TERMS.*

FOOD
See *FEED; FEEDING; COLTS, Feeding of.*

FOREARM
See Figure 51, page 150, *THE HORSE, Points of.*

FORELOCK
The forelock or foretop is the strand of hair which grows at the poll and hangs forward over the forehead. Thoroughbreds and Saddle horses usually have the forelock left on but standardbreds and harness horses usually have the forelock clipped off.

FORGING
When a horse hits his front shoe with the back in traveling at a trot or pace he is said to be forging. The cure for this lies in corrective shoeing. Have the blacksmith shorten the front toes as much as possible and set the front shoes back a little. This will cause the horse to turn his front feet over more quickly and pick them up sooner. At the same time have the back toes left long and the back shoes set a little in advance of the toes. This will cause the horse to dwell slightly on his back feet and not pick them up so soon, giving the front feet time to get out of the way. The horse that forges so badly as to cut the quarters of his front feet is said to be overreaching. He should wear quarter-boots until his stride has been corrected. Another method of correcting forging is to have the blacksmith put on a "feathered shoe." In this type of shoe the toes are rolled on the front shoes, thus encouraging the horse to get his front feet out of the way faster. See also *SHOES, types of; SHOEING.*

FORMATION RIDING
When extensive and interesting trails are not available to groups of riders who like to ride in company, variety may be introduced in the form of Formation Riding. This also has the advantage in improving the skill of the rider and the

obedience of the horse. Formation Riding may be classified as follows: Memorized Rides such as Mounted Square Dancing, Quadrilles and Musical Rides, and formations done on oral command. The latter can again be subdivided into Close- and Open-Order Mounted Drill and Equitation Exercises done on command in formation. For exact movements, see the various formations mentioned above, as listed alphabetically.

FORRARD
See *HUNTING TERMS*.

FORT RILEY
The United States Cavalry school in Kansas.

FORT RILEY SEAT
Although all modern ideas of riding are based on the conception of what is called the "forward" seat the military seat of each country differs slightly from the others. The Fort Riley seat, sometimes called the "Balance" seat, is the version adopted by the United States Cavalry. It most nearly approximates the "Saumur" or French Cavalry seat.

FORWARD SEAT
The Forward seat as opposed to the Classical seat was first advanced by the Italian, Caprilli who, studying loose horses in the field, came to the conclusion that the horse could go fastest and jump highest if he were allowed to extend his neck and to carry the weight of the rider just behind the withers rather than in the middle of his back. It differs from the classical seat in that the stirrups are shorter, enabling the rider to rise out of the saddle very readily. The rider's feet are carried back so that the point of the toe is on a line with the knee, and he sits well forward in the saddle. In addition, as the speed of the gait is increased the upper part of the rider's body is carried more to the front. All military organizations have adopted some form of the Forward Seat and one sees only this seat over jumps

in the horse shows. The only riders who do not use it for jumping are the older hunting enthusiasts. Some think the five-gaiter can be ridden more easily and will show off to better advantage if the rider is not too far forward and professionals in the saddle classes adopt a ridiculous position from the point of view of horsemanship, sitting almost on the cantle of the saddle with the feet stuck out in true "feet on the dashboard" style. The rider does not post but sits all the gaits. That this is good horsemanship no one pretends, but it makes the horse look more short-coupled than he actually is and accentuates his front.

One still sees the old English seat on the hunting field mainly because its exponents learned to ride before the modern seat came into use. It is being replaced by a more forward position by the younger riders and will probably disappear completely in time.

FOUNDER
See *LAMINITIS*.

FOUR HORSEMEN OF THE APOCALYPSE
See *APOCALYPSE*.

FOX TROT
A slow, shuffling trot, the fox-trot is one of the gaits permitted in a five-gaited Saddler as a "slow-gait."

FRESH FORAGE
See *FEED*.

FRESHNESS (in horses)
Sometimes called "stall courage" this is merely high spirits induced by too little exercise together with a plentitude of good food. Horses are much more inclined to be fresh in cold weather than in moderate. If a fresh horse has to be ridden by a beginner he can best be quieted down by saddling and bridling him and then turning him loose in a small paddock or indoor hall. He must not be allowed to roll but he should be

encouraged to fling up his heels and play around until he works out all this excess energy. The best way to take out freshness under the saddle is to ride the horse at a strong trot.

FRONT

The chest of the horse is often referred to as his "front." It should be broad with the muscles well defined. A narrow chest means poor staying power.

FULL CRY

See *HUNTING TERMS*.

FUTURITY RACES

Races for young horses, i.e., two-year-olds, three-year-olds and four-year-olds. The entries are made long before the race, sometimes before the birth of the foal.

G

GAITED HORSE

A Saddle horse which has been schooled to the artificial as well as the natural gaits. See *GAITS*.

GAITS.

The natural gaits of the horse are the walk, trot and gallop, though the trot is less natural than the walk and gallop. The artificial gaits are the running walk, amble and broken amble, rack or single-foot and the pace. The canter is a collected gallop. The three-gaited or "walk-trot" horse is required to show the walk, the trot and the canter. The five-gaited horse must, in addition, show a "slow-gait" (running walk, fox-trot or amble) and a fast rack. Plantation walkers must show the slow gait, the walk and the canter. For detailed description of each gait refer to it in this text under its name.

GALLOP

The gallop is a three beat gait in which the horse moves forward in a leaping and bounding motion. The feet touch the ground in the following sequence, (left lead) right hind, left hind and right fore almost simultaneously, left fore, then a period of suspension. The canter is a collected form of the gallop. In an extremely collected form of the canter where most of the movement of the horse is in elevation and there is little forward progress the cadence is one of four beats. Also in the extremely extended form of the gallop there is a longer interval between the placing of the right hind and left fore and the cadence again is one of four beats. See also *LEADS: CANTER; GALLOP DEPARTS; FLYING CHANGE; COLTS, Breaking and Training of.*

GALLOP DEPARTS

The taking up of the gallop or canter from the halt, walk, or trot is known as the "gallop depart." In show riding the gallop depart is always demanded at the walk. In dressage work it is frequently demanded at the halt. In military riding the trot usually precedes the gallop. The gallop depart and the correct method of demanding it from the halt and walk is described under *RIDING*.

Xenophon, who wrote the earliest preserved book on equitation, laid down the rule of demanding the correct lead from the trot by pointing out that if one desired a left lead, one should give the command for it at the instant that the horse stepped upon his right fore-foot and was about to raise the left. Frequent practicing of gallop departs is of great benefit both to the horse and to the rider.

GALLOWAY

A small, hardy breed of horse developed in Galloway, Scotland. This term was often used to describe any cobby type of horse.

GALLS (saddle and harness galls)

These are sores caused by rubbing of the harness or saddle. The horse should not be used until the sores have completely healed. Methylene blue (blue gall remedy) is usually very effective.

GARRISON FINISH

A horse coming from behind to win in a last-minute burst of speed. The term is derived from the characteristic method of racing of the jockey "Snapper" Garrison.

GASKIN

See Figure 51, page 150, *HORSE, Points of.*

GELDING

A male horse that has been castrated.

GIRTH

The circumference of the horse taken just behind the withers and forelegs.

GIRTHS

The strap which goes under the horse's belly to hold the saddle in place. The most common type is the folded leather girth with two buckles on each end. Web girths with one or two buckles are also common. The Fitzwilliam girth is one of two buckles with a narrow, one buckle girth which runs over the wide one. The Balding girth is a leather girth which has been split and stitched together to narrow it. This girth is used for horses which develop girth sores easily and is very popular for polo. Western girths are called cinchas. They have iron rings instead of buckles and fasten by means of straps attached to the saddle.

Adjustment of

The girth should not be so tight that it pinches the horse nor so loose that there is danger of the saddle turning. The exact adjustment will depend on the conformation of the animal but the usual test is to insert three fingers at the side and slide them down towards the bottom. The girth should feel tight where it passes under the horse but should have a little slack at the side. Always examine the girth from both sides before mounting.

GLANDERS

This is an extremely dangerous disease which must be reported at once to the Board of Health. It is almost always fatal and may be communicated not only to other animals but also to man. Before entry many states require that a horse be tested for glanders.

The symptoms are abscesses in the mucous membranes of the nostrils and between the angles of the lower jaw.

GLOVES

Leather or string gloves are the only kinds which are practical for riding as fabric and wool gloves slip on the reins. String gloves are particularly good for wet weather. Unlined pigskin are good for cold weather being warmer than calf or kid. Lined gloves are generally too bulky for riding. For gloves required in the show ring and hunt field see *APPOINTMENTS, Hunting.*

GODOLPHIN BARB

One of the three foundation sires imported into England about 1725 from which was developed the Thoroughbred horse.

GONE AWAY

See *HUNTING TERMS.*

GOOD HANDS

A rider is said to have good hands when he keeps a light contact with his horse's mouth at all times. Good hands are most difficult to develop. Many riders after years in the saddle have not achieved them. It is very easy to tell the rider with good hands for he seems able to demand any movement from his horse with no apparent effort and both he and the horse appear relaxed and comfortable. See also *HANDS, of the rider.*

GOOD HANDS CLASSES

Classes, usually for juveniles, which are judged on horsemanship alone.

GOOD HANDS HORSE

A horse or pony suitable for equitation classes. He should be a suitable size with perfect manners, good appearance and be especially schooled for the requirements of the "good hands classes."

GOVERNESS CART

See *CARTS*.

GRASS

See *FEED, Fresh Forage*.

GRAVEL

Occasionally a grain of sand or gravel will work its way under the wall of the hoof. It will continue to push upwards until it comes out at the coronet. The horse may have fever in his foot and be quite lame. When the gravel reaches the coronet the abscess which will form there may be opened, the gravel removed and the wound treated as for an infection. The horse usually recovers though sometimes the lameness persists.

GRAY

See *COLORS OF THE HORSE*.

GREEN HORSE

A dealer's term meaning one which has recently been shipped in from the West and may or may not be acclimated.

GREEN HUNTER

A horse-show term meaning a hunter that has not been hunted with a recognized pack and that has not won a first ribbon at a recognized show prior to Jan. 1st of the current year.

GREEN HUNTER CLASSES

Classes open to green hunters only where the jumps do not exceed three feet six inches. See also *HORSE SHOW CLASSES, Hunter Division*.

GRETNA GREEN RACE

This is a good gymkhana game for intermediate or advanced riders. The riders race in pairs from one end of the ring or hall to the other, holding hands. Having reached the far end one of the pair dismounts and signs both their names on a piece of paper. He then remounts and the two race back to the starting post. If any pair drops hands it must begin over again. As a rule a boy and a girl make each pair. The game derives its name from the famous "Gretna Green" of England which was where runaway couples went to be married.

GRIFFIN

The Griffin is the tough little Mongolian pony which is used in China for polo. He is ugly, mean tempered and almost as tough as a donkey. He is also incredibly speedy and maneuverable. It is questionable whether polo would ever have been adopted by the English had it not been for the Griffin.

Attempts have been made to improve the size, appearance and condition of these ponies by feeding and stabling. Invariably this has resulted in a loss of speed and stamina. See also *MONGOLIAN PONIES*.

GROOM (*v.*)

To groom a horse is to clean and brush him. Every horse should be thoroughly groomed every day. If worked he should be groomed again after he has cooled out. Race horses are frequently groomed two or three times a day. Grooming not only makes the horse look well but by stimulating the circulation it benefits his health. The following is the usual procedure in grooming: with a rubber curry comb and using a circular motion go over the horse thoroughly from head to tail. Follow this with a brisk brushing with a dandy brush. Next, brush the horse off with a body brush. The mane and tail should be brushed with the dandy brush and may be combed with a metal mane comb. The horse's feet should be thoroughly cleaned out with a hoof pick and carefully examined for any signs of thrush or corns. Lastly, wipe the horse all over with a soft cloth. To test the thoroughness of the grooming run the fingers in furrows against the hair. If gray tracks show the horse is still dirty. Horses that have just been clipped may be galloped until they sweat, then washed with hot water and soap, rinsed off with cool water, thoroughly hand-rubbed and walked until dry. This will take out the dandruff but the horse's coat will not be glossy for several days afterwards due to the lack of oil.

GROUP RIDING

Riding in company through country trails is one of the pleasantest forms of exercise but one should be careful to observe the various courtesies that make such riding safe. See *COURTESY*. For advanced riders, military drills, formation rides and music rides will provide entertainment and improve the horsemanship of the group. Games may also be used to stimulate interest in groups of riders. Paper-chases are fun and, even better, in country not suited to fox or drag hunting, a bloodhound hunt may be formed and will be found to be intensely interesting to all classes of riders. See *FORMATION RIDING, MUSICAL RIDES, MOUNTED DRILLS*.

GUESSING GAME

This is a most useful game for use during instruction periods to teach the points of the horse and the parts of the saddle and bridle. It is suitable for all ages of children even as young as four or five years old. The instructor begins by naming a few terms such as the parts of the bridle alone. The class repeats each name and the part is pointed out to them. Then one child is chosen to be "it." He stands, dismounted, by a pony and thinks of one of the parts that have been named. The other players each guess in turn until one names the part of which the child who is "it" is thinking, then takes his place and in turn

thinks of a part. As each part is guessed the child who is "it" must point to the part named or lose his place. When the parts of the bridle have been learned the instructor may go on to the saddle, taking up a few new terms at each lesson until the children are familiar with the seventy or more parts of bridle, saddle and horse.

GYMKHANA

A gymkhana is a riding meet in which most of the classes consist of games or contests rather than regulation horse-show competitions. Gymkhanas are excellent for childen and do much to spur them on to improving their riding. In arranging a gymkhana try and vary the classes so that the horses may have a little rest and not be kept going continually. This may be done by making certain classes open only to horses of a certain size or by following an energetic game such as the "Water Race" with an "Egg and Spoon Contest" or a "Bun Eating Race" which is not so strenuous. The main thing is to organize your gymkhana so well that there is no delay between classes. The age and experience of the riders must be considered also.

GYMNASTICS (mounted)

Also called "Monkey Drill." These are active exercises which develop suppleness, boldness and muscle in the rider. The most famous exponents of mounted gymnastics are the Cossack Riders who, in their Cadet Corps, spend a year or two learning to vault on and off horses at all gaits, to pick up objects from the ground at a gallop, to stand in the saddle or on a pad at all gaits, to ride two or three horses, standing, with one leg on each in the former case and, in the latter, straddling the middle horse while bracing the legs on the outside horses, to execute "pyramids" in which riders stand on each other's shoulders, etc. These mounted gymnastics were also part of the training of the American Indian lads. They may be adapted to the ability of the learner and will form an interest-

**FIGURE 34.
VAULTING OVER THE PONY.**

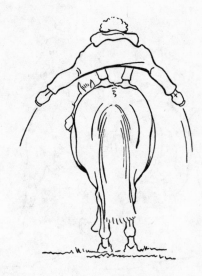

**FIGURE 35.
VAULTING ON FROM THE REAR.**

**FIGURE 36. VAULTING INTO POSI-
TION FROM THE SIDE, "NO
HANDS."**

**FIGURE 37a. VAULTING OFF AND
OVER A GALLOPING HORSE. FIRST
PHASE: RIDERS SIDE BY SIDE.
RIDER ON RIGHT CONTROLLING
BOTH HORSES.**

FIGURE 37b. VAULTING, SECOND PHASE: RIDER VAULTS OFF HORSE AND BOUNCES ON THE BALLS OF HER FEET ON THE GROUND.

FIGURE 37c. VAULTING, THIRD PHASE: RIDER, IMPELLED BY THE MOVEMENT OF HER HORSE, SPRINGS OVER IT ONTO THE OTHER ONE. IN LEARNING THIS MOVEMENT, THE RIDER SHOULD FIRST PRACTICE SPRINGING BACK ONTO HER OWN HORSE. HORSES MAY BE COUPLED TOGETHER AT THE BITS TO HELP KEEP THEM TOGETHER.

FIGURE 38. TURNING A SOMER-SAULT OFF RUMP OF PONY. IN-STRUCTOR HELPS WITH A QUICK LIFT ON THE BACK OF THE BOY'S HEAD IF HE DOES NOT SPRING HARD ENOUGH.

FIGURE 39a. THE SCISSORS. THE RIDER STARTED FROM A NOR-MAL SITTING POSITION FACING FRONT.

FIGURE 39b. THE SCISSORS COMPLETED, THE RIDER IS NOW FACING THE REAR. HE MAY REPEAT THIS MOVEMENT TO FACE FRONT.

FIGURE 40.
PYRAMIDS, ONE OF THE FEATS IN MOUNTED GYMNASTICS.

ing part of his program. Any active boy or girl of ten or twelve on a small, quiet animal can learn to vault on and off at the various gaits, to stand, a foot on each horse while another rider guides them, to vault on over the hindquarter, to reverse his position by swinging his legs up behind him, crossing them and turning quickly (the scissors) and to balance on one shoulder in a "hand-stand." The greatest problem is not in teaching the child but in finding a pony small enough and gentle enough to put up with these "monkey shines."

H

HABIT (force of)

How fortunate it is that force of habit can be so strongly developed in the horse! With his tendency to grow hysterical and his great strength the horse would be totally unmanageable by man were it not for this force of habit. Reactions are faster than voluntary actions, hence, the horse, schooled by carefully established behavior patterns, obeys his master when he receives the familiar aid signals even though it may go against his instinct.

But if force of habit is our means of training horses to obey us it can also work the other way. Horses, ridden by careless or inexperienced riders, easily develop dangerous vices. A horse that is always permitted to take up the gallop at a certain point in the trail may readily develop into a runaway. The horse that is allowed to "get away" with a vice such as turning to go home when he wants to will become a "barn rat," etc. Always demand obedience from your horse, and never let him form a bad habit, by so doing he will remain your servant, otherwise you will find him in the Master's seat. See also *COLTS, breaking and training of.*

HABIT (riding)

Women's riding apparel is generally spoken of as a "riding habit." Styles have changed considerably in riding habits and though the present ones may not be so romantic as those of a previous generation they are certainly far more comfortable. For many centuries all women rode side-saddle. Those were the days of sweeping ostrich plumes and velvet skirts so long that the hems had to be lined with leather because, when the rider was mounted, they very nearly dragged on the ground. As women became more active equestrians the danger of these long, trailing robes with their propensities towards getting hung in the saddle horn was recognized and for them was substituted the "safety skirt." This latter is an apron type of garment, worn wrapped around when the rider is on foot, but opened out so that there is less danger of its catching when the rider is mounted.

In the West, where the western saddle was used, women took to riding astride. The accepted form of riding habit in that part of the country became the divided skirt. These skirts worn by the "cow-girls" were often very elaborate leather affairs with beaded work and fringes, etc. Hawaiian Amazons had still another version of the correct habit for a woman riding astride. This consisted of long, loose trousers which, when the rider was mounted, hung below the stirrups and touched the ground! The toes were thrust into the stirrups through the material. On the ground the wearer of these strange garments looked like nothing so much as an extremely long-legged man walking on his knees! Turkish women also rode astride and wore simply very full men's trousers.

When the first version of what is now considered correct apparel for riding astride appeared it was certainly homely! It is not to be wondered that men, everywhere, and women as well, prophesied that the mode of riding astride for women would be short-lived. The coats, cut of heavy material, were bulky and hung to the rider's knees. The breeches were anything but smart. But times have changed and the smartly cut riding habit of today is most becoming and as practical as a man's. See also *APPOINTMENTS, Hunting; DRESS.*

HACKAMORE

A bitless bridle used in the West for training horses. The word is derived from the Spanish *"jaquima."* Special classes for horses shown in the hackamore, known as jaquima classes, are held. See *HORSE SHOW CLASSES, Stock Horse Division.* For use of *HACKAMORE* in training, see *COLTS, breaking and training of.*

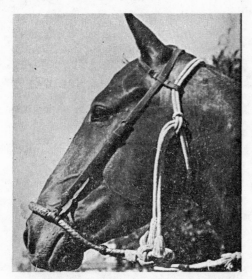

FIGURE 41. THE TRAINING HACK-AMORE, WESTERN TYPE. *FROM PRACTICAL HORSE BREEDING BY JACK WIDMER, PUBLISHED BY CHARLES SCRIBNER'S SONS. USED BY COURTESY OF THE AUTHOR AND PUBLISHER.*

FIGURE 42. THE HACKAMORE WITH THE SPECIAL HACKAMORE BIT. *FROM PRACTICAL HORSE BREEDING BY JACK WIDMER, PUBLISHED BY CHARLES SCRIBNER'S SONS. USED BY COURTESY OF THE AUTHOR AND PUBLISHER.*

HACK (*n.*)

Term used to describe the horse used for ordinary pleasure riding as distinguished from a hunter, Saddler, cow-pony, etc.

HACK (*v.*)

To ride for pleasure. This term is also used in connection with hunting in regard to moving from one covert to the other. At this time, of course, hounds are not running and the Master, field and hunt servants move at a slow jog trot.

HACK, BRIDLEPATH HACK

Classes for bridlepath hacks demand that the horse enter on a loose-reined, flat-footed walk, that he show speed and steadiness at the trot and that he have a comfortable canter. It is customary for the horse to be shown at all gaits on a very loose rein to demonstrate his manners. The horse is judged on his apparent ability to give an easy, comfortable ride. Any show of nervousness or high spirits would disqualify him. See also *HORSE SHOW CLASSES.*

HACK, HUNTER-HACK

The hunter-hack is judged both on his ability as a hunter and as a hack, hence he is required to have good manners, to show a good road trot and easy canter as well as a flat-footed, quiet walk and to jump not higher than three feet six inches. See also *HORSE SHOW CLASSSES.*

HACKNEY

The word *hackney* and its abbreviation, *"hack"* derived from the Latin, is very old and for many years has meant a general purpose horse and general purpose vehicle. During the "Dark Ages," a breed of horse known as the "Great Horse" was developed in Belgium and Holland. These horses, large and rotund in relation to height, were primarily used for carrying the tremendous weights of the knights in armor. However in Norfolk county there was developed, by means of the introduction of Thorough-bred and desert strains, a lighter horse known as the "Norfolk Trotter." From him, in turn was developed the Hackney.

As the roads in England improved, the diligences of France and the lighter Hackney coaches of England took over the transportation problems of the people, a breed of horse less weighty than the Percherons and faster became desirable. The country gentleman also wanted a horse with good, breedy lines, high action and quality. For him the high-stepping Hackney was bred. The better the roads, the less weighty the horse, so we find that though the early Hackneys were in reality coach horses, as time went on a smarter, more sport-ing type of horse and pony came into being.

In Ireland, land of Thoroughbred hunters, the Irish Cob, a pony with a good deal of Hackney blood plus some Thoroughbred became popular for gen-eral use and hunting. When the auto-mobile usurped the place of the horse on the highway the Hackney, no longer useful as a work animal, became the pet of the breeders for horse show purposes. But now from being a rather rotund ani-mal of from 900 to 1,100 pounds, the popular model for showing had become a dainty, high spirited flash of horse flesh weighing nearer 700 or 800 pounds.

The Hackney is noted for his exag-geratedly high action which makes him sometimes a little rough for saddle work. The modern, highly bred specimens are too nervous and spirited for any except show work. The larger specimens some-times show great jumping ability. Sir Gilbert, a well known Hackney stallion of the larger type was blinded in one eye destroying his usefulness for show ring purposes as a driving horse. But later it was discovered that Sir Gilbert had ex-traordinary talent as an open jumper and he resumed his show career in that role taking many prizes. Not only that but he was bred to Thoroughbred mares and his get also proved to be good over the hurdles. That the Hackney takes

readily to jumping is not to be wondered at when one remembers that the Founda-tion Sire of this breed was Blaze (foaled 1733), grandson of Darley Arabian from whom nearly all modern steeplechase horses are descended. And, in remember-ing the speed and stamina of the Hack-ney as a road horse one should also bear in mind that Blaze was also a direct ancestor of Messenger, the flea-bitten English Thoroughbred from whom are descended the Morgans, Hambletonians, pacers and Saddlers of this country.

HACKNEY HORSE SOCIETY
See *AMERICAN HACKNEY HORSE SOCIETY*.

HACKNEY PONIES
Although the Hackney Association in which all animals of purebred Hackney stock are registered is called the Ameri-can Hackney Horse Society, by far the largest number of animals registered are ponies. That is, they are under fourteen hands, two inches (56 six inches at the top of the withers). Through years of selective breeding these little animals have become the most fiery, with the most spectacularly high action, of any breed. They are generally used for driv-ing, as their high action makes them unsuitable for riding. The advent of the machine age has relegated them almost entirely to the show ring and training track. But in the former there are a great variety of classes for them, espe-cially in certain parts of the country, where there is much interest in breeding and showing them. Hackneys are shown singly, in pairs and tandem, as well as "in hand." The classes are often divided as to size, and sometimes further limited, as, for instance, "lady to drive."

Hackney blood, to give flashiness, is being introduced into other pony breeds, mainly American Shetland, and these little ponies, originally bred to work in the coal mines or as children's mounts, are so changed as to become unrecog-nizable. See also *SHETLAND PONY*.

FIGURE 43.   THE HACKNEY PONY CASSILIS GLEN IDEAL, OWNED BY MRS. J. MACY WILLETS, CASSILIS FARM, NEW MARLBORO, MASS. *COURTESY OF THE OWNER.*

HALF HALT

In changing leads on a figure eight one often employs the half halt. The horse, being on one lead for the first circle, is closely collected as he completes it. There is an instant of suspension as the collection is increased and the signals for the change of lead given. Then the horse steps out on the second circle employing the new lead. The horse must not be held at the half halt for more than an instant or he will become heavy under the hand, lose animation and come to a complete halt.

HALF TURN

This is an equitation exercise. The horses being on the track without regard to distance, the command is "half turn." Each horse individually turns toward the center of the ring in a half circle. He then returns to the wall on a diagonal and continues going in the opposite direction from which he started. The track of a horse executing a half turn resembles half of a heart. The movement should be executed at whatever gait the horse was on when the command was given, without any increase or decrease in speed. The rider should use his direct or indirect rein, his outside leg and shift his weight towards the center of the half circle. If the horse is at a walk the diameter of the half circle should be two yards, four if he is at a trot and six at a canter. All horses should execute the movement in such manner that they reach the wall and take up the new direction simultaneously. See also *RIDING, Equitation Exercises.*

HALF TURN (in reverse)

In this turn, the riders being against the wall and riding without regard to distance, first pull away from it on a diagonal and then turn a half circle towards it. The track is the same as that of the half turn but the rider follows it from the opposite direction.

HALT (n.)

At the halt the horse should stand quietly, the rider should sit relaxed but straight. There should be no tension on the reins. In saddle and fine harness classes the horse is usually required to "camp" or "stretch" when he is at the halt. See CAMPING. Hunters stand in a normal position with their weight evenly distributed and the hind legs well under the rump. Trotting horses usually stand with the hind legs slightly behind the croup.

HALT (v.)

A horse should not be jerked to a halt. If he is on a trot or a canter his gait should be decreased to the walk before he is halted. The rider, in halting, should cease posting, sit down in the saddle, apply a slight grip with his legs and tension with the reins bringing the horse's chin in and causing him to flex at the poll and relax the jaw. As soon as the horse has obeyed and come to a halt the tension should be discontinued and the rider's legs relaxed.

In Dressage competitions the horse is required to halt at least twice and stand immobile. He must not swing his hindquarters off the track nor take more than two walking steps in stopping from the canter or from the trot.

HALTER BREAKING

See COLTS, Breaking and Training.

HALTERS

Halters, sometimes called "head collars," are used for leading the horse and tying him. There are several types made of a number of different materials for many purposes. The "Johnson" halter which is of rope is very strong and inexpensive. It will outlast the average leather halter and is easy to put on and take off but care must be taken to fit it very loosely as it has a tendency to rub the cheek bones. Show halters usually have brow bands and are of finer, lighter leather than the ordinary stable halter. The dealer's halter of hemp is unsatisfactory in the stable as it cannot be adjusted properly and consequently is easily removed by the horse. Colored web halters, though cheap and pretty, especially for ponies are not satisfactory as they break very easily.

The novice sometimes has great trouble in figuring out how to put a halter on. If you will take the buckle in the left hand and the strap in the right hand, making sure that the three short parallel straps are on the bottom it is easy to slip the horse's nose through the noseband, then swing the strap over from the far side behind the ears, catch it with the left hand, bring the right hand back and buckle it snugly enough to prevent the horse getting it over his head.

HALTER SHANK

This is the rope which attaches by means of a clip to the ring in the halter and is used to lead or tie the horse.

HALTING (a group of riders)

When it is necessary to halt a group of riders some warning should be given to prevent their piling up on each other. This can be in the form of a warning hand held up by the leader a few steps before he halts or by a command. All riders should be careful to stop four feet from the horse in front of them. If a horse is restless and tries to back up or go forward he should be turned so that he faces sideways, his rump away from the trail. If the leader's horse is restless he should be turned to face the other riders when he will be contented to stand.

HAMBLETONIAN (Rysdyk's)

Rysdyk's Hambletonian was the foundation sire of that great breed of trotters which are known by his name. He was foaled in 1849. His father, Abdallah, was a thoroughly disappointing horse. By Messenger's Mambrino out of Amazonia, a granddaughter of Messenger, he was ugly with a bad disposition. He was so ungainly that, in spite of his royal breeding, the farmers would not send their mares to him. Finally he was sent up to Orange County where Jonas Seely, a well-to-do farmer bred him to a crippled mare. This mare was by Bellfounder out of One Eye. One Eye had belonged to Seely's father and when he found the daughter in a butcher shop, crippled

from a runaway, he bought her out of sentiment and brought her home. She was known as the "Kent Mare." In 1849 she dropped her foal. Seely evidently had no great faith either in her ability to produce a winner nor in the breeding of the foal (four lines of his pedigree through Silvertail, Bishop's Hambletonian, Amazonia and Mambrino ran back to the imported Thoroughbred, Messenger) for he sold mare and foal to his hired man, Bill Rysdyk for a hundred and twenty-five dollars, who, having no cash, gave him a "promise to pay."

Rysdyk now retired and set up a

FIGURE 44. RYSDYK'S HAMBLETONIAN, PAINTED FROM LIFE BY J. H. WRIGHT, N. Y., 1865. CURRIER AND IVES, 1880. *COURTESY OF WHITNEY COLLECTION OF SPORTING ART, YALE UNIVERSITY ART GALLERY.*

breeding farm. Two years later, Hambletonian won his first prize as the best two-year-old stallion in the Orange County Fair. The following year he was awarded five dollars as the best three-year-old stallion but neither of these winnings contributed especially to his fame. Three years from that time some of his get began winning at the fairs. But even

then some critics considered the Hambletonian stock as lacking in muscular development. Perhaps it was prejudice, perhaps it was blindness or lack of knowledge, but the fact remains that Hambletonian, whose get became the greatest and still are the greatest trotters ever bred, was not recognized as an important sire until he was twelve years old! Greyhound, the horse which today holds the record in harness racing of a mile in 1:55¼ ably demonstrates the predominance of Hambletonian blood. For four generations all his sires and for three generations all his dams have been direct descendants of that great horse.

Hambletonian was a bay horse with black points and two white socks. He had the neck and throttle of a Thoroughbred. His muscular development was tremendous. His croup was higher than his withers, a characteristic of all fast trotters and his great, driving, hind legs were placed behind the croup rather than under him. It was the smooth, piston drive of those hind legs which made the descendants of Hambletonian, son of the "no-good" Abdallah, out of a worthless, crippled mare able to pass all other breeds on the track.

HAMBLETONIAN (Society)

In the early nineteen-twenties harness racers realized that something must be done to spur the interest in trotters. At Churchill Downs great purses were being offered for running horses. The automobile had usurped the place of the roadster. The registration of colts of trotting blood was diminishing. The trotting interests took a leaf from the Kentucky Horse Breeder's Association. Not many years before the Kentucky Derby had all but been discontinued. For years it had been run at a loss. Finally Colonel Matt Winn was persuaded to buy Churchill Downs for forty thousand dollars. His method of bringing back interest in horse racing in Kentucky was to offer big stakes and to advertise. The Hambletonian Association was formed in nineteen twenty-three for the purpose of offering a stake for three-year-old trotters and thus create a market for trotting colts.

HAMBLETONIAN

Leading three-year-old stake race for standard bred horses. It was first raced at Syracuse, N. Y. in 1926. From there it was moved to the Good Time track at Goshen, N. Y. However, a few years ago it was removed to DuQuoin, Ill. In 1962 the Yonkers Raceway put in a bid of $50,000 for the race, later raising the bid by an additional $125,000. The latter increase was not admitted, as the bids had already been closed, and the Hayes Brothers of DuQuoin retained the race in Illinois.

HAMSTRING

The tendon running behind the cannon bones.

HAND

The horse is measured by "hands." A hand is four inches. Thus a horse measuring sixty-two inches is fifteen hands and two inches (15:2). One may suppose that, in the old days, a horse was measured by a man placing his hands one above the other from withers to ground, to ascertain the height. As a man's hand is about four inches in width that measurement was later taken as standard and remained known as a "hand."

HAND UP (when mounting)

There is only one proper way to give a hand up when mounting a rider. Have the rider stand opposite the horse's shoulder and facing it. Now bend your left knee, put your left hand on it, palm up. The rider next places his left foot in the open palm. The foot may be grasped by the ankle. At a word from the person on the ground the rider springs, at the same time the person giving the hand up straightens his legs and lifts. The rider should settle into the saddle without a jolt. By using the body as well as the arm to lift the rider there is little danger of strain and even a woman can mount a rider weighing somewhat more than herself.

HANDICAP JUMPING

In informal shows where there is a dearth of jumpers of the same size or where it is desirable to encourage jumping for children, the handicap jumping class may be resorted to. In this class the height of the jump depends on the size of the horse or pony and the ability of the rider. Jumps may be as low as eighteen inches or two feet for the little Shetlands and as high as three feet or three six for the older riders on horses. In judging such a class, performance, horse and rider only should count. If a pony negotiates a two foot jump better than a horse over a three foot six, the pony should win.

HANDICAPS (in racing)

The present system of handicapping by the addition of weights carried by the horse was not always used. At first horses were handicapped by a system of head starts. This proved very unsatisfactory, however. The Kentucky Association, formed in 1826, standardized the length of races and introduced handicapping as we know it, i.e., horses known to be faster than others were required to carry more weight. It must be remembered that whereas the addition of live weight, balanced as it is over the axis of the center of gravity, makes little difference to the speed of a horse, dead weight in the form of lead carried in the blanket on the barrel definitely slows him down.

In harness racing also, handicapping was first done by head starts. Later, the present system of having a horse graded according to his previous track records was introduced. Thus horses, all of whom are known to have trotted a mile in 2:10 will race together, while those which can do a mile in two minutes flat will be in a different class. See *RACING, Scale of Weights* (appendix).

HANDKERCHIEF (teaching pony to pick up)

This is a pretty parlor trick for a child's pony or a pet Saddler. Wrap a piece of apple loosely in a handkerchief. Let the horse smell it and then put it on the ground in front of him. He will nose it until he gets the tidbit. Presently he will pick up any handkerchief hoping to find the apple within. He can also be taught to untie a handkerchief fastened to his back ankle in the same way.

HANDS (of the Rider)

The hands of the rider are one of the "natural aids" with which he controls the horse. According to his skill and ability the rider's hands may be classified as "heavy" or "pulling" hands, "light" hands, and "good" or "educated" hands. Heavy or pulling hands are characteristic of the beginner who uses his reins to maintan his balance and who, as yet, has developed no sensitivity in his hands. He does not know how strongly to use his hands on a given horse in a given situation, or when to stop using them. Heavy hands are very painful to the sensitive horse. Yet this is a stage through which all riders must pass, and that is why horses used by beginners are chosen for their lack of sensitivity.

Light hands are characteristic of the intermediate rider who is no longer dependent on his reins as "life lines." He can keep his seat in the saddle under all ordinary circumstances independently of his hands and reins. Good or educated hands are those of the truly experienced rider. Such a horseman is able to sense, through his hands, exactly how strongly he must use them and exactly how soon they should become passive after being used actively in any situation and on any horse. Only when a rider has developed educated hands can he expect to keep a horse "on the bit" and to hold him correctly "between his legs and hands." Of all the people who consider themselves good horsemen, probably only one-tenth of one per cent ever develop really educated or good hands. See also *RIDING*.

HANDS (position of in riding)

The hands should be held from six to ten inches apart, about three inches in front of the saddle and three inches above the withers. The knuckles should be almost perpendicular, the thumbs elevated and resting on the bight of the reins. There should be a straight line from the rider's elbow to the horse's bit. The hands should be flexible, never stiff. The edges of the reins are held by the fingers. The hands should not move perceptibly and commands through the reins should be given by movements of the fingers and wrist, not of the arm. In jumping the hands are extended and lowered as the horse extends his head. The rider is thus enabled to retain control of his horse through a continued light contact between hands and bit.

HANDY HUNTER

Classes for the handy hunter require that he have good manners, taking all his gaits on a loose rein, that he be quiet at his jumps, appear to be easy to sit to and have comfortable gaits. In addition to the ordinary show jumps he is asked to negotiate obstacles which approximate trappy country. For example he may be asked to stand while the rider opens and goes through a gate, or to walk up to a jump and stand quietly while the rider dislodges the top rail. He must then back a step and take the lowered jump from there. The rider is also required to dismount, lead the horse over a jump. This class is held inside the ring; the jumps are not more than three feet six inches and the horse is judged on his promptness, manners, way of going and general "handiness." See also *HUNTERS, How Classified; HORSE SHOW CLASSES.*

HARK FORWARD
See *HUNTING TERMS.*

HARNESS (care of)

Harness should be kept cleaned and well oiled. It should never be allowed to dry out nor to remain wet or muddy. Buckles and chains should be kept polished. If it is to be stored it should be wiped with some mildew preventive. When not in use it should be hung on special harness racks. Unbuckle the buckles for cleaning every once in a while. This will help to prevent wear on the leather.

HARNESS (first lessons in)
See *COLTS, Breaking and Training.*
Fitting of.

Each horse should have his own harness which is carefully fitted to him. The girth should be quite tight but the belly band loose. The crupper should not be so tight as to irritate the tail nor so loose as to flop. The bearing rein must be adjusted according to the natural carriage of the animal's head. The bit should fit snugly and the chain should not be twisted nor too tight. If blinders are worn they should not hug the horse's eyes so closely as to impede his vision nor should they waggle at each motion of his head. The collar, especially, must fit the horse correctly or he will be miserable from collar galls. If a breast-harness instead of a collar is worn it must not press on the windpipe. For correct names of parts of the harness see Figure 45, on opposite page.

HARNESS CLASSES

Harness classes are divided into three divisions, *Fine Harness,* horses which are of the American Saddle Breed to be shown to a four wheeled show wagon; *Light Harness,* roadsters shown to road wagon or bike, and *Heavy Harness.* The Fine Harness horse wears his mane and tail long and full. He is shown at an animated part trot. Speedy trotting is penalized. He must stand quietly and back readily and his manners must be perfect.

The Light Harness horse or Roadster is a horse of good appearance with a natural tail and pulled mane. His forelock is usually clipped. He must be solid color, between fifteen:one and sixteen hands, weighing 1,000 to 1,150 pounds. He must have good manners in a light bit and must show speed at the trot going both ways of the ring. He need not have high action. Roadsters enter the ring clockwise at a jog. They then turn counter clockwise, show a road gait and then speed. The Roadster is sometimes shown under a saddle.

Heavy Harness Division:
In this division horses are expected to

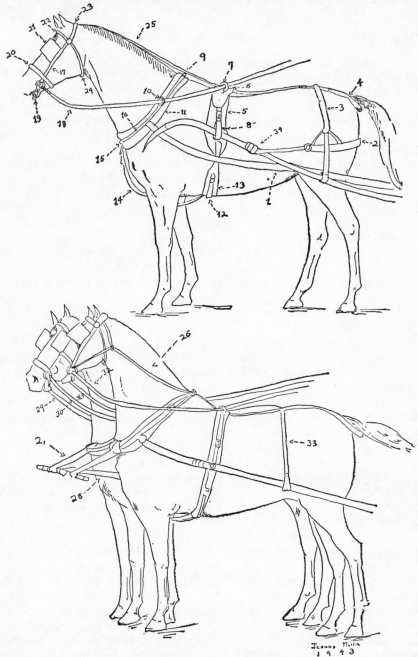

FIGURE 45. PARTS OF THE HARNESS. 1. TRACE. 2. BREECHING.
3. KICKING STRAP. 4. CRUPPER. 5. BACKBAND. 6. PAD. 7. TERRET.
8. TUG. 9. HAMES STRAP. 10. HAMES TERRET. 11. COLLAR. 12. BELLY-
BAND. 13. GIRTH. 14. BREASTPLATE. 15. KIDNEY LINK. 16. HAMES.
17. CHEEKPIECE. 18. REINS. 19. LIVERPOOL BIT. 20. NOSEBAND. 21.
BLINKERS. 22. BROWBAND. 23. CROWN PIECE. 24. THROAT LASH.
25. OVERHEAD CHECK. 26. SIDE CHECK. 27. POLE STRAP. 28. POLE.
29. OFF REIN. 30. OFF COUPLING REIN. 31. NEAR COUPLING REIN.
32. NEAR REIN. 33. LOIN STRAP. 34. HOLD BACK. NOTICE THAT IN
DOUBLE HARNESS NO HOLD BACK STRAP IS WORN AS THE HORSES
HOLD BACK BY MEANS OF THE POLE STRAPS ATTACHED TO COL-
LAR AND POLE PIECE.

show animation at the trot, speed is not required. They are shown to an appropriate vehicle and must go both ways of the ring.

Heavy harness classes are as follows:

Single Maiden Harness Horse, to be judged on quality, performance and manners.

Single Novice Harness Horse, to be judged on quality, performance and manners.

Single Limit Harness Horse, to be judged on quality, performance and manners.

Open Single Harness Horse, to be judged on quality, performance and manners.

Lady's Single Harness Horse, Mare or Gelding, to be shown to a phaeton:

Manners must be paramount, horse should be notable for beauty and quality, of solid color without flashy markings. The darker colors are preferred. Should show good action at a park gait, should stand quietly and back easily. For appointments see *APPOINTMENTS, Harness.*

Gig Class, single harness horse, stallion, mare or gelding:

Horse to be not under 14:3 nor over 16 hands. Should have good action but excessive speed not required. To be judged on presence, manners, performance and quality.

Amateur Class, single harness horse driven by amateur.

Stallions in Harness:

Limited to stallions, judged on quality, manners, performance.

Championship Harness Horse Stake:

Single Harness horse judged on performance, presence, quality, conformation and manners. Must be entered in show in at least one other class in this division other than breeding class.

Pairs, Maiden, Novice, Limit, Open, Lady's:

See description of each of above in single horse classes. In addition to performance pairs should be mated as nearly as possible in color, size and way of going.

Tandem:

To be shown to a gig or other suitable vehicle. The wheeler should have substance and power, the leader more brilliance and be slightly smaller. They need not match in color though matching is preferred.

Collection of Three Harness Horses:

To be owned by one person and shown as a pair and single. To be judged on performance as a unit, uniformity and quality.

Selection of Three Harness Horses:

To be owned and exhibited by one person. To be judged on basis of three best animals of one exhibitor, uniformity not to count.

Four-in-Hand Park Drag of solid color:

To be drawn by four matched horses with park harness, two servants in livery. To be judged on performance, quality, manners, uniformity and appointments. Appointments include extra collar, traces, reins, brake shoe, quarter blankets and coolers, lap robes, water pail, tool kit.

Road Coach:

Of bright or variegated colors to be drawn by team not necessarily matched with road harness to carry a guard in livery. To be judged on performance and substance.

Harness Ponies:

Rules for Harness classes apply in pony classes except that Gig, Lady's Pair of Harness Ponies, and Lady's Single Harness Pony are not appointment classes. Harness pony classes may also be limited to a certain size, i.e., for ponies over ten:two and under twelve hands, or over twelve and under fourteen:two, etc.

HARNESS RACING

The history of harness racing and of the development of the roadster is intensely interesting. The rise and fall in the popularity in this country and in England of the trotters and pacers, and the reasons for these declines and increases in interest form a fascinating study. Take the matter of roads. The light trotting horse came into fashion in England only after the days of coaching

FIGURE 46. FAST TROTTERS ON HARLEM LANE, N. Y. CURRIER
AND IVES, 1870. *COURTESY WHITNEY COLLECTION OF SPORTING
ART, YALE UNIVERSITY ART GALLERY.*

and the improvements of the roads had taken place. In this country one of the reasons why trotters and trotting races made their appearance in New England long before they became popular in the South was because the roads were so much better in the North. Climate also played its part. In Canada and in New England the snow-packed roads made ideal footing for the roadster, while, at that season in the South the roads were a slough of mud and impassable except on horseback.

The invention of gunpowder, too, influenced the development of trotters. Up until that time the knights had required a heavy, draft type of horse. When, due to the use of firearms, the knights were superseded by the light cavalry the demand was for the speedy, light horse that could trot and, from the trot, break into a canter.

But perhaps the most important factor in the development of harness racing in

this country was religion. Since the seventeen hundreds the Presbyterians in New England had been firm in their censure of racing. By racing they meant running, not trotting. Indeed it would have been well nigh impossible for them to have forbidden contests in trotting, for every countryman as well as members of high society had his roadster. On market day it was the custom for the farmer and the farmer's lad to invite his lady or his lass to drive to town, and, meeting his neighbor, what more natural than to prove there and then which driver could throw dust in the eyes of the other? These impromptu contests were known as "brushes."

In 1802 all race tracks in the North East were formally closed by the reformers. But trotting was not racing. Presumably the reasoning of the courts was that a race was a contest to see who could go the fastest. If a horse trotted he was obviously not going as fast as he could if he were running, therefore, strictly speaking, he was not racing!

With running horses banned it is not surprising that in New England the development of the trotter and pacer as racers became of paramount interest. Previous to this time, in 1788, a flea-bitten, not very handsome Thoroughbred stallion had been imported from England. His name was Messenger and he traced his descent straight back to the Darley Arabian. Messenger had been on the English tracks before coming to America and no one, at the time, had any idea that he was to become not only a sire of runners but the foundation sire of all modern trotters and pacers.

Why Messenger should have had this trait of being able to pass down speed at the trot and pace, when he himself was a runner, has never been completely understood. One must remember, however, that the Arabian and so called Thoroughbred stallions were bred to cold-blooded English mares and it must have been through some such fortunate "nick" that the trotting strain was developed. Be that as it may it was soon noticed that the progeny of Messenger, who at the time was standing for local cold-blooded mares, were invariably the ones who outdistanced all others in competitions at the trot.

Up until 1823 all racing at the trot was done on speedways, not on tracks. In Manhattan, the Bowery was first popular for "brushes" between neighbor and neighbor. But presently the pedestrians began to complain that their lives were being endangered by the speed and recklessness of the driving, and in 1807 Third Avenue was laid out to be devoted to this sport. This was followed by the Jamaica Road on Long Island. Later, Harlem Lane became the proving ground. Currier and Ives prints give dramatic representations of these "free-for-alls." One wonders how on earth anyone survived when one considers the number of vehicles, the narrowness and condition of the roads and the excitability of horses! The drivers of that day, Budd Doble, Hiram Woodruff, the Gold-

smith brothers, etc., must have had arms and nerves of steel!

Previous to about 1830 practically all real racing of trotters on tracks for records or stakes was done not to sulky or wagon but under saddle. The main reason for this was the lack of knowledge in the building of tracks and the weight and clumsiness of the vehicles. Under the saddle the horse could trot about two seconds faster to the mile. The improvement of tracks and sulkies gradually changed this and in 1840 we find the tide swinging over to races between trotters hitched either to sulkies or to wagons. Sometimes the contests were between single horses and pairs to a variety of vehicles. Long distance endurance tests also became popular. An American horse, Tom Thumb, hitched to the very latest thing in sulkies, went to England and trotted a hundred miles over a five mile course on Sunbury Common on February 2, 1829, completing the test in ten hours and seven minutes!

Between 1830 and 1850 trotting races fell into disrepute. The Church maintained that only "fast" people kept "fast" horses. Gambling got off to a good start and in New England and New York people of high social standing stopped going to the races or competing with the "hoi polloi" on the speedways.

But the famous rivalry of Cornelius Vanderbilt and Robert Bonner, millionaire owner of the New York Ledger, restored the standing of the trotter. Both men loved to drive good horseflesh. Both men loved a contest; and both had plenty of money to spend. The result: for ten years the East was regaled by watching first one and then the other winning in informal "brushes" on Third Avenue and on Harlem Lane. If Vanderbilt lost he was not contented until he had bought a horse that could out-trot the horse that had beaten him, and the same went for Bonner. What wonderful sportsmen these were. Fair weather or foul, out they would come and for the fun of it show the world the fastest to be had in horseflesh.

Robert Bonner was a very strict churchman. He would not race for a wager. It was Vanderbilt's desire to race with him for a purse, and he put up a bet of ten thousand dollars that there was not a pair of horses in the world that could match his Plow Boy and Post Boy on the track. The Commodore hoped to draw Bonner into a contest against his team and thus give him the opportunity of proving, under racing conditions, that he, Cornelius Vanderbilt, had the fastest pair of horses in the world. But Bonner was not to be drawn. However, neither was Bonner going to concede the title. He waited until May, 1862, when the Commodore was in the stands on the Fashion course. When the regular racing had ended Bonner offered to race his mares against time, for no stakes of course, but merely to prove that he could beat the record of the day, 2:31¼. This he did, driving his famous mares, Lady Palmer and Flatbush Maid. The first mile was 2:31½, and the second was in 2:28! The fastest, by two seconds, that any pair of horses had trotted up to that time. Bonner then got back at Vanderbilt by offering to make a present of ten thousands dollars to any gentleman who had a team that could beat his record!

Naturally Vanderbilt couldn't accept a gift so there the matter stood.

A few years before the above affair "Hippodroming" or "barnstorming" came into popularity. Audiences in different parts of the country had long been eager to see these trotters that were making history and in 1857 the two outstanding trotters of the day, Flora Temple and Lancet, set out on a tour, racing against each other for a share of the gate receipts and a purse at Elmira, Springfield and Hartford. Later Flora Temple went on alone and raced against local horses at Detroit, Chicago, Kalamazoo, Sondersby, Adrian and St. Louis. This undoubtedly had much to do with popularizing the harness racer in other parts of the United States though it was interrupted by the Civil War.

So far the Southerner had looked down upon the trotter. To him the Saddler was for everyday use and the gal-

loper for racing. The trotter was the "country-bumpkin's" nag. But owners of trotters began to take their animals south to winter them and keep them in condition for racing. Presently there was a track in Florida and one in New Orleans. Slowly the interest spread though it was to be interrupted by the Civil War.

The breeding of trotters up to this time had been a pretty hit or miss affair. Beyond recognizing that the get of Messenger were to be desired above all others little was done in the matter of selection, but presently there became vogues in trotting horse families. Justin Morgan, foundation sire of the Morgan strain, was the progenitor of one Ethan Allen. Ethan Allen was of the famous Vermont Black Horse family. They were longer legged and faster than their Morgan cousins. The Black Hawks were a daintier, prettier breed than the Messengers and migrated gradually to Kentucky. The Clays were another famous trotting family as were the Mambrinos, but all these families were superseded by the get of one horse, Rysdyk's Hambletonian. (See *HAMBLETONIAN*.)

As has been seen trotting lost popularity among the fashionable class before the middle of the eighteen hundreds and was brought back by the Vanderbilt-Bonner affair. Now, in the eighteen-sixties it again fell into disfavor because of the gambling which attended all race meetings. Swindling, pickpocketing and drunkenness became the rule until finally all ladies refused to continue to attend the track meetings. Things grew to such a state that something had to be done.

Trotting had become commercialized. It had passed out of the hands of the gentleman owner-driver. Some way must be found to control the unscrupulous professional driver. The only way to do this was to form an organization which would control all principal tracks. By forbidding offending drivers to race on tracks controlled by the organization the illegal element might be eliminated. In 1870 the predecessor of the National Trotting Association came into being.

This Association was formed for the purpose of elevating and standardizing trotting racing, and preventing, detecting and punishing frauds at the tracks.

The Trotting Association was a great success. It accomplished all it set out to do and to it we owe trotting races as we know them today. The trotter, no longer a gambler's tool, came into his own and breeders became more and more interested in breeding for speed and stamina.

Among these breeders was Leland Stanford of California. The latter state, cut off from the East by mountains, had been slow in coming to the front but now she more than made up for her tardy start. At Palo Alto the greatest breeding laboratory in history was maintained by a man who, taking a leaf from Boucher, the Frenchman, insisted that his colts be reared by gentleness.

Leland Stanford, in his study of the horse in motion, was also the first to realize the motion picture. He had a series of "stills" taken of his trotter, Occident, to prove that there is a point in the stride of a trotter when all four feet are off the ground. Later he photographed all the gaits, and Mybridge, who took the pictures with a series of mechanically timed cameras, invented a projector to show them; thus was first demonstrated the principle of the motion picture.

But trotters were not being bred in sufficient quantity to satisfy the Trotting Associations. The automobile was just over the horizon and though no one believed that it could ever compete with the horse in speed or endurance, still some of the younger generation showed interest in the mechanical horse. It had been customary for some time to race running horses as two- and three-year-olds, but the training of a trotter was far more difficult. Trotting races were still long and too strenuous for the colt. Leland Stanford, with his progressive ideas, was again foremost in promoting racing for colts and early in the seventies races for the youngsters became popular.

Up until now our discussion has been about trotters. What about the pacers, the "side-wheelers" as they were called?

In the seventeen hundreds Rhode Island had developed a breed known as the Narragansett Pacer. But though they were good roadsters they became more popular as progenitors of the gaited horse of the South than as harness racers. It must be remembered that early racing was under the saddle. Although the Narragansett Pacer was supposed to have a "smooth, gliding" motion, anyone who rides knows that of all gaits the true pace is the roughest. One can post to the trot. The amble and the rack are gentle, but the pace of most horses has a churning motion that is extremely tiring. It may be that it was for this reason that the pacer did not come into popularity as a racing horse until the racing of trotters in harness had become definitely established. One other thing affected his racing career. If a trotter "broke" his stride and fell into a gallop he could be steadied down and would resume the trot, but the pacer could not do so.

However, because of their speed there were a few pacers. There might not be as many as there were trotters but the few were very fast. In Cleveland, in 1877, Sweetser paced three heats in 2:16, 2:16, 2:16¼, the fastest three consecutive heats ever up to that time raced in harness. In seventy-nine, Sleepy Tom, a blind, thirteen-year-old pacer paced a mile in 2:12¼, the fastest mile in harness in the world! The pacers gained steadily in popularity. Their one defect, their inability to go on after a break, was solved in 1885 by a railroad conductor named John Browning. Browning owned a pacer that broke. So he invented the "hopple," a leg harness that prevented the use of any gait other than the pace! It was as simple as that! Of course, when hopples first appeared on the track they were ridiculed and objected to by many but at last they were permitted.

Harness racing still suffered from the type of vehicle used and the faulty engineering of the track. In 1887 a track shaped like a kite was built and it was found that by thus moderating the angles of the turns the trotting and pacing records could be lowered by about two seconds. This led to many controversies. Was a record made on a kite track the same as a record on an oval track? It was ruled that horses that made records on kite tracks had to have the letter K written in on quoting the record. Discussions and arguments became more and more complex. It is probable that such arguments would still be going on were it not for one thing, the bicycle. Hitherto the bicycle had been the "boneshaker" with high wheels and hard tires. But now an American doctor put pneumatic tires on the wheel of his son's bicycle to save him jolts and, at about the same time, an English inventor discovered the principles of ball bearing wheels.

Budd Doble, getting older now and not too willing to try out new-fangled appliances, had received a strange-looking vehicle from England. A sulky with bicycle wheels. He turned it over to Ed Geers who was both a trotting man and a bicycle rider. Geers was delighted. He appeared on the track at Detroit in 1892 driving the contrivance and the gallery, accustomed to the high-wheeled sulky, hooted with delight. But Geers won the race and lowered the record. That afternoon, old Doble himself took the sulky back and raced four heats in it, the fastest four heats ever raced up to that time! The joke was on the audience and the race for the purchase of the new sulkies began. As a result the argument over the legality of the kite track was dropped for now the ordinary oval was perfectly satisfactory.

But harness racing had still to be standardized and many were the tricks tried to overcome natural obstacles. Recognizing that the wind resistance had a great deal to do with slowing down speed, horses were raced with a running horse in front to cut off the wind. Records were made with a running horse in front, another on one side and a third behind, the trotter or pacer completely

"boxed" in. In several instances the leading horse had a special type of "sail" to cut off the wind still more! Of course, too, the sulky was improved. The driver now sat low instead of high.

Then, too, the question of handicapping had never been solved. Headstarts were unsatisfactory. Horses pulling weight could not be handicapped by the addition of weights as is done in running races. Star Pointer, a pacer, in 1887 broke the record and became the first two-minute horse. His official time was 1:59¼. But there were no others to compete. Many horses that had made good showings as colts found themselves out of employment. The system of classifying horses according to speed had been adopted, but the method of recording the speed was faulty. Many drivers "pulled" their horses rather than let them trot themselves into a low time class. At the same time that all this was going on the automobile was coming into its own and pushing the trotter off the roads. But trotting was not to be downed. Not by the automobile, not by stricter and stricter laws regarding gambling, not by a confusion of standards and the interest in running horses.

"Matinées" or meets between amateurs at private tracks, became popular. Interest in the Trotting Circuit was revived and harness races were promoted as the drawing features at the country fairs. In addition, in 1923, the Hambletonian Society was organized offering a stake for three-year-old stallions. The interest in the harness horse spurted again. Rules were made regarding the handicapping whereby a horse need not be put in a lower time class until he had won a certain amount of money in his own class. Thus the owner of a fast youngster was assured of several good purses before being "advanced." See *RECORDS AND STATISTICS — HARNESS RACING* (appendix).

In 1810 "The Boston Horse" trotted a mile in 2:48½ at Philadelphia. A hundred and twenty-eight years later the fabulous trotter "Greyhound" trotted

FIGURE 47. GREYHOUND, UNBEATEN ON THE TROTTING TRACKS. HIS RECORD OF A MILE IN 1:55¼ WAS SET IN 1938. *COURTESY OF THE LATE G. BEEVER, HUDDLESFIELD, ENGLAND.*

FIGURE 48. ADIOS BUTLER, WORLD'S FASTEST HARNESS HORSE. IN 1960 HE PACED THE MILE IN THE LEXINGTON TRACK IN 1:54¾. NOTE THAT BOTH HE AND GREYHOUND (SEE FIGURE ABOVE) ARE SHOWN WITH ALL FOUR FEET OFF THE GROUND. *COURTESY UNITED STATES TROTTING ASSOCIATION.*

the mile in 1:55¼, at Lexington. A gain of a little less than a minute in over a hundred years! But that meant lowering the time by one-third. What effort, what ingenuity and what magnificent struggles on the part of the horse and the driver have gone into saving that all-important short space of time!

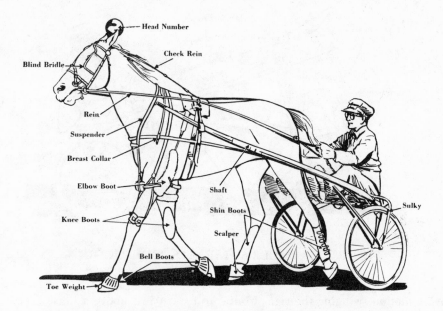

FIGURE 49. TROTTER'S HARNESS AND RIGGING.

Trotter
Diagonally gaited horse. Moves with a high-stepping, straight ahead gait with left front and right hind legs moving forward in unison. The trotter usually wears a heavier shoe than a pacer (average: 8 oz.) ; the length of his front toe is usually longer (3¾"-3⅞") ; and his angle (that formed by the front of the foot and the sole of the foot) is usually a little more acute (46-48 degrees). The trotter is generally shod "flat" in front, that is he usually wears level shoes, and usually wears a swedge shoe (a creased shoe which provides traction when the horse's hind foot hits the ground) behind.

Equipment More Often Worn by Trotters

Elbow Boots—Sheepskin lined pads worn high on front legs to protect elbows (points at rear and bottom of shoulders) from the front feet as they are folded back in top stride. Needed on high gaited trotters.

Hind Shin Boots—Leather protecting guards on the lower hind legs. Prevent cuts and bruises from the front shoes which graze the hind legs of some trotters.

Toe Weights—Brass or lead weights weighing from two to four ounces. They are clipped to the edge of the front hoofs to extend a horse's stride.

Quarter Boots—Close fitting boots on the front heel to protect the tender quarter (heel of the foot) from being cut by the hind shoes.

Martingale—A strap, running from the girth between the horse's front legs, to the reins which are threaded through the rings at the end of the martingale. Helps prevent horse from tossing and raising head.

Pacer
Laterally gaited horse. Moves with a

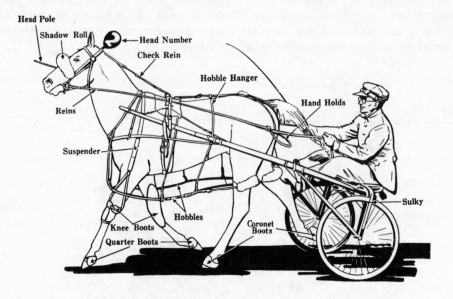

FIGURE 50. PACER'S HARNESS AND RIGGING.

swaying motion swinging the right front and right hind legs forward at the same time. The pacer usually wears a lighter shoe than the trotter (average: 5 oz.); the length of his front toe is usually shorter ($3\frac{1}{2}''$-$3\frac{5}{8}''$) and his angle (that formed by the front of the foot and the sole of the foot) is usually less acute (48-50 degrees). The pacer generally wears a flat or half round shoe in front and a combination shoe, half round in-side—swedge outside, behind. The swedge part increases traction thus widening the horse's gait and lessening possibility of the hind foot hitting a front leg. The half round portion presents a rounded edge and lessens the danger of serious injury in the event such "crossfiring" does occur.

Equipment More Often Worn by Pacers

Hobbles—Leather straps encircling the front and hind legs of a pacer on the same side to keep those legs moving in unison and to help the horse maintain its gait. The straps running over the horse's back and to the haunches are known as hobble hangers.

Shadow Roll—A large sheepskin-type roll worn just above a horse's nose and just below his eyes. It cuts off the horse's view of the track so that he won't shy at shadows, pieces of paper or other objects.

Knee Boots—Boots fitted around the knees and held up by suspenders (usually white) over the horse's withers. They protect the knees from blows from the opposite foot, especially on turns where a horse is more likely to break stride if he "brushes his knees".

Head Pole—A cue (usually a billiard cue with a hole bored in the handle to accommodate a leather thong) fastened alongside horse's head and neck to keep his head straight.

Gaiting Strap—Strap strung inside shafts of sulky to keep the horse from swinging the rear end to the right and left and traveling sideways on his gait.

HARRIERS

Hounds used for coursing hares. Beagles, which are used for hunting rabbits are followed on foot but Harriers are usually followed mounted.

HAT GUARD

This is a cord worn, especially in the hunt field, to prevent the hat blowing off. It usually runs from the brim of the hard hunting derby or silk hat to a ring inside the collar of the coat.

HAT SNATCHING

A game that is good for intermediate riders and appropriate for gymkhanas. Each rider wears a paper hat such as comes in birthday "snappers." If such hats are not available brown paper bags with the edges folded may be used. At a whistle every rider tries to snatch off the hats of the other riders in the ring while trying to prevent his own from being removed. As soon as a rider loses his hat he leaves the ring, the last one wearing a hat, wins.

HEAD

The head of the horse is not only the first thing that catches the eye, but it is used as a measure for judging the animal's breeding, spirit and way of going. Highly bred horses have finely drawn heads, the bones prominent, the lines clean cut. Intelligent horses usually have eyes set well apart. Too large a bump over the eyes may denote too much brain and consequent craftiness. The head of the running horse of breeding is a straight profile while those with an admixture of cold blood may well run to the Roman type nose. The racer, be he runner, pacer or trotter, carries his head well forward and not too high, while the Saddler and heavy harness type holds up his head and bends his crest. The so called "hammer-headed" nag is the one whose head is set on abruptly like the head of a hammer without the delicate lines at the throttle.

The horse who carries his head alertly, ears pricked forward, will rarely be mean, nor will he be so apt to stumble as the horse with flop ears and a sleepy, inattentive look. The horse with a long neck ending in a coarse, heavy head will be heavy on the forehand. The horse with deep indentations at the temples and a pendulous lower lip is an old, old veteran no matter what his teeth and the unscrupulous dealer who has used dentistry on them have to say.

Beware the horse that bends so much at the crest that his chin comes into his chest, he is a borer and will wear you out trying to get him along at a slow, even gait. Beware the horse that flings his nose up on the jumps, he is a stargazer and may readily come a cropper on a low wall. Beware the horse that carries his ears laid flat and rolls his eyes. He will take the first opportunity he can find to vent his ill-temper on either you or a companion horse.

Select the horse whose head is most nearly like the ideal head of the breed you are choosing, whose eye is alert, yet kind and whose poll, jaw and crest appear flexible.

HEAD (to head a fox)
See *HUNTING TERMS*.

HEADLESS HORSEMAN OF SLEEPY HOLLOW

Every one knows this famous character of Washington Irving which scared the wits out of the gangling schoolmaster, Ichabod Crane. It is to be found in *The Sketch Book*, written in 1819. For those wishing to compete in a costume class, that of the Headless Horseman is a simple one and always makes a hit. Just throw a sheet over your head, cut holes to see through and carry a pumpkin under one arm.

HEAT (in the stable)

Unless a horse is stabled alone he will do better if there is no heat in the stable. He must be well blanketed, of course, but he will be hardier and less subject to respiratory diseases if he becomes accustomed to a cold stable.

HEATS (in racing)

In the old days all races were run in heats. One reads of races during the Revolutionary times when the horses ran three heats of four miles each. At the present time all trotting races are in heats. The number and distance depend on the class of horse. Colts are not required to race as far as the older horses. Generally speaking, the trotter or pacer goes three heats of one mile each. There is some little time between heats and the horse is brought out long before the race and warmed up by being "scored" several times before he is raced.

HEAVES (broken wind)

A disease of the lungs in which the air vesicles of the lungs are over extended or broken down. The symptoms are a hard dry cough to start with and a slight discharge at the nose. This is followed by a lighter hacking cough, particularly noticeable when the horse is first worked. As soon as the horse takes a canter or a fast trot his breathing becomes very labored. By watching the flanks one may note that in expelling the air he appears to heave twice instead of once. The condition cannot be cured but, in its early stages may be helped by feeding the horse only wet feed and wetting down his hay. Heaves are brought on by excessive work when the horse is not in condition or by dusty or dirty feed or hay. See *FEEDS, New Hope.*

HEAVY HANDS

The rider who has no flexibility in his hands, who rides a horse by force instead of tact is said to be "heavy-handed" or "mutton-fisted." He can readily be spotted as his horse invariably appears most uncomfortable. The heavy-handed rider must first perfect his seat before he can expect to lighten his hands. The best method of doing this is to ride at all gaits with and without a saddle, with the arms folded or the hands placed on the hips, reins dangling. Having become entirely independent of his reins to maintain his balance he should then ride a well-schooled horse and practice the equitation exercises recommended in this volume and the gallop departs. It is no use putting a mutton-fisted rider on a high-strung horse as the result will be

disastrous but he must not stay too long on a snaffle-bitted borer or his hands will get worse. As his hands become lighter and his seat more secure he should be mounted on correspondingly better horses with full bridles or pelhams. See also *HANDS, RIDING.*

HEAVY HARNESS HORSE

Any type harness horse (gig, lady's phaeton, etc.) except the Fine Harness (saddle bred) or the Light Harness (roadster) types is called a Heavy Harness Horse. For classes of heavy harness horses see *HORSE SHOW CLASSES, Harness Division.*

HEDGE (black thorn)

Black thorn hedges are not common in this country but they are very prevalent in certain parts of England. They form a formidable obstacle, known as a "bullfinch" and horses must be especially trained to negotiate them.

In Hunt and Race Courses the hedge jump made of evergreens is common. The horse is allowed to brush the top of such jumps as desired. These jumps are known as "brush jumps."

HEEL (to)

When the huntsman hacks to the meet the hounds are required "to heel," or stay in a group at the heels of his horse. The discipline is maintained by the whips who ride behind and on either side.

HEEL (to run to)

See *HUNTING TERMS.*

HEELS

A good rider, who carries his heels as they should be carried, can wear long, sharp, rowelled spurs and never touch his horse with them unless he does so for a purpose. The heels are used as aids. They should be carried well below the toes and at least an inch away from the horse's side. This steadiness of heel is all important for the position of the heels, ankles and feet determine the position of the rider's thighs and consequently the security of his seat. See also *AIDS, RIDING*.

HEIGHT (of horses)

The height of the horse is measured from the top of the withers to the ground; it is estimated in "hands," there being four inches to a hand. Horses whose height does not exceed fourteen hands, two inches (58 inches) are considered "ponies" in entering them in show classes, regardless of their breeding. For many years the height of a polo pony was limited to fourteen:two and such limitations, plus the classifying of jumpers and Saddlers according to heights led to a wily trick. Owners of horses that were just a fraction over the desired measurement would teach their horses to "squat" slightly while being measured. This was done by putting a pin in a regular measuring stick. As the arm of the stick was lowered against the withers it pricked the horse who squatted to get away from it. After a few such lessons he automatically squatted whenever he felt the measure being used, thus many horses that should have been in classes for those of fifteen hands and over got into the lower classes, and many polo ponies passed inspection which should have been barred.

Although the tendency in hunters is to demand the biggest possible horse, army tests show that the horse that can endure the longest is the horse from fifteen:three to sixteen hands.

HIDE-AND-GO-SEEK

This is a game suitable only for experienced riders. The rules are much the same as those used when the game is played on foot. The person who is "it" should count to two hundred, more if the other players have to ride quite a distance to hide. The "den" should not be some specific object which the player racing for it must touch, as there is great danger in his ramming it or, his horse stopping short, being thrown against it. Rather, "den" or "home" should be a point which the player must pass such as an imaginary line between two trees or a wide gap in a stone wall.

HIDEBOUND

A horse is said to be hidebound when his skin seems tight and immovable. This condition is often indicative of worms or some other intestinal trouble. To cure it, diagnose and treat the cause.

HIGH BLOWING

A noise made by some horses when galloping which, by the amateur, may be mistaken for unsoundness of wind. As a matter of fact, high blowers are usually well-bred, spirited horses with excellent wind. The sound which slightly resembles sneezing is from the false nostrils.

HINGES (of the rider)

Imagine a steel rod run through one knee of a rider from the outside, through saddle and horse and out the other knee. The knee of the rider can now be visualized as a hinge which opens and closes but never leaves its position. If all riders could keep their knees as steadily as this how few falls there would be! The most common indication of the inexperienced rider is the little triangle of daylight which one sees between his knees and the saddle. The position of the ankle and feet largely determine the position of the knee. If you stand on the floor, bend the knees slightly and then bend the ankles in, the outside of the foot leaving the floor it will be noticed that the knees automatically bend in towards each other. Taking this position in the stirrups and making sure that it is the sharp bone on the inside of the knee, not the back of it, which comes in contact with the saddle, one can immediately notice how firm the seat feels, even without grip, and how easy it is to work the knees as hinges when it is necessary to rise out of and return to the saddle as in posting, or to keep buttocks out and let the knees absorb the shock as in jumping.

HINNY

This is a hybrid animal the father of which is a stallion and the mother a "jenny" or female donkey. The opposite cross is a mule. Neither mules nor hinnies produce young though there have been a few authenticated cases of mule foals.

HIRING A HORSE

Do not hire a horse to go riding by yourself until you are at least a moderately good horseman. Having selected your animal try him out in the stable yard before you take him on the road. And having taken him out take care of him. Remember the horse is at your mercy. He will run himself to death if you make him. He will permanently injure himself if you gallop him on hard pavements. If you get him in a lather and then tie him under a tree, while you eat a sandwich, he may injure the blood vessels in his feet and have to be shot. These are only a few of the injuries which a careless, heartless rider can cause to his willing servant, the horse.

If you are a hirer or lender of horses, judge your rider carefully before you trust him with your horse. The man or woman who comes up and says, "I want a good, fast horse" is just the kind that most probably doesn't know the withers from the croup and will kill either himself or his mount. One very good test of the horseman is to say, "There stands the horse, tack him up yourself and I'll let you take him out." The tyro won't know what you mean, and the beginner will never get beyond trying to get the bit in the mouth.

HIT OFF THE LINE (to make a)
See *HUNTING TERMS.*

HOBBLES

Hobbles are frequently used on western horses to prevent their straying. They consist of straps which encircle the pasterns or fetlock joints and are connected with a short strap or chain.

HOCK
Points of)
(See diagram, page 150.)

The hock joint is one of the most important in the structure of the horse, particularly the galloper and jumper. A horse "jumps from his hocks," i.e., he receives the necessary spring and propulsion from this joint. If the hock is weak the horse will not have the power to take high obstacles, nor will he be suitable for hunting in "trappy" country where he is called upon to lift himself over fences with little or no room for a take-off.

Viewed from the side the hock joint should appear large and flat. The distance from hock to top of haunch should appear long, which indicates a short and consequently strong cannon. A line dropped from the buttock point should fall one or two inches to the rear of the point of the hock and the back line of the cannon should be parallel to this line. The inside angle of the hock should be wide, not narrow.

Viewed from the back or front the hock should appear thick, the cannons should be straight, not bowlegged nor should the hocks bend in towards each other (cow-hocked). The bony protuberances of the hock should be prominent and there should be no puffiness or bony enlargements. If you are uncertain as to whether a hock shows deformity compare it with the other hock.

The most common injuries to hocks are bone spavins, curbs and bursar injuries. The spavin is a small bony enlargement generally due to strain or injury. Though causing great lameness at first, the lameness usually disappears. A curb is a bony enlargment on the back of the cannon just below the point of the hock. Curbs rarely cause permanent lameness but indicate weakness.

Thoroughpins are puffy enlargements on the side of the hock. Bog spavins are also bursal enlargements. Neither of these injuries cause permanent lameness but if too big will interfere with the freedom of movement. A capped hock in which the whole bursar is affected is very unsightly but rarely serious. For treatment of these injuries refer to them in this text under each name.

HOGGED MANE
A mane which is clipped entirely off is said to be "hogged."

HOLD HARD
See *HUNTING TERMS.*

HOLD ON HORSE
It is extremely difficult to explain to the learner exactly how one should hold a horse in order to control him. Belle Beach, a famous rider in the early part of this century, is said to have ridden her horses to hounds using number sixty silk thread for reins. Major Tuttle, in giving his dressage exhibitions, used thread instead of reins. An expression, common among horsemen, is the advice, "ride as though your reins were made of paper." Yet, to the tyro, this would mean that one rode always with a perfectly loose rein and never exerted pressure, which is far from true.

The amount of "hold" necessary to control a horse will depend on several factors, the way the horse is bitted, how he has been schooled and, most important of all, the skill of the rider. The rider who uses his aids too strongly will be continually tugging on his horse, and the horse wil be as persistently pulling against the rein. The rider who rides with the slack rein will find himself constantly having to pull up short. The rider with good hands on only a moderately well schooled horse should be able to make his horse take any gait, turn in any direction, without any perceptible movement of the hands or reins, everything being done with the fingers assisted by a flexible wrist. Such a rider can, indeed, control the well mannered horse under ordinary circumstances with paper or thread reins.

Until one masters this light, flexible touch one cannot really enjoy riding, nor will the horse enjoy having you for his master. See also *GOOD HANDS, RIDING, AIDS.*

HOLLOA
See *JAY; HUNTING TERMS.*

HOOD
Hoods which cover the horse's head and neck are usually used in shipping. Other types of hood with guards to prevent the horse seeing shadows, the rail, etc., are sometimes used in racing.

HOOF
See *FEET.*

HOPPLES
Hopples are a type of leg harness used in pacing and trotting races to prevent the horse from changing his gait. Pacing was never popular until the invention of the hopple by a railroad conductor named John Browning in 1885. They were at first objected to on the ground that they were "artificial" but later were permitted. See also *HARNESS RACING.*

HORSE
Characteristics of:
As explained by Count Martinengo di Cesaresco in his "Psychology of the Horse," the horse's fundamental characteristic is his "excitability to motion." This is what makes the horse fleet while the ox is merely a beast of burden. This "excitability to motion" or reaction in the form of flight, is derived, of course, from the inability of the prehistoric horse to defend himself in any other way (see *HORSE, Origin of*). Hand in hand with it goes the timidity of the horse. The natural timidity can be greatly over-overcome by handling (see *COLTS*). As the horse is handled his increased intelligence may follow one of two paths, cooperation or stubbornness. Which path is chosen will depend entirely upon the trainer. The Arab, who makes his War Mare a most important member of his family, turns the resultant increase in intelligence to such profit that these "hand-raised" Arabians seem more like

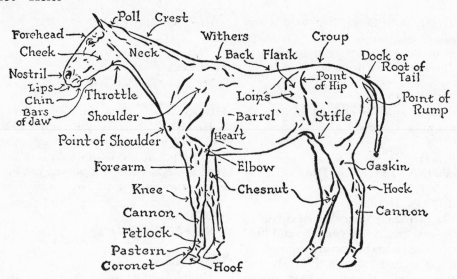

FIGURE 51. POINTS OF THE HORSE.

dogs than horses. They come at a call, kneel on command for the rider to mount, may even be trained to defend their owners with hoof and teeth if he is attacked by an enemy.

On the other hand the smart horse that is treated roughly will soon become an outlaw. Or he will become so stubborn in his resistance that only a very capable rider can handle him. The Shetland pony has acquired a bad name because of this misdirected intelligence. He is termed "tricky," "stubborn" or "mean." I have bred and raised a great many Shetlands and other ponies with a large admixture of Shetland blood in them and have never found these ponies other than safe, cooperative and easily managed. But I have given great attention to their handling and their breaking. They have never been treated roughly nor have they been allowed to "get away" with anything in their early lessons. They have not been spoiled by too much petting or too many tidbits.

Much is said and written about the horse's "intelligence." Some of our fiction writers would allow him such power of brain that were it fact, it would be we who were put between the shafts, with

the all wise, all powerful horse in the driver's seat! A horse has a certain amount of intelligence which is derived largely from instincts. He can be readily trained through his muscular reflexes but he needs constant supervision and control to direct his energies.

Our romantic writers tell us that the horse is tremendously affectionate towards his master and quotes the well-known fact that a horse will not voluntarily step on a rider that has been thrown in front of him. Any moving picture of a stiff jump in a steeplechase with jockeys rolling on the ground in front of the melée of galloping horses will prove this to be a fact but the reason behind it is not the sentimental one the writer of horse stories would have us believe. The reason goes back to the prehistoric days when the little, soft-toed *Pliohippus* knew that if he stepped on a flinty stone and cut his pad he would shortly find himself somebody's dinner.

That the horse's affection can be developed by close and intimate contact with man, is undoubtedly true. The same is true of dogs. But that the ordinary horse, stabled in a barn, loves his master, is to be questioned. When your horse, at your whistle, canters across the pasture to get the proffered lump of sugar you may think it is because of your personal attraction but more probably it is his love of sugar, and he has learned that sugar is what that whistle means.

However, if the horse is not as loving as some would have us believe, neither is he as mean or vicious. No horse was ever born mean. Some families of horses are known to develop vices more readily than others; these are the families whose members are more intelligent and more highly strung than most horses. The stallion, by some, is looked on as a naturally dangerous and not to be trusted animal. There are mean stallions, horses which would as soon take a piece out of a man's arm as not. But it is my contention that those horses were not born mean, they became so through ignorant or brutal treatment. The stallion that is treated kindly and not feared from the time he is born, that is not indulged nor allowed to develop to too great a degree such playful habits as rearing, nipping and charging, habits as natural to all colts as they are to playful puppies, the stallion that is broken to ride and drive and is ridden and driven *in company* with other horses, both mares and geldings; this stallion will never be other than gentle and cooperative for both stud purposes and general use.

To summarize, the horse is the friend and servant of man because he is high-strung and consequently "easily excited to movement," because he is not a "fighting" type of animal but one which responds to gentleness and because he has not such a highly developed intelligence that he has discovered how much more powerful physically he is than is his master.

Handling of in Stable

It is always possible, when going into a stableful of horses to judge pretty accurately the intelligence and temperaments of the stablemen and grooms in charge. If, as you enter, the horses seem quiet and unafraid—giving, perhaps, a

nicker of welcome; if you can enter a stall without its occupant bouncing to one side and glaring wildly around; if there is no attempt at kicking as you pass behind the rows of haunches in their straight stalls and no sudden shying away with a showing of heels when you open the door of the box, then you know that the man or men in charge know their business. That they have even dispositions and are neither afraid of horses themselves nor impatient with them.

It was Anna Sewell who said, in *Black Beauty*, "a bad tempered man never makes a good tempered horse." How very true! A bad tempered man with a hasty hand can ruin the most beautifully dispositioned horse in just about two days. And the horse will never again be as friendly, no matter how many years of kindly treatment follow the two short days of abuse.

Sudden noises and sudden movements are the two things which, in the stable, cause timidity in horses. Keeping this in mind, do not wave either your grooming tools or your stable implements around. The horse sees just as well behind him as he does in front, so don't swing your rake up over your shoulder or throw a strap onto a shelf behind a horse.

Never go into a stall without first speaking to the horse and, having entered, go directly to his head. (See also *ENTERING A STALL*). Never reach up suddenly to unfasten the halter, run your hand up along the neck and thence to the poll. In backing a horse out of his stall make him move quietly, and turn his head in the direction which he is to take after he is in the alley (see also *VICES in the stable*). In leading the horse into the stall walk in front of him until you reach the manger. (See also *LEADING THE HORSE into a stall, leading through a narrow passage*.)

If your horse does not want to move forward, turn him to one side and then the other when he will follow readily. Always be sure that you hold the end of the halter shank or the bridle reins in your hand, do not let them drag when the horse might step on them and give himself a "job" in the mouth. See that your horse is properly tied in his stall or, if he be in a box, that the door is properly fastened. Make sure that all grain is behind locked doors. The horse that breaks out of his stall and gets into the grain bin will eat himself to death.

Handling of in the Pasture

Train your horse to come to you when you call him. This is done by offering of tidbits and frequent petting. If you have just acquired a new horse that has never been taught to come in the pasture the following is the procedure:

Go into the pasture carrying a pail or box with a little grain in it. Shake the grain violently and give some special whistle or call to which you wish to accustom your horse. Now place the pail on the ground and move away about fifty feet. The horse will go up and eat the grain. When he has had several good mouthfuls go towards him; he will probably shy away. Pick up the pail, walk a hundred feet or so towards the stable and put it down again. The horse will follow at a respectful distance. This time do not move quite so far away. Again allow him to eat a mouthful or so and again go and take up the pail. It may be that on this first day he will allow you to pat him while he is eating; if not, get him to follow you into the stable. When he is in his stall, reward him with a good feed and stand beside him while he eats it, patting and talking to him.

In a day or so he will come running when he hears the whistle and certainly within a week you should be able to walk up to him in the pasture.

If your horse has been taught to come to a pail of grain, next teach him to come to a handful of grass. Give his whistle and *kneel down*. The horse is much less terrified if the person is lower than he. When he comes for the grass reach out very quietly for the halter strap with one hand while you proffer the grass with the other.

Do not try to corner a horse in the pasture and come up to him from behind. A kick in the face will be your reward. Do not try and chase a horse in by riding after him on another horse. The two horses will enjoy this immensely but you will not. If a wild horse or pony must be caught and he is too untamed to follow a pail of grain into a stable he should be quietly maneuvered at a walk into a corner of the field. Two people on foot then approach him, holding a fifty foot rope outstretched between them. This rope forms a barrier. The horse is now in a triangle, with the fence on two sides of him and the rope on the third. The rope should be held at about the height of the point of his shoulder and should be taut. Gradually the men at either end gather up the rope, coming towards each other and reducing the size of the triangle. They should move very slowly and talk constantly to the horse. The fact that there are two of them will confuse the horse and the rope, when it is shortened so that it touches his side will make him think that he is helpless. The man nearest his head can then reach quietly up for the halter shank. See also *LEADING, TYING THE HORSE.*

General Care

The horse must be fed correct amounts of good food on a regular feeding schedule. His stall must be kept clean. He must be thoroughly groomed each day. He must have plenty of exercise but he must not be overworked nor unwisely worked. He must be so stabled and pastured that there is little possibility of his hurting himself. Slight scratches or injuries must be attended to at once before they develop into more serious ones. Given this care, the average hardy horse will serve his master day in and day out for as many as twenty or more years with never a forced holiday due to sickness.

Study the principles of feeding. Learn what causes disease, injuries and accidents. Never demand more of a horse than he is physically capable at the moment, of giving. The horse that can readily take ten or twenty jumps at the beginning of the day will do himself irreparable harm if asked to take them after a few hours of hard work. The colt of four years cannot be expected to put in the day in the hunt field that can be expected of the seasoned hunter of seven. Think of your horse's comfort before your own, so will you have a healthy stable and a small bill from the veterinarian.

HORSE (origin and development of)

Many theories have been raised and lengthy treatises written to prove the ex-act origin of the horse. For a long time it was thought that one common ancestor sired the horse, donkey and zebra family. This theory was also advanced by Darwin on the belief that the general markings of stripes and light areas found in all three breeds were indicative of their common ancestry. But Popcock proved that the white stockings and lighter marked areas were merely the beginning of albinoism.

That the prehistoric horse was widely distributed and came into being at the same time as the other mammals is unquestionable. Traces of him have been found in all parts of the world except

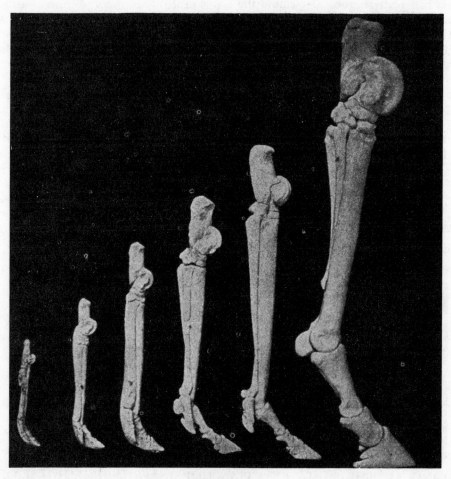

FIGURE 52.
EVOLUTION OF THE RIGHT HIND FOOT OF THE HORSE.

Australia. The fossils differ very much both in size and characteristics. The remains of a very large extinct horse, *Equus nanus* have been discovered at Walthamstow, England. These remains are said to date back to the Neolithic age. Horses of the Paleolithic age have been discovered in more than one place in Europe. The *Phenacodus Primaevus,* a tiny five-toed creature is considered an early ancestor not only of the horse but of many other hoofed animals. He existed in the Eocene age, practically before time began. In the upper Miocene age and lower Pliocene age we find the three-toed *Hipparion,* also a member of the family tree. But the most direct ancestor is the little *Pliohippus* whose leg bones had really begun to resemble the structure of the modern horse.

Thus before the dawn of history types of horses had developed in different parts of the world. These types came into being as a result of environment. *Pliohippus* was found in great numbers in North America, but here he apparently died out and left no descendants in this country. Nor were fossils found in Australia. But all over Europe and Asia horses abounded. These types have been divided as follows:

Equus Przewalskii, the steppe horse of Central Asia, similar in type to the prehistoric caveman's pony. He was a reddish brown or bay and from him have come the Japanese, Mongolian and Korean ponies.

Equus Tarpanus, the dun colored horse of Russia that was the source of the ponies ridden by the Huns, Tartars, Scythians and other invading hordes of Asia. This horse also remained in Norway and Britain and became the Celtic horse found there by Caesar.

Equus robustus, living in the forests and grassy plains of Europe remained large and massive. He was slow and cold-blooded, easily domesticated and from him developed the "Great Horse" of antiquity.

Equus agilis, the horse of the high, dry plains of Arabia and Africa is known as the "hot-blooded" horse of the south. He was probably introduced from Northern India and is akin to the Siwalik horse. It is this last horse which most closely resembles the finer types of horses today.

Horses were apparently built to carry weight from the beginning and were easily domesticated. The Hittites who lived about 2000 B.C. realized their value as a war weapon. The Hittite horse closely resembled the present day Arabian as it had the characteristic low set eye, "dish-faced" profile and high set tail. Later tribes such as the Huns also realized the value of the horse in war. The Greeks and Romans had their chariots with great scythes set in the wheels. But the Greek horses differed in

FIGURE 53. THE EARLY EGYPTIAN HORSES. *FROM* THE HORSE OF THE DESERT *BY WILLIAM ROBINSON BROWN. BY PERMISSION OF THE MACMILLAN COMPANY, PUBLISHERS.*

FIGURE 54. THE EARLY GRECIAN HORSE. *FROM* THE HORSE OF
THE DESERT *BY WILLIAM ROBINSON BROWN. BY PERMISSION OF
THE MACMILLAN COMPANY, PUBLISHERS.*

type from the Arabian, having a higher
eye, straighter profile and lower tail.

The earliest mention of the horse in
the Bible is between 1715 and 1689 B.C.
when Joseph coming into power rode in
the "second chariot." This is also the
earliest mention of the horse in Egypt.
The Egyptian horse appears to have
been nearer the Arabian type than the
Greek horse.

When turned loose the horse readily
becomes wild and propagates freely. He
runs in herds and distributes himself
over a wide territory. This, of course, is
due to his nomadic nature and the fact

that he must spend most of his time grazing if he is to sustain himself. Thus we
find evidences of wild horses of all breeds
all over Europe, Asia and Northern
Africa.

The introduction of the modern horse
in America was accomplished by Cortez
and De Soto. These horses were Spanish.
The Spanish horse had been imported
into Spain by the Arabs when, in the
throes of religious fervor, they decided
to convert the world to Mohammedanism. They succeeded in conquering the
Barbary Coast and then went into Spain.
They held Spain for many centuries but

were later forced to give it up and retired to Arabia leaving their fine Arabian horses behind them. So the ancestors of the broncho or mustang were hot-blooded Arabians.

The Arabian horse also, through war, spread to the Shetland Isles and Iceland. It is claimed by some that the Percheron breed of draft horse has Arabian ancestry. Of course the Thoroughbred was deliberately developed from the three imported Arabian sires, the Darley Arabian, the Byerly Turk and the Godolphin Barb as well as other Arabian stallions introduced into England in the seventeenth and eighteenth centuries.

The steppes horses remained small and coarse. The European "Great Horse" fathered the slow-moving, cold-blooded draft breeds. The Arabs alone used selection in breeding so the Arab horse was the first type to be improved. Some authorities claim that it is for this reason that the Arabian horse has finer characteristics than his blood cousins, the Barbs and the Turks.

As the need for specific breeds and types of horses arose the various modern horses came into being. When gunpowder was invented and the knights, previously mounted on the "Great Horse," retired, the modern type of light war horse became popular. The English wanted a fast horse for sport so they developed the Thoroughbred. Crossing the fleet Arabian with the slow-moving European mare they got a still speedier and somewhat larger animal. The great coach horses of England gave way in time to the lighter harness types such as the hackneys for the roads improved and more speed was desired.

In this country religious censure of running horses was responsible for the development of the trotters and pacers (see also *HAMBLETONIAN, HARNESS RACING*) in the North while in the South where there was no such religious feeling and also not so many good roads the easy-gaited Saddler and the running horse were favored.

The wild horses of the western plains

FIGURE 55. ARABIAN HORSES. *FROM THE HORSE OF THE DESERT BY WILLIAM ROBINSON BROWN. BY PERMISSION OF THE MACMILLAN COMPANY, PUBLISHERS.*

with their Arabian ancestry had, under the handling of the Indians, turned into tough little ponies capable of speed and with tremendous stamina. When Lord Kitchener found his own cavalry horses imported from England unsuccessful in Africa against the Boers in 1902, he sent to the United States for a hundred thousand mustangs. These tough, homely little animals bore the British troops to victory and also somewhat depleted our western stock.

The mustangs of the Pony Express riders were noted for their stamina and formed the only tie between the East and West in this country. The Criollos or horses of the Argentine have the same ancestry as our mustangs, having been introduced by the Spaniards. They closely resemble our western plains horses in their physical characteristics and in their tremendous staying power. It was two horses of this breed that Mr. A. F. Tschiffely rode on his journey of ten thousand miles from Buenos Aires to Washington, D. C. The Philippine horses were also sired by Arabian stallions imported for the purpose of improving the native breed as were the horses of Australia. These later became known as "walers" since most came from Great South Wales. They were exported in great numbers from Australia to India to be used as war horses.

So, though one may not agree with the devotees of the Arabian that he is superior to all other breeds, one must admit that it is the introduction of his blood that has been responsible for speed, sturdiness and symmetry of the lighter breeds of all kinds. But just as many alloys are stronger with finer and more valuable characteristics than their parent metals, so the breeds developed from the Arabian combined with other types have become more suited to the purposes for which they have been developed than is the pure Arabian. See also each breed under its own name as listed under *BREEDS; CAVALRY; HARNESS RACING.*

HORSE (pleasure)

Perhaps the best example of the horse that was developed purely for pleasure is the Plantation Walker. The owners of the large plantations of the South wanted a stylish, gentle breed of horse on which they could sit for hour after hour without fatigue. The five-gaited horse was developed first and the plantation owner took great pride in his fast rack but the Plantation Walker is even more specialized for he has only the flat-footed walk, the running walk and the straight canter. The latter gait was important as it enabled the rider to pass between the rows of crops without injuring them.

Also in the class of pure pleasure horses might be listed the Fine Harness Horses. These are horses of the saddle breed used in harness. The little model hackney ponies with their exaggerated action have gone past the phase of being pleasure horses and are now suitable only for Horse Show purposes and sport, but before they were bred so finely and before the automobile usurped the highway the elegantly bred harness horse was the pride and delight of his owner. The modern generation may disagree but no machine can give the suspense and exhilaration that driving or riding a spirited horse presents.

HORSE IN ART AND LITERATURE

It would be impossible in a work as limited in size as this to go into the details of the tremendous part that the horse has played in the arts from the earliest times to the present. There is nothing more beautiful to watch than a beautiful horse. No other animal, with the possible exception of the deer family, is as graceful, as free moving, as the horse and the horse in addition gives the impression of superb muscular strength and co-ordination which the deer lacks. Add to this the gentleness of his nature and his usefulness as a servant and companion and it is not surprising that one finds images of horses scratched on the walls of caves by the men of ten thousand years ago and images of horses in every other medium including the Persian drawings, Egyptian ceramics, early tapestries of medieval times and so on right down through all the ages.

Were it not for this pictorial interest in the horse our knowledge of him and his master would be very limited. As it is, we can trace him in every age and every clime.

In literature we find the horse a part of the lore of all peoples. But one very interesting fact might be noted. When horses were a part of every day living they formed the background rather than the main character of poem and story. Anna Sewell in *Black Beauty* was among the first to portray the horse as a character. But now that the horse is becoming more rare he is being studied more carefully as a creature of individual characteristics. John Bigg's *Corkran of Clamstretch*, the story of the little trotting horse, is an example of this type of writing.

In poetry we find much fine writing given over to the description of the horse in battle, in sport and as an individual. Nowhere are there more lovely lines than those of Shakespeare in his *Venus and Adonis* where he describes the respective mounts of the two lovers. The Bible gives us two particularly beautiful passages, that describing the War horse in the Book of Job, and that describing the four chariots seen by Zechariah in his vision.

The two most famous sporting descriptions of modern times are those of John Masefield, *Reynard the Fox* and *Right Royal*.

All in all, it may be said that not only has the horse changed the history of civilization by his use as a battle weapon, and brought nations together in understanding by means of their common love of sport, but he has been the inspiration of much of the best that is to be found in the arts of all nations and all times. See also *FAMOUS HORSES OF FICTION*.

HORSE IN SPORT

As nations became civilized and wars less frequent men turned to sport and sporting competitions for excitement. The Thoroughbred came into being because of the desire of the English for fast horses and horses that could carry them in the hunt field. The polo pony, not a breed to be sure, but a definite type, has been bred for his speed and flexibility. In Virginia a little, muscled up horse that could start in an instant and run a few furlongs at top speed became a popular member of the plantation owner's stable. He was called the "quarter horse." The Yankee had his fast roadster of Morgan blood. The Russians developed the Orloff Trotter. And so, all over the world, sport took a hand in standardizing and developing different types and breeds of horses for specific sporting purposes.

HORSE IN WAR

Warfare has had more to do with the development of the horse than any other one thing. That the mounted man had an advantage over the man on foot was clear to even such early peoples as the Hittites. The Greeks had their war chariots. The Knights had their "Great Horses." The Arabians cherished their War Mares. The North American Indians soon took advantage of the horses left by the Spaniards and the Indian Pony became renowned for his toughness and his speed and flexibility. The organized cavalries of Europe and America each set out to improve native stock and produce horses that would be flexible enough to fight and sturdy enough to march long distances carrying a trooper and his equipment.

When one has a specific object in view, such as in the case of the Greeks and Romans who wanted horses to pull their chariots, or the Knights who had to have great weight bearers, or the Arabians who desired speed, intelligence and flexibility, the natural result will be that horses with these characteristics will be developed. By selection and inbreeding the desired qualities are strengthened, the undesirable ones eliminated. Furthermore the general breed is often improved as has been done by the remount activities of the cavalry here (see also *CAVALRY*).

How extraordinary it is that the horse, with his excitable and fearful nature, has been, of all animals, the most use to man in warfare.

HORSE AT WORK

Several different types of horses came into being because of the work they must do. Work which was not simply sport but which contributed to the needs of the country. The heavy coach horse was one and the lighter hackney. The tremendous draft horse was another and the cowpony a fourth. Even the stunted horses of the Shetlands and other northern islands were bred and improved for their valuable services in the mines.

HORSEMAN (versus rider)

The rider is one who rides a horse. The horseman is one who not only rides a horse but knows how to look after him, how to treat him in sickness and in health and is always interested in learning as much as he can about the origin, characteristics and habits of his mount. The rider is contented to get as much as possible out of his horse with no thought as to the comfort of his mount. The horseman thinks of his horse before himself. After a hard day's work it is the animal that rates a thorough grooming and a hot mash before the man can relax in a warm bath and refresh himself with food and drink. The rider pulls his horse up on his haunches from a dead gallop at the barn door. He flings himself off the panting, lathery animal, throws the reins to a groom and rushes away to tell of the number of high jumps he has taken or boast of the speed of his horse. The horseman brings his horse in cool, having walked the last mile. If he is not his own stableman he stays around to see that the animal is properly taken care of.

When the rider is "policed" (thrown) or is unable to make his mount do what he wants, it is always the horse that is blamed. When the horseman takes a spill he looks to himself for the cause. In consequence the rider will pay dearly for his mounts. He will be forever chopping and changing them. He will be fit victim for the dealer and the laughingstock of the groom. But the horseman will always seem to be satisfactorily mounted. His horses will remain sound and his grooms contented, year after year, and if circumstances occur which prevent his owning a horse he will be offered the best of what there is to be had free and gratis by the owners of the finest horses who know that their animals will profit by the experience of being ridden and handled by a master. No matter how long he may live or how poor he may be, provided there are horses to be had, the good *horseman* will never lack a mount.

HORSEMANSHIP

Horsemanship is the science of riding the horse and of understanding his needs. No matter how far along the road one has traveled there is always more to be learned. The would-be horseman should practice constantly to improve his seat, hands and control. He should take every opportunity to ride strange horses, especially high-strung, well schooled animals. And he should read and listen to all who have anything to say on this great subject, "the horse." See also *RIDING, HORSE—General Care of, Handling of, Points of, Origin of, Characteristics of, Development of, Breeds of, COLTS.*

HORSEMANSHIP CLASSES
(good hands classes)

These are equitation classes in shows where the performance of the rider only counts. They may be for equitation at the walk, trot and canter, or they may be for jumping. They are usually limited to children who have not yet had their nineteenth birthday and are frequently more closely classified, such as classes for children under twelve and for those from twelve to eighteen. Six ribbons are usually awarded in such classes and, if the class is large, eight are not unusual.

In horsemanship jumping classes the jumps are usually limited to three feet six inches, often to three feet. The best known jumping trophy for which children compete each year is the "Maclay Cup" donated by Alfred Maclay. This is a challenge trophy presented at Madison Square Garden every November. To compete for this trophy the child must have won two Maclay Classes at registered show during the summer.

The A.H.S.A. (American Horse Shows Association) presents a trophy at each show for children's equitation, emphasis being put on the sympathy and tact with which the child handles the horse as well as on the horsemanship. See also *HORSE SHOW CLASSES, GOOD HANDS CLASSES, EQUITATION CLASSES.*

HORSESHOES

The evolution of the horseshoe is a fascinating study. Running in their native state over grassy terrain the wild horse needed no shoes, but as soon as one puts weight upon his back and takes him away from his prairies the horny protection as provided by nature is found to be insufficient. The Romans understood this and though they did not shoe their horses as we do today they provided a sort of leather boot for them with a metal plate in the bottom. Poppaea, the extravagant wife of Nero, is said to have had her horses shod in gold. And when the monument of Childeric, the father of Clovis, was discovered in 1653 it was found that his horse had been interred with him and that it wore shoes.

The Arabs have a most peculiar method of shoeing. They cover the entire sole of the animal's foot with a flat plate leaving only a small hole in the middle. According to some authorities the Arab shoes his mare on three feet only, the fourth is left bare to keep her from slipping on the pebbly inclines. He rotates the shoes so that each may have a turn at being the "brake," but this custom seems to vary with the terrain. The Syrian shoe is an even clumsier type of plate, being very heavy with both heel and toe curved. The theory behind such shoeing is wrong for the horse's frog, his natural cushion and shock absorber is thereby rendered useless.

In modern times man soon discovered that the way a horse was shod had much to do with his gaits. Blacksmiths who specialized in trotting horses came to be veritable artists at their craft, and the trade descended from father to son. Horses that had a tendency towards breaking the trot, those which injured themselves by overreaching, and those which had an awkward stride could all be helped by proper shoes. Those were the days when a blacksmith first asked to see the horse, that was brought to him, in action. Then, having observed carefully the animal's way of going, he would retire to his forge, select a bar of iron and skillfully bend it until, when finished, it fitted the horse exactly and counteracted any natural fault he might have in his stride. How different this from the average modern blacksmith who buys his shoes ready made, chops off the heels a bit, gives the shoe a pound or so and tacks it on! Indeed one is lucky if he does not trim the hoof down to fit the shoe instead of turning the latter to fit the former!

Saddle horses that must pick their feet up high wear shoes weighted in the toes. Running horses wear racing plates, as light as possible and only intended to last for one race. Colts are often shod in "tips" or "slippers," light shoes coming only half way down the hoof and leaving the frog free.

The "bar" shoe is one with a support across the heel to take the pressure off the "bars" and so relieve certain conditions such as corns. The "snow shoe" is the ordinary light shoe usually used on pleasure horses. The feathered shoe, used to correct forging, has a rolled toe which permits the horse to pick his front feet up faster and get them out of the way of the back feet.

Winter shoes may have fixed or removable cleats to enable the horse to get a grip in ice and snow. The horse should never be worked on dry pavements in these for then the full strain of weight comes on just the four points of each foot and the horse will soon become leg weary.

Generally speaking, the shoe that is light and put on with few nails is the one which will give most comfort to the horse. See also *SHOEING*.

HORSE SHOWS

In addition to the entertainment that they provide Horse Shows are a tremendous spur to the breeder. Knowing that if his horses win consecutively in the shows they will bring good prices the breeder is constantly trying to improve the conformation and performance of his colts. So, as the years go on, through the competition of these shows, the various types of horses increase in number, fineness and stamina.

The American Horse Shows Association regulates the rules and schedules of all the big shows. Horses that are bred and trained primarily for showing follow the winter and summer circuits traveling in luxurious "horse pullmans." The climax of the season, of course, is the National Show at Madison Square Garden.

In addition to the so called "recognized" shows (those which belong to the Horse Shows Association) we have the "unrecognized" shows. Though these do not present the grade of performance or of horseflesh of the big shows they are a great stimulus to the owners of pleasure horses and especially to children. The informality of a country show is delightful, with the contestants eating a picnic lunch together at the noon recess and the fat little pig-tailed girls showing their fat little ponies with as much seriousness as though the fate of a nation depended on the awarding of the coveted ribbon.

In England the Pony Club sponsors many "Pony" shows where the emphasis is put on knowledge of horsemanship as well as ability to ride, and a branch of this association has been formed over here.

By studying the horse show catalogue and familiarizing himself with the various requirements of each class, the ambitious learner can improve his knowledge of horses and horsemanship as well as pass an enjoyable afternoon.

HORSE SHOW CLASSES

Hunter and Jumper Division
Breeding Classes (shown in hand). See also *BREEDING CLASSES*.

Stallion, Thoroughbred, 3 yrs. or over with one, two, or three of get.

Mare, Thoroughbred — Other than Thoroughbred.
Suitable to produce hunters. Give registration number and breeding.

Broodmare, Thoroughbred — Other than Thoroughbred.
Suitable to produce hunters with foal at foot. Give registration number and breeding.

Yearlings, Thoroughbred.
Give registration number and breeding.

Yearlings, Other than Thoroughbred.
May be divided into colts only or fillies only. Judged on suitability to become hunters.

Two-year-olds.
Same as above.
Three-year-olds.
Same as yearlings.
Four-year-olds.
Same as yearlings.
See also *HUNTER CLASSES*.

HORSE SHOW JUDGES

To be listed as an official horse show judge one must first be recommended by two senior judges. If approved by the Horse Shows Association one becomes a junior judge. A junior judge must then judge at ten shows with a senior judge after which he may be made a senior judge. Horse shows desiring judges write to the Horse Shows Association which, from their lists recommends judges. Judges receive no pay, of course, for their services, but if it is necessary for them to travel any distance to the show their expenses are usually paid by the committee. After the show has been judged the show committee will sometimes present the judges with mementos as "thank you" gifts but it is exceedingly bad taste for exhibitors to send presents to the judges, especially before the judging has taken place.

HORSE SHOW RIBBONS AND TROPHIES

The value and colors of the usual ribbons presented at horse shows are as follows:

Grand Champion ....Blue, Red, Yellow, White
Reserve to
Grand Champion ....Red, Yellow, White, Pink
Champion ....Blue, Red, Yellow
Reserve Champion...Red, Yellow, White
First Prize ....Blue
Second Prize ....Red
Third Prize ....Yellow
Fourth Prize ....White
Fifth Prize ....Pink
Sixth Prize ....Green
Seventh Prize ....Purple
Eighth Prize ....Brown

The usual ribbons awarded are first, second, third and fourth with or without money prizes or trophies. In horsemanship classes, however, it is customary to award six or eight ribbons according to the size of the class. The ribbons to be awarded and the trophies or cash prizes are always announced on both the sheets sent to exhibitors and on the horse show programs. Money is never awarded in equitation classes. In stake classes the first four winners divide the stake according to a previously announced percentage.

Trophies awarded in classes may be in the form of silver cups or plates or they may be such things as lamps, clocks, etc. In children's classes riding crops, spurs,

etc., are popular. Some shows have a standard award for certain classes such as a special style silver goblet. As one is put up each year competitors may, over a period of time, try to win a complete set.

In war time Victory bonds and Saving Stamps were popular as trophies, especially at the local shows.

HOUNDS

"The 'orse and 'ound were made for each other and nature threw in the fox as a connecting link between the two." So says our friend Jorrocks. Certainly the music of the hounds adds much to the enjoyment of the ride. The man who hunts without trying to learn all he can about the habits of the hound and how to interpret his movements and voice misses more than he knows.

The fox-hunter, when speaking of the hound always means the fox-hound. Much thought has been given to the breeding of this sagacious animal and, during the past war, owners of packs in England sent their hounds to this country for the duration to ensure the perpetuation of their particular strains.

There is a good deal of discussion among authorities as to the relative merits of the English fox-hound as against the American fox-hound. These discussions will doubtless continue as long as there are enthusiasts for both types. The breeding, training and care of a pack of hounds is a highly specialized job and it must be remembered that the hound today, because of modern conditions, has a far harder task before him than did the hound of yesterday. Artificial fertilizers spoil the scent. Over-abundance of foxes mean that a fresh fox may readily take the place of the one he has been running. Preservation of game provides many more deer and rabbits to interfere. And more and more of the open country is being forbidden to the huntsman, who, no sooner gets his hounds running well, than he has to whip them off.

For country where fox-hunting is out of the question bloodhounds may well be introduced. With their truer noses and their greater willingness to accept discipline they can oftentimes provide great sport.

Hound shows here and in England have done much to promote interest in breeding hounds. Competitions in Horse Shows also help. It is too bad that the practice of "puppy walking" is not more prevalent in America for in that way an interest both in hounds and in hunting is promoted in the farmers and country people over whose land the hunt must run. See also *PUPPY WALKING*.

HUNTER

The horse used for hunting may be a Thoroughbred or he may be a cross between a Thoroughbred and some other breed. In countries where the going is heavy a horse with a little of the draft blood in him is considered more desirable than the straight Thoroughbred.

Thoroughbreds used for hunting differ somewhat in type from those used in racing. The latter is more the "greyhound" type with less weight-carrying ability. The ideal hunter should have strong, short, dense cannon bones that he may not tire easily nor develop weaknesses in his legs. He should have a deep chest and well sprung ribs with a well defined windpipe, thus he will be a good "stayer" and will not be subject to respiratory ailments. His back should be on the close-coupled side and his hindquarters should be sloping and pear-shaped rather than square. His hocks must be flat, thick and strong and his hind legs must be carried under him.

In disposition the hunter must not be so high spirited that his master has to be continually checking him. A fling of the heels when the run starts is not serious but the fretter, the puller, the kicker, has no place in the hunt field. The hunter must be sagacious and not easily disturbed. There is no greater crime than to injure a hound and the man who cannot trust his horse not to let fly at a forgetful puppy had best stay at home.

The hunter must be obedient and not wilful. He must be thoroughly schooled to jump where and when his master desires. He must not be clumsy and must be able to stop on the instant to avoid a fallen rider.

All hunters would be the better for a course to develop handiness. There is no more annoying thing than to be held back or lose hounds because one's horse would not stand to open or shut a gate, nor wait to be mounted when it was necessary to retrieve a lost hat.

But, given the conformation and jumping qualities, it is up to the rider and the trainer whether or not the prospective hunter becomes the perfectly mannered and schooled animal that will be the envy of the field.

How Schooled

When it has been decided by the trainer that certain of his colts are real hunter prospects their serious training begins. The colt by now has been taught to obey the rider at all gaits and he has probably had some steadying work in the breaking cart. He may even have been longed over a few jumps or have been run through the jumping lane to see how natural a jumper he is.

The next step is to give him regular work over the hurdles. The jumping lane or the enclosed pen made in a circular shape with high, solid walls is used for this. The horse is usually given his first lessons with a bridle and saddle but no rider. He may be induced to follow another horse over the course or he may simply be driven through. The jumps are not high, a foot or two to start, seldom more than three feet for the first six months. The purpose is to teach the horse to jump freely and willingly. By having the jumps quite close together for part of the training he is induced to jump off his hocks, and by having a series of them he is trained to take them in his stride.

After having a thorough course in jumping free the hunter is mounted and given lessons over very low jumps with a light rider up. He must now learn to balance himself with the shift in weight.

The rider, in the beginning, leaves the horse alone as much as possible but, as his schooling advances, the horse is taught to jump away from the lane or schooling ring over obstacles outside. Over these jumps the rider directs his mount as to speed and the exact point at which they must be taken. Great care and thought are given to seeing that the horse retains his boldness and willingness but still jumps in a disciplined manner. The jumps are raised very slowly. All varieties of obstacles are introduced, until the horse is willing and unafraid to go for the most terrifying obstacles.

The final phase of the hunter's education is his introduction to the hounds. By now he is a thoroughly accomplished animal having had from one to three years careful training. He knows how to obey rein and heel. His manners and mouth are all that could be expected. He will bring from two to five thousand dollars or more and he will be well worth it, for, with intelligent handling he will bear his rider safely and comfortably for many, many years. Hunters as old as twenty or more are to be seen in the field but they are not those which have been over-jumped and rushed through their schooling as youngsters. See also JUMPERS.

HUNTER CLASSES
See also HUNTER, HORSE SHOW CLASSES.

How Classified
There are various ways of classifying hunters when entering them in shows, hunter trials, etc. They may be classified according to weight, i.e., "lightweight" hunter, one capable of carrying up to 165 pounds in the field; "middleweight" hunter, one capable of carrying from 165 to 185 pounds, and "heavyweight," one capable of carrying over 185 pounds.

Or they may be classified according to experience as follows:

Maiden class, open to horses which have not won a first ribbon at recognized shows in the division in which they are being shown.

Novice Class, open to horses which have not won three first ribbons at recognized shows in the division in which they are being shown.

Limit Class, open to horses which have not won six first ribbons at recognized shows in the division in which they are being shown.

Suitable to Become Classes are open to horses four years or under which have not won a first ribbon at a recognized show in the Hunter Division except in classes requiring either no jumping or performance over jumps not to exceed three feet six inches.

Green Hunter Class, open to horses that have not been hunted with a recognized pack for more than one season and which have not won a first ribbon at a recognized show in the Hunter Division prior to Jan. 1st of the current year except in classes requiring no jumping or no performance over jumps exceeding three feet six inches.

Qualified Hunter Class, open to horses which have been regularly hunted with a recognized or registered pack. A certificate to this effect must be produced if requested by the Secretary of the Show.

They may also be classified according to whether or not the owner wishes them judged on conformation without performance, performance without conformation or both. The *Model Hunter* is judged on conformation and soundness alone. He is shown in hand stripped (without saddle) and is jogged merely to demonstrate his soundness. His way of going does not count.

The working and handicap classes are as follows:

Working Hunter Class, open to all hunters qualified or not qualified. Judged on performance, manners, way of going, style of jumping, pace and hunting soundness only. Conformation and honorable scars not to count.

Handy Hunter Class, open to all hunters. A special course is offered which tests the handiness, agility and manners of the horse. The rider is usually asked to open and close a gate, mount and dismount, lead over a jump, etc. Promptness and performance to count.

Handicap Hunter or Jumper Class, open to all hunters and jumpers, jumps set according to age of horses, or status (green, maiden, etc.) or in children's classes sometimes according to size of pony and age and ability of child.

Hunter Hack Class, open to all hunters, jumps not to exceed three feet six inches, horses also asked to show manners and comfortable gaits at the walk, trot and canter.

CONFORMATION HUNTER CLASSES.

To be judged on conformation, performance, manners, way of going, quality, substance and soundness. Where there are two divisions of hunters, one for Thoroughbreds and the other for other than Thoroughbreds, the emphasis for the Thoroughbred classes should be on quality (fineness) and in the other than Thoroughbred it should be on substance (stamina). In Ladies Hunter classes the emphasis is put on manners. In country shows hunters are shown over an outside course. In indoor shows the hunter course usually includes a brush, chicken-coop and post and rail jump. In-and-out or pen jumps are also popular. It should be kept in mind that in judging hunter classes the judges are interested in seeing how the horse performs over obstacles and terrain as nearly approximating the ordinary hunting conditions as possible. To win in the hunter division the horse must not only take his jumps cleanly, he must take them smoothly and in stride. Jumping too high over an obstacle is penalized whereas light ticks are often not considered. The definition of *Novice, Limit,* etc., is given in this text alphabetically. Within conformation classes for colts and *Maiden, Limit, Green, Novice* and *Suitable to Become,* the horses are usually required to show the walk, trot and canter first. Then the best eight are asked to gallop and to jump. In some classes they are not required to jump.

The requirements of each class is given in the horseshow catalogue. Prizes for these classes may be money or they may be a trophy and four ribbons. In the money classes the amount or percentage to be given for first, second, third and fourth winners is specified in the catalogue. Diagrams of jumping courses are also included in the catalogue.

Three-year-olds; four-year-olds; five-year-olds; six-year-olds and under may be further divided as follows:

Thoroughbreds; Other than Thoroughbred; Colts only; Fillies only; Lightweight; Middleweight; Heavyweight.

Jumps 3 feet 3 inches up to 4 feet 6 inches.

Performance, manners,
way of going ....60% to 50%
Conformation, quality
substance, soundness ....40% to 50%

Same classification of entries as in above class may also compete without jumping, being asked to walk, trot and canter. Best eight to be asked to gallop.

Maiden Hunters

Walk, trot, canter and/or jumps 3 feet to 3 feet 6 inches.

Performance, manners,
way of going 50%
Conformation, quality,
substance, soundness 50%

Novice Hunters

Same as Maiden but performance, manners and way of going to count 60%, conformation, etc., 40%.

Limit Hunters

Same as Novice.

Suitable to Become Hunters

Same as Maiden.

Green Hunters

3 feet 6 inches or 4 feet course.

Performance, manners,
way of going ....60% to 74%
Conformation, etc. ....40% to 25%

Model Hunters

To be shown in hand (led in with bridle only). May be divided into *Thoroughbred* and *Other than Thoroughbred.* Judged on conformation, quality, substance and soundness. Horses to be moved on a line, i.e., judge may ask horse to be trotted in a straight line past him so that he can judge him in action. Horses are then formed one behind the other in single file.

Local Hunter Hacks

Horses owned by exhibitors living within a specified number of miles of the show. Must walk, trot, canter and gallop. Back easily and stand quietly while rider dismounts and mounts. To jump two or four jumps of 3 feet 6 inches.

Performance, manners,

way of going 60%
Conformation, quality,
  substance and soundness 40%
See also *HUNTER HACKS* as listed alphabetically in this text.

Local Bridle Path Hacks

Same qualifications as above but horse not required to jump. Emphasis put on actual suitability to purpose.

Performance, manners,
  way of going 75%
Conformation, substance
  and soundness 25%

FIGURE 56. BIM BEAU, REGISTERED HALF BRED BY THOROUGH-BRED STALLION RUNCLAR OUT OF HALF BRED MARE BLUE BIRD BY CHIEF OF LONGVIEW. THIS IS A TYPICAL HUNTER-TYPE HALF BRED. *COURTESY MRS. SYLVIA LINKHART.*

HUNTERS
Lightweight ....up to carrying 165 pounds
Middleweight ....up to carrying 185 pounds
Heavyweight ....up to carrying over 185 pounds
Jumps four feet or four feet six inches.

Performance, manners and
  way of going 60%
Conformation, substance
  and soundness 40%
  Thoroughbred Hunters (give registration number and breeding)
  Judged as "Hunters" with emphasis on quality.

Registered Half Bred Hunters; Other than Thoroughbred Hunters

Judged as "Hunters" with emphasis on substance.

Ladies' Hunters

Amateurs to ride. Jumps 4 feet.

Performance, manners and
way of going 75%
Conformation, substance
and soundness 25%

Amateurs' Hunters

Same as *Ladies' Hunters.*

Open Hunters

Jumps 4 feet to 4 feet 6 inches.

Performance, manners,
way of going 60%
Conformation, substance
and soundness 40%

See *Open Hunters* as listed alphabetically.

Qualified Hunters; Lightweight; Middleweight; Heavyweight

Same specifications as "Open Hunters."

Local Hunters

Owned by exhibitors stabling or residing within specified number of miles of show, which have been hunted regularly with local pack in past season.

Jumps 4 feet.

Performance, manners,
way of going 75%
Conformation, quality,
substance, soundness 25%

Handy Hunters

Jumps 3 feet 6 inches, 4 feet, or 4 feet 6 inches, on special course, details of course to be withheld until the hour for the class. Obstacles to simulate trappy country. Riders will be required to lead over one fence.

Performance, manners, way of going
and promptness 75%
Conformation, quality,
substance and soundness 25%

Emphasis on manners. See also *HANDY HUNTERS* as listed alphabetically in this text.

Corinthian Hunters

Jumps 4 feet to 4 feet 6 inches. To be ridden by amateur members of a recognized or registered hunt in hunting attire.

Performance, manners, way of
going and brilliancy 60%
Conformation, quality,
substance, soundness 25%
Appointments 15%

Emphasis on brilliancy. See also *APPOINTMENTS.*

Hunter Sweepstake, Hunter Stake

In these classes, judged as regular hunter classes, the amount of the entry money is divided according to the announced percentages into six prizes. The exhibitor may be asked to pay an additional entry fee if not enough entries are made to make up the stake. In some cases the exhibitor need not name his horse until an hour before the class. Post entries will be accepted up until an hour before class.

Pair of Hunters Abreast

May be either combined ownership permitted or required to be owned by same owner. Jumps 4 feet.

Manners, way of going as a pair....75%
Conformation, quality, substance,
soundness, resemblance 25%

Pair of Hunters Tandem

Same as *Pair of Hunters Abreast* except that hunters follow one behind the other with about three horse lengths between them. They may be required to change position between certain designated fences.

Team of Three Hunters Abreast

Same as *Pair of Hunters Abreast.*

Team of Three Hunters Tandem

Same as *Pair of Hunters Tandem.* In changing position the third horse takes the lead.

Hunt Teams

Representing a hunt, riders to be in hunt livery.

Performance, manners, way of
going as a team 60%
Conformation, quality, substance,
soundness, resemblance 25%
Appointments 15%

In Hunt team classes the horses are ridden in single file with suitable distance between them and, as a rule, are not required to change position while on the course. See also *APPOINTMENTS, hunting.*

Sporting Tandem (a turnout used for proceeding to a meet of hounds).

Wheeler suitable to be driven in a dogcart or other appropriate vehicle; leader of hunter type, shown together as a tandem suitably harnessed; leader to carry a hunting saddle and bridle, breast collar with long traces and long reins; wheeler should trot while leader should canter. To be judged on suitability of wheeler and leader as a sporting tandem, manners, pace and way.

Ability of exhibitor as a driver and rider for best all around performance to be considered. Leader to be judged as a hunter over appropriate jumps. To be shown by an amateur member of a recognized hunt in hunting attire. To be accompanied by one groom.

Working Hunters

General rules for judging. The judges are to pick the horses, apparently the most agreeable mounts to hounds, the main consideration being even hunting pace, manners, way of going and style in jumping.

Ticks will not be scored, unless the fault of bad jumping. Conformation will not be considered. Hunting soundness only required.

Working hunters may be divided into classes according to weight as in hunters.

Additional Classes for Working Hunters

Working Hunter Trials

Jumps 4 feet to 4 feet 6 inches. On special course. Details of course to be withheld until one hour before class. Rider to lead over one jump.

Non-Winners

Of any ribbons at any recognized horse show prior to the closing of entries. Jumps 3 feet 6 inches to 4 feet.

Consolation Working Hunters

For non-winners of first or second prizes at this horse show. Jumps 3 feet 6 inches.

JUMPERS

Horses to be mathematically scored on actual jumps (see *JUMPING FAULTS, Scoring of*). In case of ties the jumps are to be raised or made wider at the

discretion of the horse show judges. The Championship will be awarded to the horse having won the highest number of points throughout the jumper division.

All classes listed below are judged on performance 100%. Descriptive terms (*Maiden, Novice,* etc.) are listed in this text alphabetically. See also *CHAMPIONSHIP.*

Maiden Jumpers
Novice Jumpers
Limit Jumpers
Local Jumpers
Amateur Ladies' Jumpers
Open to All (also called "Open") Jumpers
Handy Jumpers Special course, performance, promptness 100%
Scurry Jumpers

This class is judged on time with one second added for each fault instead of the usual scoring. Winner is one whose score is lowest in seconds. Those exceeding time limit to be disqualified.

Jumper Sweepstakes (See also *HUNTER SWEEPSTAKE*).

Five foot; Five foot six inches; Six foot class.

Triple Bar

Jumps 4 feet. Course for consecutive triple-bar jumps. Ladies not permitted to ride.

Touch and Out Class

Winners decided by the most obstacles cleared without a touch. Horse excused from the ring by bugle as soon as any bar is touched. Slip-fillets are usually used for this class.

Knock Down and Out Class

Winner is horse taking most obstacles without a knock-down. Touches do not count. Horse excused from ring as soon as knock-down occurs.

Jumper Championship
Team of Three Jumpers Abreast
Team of Three Jumpers Tandem
Pair of Jumpers Abreast
Pair of Jumpers Tandem
Bareback Comic Class

Jumps 3 feet 6 inches. Performance 100% *or* to be judged on horsemanship only, *or* winners determined by applause of audience as each entry parades singly after performance.

SADDLE HORSE DIVISION

Three-Gaited Saddle Horses

General Specifications

Horse to enter ring to the right at a trot. When ordered to line up horses must stand in single file, one behind other on long axis of ring.

Classes

Three-Year-Old Three-Gaited Saddle Horse To Be Shown Under Saddle

To be shown at a walk, trot and canter, both ways of the ring. Judged on quality, performance and manners.

Novice Three-Gaited Saddle Horse

Judged as above.

Three-Gaited Saddle Horse To Be Ridden by Amateur

Judged as above.

Three-Gaited Saddle Horse, Mare or Gelding

To be shown in a full bridle and ridden by a lady. Judged as above.

Three-Gaited Park Saddle Horse

Judged on style, finish, quality, manners and all around brilliance.

Three-Gaited Saddle Horse Open

This class may also be divided as to height for horses over 14:2 and not exceeding 15 hands; horses over 15 and not exceeding 15:2 and those over 15:2.

Combination Saddle Horse

To be shown first to an appropriate four-wheeled vehicle at a walk and trot. Then to be shown under saddle at a walk, trot and canter both ways of ring. To be judged on suitability for saddle and harness work with emphasis on trot.

Three-Gaited Local Saddle Horses
Road Hack

To be shown with a loose rein at a flat-footed walk, trot, extended trot, easy canter and gallop. Must stand quietly when rider mounts and back readily. To be judged on performance, substance and manners.

Three-Gaited Saddle Horses, Pairs

To be shown at walk, trot and canter riding abreast, both ways of ring. When lined up horses to face long side of ring, each pair to stand in single file one be-hind other. To be judged on uniformity, performance as a pair, quality and manners.

Championship or Stake

To be eligible, horses must have been entered and shown in at least one class in this division. To be judged on performance, presence, quality, conformation and manners.

Three-Gaited Saddle Pony To Be Ridden by Child Under . . . Years.

To be shown at walk, trot, canter both ways of ring. Judged on manners, quality and performance.

Three-Gaited Local Ponies

Judged as above.

Three-Gaited Saddle Pony Under 13:2

Three-Gaited Saddle Pony Over 13:2 but Under 14:2

Saddle Pony Under 11:2 To Be Shown by Child Under . . . Years

Note: The Horse Shows Association recommends the above classification for small ponies rather than designating them as a particular breed such as *Shetland.*

Three-Gaited Saddle Pony Open

Championship or Stake

All ponies elegible must have been shown in one class of this division.

Five-Gaited Saddle Horses

General Specifications

Horses to enter the ring to the right at trot. When ordered to line up must stand in single file one behind the other on the long axis of ring. Horses entered in three-gaited classes not eligible. Must be shown without artificial appliances.

Classes

Junior Five-Gaited Stallion, Mare, Gelding, 4 Years Old or Under

To be shown at walk, trot, canter, slow gait and rack. To be judged on quality, performance and manners.

Junior Championship or Stake

To be eligible, entries must have been shown in one other class in this division. Judged on performance, presence, quality, conformation and manners.

Five-Gaited Saddle Horse To Be Ridden by Amateur

Judged on manners, quality and performance.

Five-Gaited Saddle Horse, Mare or Gelding To Be Ridden by Lady

Judged as above.

Five-Gaited Local Saddle Horse

Judged as above.

Five-Gaited Stallion, Mare or Gelding

Judged as above.

Championship or Stake Horse

To be eligible must have been shown in one other class in this division. To be judged on performance, presence, quality, conformation and manners.

FINE HARNESS HORSES

General Specifications

Horses to wear long mane and tail and to be shown in light harness with a snaffle bit to a four-wheeled show wagon without top or with top down.

Classes

Fine Harness Horse To Be Driven by Amateur

To be shown at an animated park trot, extreme speed to be penalized; to stand quietly and back readily. To be judged on quality, manners and performance.

Fine Harness Stallion, Mare or Gelding

To be shown and judged as above.

Championship or Stake, Fine Harness Horse

To be eligible, horse must have been shown in one other class in this division. Shown as above, judged on performance, presence, quality, conformation and manners.

LIGHT HARNESS DIVISION

Light Harness Horses

The light harness horse as distinguished from the *fine* and *heavy* harness horses is a roadster. He is required to show speed and is usually shown in a racing sulky.

General Specifications

Light Harness Horse to be shown to a road wagon or bike. Horses to enter ring to the left at a slow trot. Should stand well and back readily.

Classes

Single Roadster

To be shown at a slow and then a fast trot. To be judged on performance, quality and manners.

Single Roadster, Appointments

Shown as above, judged on performance, quality, manners and appointments. See also *APPOINTMENTS.*

Pairs of Roadsters

Shown as above, judged on performance, manners and quality.

Pairs of Roadsters, Appointments

Shown as above, judged on performance, manners, quality and appointments. See also *APPOINTMENTS.*

Single Stallion or Gelding Roadster To Be Shown to a Bike

To be shown at jog trot and at speed. Drivers must wear stable colors, cap and jacket to match. Judged on performance, quality and manners.

Roadster Under Saddle

Riders must wear stable colors, cap and jacket to match. To be shown under saddle at a jog trot and at speed. Judged as above.

Championship or Stake, Single Roadster

To be shown to a road wagon or bike with drivers to wear stable colors, cap and jacket to match. To be eligible, horses must have been shown in at least one other class in this division. To be judged on presence, performance, quality, conformation and manners.

HEAVY HARNESS DIVISION

General Specifications

All horses to be shown at a trot at least three rounds of the ring and to reverse and do at least three rounds in other direction. Excessive speed not expected nor required. To be shown to appropriate vehicle. Horse showing evidence of lameness or unsoundness of wind to be refused an award.

Classes

Descriptive terms such as Novice, etc., are defined in this text alphabetically.

Single Maiden Harness Horse

Judged on quality, performance and manners.

Single Novice Harness Horse

Judged as above.

Single Limit Harness Horse

Judged as above.

Single Harness Horse To Be Driven by Amateur

Judged as above.

Lady's Single Harness Horse, Mare or Gelding Shown to a Phaeton

Manners paramount. All around action at a park pace. Speed not required. Must stand and back quietly. Must not pull. To be judged on manners, quality, performance and appointments. See also *APPOINTMENTS.*

Single Harness Horse To Be Driven by the Owner or Member of His Immediate Family

Judged on quality, manners and performance.

Single Harness Horse Open

Judged as above.

Single Harness Horse Under 15 hands; Over 15 and Under 15:2; Over 15:2

Gig Class Single Harness Horse, Stallion, Mare or Gelding Shown to a Gig

To be driven by gentleman amateur. Shown at walk, park pace and smart trot. All horses to be required to back. To be judged on presence, manners, performance, quality and appointments. See also *APPOINTMENTS.*

Single Harness Stallion

Judged on quality and performance.

Tandem, Open, Amateur, Specified Height

To be shown to a gig or other appropriate vehicle. A smart leader is essential. Variance in color will not eliminate but uniformity will be considered. To be judged on quality, performance, uniformity and manners.

Championship or Stake, Single Harness Horse to an Appropriate Vehicle

To be shown at a park pace and a smart trot. To back readily. To be eligible, horses must have been shown in at least one other class in this division other than breeding classes. Judged on performance, presence, quality, conformation and manners.

Maiden Pairs of Harness Horses

Judged on quality, performance, manners.

Novice Pairs

Judged as above.

Limit Pairs

Judged as above.

Lady's Pair of Harness Horses, Mares or Geldings

To be driven by lady to phaeton or viceroy with appointments. To show all around action at park pace, not faster. To stand and back quietly. Horses must have perfect mouths and never pull. To be judged on manners, quality, performance and appointments. See also *APPOINTMENTS.*

Collection of Three Harness Horses

To be shown in single harness or as a single and a pair. Each animal to be bona fide property of the exhibitor. Animals need not be named. Each exhibitor to give solo performance of his three horses as a unit both ways of ring. To be judged on performance of horses as a unit and ability to maintain proper distance between horses, uniformity and quality. Or to be judged on basis of the three best animals of one exhibitor without regard to uniformity.

Pairs of Harness Horses Open

To be judged on performance, quality and manners.

Pairs of Harness Horses under 15 Hands; Over 15 Under 15:2; Over 15:2

Judged as above.

Championship or Stake, Pairs of Harness Horses

To be shown to appropriate vehicle. Horses to be eligible must have been shown in at least one other class in this division other than breeding. Judged on performance, presence, quality, conformation and manners.

Four-in-Hands, Park Drag

Of solid color to be drawn by four *matched* horses with park harness, two servants in livery. To be judged on performance, quality, manners, uniformity and appointments. See also *APPOINTMENTS.*

Four-in-Hands, Road Coach

To be drawn by team not necessarily matched with road harness. To carry guard in livery. To be judged on performance and substance. Appointments.

Marathon

Coach to be driven over a specified course and to carry at least six persons. Contestants must finish the course within the stated time but otherwise speed not to count. To be judged on performance and substance, with emphasis on condition of horses at finish.

BREEDING CLASSES

General Specifications

Horses shown in hand, judged on conformation only.

Classes

Stallions
Mares   } Various ages.
Model

Heavy Harness Ponies over 11:2

Classes correspond to Heavy Harness Horses except that appointments do not count.

Heavy Harness Ponies under 11:2

Classes correspond to Heavy Harness Horses except that appointments do not count. The Horse Shows Association recommends that classes for small ponies be designated according to size rather than as to any particular breed.

POLO DIVISION

General Specifications

All ponies to be shown collectively at a walk, trot and canter. Then individually to do a figure eight, to gallop a given distance, stop, reverse, gallop back and stop. To ride off and to perform other tests of handiness at the command of the judge.

Note: Polo ponies are shown by riders in polo dress carrying mallet.

Classes

Polo Pony

May be divided into weight divisions, i.e., lightweight to carry up to 165 pounds. Middleweight to carry up to 185 pounds. Heavyweight to carry over 185 pounds.

All classes to be judged on handiness, performance, manners, mouth and conformation.

STOCK DIVISION

General Specifications

Horses to be serviceable sound stock-horse type, no penalty for wire cuts. Entries in all classes should be open to stallion, mare or gelding with no discrimination. Horses to be 14:2 to 16 hands.

General Rules for Performance in Ring and Judging.

Instructions to Riders.

Quirt, ramal or spurs not to be used in front of cinch. No roughness of handling permitted. Two hands may be used to balance horse in stopping. Hands to be kept clear of saddle at all times.

Showing

Horses shall all enter arena at a walk taking slow lope when asked to do so; they shall then be lined up in arena or retired therefrom at the discretion of the judge. Horses shall be worked one at a time.

Working

Start with figure eights, easy turns, no choppiness of gaits. The looser the rein and smoother the gait the better. Horse then to be walked to end of arena, turned and run full length of arena to sliding stop, turns to be made away from rail. Horse then to come to center of arena at slow gallop and make easy stop. He shall then be turned once each way with the weight on the hindquarters and hind legs in place. To back not to exceed twenty-five feet. Must not be spun or run backwards. To be brought back to judges and standing with weight on hindquarters, hind legs in one position, to make quarter turn left, half turn right, half turn left, quarter turn right. After all entries have been shown as above each horse is worked on roped sack.

The sack is to be roped, the horse run from side to side, turning squarely back as end of rope is reached with not to exceed 25 feet of rope out, the purpose being to show that the horse can work accurately and fast after an animal has been roped. The rope shall then be tied between twenty and twenty-five feet, rider shall dismount and place foot on sack; horse must hold rope tight without indication from or aid of rider or snubbing of reins.

Faults

Judges are to consider the following characteristics as faults: Switching tail. Exaggerated opening of mouth. Slackening of reata when holding sack. Turning away or exhibiting lack of attention when holding sack. Nervous throwing of head. Lugging on bridle. Halting or hesitation when being shown, particularly when being run out. Horse approaching rider in order to allow reata to be taken off animal or sack.

Classes

Lightweight Stock Horse 850 to 1,100 pounds

Heavyweight Stock Horse

Green Jaquima Class

Open to horses not more than five years old and that shall not have been ridden more than five months. To be shown in Jaquima (hackamore) only. Horses shall not be required to work fast nor to back over ten feet.

Advanced Jaquima Class

Open to horses not more than six years old who have not been worked or shown as a bridle horse.

Championship or Stake

Horses to be eligible must have been shown in at least one other stock horse class.

WALKING HORSE DIVISION

General Specifications

Horses to be between 15 and 16 hands high, of good bone and able to carry weight.

All horses enter ring to right at the running walk and continue at running walk until ordered to change.

Entire class to be worked at least once around ring at each gait, then reversed and worked as judge deems advisable.

Horses shall be lined up and individually asked to back.

Saddles to be removed for judging of conformation in championship classes. The qualifying gaits for the Walking Horse are as follows: *Flat-footed walk,* should be true, square and flat-footed. *Running walk,* should be smooth, gliding, overstepping and four cornered. The horse must have stride and head

motion. *Canter,* should be smooth, slow and straight on both leads with a rolling motion with chin well tucked in, comfortably in hand.

Judging

All classes to be judged on quality, manners and performance. Championship and stake class to be judged on above plus presence and conformation.

Classes

Junior Walking Horse, three years old

Novice Walking Horse

Walking Horse To Be Ridden by Amateur

Walking Horse, Mare or Gelding To Be Ridden by a Lady

Local Walking Horse

Championship or Stake Horse

To be eligible must have been shown in at least one other class in this division.

DRAFT HORSE DIVISION

General Specifications

Draft horses may be shown singly, in pairs or in teams of four or more. They are judged on the qualifications of the breeds being shown. They should be shown to appropriate wagons. In teams of four or more the wheelers may be heavier. They are judged on conformation, style, handiness and manners. In pairs or teams they should be matched.

Classes

Draft horse classes may be divided as to weights or as to breeds of horses.

Breeding classes are shown in hand and judged on conformation, quality and type.

MILITARY CLASSES

General Specifications

Military classes, unless otherwise specified, are judged according to the Rules of *Federation Equestre Internationale.* See also *F.E.I.*

Riders must be in uniform.

Horses must be *bona fide* property of an officer, enlisted man or the United States Government.

Classes

There are many types of military classes but those most often encountered are as follows:

Officer's Jumping Classes

Enlisted Men's Jumping Classes
Officer's Chargers

Shown mounted or in hand. See also *CHARGERS, Officer's,* as listed alphabetically.

Trooper's Mounts

Shown mounted or in hand.

Artillery Gun Teams

Shown in draft or in hand.

Police Mounts

EQUITATION CLASSES

General Specifications

These classes are for amateurs, children or adults according to the age qualifications announced in the catalogue. Money is not given as awards as this would make the riders professionals. It must be understood that whereas in other than equitation classes the rider is exhibiting whereas the animal is competing, in equitation classes the rider is competing. Classes are judged on performance of the rider only, jumping faults not to count unless fault of rider.

Riders should be suitably mounted on horses fitted for equitation classes. No exaggerated type of saddle should be used. In classes other than jumping classes four-rein bridles should be used.

Classes may be divided in Maiden, Novice, etc., also into age groups. Under eight years, eight to twelve, twelve to nineteen. Or simply under nineteen.

In addition to the requirements listed under *GOOD HANDS* classes, this text, riders may be asked to do the following at the discretion of the judges:

Championship Equitation Tests

Open only to first- and second-place winners in this section or division. To compete over a minimum number of six jumps at approximately 3/6 without wings. Judges may also ask for any of the tests given below:

1. Back
2. Dismount and mount
3. Gallop and stop
4. Figure eight at trot, demonstrating change of diagonal
5. Figure eight at canter, with flying, interrupted or stationary change of lead if on a suitable horse
6. Jump low fences at walk or trot as well as at canter
7. Pull up in turns between fences
8. Jump fences on figure-eight course
9. Jump fence in middle of ring at right angles to course
10. Change horses.
12. Jump serpentine course, demonstrating change of lead at each change of direction
13. Jump strange horse supplied by committee
14. Answer questions

In recent years it has been customary in judging a championship of such advanced jumping competitions as the MacClay Trophy Finals at Madison Square Garden, to have all contestants ride over the course without stirrups, with a fixed leg, on their own horses; then have them exchange horses and repeat the procedure; and finally to have a few surviving contestants jump a selected horse. These stiff tests have become necessary because the standard of riding in Junior Horsemanship and Equitation competitions has become so high.

Riding Classes

Pick up reins.

Mount and dismount.

Back.

Individual performance around ring.

Extended trot.

Gallop and stop.

Change horses.

Figure eight at trot demonstrating change of diagonal.

Figure eight at a canter, stopping on each change of lead.

Individual performance away from rail.

Change leads on straight line down center of ring stopping at each change.

Ride strange horse supplied by committee.

Flying change if put on suitable horse.

Adjust stirrups at trot or canter, also canter or trot without stirrups.

Jumping Classes

Back.

Gallop and stop.

Change horses.

Pull up on turns between fences.

Jump fence in middle of ring in line with course.

Jump fence in middle of ring at right angles to course.

Jump low fences at a walk and trot as well as canter.

Jump strange horse supplied by committee.

Stock Classes (equitation)

To be judged on hands, seat, performance of horse, correct appointments for horse and rider. Rider should be able to do regular stock routine and answer questions concerning additional evolutions. Method used to obtain results more important than performance of horse.

See also *APPOINTMENTS (stock); EQUITATION; GOOD HANDS; A.H. S.A.; MACLAY CUP.*

HUNTER TRIALS

These are competitions for hunters over an outside course that, as nearly as possible, represents actual hunting conditions. The obstacles are natural ones such as would be met within the hunt field. The course is usually laid in a circle with inclines to be negotiated, etc. Horses must keep a hunting pace and are judged on manners, performance, way of going and sometimes conformation. There are also competitions for hunt teams or pairs of hunters. These ride in single file at a safe hunting distance. Sometimes, at the sound of the horn, they are required to pull up and wait a moment or two to change the order so that the horse that was riding last is now put in the lead. Contestants ride in hunt livery, the classes are generally limited to amateurs and the prizes are trophies rather than cash.

HUNTING

The spirit of the chase is fundamental in mankind. Coupled with its companion and opposite characteristic, the will to survive, it may be traced back a hundred and twenty-five thousands years to the Paleolithic man who pursued animals weaker than himself in order to eat and ran from those stronger in order to escape being eaten himself. Forty thousand years ago the Neanderthal man had introduced hunting into his conception of his future life for he was buried with the tools of his chase beside him.

Throughout Greek mythology we find hunting myths very prominent. Xenophon, five centuries before Christ, was one of the earliest and most thoughful students of equestrian arts, among them hunting. Romans, Gauls, Hittites and all the other early races hunted both for sport and for food. Nimrod was a "famous hunter before the Lord," *Genesis X.* Persian paintings, early Egyptian relics, the stone monuments of forgotten races in Africa and Central America, all record hunting scenes, some most beautifully rendered. The quarry varied tremendously and included wild boar, elephant, lions, ostrich, fox, wolf, etc., but stag hunting seems to have been the favorite. Hounds and falcons were used quite early and the hunters might be afoot, mounted, or in chariots.

In the eighth century hunting came to be associated with the Christian religion and St. Hubert, who became converted to Christianity through the vision of a milk white stag bearing a flaming cross on his antlers, became the patron saint of hunting.

Hunting, throughout the middle ages, was indulged in by people of all walks and professions. The clergy especially, were ardorous *"chasseurs,"* even abbesses taking to horse. In 1387 Gaston de Foix wrote one of the earliest hunting books called *Livre de Chasse.*

Even during war time hunting was not forgotten for between battles, knights, crusaders and kings hunted. Nor did this custom end with the crusades for we find the Duke of Wellington conducting his campaign and his fox-hunting simultaneously, even to the extent of having the earths stopped over the countryside as he retreated before Soult in order that he and his officers might have plenty of sport!

FIGURE 57. HORSES AND MEMBERS OF THE HUNT STAFF HACKING ALONG A COUNTRY ROAD. NOTE COUPLES ON HOUNDS. *CHARLES PHELPS CUSHING.*

Perhaps one might suppose that the combining of hunting and war had disappeared with the coming of modern weapons but it hung on through World War I during which time several British regiments kept hounds in France and one pack got as far as Italy, while American troops under Major-General Allen both hunted and played polo at Coblenz. I have not been able to ascertain whether or not there were any packs maintained in the field during World War II but I do know that plans were made by troops stationed in the recaptured Philippines and other Pacific posts to start polo.

The French sovereigns were among the most enthusiastic followers of the chase and the earliest pack of foxhounds maintained especially for hunting in that country was kept by Louis XIII. In Italy, too, hunting was much appreciated by the ladies of the court. In Russia it was customary not only for the various hunts to be uniformly costumed but each nobleman had his horses matched in color. The Russians especially were given to great pomp and ceremony in connection with the sport of hunting.

Hunting in North America paralleled that in Europe and Asia and one of the most enthusiastic hunters was George Washington whose diary records his almost daily efforts to run down a fox or two.

According to the American Turf Register there were established packs in Baltimore, Washington and Virginia as early as 1730 but the first foxhunting club was the Gloucester, founded in 1766. The Montreal Hunt, founded in 1826, is the earliest hunt on the North American Continent to be still active.

Since the founding of the Gloucester pack the number of active hunts in the United States have grown to over a hundred. A complete list of these will be found in the Appendix.

FIGURE 58. AN OLD ENGLISH HUNTING PRINT SHOWING HOUNDS IN FULL CRY.

But the British Isles is still regarded as the home of hunting foxes on horseback. The "English Print" brings to mind scarlet-coated gentlemen scrambling over fences. The favorite fictitious character connected with hunting is surely our friend Jorrocks, with John Peel sharing the honors. Masefield gives us the most beautiful and complete description of the chase in his magnificent narrative poem, *Reynard the Fox*. No one, whether he be interested in horses, hounds or foxes can read these stirring lines without appreciating the part which hunting plays in the heart of the Britisher, be he young or old, rich or poor.

Because the horse and the hound are no longer a part of everyday living and the younger generation do not imbibe the traditions and customs of the hunt along with their breakfast cereal, the whole concept of hunting is often most woefully misunderstood by the majority of the beautifully habited and mounted riders one sees at the covert side. There have always been those who "hunted in order to ride (and particularly to jump)" as opposed to those who "rode in order to hunt" but fewer and fewer are the riders who take an interest in the scientific side of hunting.

Yet if the members of the field could be prevailed upon to study up a bit and take a real interest in hound work not only would they derive much more pleasure from their hobby but the task of the hunt staff would be tremendously lessened.

Many of the younger generation are frankly bored at the long waits while hounds are casting. For them should be reserved the steeplechase course of the drag-hunt. Perhaps one cannot really blame these young enthusiasts for they have not had the opportunity of learning anything about the science of hunting. Perhaps the fault lies with the officers of the Hunt. They should in some way strive to educate the members of their field either by way of lectures or by the distribution of literature which would tell something about the real purpose of hunting (which is to kill foxes, not to give young thrusters the opportunity of showing off their skill over fences), how hounds are bred, the difficulties of following a line, what the various sounds of voice and horn which issue forth from the covert mean, and how the field may help the staff rather than hinder it.

Hunting is one of the few active sports which may be indulged in throughout a lifetime by men and women alike. There have been Masters and Huntsmen, both male and female, who were still hunting their hounds when they were well into their eighties and children as young as two or three make their appearance at the meets in England on donkeys and ponies, securely strapped into basket seats!

As has been most aptly said, "Hunting is the sport of kings, the image of war with only five and twenty per cent of the danger."

See also *HUNTING COUNTRIES; HOUNDS; HUNTSMAN, duties of; COURTESY; HUNTING HORN; HUNTING CALLS; APPOINT-MENTS, hunting; HORSE SHOW CLASSES, hunter and jumper division.*

HUNTING CALLS
The hunting horn used in England and America will produce one note only. Yet, with this one note, the huntsman must be able to communicate much information to his hounds and his field. He does this by distinctive rhythms and tonal variations. When hounds are looking for the fox either in covert or in the open, then the huntsman's call consists of long, languid notes or several notes "tied together," i.e., the note weakens and swells in sound again. When hounds are running the notes are short and staccato. In certain instances short staccato notes are combined with longer but equally staccato notes. It must be remembered that the huntsman's voice is as important as his horn and, though he speaks in such fashion that it is rarely possible to understand what he is saying, the tones will tell the intelligent listener exactly how the hunt is going even though he may be able to see neither hounds, fox nor huntsman. Below are some of the instances in which the horn is used and the manner in which it is usually blown. Huntsmen vary these calls to suit themselves, but the basic principle remains the same.

Hounds in Covert
One short but not staccato note blown at intervals to tell them that the huntsman is with them and to keep trying. This is accompanied by much use of the voice.

Several long, doleful notes tell field and hounds that the covert is blank and they will have to go and try somewhere else.

Little sets of short, quick notes (known as "doubling" the horn) accompanied by one or two shrill screams and holloas tell hounds that the fox has been seen and call them to him.

A loud "cheer" and a tremendous scream tell the field that the fox has "gone away," i.e., left the covert. As soon as hounds are properly on the line and running the huntsman "blows them out." This is a series of staccato notes. They may be either quarter-half-quarter-half, or half-quarter-quarter, half-quarter-quarter, etc. The huntsman must always "blow his hounds away" with this special call or the field will lose confidence in him and try to pick out the line for themselves, resulting in headed hounds and spoiled hunting. If hounds stay on the line until they mark their fox the huntsman may put his horn away and do nothing but ride, but this rarely happens and the chances are that after a short run of ten minutes or so the scent will be lost, hounds will "throw up" and the huntsman will have to get them on the line again.

Hounds in the open

When hounds are casting themselves the huntsman and, let us hope, the field, sit perfectly quietly and make no noise at all. But if they seem at a loss and the huntsman has a pretty good idea of where the fox has gone he may "lift" his hounds, i.e., call them to him and lead them away to where he thinks the fox has just run. He does that with a whistle, a quiet word and perhaps one short toot on his horn. If they pick up the line he gives them a short cheer and a half dozen short notes on the horn to tell the stragglers that the main pack is away and they had better join up if they don't want to miss all the fun.

If the hounds have completely lost their fox and the huntsman wants to take them some little distance away he will collect his pack and canter away with them at his heels, the whipper-in coming up behind to keep their heads up. In this case he will probably "double" his horn every half minute or so in order to keep in touch not only with the hounds but with the field as well.

Eventually the hunt will end either with a kill or with the fox being marked to ground. In either case, having made sure that it is a fox and not someone's pet cat that has been killed, the huntsman jumps off his horse, either ties up the latter or hands him to someone to hold and there follows a riot of sounds. The shrill *whoo-whoop* which tells of the fox's death is interspersed with exultant notes of the horn, long and short "a-way-

away-way-way-a-way" with perhaps a long tremolo at the end.

One more call is given at the end of the day. The huntsman "blows home" a series of long, connected notes which last until the huntsman has no wind left. This tells hounds and field that the day's sport is over. It is time to wend their various ways homeward. A few hundred yards from the kennel the huntsman "blows home" once again to warn the kennel man that hounds are coming and to pour the hot broth over the porridge and flesh which is waiting in the trough.

HUNTING CAP

The hunting cap originated in the days when there was a "hat tax," or "capping fee." This fee was exacted of all who went out with the hounds except children under eighteen, farmers (since it was due to the courtesy of the farmers that hounds were permitted to hunt it was not considered fair that they should be taxed for following hounds on their own or their neighbors' lands) and the official hunt staff consisting of the Master, Huntsman, Whips and Field Master. All the above persons wore specially designed velvet caps, reinforced with cork to make them hard and decorated with grosgrain bows at the back and a high button on top. In passing his cap to collect the fees the Hunt Secretary could tell by the headgear exactly who owed and who didn't. Today one sometimes sees women and occasionally men wearing the velvet cap, but this is not strictly *de rigeur*.

HUNTING COUNTRIES

The method of hunting the fox, the type of horse used and the type of hound are almost entirely governed by the type of country to be hunted. England and Ireland, of all countries, are best suited to the sport. Nothing even faintly resembling the Irish hunting country exists in North America. In England the coverts are very small and generally surrounded by pastureland. Furthermore they are much more open and more readily ridden through than those in many parts of the United States and Canada. Wire is not as prevalent as here, hedges and ditches being the most common barriers. Foxes are protected and it is against the law to shoot them; consequently they are very numerous. Earths and drains are stopped the night before a hunt, so kills are much more common there than in America, where a fox may circle for hours in a covert so rough that the huntsman cannot ride in to encourage his hounds, and then, after a brief run, take refuge either in his own den or in a convenient woodchuck hole.

The scenting conditions are also far better in England, due to more moisture, and the milder climate gives a much longer season. The fact that hunting is better and therefore more popular in England than here also has its disadvantage for fields of from five hundred to a thousand people, some mounted, some on foot, on bicycles or in motor cars, are not uncommon, while in the United States a field of over a hundred is considered large.

In Ireland and Scotland the hunting conditions more nearly resemble those of the United States in that the country is much steeper and rougher. The variety of jumps in Ireland is great but the one most typical of the country is the Irish bank. These are often of great height and the horse negotiates them by leaping part way up, scrambling the rest, changing legs on the top and leaping down again. Double banks sometimes necessitate a jump from the top of one to the top of the other. To the American, accustomed to his stiff timber which he flies with utter nonchalance both the Irish bank and the English bullfinch seem terrifying while the Englishman, who thinks nothing of flying a double oxer, goes at timber with his heart in his mouth.

Even in America the types of countries differ tremendously. In New England, stone walls are the normal barriers of fields. The fields themselves are very small, the coverts enormous. When paneled the panels are narrow and must be negotiated by one rider at a time, the rest holding back. The countryside is strewn with rocks, the tiny trails leading through the woods so steep and narrow and so winding that it takes a good rider and a good horse to negotiate them at a gallop. Imagine the trepidation of the French *"chasseur,"* accustomed to his beautifully groomed forest "rides" where the turf is like a putting green and the whole thing looks like a set on the Metropolitan stage, when called upon to follow the chase through a boggy, rocky, New England trail!

In Virginia the country more nearly resembles the English countryside, the pastures being much larger and more rolling. But there is a prevalence of wire necessitating paneling which means that the field may be held up and must make up for the delay by increased speed on the other side or lose hounds. The South Carolina country is sandy, making the scenting difficult, partially wooded and as there are few fences it is generally artificially paneled for those who like to jump. In Long Island, long a scene of hunting, the packs are being literally pushed into the sea by the extension of the metropolitan district of New York. It is only because of the tremendous enthusiasm of the large landowners that hunting has survived at all in that country.

Some of the oldest packs are in Pennsylvania and Maryland. The country here is more open than the New England country and less built up than Long Island. Stone walls abound but there is not so much bog. In many places a great effort is made by the officers of the hunts to interest the local farmers in the sport. This practice, understood to be important by the English, is too often neglected here.

The Western hunts are of more recent origin than those of the South and Eastern Seaboard, but the country is much more suited to the chase and it is quite possible that, with the coming of air transportation, ardent huntsmen will commute by air to the wide open spaces where they may enjoy a really good gallop.

Whether the American or the English Foxhound is the better has long been the point of much discussion. But most authorities who have hunted extensively in both countries, will pretty readily admit that each type is the better suited for his own environment. The American hound is not as disciplined but on the other hand he has more initiative and usually a better voice than his English cousin. This latter quality is imperative in the United States where the hunt staff must rely on the voice of the hounds to tell them what is afoot. The open country of England makes hounds readily controlled, and the huntsman hunts the hounds rather than the hounds hunting the fox for themselves. All these things should be taken into consideration when discussing the respective merits of the two types.

It is most essential that the horse used in any given country be suitable and schooled for that country. The American horses, unused to the English bullfinches and double oxers will invariably come a cropper when first faced with them. The English hunter, unaccustomed to the rocky hillsides of New England, has to learn to pick his way and avoid the rolling stones. If one wishes to enjoy hunting in strange countries it is far wiser to get horses in the neighborhood than to trust ones limbs to an animal totally unschooled for that particular country and fence, no matter how fine a jumper he may be. But if you take your favorite with you, at least spend a few days schooling him over the surrounding territory before you present him at the covert side.

HUNTING HORN

The hunting horn used by fox hunters is of brass, copper or silver. It is short with a small bell and capable of only one note. The Master or Huntsman carries the horn either in a leather case attached to the front of his saddle or he may wear it tucked in his vest. The horn used on the Continent for stag hunting is a vastly different affair, being coiled and capable of many different notes. Huntsmen of stag hounds are veritable musicians but the clever M.F.H. can communicate readily with his small horn and let his servants, hounds and field know all that they should. See also *HUNTING CALLS.*

HUNTING TERMS

Most hunting terms come down to us from the English. A few are taken from the French, especially those referring to stag hunting, and America too has contributed a number. Hunting terms are often completely unintelligible to the tyro but they should be studied as the knowledge of what the hounds are doing and why will add greatly to the pleasure of members of the field.

ACCOUNT FOR

A fox or other hunted game is said to be "accounted for" when killed or run to ground by the hounds.

BABBLER

A hound that bays and flings its tongue around when not on the line is called a "babbler."

BAGMAN

In countries where foxes are scarce it is sometimes customary to bring a fox to the meet in a sack and turn him loose. As this practice is frowned upon as being unsportsmanlike, particularly when the fox has been handicapped by having his pads cut to prevent his running too fast, the "Bagman" or bagged fox is usually introduced surreptitiously.

BARBARY PACK

A rough, scratched together pack of hounds not normally kenneled together but rounded up for the occasion with the hope that they will have sufficient nose and stamina to provide sport is known as a Barbary Pack.

BEAGLE

Beagle hounds are a small breed of hounds used for hunting rabbits. They are hunted on foot. Beagle hunting is very old and, as rabbits tend to run in circles, the field does not have to move about too much.

BILLET

The droppings of the fox.

BINDER

The top of a cut and laid fence. A sapling woven between upright stakes is known as a "binder."

BLANK (To draw blank)

A covert is blank or drawn blank when no fox is found within. A blank day is one in which hounds fail to start a fox.

BLIND COUNTRY

Blind country is terrain so overgrown with weeds and underbrush that it is not possible to gauge the jumps and footing.

BLOOD, BLOODED

Hounds are said to be blooded when they kill their first fox. "Young entry" of the human race are blooded at their first kill by being dabbed on the forehead with blood from the fox.

BLUE TICKED

A hound is said to be "blue ticked" when it is mostly white with small splashes of black mixed in giving a "blue" appearance.

BOLT A FOX

"To bolt a fox" is to make him leave his earth or the drain in which he has taken refuge by putting a terrier in behind him.

BOTTOM

A big ditch or drain with a fence on one side. More common in England than in America.

BREAST HIGH SCENT

Scent is said to be "breast high" when it is so strong that hounds do not stoop to it but run with their noses off the ground.

BRUSH

The tail of the fox. The brush together with the mask and pads are awarded by the huntsman to those of the field who are first in at the kill.

BULLFINCH

This is a type of jump found in England. It consists of a thick hedge, often of thorn, too high to be jumped and through which the rider must bore.

There are often ditches and guard rails on one or both sides. The bullfinch is terrifying to one not used to it and to horses from foreign parts but it is very common in certain parts of England. A black bullfinch is one so thick that one cannot even see through it.

BURNING SCENT

"Burning" or "screaming" scent is scent so hot and strong that hounds tear along the line without hesitation.

BURST

When hounds get away quickly on their fox or when there is a fast run during a hunt it is known as a "burst."

BYE DAY

Sometimes the Master or Huntsman takes hounds out on a day not regularly scheduled on the fixture card: this is known as a "bye day."

CARRY (to carry ground)

After a heavy frost the ground sometimes sticks to the pads of fox and hound alike. They are said then "to carry." And ground so carried is known as "carries."

CARRY (to carry a good head)

When hounds run abreast in following a line they are said to "carry a good or wide head."

CARRY (to carry a line)

This is the same as to "work a line," i.e., follow the track laid by the fox.

CAST

The Huntsman casts hounds when he leads them over the ground where he thinks the fox has recently traveled. He may encourage them to "cast" themselves in covert or in the open, i.e., to spread out and search for the scent. This he does with voice and horn. Good hounds cast themselves and, especially in America, where the ground is unsuitable or the covert too thick to permit the passage of the horse and rider, hounds hunt free and make their own casts. In England the hounds are kept more closely under the Huntsman's control and he casts them himself when they lose the line.

CATCH HOLD

A huntsman is said to "catch hold"

when he collects his hounds and takes them forward at a check or in answer to a halloo indicating that the fox has been seen.

CAT FOOT

A hound is said to have a "cat foot" as it is rounder than the more elongated pad of the fox and hare.

CHALLENGE

When a hound first "owns" or "speaks to" a line he is said to "challenge" it.

CHANGE (to change foxes)

When hounds leave the line of the hunted fox and take up the line of a fresh fox they are said to have "changed." This practice is highly undesirable and is prevented whenever possible by the Huntsman.

CHARLES, CHARLES JAMES

An old English term for the fox.

CHECK

When hounds lose the scent and stop they are said to "check." A check is a period in the hunt when the field sits quietly while hounds search for the line or are cast by the Huntsman.

CHEER

The Huntsman "cheers" his hounds by calling to them. The cheerful, encouraging hunting cry is called a "cheer." See *Hunting Horn*.

CHOP (to chop a fox)

When the fox is caught and killed before he has got away and there has been no run, he is said to have been "chopped" or "mobbed."

COCKSTAIL

This is an English expression meaning a "cold-blooded" hunter, i.e., one that is not a Thoroughbred. Such horses were frequently docked in England.

COLD LINE

The faint scent of a quarry which may have lain for some time. In certain scenting conditions a scent may be quite "fresh" but still so faint as to be termed "cold."

COUNTER

When a hound runs a line in reverse he is said to "counter."

COUPLES

Hounds are counted in couples. This grew out of the custom of keeping hounds coupled together with short chains on swivels. A hunting man would never speak of twenty-four hounds, he would say "twelve couple." Thirteen hounds would be known as "six and a half couple."

COURSE

Certain species of hounds such as greyhounds run their prey by sight rather than by scent; they are then said to be "coursing" it.

COVERT (cover)

Any wooded area in which a fox might hide is known as a "covert."

COVERT-HACK

A horse which is ridden to the covert side but not used in the hunt is known as a "covert-hack."

CRASH

When the hounds all give tongue at once on finding a fox they are said to "crash."

CROPPER (to come a cropper)

When a rider falls he is said to "come a cropper." The Westerner says he has "taken squatter's rights" in like circumstances, while the military man will tell you that he has "been policed."

CRY (voice, tongue, music)

The bay of a hound is quite different from that of other dogs and his cry also varies according to whether he is running a hot or a cold scent. The sound the hound makes when he has run his quarry to earth is known as a "den cry." A noisy hound which gives tongue unnecessarily is known as a "babbler." One which runs without baying is said to "run mute." Neither of these last two are desirable in a pack. The beagle's cry is higher than that of the fox-hound while the bloodhound has a deep, resounding, bell-like voice.

CUB

The young fox is called a cub.

CUB HUNTING

Informal hunting of young foxes before the regular hunting has started is known as "cub hunting." Its purpose is to break up the litters of young foxes and teach them to run out of covert when they hear the hounds, also to teach the young hounds their business. See *CUB HUNTING* (main heading).

CURRANT JELLY

An English expression meaning hunting hare. Harriers are sometimes called "jelly dogs."

CUT AND COME AGAIN COUNTRIES

Our friend John Jorrocks was not overly fond of stiff jumps. Country which abounded in such jumps he called "cut and come again" countries.

CUT AND LAID FENCE

This is a type of thorn fence which has been partly cut through and then turned back and bound to form a firm barrier.

DEN

The home of the fox is his den.

DEN BARK

The peculiar cry which hounds give when they have run their prey to ground is known, in America, as the "den bark."

DEN DOG

A hound which is particularly keen on worrying an earth and who is useful to the Huntsman because of the distinctive cry he gives at such a time is known as a "den dog."

DEW CLAW

The false toe and claw to be found on the forelegs of hounds. In England these are often removed but in America they are usually left on.

DEWLAP

The dewlap is the pendulous skin under the neck of the hound which is a great protection from bites which might sever the jugular vein. The bloodhound has the most pronounced dewlap.

DOG FOX

The male fox. The female is the vixen.

DOG HOUND

The male hound as distinguished from the bitch-hound. Males used for breeding are sometimes called "stallion hounds."

DOUBLE

When the fox or other quarry turns back on its course it is said to double.

DOUBLING THE HORN

A series of trilling notes made by using the tongue is called "doubling the horn."

DRAFT

To remove hounds from a kennel or pack is to draft them. Draft hounds are those which have been taken from their regular pack.

DRAG

The scent which the fox leaves when he returns to his lair in the morning is known as the "drag." This is also called the night-line.

DRAG (Drag-Hunt)

This is a form of hunting in which an artificial line is laid. It is more common in America than in England. See *DRAG HUNT* (main heading).

DRAG HOUNDS

Hounds used for drag hunting. As the scent is always good drag hounds need not be as wise and experienced as those used to trail the wily fox but they must be fast.

DRAIN

Any underground water course or big ditch in which the fox may take shelter is called a drain.

DRAW (draw a covert)

To search for a fox in a covert. This is usually done by casting hounds in the covert and then having the Huntsman ride up wind through the center, flanked by a whip on either side.

DRAW BLANK

An unsuccessful draw.

DROP FENCE (drop jump)

This is a jump in which the landing side is lower than the take-off.

DROPPED FOX (see *Bagman*).

DWELLING

A hound is said to "dwell" on the line when he lingers unnecessarily on it instead of going forward.

EARTH

Any hole in which the fox takes refuge is called an "earth." Woodchuck holes are the favorite earths of foxes in America; badgers provide M. Reynard with his earths in England.

EARTH STOPPER
A person employed to stop earths.
EARTH STOPPING
In England it is customary to stop all earths (block them up) in a given territory the night before hounds are to visit that territory. The fox then, on his return home, finds himself blocked out and is forced to take to his heels. The practice is not so common in America.
ELEUIN
One of the many cries used by the huntsman to encourage his hounds. This particular one tells them to draw a covert.
ENTER
Hounds are "entered" when they are first put into the pack during the cubbing season. Young riders are "entered" by being brought by their fond parents to the covert side. Both are known as "Young Entry."
EYE TO HOUNDS
A man is said to have a good "eye to hounds" when, by watching their actions and listening to them he can tell about what the fox has done and about what they are going to do. It is an ability greatly to be cultivated but requires many hours of hunting and close attention.
FAULT
See *check.*
FEATHERING
When a hound follows along a line moving his stern from side to side but giving little if any tongue indicating that he is not yet sure of the scent he is said to be "feathering."
FIELD
The followers, whether afoot or on horseback, of the hounds other than the Master and Hunt Staff.
FIND
When hounds first smell the scent of a fox they are said to "find."
FIXTURE
The "fixture card" is sent to all members of a hunt and tell them what coverts are to be drawn on what days.
FLASHY
A flashy hound or a flashy pack is one which is unsteady and wild and is apt to overrun the scent. Even the steadiest pack will be flashy under certain scenting conditions.
FLEWED
Having pendulous flews (upper lips).
FLIGHTY
Both hounds and scent may be termed flighty if they are undependable and changeable.
FLING
Hounds which drive or are driven to the right and left at the first indication of a check are said to "fling."
FOIL
When the quarry returns over its own tracks it is said to "foil." The word is also used to mean the scent of another animal which might obliterate the scent of the fox. Wily foxes will often run deliberately through a field of sheep or cattle in order that the "foil" of the other animals will cause a check.
FORRARD
Forward. The Huntsman often so directs his hounds.
FOX
There are many synonyms for our friend the fox, *Charley, Charles James, Uncle Remus, varmint, the old gentleman, Reynard* are among the most common.
FRESH LINE
The opposite of "cold" or "stale" line.
FULL CRY
The heart warming chorus that arises when the pack is hunting joyously and noisily. In England hounds sometimes run very nearly mute when close to the fox but if all are running they are still said to be "in full cry."
GIVE TONGUE
See *Cry.*
GONE AWAY
The familiar call when the fox has been routed out of his lair, hounds are running in full cry and the field settles itself down for a bit of hard riding.
GONE TO GROUND
The fox that takes refuge in an earth, drain or other shelter is said to have "gone to ground."

HALLOO (holloa)
See *VIEW HALLOO*

HARK FORWARD
Another oft used phrase of the Hunts-man to cheer his hounds into covert or to encourage them on the scent.

HARRIER
Originally to worry or harry game (med. English *harien, harren*). The term now means a medium sized hound used to hunt hares. There are six or seven packs of harriers in America. The usual color of the coats is green rather than the pink of the fox hunter.

HEAD
See *carry a head*.

HEAD A FOX
To turn back a fox. Ignorant mem-bers of the field are often guilty of this heinous offense!

HEADED TO DEATH
A fox that has been killed unfairly by being headed.

HEADS UP
When hounds, losing the scent, raise their heads to search for it they are said to "have their heads up." It is almost as great a crime to head hounds and so cause them to get their heads up and lose the line as it is to head a fox.

HEEL
When hounds hit the line and run it backwards they are said to "run heel."

HILL TOPPER
A rider who follows the hunt by ob-serving from the hill tops and so guess-ing how hounds will run and where the kill will take place. A point-to-pointer.

HIT OFF THE LINE
When hounds recover the line after a check.

HOICK (yoick, yoicks, huic) pro-nounced, hike. A cheer to hounds.

HOLD HARD
The warning of the huntsman to the field that they must not override his hounds.

HOLD THEM FORWARD
To take hounds forward in hopes of picking up a lost line.

HONEST HOUND
A trustworthy, dependable animal.

HONOR A LINE
When a hound speaks on a scent he is said to "honor" it.

HUNTSMAN
The person who hunts the hounds and is in charge of the kennels. See *HUNTS-MAN* (main heading).

INBREEDING
Producing from closely related par-ents.

JACK HARE
The male hare.

JUMP
When a pack has been hunting slowly but suddenly presses its quarry it is said to have "jumped" it.

KENNEL
The fox's lair is known as his "ken-nel," "earth" or "den."

KENNELS
The place where the hounds are kept. The *KENNEL HUNTSMAN* is the per-son who has charge of them in the ken-nels. He may be assisted by a "kennel man" who does the cleaning, feeding, etc. The Kennel Huntsman may also double as Whipper-in.

KILL
When the fox or other quarry is killed by the pack it is called "the kill."

LAIR
Where the fox lies in the day time.

LARKING
Jumping fences unnecessarily. A prac-tice often indulged in by the type of hunting man who "hunts in order to jump."

LEVERET
The young of the hare.

LIFT
A huntsman "lifts" hounds when he takes them away from the lost line and casts them forward in hopes of hitting the line further ahead.

LINE
The track taken by the quarry.

LINE BREEDING
Producing from parents having com-mon ancestry.

LINE HUNTER
A hound that keeps close to the scent.

LIVERY
Professional members of the Hunt Staff are said to wear "Livery." Members of the field wear "uniforms."

LOSS
When hounds cannot hold the line they are said to be "at loss."

LYING (scent)
A lying scent is one which is strong at ground level.

MAIN EARTH
The fox's principal den and breeding place.

MANNERS
The deportment of hounds and horses.

MARK TO GROUND
To run a fox into his earth and then give the "den cry."

MASK
The fox's head.

MEET
The rendezvous of hounds, followers and Hunt Staff.

M.F.H.
Master of Foxhounds.

MIXER
An English tool used to mix hounds' food.

MOB
To surround and kill a fox before he has a chance to run.

MOUTHY
A hound that is noisy and a babbler is said to be "mouthy."

MUSIC (Hound)
Hound music is the cry of the pack. One of the best known jokes is that to be found in *Handley Cross* in which Jorrocks who has been offered the Mastership of a newly formed pack writes to ask if hounds are "musical" meaning whether they have good voices. "Yes," writes back Captain Doleful, who is the secretary, "they must be for they are stabled near the chapel and seem to enjoy the hymns."

MUTE
Hounds are said to run "mute" when they fail to give tongue when following the line.

NIGHT LINE
The scent left by a fox in returning to his lair in the morning is called "the night line."

NOISY
Mouthy, babbling.

NOSE
The scenting ability of the hound.

OUT-CROSS
The infusion of new blood in line breeding.

OVERRIDE
To override hounds is to press them too closely, especially at a check.

OVERRUN
When hounds shoot past the line when the scent has been diverted by a change of course or foil they are said to "over-run" the line.

OWN
To own the line is to speak to it or honor it. See *HONOR*.

OXER
A hedge with a ditch and a guard rail. A ditch and guard rail on both sides makes it a "double oxer." This is a common type of obstacle in England but rarely seen in this country except in specially made hunt courses.

PACK
A number of hounds hunted together regularly.

PACK SENSE
The trait in hounds of working well together as a pack, honoring each other and running in a mass.

PAD
The foot of the fox.

PAD-GROOM
The groom who slowly rides the hunter to the meet and brings back the covert-hack ridden there by the owner.

PATE
The fox's mask.

PIE
This refers to certain colors and markings of hounds. A "Badger pied" hound is one which the head, legs, belly and tail are cream or fawn, the ears and back shading into black with lighter "badger colored" tips on the hairs. Hare pie is similar but the hairs shade to brown rather than black and the ends are lighter resembling a hare.

PINK (hunting pinks)

The scarlet livery of the Hunt Staff are commonly called "Pinks" after a famous British tailor.

POINT

The distance in a straight line between the two most widely separated localities in any hunt.

POINT RIDER

See *HILL TOPPER*

POINT-TO-POINT

Originally a type of race in which the contestants might choose their own courses being required to go from one designated point, such as a church steeple, to another. Modern "point-to-points" held by many Hunt Clubs are usually flagged and require that the riders follow a definite course.

POTTERER

A hound that "dwells." See *DWELLING.*

PUSS

English expression for hare.

PUT DOWN

To put to death.

PUT TO

In England gratings are placed across drains by the earth stoppers and thus the expression "drains put to."

QUARRY

The hunted animal. Originally the reward of the hounds and called *"Quyrreye"* because eaten on the deer skin, *"sur le quir."*

RACK

A way through a hedge.

RASPER

A big fence.

RAT CATCHER

Referring to the informal dress worn during the cub hunting season.

RATE

The Master or Huntsman "rates" his hounds when he punishes them with the thong or a sharp word.

RAT TAILED

Having few long hairs. May be applied to horses or hounds.

RECOVER

The scent is "recovered" when it is picked up again after a check.

REFUSE

A horse that stops in front of a jump is said to "refuse" it. See *REFUSALS* (main heading).

RIDE

A lane cut through a forest or a path through a covert is called a "ride."

RIDE IN THE HUNTSMAN'S POCKET

When the greenhorn, wishing to avoid losing himself or hounds follows at the heels of the huntsman he is said to "ride in his pocket." Needless to say it is a habit to be deplored. The Huntsman has something better to do than act as guide.

RIDE STRAIGHT

The person who takes his fences as they come, riding as the crow flies is said to "ride straight."

RINGING-FOX, RINGER

A fox that runs in circles instead of taking to his heels in proper fashion.

RIOT-RIOTOUS

Hunting other than the designated game is riot. Riotous hounds are undisciplined members of the pack that persist in riot.

RISING SCENT

Scent is said to be rising when it is poor at ground level but ground odors can be smelled by a mounted man.

ROACH-BACKED

An arch backed hound. A horse with similar conformation is said to be "hogbacked."

ROAD-HUNTER

A hound that can follow a line along a road.

ROUNDING

English hounds are sometimes "rounded," i.e., have their ears rounded or trimmed off to give a more uniform appearance and save them from injury. Many look down on this practice claiming that the pendulous ears of the hound enclose and amplify the scent.

RUN

The chase of the fox.

SCENT

The odor given off by the fox and by which he is trailed. Little is definitely known about scent. Many are its peculiarities. Close pressed foxes are said to lose their scent completely. Scenting conditions may be splendid one minute and terrible the next. Scent is known to drift and in some cases to linger for days. Not only the ground but grass and bushes retain it. Facts relating to good or poor scenting may be true in certain countries while the exact opposite may prevail in others. See also, *BREAST HIGH, LYING, RISING, BURNING.*

SCORE

Hounds score when the whole pack speaks to a strong scent.

SCUT

The tail of the hare or rabbit.

SECOND HORSEMAN

The groom who meets his master at a designated point with a fresh horse to take the place of his weary hunter.

SETTLE

When hounds, coming from different points, go off on a line together they are said to "settle to it."

SINKING FOX

A nearly beaten fox.

SKIRTER

A hound that hunts on the outskirts of the pack, allowing the other hounds to do all the work. A shirker.

SLING HIS TONGUE

A babbler, a noisy hound who gives tongue unnecessarily is said to "sling his tongue."

SOFT MOUTH

A low-voiced, bell-toned hound.

SO-HO

The cry raised when the hare is viewed.

SPEAK

To cry when on the scent.

SPOTTY SCENT

Uneven.

SPOUT

English expression for rabbit earth.

STAINED

A line is said to be "stained" when it is foiled by cattle, etc.

STALE LINE

Opposite of a fresh line.

START

To "start" a fox is to find him.

STAYING POWER

The stamina and endurance of horse or hound.

STEADY

A steady hound is one that is not flighty or flashy. The huntsman steadies his hounds with his voice when they are uncertain.

STERN

Only the uninitiated speaks of the "tail" of a hound. To old timers it is the "stern."

STICK

The ability to "stick" is the gameness of the hound.

STIFF-NECKED FOX

The stiff-necked fox runs in a straight line.

STOOPING TO SCENT

Hounds are said to be "stooping to scent" when they have once taken up the cry on the line.

STOP (earth)

See *Earth Stopping.*

STOP-HOUND

A hound that stops and squats to impart a deeper note in his baying on honoring the line.

STOP HOUNDS

It is sometimes necessary to call hounds off the line because they are running into impassable or forbidden territory. The Huntsman "stops" them with voice and thong and with the aid of his "Whippers-in."

STREAMING ALONG

Going across country at a fast pace.

STRIKE (a fox)

Find, start (American).

STUB-BRED

In certain English districts foxes have their young in bushes or stumps instead of earths. These are said to be "stump-bred" or "stub-bred" or "stubbed."

SWINE-CHOPPED

When the lower jaw of a hound protrudes beyond the upper he is said to be "swine-chopped."

TAG

The white tip on the fox's tail is known as the "tag."

TAIL HOUNDS

Hounds running at the rear of the pack.

TAILING

This is the opposite of "carrying a good head." When the pack, because of being ill-matched in age, speed or ability tends to straggle out they are said to be "tailing."

TALLY-HO

This is the cheer which announces that the fox is viewed. The bearer of the news should also stand with his horse's head pointing in the direction which the fox has taken and hold out his hat, pointing with it in that direction. The word "tally-ho" to mean a vehicle drawn by four horses came from the fact that a well known English coach imported about seventy-five years ago bore this name, so all coaches took the name from then on.

THROW OFF

To cast hounds at the beginning of the meet. This is derived from the early practice of taking hounds to the covert side coupled together. When the time came to start the hunt the couples were "thrown off."

THROW UP

An English expression meaning that hounds have lost the scent and given up, hence have "thrown up" (their heads).

THROWN OUT

A horseman or hound that loses his position in the hunt is said to be "thrown out."

THRUSTER

Usually "young thruster." A thoughtless, inexperienced rider who makes a nuisance of himself by "overriding" hounds and "larking."

TIE

Hounds are said to "tie to the line" when they hunt it closely and are difficult to lift.

TIMBER

Any jump or obstacle made of wood such as a gate, hurdle, fence, stile, etc.

TONGUE

To give tongue is to bay or cry. See *CRY*.

UNIFORM

The prescribed dress worn by the followers of the hunt. For complete description see *APPOINTMENTS, hunting* in the body of this text.

VIEWED AWAY

A fox is said to be "viewed away" when he is seen to leave the quarry. This occurrence is rare in America though common in the more open country of England.

VIEW HALLOO

Sometimes a peculiar piercing scream uttered by the huntsman when the fox is viewed. Some hunts use whistles. The usual term is "tally-ho."

VIXEN

Female fox.

VOICE

See *CRY*.

WALK

In England puppies are "walked," i.e., put out on farms to be raised at liberty and be broken of chasing farm animals and poultry. See *PUPPY WALKING* (main heading).

'WARE HOLE, 'WARE WIRE! etc.

Warning given by advance followers in field to those behind.

'WARE HOUNDS

If a hound comes up from behind or the side the followers are thus warned so that they will avoid stepping on him. Sometimes it is necessary for the Huntsman to lift his hounds and make his way through the field when he would call " 'Ware hounds, gentlemen, please."

'WARE RIOT

The warning to the hounds when they show signs of riot.

WARREN

A colony of rabbit burrows.

WHELP

A very young puppy.

WHIPPER-IN

Member of the hunt staff who assists the Huntsman. For his duties see *HUNTSMAN* (main heading).

WHOO-HOOP

The cheer announcing the death of the fox.

WORK A LINE
Search for the scent and follow it along the line the fox took.

WORRIED
Torn to bits by hounds.

WORRY
The reward given to drag hounds at the end of the hunt.

YOICK, YOICKS, HOICK, HUIC (pronounced "hike") old English hunting cries.

YOUNG ENTRY
Young hounds and young riders just "entered."

HUNTING THONG

The hunting thong is the braided lash attached to the hunting crop. It is very long and is used to rate hounds. The professional rides with his thong hanging along his horse's shoulder. The amateur keeps his coiled in his hand.

HUNTING WATCH

The old fashioned hunting watch had a crystal which was solid metal, usually gold except for a very small area of glass in the center.

HUNTSMAN

The huntsman is the all important member of the hunt staff. Many Masters hunt their own hounds, thus holding both positions, but often the Master prefers to hire a professional huntsman. The huntsman's sole obligation in the field is to his hounds. He it is who decides on the strategy of the hunt, who governs the actions of hounds, whips and field. If hounds consistently fail to find and kill their fox the blame must be laid on the huntsman. Likewise, if throughout the season, hounds account for a goodly number of foxes it is the huntsman that must receive the credit.

In the kennel the hounds are taught to come to the huntsman for protection, never to fear him. The huntsman rarely rates his hounds, he leaves that to his whippers-in. He is a friend to all his hounds and sees to their welfare, never retiring after a hunt himself until making sure that all is well with his darlings.

In the field the huntsman rides first, keeping in close contact with the hounds. In the covert he encourages them to hunt out the fox with voice and horn. When they are away he cheers them on and at the kill he congratulates them on their fine work. The huntsman must never be bothered with matters pertaining to the Field. This is up to the Field Master. But you may be sure that if a member of the field offends by larking over jumps, riding over hounds or not keeping silence when hounds are being cast the huntsman, through the Master, will let them have his opinion of such conduct in no uncertain terms!

HURDLES

Obstacles used in jumping are often spoken of as "hurdles" or as "fences" no matter what type they may be. By hurdles one also may mean a specific type of fencing used for enclosing sheep. Hurdles used in racing are not solid.

I

ICELAND PONY

A stocky, draft type of pony similar to the Fiord pony of Norway. It is supposed that this pony in common with the Fiord and Shetlander is a descendant of the pure bred desert horses brought from Constantinople by the returned Varangians in the eleventh century. See also *PONIES*.

IDEAL HORSE

The Ideal Horse has been the subject of many a poet including Shakespeare who, in his Venus and Adonis, describes both the ideal mare and the ideal stallion. Or if one would go further back there is Job's magnificent description of the War Horse.

An anonymous Arabian poet describes his Ideal of a horse as follows:

Sparse is her head and lean her head,
and lean her ears pricked close together,
Her fetlock is a net, her forehead a
lamp lighted
Illumining the tribe; her neck curves
like a palm branch;
Her withers sharp and clean. Upon
her chest and throttle
An amulet hangs of gold. Her forelegs
are twin lances;
Her hoofs fly faster even than flies the
whirlwind.
Her tail-bone borne aloft, yet the hairs
sweep the gravel.

Our friend Jorrocks also had something to say on the "Ideal Horse" but,
as one might suppose, his advice is not
to be taken too seriously. For example,
he recommends a horse with a very long
back as then the whole family can
ride, and one with long, flopping ears,
for it is easy to steer between long ears,
and by having them flopping the rain
doesn't get in them causing the horse
to shake his head violently and perhaps
bring on the blind staggers! Each breed
has very definite specifications of its ideal.
These differ with the work the horse is
expected to do. Before buying a horse it
might be well to send to the association
which registers that breed and they will
gladly send you the literature. The Horse
and Mule Association gets out a booklet
with a brief description of each breed.

As in humans, there is no perfect specimen. Every horse is a compromise and
the buyer would do well to weigh the
faults against the assets of each animal
he considers, realizing that the animal
which will meet the standards he has set
for size, type, disposition and performance most certainly has yet to be foaled.

IDEAL RIDER

One often wishes that the horse might
be allowed to express his opinion as to
desirable qualifications in riders. If he
were a wise horse he would ask for the
rider who had kindness yet firmness.
Whose thoughts were not solely on the
pleasure or profit to be derived from his

mount but also on its future health and
useful longevity. Knowledge would be
paramount in desirable attributes of the
horseman. Ignorance can cause as many
equine deaths as cruelty. And finally the
skill of the rider will determine the comfort of the horse. So if you would be a
hero to your horse, develop sympathy
and skill and broaden your knowledge
as fast as ever you can.

INCLINATION OF THE BODY

At the halt the body is carried very
nearly perpendicular. A line running
from the ear would pass through the hip
bone to the ankle. But as the horse
moves forward it is necessary to incline
the body forward in order not to be "left
behind." The rider's body should anticipate the forward movement of the horse
rather than be continually "catching up"
to it. The faster the horse moves the
more inclined must the rider be. Anyone
with a practiced eye can readily spot the
rider who is "behind" his horse at the
walk, trot or canter. An even less practiced eye will notice the horseman who
is behind at a jump, for here the plunge
of the horse, catching the rider off balance, throws him back with a bounce,
his hands fly up and the poor animal receives a "job" in the mouth.

The best exercise to promote this forward inclination of the body is to fold
the arms, rise in the stirrups and, keeping this position, trot and canter. The
knees should not be unduly gripped but
should be well bent and thrust forward,
the rider's heels must be below his toes,
toe and knee on a line and the balance
on the inside knee bones. Once the easy
balance on the knees is obtained the
rider will have no difficulty in remaining out of the saddle, arms folded.

INCLINES (maneuvering steep)

Thirty-five years ago all riders went
down "slides" and other steep inclines
with the body so far back as to be virtually lying on the horse. I have before
me such a picture of an Italian officer
taking the slide at "Tor di Quinto." By
contrast is the picture of the same slide

in Captain Littauer's "More About Riding Forward," published in 1938. In this second picture one sees a group of Italian cavalrymen with hands very low, backs rounded, weight very far forward, completely out of the saddle. That the first method mentioned was the natural one is easy to understand, it goes with another picture which is entitled, "The Faultless Horsemanship of the Italians"

FIGURE 59.
THE SLIDE AT TOR DI QUINTO. *COURTESY CAPT. V. S. LITTAUER.*

and shows a squad taking a three foot hurdle with every man hauling back on the reins for all he is worth. But when the modern style of jumping came into prominence, horsemen reasoned that in taking steep inclines two factors were important: the horse should be able to dig his front toes in and he should have his hindquarters free. By having the rider throw his weight forward the horse is helped to accomplish both these things.

In going up a steep incline the rider should again keep as far out of the saddle as possible for by doing so he relieves the horse of a certain portion of the weight and makes it easy for him to use his hindquarters freely.

INDEPENDENCE (of the rider's seat as opposed to his hands)

It sounds impossible but it remains true that there are some people who believe that the purpose of the reins or the saddle horn is to give the rider support! Though one may not be quite so ignorant as this yet many riders depend on their reins to maintain their seats without knowing that they do so. Watch the horse, he will soon let you know whether or not his rider is using the reins to pull himself up on the trot or to keep from bouncing off on the canter.

There is only one sure method of developing an independent seat, and that is to ride constantly at all gaits without the use of the reins. Most horses are willing to follow a leader. If you are not sure of your own independence, have a friend ride ahead of you in a ring or on the trail, knot your reins and, putting your hands on your waist or folding them, follow your leader at all the different gaits. Even better, drop your stirrups as well. Long hours of practice at this will soon make you depend on balance rather than your reins or stirrups. Just make sure that you do not clutch your legs up but ride completely relaxed.

INDIAN METHODS OF TRAINING HORSES

The American Indians, being a primitive people, are often considered brutal and cruel in their treatment of animals and of each other. It is true that they do not have the sensitivity to pain and the sympathy that civilization is supposed to develop. To them the ability to endure pain is a sign of manhood and bravery. However, they are close students of nature and modern horse trainers would do well to study their methods of breaking and training. In a story called *The Ghost Horse*, Chief Buffalo Child Long Lance, a well-known Canadian Indian, gives a very clear and detailed description of the Indian method of capturing and training the wild horses of the prairies. Scouts first locate a desirable herd. They then find a terrain which will lend itself to the building of a funnel-shaped enclosure. This terrain is often many miles from the grazing grounds of the herd. A stockade fence is built to enclose the area to which the herd is later to be driven, which terminates in a narrow dead end. This funnel can be readily closed off after the herd has been driven in.

The scouts now surround the herd of horses. At first they allow themselves to be seen and scented only at a distance. Their purpose is to allow the horses to become familiar with the sight and smell of human beings.

As the days pass the horses become more and more accustomed to the sight of Indians peering at them, until finally they no longer run away when they see them.

The Indians now begin to drive them slowly towards the prepared chute. They also start shouting while some distance away, until the horses learn not to fear these sounds.

When the herd has approached to within a few miles of the stockade a runner or smoke signals are sent to the main encampment, which has settled down around the prepared chute. During the night every member of the encampment, from the toddler to the oldest grandmother, is given a position around the enclosure. In a leisurely fashion the horses are driven into the mouth of the chute. At this point all the Indians assist in driving them into the open plain inside it, standing on the stockade sides of the funnel and shouting, but doing nothing to hurt the horses. As soon as the whole herd is in the chute the barriers are closed and the animals are allowed to quiet down. The next day the skilled horsebreakers decide which animals are worth capturing and those not considered valuable are separated and allowed to escape.

Now comes the interesting part of the training. The horsebreaker sets out to prove to the wild horse that no matter how fearful he may be of the Indian the latter will not hurt him provided he remains docile and does not fight.

The trainer's first step is to throw a lariat around the animal. When this is fast a helper holds the terrified stallion (or mare) while the horsebreaker moves up to him and slips a rawhide shoelace over his poll and around his muzzle. At the poll there is a special nerve and the experienced horsebreaker can control the strongest stallion with this slender bit of rawhide placed in contact with this nerve. The helper removes the original lariat and leaves. When the horse has learned that attempting to pull away brings a painful jerk but that when he stands still he feels no pain and has nothing to fear he is ready to receive the next stage of training. This consists in learning to allow the horsebreaker to run his hand over every part of his body and to pick up all his feet.

Starting with the less sensitive parts, such as the neck near the withers and the shoulders, the patient Indian pats and strokes the animal with one hand while controlling him with his rawhide string with the other. This stage may take several hours, but finally the horse learns that man brings him only pleasure and not pain provided he remains quiet. When this lesson is learned the Indian takes up a folded blanket and begins over again, first patting and stroking, later shaking out the blanket and flapping it and striking the horse with it. He continues this until the horse loses all fear.

Noise is now added and the Indian shouts and makes sudden sharp sounds and motions. When the horse is thoroughly accustomed to these the Indian puts his weight across his back, leaning on his arms. Finally he mounts, and the horse, no longer afraid of man, is willing and ready to be trained.

How different and how much more humane is this method of training than that of breaking by fear and force!

INDIAN PONIES

The Indian pony is the descendant of the Spanish horses imported into Mexico by Cortez and others. The Spanish horses, in turn, were the descendants of the Arabian horses which the Arabs took with them on their religious war against Spain in 710 A.D. When the Arabs were pushed out of Spain their horses remained to be justly prized and protected by the Spaniards.

The Indians of the Americas had never seen horses until the Spanish invaders brought them with them. At first they took horsemen to be a new beast, a centaur. But it did not take the savages long to discover that they too could become "centaurs." Phil Stong in his "Horses and Americans" brings out the fact that it could not have been just a few horses escaped from the Spaniards, which are the progenitors of all our wild horses and ponies, but that the Indians must have protected and promoted the increase in their new and very valuable weapon.

The Indian did not practice selective breeding to any great extent. Neither did they do other than allow their animals to live off the country. Consequently the Indian pony is tough, hardy, fast and not very big.

INDIANA PANTS

The hopples used on pacers to prevent their breaking into a trot or gallop were known as "Indiana Pants."

INDIANS (as riders)

Indian boys had much the same sort of training in competitive riding as the Cossack youth. Picking articles off the ground at a gallop, vaulting on and off, etc., were commonplace. The Indian, especially before he adopted the White Man's saddle, was the nearest thing to a centaur that has ever been seen.

INDIRECT LIGHTING (in the stable)

The horse should never stand with the light directly in his eyes. Windows should be set high and electric fixtures should be so placed that they do not glare in his eyes. The stall should have plenty of light as horses kept in dark stalls easily develop agoraphobia. (See also *BOX STALLS*.)

INDIRECT REIN, INDIRECT REIN OF OPPOSITION

See *REINS, Use of.*

INDOOR RIDING

When winter sets in and the trails become rutted and icy the rider who has access to an indoor riding hall is fortunate. Many people feel that riding indoors is boring. This is not necessarily so. Indoor riding should be adjusted to the ability of the riders. If beginners and advanced riders try to ride at the same time, the riding will be very limited and neither can be satisfied, but if it can be so arranged that the beginner who is just learning to post comfortably or who is studying the gallop departs rides only with those who have reached the same stage in equitation ability as himself he will enjoy himself and profit far more than if the hour is spent simply following a trail. The more advanced riders have a variety of possibilities open to them. Formation riding, either in the form of memorized music rides or mounted drills, is most profitable. All sorts of games up to and including polo can be arranged according to the ability of the riders. Young horses can be schooled and the education of more finished horses along the line of *haute école* may be undertaken. Groups interested in jumping can get together and not only do the ordinary jumping but practice jumping in pairs, or in pairs coming from opposite directions, etc.

Music is a great stimulus both to the rider and to the horse and, particularly with younger riders, it should be a part of every hour's ride. Look on your hours spent riding indoors not as a way of marking time while waiting for the weather to break but rather as an opportunity to increase your skill as a horseman.

In riding indoors certain rules of etiquette must be observed if every one is to be kept happy. Do not go charging around at a gallop, changing direction without notice. If you are walking, stick very close to the wall so that faster riders may pass you. If there is a jump set up in the middle for schooling, be careful not to interfere with riders at the opposite end by allowing your horse to get out of hand after he has landed. Do not allow your horse to kick or bite at a passing horse. If you must stop for any reason pull into the center but don't remain standing there any longer than is necessary. Pass always on the inside of the ring, never between another rider and the wall. For suggestions for games, music rides, etc., see *GAMES; DRESSAGE; JUMPING; FORMATION RIDING; MUSICAL RIDES; SQUARE DANCING; QUADRILLES; MOUNTED DRILLS.*

INDOOR RIDING HALL

The professional size riding hall, one which will accommodate fifty or more riders, is usually about a hundred and fifty feet wide by three hundred feet long. Such a hall is only necessary in a community where there is much interest in riding. For smaller groups it may be divided into sections by means of canvas curtains.

A riding hall to accommodate from ten to eighteen riders should be from sixty-six to seventy-five feet wide and from a hundred to a hundred and thirty-six feet long. Such a hall is large enough for jumping yet in teaching small groups of six or ten young riders the instructor will have no difficulty in keeping the riders under control.

Windows in a riding hall should be as many as possible, set high, the lower edge at least five feet above the flooring. There should be a solid kick-board all around the walls, slanted if possible though that is not absolutely necessary.

Beams and trusses should be at least fourteen feet above the flooring and the loft should be left open for ventilation.

A visitor's gallery is very important, else you will have interested spectators under the horses' feet.

All corners should be square and not rounded so that the horse may be pushed into them.

Lights should be placed high and should have reflectors which throw the light downwards and spread it.

Tan bark is the ideal flooring for riding, but it is very hard to obtain. A foundation of ten inches or so of cinders well packed, with another ten inches of soil, shavings and some sand is about as good as one can find. This should be kept well watered and cleaned out and renewed frequently.

Doors should always open outwards so that there is no danger of a door being opened into a passing horse. The kick-board in front of the visitors gallery and in the corners may be about three feet six high with sections opening out in the form of doors. At least one door at each end should be wide enough to accommodate several riders abreast. Twelve to sixteen feet is advised.

For the main construction of the building one has the choice of metal, wood or concrete blocks. The latter is probably the best. Metal rings are terribly cold. Wooden construction with either wooden or metal trusses is good, particularly if it is covered on the outside with one of the asbestos shingles which come impregnated with white and do not need to be painted. These are also a fair insulation.

Airplane hangars are sometimes to be bought and make excellent halls though they are apt to be of metal and so very cold. However, they have plenty of head room and plenty of windows.

INFECTIONS

The horse infects very easily, especially when the wound is anywhere on the leg. It must be remembered that only one artery feeds the leg and there is very little flesh. Consequently, any deep wound in this area is extremely difficult to heal and easily becomes infected.

The symptoms of infection are tenderness and soreness, swelling and heat. The first treatment is to bathe the affected part with very hot water in which Epsom salts has been dissolved. Take a clean pail, fill it with water as hot as you can bear and put in a handful of Epsom salts. Next, take a clean turkish towel, dip it in the solution and then wrap it quickly around the infected area. When it begins to cool dip it in the water and repeat. Continue this treatment for twenty minutes. Next, wrap the part with a thick wadding of cotton, apply a dry bandage over that and soak the whole in the hot Epsom salts. Keep wet for twenty-four hours. At the end of that time one of two things will have occurred. The swelling will have subsided, showing that nature has taken over and is killing off the infection, or the infection will have "come to a head." In this latter case it will probably be necessary to open the part and allow the pus to drain out. Unless you are very experienced you had better call a veterinarian for this as it is imperative that an incision sufficiently large to relieve the congestion be made. When the incision is made the veterinarian may suggest that you continue with the Epsom salts, or he may recommend one of the sulfa drugs or silver oxide remedies. These oint-

ments cut in half the time that was formerly required to heal infections. But it must be kept in mind that an infection must heal from within. If the skin over the incision closes too quickly it will only have to be opened again as the pus will pack up behind it.

INFLUENCE

After the horseman has learned to feel what the horse is doing and to interpret what he feels he must learn to "influence" or control his horse. This is the hardest and longest lesson that must be learned. The best horseman is one who can get the most out of a given horse with the least effort, both on his own and his horse's part. Such a rider has clearly learned the three basic lessons—to feel, to interpret and to influence. See also *AIDS; DRESSAGE; COLTS, Training of; RIDING; HORSEMAN, versus rider.*

IN HAND

A horse is said to be "in hand" when he is collected and both ready and able to move in any direction or at any gait in accordance with the wishes of his rider. Most horses should be kept in hand at all times though it is permissible to walk a horse on a very loose rein by way of giving him rest after work. In hand does not mean that the rider is constantly pulling on his animal's mouth, but merely that he has contact with him and that the horse is alert.

INJURIES

Whereas sickness and disease in horses are comparatively rare, injuries occur constantly. This is particularly true where the horse is used for jumping or hunting or where a number of horses are turned out together to pasture. Ill-fitting equipment is also a common cause of injuries as is overwork or unaccustomed work.

Injuries may be roughly classified as follows: wounds, bruises, injuries to the tendons or joints.

A wound is an injury in which the

skin has been broken. The two major dangers in wounds are bleeding and infection.

A *puncture wound* is a small deep wound such as one made by a nail. Puncture wounds are common in the sole and frog and also occasionally on the legs. The great danger of a puncture wound is infection, particularly tetanus or lock jaw.

Puncture wounds should be syringed out with a disinfectant solution using a small, rubber ear syringe. Packing the wound with one of the sulfa ointments or with silver oxide (neosilvol) will generally clear up septic conditions and prevent its reoccurrence. If the area around the wound is badly swollen and very sensitive, hot applications should be applied (see also *INFECTIONS*) and the veterinary surgeon should be called. In all cases where the wound is deep, and where there is known to be tetanus in the soil an anti-tetanus shot should be given.

Lacerations are wounds in which the skin is badly torn. If these injuries occur on the legs, particularly the knees, the horse will have to have careful nursing as they are very slow to heal. But if they occur on the body they heal rapidly and rarely leave a bad scar. Lacerations, except when on the legs, do not infect as readily as puncture wounds. If a vein is torn the blood will flow in a steady, dark stream. Cold applications with a moderate amount of pressure on the wound will control this flow. If an artery has been torn the condition is much more serious as the horse may lose a great deal of blood in a very short time. Arterial bleeding is characterized by a steady spurting of bright red blood. A tourniquet is usually necessary. The tourniquet should be made of a roller bandage, never wire or cord, and a small gauze pad. If the injury is in the lower leg the tourniquet may be applied above the joint. The artery runs down the inside of the leg. If you can feel a pulse anywhere along the leg put the gauze pad on it and then apply the tourniquet,

using a short stick to tighten it. If the bleeding does not stop at once, apply the tourniquet directly on the wound. Tighten only enough to stop the spurting. Apply cold water on the outside of the tourniquet and loosen the latter at the end of fifteen minutes. If the bleeding has stopped entirely the tourniquet may be removed, but the gauze pad should be left in place and a tight, constricting bandage placed over it. If the spurting continues the tourniquet must be tightened again for twenty minutes when it should be loosened. By all means send for a veterinarian.

Lacerations in which there is a flap of skin hanging loose will need surgical treatment as the skin must either be cut off or stitched up. If the wound is on the body it will often heal with barely a trace of a scar, particularly if it can be kept clean and free from infection. But often the edges of the wound "granulate" and we have a condition known as "proud flesh." In this instance, the rough, unhealthy tissue will have to be burnt away. Silver nitrate may be used. Powdered alum applied several times will often take care of the situation.

Incisions are clean cuts such as those caused by wire. They do not infect easily but may be so situated that they injure a vein or artery.

Abrasions are wounds in which the surface of the skin has been rubbed off. Galls from badly fitting saddles or harness are painful and difficult to heal. Girth sores, especially, will lay a horse up for a number of days and great care must be taken not to irritate the skin again when the horse is put back to work. Prevention is the important thing in galls. It must be remembered that the skin of young horses or horses that have been turned out is not toughened, and it should be allowed to become accustomed to the pressure of the saddle slowly.

The fitting of the saddle is most important. If the tree is cut back or is high and does not touch the withers when the rider is mounted, if the center of the cantle does not rest on the spine, then, in all probability, the horse will not have trouble with his back, though, if the horse has been turned out or is green he should wear a thick saddle blanket for a while. If the saddle does touch the parts mentioned he should certainly have a heavy pad.

In tightening the girth make sure of two things, that the skin is not wrinkled up under it, and that the girth is not pulled too tight. Slip three fingers in the side of the girth below the billets and slide them down, the girth should feel tight at the bottom but should not be too snug at the side. Do this on both sides and you may be sure that skin and hair will lie smooth.

If a horse is known to have tender skin, bathing it with cold salt water when he comes in after work will help to toughen it.

Treatment for abrasions and galls is as follows. Make sure that the wound is clean. Wash carefully with a disinfectant. Pick out any loose gravel or sand. Paint the area with methylene blue or dust with a good antiseptic powder. Do not allow any pressure on the area until the wound has healed entirely.

Another type of wound caused by ill-fitting equipment or by pressure is the boil type. Shoe-boils, poll evil, sit-fasts and fistulas come under this heading. The horse receives a bruise from the saddle or headstall, or he may be bitten by another horse or receive a blow. In the case of the shoe-boil which occurs on the elbow the injury is caused by pressure of the horse's shoe when he is lying down. In all these cases there is considerable swelling and great soreness and pain. The skin is not broken. When the condition has reached a head it must either be opened by a veterinary surgeon, which is the best method, or it may be induced to burst by the application of hot fomentations or antiphlogistene. In either case there will be a flow of pus and infected material. The pocket must be thoroughly syringed with disinfectant, using a small rubber ear syringe. In the

case of the fistula the veterinary surgeon will have to cut away the infected tissue inside. The wound may then be treated with sulfa ointment or silver oxide. As it will be draining freely for some days the whole area around the wound should be thickly covered with vaseline to prevent loss of hair. B.F.I. (bismuth formic iodide) powder may be kept dusted on the wound and will help keep away flies. In the case of shoe-boils the horse should wear a shoe-boil boot (see illustration)

FIGURE 60. SHOE BOIL BOOT.

when he is in his stall. This is attached around the ankle of the leg on which the boil has occurred and prevents his getting his foot doubled up under him. If he is in a straight stall a piece of two-by-four nailed on the floor across the stall, about three feet back from the front, will encourage him to spread out his legs. *Do not squeeze or press any type of boil injury.*

Quarter cuts are cuts on the back of the heel caused by overreaching. They cause great lameness and pain and are slow to heal. Treat as recommended for lacerated wounds. The horse should wear a quarter boot when he goes back to work and he should be shod to correct the condition.

Speedy cutting is where the horse cuts the inside of his knee or hock with the shoe of the other foot. This is more common in the back legs than the front. The blacksmith should shoe the horse accordingly and he may have to wear boots.

Nail-in-the-foot is common where horses are turned out. As there is great danger from infection, especially tetanus infection, the wound must be handled carefully. The sole should be pared away around the injury and the whole foot soaked in a carbolic solution with very hot water for at least half an hour. It should then be painted with Churchill's Iodine. A clean bandage covering the whole sole and tied around the pastern should be kept on until the wound has healed and the horse shows no signs of tenderness.

Cracked heels or scratches. This is a condition of the area at the back of the pastern. It is sometimes a result of working in mud (hence its other name, "mud fever") but, since only horses in certain parts of the country seem to develop it, it must also be the result of an infection or virus. The symptoms are open running sores which refuse to heal. Some authorities advise keeping the parts clipped short, so that they may be well dried out as soon as the horse comes in from hunting, as a preventive. Others prefer to leave the fetlocks long and never clip the back of the pastern, on the theory that the long hair acts as a protection.

Once the condition has started it is best cured by soaking until soft, removing all scabs, drying thoroughly and then soaking with cod liver oil. The horse should not be allowed in the mud again until the area is entirely healed. When this has occurred, dust the part after hunting and when it has been washed and dried with B.F.I. or other good antiseptic powder.

Rope burns are common occurrences if care in tying and picketing the horse is not used. All too often he is tied with a rope so long that he wraps it around his back pastern. The skin is quickly rubbed off and the horse will be laid up for some little time as, due to the location of the injury, it will heal very slowly.

The foot should be soaked as for scratches, then a thick ointment applied. Resinol is good or one of the sulfas. Keep the injury bandaged to prevent infection and do not use the horse until he has recovered. He should be kept as still as

possible as movement prevents healing, and it is well to cut out his grain.

Bruises where the skin is not broken should be treated with cold water packs. Injuries to ligaments, tendons and the tendonous coverings of the joints are all too common. They usually cause severe lameness which may or may not be permanent. They often leave permanent enlargements which are disfiguring.

Sprains and strains occur frequently when the horse is asked to do work for which he is not prepared. Young horses brought in from pasture and put immediately on a working schedule which calls for jumping, fast turning, etc., are the greatest sufferers from this type of injury. An awkward landing over a jump is also a common cause of tendon injuries.

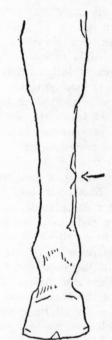

FIGURE 61. A SPLINT.

The symptoms of sprains and strains are severe lameness, heat and swelling. The best remedy is continuous cold water applications. The horse may be led into a river or a brook and kept standing in the running water for an hour or two. Or he may have a hose run over his back, the nozzle tied just above the injury. After the water treatment he should have a wet compress with some cooling lotion such as "White Lotion." He should not be allowed to move around and should be fed a light diet. If the condition becomes chronic he may have to be blistered. See *BLISTERING*.

Thoroughpins and *wind-galls* are swellings of the tendonous tissue surrounding the joints. They are hard, rubbery puffs and do not usually cause lameness. Mild treatment such as cold applications or painting with iodine is advised.

Splints are injuries to the splint bones. Young horses put to work usually throw splints which cause temporary lameness. When the splint has become set the lameness usually disappears and often the splint itself as time goes on. The treatment for splints is blistering or, if necessary, pin-firing. The veterinary will have to be called for this treatment.

Spavins are of two kinds, *bone spavins* and *bog spavins*. Ordinary bone spavins are bony enlargments below the hock. They are usually not very serious. *Occult spavins* which affect the bone are more serious and not as readily diagnosed; these need blistering and firing. *Bog spavins*, are soft, puffy enlargements on the inside and a little below the hock. They are rarely serious though they are unsightly. *Knee spavins* are usually caused by injury. They are more painful than spavins in the hock and need more drastic treatment. There will be a bony enlargement on the inside of the knee and the horse will show pain when the knee is bent.

The *stifle* is subject both to sprains and dislocations. In the former case, treat with cold fomentations as recommended under *sprains*. In some cases of dislocation the stifle will spring back immediately of itself. The horse will be dead lame for a step or two and suddenly all right again. In other cases the veterinary will have to reduce the dislocation by means of pulling on the joint.

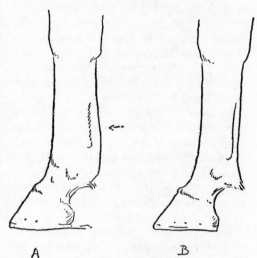

A   B

FIGURE 62. TENDON INJURY. A. A "BOWED" TENDON. B. NORMAL TENDON.

In either case the horse should then be treated as for sprains and, if the injury repeats itself he should be blistered in the area of the stifle which will serve to tighten up the ligaments. See *BLISTERING*.

Shoulder injuries are common, particularly in horses that do a lot of jumping. Tests for shoulder lameness consist

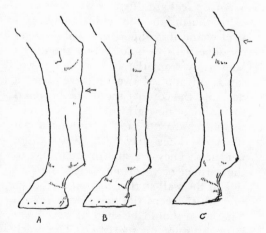

A   B   C

FIGURE 63. HOCK INJURY. A. "CURBY" HOCK. B. NORMAL HOCK. C. CAPPED HOCK.

of picking up a foot and stretching it forward and back, backing the horse over a low log when he will drag his toe rather than lift it up, and turning the horse in short circles first on one side and then on the other. Shoulder injuries usually call for blistering.

Injuries to the corners or bars of a horse's mouth may be due to badly fitting bits or to heavy hands. They should be bathed with salt solution and the horse should not be used until the animal has recovered. Bits that are too large should be fitted with little leather disks.

Injuries to the horse's feet are many and of various natures. In addition to wounds of different types we have conditions of the wall itself. *Seedy toe* is an affection of the foot in which the middle layer of horn becomes separated from the sensitive layer underneath. In this space a soft, mealy kind of horn is formed. Bad shoeing is usually the cause though this condition may also occur after laminitis. The seedy formation should be pared away. The whole area dressed with tar and tow and a shoe put on which does not press on the damaged tissue. A blister may also be applied to the coronet to stimulate the forming of new horn.

Brittle feet are due to a dry condition of the horn. The foot chips and breaks readily and it is almost impossible to get the shoe nails to hold. Water should be kept away from the feet, a hoof oil or castor oil applied two or three times a day, and the coronet should be blistered to stimulate new growth.

Sand cracks are cracks running down the wall. They may or may not cause lameness. They are due to an injury to the coronet or to rasping away the outside of the wall so that the natural secretion which keeps the hoof moist is lost. The horse should be shod so that there is no pressure on the crack. The crack may be prevented from spreading by means of a clasp or clip across it. If the sand crack suppurates, the horn must be cut away to allow the pus to escape. The coronet should be blistered.

False quarter is a horizontal crack in the wall caused by injury to the coronet. New horn formation is encouraged by application of a blister to the coronet.

A *quittor* is a fistulous type of injury on the coronet. It may be caused by bad shoeing, infections in the foot due to a foreign body, a neglected injury from a nail or an injury to the coronet itself. The area is very sensitive, the swelling obvious. Later there will be considerable discharge. Apply hot antiphlogistene and send for the veterinarian at once.

Corns are caused by bad or neglected shoeing. The corn should be pared away and a special shoe applied.

Contracted heels are also due to bad shoeing. The shoe is too narrow and the horse's heels are consequently pinched, elongating the foot. The horse may have his shoes removed and run barefoot for a time, or he may have special shoes put on to spread the heels. Contracted heels are serious and a frequent cause of lameness.

Ring Bones and *side bones* are bony enlargements around the top of the hoofs or on the pastern bones. They may be hereditary or caused by too much work at too early an age. As these conditions are often extremely serious the veterinarian should be consulted at once.

INSANITY IN HORSES

Some few horses are insane just as there are maniacs among humans, but they are rare. The horse that is insane literally has no sense. He is dangerous and should be put out of the way.

INTELLIGENCE IN HORSES

The intelligence of an animal is usually judged by the size of its brain in relation to its body, and by its ability to learn to find food. Judged by these standards the horse is very low indeed in the scale of animals, as far as intelligence goes.

But it is my contention that the testing of an animal's intelligence should take into consideration its prehistoric background. To test a horse's intelligence by giving tests which require that he solve a maze in order to find food is not suitable, for the prehistoric horse, whose natural food, grass, lay all around it, never needed to develop this type of intelligence.

The horse is not an animal of aggression. The stallion fights to keep his leadership in the herd and to protect his herd from marauding animals. But except in the case of a stallion that challenges another because he wants to take over the latter's mares the horse defends himself in case of danger, rather than attacking. Let us see what skills and instincts the prehistoric horse found necessary.

He learned to be ever alert and to interpret the slightest rustle of a leaf, the faintest whiff of an unknown scent. He remembered, from month to month and from year to year, the best grazing pastures, the safest water holes and the more protected areas. These he returned to with the seasons. He learned to communicate ideas concerning danger and movement, so that a herd could stick together in its flight. He learned to free himself when trapped in boggy or craggy country.

The modern horse, though often apt to become hysterical if he finds himself helpless and unable to flee in the face of danger, nevertheless retains his primeval instincts and has a highly developed but very specialized degree of intelligence.

He has an excellent memory. He has a homing instinct, whether through sound, scent or some sense of which we do not know, which enables him to find his way back to his own stable over many miles of unknown and previously untraveled territory. He can associate the idea of punishment and reward with actions. He develops definite likes and dislikes, both as to other horses and to human beings. He can communicate very complicated ideas to his companions. When a strange horse that has never seen an electric fence is brought into a stable of horses accustomed to one, the latter, who have learned to respect the apparently weak strand of wire, will acquaint the newcomer with its properties, and the latter

will not need the trial and error method to teach him to keep clear of it.

I have known horses, and especially donkeys and ponies, to figure out how to undo knots and latches of the most complicated sorts in order to escape from their stalls or paddocks.

In fact, it is lucky for us that the horse is not an aggressive animal and that, once conditioned through training to respond to the behests of the rider, he continues to do so; else, with his great strength, we might find ourselves between the shafts.

INTERFERING

When a horse strikes his front feet with his hind in traveling he is said to be "interfering" or "forging." This is a common fault, especially in trotters. Horses that are road weary will sometimes interfere when normally their gait is perfect. The cure is to extend the shoes on the back feet in order to cause the horse to "dwell" or delay slightly in picking them up, at the same time cutting off the toes and setting back the shoes on the front feet. See also *FORGING*.

INTERNATIONAL ARABIAN HORSE ASSOCIATION

Headquarters, 224 East Olive Ave., Burbank, Cal., publishes the *Arabian Horse Yearbook* as well as several other very interesting brochures. Their *Arabs and What They Can Do* gives a complete picture of the Arabian horse as parade horse, ranch horse, English pleasure horse, harness horse, children's mount in both English and Western tack, jumper and hunter, show horse in native costume classes and as a dressage horse. This same brochure gives rules for judging Arabian horses. Other brochures are *The Arabian Horse Halter Classes* and the *Directory of Arabian Owners*. The pedigrees of purebred Arabian horses are recorded with the Arabian Horse Club Registry of America, 120 South La Salle St., Chicago, Ill. The International Arabian Horse Association has acquired the Half-Arabian and the Anglo-Arabian

Registries from the American Remount Association.

INTERPRET

When the beginner has learned to feel what the horse is doing under him he must then learn to interpret what he feels. This is comparatively easily learned through experience.

IRISH HUNTERS

Nowhere will one find such magnificent specimens of horseflesh as in Ireland. And nowhere is there a more horse-loving people. Nature seems to have supplied the ideal type of grass and water for the development of horses and then endowed the natives with a love and an understanding of them.

The Irish hunter is characterized by his great bony structure which includes his feet. He has a heart to match, and from all over the world buyers gather in Dublin to select the champion hunters, jumpers and running horses. The Irishman will forget his love or his quarrel to attend a race. His "lepper" as he calls him, is the pride of his heart and he will sing his praises loud and long nor will he ever admit that there could be aught to be criticized. Every obvious fault has some explanation. The capped hock is "but a bit of a bruise he got last week and what could you expect the way he was leppin' the green timber." The cloudy eye is "just because he's after staring in the sun," etc.

The Irishman knows his horses are supreme and, if he has anything to say about it, you and all the world will soon know it too.

Irish ponies are very satisfactory also, being hardy yet not so coarse as ponies of other lands. They are usually good jumpers and make fine mounts for the "young entry" in the hunt field.

Mention should also be made of the Irish cob. These little horses are of no special breed. They are about the size of, and many of them resemble in conformation, the American Stock Horse. They are excellent hunting mounts, scrambling over the banks and walls, pulling themselves out of mudholes, avoiding bogs. They usually go best if ridden on a long rein and allowed to make all their own decisions as to pace, etc. Some of the best hunts I have ever had in Ireland were on top of an Irish cob.

ITALIAN INFLUENCE (on horsemanship)

Early in the twentieth century an Italian named Caprilli made exhaustive studies regarding the horse's balance and axis of gravity. His conclusion was that if the rider sat well forward in the saddle with a shorter stirrup than had hitherto been in vogue, and, using his ankles and knees as hinges rode on balance, the horse would be able to travel and jump with greater freedom. Since that time these theories have been pretty well accepted though each country has its own version of the "forward seat."

The Italian seat differs from the American in that it requires that the foot be thrust "home" at all times. Both seats call for flexibility in the rider, the ear, hip and heel to be on a line, the rider's body from the waist up to be inclined further forward as the horse increases his gait. Both seats favor the bending in of the ankle and the pushing away from the horse's body of the rider's heel. The Italian holds his hand with his knuckles horizontal to the ground and feels that the impulse of control should come from the shoulder. The American school recommends knuckles nearly vertical with the flexibility of the fingers being responsible for the control of the horse.

But whether or not one believes wholeheartedly in the Italian seat one must admit that they have revolutionized the modern conception of riding and jumping, and that their performance in contests is always spectacular. See also *FORWARD SEAT*.

ITALIAN SCHOOLS OF HORSEMANSHIP

The two most famous schools of horsemanship in Italy are Pinerolo, near

Turin and Tor di Quinto near Rome. Student officers in the Italian Cavalry go first to the former and then take a finishing course consisting mainly of cross country work, steeplechasing and hunting with the Roman Hounds at the latter.

J

JAQUIMA

Spanish for hackamore. This is a bitless type of bridle used for breaking horses. It is also used on stock horses and there are special Jaquima Classes. See also *HACKAMORE; HORSE SHOW CLASSES, Stock. COLTS, breaking and training of.*

JAY

Jay birds and black birds are of use to the foxhunter in that they often give away the presence of the fox.

> A blue, uneasy jay was cackling
> (A swearing screech like tearing sacking)
> From tree to tree, as in pursuit
> He said, "That's it, there's fox afoot."
> *Masefield*

Colts will also run a fox. It is these signs as well as by the "holloas" given by whips or bystanders that help the huntsman to recover his fox and tell the sagacious member of the field what is going on in the covert.

JENNET

This term is rather loosely used. Originally it was a small Spanish horse very popular for ladies' mounts. They were noted for gentleness and easy gaits. Shakespeare describes the horse of Venus as follows:

> But, lo, from forth a copse that neighbors by

> A breeding jennet, lusty, young and proud
> Adonis' trampling courses doth espy,
> And forth she rushes, snorts and neighs aloud:

Jennet is now sometimes confused with "Jenny" or with "hinny."

JENNY

A female ass or donkey. A mule is a hybrid resulting from a cross between a mare and a male ass. A hinny is a hybrid resulting from a cross between a Jenny and a stallion.

JEWELRY (for riding)

The only permissible jewelry is the perfectly plain gold bar or gold safety pin worn in the stock. Ornate or elaborate stock pins are very bad taste. Incidentally in fastening the stock pin it should be placed horizontally. Placing it perpendicularly invites severe injury to the chin in case of a bad fall.

JIGGING

The horse that refuses to take up a flat-footed walk but jiggles and joggles along is a most uncomfortable mount. Such an animal has not been properly trained as a colt. He was probably ridden before he had learned the lessons on the longe of taking up a desired gait and keeping it on a voice command. He should begin his schooling all over again and be ridden and longed for many hours at the walk, in an enclosed arena if possible, away from the excitement of other horses. Work on the shoulder-in, the leg-yield and the traversal at the ordinary and collected walk will eventually put the horse "between the rider's hands and legs" so that he will maintain his walk. The horseman who finds himself mounted in company on such a beast should use an active hand, squeezing slightly at each step and then releasing in cadence with the stride. This is in effect a series of "half-halts," and by this method the confirmed jigger can often be persuaded to step out calmly.

JOCKEY (*n.*)

The rider of a horse in a race. Jockeys are licensed and subject to very strict regulations by the Jockey Club.

JOCKEY (*v.*)

To jockey for position is to maneuver skillfully for an advantageous position. To jockey is also used to mean to trick or cheat at trading horses and dealing in them.

JOCKEY CLUB

The Jockey Club succeeded the Board of Control as the governing body of racing. It came into being at a meeting held by owners and trainers in December, 1893. Its organization and methods were based on those of the Jockey Club of England which had been formed at Newmarket in 1750. Its avowed purpose was to encourage the development of the Thoroughbred horse and to establish racing on a footing which would command the interest, confidence and favorable opinion of the public.

To the Jockey Club was given the task of revising the racing laws and of arranging race meetings so that they would not conflict. Its rules and regulations were compiled and given wide publicity in May of 1894. The Percy-Gray Racing Law of 1895 provided that any association conducting a race meeting must first secure a license from the State Racing Commission and that that license require that the racing be subject to the conditions and race laws of the Jockey Club.

The first chairman of the Jockey Club was John Hunter and the first vice-chairman, James R. Keene; Frank K. Sturgis was the first secretary-treasurer.

The Jockey Club functions in New York and Delaware but it has helped with the forming of race associations all over the Eastern Seaboard. Its publication, "Rules of Racing" governs all racing on recognized tracks. This publication gives the accepted definitions of the various types of races, the duties of the different race officials, the "weights-for-age" scale of handicapping, the rules governing the conduct of jockeys, the bonuses and wages they receive, etc., and the insurance that their employers must carry. The penalties for infraction of rules may run from a fine to a suspension, temporary or permanent, of the license of the trainer or jockey.

The Jockey Club has charge of the American Stud Book in which all American Thoroughbreds are registered. No horse may be registered in the Stud Book unless he is purebred and both his sire and dam are registered therein. No horse may race on a recognized track unless he is registered in the Stud Book.

To every meeting the Jockey Club sends Race Stewards, a Handicapper, Patrol Judges (who, distributed around the course, watch for fouls) and a veterinarian. The latter inspects each horse closely for signs of foul play. Under the supervision of the Clerk of the Scales, a Jockey Club official, each jockey is weighed before he mounts to insure that he carries the weight he is required to carry and no more, and he is weighed again at the end of the race to make certain that he has finished with the required weight.

The Handicapper studies each race and the history of each horse. As the horse continues his career, winning or losing races, his handicap is increased or decreased. All this is under the supervision of the Jockey Club.

The Jockey Club now forbids the admission of bookmakers or auctioneers to track meetings and permits betting only by means of the Pari-Mutuel or "totalizer" system.

The Jockey Club, in consultation with the Racing Commissions, fixes the race schedules in its territory so that major races do not conflict. In its Breeding Bureau it has acquired the use of stallions and mares and placed these in districts where it feels that they might improve the breed of local horses. It also formed the "Jockey Club Foundation," created for the benefit of indigent horsemen, and others connected with the turf.

The Jockey Club occupies a suite of offices at 300 Park Avenue, New York City, where it has collected a large library and some of the most famous Thoroughbred paintings of the world.

The following are the present officials of the Jockey Club:

George D. Widener, Chairman
Ogden Phipps, Vice Chairman
James Cox Brady, Secretary
Marshall Cassidy, Executive Secretary

JOCKEY SEAT

The flat racing jockey uses incredibly short stirrups so that he may keep all

FIGURE 64. CLOSE-UP OF A JOCKEY IN ACTION SHOWING THE CHARACTERISTIC SEAT. *CHARLES PHELPS CUSHING.*

weight out of the saddle. Steeplechase riders use a longer stirrup.

JOG TROT

Sometimes called "dog-trot" or "hounds pace." It is a slow trot, not collected and with little animation. Used in hunting to hack from one covert to another it can also be very valuable in the equitation classes, the riders jog trotting for long periods without reins and stirrups in order to develop independence of the seat.

JOINT EVIL

A disease affecting foals from birth to eighteen months. It is due to an infection in the uterus or may be caused by bacterial infection of the navel cord or through the mare's milk.

The general symptoms, varying in degree according to the virulence of the disease are an indisposition to suckle, a rise in temperature to about 103 F., stiffness of movement and possible swelling of the large joints, signs of infection at the navel, bowel irregularity and a marked inclination to lie down. Death often follows and a veterinarian should be sent for at once. Prevention is the best cure, especially if the disease is known to be prevalent in the district. The box-stall to be used for the foaling should be thoroughly disinfected. A foaling sheet may be used to receive the foal. The navel should be thoroughly painted with iodine. If infection is considered probable, due to cases in the vicinity, the mare may receive vaccine treatment before foaling.

JORROCKS

John Jorrocks, famous tea-selling cockney huntsman, figment of the fertile imagination of Robert Smith Surtees, is perhaps the best loved of all foxhunting characters of fiction. He is noted for his wit, his bad horsemanship and his practical and philosophical approach to life. Mr. Surtees has used this character in several of his works, among them *Handley Cross*. In this latter we find Mr. Jorrocks taking over the Mastership of a thoroughly disorganized pack of hounds. His advice to his new Hunt Secretary is characteristic:

"Now you see, sor," said he, "I dosn't want one of your fine auditing Secs., what will merely run his eye over the bills, and write his initials on the back, right or wrong as many do, but I want a real out-and-out workin' chap, that will go into them hitem by hitem, and look sharp arter the pence, without leavin' the pounds to take care of themselves. A good Sec. is a werry useful sort of h'animal, but a bad un's only worth 'anging. . . . you can't do better nor follow the example of the Leamington lads who string up all the tradespeople with the amount of their subscriptions in the shops and public places. It's clearly the duty of every man to subscribe to a pack of 'ounds—even if he has to borrow the money. "No tick," mind, must be the order of the day. . . . You must be all alive, in fact. Not an 'oss must die in the district without you knowin' it—you must 'ave the nose of a wultur, with the knowledge of a knacker.

Should you make an 'appy 'it (hit) and get one with some *go* in him, I'll let you use him yourself until we wants him for the boiler. In the field a good Sec. ought always to be ready to leap first over any awkward place or catch the M.F.H.'s 'oss, if he 'appens to lead over. In all things he must consider the M.F.H. first, and never let self stand in the way. Then you'll be a good Sec., and when I dosn't want a Sec. no longer, why you'll always be able to get a good Sec.'s place from the character I shall give you."

Perhaps Jorrocks' most familiar saying was his definition of hunting. " 'Unting is the sport of kings, the image of war without its guilt and only five-and-twenty percent of its danger!"

Jorrocks' advice on the selection of a horse has some wonderful recommendations! "Some people object to high-blowers, that is, 'osses wot make a noise like a steam engine as they go. I don't see no great objection to them myself and think the use they are of clearin' the way in crowded thoroughfares, and the protection they afford in dark nights by preventin' people ridin' against you, more than counterbalance any inconwenience. . . ."

He who has not made the acquaintance of the good Jorrocks should by all means do so and, though we may not admire him as a rider the situations in which he finds himself are only too familiar to the present day follower of the field.

JUMPER

A jumper, as distinguished from a hunter, is a horse that is judged on his performance over jumps only. Only actual faults are scored against him. The jumper may be of any breed and any conformation. Sir Gilbert, a hackney stallion, blinded in one eye, was a famous jumper; so was, or is, Little Squire, a thirteen hand Welsh pony. The open jumper is the jumper which is entered in the open (open to any horse) classes. Jumpers may also be classified as "green," "novice," "limit," etc. (consult

FIGURE 65. SCHOOLING THE JUMPER ON A LONGE. THIS IS PART OF THE EDUCATION OF EVERY JUMPING HORSE. IT TEACHES HIM TO JUMP FREELY, WILLINGLY AND WITHOUT EXCITEMENT. FEW HORSES ARE SCHOOLED TO JUMP "LIVE OBSTACLES," HOWEVER. *CHARLES PHELPS CUSHING.*

this text alphabetically for definitions of these terms).

It is to be regretted that most jumpers are owned and ridden by professionals interested only in the amount of money they can win. For this reason the open jumper is often very cruelly used at the horse shows. Between classes he is kept repeatedly jumping over fences that are put higher and higher and, whether he clears them or not he only too often receives a sharp rap from the rapping pole. At one show the A.S.P.C.A. confiscated a rapping pole with nails placed in it to make the punishment more severe. Because manners and ways of going do not count the professional rides as roughly as he chooses, often getting his mount over by strong arm methods alone. The life of the open jumper is often not too happy; humane societies would do well to pay more attention to the treatment these horses receive. However, since the Olympic Trials were opened to Amateur civilians, leading to many more and

stiffer stadium-jumping and cross-country competition in horseshows, the quality of riding and training of open jumpers to compete in these classes is beginning to change. At the top shows and in the high jumping classes one no longer sees horses being forced over fences at a full gallop. Trainers have found that if the horse goes too fast, jumps with his head high or jumps out of fear he has no hope of negotiating the sharp turns and the high and wide obstacles which make up the courses.

JUMPING

Jumping is not only great fun but it is one of the best ways to change an intermediate rider into a first class rider. Riders may be classified as follows: The beginner, who is uncomfortable even on the most placid and obedient horse; the intermediate rider, who has learned the fundamentals of form and control and who does well as long as his horse is not spirited or inclined to shy,

FIGURE 66. THE OPEN JUMPER. *CARL KLEIN*.

and the first class rider who prefers the spirited horse and is at home in the saddle no matter how his horse behaves.

It is comparatively easy to carry the learner through the beginner and intermediate stages, but when one comes to the advanced stages there are problems to be met. One cannot put him on a really spirited horse for his hands are not good enough. Yet one cannot say to a school horse, "Now shy or do something else sudden so that this rider may learn to keep his balance." The answer is much practice in low jumping, for here the lurch of the horse gives the rider exactly the practice he needs. For this reason parents should not look on jumping lessons for their children as something to be avoided because they are dangerous. Jumping lessons, correctly given, lessen the probability of the child being hurt.

Learning to Jump

It is assumed that the learner has been taught to walk, trot and canter. To do the equitation exercises such as turns and half turns. To ride without stirrups and reins at all gaits. He should also have been taught to take the forward seat at the gallop, and to do circles and such exercises as weaving in and out of posts at this gait and keeping the forward position. His seat should not be dependent on his hands. He should not mind if he loses a stirrup but should be able to catch it quickly at any gait. He should be mounted on a quiet, well schooled animal that has an easy jump and will not attempt to refuse or shy out.

The first lessons may well take place in the schooling pen or jumping lane. The horse has been taught to take the jumps without any help from the rider. The bar is set at one foot. The horse should have a stirrup leather around his neck just in front of the withers. The rider is required to hold on to this leather until he has learned to balance himself properly and take the jolt of the horse's landing with his knees. He should go through the lane several times at each lesson. When he can balance well he should be asked to drop his stirrups and take the same low jumps without stirrups. Next, he should practice letting go both strap and reins and extending his arms as the horse jumps.

When he can do this and at the same

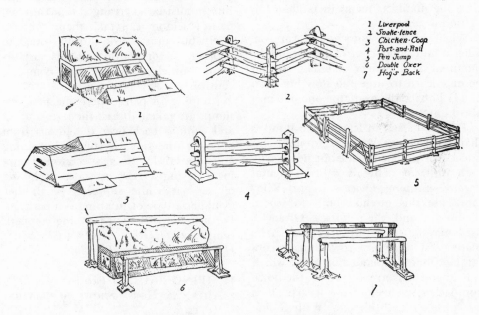

1 Liverpool
2 Snake-fence
3 Chicken-Coop
4 Post-and-Rail
5 Pen Jump
6 Double Oxer
7 Hog's Back

FIGURE 67. TYPES OF JUMPS.

time ride without stirrups the strap may be dispensed with and the rider may hold the reins in the usual manner. He should be cautioned about keeping his hands well separated and down. The jumps may be raised slightly as the rider progresses in skill but they should not be higher than three feet.

Lessons in the lane will take about a month, at the end of which time the rider should be proficient at low jumps. The rider now comes into the regular riding hall or outdoor ring. Bars are laid all around the ring and the rider is required to gallop his horse over them, not necessarily in succession, but rather to gallop, retaining his seat, in and out among them, taking those indicated as demanded. The purpose is to teach him to steer and control his horse while still keeping a jumping position.

When he shows good control, the jumps may be raised but no wings should be used. The instructor should make it a point never to allow the jumps to be raised even an inch until the previous height has been negotiated successfully and in good form. Nor should the learner be permitted to jump more than ten or twelve jumps in one lesson.

Jumping in the ring may be followed by cross-country work or by jumping outside courses. Here emphasis should be put on the control of the gait of the horse. It is best to have several pupils at a time so that they may be asked to negotiate the jumps as teams in tandem formation or abreast.

When the rider shows good form, confidence and good control he should be mounted on a variety of horses so that he may learn to urge the slow horse on and hold back the excitable one. He may also hunt.

The final stage in learning to jump is that of teaching the rider to jump his horse over a difficult but not necessarily high obstacle. This is called "mental hazard" jumping. Officers at Fort Riley often use this method both to school themselves and their horses. Obstacles used may be such things as two chairs placed seat to seat, a row of pails containing stones suspended on a bar which is held and shaken violently as the horse approaches; a wheelbarrow; a carpenter's saw-horse; a bathtub, etc. With a fine jumper and an expert rider such difficult things as a table with four men sitting around it, a small automobile or a man held in a horizontal position by two other men, may be negotiated.

When the former intermediate rider has learned to control himself and his horse over difficult obstacles, to ride a variety of animals and to jump in teams and pairs, it will be found that he no longer minds it if his horse gives an un-expected buck now and again. He may now be considered to have reached the advanced stage!

JUMPING COMPETITIONS

There are many possible ways of competing over jumps in addition to those seen at the ordinary show. The "mental hazard" type is one. See *MENTAL HAZARD*. Maze jumping is another. Here the course is set up with a variety of jumps placed around the hall or ring. At least ten jumps should be used. To one upright or another is attached a red flag. The competitor does not see the course until he enters the ring. He must take each obstacle at least once with the flag on his right. He is timed as in a scurry and the winner is the man who completes the course the fastest. The jumps must be so arranged that the competitor seldom can take them consecutively but must cross from one to another. A competition of this sort demands quick thinking and complete control.

Jumping in pairs where the first two jumps are taken abreast then, separating and coming back over the jumps from opposite directions is splendid training and entertaining to the spectators. Jumping carrying a glass of water or taking off a coat while jumping is another gymkhana type of jumping competition. For a list of orthodox jumping competitions see *HORSE SHOW CLASSES; Hunter and Jumper Division*.

JUMPING FAULTS (scoring of)

AMERICAN HORSE SHOWS ASSOCIATION RULES.

When a horse makes two faults at one obstacle only the major is counted except in the case of a refusal plus another fault when both are counted.

When an obstacle is composed of several elements in the same vertical plane a fault at the top element only is penalized. Faults at obstacles where the vertical planes differ such as oxers, triple bars, etc., are penalized as one fault only.

In judging hunters light touches are

not considered except when elimination is difficult. In this case they may be scored for reference as follows:

Touch with any part of horse's body behind stifle .. ½ fault
Touch with any part of body in front of stifle .... 1 fault
Touch of wing or standard of obstacle, no fault. Bad style is penalized by judges in hunter classes.

Knock-downs

An obstacle is considered knocked down when its height is lowered by horse or rider.

Disobediences

It is considered a disobedience if the horse runs out, bolts or refuses a jump.

Falling of Horse or Rider

A horse is considered to have fallen when the shoulder and haunch of the horse touch the ground. A rider is considered to have fallen from his horse when he becomes separated from him and has to remount.

Scoring of Pairs, Teams, Unicorns Abreast or Tandem

The two or three horses will be considered as one, i.e., the major fault at an obstacle only will be counted. In tandem formations and in abreast formations, where correct distance is not kept, a fault of ½ point will be scored for each one half horse's length and considered cumulative at each obstacle as well as at each end of the ring or between obstacles on course.

Scoring of Jumpers

Jumpers are scored as in table below unless being judged by F.E.I. rules.

Scoring of Working Hunters

Working hunters are judged on manners, hunting pace, way of going and style of jumping. Faults are penalized as given below. Ticks are not counted. Conformation is not counted, hunting soundness only will be considered.

Jumpers are penalized for touches as in table above, but are not penalized for style, gait or manners. Slip fillets may be used to determine whether or not the horse has touched the jump.

Scoring Table

Knock-down with any part of the horse's body behind stifle	3 faults
Knock-down with any part of horse's body in front of stifle	4 faults
Knock-down of obstacle by rider	4 faults
Horse and/or rider falling while in competition	Debarred
First refusal, runout or bolting on course	3 faults
Second cumulative refusal, runout or bolting	6 faults
Third cumulative refusal, runout or bolting	Debarred
Jumping an obstacle before it is re-set	Debarred
Horse bolting from ring mounted or riderless	Debarred
Circling horse between obstacles except before first obstacle or to regain course after a runout	1 fault
Failure to keep proper course	Debarred
Stepping between first and second element with hind legs of obstacle such as a Liverpool and then jumping second element	2 faults

F.E.I. SCORING TABLE

First disobedience	3 faults
Obstacle knocked down	4 faults
Flag knocked down, or, both obstacle and flag knocked down	4 faults
One or more feet in the water, or on the marking lath	4 faults
Second disobedience	6 faults
(Faults for disobedience are cumulative, not only at the same obstacle, but throughout the same round.)	
Fall of horse, or rider, or both	8 faults
(Faults for the fall are in addition to any	

other faults incurred
at the same time.)
Third disobedience, or
other occurrences listed
in paragraph 259 ....Elimination
Exceeding the Time Al-
lowed—for each com-
menced second .... ¼ fault
(Unless it is stipu-
lated in the condi-
tions that this incurs
elimination.)

JUMPS (types of)
See illustration, page 211.

JUSTIN MORGAN
Perhaps the best known sire of all time
was a little bay pony-like creature with
the muscles of a Hercules, the spirit and
fleetness of an Ariel and the disposition
and the patience of a Job. His name was
Justin Morgan and he belonged to a consumptive schoolteacher-singer of the
same name from Randolph, Vermont.
Mr. Morgan brought the colt down from
his farm in Springfield, Mass. to Vermont in the fall of 1795. Justin Morgan
the colt was then two years old, completely unbroken but so amiable that he
followed a three-year-old which Mr. Morgan rode. Noticing the animal's nice
manners and way of going Morgan broke
him to the saddle and rode him for the
next three years until he (the man) died
in 1791, the colt then being a five-year-
old. Although Justin Morgan the colt
was known to be a good hack with
plenty of stamina his owner had no idea
that he would be the founder of one of
the best known and loved breeds of road
horse in America. He therefore neglected
to write down his exact pedigree. But his
relative, John Morgan and his son Justin
Morgan both state that the sire of the
colt was Beautiful Bay (also known as
True Briton). Beautiful Bay was reput-
edly sired by the imported horse
Traveller and was out of another imported mare, Cub. He was the war
charger of General De Lancey and was
stolen from him at Kings Bridge and
brought up to Connecticut. Justin Morgan's dam is supposed to have been a
mare of the Wild-air strain belonging to
Justin Morgan the man at the time. She
in turn was Thoroughbred on the male
side but had some cold blood in her
through her dam. But whether Justin
Morgan was mostly a blood horse or
whether he was mostly cold-blooded, the
fact remains that he soon made a name
for himself as a general utility animal.
Mr. Morgan lent him for a year to Robert Evans, a hard worker but a poor
provider. Evans used him for hauling
timber and pulling out stumps. According to an eye witness it is said that Evans
matched his little, fourteen hand horse
against all comers when it came to pulling weights and in one instance moved
a log that work horses weighing twelve
hundred pounds had been unable to
budge! And this after a day of work in
the woods.

After Mr. Morgan's death the horse
was sold to William Rice of Woodstock,
Vermont. Mr. Rice used him for about
two years on his farm and then Evans,
who had been on the lookout for an opportunity to purchase the little horse
that had proved so willing a worker,
bought him back. He kept Justin Morgan for four years, working him very
hard but taking good care of him, then
he was sued for a debt and the horse
was taken over by Col. John Goss. Col.
Goss sold him to his brother, David Goss
for a hundred dollars and David Goss
kept him for seven years. He was used
for ordinary farm work and as a stallion
for two months in the spring. David Goss
then sold him to his son Phillip and by
now, being nineteen years old, his
owners seemed not too keen on keeping
him for fear that he might die on their
hands. Nevertheless some of his colts
were making names for themselves and
he was in demand. Robert Evans, his
former owner, now took charge of him
for a year and it was while he was with
him that Bulrush was sired. Phillip Goss
next sold him to Jacob Sanderson who
sold him to Mr. Langmade. And now

for the first time the courageous little horse found himself being asked to do more than his age and condition could manage. Langmade worked him for some time in a six horse team hauling freight and Justin Morgan became thin and poor, finally being bought by a Mr. Chelsea. The latter then sold him to a Joel Goss of Claremont, N. H. who kept him one year and sold him to Samuel Stone of Randolph. Mr. Stone kept him two or three years and then he went to his last home, that of Levi Bean who owned him until his death in 1821. He died at the age of twenty-nine from a neglected kick on Mr. Bean's farm at the village of Chelsea, Vermont.

As illustration page 234, shows, Justin Morgan was a powerfully built animal with a breedy head. He is said to have had an unusually fast, short stepping trot, tremendous speed as a sprinter, incredible strength as a weight puller and plenty of presence as a parade horse. Certainly his most outstanding characteristic was his prepotency as proved by his countless descendants. In addition to his physical traits Justin Morgan has also passed down his docile and mild disposition. He is said to have disliked dogs, however, and would chase any dog out of his paddock that had the temerity to appear there. He remains the only horse ever to sire an entire and distinctive breed and his get have changed the agricultural history of the United States. See also *MORGAN HORSE, JUSTIN MORGAN*.

L

LAMENESS
The lame horse, though he may be perfectly sound in wind and eye and with a constitution that will keep him going until a great age, is useless. Therefore every precaution should be taken both to prevent lameness and to diagnose and treat it correctly, should it occur.

Prevention
It must be remembered that the front legs of a horse carrying a rider take tremendous punishment, especially if he be trotted fast or galloped on hard or rocky terrain. Jumping, also, puts excessive strain on the legs. The rider can do much to ease this strain. He can consistently refuse to ride his horse at a rapid gait on bad terrain, especially a gallop where the weight comes hard on the forehand while the hindquarters are freed. He can be careful never to overwork his horse and if the animal, at the end of a long day's hunting, shows by stumbling or interfering that he is leg-weary, the rider should dismount and lead him in rather than risk injury.

The blood in the legs of a horse circulates slowly. If the horse be trotted or galloped as soon as he is brought out from his stable, the walls of the capillaries and the sensitive tissue will be injured and the horse will develop laminitis or founder. There is no cure for severe cases and the horse will have to be shot. Allowing him to stand when he is brought in hot and lathered will also bring on this condition. The old English adage, "Walk the first mile out and the last mile in," is excellent advice and should be strictly adhered to. If you're not sure how long a mile is, remember that a walking horse covers about four miles an hour so fifteen minutes of walking will equal a mile.

Proper shoeing will do much to prevent lameness. The shoe must be made to fit the horse, not vice versa (see also *HORSE SHOES; SHOEING*). The horse should not spend day after day in a stall with a board floor, his feet will dry out and become hard and flinty. Dirty stalls may cause thrush, a disease of the frogs.

Proper feed has something to do with lameness also. Horses that are fed dirty grain or musty hay may develop laminitis or a weakness in the hindquarters.

To summarize; be careful of the amount and kind of work, have a good and honest blacksmith and see that your horses are properly housed and fed.

Diagnosis of Lameness

If a horse suddenly starts limping on the road or when he has just been brought out of his stall look at his feet first. One of the most frequent causes of lameness is a stone becoming wedged in the foot. It is sometimes very difficult to extract such a stone and, if no implement such as a hoof pick is handy the easiest way to loosen it is to hammer it with another stone. The chances are that if the stone has been discovered at once, the sole and frog will not be bruised and the horse will walk sound.

If there is no stone in the foot, starting at the elbow or hock, run the hand down the horse's leg feeling for any unusual swellings or hard lumps, for heat and for signs of tenderness. If there is some question as to the presence of heat feel both legs. Sometimes it is difficult to determine exactly which leg the horse is favoring. Remember that if he is lame in front he will nod or duck his head when the *sound* foot touches the ground, but if he is lame behind he will nod when the lame foot bears the weight. The best gait at which to determine lameness is the trot. By listening to the cadence of the feet any variation will be easily discovered.

If there is no undue swelling nor excessive heat in the leg examine the feet closely once more. Founder, or laminitis is characterized by heat in the wall itself. As both front feet are usually affected equally the temperature of the walls of the front feet should at once be compared with those of the back feet.

The sole and frog should next be carefully checked. If the sole is very hard and flinty it may be this which is causing the lameness. The horse may have a corn or a stone bruise. Tap the sole with a hammer and watch for signs of flinching. Thrush is a very common disease and

causes great and sudden lameness. The split in the frog will be soft and moist, there will be a discharge which may be watery or it may be heavy. There will be an excessive odor. It is important to examine this injury immediately and apply the proper treatment.

In neglected cases the whole frog will be so affected that it will bleed readily when the hoof is cleaned and be extremely painful. Contracted heels owing to bad shoeing are also cause of lameness. The horse's foot appears elongated and the heels of the shoes are too close together.

If there is no apparent sign of injury or ailment in foot or leg, the seat of discomfort must be the shoulder if the horse is lame in front, the stifle, hip joint or spine if the horse is lame behind.

Tests for shoulder lameness include pinching the muscle along the shoulder blade for signs of sensitiveness, backing the horse over a low log, when he will drag the lame foot rather than lift it, and turning him in very short circles when he will favor the affected side very noticeably.

Tests for stifle lameness include picking up the leg and pulling it forward and high. If you suspect injury to the hip or pelvic bones, compare the two sides of the horse's quarters as seen from behind; if one is distinctly lower than the other you may search further there. Horses that go stiffly on both back legs may have some spinal fault. In some cases the vertebrae in the spine may actually become fused.

Fodder poisoning causes great weakness in the hindquarters. They sway and are so uncontrollable that the horse may fall down every step or two. A horse that has kidney trouble shows great sensitiveness over the loins and may go weakly behind as a result.

After discovering the exact extent and position of the injury or ailment, the horse should receive appropriate treatment. If he does not respond to the treatment within a reasonable length of time, by all means send for the veterinarian. Treatment for common ailments and injuries are given in this text alphabetically. See also *FEET, Diseases of; INJURIES.*

LAMINITIS or FOUNDER

A disease of the foot affecting the blood vessels and sensitive tissue under the walls of the feet. This is an exceedingly painful disease and many times incurable as the tissues are permanently injured. The tissues swell, and, as they cannot expand due to the hard covering of the wall, the pain is excessive. Horses suffering from a bad case of laminitis will groan and sweat and refuse to stand.

Cause

Laminitis can come from a variety of causes. Bad food, too much heatening food when the horse is not receiving sufficient exercise, overwork, too fast work before the horse is warmed up or allowing him to stand, particularly in a draft, when he is hot.

Symptoms

Great heat in the walls, excessive lameness. If the horse is willing to walk at all he puts his feet down very gingerly as though walking on eggs.

Treatment

Soak his feet in cold mud or clay which is kept wet. Give him a Physic ball, remove his shoes and do it gently. Send for the veterinarian who may give adrenalin injections to reduce the swelling. Keep the horse on bran mashes.

LAMPAS

This is a swollen condition of the roof of the mouth caused by a bad blood condition. The old remedy used to be to slit the affected area, to rub it with salt or to burn it with a hot iron. None of these methods are now recommended. A laxative such as Glauber salts should be given, a more laxative diet introduced and a little Epsom salts added to the drinking water for several days.

LANDING

The far side of a jump as the rider approaches it is known as the landing.

LARK *(v.)*

To "lark" over jumps in the hunting field is to jump them unnecessarily. Young "thrusters" who do this repeatedly will bring the wrath of the M.F.H. down upon their heads. No jumps should be taken unless hounds are running and then only if by taking the jump the rider is enabled to "ride straighter" than would be possible if he used a gap.

LARYNGITIS

This disease is similar to sore throat in humans and can be very serious in horses even to the extent of causing death owing to a blocking of the air passages. The horse's throat will be swollen, he will have a discharge at the nostrils, a dry cough and appear reluctant to swallow. He should be warmly blanketed, steam inhalations containing eucalyptus should be given, he should have belladonna electuary and camphor smeared on his tongue three or four times daily, and liniment rubbed on the outside of his throat. As he will probably refuse to eat he should be coaxed with linseed tea and gruel made from oatmeal. Green feed will appeal to him more than hay, but if grass cannot be procured have the hay thoroughly wetted down. Send for the veterinarian.

LATCHES (for the stable)

Latches used on box stall doors or on stable doors should be such that the horse cannot open them. They should not project nor have sharp corners against which the horse might scratch himself. Specially designed latches for stables may be purchased and whenever possible they should be used.

LAXATIVES

Before giving the horse a purgative he should be kept on bran mashes for forty-eight hours. The commonest purgative is an aloes ball. This should be given by a veterinarian as the size will depend on the animal.

Common laxatives to be kept at the

stable are Epsom salts, Glauber salts and linseed oil. Epsom salts may be given in the feed, a half pound acts as a purgative; a quarter of a pound given before a day of rest to stabled horses will keep the bowels open. Glauber salts may be given the same way. Linseed oil is very safe, a pint to a pint and a half according to the size of the animal is correct. Bran mashes are mildly laxative, and when a laxative diet is recommended it is meant that the horse be kept on bran mashes with a little Epsom salts added, plus a little hay.

LEAD REIN (use of)

The lead rein, in teaching children, is more often misused than not. The tendency is to put the young beginner up on an animal too large or too spirited and then, by means of the lead rein, leave the control to the instructor. Although this accomplishes its purpose in one way in that it gives the pupil time to get his balance before he has to worry about managing his horse, he is apt to build up a false confidence in his own ability. When the lead rein is removed, the child suddenly finds that he is not master of his horse at all and may readily lose all self confidence. The better way is to mount the child on an animal which needs little controlling, and let the pupil know what it is to handle his own horse or pony from the start.

In my classes I only use a lead rein if a child joins a class after the other members of it have learned to post and are out on the trails. I put the new pupil on a lead and let him ride in the line with me beside him until he has learned to post, usually a matter of minutes with a child over seven. I then remove the lead and let him finish the ride on his own. Naturally he has been given a thoroughly reliable mount.

LEADING THE HORSE

If the horse is bridled and to be led only a short distance the rider should first make sure that the reins are not caught behind the cantle or stirrups. Then, grasping all reins in his right hand six inches from the bit, his forefinger between them, he should walk straight forward without looking at the horse. In leading horses as in working around them the man on foot always walks on the horse's left or near side.

If the horse is to be led some little distance, or if he is high spirited and there is danger of his trying to break away the rider should pull the reins forward over his head. He should then take the ends of the reins in his left hand and with his right hand grasp them as described above. Thus, if the horse pulls he will have both hands on the reins for control. Never allow the ends of the reins to drag as the horse may step on them and break them.

Horses wearing a halter and halter shank rope are led the same way. It is always best to have a rope as well as the halter, for a horse that rears suddenly can always break away from the man if the latter is only holding on to the halter itself.

Leading a Balky Horse

If the horse stops and refuses to go forward either through fear or subborness turn him first to one side and then to the other. He will forget that he does not want to advance and will turn readily. In an emergency where there is little room such as coming out of a stall, turn the horse around several times.

Leading by the Foretop

This is not a very safe way to lead a horse but if it must be done, take the foretop in the right hand and put your left hand over the horse's nostrils. Thus, if he tries to plunge forward you can control him.

Leading with a Rope or Strap

If the horse has no bridle, halter or foretop take a short length of rope or a leather belt, slide it over the crest directly behind the ears, grasp the two ends close to and under the throat. Place your left hand on his nose. This will give you good control.

Leading Through a Narrow Passageway or Over Rough Terrain

Face the horse, take the bridle reins in each hand, raising the hands to about the height of the bit, then walk backwards steering and controlling the horse so that he does not hit his hips or plunge forward.

LEADS

At the canter and gallop the horse always "leads" with the legs on one side or the other. The shoulder of that side is freed and as the horse's feet strike the ground it will be seen that either the right or left foot, as the case may be, is in front of the others. It is most important in riding in circles and making short turns that the horse lead with his inside legs as otherwise he has little support for his body. See also *CANTER; GALLOP; GALLOP DEPARTS.*

LEAPING POWDER

Hunting term for a good stiff drink taken before the meet.

LEATHER (care and selection of)

In choosing your saddle and bridle get as good leather as you are able to afford. Generally speaking the more flexible the leather the better. If second-hand tack is being bought examine it closely for signs of dry rot or cracking. Having gotten good leather take care of it. Each time it is used the tack should be wiped off with saddle soap. Neats-foot oil applied about once a month will do much to keep leather in condition or bring back to condition leather that has been allowed to dry out. Before storing leather oil it thoroughly and wipe it off with a mildew preventive. Do not leave it stored for too long without re-oiling it. See also *BRIDLES, Care of; SADDLES, Care of.*

LEATHER (to reach for or grab)

A Western expression meaning that the rider has lost his seat and has to hold the saddle horn to keep from being thrown.

LEATHERS (n.)

The stirrup leathers are often known as "leathers." Hunting breeches made of leather are also called "leathers."

LEGS (of the horse)

The legs of the horse are of paramount importance. Together with the feet they are the part of the horse most likely to sustain injury. The forelegs carry most of the weight and act as shock absorbers. The hind legs provide propulsion. For this reason injuries to the forelegs are more common than to the hind though injuries to the hock are common.

In judging a horse's legs one should look for defects due to injuries, splints, spavins, enlargements of the joints or tendons, etc., and for defects due to malformation. The well made horse's legs are straight and sturdy. The space between them at the brisket is neither too wide nor too narrow. The feet are neither turned in nor do they point outwards. The cannon bones are of equal width at the top and the bottom. They are short, wide and thick. The tendons are well defined. The large joints are bony without enlargements. Seen from the side the foreleg should be so placed that a line dropped three inches forward of the elbow will pass towards the front of the fetlock joint and end at the back of the frog. With thoroughbreds and hunters a line dropped from the buttock point should pass two inches behind the hock and should be parallel to the back cannon.

The trotting horse carries his hind legs further behind his body than does the hunter. Here the line dropped from the buttock point would touch the point of the hock. Saddlers and harness horses are taught to "camp" or "stretch." This is an artificial position and does not mean that the horse has weak or wrongly placed legs.

Details of the construction of the legs of the horse are given in accompanying diagram. For injuries to the legs see *INJURIES.*

Legs of the Rider

The position of the rider's legs when mounted determines the secureness of his seat. From the very first time he mounts a horse the pupil should work to attain the correct position. Once attained he will be able to keep it without conscious

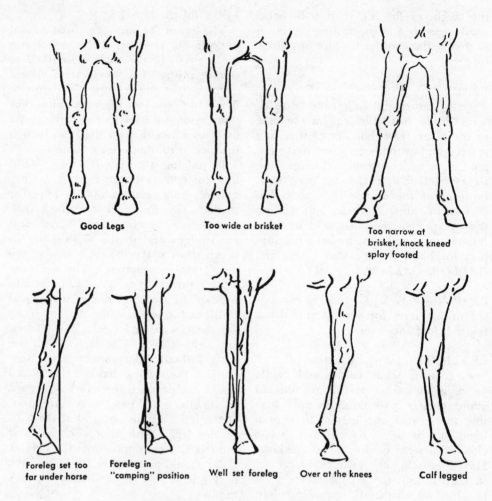

Good Legs   Too wide at brisket   Too narrow at brisket, knock kneed splay footed

Foreleg set too far under horse   Foreleg in "camping" position   Well set foreleg   Over at the knees   Calf legged

FIGURE 68. LEGS OF THE HORSE.

effort, and his seat will be secure without his having to contract his muscles.

The leg must be so rotated at the hip that the sharp bone on the inside of the knee is in contact with the saddle at all times. The knee joint should not move from this position regardless of changes in position of other parts of the leg or of the body. The rider should visualize the knee as a hinge, an imaginary bar running through the knee joints of the rider and through the horse provides the pin upon which the hinge works. There should be perfect flexibility in the joint with no cramping of muscle. When the rider is down in the saddle the inside of the thighs rest on the saddle. Until the rider's muscles have become flattened by riding he will find it difficult to keep his thighs firmly against the horse and still not tighten the muscles in doing so. From the knee down, below the top of the rider's boot, the inside of the leg remains in contact with the saddle. Beginning about half way down the calf the leg and heel are thrust out from the side of the horse. The ankle joint is bent in so that the foot of the rider is resting on the inside sole of his boot, the tread of the stirrup being across the ball of the foot and the outside edge of the tread higher than the inside edge. The toes should not be turned exaggeratedly in nor should they turn sharply out. If they are turned in the knee will be pushed out, if they are turned out the heel will go back against the horse and the rider will be holding on with the back of his calves. Remember that the actual position of the feet depends on the angle of the ankle joint and on the leg being rotated at the thigh. The heel should be well below the toe. The lower leg should be so held that, when seen from the side, a line dropped from the point of the knee will just touch the point of the toe.

Common faults in the position of the leg are as follows:

Knees turned out showing a triangle of light between the point of the knee and the saddle.

Back of the calf gripping the saddle.

Heels touching the horse.

Toes pointed too far in or too far out.

Feet pushed forward so that the toe extends in front of the knee.

Heel on a level with or above the toe.

Legs carried too far back.

See also *RIDING*.

LEG UP

When a rider is assisted into the saddle by someone on the ground, he is said to be given a "leg up." Some schools of thought feel that one should always either be given a leg up or vault into the saddle without using the stirrups as in the normal way of mounting the saddle may be pulled out of line. Colts being mounted for the first time will be less frightened if the rider is given a leg up.

In assisting someone to mount in this fashion stand by the horse's neck facing the rear. The rider should stand opposite and facing the animal's shoulder. He should gather up his reins and put one hand on the horse's neck, the other on the pommel of the saddle. The person who is assisting bends his own left knee and cups his left hand on it. The rider places his left ankle in the cupped hand. At a signal from the assistant the rider springs, at the same time the assistant straightens his knee and lifts the ankle. By this system of supporting the weight with the body as well as the hand a person can mount a rider somewhat heavier than themselves and run no risk of strain.

LEPPER

Irish for good jumper.

LEUCODERMA

This is a name given to the white patches which sometimes appear on the hairless parts of the horse. They simply mean lack of pigment and, though unsightly, are not indicative of injury or disease.

LEVRETTE (*Cheval levrette*)

This is a French term meaning that the horse has a belly like a greyhound.

LIBERTY HORSES

Liberty horses are those which perform in the circus without a rider. They are taught to turn in unison, bow, rear, etc., also to find their correct places in the line. One of the prettiest and most unusual performances of Liberty horses was that given in the Ringling Brothers Circus some years ago. Into the arena walked a beautiful black draft horse. His coat was shining, his great muscles bulged. On one shoulder and one flank was a little white patch. His mane and tail were braided with pink rose buds and he wore a white buckskin bitting rig. Beside him walked a tiny Shetland pony, an exact counterpart in miniature of the big horse, even to the white patches. After going through the usual routine the big horse went to the center of the ring and stretched. The pony then ran in figure eights passing under the big horse at each change of direction! One is always pleased with the performance of these Liberty horses for they work without constraint or force.

LICE

Horses in poor condition or those turned out in the winter often have lice.

These parasites do not pass to human beings nor will they go from one horse to another if the second is in good condition and being worked. The natural sweat of a horse seems to discourage lice to such an extent that, if a horse is used for fast work the lice will leave.

To get rid of lice first clip the horse. Then wash him thoroughly with a lysol solution. Rub a little kerosene in his mane and tail but not too much nor too hard or the hair will come off. He may be dusted with lice powder once or twice, but as a rule just the bath and the lysol will get rid of the undesirables at once.

LIFT (v.) To Lift Hounds

If the hounds are unable to pick up the scent of the fox the huntsman may "lift" them, i.e., call them to him and ride to where he thinks the scent will be better. The whips will come in behind to keep the hounds' heads up and keep them at the heels of the huntsman.

LIGHT DRESSAGE
See *DRESSAGE*.

LIGHT HANDS
See *HANDS*.

LIGHTING (in the stable)

Lights in the stable, both artificial and natural, should be placed above the eye level of the horse. If bulbs are placed inside the stalls, they should have a wire covering to prevent injury to the horse should he rear and strike them.

LIGHTWEIGHT HUNTER

A lightweight hunter is one capable of carrying a hundred and sixty-five pounds in the field. See also *HUNTERS, Classification of*.

LIMIT CLASSES

Limit classes are those open to horses which have not won six blue ribbons in recognized shows in the division in which they are competing. Equitation classes may call for riders that have not won more than six blues in other equitation classes. Horses which win in team, tandem or pair classes do not have to count these ribbons in qualifying in limit classes where they are shown as individuals. Horses shown in Limit Classes are known as "Limit Hunters," "Limit Jumpers," etc.

LINE (hunting)
The course taken by the fox.

LINIMENT

Solutions known as liniments are often used to relieve muscular strains. Sprained tendons are also treated with liniments. The effect of the liniment is to bring the blood down to the affected part. There are many liniments on the market. It is advisable to keep one or two in the medicine chest. The old fashioned "white liniment" contains white lead. The veterinarian can supply the tablets from which this is made. Rubbing liniments usually contain turpentine and alcohol. Plain rubbing alcohol is also good.

LINSEED

Linseed either as a meal or whole is useful as a laxative. A handful added to the horse's feed two or three times a week will keep the bowels in good condition and make the coat shine. Linseed or flaxseed may also be used as a poultice. Get the whole linseed from the druggist. Pour hot water over it to make a gluey consistency. Apply to the affected part, cover with a heavy dressing of cotton and bandage.

LIPIZZAN

The early Greeks, as proved by the famous Parthenon Frieze, were expert horsemen and taught their mounts all the airs and graces of the *haute école*. They rode bareback with a bent knee on small, lightly built animals whose exact breeding has never been determined.

In the early days of chivalry a gentleman was considered well educated if he was expert in only two fields—the use of the sword and horsemanship. Indeed, in many languages the very term "horseman" is synonymous with "gentleman" (*cavalier, caballero,* etc.) .

With medieval times in Europe came the knight in armor. The heavy armor was now necessary because of the development of the longbow. The knight still practiced the art of advanced horsemanship and depended on his own skill and the training of his horse in executing difficult movements, such as the *levade,* both in battle and in tournament. However, the fact that he wore the heavy, inflexible armor rendered necessary a much heavier type of horse. Also, since he could not bend his knees readily, he was forced to ride with stiff legs pushed in front of him. This made it difficult for him to balance himself and took away one of his most important aids, the use of his heels as a means of communicating with and controlling his horse.

At this time, however, in one part of the world horsemen continued to ride with the bent knee. This was in Arabia, for the Bedouins of the desert did not use bows and thus armor was unknown.

In the eighth century the Arabians conquered Spain, taking with them their desert-bred horses and their methods of riding. They ruled for five hundred years, until they were finally conquered and driven out. But they left behind them their methods of training and riding and several fine strains of horses.

In Italy at this time there was a tremendous revival of interest in the art of equitation, especially in what we today call "dressage" and in the "off-the-ground" movements. Even before the advent of gunpowder made armor useless, the crossbow, a much stronger weapon than the longbow, was invented and found to be practical against the

FIGURE 69. LIPIZZANER HORSE, PERFORMING THE CAPRIOLE. *COURTESY MATHILDE WINDISCH-GRAETZ.*

heaviest mail. This meant that the heavily armored knight on his tremendous, draft-type charger, was becoming useless in battle. A lighter type of mounted soldier was needed on a lighter and more agile type of horse.

Federico Grisone and Giovanni Pignatelli were among those Masters in Naples who endeavored to carry the torch of adherence to the early methods of training and riding and who were forever on the lookout for suitable horses. More and more they turned to the Arab and the Barb. Meanwhile, the Spanish had developed a breed known as the Andalusian and had earned tremendous reputations as "Jinates" (riders who used the "bent" knee of the Arab in riding).

Ganzalo Fernández de Córdoba, who had introduced reforms in cavalry training, had imported a number of these Andalusian stallions and founded a breed in Naples known as the Neopolitan.

In 1562 Ferdinand I imported Andalusian mares and stallions and with them started a stud farm at Kladrub, Austria, whose purpose was to breed horses to draw the royal carriages.

In 1580 one of Ferdinand's sons, the Archduke Charles, decided to move some of the Spanish horses from Kladrub to a small town east of Trieste called Lipizza. He also imported some fresh stock from Spain, among these being six young stallions. It was these that were destined to be the foundation sires of the famous white horses known the world over as the Lipizzan Horses or Lipizzanners of the Spanish Riding School of Vienna.

Though Lipizza lacked an adequate supply of water and, because of its high altitude and hilly terrain was not precisely what one would normally look for in choosing the locale for a stud farm, from the beginning the colts were nevertheless outstanding in strength and stamina. They also proved intelligent, readily trained and with unusual aptitude for the "off-the-ground" airs of the advanced dressage training.

Born black or brown, the majority of these colts turn white between the ages of four and seven. They have rather long bodies and short legs and, considering their Barb and Arab ancestry, the unusual feature of the "ram" type profile rather than the dished profile of their ancestry. Before training and under saddle on the long rein, they move freely but more like hunters than one would suppose. Collected and ridden in hand, the whole picture changes and what one took to be a rather heavy-type animal suddenly becomes light and balanced as a ballet dancer.

The first severe disturbance of the stud at Lipizza came when Trieste fell into Italian hands during the first world war. The horses were moved out to escape the invaders, some going to Kladrub, others to another imperial stud at Luxemburg. Later many were confiscated by the Czechoslovak Republic and others handed over to the Italian government. However, after the Treaty of Versailles many were reunited at Piber, near Gratz. With the exile of Emperor Charles, the Spanish Riding School lost its patron, and for many years, while the new government was struggling to resolve its economic problems, the burden of the support of the horses and the School fell on the shoulders of its chief, Count Rudolph van der Straten.

In 1942, with the invasions of the second world war, it was again necessary to remove the School to Czechoslovakia. There, however, they were soon threatened with confiscation by the Russians. It was at this point that General Patton of the United States Army, himself a Cavalry man, stepped in and insured the safety and preservation of the Lipizzan Stud and the Imperial Riding School and their return to Piber.

At present, during the winter months, the Spanish Riding School is located at its original headquarters in Vienna. Here stallions in training are kept. The School is active and men and women come from all over the world to study advanced riding under the Masters of

Equitation headed by Colonel Louis Podhajsky. The mares and young stock remain at Piber. Every animal is a direct descendant of one of the original six stallions imported by the Archduke Charles. These form the six families—Pluto, Conversano, Neopolitano, Favory, Maestoso and Siglavy. Each foal receives a double name, the first indicating its ancestry and the second its personal name. Each family also has its distinctive brand.

Only those young stallions which are outstanding in aptitude and conformation are chosen for training. This training begins at the end of the third year or the beginning of the fourth. For one year the colt is taught only basic movements with emphasis on extension. He is thoroughly schooled on the longe and on the long reins, the trainer walking behind. Not until he has learned to take up all the natural gaits and to change them on voice command is he mounted. Under the saddle he is ridden on light contact with no effort at collection, on straight lines and on large circles, with intensive work on the strong walk and trot.

At the end of the year, if he is deemed ready, more advanced work to improve his lateral and longitudinal flexibility is begun, again on the long reins and between the pillars. The young stallion now learns the intermediate dressage figures, the shoulder-in, leg-yield, renvers, travers, traversal, etc. Also the flying change of lead—all this with the trainer walking. To see one of these horses at the collected canter, exactly cadenced and with the trainer at an active walk almost touching the animal's hocks, make a perfect flying change as the trainer crosses behind him from one side to the other is like watching something magical.

From the above figures the stallions go on to the more difficult piaffe, passage and pirouette. Having been perfected in the long reins the trainer now continues the training under the saddle.

As their training continues, individual horses show an aptitude for certain of the off-the-ground movements such as the levade, croupade, ballotade, capriole and corbette. However, few horses are trained for more than two or three of these movements and some are trained for but one or two. It is interesting to note that whereas in the simpler movements the trainer rides with stirrups, in the off-the-ground airs he always rides with a fixed leg without stirrups.

To some these movements may appear simply artificial gymnastics. Actually they are distinguished from the "circus" type of *haute école* by the fact that horses at liberty spontaneously execute every one of them, and it was through the study of natural movements that they were developed.

LIPS (of the horse)

The horse's lips should be flexible and not pendulous. The latter condition where there is much relaxation of the lower lip denotes extreme age.

LONGE

The longe is a long rein used in schooling, breaking and training the horse. It should be at least thirty feet long, be flexible and have a swivelled snap at one end. For use of the longe see *COLTS, Breaking and training, JUMPERS.*

LOOSE REIN RIDING

Although the rider should habitually ride with his horse in hand it is very restful for the latter to be allowed to walk out with a loose rein occasionally. This should never be done when traversing rough terrain or going up and down inclines. When riding with a loose rein the rider should be constantly alert for signs of misbehavior or fright on the part of the horse, and he should also keep his eyes open for sights which might startle his horse, gathering him well before he comes to such disturbances.

In certain classes in horse shows the horse is shown on a loose rein to prove that he is not excitable. Road hacks and hunter hack classes are typical of those requiring the rider to show his mount on a loose rein.

LOPE

This is a gait widely used in the west. It is not a true canter, being a movement in which the horse canters in front and trots behind. It is encouraged in the stock horse because it is very smooth, but it is not a gait to be encouraged in horses used for jumping or dressage.

LOU DILLON

A famous trotter. See *RECORDS AND STATISTICS—HARNESS RACING* (Appendix).

M

MACLAY CUP

This is also known as the ASPCA Trophy. The trophy is donated by Alfred Maclay in the name of the American Society for the Prevention of Cruelty to Animals. Throughout the year Recognized Shows offer Maclay classes. The competition has now become so stiff that, whereas it was only necessary to win one blue in a Maclay to qualify as a contestant for the Maclay Trophy at Madison Square Garden in November, it is now necessary to win at a small show three times in order to qualify. Even after thus weeding out the contestants it is still necessary to hold an elimination contest at the Garden in the morning and to select from a field of from sixty to ninety competitors twelve or fourteen to compete in the afternoon. The tests are stiff and competitors are sometimes required to take the complicated course without stirrups and riding another competitor's horse before the winner is finally chosen.

MAIDEN CLASSES

A maiden class is one open to horses which have not won a first ribbon at a Recognized Show in the division in which they are showing. Ribbons won in pair or team classes are not counted when estimating ribbons for individuals. Hunters, jumpers, Saddlers who have not won a blue are known as Maiden Hunter, Maiden Jumper, etc. This term also applies to contestants in equitation classes who have not yet won a blue.

MAKING A CAST

This is a hunting term meaning that hounds, encouraged by the huntsman, search a given territory in order to pick up the scent of a fox. When the line has been lost the huntsman will very often "lift" his hounds, carry them to where he thinks the scenting is better or where it is known that the fox has passed and "make a cast" for the line again. See also *LIFT*.

MALLENDER

The Mallenders are the chestnuts or small callosities appearing on the insides of the horses's legs. There is some disagreement as to exactly what these are, though some authorities feel that they are all that remains of the fifth toe of the prehistoric horse.

MAMBRINO

Sire of Messenger who became the foundation sire in this country of the trotting, pacing and saddle strains. Mambrino himself was the foundation sire and head of the most famous family of English coach horses. He was a direct descendant of the Darley Arabian. Messenger also had a son, Messenger's Mambrino, who sired Abdallah who in turn sired Rysdyk's Hambletonian, the founder of the great trotting horse family, the Hambletonians.

MAMBRINOS

The descendants of Messenger's Mambrino were known as the trotting family of "Mambrinos." This family was particularly popular in Kentucky, vying for first place with the Clays, the Morgans

FIGURE 70. MAN O' WAR, AMERICA'S BEST-KNOWN AND BEST-LOVED RACE HORSE. SHOWN WITH HIS TRAINER, WILL HARBUT AT FARAWAY FARM, LEXINGTON, KY. *BERT CLARK THAYER.*

and the Hambletonians, all of whom trace their ancestry back to old Messenger and thence to the Darley Arabian.

MANE (care of; styles in)

The mane and tail of a horse indicate to some extent his breeding; the "hot-blooded" horse having a finer, thinner, shorter mane than the "cold-blooded." It is customary to keep the mane of the Thoroughbred pulled and shortened if Nature does not do so. This is done by pulling the hair out by the roots. As the horse's nerves in his neck are very insensitive he will not object to this procedure though it may sound cruel. Grasp the hair in a little tuft, perhaps a dozen hairs at a time, choosing always the longest, and pull. Continue working up and down the mane until it is of a uniform length (about five or six inches)

and thinness. The tail may be thinned the same way. For hunting and showing, the Thoroughbred usually wears his mane done up in little pigtails which are braided with either thread or wool, turned under and tied with a rosette at the top.

Hunters other than Thoroughbred usually have their manes clipped entirely off with the clippers (hogged).

Five-gaited Saddlers, including the Plantation Walkers, wear their manes and tails as long as they will grow. For showing, the forelocks are braided in three long pigtails as in the mane just back of the poll. Unlike the hair-do of the hunters these pigtails are not folded under and the colored wool is allowed to hang down in streamers.

Three-gaited Saddlers wear their manes hogged. They also have their tails pulled leaving very little more than a plume at the end, the hair of the whole dock being pulled short and scanty.

Roadsters and other harness types other than the "Fine Harness" horses wear their manes shortened like the Thoroughbreds but with the foretop clipped off entirely. Draft breeds usually wear their manes braided with rosettes.

MANEGE

A French word meaning a riding hall, riding academy or school for teaching horses. Also used to indicate "High School" type of training for horses as well as the gaits which he uses in such training.

MANGE

Parasitic mange is one of the most contagious of skin diseases. Fortunately it does not often occur in well regulated stables. If it does occur, the veterinarian should be sent for at once as in some cases the Sarcoptic form is almost impossible to eradicate and will spread through the stable like wild-fire.

There are three forms of mange: Sarcoptic, the most serious, Soroptic, which is due to a different type of mite and is more easily cured, and Symbiotic. The latter is usually only present under the tail and inside the legs. The symptoms are an intense itchiness and desire to be scratched. The hair gradually falls out, leaving the skin thickened, wrinkled and covered with small scabs.

Isolate the horse, put him on a cooling diet, clip him and burn the hair. Disinfect the stall, burn the bedding as it is taken out. Wash the horse all over every three days with the following solution: 1 lb. lime, 2½ lbs. sulphur, 8½ gals. water. *Send for the veterinarian.*

MANNERS

The manners of the horse are extremely important. A bad-mannered horse is a nuisance both to his rider and to others riding with him. A horse should never be allowed to kick or bite at another horse but should receive a sharp slap with a riding crop the instant he shows such tendencies.

The well-mannered horse shows himself willing and obedient. He does not rear, buck, jig or balk. He responds immediately to the demands of his rider. In jumping he neither rushes his jumps nor slows up so much as to require exaggerated use of the legs or crop to get him over. In the field he does not pull nor try to pass other horses. If it is necessary to wait at a panel he does so without fuss.

The well-mannered horse stands quietly while being mounted. He is quiet in the stall and follows readily when led by the bridle reins or halter shank. In judging hunters, ladies' hunters and hacks, ladies' harness horses and children's ponies, manners are considered of paramount importance. Even though you may never want to show your horse he will give you far more pleasure if you give him a thorough course in good manners. See also *VICES*.

MAN-O-WAR

Famous thoroughbred chestnut horse, foaled 1917. Owned by Glen Riddle Farm. Bred by August Belmont. Raced 1919, 1920. Started twenty-one times, came in first twenty times. Won $249,465.

MANURE (care of)

Manure that is allowed to remain near the stable is a breeding ground for flies as well as being disagreeable to the sense of smell. When the stalls are cleaned in the morning the manure may be dumped near by, but it should be hauled away to the compost heap as soon as possible. If one has the facilities, loading the manure directly into a manure spreader or into a dump cart is the simplest way of handling it. The addition of lime will help kill off the flies and make the manure more valuable as a fertilizer. When the cart is filled it can be hauled away and disposed of either by spreading directly on the fields or piled for use later. If manure must be kept near the stable it should be thoroughly sprayed once a day with a solution of D.D.T., ten percent strength.

MARE

A mare is a female horse over the age of four years. Unaltered male horses over four are known as stallions; stallions that have been castrated are known as geldings.

MARILES

General Humberto Mariles-Cortes is one of the outstanding contemporary horsemen. He was born in Parral, Chihuahua (Mexico) in 1913. He was slated for a military career, joining the Academy of Parral at the age of 13 as bugler. He showed great aptitude both in riding and in training, and after graduation was kept on at the Academy as riding instructor. At the end of three years he was transferred to another military school, the "Application School," where he continued training officers for international competition. In 1938 he was put in charge of a new Military Riding Academy whose sole purpose was to train Army Officers for international and Olympic competitions.

In 1941 General Manuel Avila Camacho, then president of the Mexican Republic, established an *Asociación Nacional Equestre,* an Association the purpose of which was to develop both riders and horses for international competition. This Association was not limited to the military. It soon became a very popular organization, with members from many countries, who came to study under the General.

In 1962 the Association was closed by the political regime, which was not in favor of a riding program. General Mariles is now in the process of reorganizing his instruction program, as a private individual.

Methods of jumping and teaching. Early in the 1920's most international riding teams, in those days generally limited to the military, especially in Olympic competition, adopted the Italian Forward Seat for jumping. The rider remained balanced in his stirrups from the time he entered the ring. The horses were able to maintain a much higher rate of speed than is possible today, for the courses in those days were simpler. Since all such competitions were judged on time as well as on faults, speed was important.

In 1938 the Olympic competitions were held in Italy. The Italians had been winning consistently in all stadium jumping events in international jumping competitions. Their horses were extremely obedient, swift and agile. All training in Dressage had been discontinued and the whole position of the rider was the opposite of the deep-in-the-seat, classical position which utilized the use of the back and which emphasized complete control of the horse with a slow approach to the jumps. When the Mexican team, led by General (then Captain) Mariles, entered the ring the audience and other competitors were astonished to see that though the riders used the forward position on the take-off and through part of the flight of the jump, as soon as the hindquarters of the horse had cleared the obstacle the rider sank back into the saddle, and, keeping the horse strongly on the bit, maintained a much slower rate of speed. However, this permitted very much sharper turns and, because of the slower approach, the horse was able to judge the obstacles more correctly and consequently made fewer jumping faults. At the end of the competition the Mexicans were far out in front in the top honors, with Mariles himself holding highest points for the Individual Championship.

Until 1958, when the General was temporarily incapacitated by an automobile accident and then later superseded, the Mexicans were consistently outstanding in all international jumping competitions.

The Mariles method of training the horse includes constant training and work on Dressage through the intermediate phases, with emphasis on extension and collection of the gaits, especially the trot. There is much cross-country work over rough terrain, using the native "barrancas" (sand slides) to develop boldness, strength and agility, and daily practice over every conceivable type of obstacle. Cavalletti of varying heights and distances apart, beginning at bars set at six inches, four feet apart, and going to those four feet in height at twenty-four to thirty-six feet apart, are permanent features of the schooling ground and every horse jumps the cavalletti each day before going on to the individual jumps.

The General believes in firmness with gentleness. This is contrary to the opinion many people have of his methods, but the author spent a month at the Asociación in 1959 and was impressed by the calmness of the horses, both in the stables and under saddle.

MARK A FOX (mark to ground)
See *HUNTING TERMS*.

MARTINGALE
A part of the tack. The most common types of martingales are running and standing, see Figure 71. The standing martingale is attached to the noseband at one end, the girth at the other. Its purpose is to prevent a horse from carrying his head too high or to cure him of tossing it. The running martingale is used to give the rider more control with a snaffle bridle. The reins of the snaffle are run through the rings in the martingale, the other end being attached to the girth. The length of the martingale is so adjusted that there is no pull on the bit when the horse carries his head at a normal level. When the horse puts his head high the pull on the bit is from below, so that the action is on the bars of his mouth, as with a bar or curb bit, instead of the normal action of the snaffle which is on the corner of the lips only.

French and German Martingales. See *DRAW REIN*.

Irish Martingale
This is a short strap with a ring at

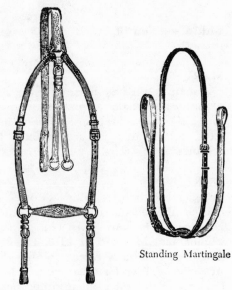

Standing Martingale

Running Martingale with Hunting Breastplate

FIGURE 71. MARTINGALE AND BREASTPLATE.

each end. The reins of the snaffle bridle run through the rings and the strap slide up to about six inches from the bit. It gives additional control and prevents the snaffle being pulled too far through the animal's mouth.

MASHES
Hot bran mashes are excellent for a horse if given once a week before a day of rest. Put three or four quarts of bran, a handful of salt, a few carrots or a handful of linseed meal into a clean pail. Pour on boiling water. Cover with a burlap bag and allow to steam until cool enough to eat.

Horses with bad teeth may have to have all their food in the form of mashes. Whole or crushed oats can be used and the mash should be allowed to stand long enough to soften the grain thoroughly.

MASK
The head of the fox is known as the "mask." At the kill it is cut off by the huntsman and presented to one of the field. Tied to the pommel it indicates

to all and sundry that the rider was present at the death. The brush and pads are similarly presented as trophies.

MASSAGE

Hand massage of the horse's legs is very valuable in certain conditions and injuries. It stimulates the circulation and so promotes the healing of the tissues. It is particularly useful in treating "stocking" where, due to bad circulation or to an old injury the horse's back legs swell when he stands in his stall. The leg should be rubbed towards the heart. In cases of colic or prostration where the limbs become cold they should be well massaged.

Massaging with a bandage is also good. In this the horse's flexed lower leg is held across the worker's knee. A straight bandage is put once and a half around the cannon. By holding the end the worker can "see-saw" them back and forth, creating friction.

MASTERS OF FOXHOUNDS ASSOCIATION OF AMERICA

The Master of Foxhounds Association of America was established in 1907. Among its other functions it assigns territories to the various hunts. Hunts registered with this Association are considered "recognized" hunts and may send teams to Horse Shows as such. Recognized hunts frequently show their hounds in competition also. Hunters, to be qualified, must have hunted regularly with a Recognized Hunt.

The address of the Association is 112 Water Street, Boston 9, Mass.

MATINEES

In the late eighteen-sixties professional harness racing got into bad repute due to the gambling element and the undesirable practices of the bookmakers and drivers. To offset this and to bring trotting and pacing races back into favor with the higher class of driver-owner, in 1871 the Waverly Park Gentleman's Pleasure Driving Association started the matinees. There was a formal calendar of weekly events for members and guests of the club. The events became very popular and amateur matinee racing spread all over the country. The prize was always a trophy, often a badge made up of the club's crest together with the heads of a mare and her colt enameled on a gold background with diamond eyes. See also *HARNESS RACING*.

MAZE JUMPING

A form of jumping competition to test the alertness of the rider and the handiness of the horse. The course consists of a variety of jumps laid out in the ring at odd angles and intervals. A red flag is attached to one standard of each jump. The rider must take each jump at least once with the flag on his right. The rider to complete the course in the shortest time wins, jumping faults do not count. For suggested layout of jumps see illustration, page

McCLELLAN SADDLE

The saddle-tree used by the army. It has a split tree and a high pommel and cantle. It is very easy on the horse, is practical for carrying field equipment but is not so suitable for equitation, polo, jumping, etc.

MEET

A hunting term meaning the gathering together of those intending to participate in the hunt. The time and place of the meet is always announced in advance.

MEGRIMS or STAGGERS

This is an affection of the brain corresponding to fainting in human beings. The horse falls down unconscious. It is due to defective circulation caused by a weak heart, or by undue restraint of throat lash or collar. It can also come from impaired digestion due to bad food or incorrect feeding; worms; or a congestion of the brain.

It usually attacks the horse while he is at work, especially if the weather is hot and he is in the sun. The horse will regain consciousness in a few minutes but will appear dazed. Immediate treatment is to loosen his tack and to put cold water on his head. The veterinarian should be called and a purgative given.

MENTAL HAZARD JUMPING

A jumping competition which tests the training of the horse. The jumps are not high but are peculiar. They may be such things as a wheelbarrow, a pair of chairs set seat to seat, a baby's bathtub filled with water, a bassinet, a row of pails hung on a rod which are rattled as the horse approaches, etc. One way of scoring this competition is as in golf. Each time a horse approaches a jump it is one "stroke," if he shies out or refuses it will cost him another "stroke." Thus the par of a ten-jump course would be ten.

FIGURE 72. IMPORTED MESSENGER, THE FOUNDATION SIRE FOR ALL TROTTING, PACING, AND GAITED HORSES IN AMERICA.

MESSENGER

Messenger was the foundation sire for all trotting, pacing and gaited horses in America. An English stallion imported in 1788 he was an ungainly and ugly flea-bitten gray. He had had an undistinguished record on the English tracks and no one suspected that he was to become such an outstanding foundation sire. There has been much speculation as to why Messenger, a running horse, should have handed down trotting and pacing speed to his descendants, but it must be remembered that the English Thoroughbred was derived from the Arabian plus the native mares. Some happy nick in Messenger's immediate ancestry was undoubtedly responsible for the propensity of his get in the harness and saddle categories. See also *MAMBRINO*.

M.F.H. MASTER OF FOX HOUNDS

The "Master" is ruler and, where his

pack is concerned, his word is law. He may or may not hunt his own hounds. Sometimes a professional huntsman is employed for that purpose, but he is responsible for the routine of stable and kennel, for deciding what terrain is to be worked and when, and for all things pertaining to the Hunt. The Master must be a man of great diplomacy for he has to blend two opposing points of view to his purpose. The members of his hunt, for the most part, are interested only in the sport he can show. The farmers over whose land he hunts want the foxes exterminated with the least possible danger to their crops and fences. It takes a man of strong character and persuasive tongue to satisfy both factions.

Certain rules of etiquette are observed in the hunt field. One of these is that gentlemen always tip their hats to the Master. Another, that one does not pass him when hounds are running except at his suggestion. It is also *de rigueur* to thank the Master at the end of the day for the sport he has provided. It is probably the ambition of every enthusiastic young "Thruster" to some day be Master of his own pack. Perhaps if he knew the trials and tribulations which the exalted position carries with it he would not be so anxious. See also *APPOINTMENTS, Hunting; HUNTING.*

MIDDLE DISTANCE
A medium-length run, up to 1¼ miles.

MIDDLEWEIGHT
Hunters that are capable of carrying a hundred and eighty-five pounds to hounds are classified as "middleweight" hunters. See also *HUNTERS, How Classified.*

MIXED GAITS
Many "gaited" horses have a tendency to mix their gaits, breaking from one to the other. They should be carefully schooled out of this habit and taught to take and keep the desired gait on command.

MOLARS
The molars are the large grinding teeth of the horse. There are twelve in each jaw. The upper jaw is wider than the lower and the upper molars grow downwards and outwards, the lower molars inwards and upwards, consequently, the outer side of the upper and the inner side of the lower molars get no wear; hence the enamel grows into sharp points which lacerate the cheeks and tongue and prevent mastication. This is one of the most common causes of poor condition in horses. The horse can only digest what he has properly chewed. If the grain goes into his stomach still whole or only slightly broken up, it will pass right through him and do him no good. Horses should have their teeth examined and "floated" (the sharp edges filed off) every six months. A molar may sometimes split and become decayed. In this case the molar below or above it will grow to a superfluous length causing great pain and perhaps entirely preventing the horse from chewing. See also *TEETH.*

MONGOLIAN PONIES
These incredibly tough little beasts are certainly not pretty but they are exceedingly strong and fleet. Something of their stamina is made apparent by the custom of the owner, often a heavy and large man, who mounts his thirteen-two animal, rides him at a dead run for mile after mile until he is in a full lather though the temperature may be many degrees below zero, and halts from the gallop at his destination. His host appears, carrying a pail of water. This is flung over the pony and promptly freezes into an overcoat of ice. The animal is now tied outside, but his ice overcoat keeps the heat of his body inside and he apparently thrives on this treatment. See also *GRIFFIN.*

MONKEY DRILL (mounted gymnastics)
A system of exercises to induce confidence and suppleness in the rider. The Cossacks were the original exponents of

this branch of horsemanship and the American Indians were also noted for their feats of skill along these lines. Vaulting on and off galloping horses, standing on one or two horses or standing on two while straddling a third, riding in pyramid formation (see Figure 40) are among the most familiar of these exercises. See also *MOUNTED GYMNASTICS*. See *GYMNASTICS—mounted*.

MORGAN HORSE

In 1747 at West Springfield, Mass. a man was born whose name was destined to become familiar throughout the United States as well as in far countries wherever knowledge of the horse was deemed valuable. Schoolteacher, singer, consumptive, with little physical stamina Justin Morgan the man is famous for one thing only, that of having been the owner and breeder of Justin Morgan the horse. And Justin Morgan the horse is the only horse whose name has been given to a recognized breed. Other names such as "Hambletonian" are strains or

FIGURE 73. STATUE OF JUSTIN MORGAN, THE FAMOUS SIRE OF THE BREED THAT BEARS HIS NAME. *COURTESY MORGAN HORSE CLUB.*

families but the progeny of Justin Morgan are a breed different from every other.

There is and will always be some difference of opinion as to the exact lineage of Justin Morgan the horse, but the consensus of opinion seems to be that he was sired by Beautiful Bay (also known as "True Briton") . The dam is nameless though she is supposed to have been of the "Wild-air" breed, sired by *Diamond* son of *Wild-air* who was also known as the *Church* horse. That Justin Morgan was mainly of Thoroughbred and thus Arab blood is unquestionable, and that he also had some cold blood in him **is** shown by his shaggy fetlocks and the type of muscular strength for which he was famous. The characteristic which has made Justin Morgan the best known sire in the world is his extreme prepotency. Every Morgan horse is descended directly from this one stallion, and though there is obviously no such thing as a "pure-blood" Morgan, for one cannot have a pure-blood horse from any one animal, yet so prepotent was Justin Morgan that his get retain his physical characteristics and temperament generation after generation.

FIGURE 74.
THE MORGAN OF TODAY. *COURTESY MORGAN HORSE CLUB.*

The Morgans are a small breed. Originally they were from fourteen to fifteen hands in height weighing from eight hundred to a thousand pounds. Justin Morgan himself was fourteen hands, a mere pony. They have delicate heads, tapering necks, short legs, extremely heavy shoulders with great width at the brisket, short backs (one skeleton of a Morgan shows the absence of a lumbar vertebra, proving the Arabian ancestry) , heavy, well-set tails and good quarters. In disposition they are gentle and docile. Although Justin Morgan the man used his colt mainly as a Saddler it is as a roadhorse that the Morgans have become famous. They antedated the Hambletonians and were among the speediest of harness horses. Their gait is smooth and quick stepping with little elevation. Justin Morgan the stallion was also noted for his weight pulling abilities and for his prowess as a sprinter under the saddle. He was reputed to have been unbeaten in his neighborhood as trotter, sprinter and weight-puller, and on holidays he appeared as a parade horse!

Justin Morgan begat three stallions of whose progeny there remain enough to be termed "families." These families are the "Bulrush," the "Sherman" and the "Woodbury." The Bulrush family, mostly bays and browns with black points and a complete absence of any white marking such as stars or socks were common in Vermont and in upper Connecticut. They were very strong but had not the fineness of the other families. The Woodburys, coming from Vermont also, were deemed the best types for years. They were much finer and had a more commanding appearance than the Bulrushes. They ran to bays and chestnuts often with a white blaze.

The third family, the Sherman family, though smaller than the other two, were the foundation stock for another great family, the "Black Hawks." And from the Black Hawks came one of the world's most famous trotters, Ethan Allen.

As generations of horses succeeded each other and the speed of the Morgans was superseded by that of the Hambletonians, the former lost their position as top harness racers but remained favorites as generally useful light horses. Where at first they had been native only to New England, California and Texas took them up and today there are more Morgans bred in the West than in the East. By mixing the blood with that of other strains several types of Morgans have been developed. We have the general type, the Saddler and the cowpony. Though they vary somewhat in appearance yet they all have old Justin Morgan's splendid physical development, stamina and even disposition. See also *JUSTIN MORGAN, HARNESS RACING; RECORDS AND STATISTICS— HARNESS RACING* (Appendix).

MORGAN HORSE CLUB
Address 90 Broad St., New York City.

Publisher of the Morgan Register, est. 1894. Registrations from 1930 to 1942 incl., 2,414, yearly average 186.

MOUNT (v.)

There are several systems of mounting and one should use that which is most suitable for the horse. The accepted method for horsemanship classes is for the rider to stand at the near shoulder of the horse facing rear. The reins are grasped in the left hand, short enough to give the rider control if the horse should move. If the horse has a tendency to wheel away from the rider with his hindquarters, the off rein may be held tighter than the near with the horse's head bent slightly away; this will help prevent the movement of the hindquarters. The rider takes a lock of the mane in his left hand together with the reins. Holding his stirrup with his right hand he puts his left foot into it, bending his knee and bracing it against the horse's shoulder. He should be careful not to dig the horse in the belly with his toe. He then puts his right hand on the pommel of the saddle and springs from the ball of the right foot. The right foot is carried well over the quarters to avoid touching them and the rider should endeavor to keep the weight on his left foot landing very lightly in the saddle.

The above method is good for several reasons. If the horse has the habit of moving forward when he feels the weight of the rider the latter will not be "left behind." Some horses have the unpleasant habit of kicking forward with the back foot at the rider as he stands preparing to mount. If the latter is foolish enough to face front he is apt to get the kick in the small of his back. The army method of mounting is similar to that described above, except, that the man stands with his head turned to the front in order to watch his leader, and rests his right hand on the cantle. The objection to this method is that if the rider pulls too hard on the cantle he is apt to displace the saddle; furthermore he must move his hand while in mid-air as otherwise it will be in the way of his leg.

A short person mounting a tall horse, especially one which has the habit of backing away from the rider will be able to mount more readily if he stands about even with the cantle of the saddle facing front, the reins in his right hand. But this method should never be used unless absolutely necessary and certainly never unless the horse is known not to kick.

When mounting colts or very restive horses it is best to be given a "hand up" rather than use the stirrups. An assistant takes the left ankle of the person mounting and gives him a quick lift. (See also *HAND UP*). It is also possible to mount the horse both from the side and from the rear by vaulting. In the former the rider puts one hand on the withers and the other on the back or seat of the saddle and springs up straightening his arms. He then swings his leg over. In vaulting on over the hindquarters the rider takes a run and puts a hand on either side of the rump, springing up and forward. A very active rider can vault on from the rear and land standing up. Needless to say, the horse must be well schooled for this type of vaulting which is one of the exercises in "Monkey Drill."

Whatever method of mounting is used certain principles must be followed. The rider should coordinate his spring and his lift putting as little weight as possible on his hands to avoid shifting the saddle. He should be careful not to touch saddle or horse as he swings his leg over and he should settle into the seat as lightly as he possibly can.

MOUNTED DRILL

The primary purpose of mounted drill is to enable leaders to conduct a large body of mounted men from one point to another without confusion. However, for the ordinary horseman it has a second purpose, for there is nothing to equal this type of formation riding in teaching control of the horse. On an oral com-

mand each rider must execute a figure which requires that he increase or decrease his gait or change his position in relation to the other riders, and that he maintain exactly this new gait and position. Any rider beyond the earliest stages of his experience can manage a quiet horse if he is not required to maintain this exact control, but in learning to do so the neophyte will find many problems the solution of which will increase his own skill and enjoyment.

Mounted drill also provides variation for groups of riders, both in an indoor arena and outside in a wider area. To be successful, however, there are a few rules which must be adhered to.

Leaders. The leader or director can either ride at the head of the column, which would be his normal position in army maneuvers, or he can ride on the flank and give commands which are repeated by another leader riding at the head of the column. By so doing he can make corrections and teach the movements as needed.

Commands. The commands are given in two parts—the command of preparation, which tells the riders what they are about to do, and the command of execution (the word *HO*), which tells them to do it. For example, when the riders are in single file (column of troopers) the commander wanting to get them up into twos gives the command *Column of twos* (the command of preparation) then after a pause gives the command *HO*. (Sometimes the command *NOW* is used instead of *HO*.)

Voice. The tone of voice used in giving the commands is extremely important. The command of preparation is given in a sustained tone, the command of execution in a tone of finality. Where the gait is being decreased the command of execution is given in a lower tone of voice to indicate this.

Definition of Terms

Army terminology is very exact and simple. The following are the most commonly used terms:

About. Any command containing the

word *about* means that when the movement is completed the riders will be moving in the opposite direction from the original one.

Column. A file of riders, one behind the other.

Column of troopers. A single file.

Columns of twos or fours. A file of riders, riding in pairs or four abreast.

Distance. The space between riders when measured from the front of the column to the end of it. The normal distance is four feet from one horse's tail to the nose of the horse behind him.

File Closers. One or two riders not assigned to a regular squad who ride last in the column. They are usually sergeants or corporals and, in military maneuvers, have special duties, such as acting as road guards, when they ride to the front and station themselves at cross roads to control traffic while the column rides between them. They also repeat the oral commands and make corrections or relay information when the director is also the leader and riding at the head of the line. In practicing in an area enclosed or marked-off for instruction purposes it is sometimes wise to let the least experienced horsemen ride as file closers without assuming any of the duties mentioned above, as this is an easier position than riding in the ranks.

Decrease the front. Reducing the number of riders riding abreast. (Coming down from *line* to *column of fours* or from the latter to *column of troopers* would be *decreasing the front.*)

Increase the front. To change formation so that the number of riders riding abreast is increased (*column of troopers* to *column of fours,* for example).

Interval. The space between riders going from flank to flank. The normal interval between horsemen riding side by side is three inches from toe to toe, six inches from knee to knee. Both intervals and distances may be increased on command of the leader.

Move to the flank. To move at right angles of the line of march. Thus if riders are in a column of troopers and the command "By the right flank . . . *ho-o-o!*" is given, all riders turn to the right and continue across the hall to the opposite side.

Platoon. A platoon consists of three or more squads.

Squad. A normal squad is eight riders. The squad leader is number one of that squad. For groups of riders of sixteen or less it is more practical to drill with half-squads, in which case a squad consists of four riders.

Mounted Drill may be classified as *"open order drill"* or *"close order drill."* In the latter the intervals and distances are as stated (six inches knee to knee between riders riding abreast and four feet from nose to tail between horses following each other). In open order drill the distances are increased so that a platoon riding in line becomes a line of skirmishers, etc.

General Rules

All commands are given in two parts, as stated. The command of preparation, having been given by the leader (or by an instructor), is repeated by each squad leader. The command of execution is then given and the movement is executed.

In increasing the front all the riders except the leader and the rider (or riders) in the first element directly behind him increase the gait instantly and continue at the increased gait until each individual comes into his new position, when he resumes the original gait.

In decreasing the front all riders except the leader and the first element behind him decrease the gait one degree (trot to walk, walk to halt, etc.) while the leader and the first element move out at the new order at the original gait, being followed by the succeeding elements in the new order at the original gait.

MOUNTED GYMNASTICS

A system of exercises used in all modern cavalry training to induce confidence and flexibility in the rider. The horses

FIGURE 75. TEACHING THE BE-
GINNER TO PICK UP HIS REINS
AND GET THEM THE RIGHT
LENGTH BEFORE MOUNTING.

FIGURE 76. POSITION OF RIDER
AT "PREPARE TO MOUNT."

FIGURE 77. MOUNTING BY NUM-
BERS. POSITION AT THE COUNT
OF "ONE."

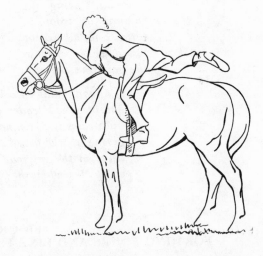

FIGURE 78. MOUNTING BY NUM-
BERS. POSITION AT THE COUNT
OF "TWO."

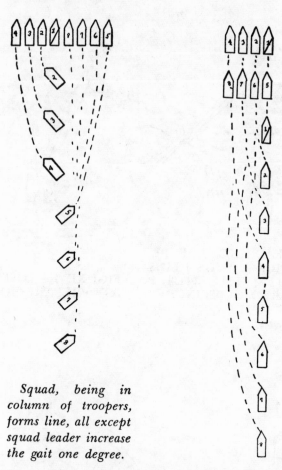

Squad, being in column of troopers, forms line, all except squad leader increase the gait one degree.

Squad, being in column of troopers, forms fours, all except squad leader increase the gait one degree. In both cases if a command to decrease the gait has been given only the squad leader slows down, the others continue at the original gait until the new formation is completed when they take up the new gait.

FIGURE 79.
FORMING FOURS AND LINE FROM COLUMN OF TROOPERS.

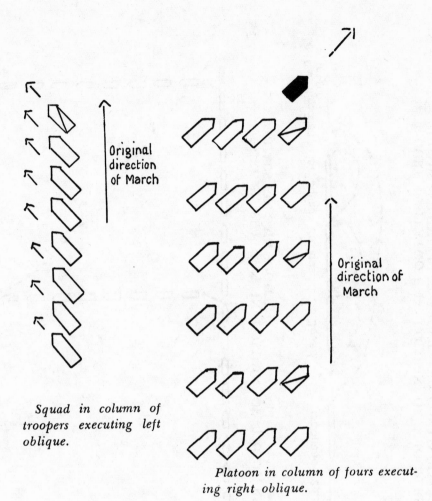

Original
direction
of March

Original
direction of
March

Squad in column of troopers executing left oblique.

Platoon in column of fours executing right oblique.

FIGURE 80. THE OBLIQUES.

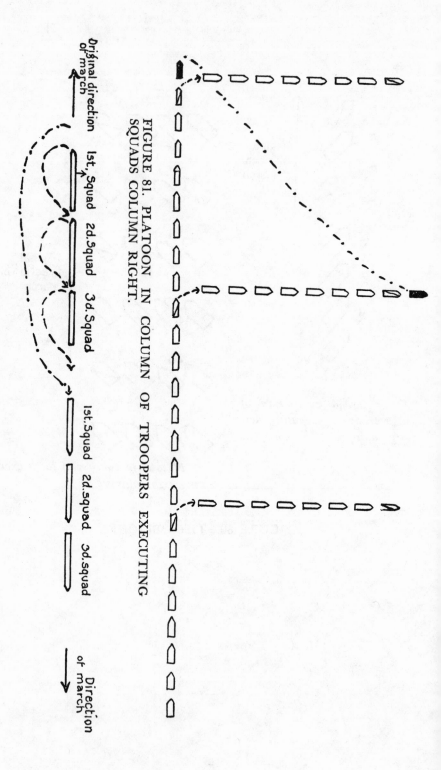

FIGURE 81. PLATOON IN COLUMN OF TROOPERS EXECUTING
SQUADS COLUMN RIGHT.

FIGURE 82. PLATOON IN COLUMN OF TROOPERS EXECUTING
SQUADS COLUMN LEFT ABOUT AND CONTINUING THE MARCH.

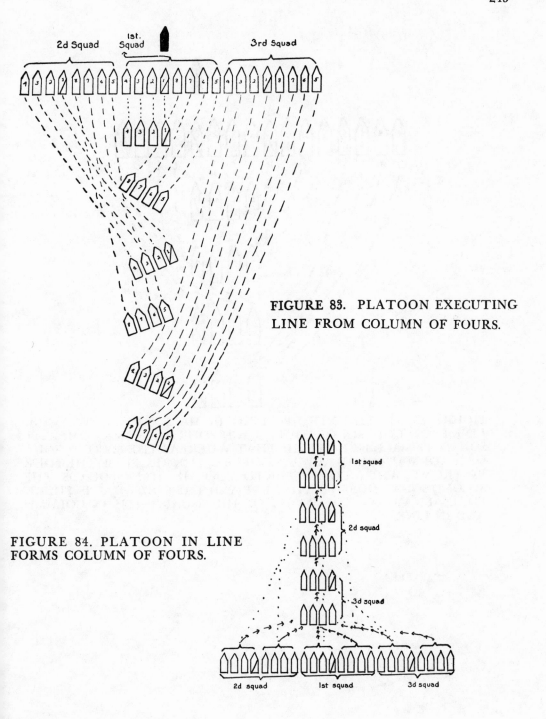

FIGURE 83. PLATOON EXECUTING
LINE FROM COLUMN OF FOURS.

FIGURE 84. PLATOON IN LINE
FORMS COLUMN OF FOURS.

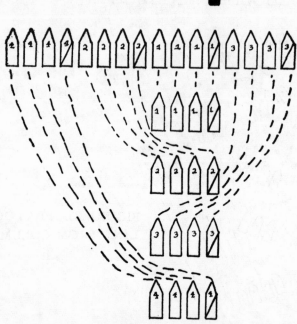

FIGURE 85. SMALL UNIT DRILLING IN HALF SQUADS. FORMING
LINE FROM COLUMN OF FOURS. EACH FOUR ACTS AS A COMPLETE
SQUAD. IT WILL BE NOTICED THAT WHEREAS THE SECOND FOUR
OF A NORMAL SQUAD ALWAYS GOES TO THE RIGHT OF THE FOUR
IN FRONT WHEN COMING INTO LINE, IN HALF SQUADS THE
SECOND SQUAD GOES TO THE LEFT AND THE CORPORAL IS THERE-
FORE ALWAYS ON THE RIGHT OF HIS SQUAD BOTH IN COLUMN
AND IN LINE.

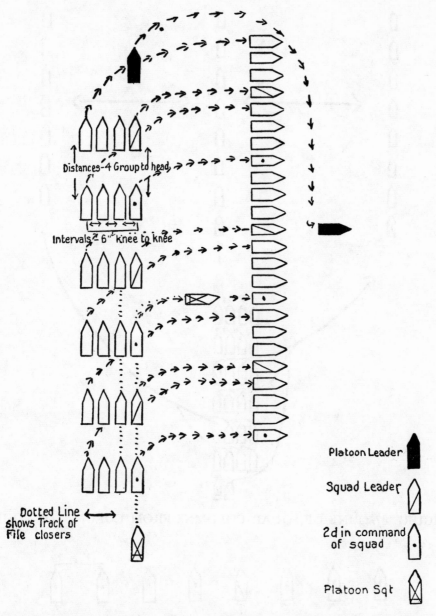

Distances—4 Group to head

Intervals 2 6" knee to knee

Dotted Line shows Track of File closers

Platoon Leader

Squad Leader

2d in command of squad

Platoon Sgt

FIGURE 86. FOURS RIGHT. PLATOON IN COLUMNS OF FOURS EXECUTES FOURS RIGHT AND CONTINUES THE MARCH.

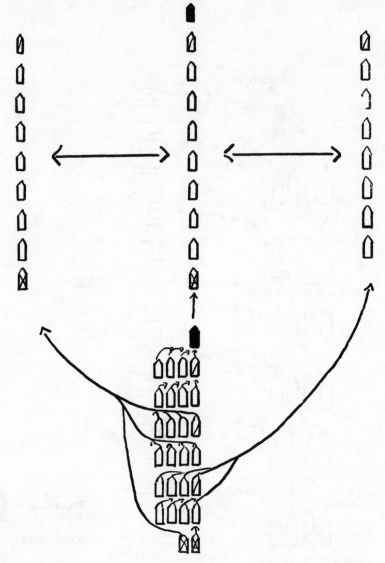

FIGURE 87. LINE OF SQUAD COLUMNS FROM COLUMN OF FOURS.

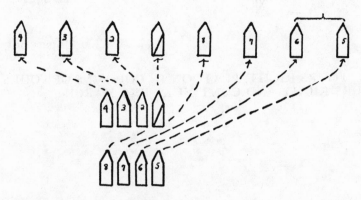

FIGURE 88.

FORAGERS FROM COLUMN OF FOUR FORMED BY SQUAD.

FIGURE 89. ARM SIGNALS USED IN MOUNTED DRILL.

are specially schooled to allow the riders to vault on and off over the hindquarters or from the side at all gaits. The riders ride standing at a gallop on one or two horses, or on two while straddling a third. Pyramid riding (see illus. 40, page 125) is also popular. The "scissors" in which the rider crosses his legs behind him and, with a sudden twist of his body, lands facing in the opposite direction, somersaulting off over the tail, doing a handstand on the withers, etc., are all familiar movements. The Cossacks and the American Indians were the two foremost exponents of this form of riding. See also *MONKEY DRILL; GYMNAS-TICS—mounted.*

MOUNTED TROOPS

Organized riding for children in the form of mounted cavalry troops is excellent for stimulating interest and developing both good horsemen and good citizens. There are a number of these in different parts of the country and the work they do is very beneficial. For complete description of the formation and running of such a troop see *The Complete Book of Horses and Ponies* by the author of this encyclopedia.

MOVING PICTURES (use of in teaching)

One of the most satisfactory methods of showing the rider both his good and his bad habits in riding and in jumping is by the method of moving pictures. The instructor should carry the camera slung around his neck and take frequent shots so that the riders lose self-consciousness. He may even pretend to be taking pictures when actually he is not doing so until his class hardly notices when the camera is focused on them. When the pictures are shown suggestions may be made as to improvement. Slow motion pictures are especially valuable for this purpose.

It is interesting to note that Leland Stanford in proving that there is a period at the trot when all four feet of the horse are off the ground at the same time, was really the originator of the moving pictures. He had a series of stills taken by mechanically controlled cameras and then flashed them quickly on a screen one after the other. The effect was jerky but it showed that the appearance of movement could be obtained in this way.

Modern race tracks are equipped with a most unusual type of moving picture camera. This camera has an open shutter and registers only moving objects. It is focused on the finish line. See also *DEAD HEATS.*

MUD

Mud is both a fine therapeutical agent and the cause of much trouble in the stable. The horse whose feet are not cleaned properly may easily develop a condition known as "scratches" or "mud fever" at the back of the pastern. This condition is extremely painful and may well lay the horse up for some little time. On the other hand horses which are lame from hard, dried out soles may be helped by having the feet packed with mud. Horses with laminitis are greatly benefited by being allowed to stand in thick, cold mud baths.

MUD FEVER

See *INJURIES, Cracked heels or scratches.*

MUSCLES (of the horse)

The type of muscles desirable in a horse depend upon the kind of work he is expected to do. The draft horse should have bunchy, thick muscles. These are most capable of intense strength and weight pulling qualities. The running horse needs long, flat, flexible muscles. These give greater speed and jumping ability. The muscular development or potential development is extremely important in judging the conformation of the horse. The horse whose muscles are flabby and slack will simply not have sufficient stamina to stand a day's hunting or a long pack trip. The muscles are attached to the bones by means of the tendons. By contraction of the muscle and consequent shortening of the tendon, movement is made possible. Weak muscles mean weak tendons, weak legs and a useless animal. A horse that has just been brought in from a season of freedom must be "muscled up" slowly. Otherwise irreparable injury will be done to the tendons. Much slow work at a walk or a jog trot will do more to muscle him up than short quick gallops. Walking up and down hill is especially valuable for this purpose. Frequent and thorough grooming is also a great "toner up" of muscles. Be sure your horse is in good muscular condition before you call on him for strenuous work, it is far more important than mere fat. See *DRESSAGE, COLT, Training of.*

MUSIC (hound)
See *HUNTING TERMS.*

MUSIC (use of in teaching)
In work in a riding hall, especially with young beginners, music can be very stimulating. Horses have a tendency to keep time to music. If your class is practicing the jog trot without stirrups a slow rhythm will insure a steady, slow pace. A more vigorous trot will be induced by livelier music. The waltz is the proper music for the canter or gallop as the latter is a three-beat gait. Gay polkas and fast marches will inspire rider and horse alike. Children relax better and seem to be able to post more easily when there is music. The easiest method of introducing music in the riding hall is by means of a public address system with loud speakers. The victrola attachment should be in one piece with the amplifier, and the loud speakers should be distributed around so that the music may be heard at every point. The microphone will also be useful to the instructor, particularly for directing music rides, etc.

MUSIC RIDES or MUSICAL RIDE
A music ride is a formation ride in which the riders go through previously rehearsed figures to music. There are any number of these figures and the ingenious person can make up others. Riding in twos and fours, separating and coming together again, crossing the ring from opposite corners, the riders alternating as they cross; wheeling, etc., are a few of the most common. The music ride differs from mounted drill in that the figures are rehearsed and not simply executed on command. The figures are also much more diverse. Music rides are very beneficial for teaching control of the horse, they are a pleasant diversion for groups that must ride indoors during bad weather and are good for exhibition purposes. Various cavalry units often give beautiful exhibitions of music rides at the National Horse Show at Madison Square Garden. The horses are matched in color, the riders in fancy dress carrying lances and the whole is as beautiful as a ballet.

MUSICAL CHAIRS
This is a game suitable for gymkhanas. A circle of chairs is placed in the center of the ring. The riders ride in pairs and there is one chair fewer than pairs. The music starts and the riders follow each other around the chairs. When the music stops one rider of each pair dismounts and runs to get in a chair. Each time one pair loses, it leaves the ring and a chair is removed. The game may also be played with the riders not in pairs in which case the rider must lead his horse to the chair before sitting in it.

MUSICAL STALLS
This is a game suitable for intermediate riders. Bars are placed on the ground to form stalls. They should be about eight feet long and be placed parallel to each other in a row, each bar about four feet from the next. There should be one fewer stalls than riders. The riders ride around the ring or hall keeping to the wall. When the music stops they race for the stalls, ride in and stop. They should only be allowed to come into the stalls from a specified side and should all be facing the same way. They are not al-

lowed to cross through the center but must go around an end. As one rider is left out each time he leaves the ring and a bar is removed. When the riders are reduced to two or three they should be required to separate and to canter as long as the music is going.

MUSTANG

The small hardy horse of the Western plains is known as the mustang. He is a direct descendant of the Spanish horses brought over by Cortez. He therefore, as do all modern light breeds, goes back to the desert stock. He is not to be confused with the wild horses so often found in the West which are a mixture of breeds and have greatly deteriorated in stamina and appearance.

N

NAIL IN THE FOOT

This constitutes one of the more serious puncture wounds in as much as the horse's foot is in contact with the ground in which is found the tetanus bacillus. If the nail goes in deeply enough to draw blood the blacksmith should be called and the wound well cleaned out and opened. The foot may then be soaked for a short time in Epsom salts or lysol solution after which Churchill's iodine should be poured into the wound. The foot and wall should be felt every few hours for signs of fever. Do not delay in calling the veterinarian if such a symptom occurs as he may consider it advisable to give the animal a tetanus shot.

NARRAGANSETT PACER

In Revolutionary times racing was forbidden by law and religion in all the New England states except Baptist Rhode Island. Here a noble breed of horses was developed, namely, the Narragansett Pacer. They are said to have had a smooth gliding motion rather than the usual "side-wheelers' " churning gait and were very popular not only in the state where they were bred but also with the Virginia plantation owners who imported them into their state. However, though the Virginia gentleman was glad to have a pacer for riding purposes, he did not care to race them, feeling that the Thoroughbred was the sporting horse, but the Rhode Islanders enjoyed racing them though no very accurate accounts of their speed were kept.

NATIONAL CUTTING HORSE ASSOCIATION

P. O. Box 12155, Fort Worth, Texas. Organized in 1946. Its purpose is to formulate and supervise the enforcement of rules for competitions for Cutting Horses, to encourage and promote interest in the breeding, training and competition of the Cutting Horse and to assist the operation of such competitions by providing qualified judges, assistants, etc. It publishes a monthly magazine, *Cuttin' Hoss Chatter,* which is distributed to all its active members. Also an annual booklet, with complete rules for judging Cutting Horse Competitions, lists of current and past champions, list of members and other pertinent information. This booklet may be obtained by writing to the Association. The present Officers of the National Cutting Horse Association are:

H. L. Akin, *President,* Route 3, 1320 North 14th Street, Frederick, Oklahoma;

J. D. Craft, *Vice-President,* P. O. Box 825, Jacksboro, Texas;

Dean Sage, *Regional Vice-President,* Triangle T Ranch, Sheridan, Wyoming;

Leslie H. (Les) Geddes, *Regional Vice-President,* 2220 Clinton Street, Rockford, Illinois;

Zack T. Wood, Jr., *Regional Vice-President,* Tillar, Arkansas;

Byron Matthews, *Chairman Executive Committee,* 412 North Fielder, Arlington, Texas;

Beverly Thompson, *Acting Secretary-Treasurer,* NCHA Business Office, P. O. Box 12155, Fort Worth, Texas.

NAVEL (treatment at birth)

When the foal is born the navel should at once be painted with iodine; failure to do this may result in a serious infectious disease known as *joint evil.* See also *BIRTH, COLTS; BROOD MARES; JOINT EVIL.*

NAVICULAR DISEASE

This is a corrosive ulcer on the navicular bone in the foot. It is incurable and eventually the horse will have to be destroyed. It may be caused by a variety of things including improper shoeing, too much fast or strenuous work on hard ground, contracted heels, conformation (horses with short, upright pasterns are more prone to navicular disease than the long sloping type which are better as shock absorbers) or it may be hereditary.

The symptoms are a tendency to "point" one foot and then the other in the stable, a narrowing of the foot and turning in of the toes, lameness when the horse first leaves the stable, and heat in the foot after use. The horse may be shod with pads or he may have his feet packed with white rock or clay. Cold wet packs also relieve the pain but there is no cure and the horse will become worse and worse.

NEAPOLITAN NOSEBAND

The Neapolitan noseband is similar to the Western hackamore but even more severe. The loop encircling the nose is of metal with two metal shanks. The leverage is such that it would be easily possible to crush the bones of the lower part of the skull. This same type of noseband was used by the Libyans and a less severe type but one on the same principle is to be seen in Arabia today.

NEAR SIDE

The left side of a horse is known as the "near side." In England the traffic keeps to the left, therefore in working around a horse the coachman usually stood on the left side if possible to be on the side of the road. The custom of mounting on the near or left side originated in the early days when horsemen wore swords. The latter, hanging on the left for convenience, would have interfered with the rider by hanging between his legs should be mount from the right. As the horseman was therefore most often on the left side of his horse this came to be known as the "near" side. The right side is known as the "off" side. In a pair of horses the one on the left is known as the "near" horse, the one on the right the "off" horse.

NECK

The shape and carriage of the horse's neck varies with his breeding as well as with his individual conformation. In a horse that must travel at speed such as a Thoroughbred or a roadster the neck should be slender and flexible with not too much of an arch. It should be remembered that the longer the neck the smaller should be the head or the horse will be heavy in the forehand and badly balanced.

The Saddler has a thicker and more arched neck than the roadster or racer and he has much more flexion at the poll. This should not be too exaggerated, however. The draft horse has great strength in his neck.

In selecting the children's pony the one with the draft type of neck should be avoided as he will be a puller. Rather, choose the pony with the fine neck indicating flexibility.

A ewe-neck is one in which the curve is reversed and the neck dips down from crest to withers. The ewe-necked horse is generally hammer headed and sometimes holds his head in such a peculiar position that his ears will very nearly brush the rider's chin.

The windpipe should be large and

well defined as this makes it easier for the horse to breathe when he is running. The neck should be tapering towards the head and well muscled up at the shoulders and withers.

NECK REINING

This is a method of asking the horse to turn by carrying the reins, which at the time are held in one hand, to the side towards which the horse is intended to go. The touch of the rein on the opposite side of his neck tells him to turn. It is a Western term and a Western method of using the reins, and should not be confused with the ordinary use of the indirect rein as described under *REIN EFFECTS*. A horse that "neck reins" is also said to be "bridle wise." The difference in this use of the rein, essential in the control of stock horses, polo ponies, etc., where the rider must keep one hand free for his work, is that there is no continuous contact with the horse's mouth and therefore no exact communication and control of the horse. The horse turns in the easiest way possible; it can be on his center, forehand or hindquarters, depending on how fast he is going. Teaching the horse to neck rein is very simple. The trainer uses his legs and his direct rein as well until the horse learns what is wanted.

NECKWEAR

For informal hacking and cubbing, as well as for country shows, there are a variety of types of neckwear available, ranging from the turtleneck sweater to the colored stock, and including special shirts with bow ties of self material and simple but colorful "chokers." For even more informal riding, an open-neck shirt or an ordinary shirt with a man's tie is correct. For formal hunting and for Hunter classes one of course wears the regulation white stock tied in an Ascot knot. Saddle Horse riders wear white stocks also but do not use the Ascot knot.

NEW FOREST PONY

This pony is native to Hampshire, England. Its origin is somewhat obscure though native ponies have lived in the New Forest for many hundreds of years. Queen Victoria, wishing to refine and improve the breed, allowed her Arabian stallion "Zorah" to run wild there for eight years. Inasmuch as the terrain is very rough and often boggy and the forage is sparse, these ponies are among the hardiest, most easily kept and sure-footed of all. They are bigger than other shire breeds, running from twelve hands to fourteen-two. Since many roads cross the moors the ponies are accustomed to traffic from birth and are not afraid of it; they are also more used to seeing people and so are more friendly and more easily trained, and make unusually steady, comfortable "family" ponies, both for riding and driving.

NEW HOPE
See *FEEDS*.

NIPPING
See *VICES*.

NOSEBAND
See Figure 45, page 135, See also *CAVESSON*.

NOSE
See Figure 51, page 150, *HORSE, Points of*.

NOSE BLEEDING

This is a fairly common occurrence and is due to a broken blood vessel. Usually it will stop of itself. Cold compresses may be applied to the outside of the nose and cold water may be syringed up the nostrils. If the bleeding persists the horse may be given a shot of adrenalin and he may have calcium lactate added to his food. Sudden gushing of blood at the nose if the horse has just hit his head is an indication of a fractured skull.

On no account try and stop bleeding at the nose by plugging the nostrils as a horse cannot breathe through his mouth and will die of suffocation.

NOVICE

A horse or rider is considered a novice until he has won three first ribbons in the division in which he is being shown.

NOVICE CLASSES

Novice classes are open to novice horses or riders. The jumps in these classes do not generally exceed three feet six inches. See also *HORSE SHOW CLASSES, Novice.*

NURSING

It is important that the foal nurse as soon as he is strong enough to stand which will be a few minutes after birth. The milk at this time contains vitamins and also a laxative element which will help to clean him out. Sometimes the foal seems unbelievably stupid. He will try everywhere except the right place for his food. He may even go over and start sucking on the stall door. Sometimes too, the mare is impatient especially if her bag is very full or if it is the first foal. In difficult cases one person should hold the mare while another helps the foal. If the person who is handling the foal will stand behind him bracing his body against the foal's hindquarters he can then use both hands to direct the head and if necessary milk a few drops into the mouth. Patience and persistence is necessary and on no account should the mare and foal be left after foaling until the foal is standing and sucking. See also *COLTS; BROOD MARE; BIRTH.*

O

OATS

Oats usually form the major portion of the grain ration of horses used for fast work. They should be plump, heavy and sweet. They should not be discolored nor dusty. Oats are more easily digested and assimilated if crushed or "crimped."

Many large stables have their own oat crushers; if crushed oats are bought it should be from a firm or dealer that guarantees its produce as the tendency is to use the less good oats for this purpose. Oats may be mixed with bran, three or four parts oats to one of bran by bulk. The normal feed for a horse weighing a thousand pounds and doing ordinary work is from nine to twelve pounds per day of oats or oats and bran mixed, given in three feedings. See also *FEED.*

ODDS-ON

A bet in which the bettor risks more money than he can win. If the bettor makes and wins a bet of ten dollars at one to two for example, he will get back his original ten plus five more, making fifteen dollars in all.

OFF SIDE

The right side of the horse is known as the "off" side. In a pair or team of horses the one on the right is known as the "off" horse. See also *NEAR SIDE.*

ON THE BIT

The horse is said to be "on the bit" when he works willingly and at the desired gait and pace through instructions given him by the rider who maintains a constant and light pressure on the bit and a light feel with his legs. It takes a great deal of training to teach the horse that he must accept this light pressure and learn to push against it rather than avoid it. In the extended gaits, for example, the horse actually learns to depend on a stronger and stronger pressure of the bit and lean on it to keep his balance as he takes longer and longer strides.

OPEN JUMPER

An "open jumper" is a horse considered suitable to compete in the "open" classes. Such a horse is judged on performance alone. A hunter is judged on manners and conformation but the jumper in an "open" class that gets over the most jumps with the fewest "faults" wins regardless of how he behaves or what he looks like. See also—*JUMPERS— JUMPING; HORSE SHOW CLASSES, hunter division.*

OPEN JUMPING CLASSES

An open jumper class is one that is open to all horses regardless of breed, age, size, experience or conformation. See *HORSE SHOW CLASSES, hunter division.*

OPHTHALMIA

Ophthalmia is a very serious disease of the eyes about which little is known. It is an infection or abscess behind the eye ball. Some veterinarians believe that the trouble starts from a clogged up tear-duct and advocate syringing this out with a boric acid solution followed by application of a silver oxide product or a sulfa ointment in the eye. To syringe out the tear-duct the tiny opening in the nostril must first be located. By opening the nostril it will be seen several inches up the nose against the center wall of the nostril. A hypodermic syringe fitted with a special blunt end or point should be used and the solution sprayed up the tear-duct until it is cleared. This is indicated by clear water running out of the other end of the duct at the eye. The ointment is then put inside the lower lid. Vitamins are also prescribed. The symptoms of ophthalmia are first a watering of the eye which would confirm the theory that the duct is clogged, followed by the whole eye turning a greenish opaque color. The opaqueness gradually reduces in area until there is a small spot behind the pupil. This disappears in a few days but the eye ball is left with a bluish tinge and the sight is more or less impaired. Ophthalmia is usually recurrent and often passes from one eye to the other, the horse, after a series of attacks, going blind. It is very painful and the animal should be kept in darkness until the acute stage has passed.

OPPOSITION (reins of)
See *REINS.*

ORNAMENTS (bridle)

Bridle ornaments are common on driving bridles and on the type of riding bridle where the throat latch is separate from the crown-piece. In the latter case they are essential to keep the brow-band from falling down over the nose. Cavalry horses usually wear copper ornaments with the seal of the United States embossed on them. In Victorian times some of the bridle ornaments were very elaborate, being of metal, glass or china with colored flowers or other designs on them. They are often bought by antique shops and made over into curtain tie-back holders. A well turned out carriage horse generally wore metal bridle ornaments with the initials or monogram of the owner thereon.

OUTLAW

A horse that cannot be ridden or is so wild as not to be worth the breaking is termed an "outlaw."

OVERFEEDING

Horses have small stomachs and, unlike ponies and mules, will eat themselves sick. Furthermore, a horse that from illness or some other cause is not being exercised will overeat and should have his normal ration reduced by at least a third.

OVER RUN (to over run the scent)
See *HUNTING TERMS.*

OWN (to own the scent)
See *HUNTING TERMS.*

P

PACE

The pace is a two beat gait in which the lateral legs move together. As a rule it is a rough gait under the saddle with an uncomfortable rolling "side to side" motion though there are exceptions to this. The very slow pace is permitted as a "slow gait" in the five-gaited Saddler. The fast or racing pace is often faster than a trot, but it has one disadvantage in that if the horse breaks into a canter he cannot get back into the pace. It was not until "hopples" were invented in 1885 that the racing of pacers became really popular.

PACERS

The pacing stock came from the same stock as both the trotters and the five-gaited Saddlers, tracing their descent back through Rysdyk's Hambletonian to old Messenger. Rhode Island developed a breed known as "Narragansett Pacer" (see this text) which had an unusually smooth gait and many of which were sent to Virginia for the plantation owners. Sleepy Tom, a totally blind pacing horse which had been bought at the age of twelve for goods amounting to an estimated valuation of about thirty dollars was one of the early pacing champions. His owner, Stephen Phillips, had great confidence in him and it would seem that the confidence was returned, for Sleepy Tom was willing to rely entirely on his driver and in two successive years broke the harness racing records. In 1878 he did the mile in 2:22½ and the following year he did it in 2:12¼! After this race he was sold for six thousand dollars but Phillips continued to drive him.

One of the most famous families of pacers is the "Direct" branch which came down from Dictator, he being a Hambletonian. Tennesseee produced the "Hals," others were "The Blue Bulls," the "Hiatogas" and the "St. Clairs." Directum I in 1916 paced a mile in 1:56¾ which is still the record. See also *HARNESS RACING*. Trotting men were rather scornful of the pacers at first, calling them "wrigglers" or "sidewheelers" but after the invention of the "hopple" they came to respect them!

PADDLING

When a horse travels behind with his toes turned out and his hocks bent towards each other he is said to be "paddling."

PADDOCK

A paddock adjoining the stable is a great convenience. Horses may be turned into it while the boxes are being done up and animals which are turned out in a field are more easily caught if they are first driven or coaxed to follow the owner into an enclosed paddock. If a ton of sand be spread in one corner it will be greatly appreciated as nothing is so delightful to a horse as a good roll in sand. Another corner, possibly fenced off, might well contain clay which, when soaked with the hose, could be used for horses which would benefit by being allowed to stand fetlock deep in mud. See also *MUD*. The fencing of the paddock should be very strong and the gates should have good catches. No nails, wire or glass should ever be allowed to collect in it. If the paddock borders on the road, turn the brood mares with their young foals in it that the babies may become accustomed to passing traffic.

PAIR CLASSES

These may be for hunters, Saddlers, jumpers or equitation events. In some uniformity is stressed, in others general appearance and performance. For complete description of each class see *HORSE SHOW CLASSES*.

PALOMINO

The outstanding and deciding characteristic of the Palomino is his color. He must be of a cream, golden or very light chestnut with a "flax" (nearly white) mane and tail. His eyes and skin must be dark, he may and usually has white socks or stockings and a white blaze. In type he shows Arab characteristics but is larger, heavier and with a coarser head.

The original stock was developed by selective breeding in Mexico from the Spanish stock imported by Cortez. Of late the breed has been much improved

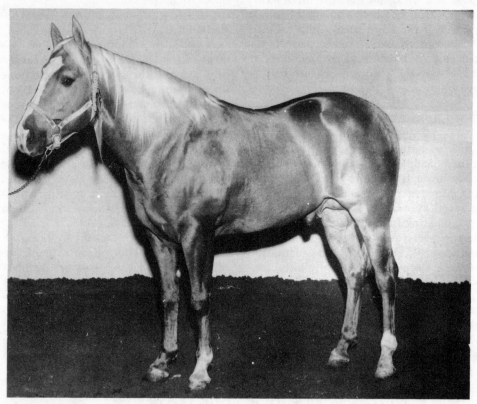

FIGURE 90. THE PALOMINO HORSE. *COURTESY JAMES CATHEY.*

by crossing with Arabian and Thoroughbreds of a light chestnut color. Three different types are recognized. The Park Hack, a general utility Saddle horse with emphasis put on manners and gaits. The parade type, with emphasis on showiness, and the stock horse with emphasis on flexibility and general utility as a working horse for stock purposes.

Inasmuch as there is a good deal of confusion regarding the requirements for registration, the complete rules for registration as set up by the Palomino Horse Breeders of America (PHBA) are printed below, with their kind permission.

1. All Applications for registration shall be made in triplicate. The white copy is for the National Office, the Blue copy is for the State Secretary and the pink copy is for the owner of the horse.

2. Applications from states having affiliated associations must be submitted in duplicate to the State Secretary with the required fee. Applications from non-affiliated States must be submitted direct to the National Office with the proper fee.

3. The application must be filled out in detail by the owner as to color of skin, eyes, mane, tail, body color and etc.

4. The body coat color must be as nearly as possible, that of a newly minted gold coin. It shall vary not more than three shades lighter or darker.

5. Mane and tail must be white, with

not more than 15% of dark or chestnut hair in either.

6. A Palomino may have white markings on the face or may have white socks or stockings below the knees or hocks. It must be free of white spots on the body except those caused by saddle rubbing or accident. All markings must be clearly shown in ink or indelible pencil on the chart printed on the front of the application exactly as they exist on the horse.

7. The skin of a Palomino must be basically dark. (A horse shall be considered to be basically dark skinned when the eyes are dark, and the color of the skin around the eyes and nose is dark or black).

8. The eyes must be dark brown, hazel or black, and both of the same color.

9. The Palomino horse should be from 14-to-16 hands and should weigh from 900 to 1300 pounds.

10. Applications will not be considered unless the pedigree chart on the application is properly filled out, showing the pedigree of animal. Such pedigree shall show the registration numbers and registration initials of all registered ancestors shown therein and the coat colors where possible.

11. All registration numbers of recognized breed associations shown on the application will be verified by the National Office.

12. All horses must be registered in the name of the owner, or owners, as such name is carried on the membership certificate, except that a joint membership of husband and wife, or Mr. and Mrs., the horse may be registered in the name of either the husband or the wife.

13. The breeding certificate on the reverse side of the application must be filled out in the handwriting of the owner of the sire, and must be signed by him, or his authorized agent. If the registration of the animal concerned depends entirely on the registration number of the dam, the owner of the dam must sign the breeding certificate. A separate breeders certificate properly executed will be accepted in lieu of the certificate on the back of the application when such original breeders certificate is available.

14. The signing of an application for registration is an agreement by the owner to conform to all rules and regulations and requirements of this Association regarding registrations.

Regular Registry

1. No Palomino, except a gelding, is eligible for registration in the Regular Registry unless its sire or dam is registered in PHBA, or unless the animal itself, or its sire or dam is registered in one of the following recognized breed associations:

American Remount Association (ARA); Arabian Horse Club (AHC); American Quarter Horse Association (AQHA); American Saddle Horse Breeders Association (ASHBA); Jockey Club (JC); Morgan Horse Club (MHC); National Quarter Horse Breeders Association (NQHBA, absorbed by AQHA by consolidation); Palomino Horse Association (PHA); Tennessee Walking Horse Breeders Association (TWHBA); United States Trotting Association (USTA).

2. A gelding is acceptable for registration strictly on color and conformation, regardless of whether or not it has a registered sire or dam.

3. No Palomino is eligible for registration in this Association if its sire or its dam is a draft horse or pony, or if its sire or dam is a piebald or an albino.

4. No application is acceptable on a stallion under two years of age or a mare or gelding under one year.

5. The fee for registering a stallion, mare or gelding shall be $11.00 for members and $16.00 for non-members.

Palomino breed registry

1. No Palomino is eligible for registration in the Palomino Breed Registry unless the animal qualifies either by pedigree or by its progeny.

2. To qualify by pedigree, both the sire and the dam must be registered, one of which must be registered in the records of Palomino Horse Breeders of America. The other parent, either the sire or the dam, not registered in PHBA shall then qualify as to bloodline, such bloodline to be registered American Quarter Horse, Arabian or Thoroughbred.

3. To qualify by its progeny, a Palomino stallion must be registered in Palomino Horse Breeders of America and must also have five of his get registered in PHBA. A mare to qualify, must herself, be registered in Palomino Horse Breeders of America and must also have three of her produce registered in PHBA.

4. The fee for registering a stallion in this registry is $20.00 for members and $25.00 for non-members.

5. The fee for registering a mare or gelding in this registry is $12.00 for members and $17.00 for non-members.

Junior registry

A Junior Certificate of registration may be issued on any Palomino stallion under two years of age or any Palomino mare under one year of age, providing such Palomino stallion or mare qualifies for registration upon bloodlines, pedigree and color as specified under the registration rules of this Association.

The fee for a Junior Certificate shall be $5.00 which fee may be applied on a regular registration certificate when the horse becomes old enough for registration. A Junior Certificate must be surrendered to the Secretary of the National Association within 60 days after the horse reaches the age for proper registration, after which the certificate shall become null and void and the $5.00 fee shall be forfeited.

PALOMINO HORSE BREEDERS ASSOCIATION

Headquarters: Mineral Wells, Texas.

PANEL (*n.*)

In the hunt field obstacles whether timber or stone are often spoken of as "panels."

PANEL (*v.*)

In hunting country where the natural fences and walls are not suitable for jumping it is customary to panel them. In timber country "chicken-coop" jumps are often erected. In stone wall country a section of the wall with a good landing and take off is selected and a "rider" or rail is put on top of the wall to reduce the danger of broken knees if the horse should graze it.

PAPER CHASES (hare and hounds)

A paper chase is great fun. The "hares" should be equipped with big sacks containing rolled oats rather than torn up paper. This has several advantages; it involves no preparation, it does not fly around and the birds will see that none is left to disfigure the countryside. As a rule two "hares" go together. They must drop a handful of oatmeal at least every twenty feet or so and always at forks. They may lay as many false trails as they wish. The length of time they are given for a head-start will vary with the terrain and the ability of the riders; fifteen or twenty minutes is usually plenty. The first of the "hounds" to sight the "hares" wins.

PARK HACK

A park hack is a horse suitable for general riding. In a show he is required to have easy gaits, good manners and a showy appearance.

PARK RIDERS

This term, to horsemen, means the person who has perhaps taken a few lessons in equitation but who really knows very little about horses, his only interest being in the stylish figure he thinks he cuts while riding in the park. The typical park rider usually wears clothes which, from their very newness, give him away and unless mounted upon the very mildest of horses will come a cropper.

PARLAY

To increase the amount of money bet on a race by adding to the bet money won on a previous race.

PARROT MOUTH

A parrot mouth is one in which the upper jaw is over shot and the upper incisors extend in front of the lower incisors. See *TEETH*.

PARTHENON HORSES

One of the most famous friezes in the world is that of the horses on the Parthenon. See Figure 54, page 155.

PAS DE CÔTÉ

A French term meaning "step to the side." In the direct *pas de côté* the horse moves sideways without moving forwards, crossing his legs to do so. This step is used in aligning a row of horses when they are abreast but not at the required intervals one from the other. Horses that compete in shows are all taught the *pas de côté* even though the riders may not know it under this name, for in lining up for the judging the rider causes his horse to move either to the right or to the left, if he is too close or too far from the horse on his flank. Cavalry horses also learn to do this for purposes of mounted drill.

The *traversal,* sometimes called the "two-track," is also a form of *pas de côté,* but in this case the horse moves forwards on a diagonal line as well as to the side. See *DRESSAGE; RIDING, The Advanced Rider.*

PASSAGE DES CINGLES

This is the space just behind the elbows along which the girth passes. It should be broad enough so that the flaring of the ribs and belly does not force the girth against the elbows.

PASSENGER

A person who rides with no control, i.e., who lets his horse decide gait, speed and direction, is known as a "passenger."

PASSING OTHER HORSES

It is often necessary to pass one or more horses while riding on a narrow trail or along a hard road. The "passer" should warn the other riders and ask permission to pass, and he should do so at a gait only slightly faster than theirs. Those being passed should turn their heads towards the person passing, if necessary, backing off the trail. See also *COURTESY.*

PASTERN

See Figure 51, page 150, *HORSE, Points of.*

PASTURES

A good pasture is very valuable. It should be well fenced, not muddy, with a good stand of grass and preferably a brook. Horses that have had a hard season of hunting will benefit greatly by a few weeks or months at pasture.

PATO

This is a mounted game similar to mounted basket-ball which originated in and is very popular in South America. The ball used is of leather and is in a rope harness with handles. The riders ride small native horses and wear the full, loose trousers of the *gauchos.* They are very adept at leaning over and picking the ball up off the ground while going at a full gallop. The Spanish word *pato* means "duck," and the game was originally played with a live duck, which was picked up by the neck. Because of its cruelty the game was banned for some years. Later the ball was substituted for the unfortunate bird.

PECKING

When a horse hits a jump lightly with his front feet he is said to "peck."

PEGASUS

See *FAMOUS HORSES OF FICTION.*

PELHAM

A bit with a bar mouthpiece and double rings. See *BRIDLES.*

PERCHERON

The Percheron is the most popular

and most widely distributed of any of the draft breeds. It originated in the district known as "Le Perche" in France. This district is ideal for raising horses and together with Normandy has been recognized for centuries as the land of the draft breeds. The Moors, mounted on Arabian and Barb stock, first conquered Spain and then overran France, to be defeated in 732 at Tours by Charles Martel. Tours is in one corner of "Le Perche," so it is not surprising that the Percheron shows definite traces of Arab stock.

FIGURE 91. A TYPICAL PERCHERON SIRE. *COURTESY PERCHERON HORSE ASSOCIATION.*

The Percherons were first used as chargers by the knights and for other military purposes. Later they became the most popular breed for pulling the "diligences" or French stage coaches. Because the grays were more readily visible at night this color was preferred. The first four Percherons to be brought into the United States were imported in 1839 by Edward Harris of Moorestown, N. J. Three of the four died but Mr. Moore went back and brought over four more. In 1851 two more stallions, *Normandy* and *Louis Napoleon,* were imported and the former, especially, was responsible for a great many colts. It is claimed that he averaged sixty colts a year; he died at the age of twenty-six.

Canada also became interested in Percherons, and the Lane ranch, during 1914, 1915 and 1916, bred them very extensively having over four hundred head of registered Percherons. The Normandy horse which was somewhat similar to the Percheron was, for a while, registered in this country in the same book, the horses being called Percheron-Norman, but in France the true Percheron, to be registered in the French book, must have been born within the district of Le Perche.

The Percheron is noted for his mild disposition, his tremendous muscular development and strength and his stamina. The average size is 16.1 to 16.3 and the weight 1900 to 2100 pounds. The preferred colors are dapple gray or black. He is a very agile horse considering his great weight and withstands both heat and cold very readily. He is very long lived, often attaining the age of thirty and is desirable for all draft purposes. See *AMERICAN PERCHERON STUD BOOK.*

PERFECT HORSE

There has never been nor will there ever be the "perfect" horse. In selecting the horse, perfection must be kept in mind, but compromises will have to be made. If one could form a "composite" horse as one makes "composite" photographs, perhaps the ideal could be attained; until then the best thing to do is get the animal which is nearest in perfection to your needs, and then try and improve him.

PERFORMANCE

Many jumping classes are judged on "performance" only. This means that the horse that has the fewest jumping faults as scored by the A.H.S.A. or the F.E.I. rules will win the class. Children competing in horse shows should be made to realize that obviously everyone cannot win the blue and that if they put on a good performance, riding as well as they can and getting the most out of their mount, they should be satisfied.

PETIZO

The Petizo is a pony native to Argentina. The origin of the Petizo is unknown. He is completely different from any other breed of pony, being cobby in type but extremely short legged. He is handy, good-tempered, an excellent weight-carrier and averages thirteen hands in height.

PHAETON

This is a type of carriage often required in lady's harness classes.

PIAFFE

Piaffe is a dressage movement in which the horse trots in place with a light high action of both the front and hind legs. See *DRESSAGE; RIDING, The Advanced Rider.*

PICK-ME-UP

The horse which is suffering from exhaustion after being over-ridden will benefit by a "pick-me-up" consisting of half a pint of whiskey in a pint of warm water or milk. The mixture can be put in a bottle, the horse's head tipped up and back and the liquid poured down his throat. He should then be groomed quickly, well blanketed and left alone. A little later he may be given a hot linseed or bran mash.

PIGEON TOES

When the front toes of the horse point in he is said to be "pigeon toed." This is a bad fault as it often causes stumbling; it may also be an indication of navicular or other trouble.

PINK COAT or HUNTING PINKS

The customary color for coats of the gentlemen members of a hunt is a light scarlet though there are exceptions. These are commonly called "pink" but not because of their color. A famous London tailor named "Pink" or "Pinke" gave his name to the hunting coat and they have been called "pinks" ever since.

PINTO HORSE ASSOCIATION, Box 155, R.F.D. 1, Ellington, Conn.

Leo W. Carrier, *President*
Harold E. Cottrell, *Vice-President*
Miss Helen Hammond, *Secretary*
Herbert H. Teller, *Treasurer*
Mrs. Perry Wright, *Registrar*
Aaron G. Olmstead, *Editor, Chairman, Board of Directors*
Present registrations about 1600.
This Association was formed in 1956

FIGURE 92. IN THE PIAFFE, SHOWN HERE, THE HORSE "MARKS TIME" IN PLACE. IT IS FIRST TAUGHT BY THE TRAINER WALKING BESIDE AND A LITTLE IN FRONT OF THE HORSE. THIS MOVEMENT REQUIRES GREAT ENGAGEMENT OF THE HAUNCHES AND SUPPLE-NESS OF THE LOINS.

and incorporated the same year. Like the Palomino, the Pinto is a color rather than a breed, though the Association is standardizing its registry as a breed and it is so recognized both in the United States and Canada. The term "Pinto," which is Spanish for "painted" or "colored," was chosen over "Skewbald" or "Piebald," since it covers both these descriptions.

There is also a Pinto Pony Registry for animals not larger than 14:1. Color markings, a history of the breed and classifications of markings are published here by courtesy of the organization.

PINTO

(Text for this article has been adapted from *A Primeval Horse*, by Carl E. Raswan.)

The Pinto as we know him today is recognized the world over as a distinctive American horse, whose offspring roam from the pampas of Argentina to the forest-meadows of Alaska. His merits and good qualities have been notable to such a great extent that at other times of history and in other lands (in Europe, Asia and Africa) the Pinto played a prominent and romantic role as a war and pleasure horse.

Modern Pintos of the Americas have degrees of excellence which match the endurance and intelligence of the Arabian; the general utility of the Morgan; the workability and "cow-sense" of the stock-horse, as well as the docility and usefulness of a children's pony.

The Pinto has to be regarded as a mixture of (or as a very close relative to) the Arab, Morgan, stock horse, Welsh or Shetland pony, or of any other of the various horse and pony types. This knowledge should encourage us to breed Pintos not aimlessly (leaving results to a mere "chance"), but intelligently to create *distinctive types of Pintos*. At the present most Pintos are only considered

FIGURE 93. PAINT McCUE, BLACK OVERO STALLION OWNED BY RALPH THOMAS. THE OVERO IS ONE OF THE TWO COLOR-PATTERNS RECOGNIZED BY THE PINTO HORSE ASSOCIATION. *COURTESY OF THE PINTO HORSE ASSOCIATION.*

FIGURE 94. COLONEL, BLACK-AND-WHITE TOBIANO STALLION OWNED BY JOHN CELORIA. THE TOBIANO IS THE SECOND OF THE TWO COLOR-PATTERNS RECOGNIZED BY THE PINTO HORSE ASSOCIATION. (SEE ALSO ABOVE ILLUSTRATION.) *COURTESY OF THE PINTO HORSE ASSOCIATION.*

members of a color and markings breed, but we can easily improve this situation by elevating our Pintos to be representatives of *distinguished* types.

As breeders and horselovers we make use of our animals for special purposes: cow-work, show ring, polo, dude riding, cavalry, etc. We should "sit back" and think those precious opportunities over which have been thrown into our laps with the possession of tens and even hundreds of thousands of Pinto horses in North and South America. The Pinto as a "wild Mustang" and "Indian War-Horse" is a creature of the American past, of a bygone age which hardened the Pinto in the pioneer work of our forefathers: Anglo-Saxons, Indians and Spanish-Americans. The weak foals died, only the strong survived. Thus, the average Pinto of our time is still a living and outstanding example of the survival of the fittest horse that has ever existed in any country.

To succeed in selective breeding of better Pintos we should classify the various distinguishable types of Pintos in America. The Arabians as the original light Saddle and harness horses in any country of the world, may serve us well as examples, and the Pinto horse (like the Arabian) does not belong to just one established type, but may be recognized to belong to one of the three following classifications:

1. A masculube (muscular) horse; rather broad, that is, wide from the front —across back, through fore arm and gaskin, and deep through girth and loin. (Morgan type).

2. A feminine (graceful, handsome) horse, but wiry, though longer, more slender lines prevail; and more refinement, rather elegant and lighter in frame (bone) and general conformation. American Saddlebred type.

3. A race (speed) horse type, long, angular (instead of rounded outlines) and sometimes high legged, or somewhat coarser in head and body (a "plain," but useful horse with more size, bone and speed, though perhaps less intelligence).

If we keep in mind that Pintos are not uniform in type, but that a Pinto may represent a Morgan, American Saddlebred, Quarter Horse, Thoroughbred, or one of the three Arabian types, we should find it easy to match our Pinto mare to the proper sire of the other breed, so that a Pinto foal of a distinguished type can be produced.

The original Pinto, like the authentic Arabian, has to be considered a primeval horse—a creature of the "first" age of our world. The mimicry (or mimesis), the close resemblance in spotted markings (mostly coloring) of the Pinto to its sun-spotted and shade-spattered surroundings, is nothing but a natural camouflage to screen itself with dark and light splashes of color from the eyes of their enemies. The American Indian preferred a "painted" horse to a plain colored one, because he had learned the advantage of color-disguise.

The ancient Pinto was not just a color and marking breed, but of distinctive types. The *Kathiawari* of India, and the *Tanghan* of Tibet (and the region of the Himalayas) were like the early American Indian "paints" small horses of Arabian characteristics. Later these Himalaya and Tibet Pintos were misbred to Mongolian and Mongrel European horses, but with the introduction of fresh blood of Arabian sires, imported through Moslem Indian Princes and the British Indian Government, the original (refined and harmonious) types of strength and beauty were restored, thus revealing again endurance and intelligence, docility, and good health in the extreme.

In India and Arabia, among the Moslems, the Pinto is called *Kanhwa* ("blotched" with chestnut, white and black). In India a *Phulwari* is a "flowering" horse, that is a white horse covered with small flowers of black spots.

Colors Of Registered Pinto Horses and Ponies

The Pinto coat color is always a combination of white and one of the ten basic coat colors. The Pinto comes in two patterns, overo and tobiano. Therefore, in describing the color of a registered Pinto, the Pinto Horse Association of America, Inc. has adopted the system of using the basic coat color, other than white which is common to all Pintos, combined with the pattern. For example, the Association's description of a black and white horse with clear, even markings divided about half and half, having white legs, would be "Black Tobiano Pinto." The color black tells us the color other than white, tobiano tells us the pattern, and Pinto indicates the horse is spotted. The system of description lends itself easily to abbreviation—the above description of "Black Tobiano Pinto" being abbreviated as "BLKT."

The ten basic coat colors adopted as standard within the PtHA, along with their abbreviations, are listed below. These are the only colors that will be used in official studbooks and publications.

Overo (O). A colored horse, roan, dun, sorrel, bay, brown, or black, with white extending upward and irregular in pattern. Mane and tail dark or mixed, head usually white or bald. Legs usually have a combination of white and solid color.

Tobiano (T). Clearly marked pattern with white as a base and another color usually divided about half and half throughout the coat. Mane and tail are the color of the region from where they stem. Legs are usually white; head dark or combined with markings such as star, stripe, snip or blaze.

Bay (Bay). A mixture of red and yellow, being probably as much the color of a well-baked loaf of bread as anything. A light bay shows more yellow, a dark bay more red. The darkest, a mahogany red overtone. Bays always have black points. A Bay Pinto may have black areas in mane and tail.

Black (Blk). A black horse is black and almost invariably has black eyes, hoofs and skin. The points are always black, though socks, boots, and stockings are common. Black Pintos must have only black and white markings, especially around the muzzle and body open-

ings and may have either black, blue or glass eyes.

Blue Roan (Blr). A Roan horse is any horse whose coat carries white hairs intermingled with one or more of the base colors. A blue roan is best described as being the color of gun metal.

Brown (Brn). Many brown horses are erroneously called black because they are so dark. A close examination of the hair on the muzzle and lips will usually determine if the horse is brown or black. A brown Pinto will invariably have a brownish cast to the coat at the base of the hairs when well groomed and in bright sunlight.

Chestnut (Cnt). A chestnut is one that has a coat that is basically red. His mane and tail are the same shade as his body. A liver chestnut can be almost black, except for the red tint seen on a well groomed coat.

Dun (Dun). The dun horse is one whose dominant hair is some shade of yellow. He may vary from pale yellow to a dirty canvas yellow. He always has black points. A palomino is a dun with white or light colored mane and tail and light colored points.

Grulla (Gla). Pronounced *Grewya*, this describes a horse that is dun with roan characteristics—yellow hair mixed with brown or black. He always has black points. It is a smooth, grayish-blue color of that of a mouse. It is *not* a blue roan (which is white mixed with black), as the color is more suave and is always permanent. Some almost seem purple or smoke colored.

Palomino (Pal). A dun with white points. The dominant color is yellow and runs from a light cream color to a rich oak color. The Palomino is often described as the color of a newly minted gold coin. The distinction lies in the fact that the points are always white.

Red Roan (Rdr). As with the blue roan, the hairs of white are mixed with chestnut. This horse has often been described as strawberry roan.

Sorrel (Srl). A sorrel is nothing more than a red chestnut, with a flaxen mane and tail. The distinction here lies in the fact that the mane and tail are always a lighter shade than the body color.

These, then, are the ten basic coat colors used by the PtHA to describe registered Pinto horses and ponies. These standard colors enable the Association to insure uniformity in Pinto descriptions in Association publications and correspondence with PtHA members. When the basic coat color is combined with the pattern it promotes universal understanding and can be readily abbreviated to reduce the length of the description of any Pinto in question.

Shown below are markings that are common to Pintos and solid-color horses.

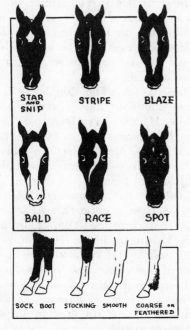

FIGURE 95. MARKINGS COMMON TO PINTOS AND SOLID-COLOR HORSES.

PIROUETTE

There are two movements described by the word *pirouette*. To the classical dressage rider it means a turn on the hindquarters, executed at the canter, in which the inside back foot is used as a pivot and is lifted and replaced almost on the same spot while the forehand of the horse revolves around it. It is an ex-

tremely difficult movement, for the horse must be completely fluid and smooth under the rider and the cadence of the canter must remain even. Yet this is one of the movements most commonly seen in horses at liberty.

To the circus rider the *pirouette* is a pivot of hindquarters around forehand in which the two front feet are held perfectly still and actually wind or twist one around the other. When the turn is completed the horse holds the pose, and then unwinds. The movement is often executed with the front feet on a stand. See also *DRESSAGE, RIDING, The Advanced Rider.*

PIVOT

The pivot is similar to the pirouette and the horse may pivot around his hindquarters, holding one back leg in place while side-stepping with the other, or he may do a "croup around forehand" which is essentially a pirouette. In performing a croup around forehand the horse is caused to move his croup away from the pressure of the rider's legs as in side stepping while the forehand is kept in place by use of the reins. In the front pivot the hindquarters are prevented from moving while the reins, especially the rein of opposition, are employed to turn the animal's forehand. See *DRESSAGE; RIDING, The Advanced Rider.*

PLACE

To come in second in a race. (In betting, second or better.)

PLANTATION WALKER

The Plantation Walking Horse, officially known as the Tennessee Walking Horse, is of recent origin. It traces its ancestry back to Black Allan who was of mixed Hambletonian and Morgan ancestry. Like Justin Morgan, Black Allan was remarkable for his potency, his progeny retaining his characteristics to a remarkable degree. The Walking Horse was developed for the use of the plantation owners of the South who want a

FIGURE 96. PIROUETTE TO THE RIGHT. RICHARD WAETJAN, IN-
TERNATIONALLY-KNOWN OLYMPIC RIDER, ON BURGSDORF.

horse with an easy ambling gait and which will canter straight so that he may be ridden between rows of crops. The Walking Horse is also heavy enough for light farm and general utility work. The Stud book for the breed was started in 1935 and large horse shows have classes for this breed. See also *HORSE SHOW CLASSES, Saddle Division; TENNESSEE WALKING HORSE BREEDERS ASSOCIATION; SADDLE HORSE*

PLATE

A race for a prize, no stake being offered.

PLATER

A horse that habitually races for prizes not being considered good enough to race for stakes. The term is derogatory and is used to mean an inferior horse.

PLATES (racing)

The thin shoes which race horses wear are known as "plates."

PLEURISY

This is an inflammation of the pleura or membranous covering of the lungs. It may come from bacteria or from a deep chest wound. The symptoms are a

FIGURE 97. THE TENNESSEE WALKING HORSE, COMMONLY CALLED THE "PLANTATION WALKER." *COURTESY TENNESSEE WALKING HORSE ASSOCIATION.*

very high temperature, appearance of distress and pain, discharge at the nostrils, excessive movement of the flanks and abdomen with little movement of the chest, fast breathing and an indisposition to lie down. The disease frequently goes into pneumonia. The veterinarian should be called at once as the disease is very serious, often resulting in death. It is sometimes necessary to tap the chest to withdraw fluid. Treatment consists of a mild blister on the chest, four tablespoons of Epsom salts and one teaspoon of nitre in the drinking water daily, and an airy box with warmth and plenty of blankets. The legs should be bandaged with dry wool bandages.

PLEURO-PNEUMONIA (contagious)

This disease which is due to bacterial infection gaining access to the lungs through inhaling is fortunately not very common. In addition to the symptoms mentioned above in pleurisy, the horse may have a cough, the membranes of his eyes will be bright red, the thin watery discharge from the nostrils will later become thick and brown in color. The patient will grunt and there will be a swelling under the chest. If the case is diagnosed at once and the horse is not worked he may recover with careful treatment. He should be given inhalations of Eucalyptus and may be fed boiled oats, steamed hay or fresh grass and linseed mashes. He should be well blanketed and a long period of convalescence is obligatory. The horse should be completely isolated and the veterinarian sent for.

PLOUGHLINES (use of in longeing)

The very long ploughline or two lines buckled together are useful for longeing

FIGURE 98. PLAUDIT, A PALOMINO QUARTER HORSE OWNED BY
LEON H. HARMS, ALBUQUERQUE, N. M.

the colt. Ordinary ploughlines may be
used for long rein driving where the
trainer is on foot. See COLTS, Breaking
and Training; Jumping.

PNEUMONIA

Pneumonia or inflammation of the
lungs is a very serious disease and often
follows influenza or strangles. The symptoms of pneumonia are a rise in temperature, shivering attacks, a cough and a
thin nasal discharge which later thickens
to a yellow brown. The mucous mem-
brane of the eye will have a distinct bluish color. The animal is constipated and
the faeces are mucus coated. The veterinarian should be called at once. Careful nursing is most important. The patient should be well blanketed and bandaged in a warm but airy box stall free
from draughts. Eucalyptus inhalations
may be given and the bowels kept open

with four tablespoons of Epsom salts in
the drinking water. A teaspoon of nitre
should also be added for the kidneys.

POINT (to make a)
See HUNTING TERMS.

POINTING

When a horse stands on three feet and
touches the tip of one front foot without
resting weight on it he is said to be
"pointing." This is a symptom of such
ailments as "navicular" disease.

POINTS OF HORSE

See Figure 51, page 150, HORSE,
Points of.

POINT TO POINT

A form of race in which the contestants are given certain specified "points"
or places to which they must ride. They

may choose their own course or line just so long as they go to each of the specified points before coming in at the finish.

POLE

Distances on the race tracks are marked with poles at each sixteenth of a mile, so that horses may be timed at these distances. The finish pole is usually painted a different color from the others to prevent jockeys from mistaking the next to last for the final one.

POLE BENDING

A popular contest in Western Shows and gymkhanas. The horses ride a course, threading between a row of light poles, turn at the end and come back.

POLICE HORSE

For many years the horse has played a valuable part in police work. And in spite of the motorcycle and the automobile he continues to be of service. For some reason the crowd of riotous rabble is far more afraid of the police horse than he is of a man armed with a much more lethal weapon. It is easier for one man to disperse a crowd by riding into them than by threatening them with an automatic.

FIGURE 99. THE POLICE HORSE, THROUGH TRAINING AND DISPOSITION, IS SAGACIOUS AND CALM. HE IS THE PRIDE OF HIS MASTER'S HEART. *CHARLES PHELPS CUSHING.*

In traffic jams the mounted officer can see over the roofs of the cars and, having discovered the cause of the trouble, thread his way neatly between them and straighten out the dilemma. For patrol work along shore lines and in parks the mounted man can cover territory more quickly than the man on foot and he does not have to stick to the highway.

The police horse must undergo a stringent examination before being accepted. Many cities require that he be of a specific color (all New York horses are bays). He must be of a specific size and between the ages of four and seven. He must have an even disposition but he must be both bold and teachable. Having been accepted the prospect is given from one to three years training at one of the police training depots. When finally he takes up his work he knows many things and he is absolutely obedient. He receives the best of treatment and when his days of usefulness are over he is retired, never sold to end his days in ignominy as is a huckster's horse.

POLICED (to be)
To be policed is to be thrown.

POLISH ARAB
Poland, from the very beginning of her existence, was the most vulnerable of all European countries to attack and depended upon her splendid cavalry for protection abainst barbaric invasion. As early as the 10th Century trade relations with the Far East acquainted the Poles with the Arabian horse. This smoothly moving, high spirited but gentle animal had the strength, endurance and intelligence they needed. Crusaders returning from the Holy Land and wars with the Turks brought home Arabian horses. The Poles' exceptional love of horses, their intelligent methods of breeding and training, together with favorable conditions of soil and climate developed Arabs with substance and quality which retained the classic type.

The Royal Division in the stud of King Zysmunt August (1548-72) bred only horses of pure Arab blood, carefully selecting stallions and mares that would produce the best. In 1803 Prince Sanguszko sent an expedition to Arabia and from that time until the World War breeding material of top quality was imported from the desert. Poland can boast of possessing female strains of purebred Arabian horses with proven pedigrees which, having survived 150 years have lost none of their vitality and still play an invaluable part in Polish breeding. From Poland the Sultan Abd-ul-Azis obtained foundation stock for his Arab stud at Stamboul in 1864. In succeeding years Polish Arabs won the Gold Medal at the International Show in Paris. The Polish stallion Van Dyke was imported and highly prized by Spain. SKOWRONEK became the chief sire in Lady Wentworth's Crabbet Stud and Champion Arabian of England.

Horse breeding was so important to Poland that in 1919 soon after she had regained her independence, Janow-Podlaski was organized to assemble as quickly as possible that part of breeding stock from the celebrated Polish studs which had escaped annihilation by the long years of captivity and World War I.

In 1931 Prince Roman Sanguszko organized an expedition to Arabia to replenish some of the breeding material. He imported the purebred Arabian stallion KUHAILAN-HAIFI. This beautiful brown stallion not only assured Janow-Podlaski a fresh infusion of pure Arabian blood but with the birth of the bay stallion OFIR (Kuhailan-Haifi-Dziwa by Abu-Mlech) in 1933, "the ardent wish of all Polish breeders and lovers of Arabian horses for a regenerator of pure Arab blood was realized."

Because OFIR's son WITEZ II had the regal bearing of his grandsire, he was given a name which means Prince. He was the favorite of the stud assistant who thought he was the most beautiful and classic of all the colts. Then in 1939, when WITEZ II was just a year old, Poland was invaded once more.

The Germans stormed in from the

west, but the Red Army arrived first at Janow-Podlaski, driving off the finest stock. Somehow on the long walk to Russia that cold winter, with stops along the way at peasant houses and country manors, WITEZ II escaped. A farmer recognized him and tried to hide him but the German Research Commission's search was successful. WITEZ II was identified by the crown and number branded on his sides and returned to Janow-Podlaski, then under German command. In 1941 he was tested for disposition, temperament, conformation, endurance in hunting, cross-country riding, trail riding and jumping. Then from many excellent stallions he was chosen for the Wolhyman National Stud, Mlynow, where most of the breeding material had originated from the world-famous stud of Prince Radziwill.

In 1943, because of his outstanding record as a sire, the Germans sent WITEZ II to their newly founded stud in Hostownia, Czechoslovakia, where he stayed until the tide of battle brought an Allied victory. As the Soviet Army again swept in, the Nazis retreated farther west, evacuating WITEZ II to Monsbach, where Patton's Third Army came riding to the rescue.

WITEZ II, with other imported horses, was sent to the Quartermaster's Depot (Remount) at the Kellogg Ranch, Pomona, California, and on June 23, 1947 was presented to the public as a Depot stallion.

POLL

Top of skull between ears. See *HORSE, Points of.*

POLL EVIL

An abscess on the poll due to a blow or other injury. See *FISTULA.*

POLO

Polo (from the Tibetan *"Pulu"* meaning ball) is one of the oldest games. Very old manuscripts in the British Museum show polo being played as early as 600 B.C. and there is reason to sup-

pose that it was played long before this. Many similarities exist between the game as played by the early Persians, the first recorded mention of polo, and as played today. Old drawings in the British Museum show that the mallets were almost identical, and there were boys standing on the edge of the field holding extra mallets in case of accident. The horses' legs were bandaged. There were two goal posts and even the types of strokes and the form used was much the same. One drawing shows the Persian ladies in ruffly dresses riding astride and using a seat which more nearly approximates the present balance seat than did that of our own grandfathers. The ball is in midair and the four Persian ladies are racing towards it at a full gallop, there is nothing delicate or frail in their attitudes and their horsemanship is excellent!

The historian Tabari who lived about 914 A.D. tells us that the game was played in the time of Darius, 521-485 B.C. Firdousi, the great Persian poet, describes in his "Sháh-náma," sometimes called the "Iliad of Persia," the first international polo match between the Iranians and the Turanians. There were seven on a side in this match and there is frequent mention of the value of "team play."

Gradually the game became more organized. The length of the field was set at 300 yards by 170 yards (early Sixteenth century) and the number of players was reduced to four on a side, etc. When the Mohammedans conquered the Persians they continued the game and also introduced it to Constantinople. At about this time the game, in Asia, underwent a temporary change. The traditional mallet was replaced by one with a small racket at the end, similar to a lacrosse racket, and for the willow ball was substituted a leather one. It was this form of racket and ball which was taken up by the Japanese. The Japanese also used a paper ball covered with bamboo fiber. The goal was boarded up and contained a hole and the player had to carry the ball down in his racket and put it into the hole. This form of polo

FIGURE 100. THE EARLIEST PICTURE OF POLO. *CULVER SERVICE.*

is still played in Japan under the name "Da-kiu." The Chinese had a similar game, sometimes varying it by having only one goal, all players striving to make a goal by putting the ball into the bag.

Polo appeared in India, having spread from Persia, in about the sixteenth century. Here it was called *"rol."* In this form of the game there were many on a side and there was little team work, each man trying, by means of dribbling, to keep the ball in his possession as long as possible.

In 1854 polo came into Bengal from Manipur and in 1862 it was played in Punjab. In 1864 a tribe of Manipuris visited Calcutta to show their skill. The year before, in 1863, the first game to be played by Europeans was staged in Calcutta.

The introduction of polo to England was pure happen-chance though it was bound to come about sooner or later. A description of the game of polo was printed in "The Field" in 1869 and Lieutenant Hartopp, member of the Tenth Huzzars, chanced to come across it. He and other members of the regiment immediately became interested. There and then they sent for their chargers and, armed with canes and short sticks, they mounted and tried to knock a ball about. As they were riding regulation cavalry horses this was rather difficult but so intrigued were they with the possibilities of the game that they sent an envoy to Ireland to get them some ponies under fourteen hands with the stipulation that they be quiet and handy. They might also be slow for none of the men conceived of the possibility of playing polo faster than a very slow trot or canter!

The ponies came, a rough field was leveled off at Hounslow where the regiment was quartered and the Huzzars sent a challenge to the Ninth Lancers stationed at Aldershot. The first game could hardly be called scientific inasmuch as there were no rules, eight men on a side and every man for himself! But fun was had by all and polo was successfully launched.

The popularity of the game spread from one military outfit to another. In 1873 it was taken up by the Hurlingham Club of London as an "attractive addition to pigeon shooting." A set of rules was drawn up reducing the number of players on a side, first to five and later to four. All England was interested and the attendance at the games was tremendous. In 1877 the "Champion Cup" was founded.

In India, too, the game was being played by both the military and civilians and the same year that saw the Champion Cup inaugurated also brought the establishment of Indian regimental tournaments.

To Mr. James Gordon Bennett goes the credit of introducing polo to the United States. He returned from England in 1876 with a supply of mallets and balls and the firm determination of interesting his friends at home in the

game he had watched being played at Hurlingham. Ponies were procured from Texas and games were started in New York City at Dickel's Riding Academy. When spring came the players moved to the Jerome Park race-track in Westchester County and shortly thereafter the Westchester Polo Club was formed.

In 1879 the members of Meadow Brook Club of Long Island took up the game and this was followed by the formation of the Brighton Polo Club under Mr. H. L. Herbert. As mallets and balls were extremely difficult to obtain croquet balls were used and croquet mallet heads were mounted on hay-rake handles.

The forming of the Buffalo club followed and then came the first real match game which was between the Buffalo team and the Westchester team. The Westchestians, being more experienced, won, but the following year, when they went to Buffalo for a return match, the Buffalonians turned the tables on them.

In 1879 the second great match was played before ten thousand spectators. It was between the Westchester team and the Queens County Club which had been started by Mr. August Belmont and it was played on the year-old playing field at Prospect Park, Brooklyn. From the descriptions one surmises that team play was still unknown, the rules very few and roughness was the order of the day.

Harvard College was the first University to organize polo and in 1885 they sent a team to play against Pelham County Team and also the Meadow Brook Team, both of whom they beat. Princeton and Yale soon followed suit with teams. Polo also spread to Pennsylvania and to the Genesee Valley in New York State.

Mr. Theodore Roosevelt became very enthusiastic over the game, was handicapped at one goal and, in 1890, was on a winning team. Polo now spread rapidly all over the East. The first rules were those of Hurlingham. The time of the "chukkers" was not limited, rather the game was for two out of three goals, and there is a record of one game in which it took sixty minutes of uninterrupted play to make the first goal!

In 1888 the system of handicapping was found necessary. By this system players are evaluated by a committee as to their worth in goals to their team. The combined values of the two teams are then subtracted one from the other and the weaker team starts with a stated number of goals which must be made up by the stronger team before they can score. Without this system polo would long since have died out for it would have been impossible for the many teams of various strengths to have competed successfully against each other.

The Polo Association was organized in 1890 and today carries on its splendid work of organization at its offices at 250 Park Avenue, New York City.

The introduction of polo to the United States Cavalry was about as fortuitous as the introduction of polo to England. It seems that in the early eighties an American Cavalry regiment was marching to a new post in the Western United States and they happened to stop at a small city for the night. Among the residents who turned out to welcome them were some men who had played polo in England. Wishing to entertain their guests these men proposed that they get up two teams and have a match. The Cavalry men were delighted. They stayed over twenty-four hours and the next day the great event took place on a field improvised on the gopher-ridden prairie. As equipment was scarce a croquet ball was used and hockey sticks, lengthened with branches cut from trees, were the mallets! Rules were conspicuous by their absence, as was any semblance of team play, but it is known that the civilians finally won, 5 to 2.

Although the British Army quickly recognized the value of polo in the training of its Cavalry officers, the American Army was reluctant to accept the game as a regular part of the training. It was not until 1900 that, under Colonel Mills and Colonel Treat, who were Superintendent and Commandant respectively of West Point, the game became well organized at West Point with ponies supplied by the government. Later the three year course of instruction in horsemanship given to the Cadets at the Point included thorough training in polo.

Fort Riley, the cavalry school in Kansas, had polo as part of its program since 1896. They later had a number of playing and practice fields and a string of from one hundred and twenty-five to one hundred and fifty ponies trained each year by the cadet officers. Other famous army teams have been developed by the Tenth Cavalry Division and the Sixth Field Artillery. Fort Bliss, Texas, develops championship teams and in 1925 sent a team under the masterly command of Major Harry Chamberlin to win the Inter-Circuit Championship as well as the Twelve-Goal Championship.

The Army Polo Association was made a member of the United States Polo Association in 1902. Steady growth has taken place since then to such an extent that Infantry as well as Cavalry units are participating.

In 1923 and 1925 the first international Army matches were played between the American and British army teams. The 1923 matches were played at the Meadow Brook Club on Long Island and to everyone's surprise the American team won. In 1925 our team traveled to London and were again successful. In 1921 the decision was made to hold international competitions with England (civilian and army players alike eligible), these matches to be held not oftener than once in three years. The United States has also played the Argentine Polo Association. It is felt that the spirit of sportsmanship evidenced at these matches in contrast to the bickering and bad feeling often shown in other sports, is of great benefit to international relations. But the great expense involved and the interruption of National Polo makes it wise to limit the matches to once every three years.

Previous to this regular organization

of international polo there had been some games between British and American teams, the first being in 1886 when Britain sent a team captained by Mr. John Watson. The American team was captained by Mr. Thomas Hitchcock and the match took place at Newport, Rhode Island. The British team was far better organized, the players more experienced with a wider variety of strokes (Mr. Watson had just returned from India where he had learned the back strokes) and the British won both games.

In 1902 a formal challenge was sent to England and a team developed at the Rockaway Club under the captaincy of Mr. Foxhall P. Keene went to England to try and win back the trophy. The match was to be two games out of three. The first was won by the American team, the score being 2 goals to 1. The second was won by the British, 6 goals to 1, and the third game went also to the British, 7 to 1.

After these two defeats, the Americans realized that team play was the most essential element of polo. They worked hard and developed a free roaming, hard hitting type of play with much passing of long shots between the members of the team as opposed to the old idea of one player clinging, by means of dribbling, to the ball as long as possible. In 1909 Mr. Harry P. Whitney took a team to England and brought back the coveted cup. In 1911 the British, under Captain Hardress Lloyd, came to America to win back the cup. The British ponies did not live up to expectations and Captain Lloyd had some difficulty mounting his team. The preliminary matches were disappointing, but when the final match came the British ability to fight with odds against them came to the front, and they were just barely defeated by a score of 4½ goals to 3 in the first game and 4½ to 3½ in the second. In 1913 the British again challenged and the score was even closer, the Americans winning on a ¼ goal penalty. In 1914 the tables were turned and the British triumphed, the final scores being 8½ to 3, and 4 to 2¾.

From 1921 on, the matches, as has been stated, were limited to one every three years and the Americans have won consistently. The games have been splendid examples of fine sportsmanship, and each team has regarded its opponents as very worthy rivals. The fitness, not only of the riders but of the ponies, plays a large part in the ultimate score, and a string of forty-five mounts is not considered too large for a team of four men.

POLO PONIES

Early polo was played on whatever native stock could be found. In India the Mongolian pony (called a "griffin") was and still is popular. When polo was first introduced to England, Irish ponies were used. The main qualifications of the pony in those days was smallness and maneuverability. The game was slow for the players were not very adept and team work, which meant forward passing, had yet to be developed.

But as the game became faster it became necessary to breed better ponies. In 1893 the English realized that if satisfactory ponies were to be bred then something more than the prevailing haphazard system of breeding was indicated. They therefore formed the Polo Pony Society and published the first volume of their Stud Book in 1894.

The records of this Stud Book shows that there were fifty-seven stallions and three hundred and sixteen mares registered. The bloodlines used were Thoroughbred, Arabian and the many types of ponies to be found in England. Of all the pony types used, the Welsh was found to be the most successful. The Welsh pony is of symmetrical conformation, hardy, handy and speedy. The interest in polo has done much to improve the Welsh ponies which are popular as children's mounts and hacks.

International polo and especially the interest that Argentine takes in polo has also effected the breed of pony. There are two types of native pony in Argentine, both of which have been used for polo. The smallest is the "Petizo" pony

FIGURE 101. MODERN POLO PLAYERS AND THEIR PONIES. *CHARLES PHELPS CUSHING.*

whose origin is unknown. The Petizo is a blocky little animal with very short legs and good weight carrying ability. He runs from thirteen to fourteen hands in height. His gait is not as free as the Criollo, the other Argentine type of pony.

In the early days of polo in the Argentine the Petizo was used almost entirely, but when the standard of height was raised the Criollo became popular. The Criollo is descended from Spanish stock. He has inherited the smoothness of gait of his desert ancestors. He much resembles the bronco of the United States and is extremely hardy.

But Criollo blood alone is not enough to make first class polo material. Breeders therefore imported from England Thoroughbred stallions whose get were known to have the desirable qualities. These have been crossed with polo mares of the Criollo stock and the result has been as good a polo mount as there is to be found.

In the United States a similar cross, that is, Thoroughbred stallions on Western polo mares is producing good ponies. Various breeds such as the Morgan, the Quarterhorse and the Arabian, lay claim to the value of an admixture of their blood in obtaining the desirable animal for polo. It has been definitely established that stunted Thoroughbreds are not hardy enough, the polo pony must have *pony* blood in him to be hardy and strong. But the Thoroughbred blood is essential if speed is to be obtained.

The training of the pony is of paramount importance. The old-fashioned method of leaving the ponies to run wild until four and then forcibly breaking them is giving way to the much more scientific methods of handling from birth. Working for long hours in the bitting rig and longe rein, before mounting, and then careful training over a period of months has been found to be the best method.

Good polo ponies bring enormous prices. When one considers the time that must be spent on them and the difference that the mount makes in the game this is not to be wondered at. The last English team to play the United States in this country brought forty ponies over with it. Men of means who have fine ponies are very generous about donating their favorite mounts to their country's team when they are needed for international polo. The good polo pony must not only be swift, agile and obedient, he must really know the game and love it, following the ball on his own account and placing himself in relation to it so that his rider can be in the best position to hit it. Furthermore, he must have great courage and be willing to put his own weight against the weight of an opponent. Rudyard Kipling, in his story, the "Maltese Cat," gives a delightful picture of the sagacity of the polo pony.

PONY

Let us start by saying that according to international rules the distinguishing feature between a horse and a pony is height. Any animal whose height measured at the withers does not exceed fourteen hands and two inches (58 inches) is considered a pony. Nevertheless certain small breeds of horses, Arabian and Quarter Horses for example, are shown as horses in classes for their breed, though they may be under the designated height. However, they may also be shown in children's pony classes. Also polo ponies and cowponies are usually referred to as ponies rather than horses, even though they may exceed by many inches the 14:2 which is supposed to be the limit.

Now let us discuss some of the actual breeds of ponies. The prehistoric drawings of horses on the walls of the Lascaux Cavern in Dordogne show ponies that are exact replicas of today's Exmoor ponies. They have the same broad chest, thick neck, short legs, flowing manes and rather delicate heads. Skeletons of such prehistoric animals have been found in Alaska. From this evidence we assume that all these ponies of the North, including the Icelandic, the Shetland, Welsh, Dülmenian and others, are descended from the Tundra pony of Alaska. A slightly heavier and perhaps larger primitive horse called the Przevalski emigrated from America into Asia, and its descendents include the Mongolian, Norwegian and perhaps the Scottish Garron.

Some of the above breeds, especially the Welsh, have been refined in appearance by the introduction of Arabian and Thoroughbred blood. Some authorities feel that, although this may make the animals more delicate and beautiful to the eye, it detracts from their stamina and ability to survive in their natural habitat. Nature and environment determine the final product, whether it be animal or vegetable. When we find a creature that has remained the same for many thousands of years we know that it is the most perfect specimen which can be produced. Then how do we reconcile the physical differences of the Arabian horse and the Icelandic pony? Both have remained unchanged for many generations. The answer is suitability to environment. Let us first take up the pony descended from the Tundra primitive pony, the Icelandic pony. It lives today in the vast stretches of the Tundra as its ancestors lived. Throughout a long winter it must dig under the snow for roots, twigs and coarse grass. No shelter protects it from the icy winds. Yet the herds survive and increase in size. What are the characteristics of this animal? Its head is large and thick, its nostrils are small and can be tightly closed. Within the head are large nasal passages and teeth with roots three inches long. Its gullet is very wide. Its body is covered by a thick mat of fur with a heavy undercoat. Mane and tail are bushy and thick. The tail is set low and close to the buttocks. All the above characteristics help it to survive in the intense cold and with only the coarse scanty forage. Because the nostrils are small and the air passages large, the animal takes in the cold air in small breaths and then warms it in the large air passages before it is carried to the sensitive lungs. The gullet is wide to permit the entrance of much coarse fodder. The teeth, which renew themselves as they are worn down by growing in from the roots, are long enough to last thirty or more years even though they are worn away much more quickly than those of the southern horse that lives only on grass, hay and grain.

In comparison to the pony the Arabian horse has wide flaring nostrils and narrow air passages. He breathes the air in great gulps and it passes directly to the lungs, where it does no damage as it is already warm. He holds his tail high and away from his body, for he does not need to keep his back to the wind and use his tail as protection. His body coat is fine with no heavy undercoat. In other words, in both animals nature has produced the perfect specimen for its environment. By crossing them we get an animal which is well suited to the needs of the breeder but which would never survive in its natural habitat.

There are a great many recognized breeds of ponies, several of which have only lately come to the fore. These latter, such as the Canyon pony, are merely stunted horses and will probably not survive, as they have no real use. Such an animal is the "toy" horse being bred in Argentina by Señor Julio Falabella. These little animals stand only twenty inches high at the withers when fully mature. They are solid-colored animals with short, weak legs and large heads. This breed has not yet found an official name, though Señor Falabella, who has a stud of about four hundred, is considering calling them *Tapemi* (an aboriginal Indian word meaning "little countryfolk").

POSING

Teaching a pony or horse to "pose" with his front feet up on a small platform is easy and good discipline. Half a nail keg is the simplest thing to use by way of a "prop." Lead the pony up to the keg, lift one foreleg and put it on the keg and then the other, immediately give him a tidbit by way of reward. Repeat this several times daily and at the end of a week it will only be necessary to bring him into the general vicinity of the keg when he will immediately walk over to it, mount and "pose" as long as desired.

POST ENTRY

Certain classes in horse shows permit "post entries," i.e., the owner does not have to enter his horse until fifteen minutes before the class is called. The term is derived from racing, where the contestants were not named until going to the "post."

POSTING

The act of rising to the trot is known as "posting." In the days of the diligences and stage coaches the "post boys" who rode the near horse of each pair soon found that they did not get as tired if they rose in their stirrups on each alternate diagonal. This came to be known as "posting." The favorite Saddler in those days was always an ambler, so the ordinary horseman merely sat quietly to that easy gait but the stage coach horses trotted. In posting to the trot one should go no higher than is necessary and the movement should be forward as well as upward. The knees should remain fixed, the heels and feet should not move and the back muscles should not be brought into play. At the trot the horse moves his diagonal legs alternately. It is more restful to him if the rider changes the diagonal occasionally, i.e., he should post for a while when the left foreleg goes forward, then switch to the right.

POTATOES (use of in feeding)

Potatoes are very useful for fattening a horse. A good sized potato cut up into small cubes and sprinkled on the top of each feed will quickly put on weight when all other methods have failed.

POTATO RACE

This is a good game for gymkhanas. The players, if too many, may play in heats, six to a heat. The potatoes should be laid in parallel rows, four feet apart, the interval between the rows being sufficient to allow the horse to travel and turn. The contestant is given a sharp pointed stick about four feet long and a pail is set at the beginning of each row. The player who first gets all his potatoes in his pail by stabbing them with the stick wins.

POULTICES

Boils and other types of infections are often helped by the application of a hot poultice. The effect, through heat and a tendency to draw, is that the circulation of the blood is increased and the infection is brought to a "head" when it may be lanced. A flaxseed poultice is simple and satisfactory. Take a pound of flaxseed and mix boiling water with it until it is a soupy paste. Cool until able to be borne and then put on the affected area. Cover with a heavy coating of absorbent cotton and several thicknesses of newspaper. Bind the poultice in place with a suitable bandage and do not disturb for twelve hours. Bran may also be used for a poultice though it is not as effective as flaxseed. If an antiseptic poultice is required, a handful of salt or a teaspoon of lysol may be added. Antiphlogistene is the best poultice as far as retaining the heat goes. It is clay-like in substance.

The can is heated in boiling water. To test the heat stir with a knife blade and then hold the blade on the back of your hand; it should be as hot as you can bear it but should not burn.

One of the most common injuries which require poulticing is nail in the foot; use flaxseed for this, put a large square of heavy cambric on the ground and spread a thick poultice on it. Wash the horse's foot thoroughly in hot Epsom salts, then have him stand on the poultice. Bring the ends up and tie them securely around the pastern. Remember that the thicker the poultice and the covering the longer it will hold the heat.

POWDERS (healing)

Healing powders are useful on abrasions and surface wounds where it is desirable to heal the wound quickly. B.F.I. (Bismuth, Formic Iodide), Asterole, and Sulfanilimide are all good.

PRAD

This is a Victorian word for horse. One finds it used in Dickens but more especially in Surtees' works.

PREPOTENCY

The ability of a stallion to pass his outstanding characteristics down to his get is known as prepotency. Some stallions are prepotent to such a degree that generations later their descendents will still display the characteristics of the original sire. Justin Morgan, founder of the Morgan breed, is an outstanding example of this.

PRESSURE BANDAGES

For horses with worn, weak or injured tendons or for horses that tend to "stock up" pressure bandages are very helpful. First apply a thick layer of dry cotton wool and then wrap firmly with an ordinary wool roller bandage. The bandage may be wrapped spiral fashion beginning at the top and going around the leg several times before beginning the spiral. It should be given a half twist on each turn and the pressure should be even and not too tight.

PRICKED SOLE

A pricked sole may be caused by careless shoeing or by stepping on a nail. In the case of the former the blacksmith has driven the nail too close to the quick. The symptoms are extreme lameness and heat in the wall and sole. Have the shoe removed at once. Soak the horse's foot in hot Epsom salts. If there is a hole in the sole which can be reached have it pared out and pour iodine into it. Put a flax-seed poultice (see *POULTICES*) on it for several days. If the injury is bad or there is known to be tetanus in the territory the horse had better be given a tetanus shot to prevent lockjaw.

PRIMITIVE HORSE

See *HORSE, Origin of.*

PRISONER'S BASE

This is a game which, with good players, can be very exciting. It is best played in a ring or enclosure. The enclosure should be marked off into thirds. The size of the enclosure will decide the number of players but usually from five to seven on a side is best.

One third of the enclosure will be the home territory of one team, let us call them the "Blues." The third at the opposite end will be "home" for the "Reds." The central portion is free ground. In the center of each "home" territory a portion of the end barrier will be a "goal." For a Blue to make a goal and consequently score a point he must ride from his own territory down and touch the Red's goal without being tagged by a member of the opposing team. If he is so tagged he is a prisoner and must remain inside the Red's home territory until freed by one of his own team mates. If more than one person on a team is imprisoned all are freed when one is touched by a member of their own team. A person freeing prisoners may not at the same time make a goal,

but he may return to his own territory without being caught.

Anyone may ride in the central "free" portion of the field, but they are subject to being tagged by a member of the opposing team if the latter has left his own territory since the cruising member has done so. Thus, if "A" on the Blue team comes out into free ground and "B" of the Red team comes out after "A" does, "B" can tag "A" and take him prisoner.

PRIVET HEDGES (for jumps)

Privet makes a good hedge for "brush jumps." When first planted it must be protected from animals or it will not grow but, once it gets going well, it is hardy and readily trimmed to a good height. It is wise to put a rail a few inches below the top as horses being schooled often get careless and brush through so often that there is little left of the hedge.

PRODUCE RACE

A race in which competitors have been nominated before their birth.

PROFILE

The profile of the horse tells much about his breeding and his potential value. It should be carefully studied before the animal is purchased. The "dished" profile, i.e., one with a depression between the forehead and the end of the nose, indicates Arab blood. Thoroughbreds sometimes show this profile having inherited it from the desert ancestors. On the other hand, a "Roman" nose indicates coarseness and "cold," possibly draft, blood. The "top" line is very revealing of the body. The Arabian's and the Saddler's croup line will be nearly straight. The Barb has a lower set tail and the croup of the Thoroughbred also slopes away. The Hambletonian will have higher croup than withers. If the back dips in badly the horse is getting on in years. If the back has a "hog bend" with low withers it will be nearly impossible to keep a saddle in place on him without having to resort to a crupper strap. The horse whose back between withers and croup appears excessively long will be a poor weight carrier and a hard keeper.

Particularly in judging colts where the muscles are not developed and the animal cannot be tried under the saddle, a careful study of the animal's profile is important.

PROPORTIONS OF THE HORSE

The desired proportions of the horse depend largely upon the work he is to be required to do. Study the photographs given in this volume of the various breeds. Notice how they differ in proportions. Before buying your horse decide which type is most suitable for your purpose and then get one having as nearly the ideal proportions for that type as you can find. See also *HORSE; PONY; PROFILE; CONFORMATION.*

PROTEST

A protest, if the owner of an entry does not agree with the Judge's decision, may be entered at a horse show but it must be in writing and a bond of twenty-five dollars must be put up and the latter is forfeited if the original judgment is sustained. Winners of races are sometimes protested also, in the case of a foul.

PROUD FLESH

This is the name given to the unhealthy tissue which sometimes forms around a wound. If allowed to remain a large scar will result. Application of nitrate of silver or of powdered alum will burn off the proud flesh and the wound will heal much more readily.

PUFFS

See *WIND GALLS.*

PULLING

See *VICES.*

PULSE

The pulse may be taken where the submaxillary artery passes under the jaw or at the radial artery inside the foreleg.

The horseman should make a practice of finding and taking the horse's pulse frequently so that in an emergency he can do so quickly. The normal pulse is 36 to 40 beats to the minute.

PUPPY WALKING

Puppy walking is more common in England than here. The expression refers to the custom of "farming out" puppies to people who are interested in the hunt. The foster parents keep the puppies from the time of weaning until they are old enough to be returned to the kennel for training.

PURCHASING THE HORSE

See *BUYING THE HORSE; DEALERS.*

PURGATIVES

As the strength and amount of the purgative will depend on the size of the horse a veterinarian should be asked to prescribe a purgative. Epsom salts and linseed oil are safe for the amateur. See *LAXATIVES.*

PUSH POLO

This is a good game but requires special equipment in the form of an inflated ball at least three feet in diameter. The riders push the ball by riding against it, each team trying to maneuver it between the goal lines of the opposing team. Ponies are particularly adapted to this game and soon learn to push the ball ahead of them with their noses.

PUTTING TO (hounds)

See *HUNTING TERMS.*

Q

QUAD

This is a Cockney slang word for a horse.

QUADRILLE (Dressage Quadrille)

The Dressage Quadrille was a very popular form of entertainment and mounted exercise in the days when kings and noblemen maintained private schools of equitation. Today we see the Dressage Quadrille performed by the Spanish Riding School of Vienna with all the beauty and exactness of execution which has descended to us over the centuries. To the stately music of the dance the maroon-coated riders with their above-the-knee black boots, two-cornered hats and white breeches, mounted on their snowy Lipizzan horses, wheel, pirouette, advance and retreat in the lofty, measured cadence of the *passage*, every rider maintaining his exact distance and interval with relation to the others.

Although no ordinary group of riders could hope to achieve such perfection, a group whose members are skillful enough to execute the shoulder-in, traversal, counter-change, voltes and half-turns at the sitting trot, and circles and flank movements at the canter can develop a very pretty exhibition and improve themselves and their horses in so doing. Special music must be selected first. Then movements to match the phrases, so that the horses change figures and gaits as the musical phrases change, must be chosen. A good plan is to use a three-minute selection suited to the cadence of the sitting trot, with a variety of figures selected and ridden at this gait, followed by three minutes of the canter, which, of course, is always done to a slow waltz rhythm, and finally by another three minutes of different figures to different music for the last part of the dance. Introduction music and an exit will also have to be chosen and rehearsed. When all has been decided upon, an LP record or a tape recording of all the music can be made. If a record is to be used and the Quadrille done as an exhibition, it is well to have two records made, one for everyday practice and one to be kept for exhibition purposes.

Although a passable Quadrille exhibition can be given with four riders, eight are better and twelve more effective still. Remember, however, that the more riders the more difficult it is to acquire a semblance of perfection. The music for the trotting phases should have the rhythm of Morton Gould's "Pavanne" or the well-known "Syncopated Clock" by Leroy Anderson. For the cantering phases use pieces such as the "Gold and Silver Waltz" or "The Skater's Waltz."

The conventional costume for performing an exhibition dressage quadrille is high silk hat, white stock tied in an Ascot knot with a gold safety pin to hold it, yellow vest, white breeches and black boots. White boutonnieres and white gloves add elegance. Though the above sounds like an exceedingly expensive outfit, and would be if tailored to measure, one can often go to a local "thrift shop" and buy the top hats and tailcoats for a song. White corduroys or gabardine breeches are quite cheap; yellow vests can easily be made by covering the front of an old vest with a heavy yellow twill and adding brass buttons.

QUALITY

The "quality" of a horse is its fineness, "substance" refers to its strength or stamina. In horse show judging certain classes put emphasis on "quality," others on "substance." Particularly in divisions where there are classes for Thoroughbreds and other than Thoroughbreds such as the hunter division, the emphasis in the class for Thoroughbreds would be put on quality while that for other than Thoroughbreds would be on substance.

QUARANTINE

It is often necessary to quarantine a horse and always wise if a new animal comes into the stable, particularly if he has been shipped from some little distance. A special stall for this purpose should be selected, preferably one which is well separated from the others.

QUARTER

The area on the outside of horse's foot,

seat of "quarter cuts." See *HORSE, Points of.*

QUARTER BOOT

This is a flexible boot attached above the coronet which extends down over the hoof and protects the quarter from injury.

QUARTER CLIPS

Horseshoes are attached by means of nails plus extensions or clips which are triangular in shape and come up over the edge of the wall. The clips may be either at the toe or at the quarters. Quarter clips are to be preferred, particularly for the back feet, as they hold very much more firmly than do toe clips.

QUARTER CRACKS

These are cracks in the hoof at the location of the quarter. See also *SAND CRACK.*

QUARTER CUTS

Cuts on the quarters caused by striking with the other foot are called "Quarter Cuts." A horse that overreaches should be protected by the wearing of quarter boots.

QUARTER HORSE

The Quarter horse derives his name from the fact that the early settlers of Virginia liked to race their horses in competition over "race paths" rather than regular tracks. These paths were cut out of the wilderness and averaged a quarter of a mile in length. Thus the Quarter horse was primarily a race horse, but he is the extreme opposite in conformation of the Thoroughbred which is the type generally thought of in connection with flat racing. The Thoroughbred has been developed for sustained speed. He is light in comparison to his height, his legs are long, permitting a great length of stride, his neck and head

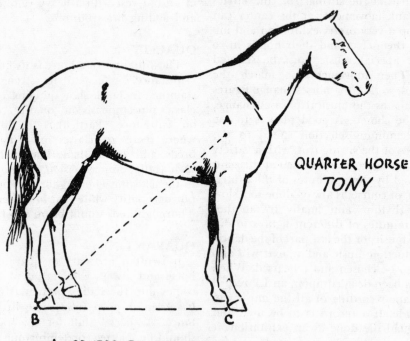

QUARTER HORSE
TONY

A—CENTER OF WEIGHT
A B— LINE OF THRUST
A B C —ANGLE OF THRUST

FIGURE 102. CHARACTERISTICS OF THE QUARTER HORSE.

are slender and long, his pasterns are sloping and long and his muscles are long and flat. The Quarter horse, on the other hand, is low to the ground with thick, short cannons. Although a full hand or more shorter than the Thoroughbred he weighs about the same, 1200 pounds. All his weight is carried in front. This reduces the "angle of thrust" in his stride making for less elevation and consequently more speed forward. His muscles, particularly of shoulder, jaw, thigh and gaskin, are lumpy and bulky. Because he is heavy and carries so much weight in front he tires easily, but he can get off to a faster start, turn more easily and develop more speed over a short course than any other breed of horse. It is therefore not surprising to find that, although his popularity as a race horse declined with the regulation tracks, he is a great favorite with ranchers as a cowpony. In addition to his build the Quarter horse is an easy keeper, he can live off the land, and he has a mild disposition. His agility, speed and weight make him ideal for roping and holding steers.

FIGURE 103. WIMPY, CHAMPION QUARTER HORSE WHOSE STATUE STANDS OUTSIDE THE HEADQUARTERS OF THE MORGAN HORSE ASSOCIATION IN AMARILLO, TEXAS. *COURTESY AMERICAN QUARTER HORSE ASSOCIATION.*

The foundation sire of the American Quarter horse was imported Janus, an English Thoroughbred that stood in Virginia between 1756 and 1780. The genealogies of all present-day Quarter horses trace back to this stallion. As has been noted in the case of Messenger, himself a Thoroughbred whose progeny were noted for their speed at the trot and for their ambling, pacing and racking abilities, the English Thoroughbred was developed from Arabian stock on native mares. Somewhere in the ancestry of Janus there must have been a happy "nick" which gave him the peculiar characteristics of the Quarter horse and also the prepotency to pass them down. Janus stood about 14.2, heavy built with bulging muscles, and was raced over four mile courses but his "get" were all known for their ability to spurt for short distances.

QUARTERING

Quartering is a modified form of grooming in which the blanket is left on. The animal's head and neck are brushed, the blanket folded back and one forequarter groomed, the front is replaced, the back folded forward and the hindquarter on the same side groomed. The groom then goes around to the other side and does the other two sections in the same way. The legs and feet are cleaned and examined. With race horses it is customary to give them a "quartering" before their work out and give them a thorough grooming later.

'QUARTERS

This is an abbreviation for hindquarters and refers to the part of the horse behind the center of gravity, which is at the girth.

QUINELLA

A bet to select the first *two* horses to finish in a race, not necessarily in the order of finish.

QUITTOR

Quittor is a fistulous sore on the coronet. It may come from a blow from the other foot, or from pus working up from a suppurating corn or from "gravel" or a suppurating sand crack. The condition is serious. Apply a poultice and send for the veterinarian.

R

RACE HORSE

The term race horse brings to mind the type of horse which has been developed specifically for flat racing, namely the English Thoroughbred. This breed was produced by crossing imported Arabian stallions with European native mares. All registered Thoroughbreds go back to one of the three original desert stallions, the Byerly Turk, the Darley Arabian or the Godolphin Barb, all imported into England between 1690 and 1725. Later, importations of Arabian stallions improved the breed still more.

Through selective breeding the Thoroughbred has steadily increased in speed, but his stamina is not as great as other breeds. He cannot "live off the land" as can the cow pony, also descended from desert stock. He cannot carry the amount of weight in proportion to his height that the three-quarter or a stockier type of horse such as the Morgan can carry.

Thoroughbreds with jumping ability are made into steeplechasers. The steeplechaser must be able to take jumps in his stride and to have speed at the gallop. He is more greatly handicapped by weight than the flat racer for the steeplechase jockey does not ride with as short stirrups as his brother the flat-racing jockey.

In speaking of race horses one should not forget the little Quarter horse. In type, he is the direct opposite of the Thoroughbred, being short legged and bunch muscled. He originated in pioneer

FIGURE 104. THE HEAD OF A RACE HORSE. THE LEAN, BONY HEAD, ALERT EXPRESSION, THIN, FINE MANE AND TINY EARS DENOTE THE THOROUGHBRED.

days where the plantation owners of Virginia, having hacked out quarter mile "race paths" from the virgin forests, amused themselves by engaging in what might be termed "sprinting races." Though the American Quarter Horse no longer races on formal tracks as, due to his build and his type of muscles, he tires at the end of his quarter of a mile, he is far from out of favor for he makes a splendid cowpony. Incidentally, the Quarter horse, though completely different in conformation from the Thoroughbred, is descended from the imported English Thoroughbred stallion, Janus, who goes back to the Godolphin Barb.

The American Standard Bred trotting horse traces his ancestry to Messenger, the famous English Thoroughbred imported in 1788 and whose pedigree goes back to Darley's Arabian. The trotter, or Standard Bred, differs in conformation from the Thoroughbred in having heavier, higher hindquarters, a straighter shoulder, longer back and somewhat

coarser head. The pacer also traces his lineage to Messenger and is similar in conformation to the trotter. The Orloffs, the Russian family of trotters, go back to the Arabian stock though the Arab himself is not a speedy trotter.

Thus, one finds that selective breeding, beginning with the same original stock (desert crosses with European) has given us three very distinct types of race horses, each the fastest to be found in his class. See also *THOROUGHBRED; QUARTER HORSE; STANDARD BRED; ARABIAN; MESSENGER; RECORDS AND STATISTICS—HARNESS RACING* and *STEEPLECHASE AND HUNT* (Appendix.)

RACING

The instinct of competition is innate in mankind. No sooner does the child learn to talk and to run than he challenges his playmates to a race.

The earliest record that we have of racing is in a papyrus letter written by Thothmes I in the 18th Egyptian Dynasty. Thothmes wrote that, having conquered Mesopotamia, he was bringing back a racing horse (an Arab). This is apparently the introduction of the Arab in Africa. Somewhat later Solomon bought a number of racing horses in Egypt, paying as much as the equivalent of $3,000 for some.

The Greeks introduced racing in the Olympic games in 648 B.C. From there it spread to Rome.

England is the birthplace of the Thoroughbred, and racing is the life of the British public. The oldest racing in England ocurred in Newmarket during the reign of Charles II. Newmarket is still the scene of racing today, as well as being the home of the Jockey Club. An English race now known as the "Roodee" and held at Chester was, under Henry VIII, known as the "Roody."

Queen Elizabeth kept a stud and racing stable and in 1587, accompanied by a vast retinue, she attended the races at Croydon. The York Plates is the oldest race which has continued each year since

FIGURE 105. WHIRLAWAY, THE TOP MONEY-WINNING RACE HORSE OF THE WORLD. *BERT CLARK THAYER.*

its founding. It was first run in 1711 under Queen Anne.

The earliest formal description of a race is to be found in Clarkson's History of Richmond. It occurred on May 6, 1622. Six horses were entered and the race was four miles long.

Royalty continued to be interested in racing and we find that George IV, as Prince of Wales, rode in and won 185 races, one of which was the Derby (1788). Racing was introduced into France from England during the reign of Louis XIV where it became very popular.

Nothing, with the exception of warfare, has been so responsible for the development of the blood horse as has been racing. When large prizes are offered for the horse that can run the fastest, it is only natural that both amateur and professional breeders are going to concen-

trate not only on raising horses but on raising the *fastest* horses. Of the original strains of horses the Arabs were the fleetest. But it was soon discovered that the crossing of the Arab with the larger mares of the European continent created an even swifter species which later came to be called the English Thoroughbred. From a number of desert stallions and mares came the founders of the three great Thoroughbred families. All present day race horses go back to one or more of these stallions. Matchem was foaled in 1748, Herod in 1758 and Eclipse in 1764. Ninety-five percent of the winners of the English Derby go back to the Darley Arabian, sire of Eclipse. Man of War, the most famous American race horse, who won twenty-one out of twenty-two starts traces his pedigree back to all three foundation sires. He is said to have inherited the speed of Eclipse, the staying power of Matchem and the heart of Herod. The interest in racing and in the breeding of Thoroughbreds in America paralleled that in England. The early settlers of Virginia and Maryland had what came to be known as "Quarter horses." Regular tracks were unknown but racing paths of about a quarter of a mile in length were cut out of the forests and sprinting races became popular.

Longer races were also popular during revolutionary times. Handicappers, jockeys, bookmakers there were none. But it was customary for one gentleman to challenge another and if they came from different states then much interest ensued, for each horse was considered to be upholding the reputation of his state. Of betting there was plenty, though no stakeholders were considered necessary for the betting was between friends. The race was started either by a pistol shot or by the dropping of a handkerchief. The owner might ride his own horse or, if he were to heavy or not too proficient as a horseman he might get a young friend to substitute. Many races were run in three heats of four miles each. If a horse didn't do so well in the first heat the owner might decide to switch jockeys for the remaining two.

Endurance rides were also popular and we read of the wager of Mr. Obalddeston of England who, in 1831, bet a thousand guineas that he could ride 200 miles in ten hours. A four miles course was laid out and, changing horses every four miles (a total of 29 horses were used) the energetic gentleman covered the distance in 8 hours and 42 minutes without any apparent effort!

Before the establishment of regular race courses certain cities were wont to give over streets or thoroughfares to racing. Third Avenue in New York was the popular scene of brushes between the owners of the fastest trotting and pacing horses. Race Street in Philadelphia was used for running horses. In 1665 Governor Nicolls of New York, an Englishman to whom the development of the Thoroughbred was important, inaugurated the first race course in America. It was on the flats of Long Island near Hempstead and the good Governor offered a silver porringer as a trophy. The race became an annual event, a new porringer being put up each year. One of these trophies turned up recently in a silver shop and is now at Yale University.

In its growth from casual infancy to formal adulthood, racing has been threatened with extinction more than once. In the United States religion has played a large part in influencing not only the geographic position of racing centers but it has also been responsible for the development of certain breeds of horses. In New England racing was forbidden entirely under the Blue Laws of the Puritans. So the breeding of the running horse moved South. Pennsylvania, New Jersey, Maryland, Delaware and Virginia continued to raise and run gallopers but the people of New England proper, with the exception of Rhode Island, satisfied their interest in seeing whose horse could go the fastest by switching to harness horses. The makers of the Blue Laws evidently realized that there was nothing they could do to prevent one farmer challenging another to a brush on the public highway; so, they ruled that trotting and pacing were not racing! Were it not for the Blue Laws it is probable that the standard bred horse would never have come to the fore as a racer but would have remained simply a utility animal.

Wars did much to curtail racing and the raising of Thoroughbreds. It also shifted the interest in racing away from the territories which were the actual scenes of battle and so spread popularity of the sport.

Without the interest of the spectators in betting racing would never have become the "big business" that it had to become in order to survive. The great crowds that go to the meets go there not only to see the horses run but in the hopes of making a little extra money. The fact that they have a personal interest involved whets their enthusiasm. It is the size of the crowds which permits the tracks to offer the tremendous prizes which they offer for the various Stakes races. Until Belmont realized this and began upping the Stakes at Belmont Park, racing bid fair to die of lassitude.

The track at Churchill Downs outside Louisville, Kentucky, where the "Kentucky Derby" takes place, lost money continuously from the time it was founded in 1875 until the early nineteen hundreds. It was about to be closed for lack of funds when Colonel Matt Winn was persuaded to buy it. Studying the success of the northern tracks he quickly came to the conclusion that the prizes being offered at Churchill Downs were not large enough to attract the owners of the larger racing stables. They would rather go to Hempstead, Saratoga and Belmont. So he upped the stakes.

But racing had now become an enormous and in some cases a very corrupt business. There was no standardization of rules between states and no method of disciplining jockeys, owners or trainers who intentionally fixed a race in order to put money into their own pockets. If the racing commission of one state forbade a certain jockey to ride or a certain owner to enter his horses, because of malpractice, the miscreant had only to cross the state line in order to continue racing.

Betting also had fallen into the hands of unscrupulous men who found it easy to make their books in such a way that the bookmaker was bound to win a large share of the money. So betting was banned in many states. One effect of this was to move the racing over the border into Mexico.

Even without war, religion and ethics, it is probable that racing would never have grown to more than a spindly child had it not been for the handicapping system. When several horses race against each other and one is obviously the fastest there is not much point in racing those same horses again until, in some way, the fast animal can be so handi-

capped that there is some possibility of his being beaten by the others.

The present system of handicapping is the result of an immense amount of study on the part of men of very keen minds. All Thoroughbreds are considered to have been foaled on the first of January of the year of their birth. They are sold as yearlings, trained the following fall and, if they have matured sufficiently, raced as two-year-olds. The younger they are the less weight they have to carry. A two-year-old in July will carry twenty-four pounds less weight than a three-year-old and thirty-two pounds less than a four-year-old over a six furlong course. This system of handicapping was originated in England by Admiral the Honorable John Henry Rous, the English racing expert. It is known as the "weight for age" system. (See appendix.)

A board of experts studies the outcome of each race and as a horse grows in reputation, winning more and more races, he is required to carry more and more weight in order that the contests may remain as equal as possible. The actual time in which a horse runs a given distance is completely immaterial until one inquires into the amount of weight he carried. For the time of one horse covering a mile can obviously not be considered better than the time of another over the same course carrying thirty or forty pounds more even though the stop-watch shows that the more lightly burdened animal covered the distance much faster.

In addition to handicap races there are specific kinds of races which limit or qualify the entrants in one way or another. We have, for example, the so called "condition races." These may be for two-year-old colts or for two-year-old fillies or for any two-year-olds which have not won a race since a certain date. Or, they may be for three-year-olds and up, none of which has won a race since a specified month. Thus the entries are limited to horses which are not topnotchers.

Allowance races are those in which the

handicap of each horse is determined by his past performance and the racing secretary informs the horsemen which of their Thoroughbreds is eligible for a given race.

Claiming races are those in which the value of a horse is limited and is declared by the owner before the race. A claim may be put in for the animal by another owner and if such a claim is put in the animal changes hands at the end of the race. Should the horse be killed during the race the claimer gets the corpse, the owner the money. Selling races are similar in effect but here the *winner* of the race is auctioned off after the race.

In 1750 the English realized that some sort of organization was necessary to control racing and the Jockey Club was established at Newmarket. In the United States each state which permits racing has a Racing Commission which governs the racing in that state. But these Commissions and other Racing Associations which were formed were not uniform. In 1893 it was felt necessary to organize a club which would have more control and which could standardize the rules of racing. At the request of the owners and trainers the Jockey Club was formed to control the racing in New York. The purpose was to give to this club the power of licensing jockeys and trainers, revising the rules, appointing officials, arranging race schedules and acting as final court of appeal in the question of disputes. The Jockey Club also took over the registration of Thoroughbred horses and became the custodian of the American Stud Book. No horse may race on any recognized course unless his name is in the Stud Book and no horse may be registered unless he is purebred with the name of both sire and dam in the book. In this way the Thoroughbred strain is kept pure.

Not only does the Jockey Club maintain control in New York State and in Delaware, but it has helped to formulate the rules in nearly all the Eastern Seaboard states. The Jockey Club uses its right to cancel licenses as a means of discipline. A jockey, trainer or owner who has lost his license because of misbehavior may not race on any track governed by the Jockey Club. In cases of flagrant malpractice such as the evidence of a horse having been doped all the horses of that stable are forbidden the track.

The Jockey Club sends a veterinarian to each track and he passes on the condition of each horse before he is allowed to race. Patrol judges watch the race from all angles through fieldglasses to prevent fouls. The jockey is weighed before he rides and immediately afterwards to make sure that there has been no tampering with weights. The shoes of the horses are inspected, for a too heavy shoe would materially lessen the probability of the success of the animal.

These and many others are the duties of the Jockey Club. But by 1942 it was recognized that an organization with an even wider scope was necessary. The Thoroughbred Racing Association was formed at the request of owners, trainers, race-track officials and others interested in all phases of racing. Its purposes as stated in its by-laws are to promote and coordinate patriotic and charitable activities of the Thoroughbred racing associations of the United States; to promote the common business interest and improve the business conditions of the Thoroughbred racing associations; to promote interest in Thoroughbred racing and to improve the operations affecting Thoroughbred racing; to prepare and distribute literature which will contain information useful to Thoroughbred racing associations.

Since its foundation the T.R.A. has been extremely active. All the major racing associations are included in the membership of T.R.A., and this widening of scope means a unification of racing rules and an increase in power.

Early in the twentieth century reforms swept the country and one of the first activities to be attacked by the reformers was that of gambling as carried on at the race tracks. Many states forbade bookmaking or auctioneering, the two forms of betting which were in use. But either some form of betting would have to be permitted or the death knell of racing would be tolled. The problem was solved by the introduction of the invention of Pierre Oller, the French perfumer. Oller, disgusted at the dishonesty of the bookmakers, had invented a new system of betting known as the "pari-mutuel" system. The "totalizer" or machine which mechanically figures out the odds was installed at a French track and became immediately popular. But it was not for some time that American tracks adopted this system. Now it is the only one permitted under the Jockey Club rules.

In order to stimulate breeding the "Futurity" or "produce races" were instituted. In these the foal is registered before its birth. The distances and weights are adjusted to the ages of the colts. The breeder is encouraged to register all his foals soon after birth for the fees are enormously increased as the foal attains maturity.

The major racing sections of the United States are the East, which includes the tracks of New York, New England and Maryland; the Mid-West, which

FIGURE 106. THE START OF THE PENSACOLA CLAIMING HANDI-CAP AT THE HIALEAH TRACK IN MIAMI. NOTE THE AUTOMATIC STARTING GATES. *WIDE WORLD.*

takes in Kentucky, Ohio, Chicago, Nebraska and Detroit; the South, which includes Florida, Louisiana and Hot Springs, and the West, California and Washington.

It has taken two hundred years to come from the informal meets between neighbors to the present day elaborate race meeting with its thousand of spectators, its enormous purses, its Thoroughbreds with their retinues of trainers, exercise boys, jockeys, etc., and the track with its automatic starting gates, its many race officials, its photographic finishes, etc. If one includes the many professions and businesses which lie behind this great spectacle one must admit that racing is one of the larger present day industries.

See also *BETTING SYSTEMS; HARNESS RACING; HANDICAPPING; THOROUGHBREDS; JOCKEY CLUB; T.R.A.; DEAD HEAT; RACING; RECORDS AND STATISTICS* (appendix).

RACING COLORS

The Jockey Club assigns colors to racing stables according to applications. They may be assigned for one year or for life. Sometimes colors are reassigned when no longer in use, but this is not the case with the colors of famous stables. Jockeys wear the colors as assigned, and the pattern of caps and shirts, as far as the colors are concerned, is also prescribed.

RACK

The "rack," *"amble rompu"* or "broken amble" is one of the gaits of the five-gaited Saddler. It is also known as the "singlefoot" by reason of the fact that it is a four-beat gait, each foot striking the ground separately. It is very fast and smooth with much elevation. It is a tiring gait for the horse though very easy for the rider. A horse should not be allowed to rack for too long a period without being rested by being shifted to another gait. Horses of saddle ancestry are easily taught to rack though the gait may be more of an amble with less brilliance. Trotters also, coming of the same original stock as the Saddlers (both descended from the imported Thoroughbred stallion, Messenger) will often break into a rack. The rack should not be confused with the pace which is a two-beat gait, the lateral legs moving in unison. This is usually a very uncomfortable gait for the rider though there are smooth pacers.

RANGE HORSE

This is the correct term for a horse or pony used for work with cattle. The common term is "cow pony."

RAPPING POLE

In training an "open" jumper it is customary to use the rapping pole to encourage him to fold up his back legs. The procedure is for the trainer to stand at one end of the jump holding a light pole a few inches above the top rail of the obstacle. After the horse has cleared the jump with his front legs the trainer brings the pole up and gives the animal a sharp rap on his belly. If trainers would use only a light pole and not punish the horse when he is doing his best, there would be no objection to the rapping pole. Unfortunately this is not the case. At the shows one sees the horses being forced over jumps again and again and no matter how high or how well they jump they are continually rapped. At a recent out-door show the Humane Society confiscated a rapping pole that had a row of sharp nails in it. Such practices are not only cruel in the extreme but, by forcing the horse beyond his natural endurance, shorten his useful life.

RASPING (the hoof)

Rasping or filing the wall of the hoof to make it fit the shoe is a practice greatly to be condemned. Examine your horse's hoofs after they have been newly shod and make sure that the line from coronet to toe is continuous and does not appear to have been rasped away.

RASSEMBLER
See *CHAMPING THE BIT*.

RATE (to rate hounds)
See *HUNTING TERMS*.

RATIONS
See *FEED; FEEDING; HORSE, General Care*.

REARING
See *VICES*.

REATA
A reata is a lariat used for roping. The word "lariat" is the English pronunciation of the Spanish "La Reata."

RECOVERY (after stumbling)
Although the natural instinct of the rider, when the horse stumbles, is to pull up on the reins, people who have studied ballistics feel that the best thing to do is to allow the horse a loose rein so that he may use his head to balance himself.

RECORDS AND STATISTICS
See Appendix.

RED ROVER
This is a game suitable for both intermediate riders and advanced riders. It should be played in an enclosed ring. One rider stands in the middle of the enclosure, the other players being lined up at one end. The player in the middle calls: "Red Rover, Red Rover, come over, come over." All the other players now try to ride from where they are to the opposite end without being tagged by the person who is "it." If tagged a player remains in the center and, the next time the others are called across, helps tag. This continues until all are caught, the last player to be caught is considered the winner and is "it" for the next game.

REFUSALS
When a horse shies out or stops before a jump it constitutes a refusal. The penalty in horse shows is three points for the first refusal, six for the second, elimination for the third.

Horses that refuse consistently are being asked to jump obstacles for which they have not been sufficiently prepared in their training. The tendency among trainers is to rush the training, obtaining the horse's obedience by force rather than by habit. In training jumpers the jumps should be kept very low until the horse automatically responds to the signals given by the rider which indicate that he is to jump. The obstacles should then be raised by degrees, an inch or two at a time, and the horse should become thoroughly confident over each new height before being asked to take the next. The jumping of peculiar looking obstacles should be introduced and the horse patiently schooled to take off on signal, no matter what the obstacle.

Another common cause of refusals is too much schooling. The horse becomes bored or tired and "goes sour." Such a horse should be started all over again, just as though he had never had a lesson in jumping.

If a horse refuses in a show, it is best to give him only a short run when bringing him up to the jump for the second time and to use the aids strongly, in this way he will not have so much time in which to consider refusing.

If a horse refuses in the hunt field, he should be pulled out of the line, all other riders who are waiting to jump the panel should be allowed to go ahead and the refusing horse should follow the last rider. This is a very strict rule, and a wise one, for taking the refusing horse back to the panel before the other riders have taken it means that he may refuse again and thereby delay the field. Letting him go last makes him the more willing to jump as few horses like to be left entirely behind.

REGISTRY OF HORSES
The seventeen American breeds of horses as listed in this volume under *"BREEDS,"* have Associations which

keep records of the horses registered as being of that breed. In some cases it is necessary that both the mare and stallion have been registered. In some the stallion only, with mare of certain other breeds being eligible. In some cases, such as the Palomino, the color is the deciding factor, and in others, such as the Quarter horse, it is the conformation and type. Owners wishing to register their horses should write to the appropriate Association for the necessary blanks.

REINING

These contests, over complicated patterns, test the flexibility, knowledge, intelligence and willingness of the horse. He is judged on time and proficiency in changing leads, turning, stopping and backing, as well as on balance, lack of excitement and obedience in the above.

REINING BACK

To rein back is to cause the horse to move backwards. The animal should first, by suppling motions of the reins, be induced to depress his chin, the rider then gives the signal for movement by pressure of the legs and causes the movement to be backwards instead of forwards by stronger suppling of the reins. As soon as the horse takes a step backwards the aids should be relaxed. He is then, in the same fashion, asked to take another step backwards. The horse should never be allowed to rush backwards or to take more steps than the rider demands; to allow him to do otherwise invites the forming of a bad "defense" habit when a horse, to escape being asked to move forwards, backs up.

REINS

The reins are the telegraph lines between the horse's mouth and the rider. Through them he controls the forehand of the horse and also learns, in advance of the performance, of unexpected and perhaps undesired actions of his mount.

Types of reins.

The ordinary double bridle has two sets of reins, the snaffle and the curb.

The snaffle reins are usually a little wider than the curb reins and are fastened together by a buckle. This is so that they may be unbuckled to allow the attachment of a running martingale. The curb reins are stitched together. The reins may be fastened to the bit either by stitching, by hooks, by buckles or by a leather slide.

Hunting bridles often have braided reins. These give the rider a better grip in wet weather. Reins with rubber over them are also sometimes used for this purpose.

On Western bridles the reins are not buckled together. Western horses are trained to stand when the rein is pulled over their heads and allowed to hang down. If the reins are not fastened together there is less likelihood of the horse becoming entangled in them. Such reins are often fastened to the bit by means of a leather loop. See also *BRIDLES.*

Use of reins.

A study of the accompanying diagram explains the effect of the reins when used in the four ways described. It should be noted that the reins should never be used alone but always in conjunction with the legs and weight. It will depend on exactly what movement is required how these aids are coordinated. For example, in the use of either the direct or indirect rein where the horse is being asked to turn while moving his hindquarters to follow in the path of his forehand, the opposite or outside leg is used. If the desire is to turn the horse in place, croup around forehand, the right rein of indirect opposition in conjunction with the right heel may be used. This turns the horse to the right and pushes the hindquarters to the left. The right indirect rein of opposition, if applied in front of the withers in conjunction with the left heel, will cause the horse to turn to the left on his center. The right indirect rein of opposition applied behind the withers and in

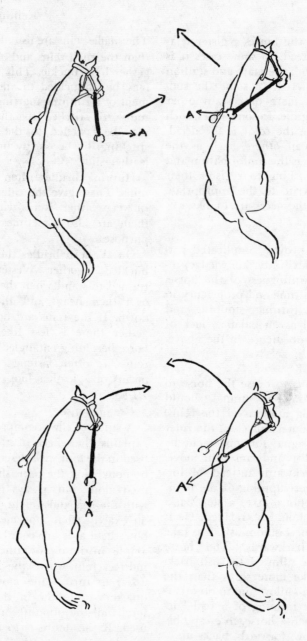

A indicates the direction of the pressure being applied to rein. *Upper left:* THE LEADING REIN. Pressure is to the right, horse's head is turned to the right and the direction of the turn is to the right. *Upper right:* BEARING REIN. Pressure is against the horse's neck to the left, horse turns his head to the right very slightly but he himself turns to the left. This is sometimes called "bridlewise." *Lower left:* DIRECT REIN OF OPPOSITION. Pressure is exerted to the right and to the rear. Horse turns to the right without advancing. *Bottom right:* INDIRECT REIN OF OPPOSITION. Pressure is to the rear and to the left. Horse turns to the left without advancing.

FIGURE 107. USE OF THE REINS.

conjunction with the right leg will cause the horse to two-track to the left.

The horse should be schooled to react correctly to the different rein and leg effects, but the lessons should not be hurried and he should not be asked to go on to the more advanced lessons until the early reflexes are thoroughly established. See also COLTS, Breaking and Training; AIDS.

REMOUNT

When the United States maintained a horse cavalry the latter had military centers in various parts of the country known as Remount Stations. Here horses to be used as replacements for discarded cavalry mounts were bought and trained. Sometimes stallions were maintained at these stations, also, and some breeding was done, although as a rule these stallions were at stud to outside mares, the get then being bought later if desired by the army.

RESTING THE HORSE

In endurance rides the horse may be rested by two methods. There should be frequent change of gait and the rider should dismount and lead the horse for five minutes out of every hour. A longer rest period at noon should be given during which the saddle is removed, the horse rubbed down, allowed to roll, be watered and fed. After a fast run in the hunt field the rider should dismount during a check and walk his horse to cool him out. "Never sit a standing horse" is old and very good advice. Rubbing down the horse after work also rests him.

REWARDS

The horse is trained on a system of rewards and punishment. By this is not meant that the horse is fed a tid-bit each time he obeys nor beaten when he refuses. In bitting the horse, for example, the pull of the reins is the punishment, the relaxing of them the reward. In halting, the tension of the reins to the rear and the pressure of the legs is the pun-

ishment, the relaxing the reward. Horses appreciate a pat on the shoulder and a word of praise. A bit of carrot may be used as a reward to teach some specific thing such as posing, or to cure a vice such as moving while the rider is mounting, but this should not be overdone. Feeding sugar or other tid-bits from the hand is apt to promote a tendency towards nipping, especially in ponies.

RIBS OF THE HORSE

The shape of the ribs is most important. The first two ribs should not "bulge" out too suddenly or they will force the girth against the elbow, but the middle ribs should spring well out thus allowing more room for lungs, heart and stomach and also making the keeping of the saddle in place much easier.

RIDE, DRIVE AND JUMP CLASSES

In these classes the horse is first shown to an appropriate vehicle. He is then unharnessed, saddled and asked to walk, trot and canter in both directions. Eight or more horses are then chosen and asked to take four jumps. These jumps do not usually exceed three feet, or three feet six inches. The horse is judged on consistency of performance and on manners.

RIDE IN THE HUNTSMAN'S POCKET
See HUNTING TERMS.

RIDE STRAIGHT
See HUNTING TERMS.

RIDER
The rail laid across a stone wall to protect the horse's knees and to indicate a jumpable panel is termed a "rider."

RIDER Versus Horseman
See HORSEMAN.

RIDING
"There is something about the outside of a horse which is good for the inside of a man." This adage is wiser

than might first appear. But one should not consider just the hours spent in the saddle as beneficial. Rather, the rider should become a horseman as well, and learn, through caring for the animal himself, what its needs are. In this way he will gain both mental and physical health.

Too often by riding the beginner thinks only of how to stay on his horse. That staying on the horse is essential one cannot deny, but there are many other and just as important things to be learned. How to stay on the horse is the first lesson and by far the easiest. From that one goes to how to make the trained animal obey one's will with the least possible effort on the part of both rider and horse. When the rider can ride a slow, dull animal or a high-spirited, light-mouthed animal with equal facility and obtain from both the utmost of which he is capable, he may be said to have made good progress with his riding. Then he may learn to take an untrained colt and turn him into a finished Saddler, hunter, jumper or polo pony.

The reason why riding is such a fascinating sport is that there is an endless amount to be learned and no matter how many years one puts on it there is always more ahead. No one knows it all. Every good horseman is on the lookout for new ideas. Every new horse represents a new problem which must be solved.

The ambitious beginner should remember that though it may take him years to become an expert, still he can have fun every step of the way. He should try and get just as much as he can out of his lessons both by listening to the instructor and by observation. He can learn much by reading the many good books which have been printed on the subject and he should never consider that he has learned all there is to be learned.

The first maxim of the beginner is "It's never the horse, 'it's always the rider." This means that if a rider fails it is through ignorance, inability or inexperience. Let us take the example of a horse that shies suddenly. The beginner finds himself on the ground. His tendency is to blame the horse. The horse should not have shied. But if the rider had been more proficient he would not have fallen off, in fact, had he been alert and a good horseman the horse might not have shied at all. Therefore the fact that he fell off, though caused by the shying of the horse, was really the fault of the rider. There is great comfort in this maxim for what it really says is that riding is by no means impossible, it is simply a question of practice and education. Having taken this thought thoroughly to heart the beginner is ready to start his career as a horseman. Choose your riding school with care. Many so called "schools" are merely livery stables, the "instructors" being very nearly as ignorant as the pupils. The good instructor will be very detailed in his instructions. He will show the pupil exactly how to hold his reins, exactly how to sit and how to demand changes of gait from the horse as well as the use of the aids in turning, etc. The pupil must now spend long hours trying to perfect himself. He should not try to advance too fast, but learn one lesson thoroughly before going on to the next. He must keep the image of the ideal position of the rider in mind until he learns to imitate it automatically. He must remember that the good rider is he whose horse obeys him immediately and yet whose commands are so inconspicuous that to the observer he appears to be giving none. Belle Beach is supposed to have gone hunting with reins made of silk thread. Major Tuttle sometimes used thread reins in giving his dressage exhibitions at Madison Square Garden. Of such lightness and flexibility are the hands of the experts.

Riding without stirrups and without reins is about the only short cut there is in obtaining a secure seat. Remember that the seat must be retained by balance when riding without stirrups, do not draw the legs up and cling with the knees. The canter is much easier than the trot when riding bareback and in coming down to a walk from a canter the rider should be prepared for the few rough trotting steps.

The following *equitation exercises* will promote balance and flexibility in the rider: Raise the hands as high over the head as possible. Now bring them down and rest them on the hips keeping the back erect. This is the correct position of the body in the saddle or bareback. With the hands on the hips rotate the body from the hips in both directions. Bend forward and touch the forehead to the horse's mane. Lie back until the head rests on the horse's croup. Fold the arms across the chest and repeat these movements. Lean forward and touch both toes. From that position go directly back again to the prone position. Sit up and extend one hand before you, now raise it over your head and look up at it, turn and point behind you, still looking at your hand, then reach down and touch first one toe and then the other. Do this with the other hand. Rotate first one foot from the ankle and then the other. Next rotate the legs alternately from the hip. Reach the right foot as far forward as possible and the left foot back, then reverse them. Bring both feet up and click the heels together over the horse's neck. Now bend forward and bring them back and touch them over the croup. Fold the arms and turn completely around in the saddle rotating first one way and then the other, bringing the legs across in front of you in turning. Stand up in the saddle and in resuming your seat rest all your weight on your hands and come down slowly. Vault off your horse first when he is standing, later at all the different gaits. For more active exercises see *MONKEY DRILL.*

Exercises to promote control:

One of the prime characteristics of horses is their liking of following their mates. It is necessary that the tyro learn how to control his mount independently of others. The following exercises will teach this:

The riders being in column formation, at a walk, at a command the leading horse takes up a trot and passes from the front to the rear of the column following the track. The other horses remain at a walk. This will test the ability both of the horse trotting and of the rider on the second horse which will want to follow his mate. The same exercise may be done on a canter. Next the rider can pass from front to rear by means of executing a half turn, traveling along the line of walking horses and falling in at the rear by means of a half turn in reverse.

The riders being lined up at one end of a corral or drill field, one rider at a time is asked to leave the ranks and canter away. At the sound of a whistle he is to pull up quickly, remain halted until the next whistle and then continue his gait to a designated spot.

The riders being in a group or column riding down a drill field at a trot or canter, one rider remains behind, preventing his horse from following his mares. When the group has come a little distance from the lone rider they take up a walk at which the rider who is waiting must bring his horse up to them at a slow trot (not a canter).

Close order mounted drills and musical rides are one of the best methods of learning control of the horse and all groups of intermediate riders should practice these constantly.

Equitation exercises:

The following exercises will train you to use your legs and reins correctly and will develop flexibility in your horse.

Half turn:

The rider, applying the leg towards the wall (the outside leg) and the opposite rein causes the horse to describe a half circle and then travel on an oblique back to the wall. He will now be going in the opposite direction. The rider's weight should be disposed towards the center of the half circle. The diameter should be six feet at a walk, nine at a trot, twelve at a canter.

Half turn in reverse:

Using the same aids as above the rider causes his horse to leave the wall on a

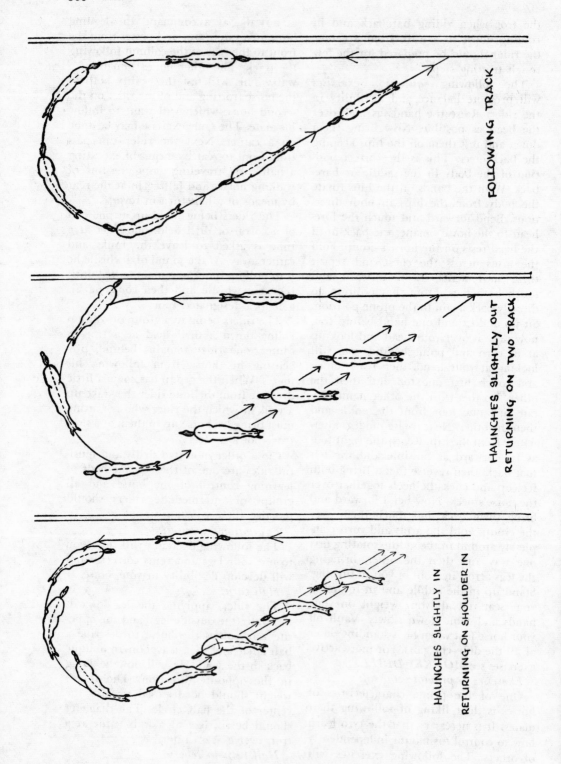

FIGURE 108. THE HALF TURN.

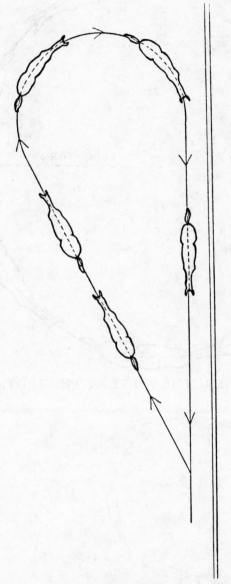

FIGURE 109.
THE HALF TURN IN REVERSE, SIMPLE OBLIQUE AWAY FROM WALL.

diagonal and when sufficiently far from it turns him towards it, resuming the march in the opposite direction.

Voltes:

Using the outside leg and the leading or indirect rein depending on how the horse has been trained, the rider turns his mount in a circle and continues the march in the original direction. In all the above exercises the original gait of the horse should be maintained.

Figure of eight:

The rider describes two circles forming an eight.

Serpentine:

The rider executes a series of half turns down the center of the hall.

Gallop departs:

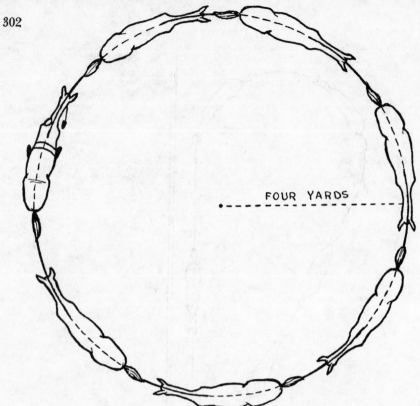

FOUR YARDS

FIGURE 110. THE VOLTE AT THE TROT.

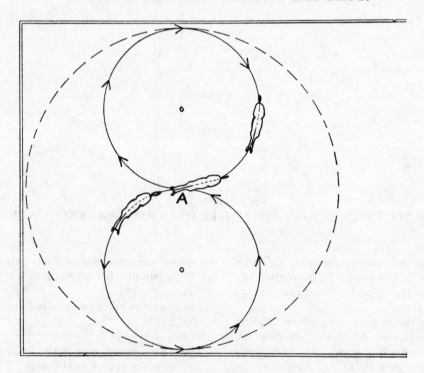

A

FIGURE 111. THE VOLTE FIGURE OF EIGHT.

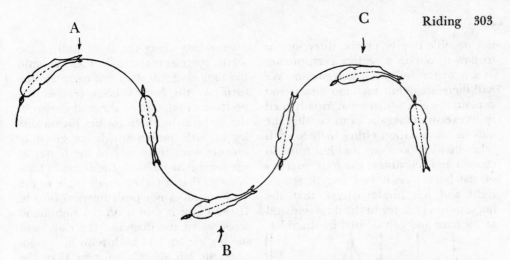

FIGURE 112. THE SERPENTINE. A. HAUNCHES FOLLOWING THE TRACK. B. HAUNCHES RANGED OUT. C. HAUNCHES RANGED IN.

There are two usual methods of putting the horse into the canter or gallop. The first is by means of the lateral aids. The rider takes up the position of the "leg-yield" on the track, the horse's haunches being pushed slightly to the center while the head is held in to the wall. To do this he uses his outside leading rein slightly in opposition and his outside leg behind the girth. With the animal collected he then pushes with his back, lifts lightly with his hand and uses his leg more strongly. As soon as the horse is in the gallop or canter he straightens him out so that he is again traveling on the track correctly. This method of taking the canter is used only by less experienced riders on less-well-trained horses. It is the easiest method of ensuring that the horse takes the correct (inside) lead, but it is not a good one, as the horse, having taken the required gait, must then be straightened out. Many horses tend to travel crab-wise anyway, and to start in this position only increases that tendency. Furthermore, unless the horse is immediately straightened out he will be bending the opposite way to that he should be, as he rounds his corners.

The better and more advanced way is the gallop depart on the diagonal aids. In this method the rider uses his outside leg to push the horse's haunches slightly off the track to the center. With this method he uses his inside *indirect rein of opposition.* (See *REINS, use of.*) This has the effect of bending the horse's head towards the center but throwing his weight onto the outside shoulder, thus freeing the inside foreleg so that the horse takes the correct lead. Trainers who wish to teach the young horse the gallop depart on the diagonal aids from the beginning first teach the canter on the voice command on the longe. The horse, being accustomed to taking the correct lead with his body curved with the circle, then readily learns to take it under the rider when he is placed in this position and when the oral command is also used.

The Advanced Rider:

It is assumed that the rider has learned a good seat independent of his hands or legs, to maintain his balance and position. He can control any ordinary horse and demand and receive a smooth performance of the equitation exercises mentioned above. It is now time for him to learn a more delicate and precise application of the aids. It is best to learn this under the supervision of a good instructor and on a horse that has been trained. Since every action of the rider will depend on the reaction of the horse it is not possible to give precise directions as to how to obtain a perfect performance of any of the following movements. We will therefore define each movement and explain the aids which are normally used in its execution. Again let us say that the aids in combination either to help each other or to oppose one another must so control and coordinate the four quarters of the horse (right and left forehand, right and left hindquarters) that the horse moves each leg in the direction and at the pace and gait desired by the rider.

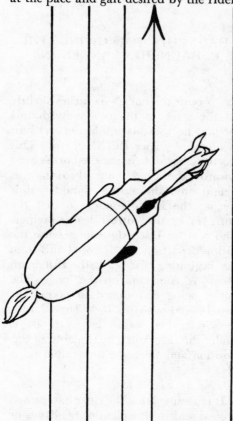

FIGURE 113. THE LEG-YIELD.

The leg-yield (see Figure 113). This is the first movement that puts the horse completely between the rider's hands and legs and it cannot be executed unless he is so ridden. To achieve this exercise, whose purpose is to teach the horse to give to the pressure of the rider's calf or heel and to move away from it, the rider,

after riding along the short wall of the arena, commences to make the turn onto the long wall but does not complete the turn. As the horse's body reaches the position in relation to the wall shown in the picture the rider applies his outside leg in little pushes which are given in cadence with the stride of the horse; at the same time he holds the animal's forehand so that it travels at an angle to the wall and does not push forward into it. If the horse is shown on the right-hand track, as in the diagram, the rider will use his left leg and both reins in opposition, the left slightly stronger than the right. But these reins should not have a steady pull but should release and grip again in cadence with the stride. In the release unless a light contact with the mouth is maintained, the horse will not be held between the rider's hands and legs. The rider's weight is down in the saddle and he uses his back if necessary. In training the young horse it is permissible to turn his head slightly away from the direction of the movement, but in the correct execution there is no bend in the horse's spine from poll to dock.

The pivot around forehand. Some trainers and instructors teach the pivot before teaching the leg-yield. Its purpose is the same—to mobilize horse's hindquarters and make them responsive to the rider's legs. As shown in Figure 114 the horse turns in a circle, moving his hind feet in a wide arc while one forefoot is lifted and replaced almost in the same spot and the other moves around it. The rider starts from the halt about two feet from the wall of the arena and parallel to it. Let us assume that he is pivoting with the quarters moving to the left. He puts the horse on the bit and applies light pressure with both legs. He then increases the pressure on the right rein and, at the same time, pushes with the heel of his right foot. He increases both these signals, bending the horse's head to the right as he does so, until his mount takes one step with his hind legs to the left. The aids are immediately relaxed and the horse given

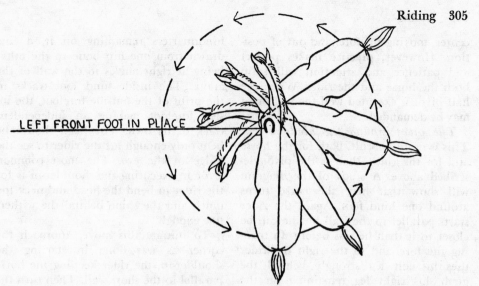

LEFT FRONT FOOT IN PLACE

FIGURE 114.
PIVOT ON THE FOREHAND. HAUNCHES TO THE RIGHT.

a word or pat of approbation. He is then asked to take another step in the same manner. This is continued until a turn of a hundred and eighty degrees (halfway round the clock) is completed. Using the opposite aids the rider then pivots him back to his original position. The less experienced rider will find that whereas it is quite easy to demand and get the first three steps, the next three are much more difficult, the horse tending either to back up or to turn on his

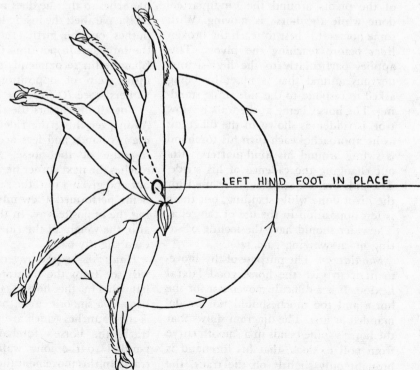

LEFT HIND FOOT IN PLACE

FIGURE 115. THE PIVOT AROUND THE HINDQUARTERS.

center, moving his forehand out of position. However, practice makes perfect and patience and attention will train both the horse and the rider. When the half pivot is executed well the full pivot may be demanded.

The pivot around the hindquarters. This is more difficult, both for the horse and for the rider, than is the pivot described above. A study of the diagram will show that here the horse turns around one hind foot. Again the rider starts parallel to the wall but he can be closer to it than he was before. In turning the forehand to the right the rider uses his left leg strongly behind the girth, his right leg remaining on the girth. Both reins, with slight opposition, are carried to the right and the horse is thus induced to take one step with his front feet to the right and stop. In both pivots the horse's feet which are moving should cross, and in the finished execution there is of course no complete stop between steps; the horse moves smoothly and unhurriedly.

Broken lines. This is an application of the pivots around the hindquarters done while the horse is moving. With some horses it is best to teach the broken lines before teaching the pivots. This applies particularly to the high-strung, nervous animal that is upset by being asked to respond to the aids while standing. The horse, being at the walk or slow trot, is ridden as shown in the diagram; as he approaches each turn his forehand is swung around his hindquarters without changing the cadence of his stride. The aids are the same as those used for the pivot done while standing, but there is less opposition in the use of the reins. The rider should have the feeling of sitting on a swinging gate.

Shoulder-in. The purpose of this movement is to give the horse good lateral flexion. It is a difficult movement for the horse and too much should not be demanded at first. The diagram shows that the horse's spine bends in a smooth curve from poll to dock, that his forehand is brought only slightly off the track, the hindquarters remaining on it, a line drawn from one hip bone to the other being at right angles to the wall of the arena. The inside hind foot tracks in the print of the outside forefoot, the inside forefoot making an independent track of its own. The head should be bent only enough for the rider to see the bulge of the eye. The most common error in executing the shoulder-in is for the rider to bend the head and neck too much and the spine behind the withers not enough.

To initiate this move, approach the corner as was done in starting the shoulder-in, the rider keeping the horse parallel to the short wall. Then turn the corner using the inside leading rein and a strong inside leg against the girth to keep the horse out to the wall. Having completed the turn, take one more step on the curve of the turn towards the center, and as the horse completes this step, which brings his inside forefoot off the track, push him along the wall in this position. The outside leg is carried behind the girth and hold's the horse's haunches so that he does not pivot them off the parallel; the inside leg gives strong pushes on the girth; the hands keep the forehand in position. Colonel Harry Chamberlin recommends the use of the inside rein of opposition *behind* the withers. (See *REINS, use of.*)

Not all instructors use this rein effect. As in everything the rider will have to use his hands and legs according to the response of the horse. As the horse reaches the next corner he is straightened out and given a rest, the same movement being performed a few minutes later going the opposite way. In this movement, also, the weight of the rider is down and even slightly back.

Haunches-in (the travers). The reader will see from the diagram that in the haunches-in the horse's spine is again bent in a smooth curve, but this time it is the haunches which are pushed off the track, the horse's forehand remaining parallel to the long wall and on the track. In this movement the rider's hands

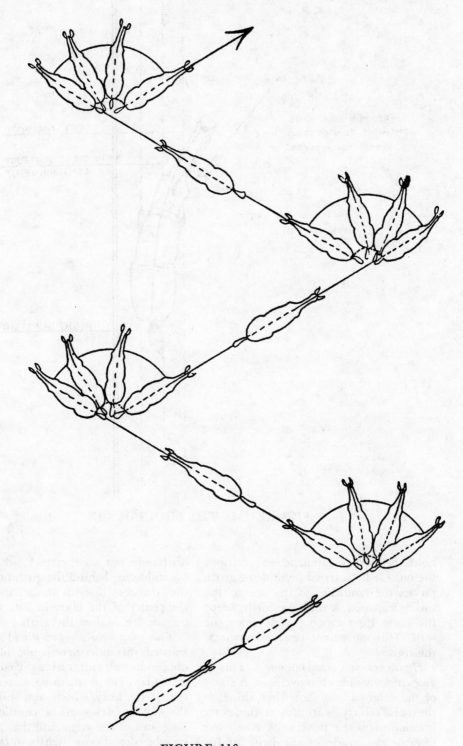

FIGURE 116.
EXECUTING BROKEN LINES WITH TURNS ON THE HAUNCHES.

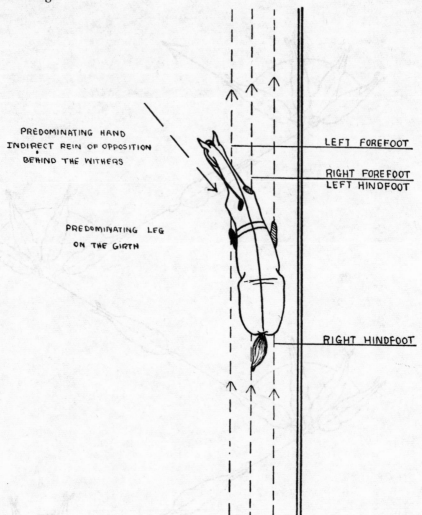

PREDOMINATING HAND
INDIRECT REIN OF OPPOSITION
BEHIND THE WITHERS

PREDOMINATING LEG
ON THE GIRTH

LEFT FOREFOOT

RIGHT FOREFOOT
LEFT HINDFOOT

RIGHT HINDFOOT

FIGURE 117. THE SHOULDER-IN.

hold the horse's forehand in position; the outside leg, carried behind the girth, pushes the haunches to the center; the inside leg, used against the girth, keeps the horse from moving away from the wall. This movement is also known as the *travers*.

Haunches-out (the renvers). This is an extremely difficult movement. A study of the diagram will show that although the horse's body is in almost the exact position as in the travers, he is moving towards the inside of the bend of his body instead of the outside. Again the rider holds the forehand straight with

his hands, but off the track, while with his inside leg behind the girth he pushes the haunches towards the wall, keeping the center of the body in line with his outside leg against the girth.

The traversal (two-track). Once learned, this movement is not difficult to obtain, but all riders have difficulty with it at first. The main thing to remember is that the horse's body and spine from the withers back *must* be parallel to the long wall of the arena and that his head may be turned only slightly in *the direction of the movement*. The tendency always is for the rider to try to move the

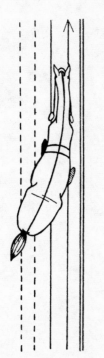

FIGURE 118. HAUNCHES-IN (THE TRAVERS).

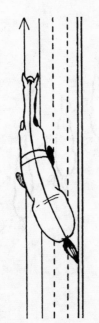

FIGURE 119. HAUNCHES-OUT (THE RENVERS).

horse sideways by turning his head *away* from the direction of the movement, thus improving the mobility of the haunches.

To correct this tendency ride the movement at first with the reins in one hand. Think of the horse as moving first his forehand and then his hindquarters a step at a time. Having turned the corner onto the long wall, start with a step of the forehand towards the center, using the inside leading rein. Immediately check the forehand and push the hindquarters to the center, using the outside leg behind the girth. Hold the hindquarters and lead the forehand another step, etc. The horse must cross both his front and his back legs; in moving to the left the right front and right hind cross in front of the left front and left hind.

The counter change of hands on the two-track. In this movement the horse is required to change, while moving in one direction on the traversal, to the opposite direction. For the horse this is difficult, as he must shift his balance completely in a fraction of a second. The rider must learn by feel and practice exactly when in the horse's stride to ask for this change. As in all such demands, before changing the aids the rider asks for a half-halt. In learning this movement, and also in teaching it to the young horse, the procedure is usually to move away from the long wall on a traversal until the horse reaches the center point of the hall, then to change the aids and move back to the same long wall, also on the traversal. Later the true counter change as shown in the diagram can be executed. This starts with the rider riding a straight line down the center of the arena. On initiating the movement he moves away from the line to the left, as shown, after a given number of steps he changes direction and moves across the line to the same number of steps beyond it, to change again and repeat, until the length of the arena is completed, when he returns to the track. This is one of the most beautiful movements when executed smoothly and, once rider and horse have learned their parts, not difficult. It is one of the best movements to use in *Dressage Quadrilles* and should be carefully matched to the musi-

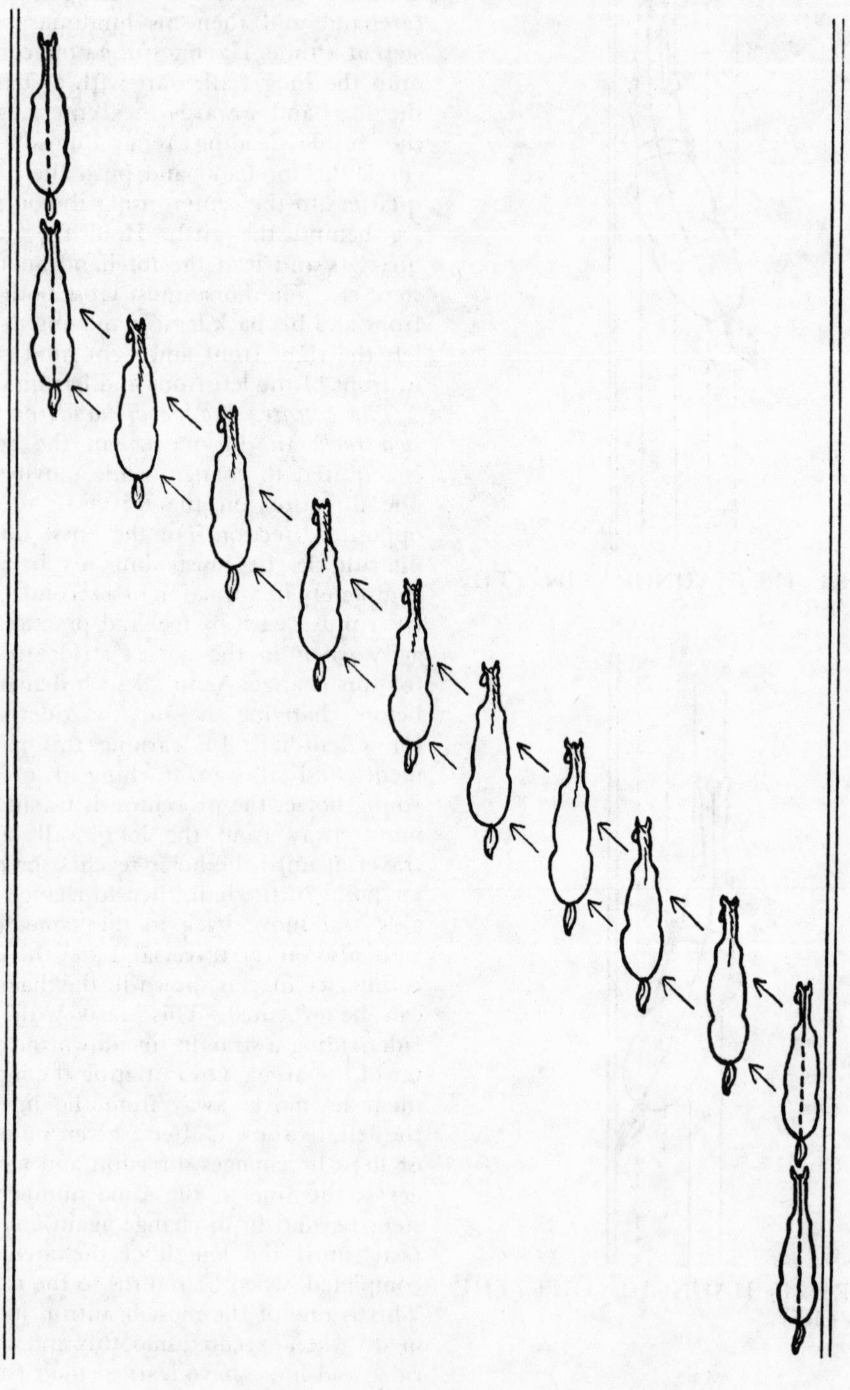

FIGURE 120. THE TRAVERSAL (TWO-TRACK).

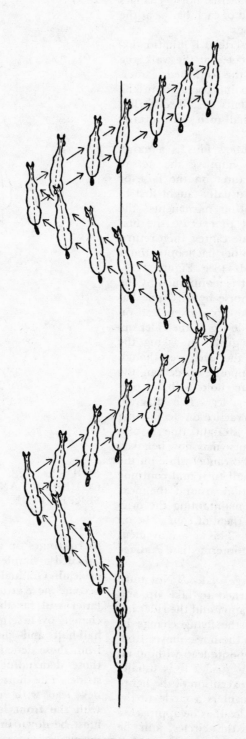

FIGURE 121.
THE COUNTER-CHANGE OF HANDS ON THE TWO-TRACK.

cal phrases, so that the horse changes direction at the end of each bar or at the end of each phrase.

All the above described Equitation exercises may be executed at the walk, the sitting trot and the collected canter. They may also be incorporated in the equitation movements described earlier (the half-turn, half-turn in reverse, circles, etc.).

The counter-canter. This is a movement designed to improve the horse's balance. It is a canter on the false or outside lead. It is usually taught first in long, flat, serpentine movements, the horse being asked to execute the first flat loop on the true canter, then return to the wall on another flat loop without changing the lead. (See Figure 122). The counter-canter is maintained by the rider's legs. The horse by this time has been taught to take up a given lead on signal of the outside leg of the rider applied behind the girth. In asking the horse to maintain the lead, even though curving in the opposite direction, the rider keeps a strong hold with his outside (now inside) leg. The diagram makes this clear. Practice on demanding either lead on a straight line is also worked on. The horse may now be asked to take a designated canter while on the straight, make a half turn and continue in the new direction around the next corner while still maintaining the original lead. He will then, of course, be on the counter-canter. This is a movement often demanded in intermediate *dressage* tests.

The flying change of lead. Not until the horse has learned to take up and keep the counter-canter and the rider has learned it should the flying change be attempted. In this the horse moves from one lead to the opposite lead without an interruption in his stride. It is usually taught first in the execution of the figure eight. The rider canters a circle to the right on the right lead; as he approaches the point where the circles join he brings the horse down to a trot for two steps and asks for the left lead, on which

FIGURE 122. TEACHING THE COUNTER-CANTER ON A FLAT SERPENTINE.

he continues on a left-hand circle. This is called a simple or interrupted change of lead. Gradually as horse and rider become more attuned to one another the latter will be able to ask for a flying change by first giving the signal for a half-halt and then changing his aids from those demanding the right lead to those demanding the left, all in one stride. The horse should instigate the new lead with his back leg, following with the front leg. The rider's weight must be down in the saddle and under no circumstances should he throw himself forward and over the shoulder on the side of the new lead. The most advanced exercise in demanding the flying change is to ask that the horse execute it changing on a given number of steps on a straight line. Starting with every sixth step the horse executes a flying change every fifth, every fourth, every third, every second and finally every step. Long before he is ready to do this he will be worked on the serpentine at the true canter, at the false canter and with a flying change.

Piaffe. In this movement the horse trots in place, highly collected and with light steps. It is usually taught on foot, the trainer leading the horse with his left hand while he lightly taps the hindquarters with a long whip to demand the steps. At first the horse is allowed to move slightly forward, later he learns to step in place. The rider usually is taught this by the instructor, the latter working from the ground. The aids are a series of half halts with strong pressure on first one rein and then the other and with the leg movements also alternating. The back is also used strongly, if necessary, to keep the horse collected. (For illustration, see general heading *PIAFFE*.)

The Passage. This movement, a very slow-cadenced extended trot with a perceptible instant of elevated hesitation in each stride, may be developed either from the strong trot or from the *piaffe*, depending on the horse. The aids are almost the same as those of the *piaffe* but the horse is not held in place. To many people it is the most beautiful of all the movements of the horse.

The Pirouette. This is a turn on the hindquarters at the canter. The horse's back legs continue the normal stride but make a very small circle while the forehand makes a larger one around them. The same aids as those demanding the ordinary turns on the hindquarters are used, the horse being at the canter. Generally it is easiest to demand the movement while doing a half turn in reverse; later it can be executed while riding on a straight line. (For illustration, see general heading *PIROUETTE*.)

RIDING ETIQUETTE
See *COURTESY*.

RIDING INSTRUCTORS
The proper choice of a riding instructor is of utmost importance, especially where very young or timid riders are to be considered.

The instructor must be a good rider himself, such a good rider that he does not have to think of himself or of his own horse even when the latter may start "playing" and acting up. He must be able to control his expression and voice in event of an emergency. If a horse and rider become frightened, the worst possible thing is for the instructor to allow any hint of fear or excitement in his voice or manner as he calls his directions. Excitable or nervous persons should never teach a sport such as riding where the first and most important factor to be instilled is that of confidence.

The instructor must have both patience and ingenuity. He must be able to maintain the child's interest through the long intermediate stages of becoming a horseman when much practice at slow gaits is essential. He must be a good disciplinarian for unless he can control his pupils they are in danger. But above all he must have a love of teaching and a sympathy for his pupils. If they do not like him they will discontinue their lessons and, unless he genuinely enjoys his profession, they will certainly not enjoy him or his teaching.

RINGER
A ringer is a horse that is entered fraudulently under a false name in a race, usually in order to procure better betting odds.

RIOT, RIOTOUS (hounds)
See *HUNTING TERMS*.

RISLING (ridgeling)
A ridgeling is a horse whose produc-

tive organs are only partially developed making it difficult to geld him.

The horse that has been incompletely gelded is also known as a risling or ridgeling. These animals, often mistakenly purchased as geldings, continue to show stallion characteristics and often a tendency to bite. It is sometimes impossible to correct this vice as rislings cling more stubbornly to the habit than does the ordinary stallion. Use of muzzles when the risling must be handled by a child, stabling where he cannot reach out and grab a passerby and alert attention at all times by the handler are musts. However, the risling that likes to take a bite at a human being seldom annoys other horses.

ROAD HACK

A road hack is a horse shown under the saddle whose outstanding gait is speed at the trot. See *HORSE SHOW CLASSES.*

ROADSTER

A roadster is a horse driven to a wagon or bike whose outstanding characteristic is speed at the trot or pace. See *HORSE SHOW CLASSES; HARNESS RACING.*

ROAN

Roan is one of the mixed colors of the horse, being any solid color with white hairs mixed throughout the coat. See also *COLORS OF THE HORSE.*

RODEO

See *WESTERN TERMS.*

ROLLER

A roller is a surcingle holding a stable blanket or sheet in place.

ROLLING UP

This is a practice originating in the German cavalry. If a horse refuses to leave his companions or to go in a desired direction, he is made to turn in

FIGURE 123. A RODEO RIDER. STEER RIDING IS ONE OF THE MORE ACTIVE EVENTS OF THE RODEO. *CULVER SERVICE.*

short circles in one direction or the other until he becomes slightly confused. He will then usually move out as desired.

ROMAN NOSE

The Roman nose is the opposite of the "dished" profile of the Arabian Horse. It usually indicates a fairly large mixture of common blood, often draft blood. It is not a desirable characteristic in hunters or Saddlers.

ROPE BURNS

See *INJURIES*.

ROPING

The cowboy depends on his rope to catch his cattle and horses. But he must be helped by his mount. The rider develops great skill in throwing the lariat; once he has roped his steer, it is the horse that keeps the rope taut while the cowboy dismounts and goes over to his quarry. The good roping horse is wise and clever and a credit to his training.

ROPING COMPETITION

In this competition the horse works as a team member with his rider. The horse judges the speed of the calf or steer being roped and times his approach to give the rider the best opportunity possible to throw his loop. He must then hold a taut roped and times his approach to give the pletes the tie-down.

ROSETTES

See *ORNAMENTS, Bridle*.

ROSINANTE

See *FAMOUS HORSES OF FICTION*.

ROUND UP

Each spring on the big ranches the stock that has been turned out for the winter is brought in to be inspected and the new calves and colts branded and castrated. This is called a "round up."

RUB RAG

After the horse is groomed he should be wiped off with a rub rag. The best of these are of raw silk or of linen. Cotton leaves lint. Light wool is not bad but not so good as the silk.

RUBBER NUMMAHS

Saddle pads are now being made of sponge rubber. They are soft but are not good for use in hot weather as they tend to cause excessive sweating.

RUBBER PADS

Horses that are driven on hard roads or that have a chronic foot or tendon ailment may sometimes be helped by being shod with rubber pads under the shoes. In buying a horse one should think twice before buying one that is so shod for it often indicates the presence of laminitis or navicular disease.

RUBBING DOWN

A good rub down rests the horse, relaxes the muscles and increases the circulation. The rubber must be sure that he really puts strength and effort into the rubbing and doesn't just dab at the horse.

RUG

The heavy wool blanket used for shipping and for daytime use in the stall is called a rug.

RUNAWAYS

See *BOLTING*.

RUNNING HIS FOIL

See *FOIL, HUNTING TERMS*.

RUNNING WALK

This is one of the "slow gaits" of the five-gaited Saddler. It is a quick-four-beat gait similar to a single-foot but with less elevation and considerably slower.

RUSHING

Rushing jumps is a common characteristic of horses whose education in jumping has been too hurried. It is a defense and should be cured by slow, patient schooling over low hurdles until the horse is no longer either afraid of them nor excited at them. Training on a longe is most beneficial.

RUSSIAN HORSES

The Russians are noted for their skill with and interest in horses. Everyone has heard of the Cossacks. Here the emphasis is on gymnastic riding. The horses are often "steppes" ponies or such horses crossed with larger stock for size. These steppes ponies are descended from one of the original prehistoric types, the *Equus Tarpanus*. This little animal was dun in color and had no callosities on the back legs.

The Russians have also developed a fine type of trotter and Saddler known as the *ORLOFF*. The Orloff is bred from desert stock and he is used both for racing in harness and, under the saddle, for cavalry purposes. He is Arabian in many of his characteristics and new infusions of Arabian blood are constantly being introduced, thus maintaining the quality of the type. Harness racing has acquired great popularity in Russia and the Russian feels that his "Orloff" is every bit as fast as our "Hambletonian."

The Russians also have an extensive Olympic Training Program. As in the United States, the country is divided into sectors, with local meets to determine which riders train for the actual competitions. In the 1960 Olympics the Russians were outstandingly successful in the *Dressage* competitions.

S

SADDLE

History of

The earliest type of saddles so far identified are those of the ancient Gauls. Small terra cotta figures found in France and dating back to the early centuries of our era show warriors carrying shields perched on stirrupless contrivances which more nearly resemble the howdah

of the camel than a saddle. How they remained there is incredible. The only purpose of this type of saddle seems to be to raise the rider above his enemy.

The Greeks, noted horsemen, rode bareback almost invariably. Alexander and his cavalry pursued Darius without benefit of saddle. The early Indian riders of this country used no saddles and only adopted them in imitation of the white man.

In medieval times the Knights had a saddle which was deep in the seat with a high cantle and pommel and very long leathers. But the Knight, with his tremendously encumbering armor was anything but flexible. On foot he was hopelessly at the mercy of his adversary, so the prime purpose of his saddle was to keep him from falling off his charger.

At about the same period the Oriental fighter also adopted the use of the saddle. Unlike the Knight, he rode with very short leathers primarily so that, standing in his stirrups, he might the more freely use javelin and scimitar.

When the American Indians first devised saddles, they contrived them of rawhide shrunk onto a frame or tree of either wood or elk-horn. These saddles were incredibly tough and strong.

Obviously the various types of saddles have come into being for specific purposes. The English, or flat saddle, is the only possible tree which can be used successfully for racing, polo and jumping. The crescent shaped cowboy saddle with its double cinches, high horn and high cantle is essential for the work of the ranch. In between these types are various modifications of each, and each modification is so made because of the purpose for which it is used.

Types of modern saddles

The Western or cowboy saddle which is similar to that used not only in this country but in all countries where men spend long hours in the saddle rounding up cattle, roping calves, steers and colts, etc., is characterized by its deep seat, high cantle and pommel. In this saddle the stirrups are set about midway and the cowboy rides with an almost straight leg. As his horse lopes and walks most of the time with an occasional fox-trot by way of variation, he does not need to "post" or rise to the trot, and so does not need a bent knee. His saddle is equipped with rings and rawhide "saddle strings" to which he may attach his equipment. The double cinches, pulled tight by the slip knots of the latigos, ensure that the saddle remains in place under the strain of a lusty steer attached, by the lariat, to the saddle horn. The sudaderos, wide leather flaps, protect the rider's legs from the pinch and play of the leathers for our Western friend rides in short boots and blue jeans. The covered stirrups are a protection against thorns, cactus and scrub. As the cowboy saddle has little padding a very thick pad is essential, and the cowboy uses a heavy blanket, preferably a hand-woven Indian or Mexican blanket. Many of these cowboy saddles are elaborately decorated with silver ornaments and leather tooling and they can be very heavy as a result of this decoration, but the tough little cow pony bears up under the weight surprisingly well. They are also fabulously expensive. The ten-gallon hat, the soft, high heeled boots and, especially the ornamented saddle and bridle, represent the most valued of the cowboy's worldly goods. He may, on leaving his employer, lose his horse, but his saddle and other equipment goes with him.

The McClellan saddle, which is the tree used by the soldier in the American Cavalry, was developed during the Civil War. It is a sort of hybrid combining the features of the cowboy and the English type saddles but it is more Western than English in type. It has a fairly flat seat with a modified cantle and pommel. The girth is held in place by latigos as in the cowboy saddle, and it has a "split tree." In other words, the tree which extends down the middle is divided so that the horse's spine is not touched by the hard tree or saddle. The cavalry man rides with shorter stirrups than does the cowboy and his saddle is good for the

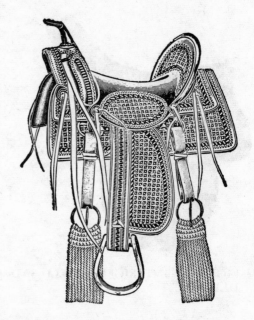

FIGURE 124. FANCILY DECORATED STOCK SADDLE.

purpose to which it is put, but it is not suitable for jumping or polo where the rider must be able to rise well out of his stirrups and bend well forward or to the side, unimpeded by a high pommel. Different types of the English or flat saddle vary greatly in cut but the basic principle of all is the same. Here both cantle and pommel are practically eliminated. The stirup is set well forward of the center enabling the rider to keep his weight over the horse's center of gravity. The rider is free to bend in any position. The seat is padded and, because the panels are also well stuffed, a well fitting English saddle needs no pad or blanket.

The racing saddle is incredibly light. The saddle designed for showing Saddlers is specially cut with a square, cut back pommel which throws the rider back in the seat and thus emphasizes the showy front of the horse while minimizing his often over-exaggerated length of back and loin.

The officer's field saddle (see illustration) is a flat saddle mounted on a split

FIGURE 125. OFFICER'S FIELD SAD-DLE.

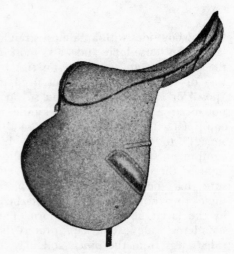

FIGURE 126. THE FORWARD SEAT SADDLE.

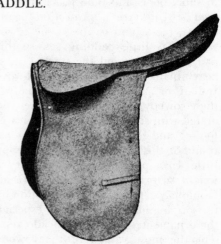

FIGURE 127. THE RACING SAD-DLE.

tree. It gives the rider freedom, yet has the advantage of providing an extended "fan tail" to which may be attached a blanket roll as well as rings for saber, pistol, etc.

The "forward seat" or Italian saddle is characterized by skirts or flaps which slant well forward and sometimes by knee rolls against which the rider may brace his knees in jumping. Special stirrups are sometimes used with this type of saddle in which the slot for the leather is set off center, ensuring that the rider's feet remain pressed against the inside edge of the stirrup. The forward seat saddle is very popular for jumping.

The modern Arabian saddle has changed little in the centuries. It remains little more than a high peaked pad affair held on by such loose girths that one wonders how on earth the riders ever managed to stay aboard!

Selection and care

In choosing a saddle one must take into consideration both the use to which it is to be put and the conformation of horse and rider. If possible take the saddle on trial and fit it on the horse before purchasing. In the old days saddle makers went from stable to stable and

each horse had his saddle especially padded to fit his particular needs; more than this, the saddle was often repadded if the horse lost or gained flesh, but such days have passed. One must now be content with "ready-made" instead of "custom-fitted" equipment.

If your horse has high withers, a "cut-back" or open throat is obligatory. If he has a protruding spine, the saddle must be so padded that, standing at either front or rear, one can look between the tree and the spine from pommel to cantle. A horse with a "double back" needs a differently constructed saddle. If

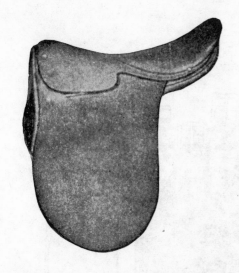

FIGURE 128. THE HACKING SADDLE.

the rider is of generous proportions, the saddle must be made accordingly, and the little child needs a specially designed tree with short skirts so that his legs may not be spread too much and may be used to some advantage.

The new saddle is a thoroughly uncomfortable affair until properly broken in. For this reason most horsemen prefer to buy used tack. If it is necessary to break in a saddle, first douse it well and frequently with some reliable saddle oil and then wear old clothes until the liquid is well worked into the leather and the latter is no longer stiff and squeaky.

For every day care it goes without saying that the saddle should be cleaned and polished with saddle soap each time it is used. The panels and the cantle especially must be well soaped and no sweat should be allowed to accumulate on the former. The billet straps need frequent applications of oil to keep them supple, as do the stirrup leathers. The girth should always be completely detached and laid across the seat after being cleaned. The saddle must be kept on a rack and should be covered with a dust cloth. A good saddle will outlast

both horse and rider. New saddles of pigskin of good quality sell for from a hundred to two hundred dollars and even the common park saddle costs over fifty, so they are well worth taking care of.

SADDLE BAGS

These are large leather pockets which are attached to the cantle of the saddle.

SADDLE CLASSES

See *HUNTER CLASSES, Saddle division.*

SADDLE HORSE

When a horseman speaks of a "Saddle horse" or "Saddler," he does not mean simply an animal which has been broken to the saddle and is used for riding purposes, he is referring to a specific breed of horse whose official name is "American Saddle Horse."

Of all horses the Saddler is the most showy. In truth, he is the veritable "peacock" of the Horse World. He is distinguished by his beautiful head, held high and proudly, his long, fine neck, his sloping shoulder and well turned quarter with a high set tail. He is elegance personified. His action, either by breeding or by shoeing, is exaggeratedly high but his back hardly moves at all, the horse giving the appearance of moving through the air on a level plane on flexible springs. His disposition is as nearly perfect as one can find among horses, but it takes a good rider to handle a highly finished five-gaited Saddler.

To understand the Saddler one must go back to the old, old law of necessity being the mother of invention. In pioneer days there were two means whereby the early settlers could travel, the water ways and the almost impassable trails and roads. In many parts of the country and for a good part of the year the roads were impassable to any but the man on horseback. No wagon or cart could get through the mudholes which were veritable bogs. Perhaps the story of the hat seen moving,

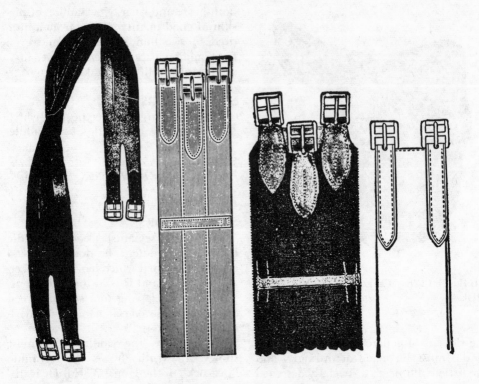

FIGURE 129. TYPES OF GIRTHS.

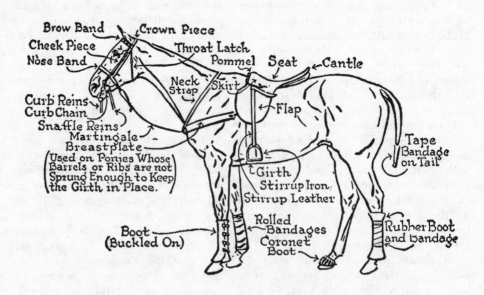

FIGURE 130. PARTS OF THE SADDLE AND BRIDLE.

FIGURE 131.
COLONEL BOYLE, REGISTERED AMERICAN SADDLEBRED STALLION.

FIGURE 132.
TECHNISTAR, REGISTERED AMERICAN SADDLEBRED MARE.

on its own volition, along the Virginia road and which later turned out to be a Virginia Planter, mounted, on his way to church, may be exaggerated but the fact remains that, with the scattered population, he who would have contact with his neighbor must ride.

In the South the plantations were vast affairs. The plantation owner who would keep an eye on his property must spend long hours in the saddle. For this he needed a horse with the easiest of gaits and the most amenable of dispositions. The trotter required too much exertion. The runner was no good, for the planter wished to ride in a leisurely fashion, discussing his problems with his overseer and taking a careful look at his crops meanwhile. Yet the planter was a man of distinction and pride. The ambling jennet, suitable for the lady in England,

was not his idea of a man's mount. But it was the amble or the "broken amble," called the singlefoot or rack, which was the desired gait. On a horse so schooled the planter could travel all day without fatigue. Combine with that a very collected canter and the type of disposition which would enable him to canter his horse between the rows of crops, add a showy, commanding appearance and the Kentucky or Virginia gentleman had something which was really pretty special. But how was such a horse, completely different from any breed heretofore known, developed? Through the tried and true method of selection, and breeding to type.

In his native habitat the Arabian horse is taught to amble and rack. His gait is not elevated but he learns it readily. The Thoroughbred descends

FIGURE 133.   WING COMMANDER, OUTSTANDING FIVE-GAITED CHAMPION OF TODAY. *COURTESY OF AMERICAN SADDLE HORSE ASSOCIATION.*

from the Arabian, so it is not surprising to find the Denmark, the official foundation sire of the American Saddle-Horse is of Thoroughbred and Arabian descent. The Mambrinos, from whom Messenger was descended, play a large part in the Saddle pedigree as do other strains such as the Morgan. The Saddler has been bred to two distinct types, the five-gaited and the three-gaited. In harness he is known as the "Fine Harness" horse. The five-gaited Saddler is of a little heavier build than his less well educated cousin. He wears his mane and tail long and flowing. In addition to the walk, trot and canter he is taught a "slow gait" which may be an amble, a running walk, a foxtrot or a stepping pace, and a speedy rack or singlefoot. He is not encouraged to pace, for that is an uncomfortable gait under the saddle but he learns it readily if encouraged. The five-gaited horse is bred almost entirely for show purposes now, for the number of riders not interested in showing who can ride with enjoyment such a highly schooled animal are very few and far between.

On the other hand, the Tennessee Walking Horse or "plantation walker," an off-shoot of the Saddler, is very popular for hacking. He resembles his cousin to some extent but is not nearly so highly finished. His gaits are the walk, slow gait and canter. (See also *TENNESSEE WALKING HORSE.*) The three-gaited show Saddler has the spirit and presence of the five-gaited but is more lightly built. He wears his mane clipped off and his tail pulled until little more than a rat's tail is left. The highly bred specimens are used almost entirely for showing but the introduction of Saddle blood into any other strain such as the Thoroughbred. Morgan or Standard bred produces animals which make fine park hacks. See also *AMERICAN SADDLE HORSE BREEDERS ASSOCIATION.*

SADDLE SORES

Saddle sores or galls are sores caused by a misfitting saddle or one which has been put on incorrectly. Riders with bad seats will often give a horse saddle sores. They come most frequently at the withers and on the spine under the cantle though sores on either side of the spine are not uncommon. To treat, bathe them in an antiseptic solution and apply methylene blue (Blue Gall Remedy). The horse should not be saddled again until the sore is completely healed. This will take ten days to two weeks. If he must be ridden in a saddle a thick pad with a hole cut in it over the sore should be used. If the sore is on the withers a saddle with a cut back throat can be substituted. If it is at the extreme end of the cantle it may be possible to fit the horse with a shorter saddle until the sore has healed. Generally speaking, a horse with a saddle sore is a disgrace to its owner and implies carelessness and improper handling or riding.

SADDLER

This is a contraction for Saddle Horse and means a horse of a specific breed, not merely one which is used for saddle purposes. See *SADDLE HORSE.*

SADDLING THE HORSE

To saddle the horse approach him from the near side carrying the saddle over the left arm, the pommel to the left. The stirrups should be run up on the leathers and the girth should be laid across the seat. If a saddle pad is used, it may be placed on the horse's back with the right hand. It should be put well in front of where it is intended to rest and should be slid back into place. This insures that the hair lies smoothly. If no pad is used the saddle itself is laid lightly on the withers and then slid back into place, which accomplishes the same purpose. The next step is to go around to the far side, take the girth off the seat and buckle it to the billets on that side, making sure that nothing is out of place or folded under. The girth is then buckled on the near side but not too tightly. The saddle should be so placed that the girth is about the width of your hand behind the elbow (this applies to English saddles only). The pommel is

FIGURE 134. THE PROPER WAY TO CARRY A SADDLE.

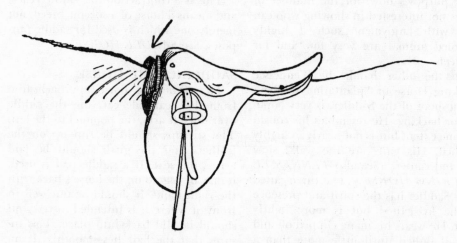

FIGURE 134a. SADDLE IN PLACE WITH POMMEL PAD.

far enough forward so that the slope of the withers bone keeps it from rocking. The general tendency of beginners is to place the saddle too far to the rear. But neither should it rest up on the shoulders where it will impede the horse's action and may cause him to stumble.

When the horse is ready to be ridden he should be led out of his stall, the

girth tightened once more and the stirrups pulled down. The girth should be just tight enough to keep the saddle in place. If it is too tight the animal will inevitably develop girth galls. If too loose the saddle will turn when the rider is mounting. A good rider can ride without a girth, if need be, for ordinary riding and he should not feel that a tight

FIGURE 135. THE BALANCE SEAT. THE FIGURE ON THE LEFT IS BEHIND THE CENTER OF GRAVITY OF THE HORSE. HIS TOE IS NOT IN LINE WITH HIS KNEE, HIS HEEL SHOULD BE DOWN, HE IS SITTING AS ONE SITS IN A CHAIR. THE FIGURE ON THE RIGHT DEMONSTRATES THE MODERN "BALANCE SEAT." A SUDDEN MOVEMENT ON THE PART OF THE HORSE WILL NOT THROW HIM OFF BALANCE AS IT WILL BE ABSORBED BY FLEXION OF THE KNEE, THIGH, AND ANKLE. *FROM* EQUESTIONAIRE, *BY HARRY DISSTON.*

girth is either essential or desirable. The usual test is to insert three fingers at the ribs and then slide the hand down towards the brisket. There should be plenty of room at the ribs but the girth should be snug at the bottom. This method has the added advantage of smoothing out the hair and helps prevent girth galls.

SALIVA TESTS

These are tests given to race horses if it is suspected that the horse has been doped to prevent him winning a race or to give him extra speed by artificial stimulation.

SALT

Horses must have salt and it is particularly important in hot weather when so much body salt is lost through excessive sweating. Ordinary salt may be mixed with the feed, given in mashes or, in either brick or lump form, kept in the stall at all times. The brick salt is rather soft and should always be kept in a container which is so constructed that the horse cannot bite off chunks. Cattle salt, which comes in large blocks and is designed to be stuck on the end of a stick is unsuitable for horses as they tend to swallow big lumps whole and may choke themselves. Rock salt, the kind that looks just like big pieces of granite, is excellent. It is too hard to be bitten into pieces and, when a lump is kept in the feed manger, it tends to prevent the animal from bolting his grain. See also *HORSES, Feeding.*

SAND CRACK

A sand crack is a perpendicular crack in the wall due to injury to the coronary band. It may or may not cause lameness and is subject to infection. If the crack is at the toe the horse should be shod with quarter clips and the crack held together with clinches. If infection is present the horn will have to be pared away to allow the pus to escape and the foot should be soaked in hot antiseptic solutions. The coronet may be blistered to encourage new growth of horn.

SANDSHIFTER

This is the trotting man's term for the pacer.

SANDWICH CASE

The sandwich case is an essential part of hunting appointments. It is made of leather with a tin box and it has leather straps with which it may be attached to the saddle. The sandwiches are usually chicken, tongue or ham. Sandwich cases are very expensive, especially in this country, but as they never wear out it is never necessary to buy more than one.

SAUMUR

Saumur is the French Cavalry school

corresponding to Fort Riley in this country and Weedon in England. Many United States Cavalry officers are sent to Saumur to study French cavalry methods and our cavalry seat most nearly resembles that developed by the French.

SCALDS

Scalds or burns due to friction or other causes may be treated with "Amertan," a tannic acid jelly soluble in water which forms a coating thus cutting off the air and relieving the pain.

SCHOOL RIDING

When the weather conditions do not permit of hunting or cross-country work, the horseman anxious to improve himself and his mount can put in profitable hours working in the riding hall. This is the time to practice the gallop departs, serpentines, etc., and the less difficult dressage figures. If your hunter is heavy under the hand and not as flexible as you might wish, some work in the turns and figure eights at the various gaits as well as the pivots will make him handier. If your hack has the habit of jibbing, you will now have the opportunity of working him out of this habit through exercises and practice in side-stepping, etc. There is no horse nor a single rider who cannot go further than he has gone with his riding education.

SCHOOLING

When a horseman speaks of "schooling" a horse, he means putting him over the hurdles.

SCHOOLS OF HORSEMANSHIP

The ordinary riding academy should never be called a "school," for generally speaking the riding instructors are very nearly as ignorant as the "drug-store cowboys" who come there to learn. There are, however, a few good riding schools which do a conscientious job. Before placing a child in such a school the parent should visit the classes several times and make sure that he is getting what he is paying for. Taking groups out on the road is not necessarily teaching them how to ride. Quiet horses will generally follow a lead horse, and though at a certain stage of riding when what the prospective horseman needs is simply practice at the walk and trot to acquire balance, trail riding is valuable, the work in the ring is even more important. In visiting the school note the size of the classes. Experienced children may well ride in groups of ten to twenty and profit by the size of the group for they can then do drills and games. But the beginner should rarely be with more than ten companions of like ability and the very small child will learn more quickly if there are only four or five others with him.

The type of mount used is also important. Horses kept in good condition and of good breeding may often present a good appearance but they are not necessarily the right type of mount for the child, especially the timid child. Beware the school that takes private pupils on high class horses on a lead rein. Your child, under such instructions, may learn to sit well but he will learn nothing of control. On the other hand, never put your child in a school where the horses are nothing but worn out plugs. Some day he will find himself on a more spirited mount and may have a bad accident.

Much can be learned from conversation with the riding master. Ask him what seat he prefers. What type of mount he considers proper to teach children. What methods he uses to teach control. Whether he has his pupils ride without stirrups, etc.

SCISSORS

This is a mounted gymnastics exercise in which the rider faces to the rear by crossing his legs behind him and twisting suddenly. See *MOUNTED GYMNASTICS*.

SCORING

This is a harness racing term and refers to the practice of warming up the horses about to be raced by trotting them for short distances on the track in a clockwise direction. As a rule, the horse is scored a number of times, each time a little faster than the last with a walk in between before he is turned counter-clockwise for the race. A trotter may well cover five or six miles before he actually races and he is scored again in between heats.

SCOURING

Scouring or diarrhea is a symptom of some internal ailment. The most common cause is bad grain. The horse should be given a purgative and kept on a laxative diet for a few days. A handful of flour added to the grain may help, but the important thing is to find the cause of the trouble. Horses given too much green feed or too rich hay, such as alfalfa, will often scour.

SCRATCH (*v.*)

To withdraw a horse from a race.

SCRATCH (to start from)

This term which has become an idiomatic expression meaning to start without handicap originated in early times. Races were informal affairs usually taking place on a village road or forest path. It was customary for the starting line to be "scratched" across the dirt of the road, horses starting on even terms thus "started from scratch."

SCRATCHES

See *INJURIES, Cracked heels or scratches*.

SCREW

This is an old fashioned term for a poor, broken-down hack.

SCURRY

A scurry is a jumping contest done against time in which each fault counts a second off. See *HORSE SHOW CLASSES*.

SEAT

The horseman's seat refers to his position in the saddle. It includes the way he carries his arms, hands, legs, feet and back. The position adopted varies with the type of horse being ridden, the type of riding being done and the country to which the rider belongs. Styles in riding change from decade to decade, as a more careful study of the horse and rider in action is made. As a rule the changes are adopted first by the military instructors and competitors at the shows.

The most common variations are the Fort Riley or balance seat, the racing or jockey seat, the steeplechasing seat, the cowboy seat, the English hunting seat, the classical seat, the Italian seat, and the Saddle-horse seat.

The balance seat or a modification of it is the one most generally accepted in this country for equitation and jumping.

To take it the rider sits in about the middle of the saddle on his pelvic bones (not his coccyx), legs hanging straight, arms at his side, back erect but not stiff. He next bends his knees and inserts his feet in the stirrups from the outside without disturbing the perpendicular line of the leathers. The feet are inserted as far as the ball of the foot only, the toes are pointed neither in nor out nor parallel with the horse's body but are at about the angle of the toe when walking. The heels are thrust down, the inside of the foot rests against the inside of the stirrup, the ankle is bent slightly in, the heel being rotated slightly out from the thigh. This throws the inside of the knee, calf and thigh against the saddle. The tread of the stirrup is now on an angle, the outside being percep-

FIGURE 136. GOOD AND BAD POSITION AS SEEN FROM THE FRONT. BAD POSITION OF BOTH HANDS AND LEGS IS SHOWN AT LEFT. NOTE THE DAYLIGHT BETWEEN THE RIDER'S KNEE AND THE SADDLE. AT THE RIGHT IS A GOOD POSITION OF THE LEGS. THE HORSE SEEMS TO BE HAPPIER TOO.

tibly higher than the inside. The knee extends forward of the stirrup leather. The exact length of the leather depends on whether the rider is hacking or jumping. In case of the former, with the legs fully extended, the tread of the stirrup should strike the bottom of the ankle bone; in case of the latter the leather should be shortened an inch or two so that the tread strikes the middle of the instep.

The rider next picks up his reins. These should be held short enough so that there is a direct line from the rider's elbow to the horse's bit. The hands should be separated from six to ten inches depending on the width of the horse's neck. The wrists should be flexible. Some schools believe that the knuckles should be held perfectly vertical, the thumbs on top, others that the wrist should be turned so that the knuckles are midway between the vertical and the horizontal. In any case the wrist should be flexible, the horse should be controlled mainly by the actions of the fingers on the edges of the reins.

The head should not be tipped to one side or the other and the rider should look straight ahead between the horse's ears. Seen from the side, a plumb line dropped from just behind the rider's ear should penetrate his hip and ankle bones. The knee and toe tip should be on a line. As the horse moves forward the rider leans his upper body slightly more forward and the faster the movement the further forward the inclination. The legs, however, remain in the same position.

The so called "classical" seat varies from the above description as follows: The stirrups are several holes longer though the rider is still pretty well forward in the saddle. The foot is held flat in the stirrup with the toes parallel to the horse's body, the knee, due to the longer stirrup, does not extend in front of the leather or very little in front and is much less bent. For this reason the seat is not as good for jumping as the rider has much less flexibility.

The Saddle horse seat calls for a rather exaggerated pushing forward of the leg, the leather no longer hanging straight. Professionals showing Saddlers exaggerate this seat to such an extent that they sit practically on the cantle of the saddle, the feet well out in front, legs perfectly straight, hands held high, and do not post. They do this to improve the showy appearance of the horse, emphasizing his front and minimizing his length of back.

The English Hunting seat differs from the balance seat in that the rider sits behind the center of gravity of his horse. The legs are not pushed as far forward as in the Saddle horse seat. Forward seat riders refer to this style of riding as "feet on the dashboard" riding.

The present style of steeplechase seat somewhat resembles the English hunting seat though some schools of thought feel that this is gradually being replaced by the more forward seat.

The Italian forward seat differs from the balance seat in that the feet are thrust home in the stirrups, the leathers are shorter, the knee of the rider still more bent and the angle of the body more forward than in the American version.

At the opposite end of the line from the Saddle horse seat is the jockey or flat racing seat. Here the idea is to get all the weight off the horse's back and loins. The stirrups are so short that the rider's knees are even with the top of the withers, the feet are home and the heels level or above the toes. The back is hunched over, the reins incredibly short. One wonders how on earth the riders stay aboard but the use of this seat is said to be the equivalent of lightening the burden of the horse by seven or eight pounds.

The cowboy rides a completely different seat from those so far described. This is made necessary by the work he does. In order to rope cattle he must ride a stock saddle. This saddle calls for a very nearly if not entirely vertical leg and a very deep seat. The cowboy does not need to bend his knees for flexibility for he neither posts nor jumps. His horse does not do an "English" trot but fox-trots and lopes. The cowboy may either sit down in his saddle or stand in his stirrups, either is comfortable. As he needs his right hand for his lariat he always holds both reins in his left hand. He rides with a very severe bit and the horse, knowing the punishment in store, stops and turns on the slightest indication from the rider, hence the reins hang in a loop. There is no such thing as contact with the horse's mouth through the reins. Though this seat is not to be recommended from an equitation standpoint it is the most practical one for the use to which it is put. See also *RIDING, JOCKEY SEAT*.

SECOND HORSEMAN

This is a hunting term referring to the groom who brings a fresh horse to the hunt in the middle of the day so that the horse that started in the morning may be taken home.

SECRETARY

The Hunt Secretary is an important member of the staff. He keeps the books and makes himself useful in many ways. Our friends Jorrocks had very definite ideas on the qualifications of a good "Sec." See page 208, this volume.

SEEDY TOE

This is a condition, usually due to bad shoeing though it may also follow laminitis, in which the outer wall separates from the inner, sensitive layer underneath and a mealy kind of horn is formed between the two. The seedy formation may be pared away and the hoof dressed with tar and tow. A shoe should be attached which does not press on the damaged tissue. A blister may be applied to the coronet to stimulate new growth of horn.

SELECTION OF HORSE

See *BUYING THE HORSE*.

SERUMS

Science has found many serums which are of use in preventing such diseases as sleeping sickness and lockjaw. If there are cases of such diseases in your neighborhood it would be wise to have all horses in the stable inoculated.

SERVANTS (hunt)

The Whips and professional Huntsman are known as the "hunt servants."

SET TAIL

The fashion of breaking and setting the tails of Saddle and combination horses to give them a more fashionable appearance is highly cruel. Many states will not allow such horses to be shown and it is to be hoped that in time the practice will die out. Not only is the operation itself very painful but the horse is forever deprived of the use of his tail as a fly whisk. Horses so disfigured will often kick their bellies with their hoofs to rid themselves of the stinging flies until both hoof and belly are running with blood. A fly sheet does not keep off the insects and few stables are entirely screened. Furthermore, horses that in their youth were well taken care of often fall into neglectful hands when their show careers are over and spend a miserable old age, unable to fight the tormenting flies in the way that nature intended. See also *DOCKING*.

SEW A BUTTON

This is a gymkhana contest. The riders race to the opposite end of the course where a team mate sews a button on the coat-sleeve, the first to return to the starting line wins.

SHADBELLY

This is a special cut of hunting coat, somewhat similar to a cutaway. It is usually worn with a top hat rather than a derby and is more dressy than the ordinary hunting coat.

SHEET

The fly sheet is worn in the stable

in warm weather both as a protection against flies and to keep dust and hay off the horse's coats. Fly sheets are usually made of porous linens; checked and plaid patterns are smart.

SHETLAND PONY

The Shetland pony in parts of the United States, particularly the North Eastern Seaboard, has undeservedly acquired a bad name as a children's pet. One hears that he is stubborn, bad tempered and mean. That there are such individuals is undoubtedly so. One finds similar characteristics in certain individuals of any breed, but anyone who has raised Shetlands knows that they come into the world with very much the same dispositions as Saint Bernard dogs.

The pony, of any breed, is unquestionably less timid than the horse, and often craftier. For this reason he is more easily spoiled. He is also far more easily trained. Certain rules must be followed and if followed the small child will have a companion, playfellow and servant all in one.

First, do not feed the Shetland any grain unless he is in very poor condition or is being used for hard work at least two hours a day. Mares in foal may have a little grain though it is usually unnecessary. Grain seems to have the same effect on ponies that alcohol has on certain people. It makes them skittish and unreliable. Ponies fed on grain and kept stabled will get stall courage very quickly, especially in cold weather.

Second, do not keep your pony shut up. A small paddock with an open shed is all the protection he needs. A tightly packed hay stack will often provide both the necessary food and the shelter in winter.

Third, never make a practice of feeding a pony out of your hand. The pony that is frequently fed tidbits will almost invariably become a nipper. If you want to give him a carrot put it in a box for him. The exception to this rule is when you are training your pony or teaching him to come to you in the pasture, then he may be given a handful of grass or an apple as a reward for learning his lesson. Don't give him sugar or sweets at any time.

The breaking and training of the pony is of utmost importance. Most Shetlands are too small to be ridden by an adult. But if they are given regular lessons in the longe, long reins and to the cart by an experienced horseman they will not be stubborn under the saddle. But do not expect a young child who has not had riding experience to manage a Shetland alone simply because the latter is small. Have your child taught to ride properly. Ride with him yourself until he learns how to manage his mount. Shetlands and other breeds of ponies go very much more readily in company. For this reason it is far better to have two ponies than one. A brother and sister aged five and seven respectively can have a great deal of fun riding in company and be perfectly safe, whereas the younger and possibly the older might not be able to make a pony leave home alone.

Eating grass with a younger rider up is one of a pony's less desirable habits.

FIGURE 137. THE ENGLISH TYPE SHELTLAND. CONTRAST WITH THE PICTURE OF THE AMERICAN SHELTLAND FOLLOWING. THE RIDER HERE DEMONSTRATES AN EXCELLENT SEAT WITHOUT SADDLE, BODY STRAIGHT, LEGS RELAXED.

The young child, under ten, will not be able to prevent this habit, especially in the spring when the grass is especially seductive. A calf muzzle put on over the bit by means of a strap running behind the ears will be found to be very useful if your pony has this habit.

The character training which a child can derive from owning and caring for a pony is very valuable. He will learn patience, initiative and courage, as well as a love of animals.

FIGURE 138. THE AMERICAN TYPE SHELTLAND. THIS IS A MORE SLENDER ANIMAL THAN THE ENGLISH SHETLAND SHOWN ABOVE. HE WILL CARRY HIS YOUNG RIDER ACROSS COUNTRY AND OVER THE JUMPS FOLLOWING THE BLOODHOUND WHICH YOU SEE AT HIS FEET.

The exact origin of the Shetland is not known though some authorities believe that he may have come originally from desert stock. The climate and environment are responsible for his small size. See also PONIES; COLTS, Breaking and Training of; HORSES, Buying of; TEACHING THE CHILD TO RIDE.

The English type Shetland, as found in the Shetland Isles, is a blocky, draft type of animal and is sturdy, untiring and enormously strong. He is particularly noted for his weight carrying abili-ties and his strong feet. But his neck is too thick and his barrel too round to make a good saddle animal.

Breeders in this country, using Shetland stock, have developed a more slender type of animal. These ponies are veritably little horses. They retain the quiet disposition but are far more active and have less clumsy gaits. Such a pony of forty-two or forty-four inches can often jump as high as three feet and makes a fine little hunting mount for a young child. The two types are known as the "English" type and the "American Shetland, pet pony" type. In horse shows the latter are shown under the saddle by children both in the "pet pony" classes and in the "hunting pony" classes, the latter, of course, over jumps. They are usually divided two and sometimes three ways. If two ways, they are shown as "large ponies," i.e., from thirteen hands to and including fourteen-two (few pure-bred Shetlands are shown in the large division though many cross-bred ponies with Shetland blood reach this height), and "small ponies," those under thirteen hands. If divided three ways, we have a "large division," thirteen-two to fourteen-two; a "medium division," twelve hands but under thirteen-two; and a "small division," under twelve hands. As a rule only jumping ponies are judged in three divisions.

SHETLAND PONY, miniature type

For many years in England and more recently in the United States breeders have been producing a miniature type of Shetland. These ponies average from nine to ten hands in height (36 to 40 inches) and many are much smaller. They are endearing little creatures with fine silky manes and tails and, properly handled and trained, are very gentle. Their only disadvantage is that they are little more than toys and are suitable only for children under four years of age, although of course they may be driven by older children.

SHETLAND PONY, show type

Of recent years a new type of so-called "Shetland" pony has made its appearance in the show ring. This is an animal with a preponderance of Hackney pony blood and characteristics which might more properly be called a "miniature Hackney." They have the very high action (due partly to breeding, partly to schooling and shoeing) and the nervousness of the Hackney. They are not suitable for a child to ride or to drive when schooled for showing. However, the less nervous ones, not trained or shod for competition, do sometimes make suitable mounts. The emphasis for showing is on flashiness and smallness. The tails and manes are untrimmed. These ponies bring fabulous prices, weanlings selling for thousands of dollars if they have a pedigree of prize-winning parents.

SHIRE HORSE

During the Middle Ages "the *Great Horse*" came into use. He was a "great" horse indeed in size and this size was needed for he it was that was called upon to carry the knights complete with heavy armor. The Shire Horse, the largest of the draft breeds, is supposed to be the direct descendant of these mountainous horses of a by-gone era, and the nearest living representative of these horses. The "Great" Horse was Norman but he was taken across the channel into England at the time of the Norman Conquest in

FIGURE 139. THE SHIRE HORSE. *COURTESY OF THE AMERICAN SHIRE HORSE ASSOCIATION.*

1066. He then became known as the "Old English Black Horse" for black was the prevailing color. Today the bays and browns with white markings predominate. At one time grays and whites were cultivated for parade purposes.

The Shire, like all draft breeds, is gentle in the extreme. He runs seventeen and more hands in height and has been known to weigh as much as twenty-three hundred pounds though the average is 1800 to 2200.

SHOE BOIL

This is a boil caused by pressure of the shoe when the horse is lying down. It forms on the elbow and is usually about the size of an orange. When it has come to a head it must be opened and drained and not allowed to close until the draining has stopped. Syringe out twice a day using a lysol solution in a rubber ear syringe. Cover the area below and around the boil with a thick coating of vaseline to prevent loss of hair. *Do not squeeze.* See *INJURIES.*

SHOE BOIL BOOT

This is a doughnut shaped boot which is attached to the fetlock joint to prevent irritation of a shoe boil (see Injuries). One can be improvised from a section of inner tube filled with sand.

SHOEING

Except around the race tracks and shoe stables the expert blacksmith who took a veritable pride in his trade is among the missing. The modern smith is contented to tack a machine-made shoe onto the hoof in a matter of a minute or two. One is lucky if he is not of the school that believes in trimming the hoof to fit the shoe rather than vice versa.

Bad shoeing can cause both temporary and permanent lameness. Good shoeing can correct many faults in gait. Corrective shoes such as bar shoes, three quarter shoes, feather edged shoes, etc., are often needed when a horse is recovering from a corn or has such habits as speedy cutting. The horse whose heels have become contracted due to too narrow shoes may be helped by being shod with half shoes which allow the heel to expand. Most veterinaries can give good advice on shoes where something out of the ordinary is needed. For the layman the thing to watch is that the outside wall is not rasped down at the toe, that the heels do not extend too far out behind nor come inside the natural line of the wall at the heels and that the horse does not overreach or go crookedly after being shod. If possible, he should be shod so that the frog touches the ground and so performs its natural function, that of acting as a shock-absorber. See also *FEET.*

SHOES (types of)

The ordinary shoes used on Saddle horses and hunters are known as "snow shoes." These are light shoes, those used on the front feet being put on with toe clips and having no calkins or heels; the back shoes being put on with side clips and having small calkins to prevent slipping.

In winter these may be replaced with a patented shoe which allows for the attachment of sharp ice calks. The horse should never be worked on dry ground with calks, however, as his tendons will surely suffer.

The *bar shoe,* which has a raised heel, was frequently used to relieve a horse that was "over at the knees" due to shortened tendons. This type has largely been replaced by a "wedge" shoe, i.e., one that, instead of ordinary heels, gradually thickens in a wedge shape towards the back. Such a shoe puts less strain on the tendons than the shoe with high calks.

The *feather edged shoe* is one which is beveled off on the inside to prevent brushing and speedy cutting. The nails in this shoe are all on the outside and toe and it is held in place with side clips.

The *tip* is used on horses turned out to pasture to prevent the wall from breaking. The *half shoe* does not extend all the way to the heel but stops half way, thus allowing for expansion of heel and frog in curing a condition such as contracted heels.

In conditions where the frog needs development a *Charlier* shoe may be used. Here the blacksmith cuts away the wall to receive the shoe which is bedded in it.

A *three-quarter* shoe where the shoe comes to the heel on one side but stops half way down the opposite side of the foot, may be used to relieve pressure from a corn. For horses with thrush where it is desirable to pack the frog and sole a simple flat strip of iron may be wedged in under an ordinary shoe across the back near the sole.

The *racing shoe* is extraordinarily light and only intended to last for one race. On the other hand, Saddlers and hackneys often wear weighted shoes to make them pick up their feet. Harness horses, both the trotters and the pacers, need very scientific shoeing to give them full speed. It is at the harness tracks that one finds the most expert blacksmiths. A good man can watch a horse in action, then, from a simple strip of steel, make him a shoe which will take seconds away from his record. Horses that tend to break from one gait to another are also helped by special shoeing.

SHOULDER

The slope of the horse's shoulder is very important. The horse with the straight shoulder will have a hard gait. He may also have trouble keeping his saddle in place. The draft horse needs heavier shoulders than the Saddler. The muscles on the race horse must be flat and stringy at the shoulder rather than bunchy.

The shoulder is often the seat of injury, and such injuries are harder to cure than are those of the leg. As a rule, a good blister is the only thing that will be effective in shoulder lameness. See also *INJURIES*.

SHOULDER-IN

This is a schooling movement designed to improve the horse's lateral flexion. This movement so places the horse that,

whereas his hind feet travel along a straight track parallel to the wall, the forehand of the horse is carried slightly to the inside; thus, in traveling on the left hand (the center of the ring being to the rider's left), the horse's right forefoot should be planted directly in line with the tracks of his left hind foot and his left forefoot should form a pattern of prints inside of this. In order to do this correctly the horse must bend his spine in an even curve beginning at the poll and ending at the dock. For diagrams and methods of achieving this movement, see *RIDING, The Advanced Rider*.

SHOW

To come in third in a race. (In betting, third or better.)

SHOWING

The showing of horses has not only become the pastime of the wealthy but a means of livelihood for thousands. It has stimulated the breeding and thus the improvement of every type of horse. One needs professional help and plenty of time and money to compete in the larger shows but local shows offer amusement and beneficial competition, especially for the ambitious young rider. See also *HORSE SHOWS*.

SHOWS

See *HORSE SHOWS*.

SHYING

Many horses shy from high spirits. Others shy from timidity and some have special conditioned "hates." The good horseman can usually tell a perceptible time before the horse is going to shy. Then is the time to prevent it by a stronger use of the aids and talking quietly to the animal. Learn to look ahead as you ride for objects which might startle your mount. Remember that he is less apt to be afraid of a fire engine or a truck than of blowing clothes, paper or a child on roller skates. What to do when your horse shies will depend somewhat on the animal. The rider should increase his leg grip and shorten his reins. Some horses will go quietly by an object if they are allowed to take a good look at it, others are less afraid if they are turned away from it. Try and keep the horse moving. If he whirls don't pull him back but turn him all the way around so that he is still facing in the original direction. If you are with a companion who is mounted on a steadier animal let the other go first. Don't use force unless you have to; beating a horse past an object may get him by but he will have two fears to combat the next time he meets the same thing. See also *VICES*.

SIDE BONES

A side bone is a condition in which the cartilage on the side of the coronet becomes ossified. It may be caused by overwork, bad shoeing or it may be hereditary. The symptoms are heat in the coronet near the heel and an enlargement in the shape of a ridge. In mild cases no lameness is caused, in bad cases it will be necessary to blister the part or even to groove the wall below the side bone to relieve the pressure.

SIDE-GALLOP

See *RIDING, The Advanced Rider (Traversal)*.

SIDE-STEPPING   (two-tracking)

See *RIDING, The Advanced Rider (Traversal)*.

SIDE WHEELER

This is a trotting man's name for a pacing horse.

SIGNALS

See *AIDS*.

SILKS

The colored blouses which jockeys and the drivers of harness horses wear are known as "Silks." They serve to identify the stable.

SINGLE-FOOT

The single-foot or rack is one of the steps required of the five-gaited horse. It is fast, showy and elevated and gets its name from the fact that it is a four-beat gait, each foot touching the ground by itself.

SIRE

The father of a horse is known as the sire. Certain stud horses are very prepotent, i.e., have the distinguishing quality of passing their characteristics down to their descendants for generation after generation. Perhaps the most noted of these "foundation sires" was Justin Morgan, the founder of the breed of Morgan horses. Though his blood has been mixed with many other breeds, his progeny still adhere to the characteristics both physical and otherwise of Justin Morgan who died in 1821. For other famous sires see *FAMOUS HORSES*.

SIT FAST

A sit fast is a type of boil which forms under the skin on the side of the back, usually below the spine. It is caused by the pressure of an ill-fitting saddle. A lump first forms and, if there has been an old wound a hard dry scabby skin will form over the sore. This will later slough off leaving the sit fast. The latter becomes larger and more painful and can only be cured by resorting to surgery.

SIZE OF HORSES

The average size of the horse varies greatly with his breed. The tendency at the moment is to breed for very large horses, particularly in the hunter line. But army tests have shown that the horse's strength does not increase in proportion to his size after the height of sixteen hands. Thus a seventeen hand hunter is literally not as strong as a sixteen hand hunter, for the additional weight which he carries is more than the increase in muscle. Many Associations limit the horses which they accept for registration to a certain size, others do not. Of course the race horse must have a certain length of stride though there have been many small racers, and in jumping the good big horse will usually out-jump the good little horse. Here again one finds exceptions such as Little Squire, the thirteen hand Irish pony that won the open jumping at Madison Square Garden year after year against the stiffest competition that the country had to offer.

In buying a horse for children the size is extremely important. Little children simply cannot do as well on a big animal. The gait is too long and the child's feet do not contact the horse where they can effectively be used as aids. Before buying a fifteen hand horse for a six or seven year old the parent should pause and consider how he himself would feel mounted on a horse the height of an elephant.

SKEWBALD

This is one of the color patterns, being a spotted horse which combines white areas with any color other than black. A black and white horse is a piebald. Both these horses are erroneously described as "paints" or "pintos." See also *COLORS OF THE HORSE*. Skewbald and piebald animals occur in Western and pony breeds, more especially Shetland ponies. Thoroughbreds and most established horse breeds are never spotted.

SKINNER

A skinner is, in dealers' language, a horse that should be sold to the knacker for horse meat.

SKULL

The difference in the skull formations of horses according to the breed is one of the ways in which the evolution of the breeds has been traced. The skull of the Arabian, for example, shows the eye set lower than in other breeds and the typical "dishing" of the nose. The Greek horses do not show these characteristics whereas the Egyptian horses do. The migration of the desert horse all over the world can be followed by the bony structure of the skeletons found, not only of the skull, but by means of other charac-

teristics such as the fact that the Arabian has one fewer vertebra than other breeds.

In choosing a horse, prominence of the bones in the skull indicates finer breeding, the coarser breeds such as the Quarter horse and the draft breeds being distinguished by the muscular appearance of the head.

SLEEPING SICKNESS
See *ENCEPHALITIS*.

SLIP FILLETS

These are little strips of wood placed on the top rail of the obstacle in open jumping competitions. If the slip fillet falls the obstacle is considered to have been touched and the fault is scored against the horse.

SLIPPER

A light shoe put on temporarily to protect the horse's feet is called a slipper.

SNAFFLE

The snaffle is a bit which is jointed in the middle and is fitted with one pair of reins, though two, buckled into the same rings, are sometimes used. It is the lightest bit and works entirely on the corners of the horse's mouth, not on the bars. The snaffle is the popular bit for hunting and jumping for even a poor rider can do his horse little harm in it, but if one would develop light hands one should ride in a full bridle. The snaffle is unsuitable for Saddle-horses or for exacting forms of equitation as one cannot convey to the horse the demand for much variety of movement. Though beginners usually ride in snaffles, the riding master feeling that until they gain their balance it is not well to subject the horse to the punishment of heavy hands on the curb, they should not be allowed to lean on the reins nor should they be permitted to use the snaffle too long or they will become "mutton fisted." See also *BITS, BRIDLES*.

SORES

Some horses, with tender skin, get sores much more easily than others. Condition also has a great deal to do with this and certain ailments, such as kidney disease, lessen the horse's resistance to infection so that every fly bite may turn into a running sore. The type of treatment will have to depend on the kind of sore. Saddle and girth galls yield readily to applications of methylene blue (Blue Gall Remedy). Infectious sores may be treated with B.F.I. powder, sulfathiazole ointment, or novoxil which is a silver oxide ointment. Sores which refuse to heal should be examined for the existence of "proud flesh" and such healing remedies as Balsam of Peru are sometimes effective after the proud flesh has been burned off. See also *INJURIES; GALLS; SADDLE SORES*.

SORREL

Sorrel is the countryman's name for the lighter shades of chestnut. See *COLORS OF THE HORSE*.

SOUNDNESS

The three things to be considered in buying a horse are, *first,* soundness of wind, limb and eyes; *second,* manners, and *third,* conformation. By far the most important of these is the soundness. If possible, have the horse tested by a veterinarian or get a warranty from the seller. For tests for soundness see *TESTS; BUYING THE HORSE*.

SPANISH HORSES

When the Arabs invaded Spain for the purpose of converting them to Mohammedanism they took with them their horses. When, five hundred years later, they were evicted, the horses had become native to Spain. It was these Spanish horses of desert heritage which were imported not only into America but practically all over the world for the Spanish were an exploring and conquering nation. Thus we find that the horses of the Argentine, the horse of Cuba, and of the Philippines, the Mustang and Cowpony of the West, all descend from the horses of the invading Spaniards.

SPANISH RIDING SCHOOL OF VIENNA

See *LIPIZZAN*.

SPANISH WALK AND TROT

The Spanish walk is one of the more difficult movements of dressage or high school. The horse raises each foot in turn and extends it forward, holding it out for a perceptible pause before placing it on the ground. The action is extremely elevated, the horse's body appears to swell in size and sway gently as he moves forward and this swaying motion is even more evident when the gait is increased to the trot. It is an extremely tiring gait and the horse should not be asked to execute it for more than a short distance.

The preliminary training for the Spanish Walk is done on the ground. The trainer, by light taps of the whip, induces the horse to raise one foot after the other and plant it again lightly. Some trainers employ ropes to achieve the desired elevation but it is best not to use mechanical aids if possible. The most difficult idea to convey to the horse is not that he must raise his feet but that he must bring them down lightly and progress forward. When the animal finally understands what is desired the trainer mounts and, still using taps of the whip on shoulder and croup, accompanied now by a gentle swaying of his body and pressure of the heel directly behind the girth, leads the horse into the new step.

Several things must be borne in mind. First, the teaching of so artificial a movement as this takes many lessons, the length of each lesson being limited to five minutes. Rewards in the form of sugar or carrots are obligatory. The horse must not be allowed to become balky or resentful as he will surely do if overtired. Also, every attempt must be made to insure that not only are the fore feet lifted and extended but the back feet too.

SPAVIN
See *INJURIES*.

SPEAKING (hounds)
See *HUNTING TERMS*.

SPEED OF HORSES
The horse walks at the rate of four miles an hour, trots at nine miles and gallops at twelve. Naturally these speeds vary to some extent but the above rates of speed are those considered the average. The running horse develops great speed and of course the harness racer also. Equipoise's record of a mile in 1.34⅖ is the world's fastest mile on an oval track.

SPEEDY CUT
A speedy cut is an injury to the inside of the hock or knee caused by the striking of the opposite foot of the horse. Shoeing can remedy the fault in most cases but the horse given to speedy cutting should wear boots as a protection.

SPLINTS
A splint is a bony enlargement on the cannon or splint bones. It may occur on front or hind legs anywhere along the cannon bone though it is more common in the front. It is caused by overwork at an early age when the horse's bones are soft. Splints generally cause only temporary lameness and often disappear entirely. The lameness may often be relieved by blistering. A large splint high up on the bone is bad as a horse with high action or a horse in poor condition will often strike the splint with the opposite leg, causing severe lameness for a short time. See *LEGS of the horse, INJURIES*.

SPLIT PASTERN
This is a fracture of the bones or ligaments of the pastern and can only be definitely diagnosed with X-rays. The horse will be very lame and a plaster of paris cast together with complete rest, preferably in a sling, is the only remedy.

SPLIT WALL
See *SAND CRACK*.

SPRAINS
See *INJURIES*.

SPRINTER
A horse that is run up to 7 furlongs is called a good sprinter.

SPURS
The spur, even the rowelled spur, as used by the expert horseman, is not in the least cruel. But, as other writers have said, equipping the tyro with the rowelled spur is like putting a razor into the hands of a monkey. The good horseman never touches his horse with his heels or spur unintentionally, and he can exactly gauge the amount of pressure which he chooses to use according to the sensitivity of the horse. The spur is used to convey commands to the horse, not simply to make him go faster as the uninitiated believe. The good horseman would consider himself disgraced if he ever put a mark on his horse with his spur.

The Western rider, unfortunately, does not use his spurs in this manner, but, when riding in competition in rodeos, spurs his horse cruelly both fore and aft to excite him into bucking so that he may be given an opportunity to show his skill. Granted that the cowpony has not the sensitivity of the hot-blooded horse, the cowboy still does not need the long rowels which he wears. On the other hand, Mexican and South American cowboys, as well as our own, often sport the long rowelled spur for looks and, if good enough riders, never punish their horses unnecessarily.

SQUARE DANCING (mounted)
Any group of from eight to twelve moderately competent riders can add variety to their riding program and, at the same time, improve their skill and the flexibility and obedience of their mounts by executing simple square-dance figures at the sitting trot or the

slow canter. Choose patterns which do not require very much "swinging." Start your dance by forming the regulation square at the command "Sets in order." If there are twelve riders, instead of eight, place two couples on each long side, thus forming a rectangle instead of a square. The gentleman always, of course, has the lady on his right. When the music starts the caller says "Salute your partners" (partners bow to each other), then "Salute your corners" (riders bow to riders on their opposite sides from their partners (ladies bow to those nearest on their right, gentlemen the opposite). Next comes "Circle right." Riders turn simultaneously to their left, thus forming a circle, single file, and all ride once around, stopping at their original places and facing center in pairs as before. The introduction over, the pattern of the individual dance follows. At the end experienced riders can do an "allemande left and grand right and left"; less experienced riders can simply do a "Grande promenade." In the latter the riders turn in pairs to their right and circle the hall in pairs, the gentlemen on the inside, the ladies on the outside.

There are on the market a number of books on traditional square dances from which suitable figures for mounted work may be adapted. Horses suitable for square dancing should have smooth, well-cadenced, slow trots and canters. The music can be played on a juke box, a record player or tape. Choose records without a recording of the calls, as these will have to be adapted.

SQUARE TROT

A horse is said to trot squarely when the cadence of the gait is perfectly regular, indicating that he is putting an equal amount of weight on each pair of legs.

STABLE

In designing a modern stable one should have the plans as functional as possible taking all factors into consideration. Not only will this tremendously

reduce the labor but it will vastly improve the appearance of the building. The location of the stable is also important; it should be near enough the main dwelling so that any commotion can be readily noticed or it should have quarters for the stable man incorporated in the design. Yet it must not be so close to the owner's living quarters as to be offensive.

Insulation of the stable in cold climates will remove the necessity of artificial heating. Not only will your horse be healthier but the fire hazard also will be greatly reduced. In hot climates ventilation is of extreme importance and the stable should be so built as to take advantage of the prevailing wind. The size and types of stalls will depend on the kind of horses to be stabled, but whether your string consists of children's ponies or of hunters, be sure that all side walls of stalls are built of two inch oak.

The location of water in the stable is important. Where more than three or four horses are kept, individual automatic water bowls in each stall will save an enormous amount of time and labor as well as insuring that your horses will never go thirsty due to the laziness or carelessness of a groom.

It is safer to store your hay and grain in the loft. Chutes into each stall or a larger chute near the center of the stable enables the groom to feed the horses easily. Holes cut in the ceiling above each stall will permit him to fork the hay down as needed.

The tack room which should be equipped with running water and a cleaning rack for saddles as well as individual bridle and saddle racks should be near enough to the horses so that it is not too much of a chore to carry the tack back and forth. The runway behind the stalls should be wide enough to allow of easy turning of the horse. The flooring of this runway should not be slippery.

The location of the manure pit or pile is important. If possible the manure should be carried entirely away from the stable each day as this greatly reduces the odor and the presence of flies. Screens should be provided on all doors and windows. The stable should also be so located that there is room for a small paddock adjoining it and it should not be directly on a public thoroughfare. If it is close to a road there should be some special place allotted for mounting and dismounting as this is one of the times when a rider has not full control of his horse and a restive horse that side-steps out into a road in front of an approaching car can cause a serious accident.

There is no reason why a stable cannot be as attractive as any other type of building. Think of the main house and the stable as parts of the same unit and see that the architecture, the pitch of the roof, etc., harmonize. See also *HORSE, Care of; TACK ROOM; STALLS; WATER FOUNTAINS; LIGHTING; VENTILATION*.

STABLE EQUIPMENT

The ordinary tools needed for the stable are the push broom, the sweeping broom, the rake, the four or five tined manure fork, the hay fork and the wheel barrow. Fixtures in the stable may vary greatly. See *WATERING, Methods of; LIGHTS*. The tack room will need a complete set of equipment for taking care of the tack and of course grooming tools of all kinds are essential. See *GROOMING*. Extra stable buckets should always be at hand for use in First Aid and for sponging off a horse. Stable buckets should be as sturdy as possible.

A wrecking bar, a hammer, pliers and wire cutters must be kept in a convenient place where they can be easily found in event of a horse getting into trouble. Most modern stables have electric clippers, and a supply of oil and kerosene should be kept with them.

The First Aid cabinet is very important and stock remedies should be replenished whenever they get low. This particularly applies to colic medicine and antiseptics.

STABLE MANNERS

The stable manners of the horse are extremely important, especially where children are in and out. Many stable vices such as crowding and kicking can be cured (see *VICES*) but the horse that is really mean or so nervous as to be completely unreliable should not be kept except under the care of an extremely experienced horseman.

The horse with good stable manners will move over readily in his stall, he will not side kick at other horses or kick backwards at a horse being led behind him. He backs out readily and does not rush in when returned to his stall. He does not crib or tear his blanket. He does not knock down his manger, paw holes in the flooring nor dart backwards the minute the halter is unfastened.

One of the most dangerous of the stable vices is that of the horse housed in a loose box stall refusing to allow a person entering his stall to come up to his head. Such a horse is better off in a straight stall. Putting the feed manger in the front of the box and, on entering, always putting a little grain in the box, will cause the horse to come up to the trainer. On no account stand behind a horse that deliberately swings his hind legs at you for his next step is to let fly and you may readily find yourself pinned in a corner unable to escape.

STABLE ROUTINE

It is very important that a regular stable routine be established, and that a new groom be trained to follow this routine exactly. The first thing in the morning is the feeding. This should be done before the groom has his own breakfast and he may then eat while the horses are eating. Immediately after breakfast the stalls are cleaned. As soon as this is done each horse, whether he is to be ridden or not, is thoroughly groomed and if there is no water in the stalls, all animals are watered. Horses to be ridden should be tacked up about fifteen minutes before they are needed, the girth left comfortably loose. The owner of the stable may choose a time just before the noon feeding to inspect the stable, discuss the condition of the animals with the man and possibly attend to anything in the way of medical treatment which is necessary.

The horses should be watered before the noon feeding and the stalls cleaned. The horses to be used in the afternoon are then tacked up. In the late afternoon the groom shakes out the bedding, sees that water pails are filled or waters the horses at the main trough before feeding them and then feeds. The tack must be done after the horses come in and if possible each horse that was used must be groomed before being returned to his stall.

STAGGERS
See *MEGRIMS; BLIND STAGGERS.*

STAKE AND BOUND FENCE
This type of fence is comon in England, not so common over here. It is a live thorn fence, the thorns of which have been cut half through and then bent over and bound down to make it stronger. It is often seen in the Shires.

STAKE CLASSES
Stake classes are those in which the prize is money. Most open jumping competitions are stake classes.

STAKE HORSES
These are horses which are exhibited in stake classes or run in stake races. To call a horse a stake horse is a compliment whereas the term "plater" meaning a horse that competes for a trophy, is derogatory.

STAKES
Stake races are often called "stakes," thus one speaks of the "Derby Stakes."

STAKES RACE
A race in which entry fees and any other added money is divided among first, second, third and fourth horses.

STAKING OUT A HORSE
Only horses which are used to being tethered can be staked out as others are apt to wind themselves up in the rope and get bad rope burns if nothing else. The stake should be in the form of a metal pin with a swivel head. Another method of staking out a horse which does prevent, to a large extent, any entangling, is that of mounting a wooden arm on a swivel post three feet high. A short rope attached to the arm is fastened to the horse's halter. As the area over which the horse grazes when so tethered is very small this method is not very practical. A better way is to build a small, portable electric fenced pen which can be moved from place to place as the horse grazes.

STALE HORSE
A horse is said to go stale or sour if, through boredom, he refuses to perform as desired. This term is especialy used in connection with jumpers. Horses get easily bored and if jumped too long or too often over the same obstacles, especially if being ridden by an incompetent horseman, will often go sour and refuse to take even a very small hurdle.

STALE LINE
See *HUNTING TERMS.*

STALL
Stalls are of two types, the box stall and the straight stall. The regulation size for the box stall is twelve by twelve. It may be larger if its occupant is over sixteen hands. For small ponies a stall eight by eight is ample. See also *BOX STALLS.* A straight stall is usually five by ten.

STALL COURAGE
The horse that stands too long in his stall without exercise develops "stall courage" and will buck and fling his heels to the sky when first mounted though, normally, he may be a very quiet animal. The best cure for stall courage, if the horse is to be ridden by a timid

or inexperienced rider, is, immediately before the lesson, to turn him, saddled and bridled, into the riding hall and let him play. He must not be allowed to roll, and the stirrups must either be detached or run up on the leathers. The bridle reins must be slipped behind the cantle or under the leathers.

The best way to take stall courage out of a horse under the saddle is to trot him steadily for a mile or two.

STALLION

The mature male horse is called a stallion. Stallions that have been castrated are called geldings. Until the male horse becomes four years old he is known as a colt, the female being called a filly.

There is a great and generally unnecessary fear of stallions in this country. The stallion is high spirited and may readily, through bad handling, become mean, but he is not born so. If handled properly, ridden regularly and in company and kept in a stall where he can see other horses, the stallion under good hands, is no more unreliable than the mare or gelding. It is not customary to alter the horses in France, Spain or the South American countries and the stallions are worked right along with the mares as a matter of course.

STANDARD BRED

Trotters and pacers are known as "standard breds." This does not imply that they are not registered or purebred according to their breed. Standard breeds are also known as "cold-blooded" horses as against the "hot-blooded" Thoroughbred. See also *TROTTERS; HARNESS RACING.*

STANDING MARTINGALE

This is a device for steadying the horse's head. See *MARTINGALES.*

STARTING THE HORSE

The horse should never be put into motion carelessly. The well trained animal stands perfectly still while being mounted and waits a signal from the rider before moving off. If he has not been so trained his education should be attended to at once. Having settled himself in the saddle the horseman holds his reins in one hand while he adjusts his stirrups. He then puts his reins into two hands. He "collects" his horse slightly by gathering the reins and exerts a little pressure of the leg. He may or may not speak to him also, but if he does it should be in the form of a word or a phrase, not the familiar "clucking" sound. The horse should step out readily but quietly at a walk. He should be walked for at least fifteen minutes before being trotted.

STATISTICS

See *RECORDS AND STATISTICS* (Appendix).

STAYER

A horse that keeps going without losing speed or staying power for 1½ miles or more is said to be a good stayer.

STEADY (to steady hounds)

See *HUNTING TERMS.*

STEADYING (the horse)

The horseman steadies his horse just before demanding a special effort on his part such as jumping. He does this by increased and steady pressure of the reins and slight, not exaggergated, pressure of the legs.

STEALING STICKS

See *PRISONER'S BASE.*

STEELDUST

The Steeldust is a term used to designate a certain family of horses which were descended from a sire of that name.

STEEPLECHASE AND HUNT ASSOCIATIONS

See Appendix.

STEEPLECHASE AND HUNT RECORDS, 1961

See *RECORDS AND STATISTICS* (Appendix).

FIGURE 140. TITON HANOVER. A STANDARD BRED TROTTER, PAINTED BY WESLEY DENNIS.

STEEPLECHASING AND HURDLE RACING

The term steeplechasing is derived from the custom of outlining the course of the race by means of church steeples. It is a race run over a course which approximates natural conditions. Its purpose is to test a horse as to his qualifications as a hunter. For this reason steeplechasers are not necessarily Thoroughbreds.

Steeplechasing and Hurdle racing have never had the extensive schedule of meets that one finds in flat racing. On the other hand, the Grand National of England, the Maryland Hunt Cup of this country are as well known as any flat race.

Steeplechasing was first officially recorded in the English Racing Calendar in 1865 though it is much older, of course, than this. The American Turf Register records the first Hurdle race as occurring at Washington, D. C. in October, 1834. It is described as being "one mile out, leaping six fences, every gent riding his own horse," for a piece of plate valued at one hundred pounds.

In 1838 the Governor General's Cup was given by the Earl of Durham, the race, the oldest still existing, taking place at Montreal, Canada.

Hurdle racing differs from Steeplechasing in that the course is usually over a dirt track, generally inside a race track, over hurdles. These hurdles are not solid.

FIGURE 141. NEJI, THE WORLD'S LARGEST MONEY-WINNING 'CHASER. OWNED BY MRS. OGDEN PHIPPS. *COURTESY NATIONAL STEEPLECHASE AND HUNT ASSOCIATION.*

The combination of flying hurdles and the dust raised made hurdle racing extremely unpopular and it was discontinued in 1900 to be started again a few years ago.

The forward seat adopted by jockeys in flat racing enormously increased the speed of horses in these races. But the tremendous jumps which must be maneuvered at speed over a steeplechase course prevented the adoption of the extreme forward seat. Riders are now using a modified forward seat and the speed has been increased as a result. In early times it was customary for the riders to hold the horses in until the jumps were taken, not getting up a real burst of speed until the home stretch. But now one finds them starting off at a full gallop.

The Grand National, which is undoubtedly the toughest of all courses, demonstrates the proportion of horses which may finish. In the year 1946 thirty-four horses entered, six finished. One was killed outright, another badly injured. The race was won by a quiet "lady's hunter," Irish bred, named "Lovely Cottage." In 1928 forty-two horses started and only one finished. In 1961, thirty-five horses started, fourteen finished. The race was won by Mr. C. Vaughan's "Nicolaus Silver," ridden by H. Beasley. A survey of winners of the Grand National showed that the majority of these horses had, at one time or another, been hunted by ladies. This would imply that manners and obedience are as requisite to the winning of this great race as are stamina and speed.

One can hardly mention the Grand National without bringing to mind the title of the famous book *National Velvet*, by Enid Bagnold. This beautifully written book tells of the riding and winning of the Grand National by a fifteen-year-old girl on a piebald horse.

Two American bred horses have won the Grand National, Rubio and Battleship. Irish horses have proved the best steeplechasers and, as a general rule, a successful steeplechaser is not a flat racer. The flat racer starts his training as a yearling. The steeplechaser runs out until he is a four year old and his tendons are strong enough to stand the grueling schooling which is necessary. The Meadow Brook Club was a pioneer of steeplechasing in this country. The Maryland Hunt Cup, the best known and favorite of the steeplechases in the United States came into being in 1894. Five gentlemen, the Messrs. Baldwin, Farber, Hopkins, Ulman and Whistler, were discussing and arguing over the respective merits of the various hunters in their district. They decided that the best method of settling the argument was to have a race over hunting country. A challenge was then forwarded to the Green Valley Hunt and so began the Maryland Hunt Cup.

In those days Hunt race meetings were very informal affairs. There were few rules and much discussion as to what these rules should be. Should one stop and help a rider who had fallen? As the riders were amateurs and gentlemen the general consensus of opinion was that one should. Happily, the presence of patrol judges has never rendered this act of benevolence necessary. But the riders often warn a competitor that he is going off the course. Modern steeplechase courses vary widely, they may be timber or brush, or both. Some clubs, such as the Meadow Brook, have two courses, one timber and one brush. But the National Steeplechase and Hunt Association has certain specifications to which all courses must conform. There must be twelve fences in the first two miles. There must be six fences in each succeeding mile, exclusive of hurdles. In each mile there must be a ditch, six feet wide and two feet deep on the take-off side of a four-foot-six fence. There must be a water jump twelve feet wide and two feet deep guarded by a three foot fence.

The steeplechasing and hurdle racing season is from November to March and so does not interfere with the racing schedules. In the appendix are given lists of courses, owners, famous horses and the weight-for scale handicap table for steeplechasers. The rules are formulated by and the meets are under the jurisdiction of the National Steeplechase and Hunt Association. Its offices are at 300 Park Avenue, New York City. See *STEEPLECHASE AND HUNT ASSOCIATIONS* (Appendix); *RECORDS AND STATISTICS—STEEPLECHASE AND HUNT, 1961* (Appendix).

STERN

The tail of the hound is known as the "stern" and always so designated by hunting people.

STIFF NECKED FOX
See *HUNTING TERMS*.

STIFLE
See Figure 51, page 150, *HORSE, Points of*.

STIFLE LAMENESS
See *INJURIES*.

STIMULANTS

Brandy or whisky is the stimulant usually used in cases of collapse or chill. It should be remembered, however, that no horse should have liquids poured down his throat if he is unconscious as there is danger of it entering the lungs.

STIRRUP LEATHERS

These are the straps by which the stirrups are attached to the saddle. They must be of the best and most flexible leather.

STIRRUPS

Metal stirrups are usually used on English saddles, wooden ones with or without leather guards on stock saddles. For children the wooden stirrup is less slippery and broader, hence easier to hold. If a wooden stirrup with a leather guard is used an additional strap should be attached to the guard and to the bottom of the tread of the stirrup so that there is no danger of the rider thrusting his toes through and getting them wedged in.

STOCK (v.)

A horse whose legs swell up when he stands is said to "stock" up. This is a circulatory ailment usually due to injury. It may be relieved by bandaging the legs and by massage. The same type of swelling sometimes appears under the belly. In this case the horse should be given a good purgative such as Epsom salts and kept on a laxative diet for a few days.

STOCK HORSE

A horse used in working with stock is called a stock horse or a cow pony. There are special classes for these horses in the shows. See *HORSE SHOW CLASSES, STOCK HORSE DIVISION.*

The well trained stock horse is a truly remarkable animal, to be compared, in training, flexibility and obedience to commands with the High School horses of circus and *Manege.*

STOCK SADDLE

See *SADDLES.*

STOCKINGS

White markings which come above the fetlock joints are known as "stockings," those which are short are called "socks."

STOMACH (of the horse)

The stomach of the horse is very small in relation to the size of his body. For this reason he should be fed often and little, especially when it comes to grain. See *HORSE, Care of; FEEDING.*

STONE AGE HORSES

See *HORSE, Origin of.*

STONE IN THE FOOT

A stone wedged in the foot is the most common cause of sudden lameness. If no hoof pick is handy it may be dislodged by hammering with another stone. Sometimes, if the horse has traveled some distance, the sole will be bruised but, as a rule, as soon as the stone is removed the horse will go sound.

STOPPING (Earth stopping)

See *HUNTING TERMS.*

STOPPING (the horse)

The horse should not be jerked to a sudden stop as this puts too great a strain on his tendons. Except in polo or roping cattle he should be brought gradually to a halt by use of the aids. Under expert hands the horse may be trained to come to a dead halt from the different gaits but he must come to this gradually and obediently, not through force.

STRANGLES

Strangles is a complication which frequently occurs in influenza, shipping fever, and other respiratory ailments. The gland under the horse's jaw becomes infected and very swollen. The horse runs a high fever and can hardly swallow. It is necessary to open the gland and drain off the pus, keeping it open until the infection has been conquered. Sometimes the gland remains thickened which affects the flexion of the head and may affect the wind.

STRAPPED LIGHTNING

When hopples were first introduced in harness racing to induce pacers to keep their gait, horses so equipped were referred to as "strapped lightning."

STRAPPER

This is an English term meaning groom. Strapping a horse means grooming it and hence a groom is called a "strapper."

STRAW

Straw is the most common material used for bedding. Rye straw is the best and if it is chopped up it will be more absorbent. Horses eat oat straw and some horses eat any straw. Such animals will have to be bedded on peat moss or shavings. Horses with heaves should not be bedded on straw.

STRETCHING

Saddle and harness horses are taught to stand with their legs outstretched. This practice originated with the ladies' harness horses to insure that they stood quietly while milady stepped into her phaeton or victoria. A horse that is stretching or camping cannot move forward or backward until he first brings his legs under him. Horses that stretch without being trained to do so have kidney trouble. See also *CAMPING*.

STRIKING

Striking is a form of brushing similar to speedy cutting in which the horse strikes one leg with the toe or side of another leg. Therapeutic shoeing will correct this in most cases though the horse should wear boots until he has been cured of the habit.

STRING HALT

This is a curious affliction whose exact cause is not known which makes the horse pick his back legs up very high and walk in a peculiarly exaggerated fashion. Some authorities think it to be a nervous condition, others attribute it to strained tendons. Surgery is the only cure, but, as it does not affect the usefulness of the animal there is no particular reason for going to these extremes except in the case of valuable show animals.

STRONG TROT

In the strong phase of the trot the horse lowers his head slightly but without pushing his nose beyond the vertical, and leans on the bit for support. At the same time he brings his quarters well under him and extends the length of his stride both with his front and his hind legs. There is a much more marked cadence, the horse balancing for a perceptible instant first on one diagonal and then on the other. This pause is not as marked in the strong trot as it is in the *passage*, but the former definitely resembles the latter. The strong trot is one of the most valuable of all exercises to strengthen the horse. It is called for in all *dressage* competitions and schooling rides. Some horses learn it very readily; others, particularly those with much Arabian blood, find it very difficult.

STUD

A stallion that is used for breeding purposes is often called a stud or stud horse. The mares and stallions together on a breeding farm are also known as a stud.

STUD BOOK

The registry in which the horses of the various breeds are registered is known as the stud book.

STUD FEES

These are the fees which the owner of the stallion collects for his services.

STUMBLING

One of the most pernicious habits in horses is that of stumbling. Jorrocks tells us that in his opinion the horse that hits the same stone with one foot after the other is just as desirable as the horse that turns out his toes to such an extent that he brushes the stones off his path! Horses will stumble because of bad shoeing, lack of condition or overwork. Bad conformation is a common cause and some horses just don't seem to care. They travel along so close to the ground that they trip over every little unevenness. A horse will stumble much more frequently at a walk than at a trot or canter, and a spirited horse is rarely a stumbler except from bad shoeing or a serious fault in his conformation.

One of the most common causes of stumbling is lack of balance on the part of the horse which has not learned to carry himself properly under the weight of a rider. These horses are usually on their forehand, with the center of gravity too far forward. If this is the cause of your horse's pernicious habit of stumbling you will be glad to know that a thorough course of basic and intermediate *dressage,* both mounted and on the longe, will usually cure it.

If the habit is due to bad or weak conformation the fault is not so easily corrected. Many horses that stumble at the walk through inattention will correct the fault when they have learned to go "on the bit" and pay better attention to the demands of the rider.

SUBSCRIPTIONS

Most hunts are financed by subscriptions. To refer again to our friend Jorrocks, it is he who said that every man should subscribe to the local hunt whether he hunted himself or not and the simple fact that he could not afford it was no excuse!

SUBSTANCE

The word "substance" in refering to horses means their apparent stamina and hardiness. "Quality" refers to their fineness. Horses in certain divisions such as hunters may be classified as "Thoroughbred Hunters" and "Hunters other than Thoroughbreds," the former being judged largely on quality and the latter on substance. See also *QUALITY; HORSE SHOW CLASSES.*

SUDADERO

The sudadero is the leather flap behind which the stirrup leather on the stock saddle runs. It protects the rider's leg from contact and friction with the leather for Western riders wear thin, loose pants and do not wear high boots.

SUFFOLK HORSE

The Suffolk or, as he used to be known, the Suffolk Punch, is the oldest of the draft breeds. He originated in Suffolk, England, and it is believed that his ancestors were the horses of the Norsemen. He is characterized by his color (all Suffolks are chestnut) and by his extreme rotundity. In size he runs from sixteen to seventeen hands and weighs from sixteen hundred to eighteen hundred pounds.

The Suffolk breed is not as well known in America as in England but there are breeders in many parts of this country. His friends claim that he excels all other draft breeds in disposition, longevity and substance.

SUGAR

Most horses like sugar though it seems to be an acquired taste. A little, offered as a reward for learning a new lesson, is permissible, though a carrot or bit of apple is better, but too much sugar makes a horse mean and develops in him the habit of nipping and biting.

SUITABLE TO BECOME

These are classes referring to colts or fillies that are to be judged on their apparent promise as future hunters. See *HORSE SHOW CLASSES, Hunter division.*

SULKY

The racing vehicle is called a sulky or "bike." The original sulkies were very high wheeled affairs. In the late eighteen-eighties at about the time bicycles came into being the new form of sulky with bicycle wheels was introduced. Later this was further improved by placing the driver very low and close to the horse. It was the introduction of the low wheeled, light sulky which standardized harness racing and made it possible for the horse to negotiate the sharp turns at

FIGURE. 142. THE SUFFOLK HORSE. *COURTESY OF THE AMERICAN SUFFOLK ASSOCIATION.*

a high speed. See also *HARNESS RACING.*

SUNFISHING

This is a Western term which means a form of bucking in which the shoulders are alternately brought close to the ground and then raised.

SUNSTROKE

Horses sometimes succumb to sunstroke though this is rare. The animal should be brought into the shade and ice packs applied to its head or a hose of cold water run over head and neck.

SUPPLING EXERCISES

For the horse

A course of suppling exercises in which the horse is required to bend his neck and raise and lower his head and to bend his croup, or carry his legs further under him than nature intended, will often improve the balance of a badly made animal and make more flexible and obedient the unschooled colt. These exercises are usually given while the rider is on foot and to be of any use must be given consistently for a short time every day. See *COLTS, Breaking and Training of; DRESSAGE; RIDING, The Advanced Rider.*

For the rider

One of the most noticeable skills to be observed in a good horseman is the facility with which he regains his balance when the horse swerves, bucks or makes some other sudden motion. This flexibility is acquired. One of the methods of developing it is by means of suppling exercises. Bending forward and touching the toes while the horse is in motion, raising the hands high in the air, rotating the head and rotating the body from the hips, lying back until the head rests on the croup, are all valuable and may be performed at all the different gaits. The rider may also turn completely around in the saddle. In teaching beginners, these exercises should form a part of all the early lessons, they will not only make the learners more flexible but they do much to instill confidence in timid, young riders. See *RIDING*.

SURCINGLE

The surcingle, sometimes called a roller, is a broad band equipped with a buckle which encircles the horse and keeps the stable blanket in place.

SURENESS OF FOOT

Horses bred in rocky, mountainous country are notoriously more sure of foot than those bred in grass lands. Lighter built animals are less clumsy than large, heavy breeds. The pony, donkey and mule are sometimes incredibly sure-footed, negotiating steep, narrow inclines with complete nonchalance. Sureness of foot is a very desirable characteristic, particularly in horses that are to be ridden or hunted in trappy country. It is one of the things for which a horse should be tested before being purchased.

SWAYING

If your horse comes out of his stall with a peculiar swaying motion of the hindquarters which increases perceptibly when weight is put on his back, look for some intestinal trouble such as fodder poisoning. Bad kidney trouble will also cause the horse to lose control in this fashion as will a twisted gut. Have the veterinarian at once as, in the case of fodder poisoning, the horse needs immediate treatment if he is to survive.

SWEATING

All horses sweat profusely when being used hard or in very hot weather. In so doing they lose a great deal of the salt which they need and unless this salt is replaced may suffer from heat exhaustion. Horses that are in soft condition will sweat more readily than those which are muscled up, for this reason the sweating should be used as a guide to the amount of work the horse can stand.

Very excitable horses will sweat even when in good shape and this, too, should be taken into consideration. A horse that is hot and sweaty may be allowed to drink provided he is kept moving afterwards, but the animal that is brought in covered with lather, watered and put into his stall will inevitably develop founder.

SWEAT SCRAPER

This is a flexible metal instrument used to scrape off the sweat or water when the horse is washed. Wooden scrapers are also common and a scraper can be improvised from a barrel stave.

SWEEPSTAKES

A race in which the winner takes all.

SWELLINGS

In cases of lameness the first thing the horseman looks for is some form of swelling or lump. The size, degree of hardness, and heat in the swelling will further help him to diagnose the trouble. See also *INJURIES; INFECTIONS; BRUISES*.

SWINE CHOPPED HOUND

See *HUNTING TERMS*.

SWOLLEN LEGS

Swollen legs may come from a variety of causes. If the horse's legs swell whenever he is not used it may be from an old injury or from a circulatory disturbance. See *STOCK; INJURIES; INFECTIONS*.

SYRINGES

Syringes of several sizes should be kept in the First Aid cabinet. A small, flexible rubber ear syringe is invaluable for washing out boils, deep wounds and infected pockets. The ordinary fountain syringe is too small for giving enemas to horses though it can be used. A better implement is to take a small pail, have a metal spout attached at the base to which a flexible rubber tubing can be attached.

T

TACK (*v.*)

To tack up a horse means to put the saddle and bridle on him.

TACK APPOINTMENTS

Certain classes in horse shows require that specific types of tack be used. See *APPOINTMENTS, Tack; Hunting.*

TACK, *Care of*

All harness, saddles, bridles and other equipment should be cleaned after use. If muddy they should first be washed with plenty of water and soap and then finished off with a semidry sponge and soap. Metal parts must be washed clean. Once a month or so bridles and saddles should be taken apart and each piece of leather wiped off with Neatsfoot Compound, an oil containing Neatsfoot Oil.

New tack should always have a treatment of Neatsfoot before use. It is difficult to do this without spotting the tack, but this is not important, as the spots will disappear in time. However, they may be avoided if the leather is dampened with a sponge and if, in the case of the bridle, each strap is dropped into a pail of oil so that it is all covered at the same time. After a moment or so it is lifted out and the excess oil drained back into the pail with a sponge.

If leather is to be kept stored it should be cleaned and oiled at least once a year to prevent dry rot.

TACK ROOM

This is the room in which the tack is kept and where it is cared for. It should be equipped with running water, enough bridle and saddle racks to accommodate the tack, a cleaning rack for saddles and an iron hook for cleaning the bridles. Saddle-soap, oil and sponges and cloths should be on a convenient shelf or in the drawers of the cleaning rack. The tack room may well contain First Aid equipment as well. A stove for heating hot mashes is also an excellent piece of equipment. See also *STABLES.*

TACK, TACKLE

The tack or tackle as it used to be called is the saddle, bridle, pad, martingale, etc., which is used in riding. For description of each article, its selection, care, etc., consult this volume under the specific name.   See also *SADDLE; BITS; BRIDLES.*

TACKING RACE

This is a contest suitable for gymkhanas. The contestants enter the ring leading a horse in a halter. They line up at one end of the ring. At the opposite end the tack for each horse is hung. At a given signal contestants lead the horses to the tack and tack them up. The first rider to finish and pass inspection wins. The judges should penalize such things as displacement of saddle, failure to fasten keepers, twisted billets, pad not in correct position, curb chain twisted, etc., the contestant being sent back to make corections.

TAG (the foxes)

See *HUNTING TERMS.*

TAG

The game of tag and variations of it may well be used in class instruction to give confidence and relaxation. The person who is "it" should be required to tag the other rider, not the horse. In Chinese tag, he who is tagged must keep one hand on that place until he tags someone else. In cross-tag, if someone passes betwen the chaser and the "chasee" the chaser must leave his original quarry and pursue the new. For beginners the game may be played at a walk only and for intermediate riders it may be played at a trot whereas the more advanced riders will play it at a gallop.

TAIL

The horse's tail is a most useful appendage as well as an indication of his breeding and a plume of beauty. The practice of docking the tail is cruel in the extreme and will, in time, be outlawed. The only excuse for docking a tail is that, in harness horses, it prevents the horse from getting his tail over the reins. The five-gaited Saddler is noted for his long sweeping, heavy tail which often drags on the ground. The Thoroughbred has a fine, thin tail; if nature didn't give him one his owner or groom will. The tail should be kept clean and free from tangles. If thinning is in order the hairs are pulled out, a few at a time, not cut out or clipped. The nerves in the dock are not sensitive and the horse will not object to the pulling provided one does not attempt to pull too mnay at once.

The so called "set tail" seen in three-gaited Saddlers and in combination horses, is to be deplored. Like docking it takes away the use of the tail as a fly switch and the horse must forever wear a harness to keep his tail elevated. The result is far from beautiful, in fact, it is downright disfiguring and it too will soon be outlawed. The practice arose from the fact that horses with tails set high by nature are supposed to have stronger backs than others, so man has tried to improve on nature and thus give the appearance of strength.

TAKING THE BIT

Some horses accept the bit readily, others put up a defense. If the horse refuses to open his mouth the rider should insert his fingers or his thumb and touch the bars or the tongue. The horse hates the taste of flesh and will immediately wrinkle up his lips and open his mouth in disgust. See *BRIDLING THE HORSE.*

TALLY-HO

This is a type of four-in-hand pleasure coach. It derives its name from a coach which was called "The Tally Ho."

TALLY-HO

See *HUNTING TERMS.*

TANDEM

Driving one horse in front of the other is called driving tandem. This is far more difficult than driving two horses as a team for the rider has no real control over the leaders. It originated in hunting countries where the meets might be some miles off and the horseman wished to get to the hunt without tiring his hunter. He therefore hitched the hunter in the lead where he would have no pulling to do, driving a hack or harness horse as a wheeler. The tandem then became very fashionable. The tandem cart was originally designed to carry the hounds along to the hunt in a box under the driver's seat. This had the added advantage of raising the driver which gave him more control over his leader.

For tandem classes see *HORSE SHOW CLASSES.* Riding tandem, i.e., riding one horse while driving another in front, became popular for a while and there were classes for such riders, sometimes with jumps, but this sport was never very widespread.

Training a tandem is difficult work and requires long hours spent on foot driving the horses ahead. In choosing horses for a tandem the leader should be slightly lighter and smaller of build than the wheeler, with greater presence and quality.

TASTE IN DRESS

By his choice of clothes shall the horseman be known. Nothing gives away the novice more quickly than loud or incorrect clothes. Correct and appropriate dress for riding was decided upon years ago and is functional in design. The cut, particularly women's riding habits, has changed somewhat but the colors remain the same. For correct clothes see *DRESS; HABITS; APPOINTMENTS, Hunting.*

TATTERSALL

Tattersall's is a famous sales stable in London. The word also refers to the gaily colored vests worn for riding and hunting.

TEACHING RIDING

The rules for teaching the child or adult to ride are much the same as those governing the training of the colt. The instructor must first gain the confidence of the pupil and establish a friendly relationship between them. Next, he must give his pupil a succession of successful experiences. His demands must be such that the pupil is able to fulfill them, if not perfectly, at least partially. The lessons must be so arranged that each is thoroughly learned before a more advanced stage is demanded. They must be kept interesting and be as varied as possible. In the early lessons every effort should be made to avoid falls or accidents. The pupil must be taught to vault off his horse, first, while it is standing, later, while it is in motion. It must be explained to him again and again that in the event that he loses control or balance he has only to vault off correctly and he will not be hurt. Later the pupil should come to take such falls as negligible.

The progress that the pupil will be expected to make will depend on his age and temperament. If a very young and timid youngster is being taught, it may be necessary to spend several hours simply leading the pony around, patting him and talking about him. An older, bolder child will mount at once and learn to post during the first lesson.

The teacher's first goal, in teaching both adults and children, is to engender in his pupils confidence in themselves and in their mounts. A love of riding and a desire to improve come next. The teacher who tries to instill confidence by making the pupil more afraid of him than he is of his horse is merely giving his pupil two fears instead of one. The teacher who makes his lessons boring, who mounts his pupils on animals that are unsuitable or who teaches them nothing about the care of the horse and his essential needs and characteristics will never make enthusiastic horsemen.

Lessons in control are as important as lessons in form and only too often they are entirely neglected. The resourceful instructor will think of many ways of teaching this control. The army equitation exercise of having the pupils in a column of troopers and then asking the lead horse alone to canter from front to rear while the other horses continue at the walk, is one of the best as it demands two different types of control and the correct use of the aids. If the group is riding in a large open area one horse may be told to remain behind while the others ride ahead, then, on command, the lone rider is to catch up at a slow trot; the tendency of the horse, of course, is to gallop back to his companions and it takes real skill to hold him down. Mounted drills and games are of paramount importance in teaching control as are musical rides. It will be seen that there is great advantage in having the pupils riding in groups rather than receiving private instruction for the private pupil has no opportunity to handle his mount and himself in competition. Furthermore, the child that is instructed in a group gains self-confidence and progresses much more rapidly than does the child who rides alone with his instructor. Later, when it is desirable to polish him up a bit he may receive some private lessons.

As has been stated, it is hard to say exactly what progress is to be expected as so much depends upon the age and natural aptitude of the pupil but below is a table of tests which will serve as a measure of progress. Children under eight should be able to pass the first group at the end of twenty-five lessons. Many of that age will be able to pass them in half that number of hours. Children between eight and fourteen should go through both the first two groups in from twenty-five to forty hours. The last group is much more difficult and will take a good many hours of hard work. Some will never reach this stage of achievement.

Beginner's Tests

Walk in good position with reins and stirrups.

Walk without reins and stirrups.

Trot with legs and hands in good position.

Jog trot without reins and stirrups.

Change hands at a walk and a trot.

Dismount at a standstill and at a walk.

Mount a suitably sized mount without help.

Adjust stirrups.

Saddle pony alone.

Lead in and out of stalls, around ring, etc.

Unsaddle, unbridle, put on halter and stable blanket.

Do suppling exercises at a walk.

Know all parts of tack and points of horse.

Canter bareback on specially schooled pony.

Intermediate Tests

Canter bareback individually and in a group.

Canter in a saddle.

Bridle horse.

Execute all mounted drill maneuvers.

Show individual control at all gaits.

Do suppling exercises at trot.

Vault off at a trot and slow canter.

Turns, half turns, circles, figure eights, change hands, broken lines at a walk and trot.

Games such as Red Rover, Musical Stalls and Tag played in a saddle.

Know leads and gallop departs.

Advanced Tests

Ride relaxed and with good form at all gaits, both bareback, in a saddle with stirrups, and in a saddle without stirrups and reins and with the arms folded.

Turns, half turns, circles, figure eights, change of hands and broken lines at a canter.

Negotiate jumps both individually and in teams, the height depending on the ability of the horse.

Be able to handle a high-spirited, excitable horse both alone and in company.

Be able to handle a stubborn horse such as a "barn-rat."

Jump low jumps without reins and stirrups.

School a horse for "mental-hazard" jumping.

Understand stable management, the steps in breaking and training colts and how to cure vices.

Change from any gait to any other gait easily and without obvious effort.

Execute intermediate dressage figures described under *RIDING, The Advanced Rider.*

TEAM JUMPING

Classes for hunt teams or jumping teams call for certain specifications as to uniformity, weights and performance. As a general rule the hunt team consists of three matched horses, one a lightweight, one a middleweight and one a heavyweight. They are required to take the course at hunting speed and maintain a safe distance between horses. In some cases the team may be halted and the positions of the riders reversed, the last horse coming up to the lead. The riders are usually required to ride in hunt livery and must have the usual hunting appointments.

Teams of three jumpers usually jump abreast and are not necessarily matched. For judging these classes see *HORSE SHOW CLASSES.*

TEETH

The horse has twelve molars and ten incisors in each jaw. Male horses also have two tushes, thus a horse with a full set of teeth will have forty-six teeth if he is male and forty-four if female. Tushes in mares are not unknown, however.

The molars, or grinding teeth, need frequent attention. They work in a rotary motion which wears away the surfaces but as the upper jaw is wider than the lower the outside edges of the upper teeth get no wear and tend to become sharply pointed. These points irritate the horse's jaw and must be filed off at regular intervals. This operation is known as "floating" the teeth. If a horse loses a molar, the one above or below the gap will continue to grow and may

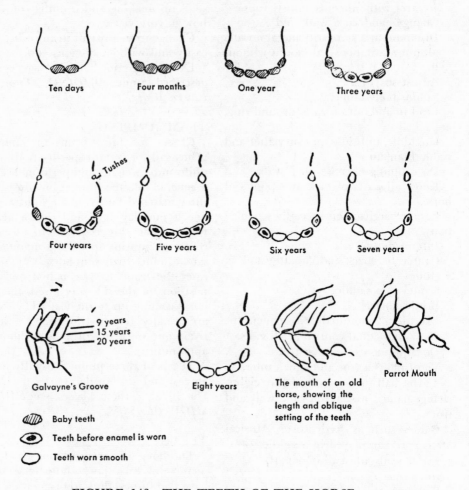

Ten days   Four months   One year   Three years

Tushes

Four years   Five years   Six years   Seven years

9 years
15 years
20 years

Galvayne's Groove   Eight years   The mouth of an old horse, showing the length and oblique setting of the teeth   Parrot Mouth

Baby teeth

Teeth before enamel is worn

Teeth worn smooth

FIGURE 143. THE TEETH OF THE HORSE.

in time prevent the horse from closing his mouth, this in turn will prevent his chewing his food properly and he may easily succumb to colic. Horses that cannot chew comfortably will swallow their food whole and even though they may not become actually sick they will lose weight rapidly. If a horse remains thin in spite of plenty of feed and good care it is probable that his teeth are causing the trouble.

Examining the incisors, or front teeth of the horse, is the best method of ascertaining his age. The central incisors appear shortly after birth, some colts being born with them. The next pair, or lateral incisors, are cut at from four to six weeks and the corner incisors come at six to nine months. These are all "milk" or baby teeth and are much smaller and shorter than the permanent teeth.

At two and a half years old the central permanent incisors push out the baby teeth, at four the lateral permanent incisors come into wear, and at five the tushes and the corner teeth are full sized. The horse is now said to have a full mouth.

If one examines the teeth of a five year old it will be noted that each tooth has a cup or depression in its center, the outside enamel being raised. With use this enamel is worn away and the cup disappears. At six years old the cavities in the central incisors have disappeared, at seven the laterals are smooth and at eight all the cups are gone. The horse is then said to be "aged" and from then on it is more difficult to determine his exact age. For this reason many a dealer will automatically give the age of his horses as "nine years."

At nine a groove appears on the upper corner teeth near the gum line. This is known as *Galvayne's Groove*. It extends gradually down the tooth with age, reaching half way down at fifteen and to the bottom at twenty. It then begins to disappear at the top and at thirty is gone.

No only do the cavities disappear with age but the teeth themselves become longer and more oblique. This gives one more measurement of age though it is not too accurate.

Wolf teeth are small, extra teeth which sometimes appear in front of the molars. They are said to affect the eyesight and should be removed.

TEMPERATURE

The normal temperature of the horse, taken rectally, is 100 degrees.

TENDONS

The tendons of the legs should be well detached and prominent. They should be straight, with no tendencies toward enlargements. Injuries to the tendons are common (see *INJURIES*) and require careful treatment and nursing.

TENNESSEE WALKING HORSE

See *PLANTATION WALKER, SADDLE HORSE*.

TENNESSEE WALKING HORSE BREEDER'S ASSOCIATION

This is located at Lewisburg, Tenn. Its register, started in 1935 is now in its fourth volume. The total registered from 1935 to 1943 is 10,800 of which about 3,300 are stallions and 7,500 mares.

TESTS FOR SOUNDNESS

The horse that is not sound is useless no matter how beautiful he may be. Hence the prospective buyer should spend plenty of time testing him for soundness of wind, limb, and eyesight.

To test the wind, gallop the horse for several minutes, then get off and look at his flanks. If they show a double heave when the air is expelled the horse is suffering from heaves. High blowing is not a defect but coughing or wheezing is. Large horses are more subject to weaknesses in wind than lighter horses so the heavyweight hunter should be especially well scrutinized from this angle.

To test soundness in legs, trot the horse on a hard surface, any variation in cadence means trouble. Trotting him up and down steep inclines will often bring out shoulder weaknesses. The gallop is not a good gait at which to ride a horse when judging for soundness as the horse can take the weight off the affected limb and, due to the triple cadence of the gait, this will not be noticed.

Have another rider ride the animal directly towards you, directly away from you as well as past you. Watch for any peculiarity of gait such as dishing or paddling and for undue motion of the head. Anything that looks wrong is wrong.

Examine the legs carefully for signs of splints, sprains or bowed tendons.

To test the eyesight wave the hand near the eye from behind. Also examine the eye carefully for any discoloration. Animals suffering from ophthalmia retain a characteristic bluish tinge in the eye. White spots may mean injuries which cause complete or partial blindness. Paralysis of the retina sometimes occurs. Bring the horse into the light and see if both pupils contract at an equal rate.

Tests for manners are also in order and the buyer would do well to handle the horse all over and pick up his legs. Watch him being saddled and bridled. Try him out alone and in company, both on the trails and through traffic. See also *VICES, MANNERS, INJURIES—LEGS, FEET*.

TETANUS

Tetanus or lockjaw is fatal if it once develops. The bacteria grows in soil, is taken into the intestines of the horse with grass and expelled again in the manure, hence tetanus germs are apt to be prevalent around stables though if the tetanus germ has never been introduced into the locality it will not necessarily be present because of the presence of stable. If the germ enters a deep wound and the wound closes too soon the horse may easily contract the infection through his blood stream. A horse that receives a bad puncture type of wound, particularly if there is known to be tetanus in the neighborhood, should at once receive the anti-tetanus vaccine which will prevent the disease. The earliest symptom of tetanus is extreme hypersensitivity. The horse jumps violently on being touched.

THONG

The long thong on the end of the hunting crop is not intended to be used on the horse but is a means of disciplining the hounds. Amateurs carry the thong coiled in the hand, professionals allow it to dangle.

THOROUGHBRED

The term "thoroughbred" is often misused. Many people seem to think that it is synonymous for "purebred." But Thoroughbred really means a distinct breed of horse. We have the Morgan and the Hambletonian, the Percheron and the Hackney and we also have the Thoroughbred.

The Thoroughbred, or English Thoroughbred, as he was first known, was bred in England. The three original foundation sires were the Byerly Turk, the Godolphin Barb and the Darley Arabian. These three desert stallions were imported into England between the years of 1690 and 1725. They were bred to native mares and their get was improved by selection and the further introduction of desert bred stallions. From these three stallions all the registered Thoroughbreds both in this country and in England are descended. It is also interesting to note that many other breeds and families of horses go back to the Thoroughbred. The imported Thoroughbred, Messenger, sired the trotters and pacers. He in turn came from Mambrino stock from which came the Saddlers and pacers. The Morgans also go back to the Thoroughbred.

The Thoroughbred was bred for racing at the gallop and for jumping. No horse in the world can stay with him on the track and no horse can outjump him in the hunt field. He is more high-spirited, timid and more delicate than the "cold-blooded" horse. He is also more sensitive and more easily excited to flight.

In conformation the Thoroughbred has a fine delicate head with a straight or dished profile, never a Roman nose. His neck is long and slender. His shoulders are sloping. His back is longer than the Arab but not so long as the Saddler or the trotter. The point of the croup is higher than the dock and, seen from behind his rump, is pear shaped rather than square. His ribs spring out from the spine in "roof shaped" angle rather than straight as do the draft breeds. His height of chest and width of brisket is large, leaving room for his great heart and his powerful lungs. His cannon bones are not as short as the Quarter horse though shortness of cannon is desirable as it means less fatigue. His muscles are flat and stringy, not bunchy. His veins are very prominent. His mane and tail are thin and fine.

Though high-spirited the Thoroughbred is seldom mean or stubborn. He is easily spoiled by rough treatment and easily gentled as a foal by kindness. He cannot live off the country as can the mustang; his skin is so thin that he suffers terribly from flies and will lose weight rapidly if turned out in hot weather. A mixture of Thoroughbred blood adds courage and quickness to the cavalry mount and the polo pony. When crossed with a heavier breed he makes a splendid heavyweight hunter for trappy and boggy country.

Some of the best Thoroughbreds are bred in Ireland. There is something there about the climate, water and pasturage which builds bone and Irish Thoroughbreds are valued all over the world for these qualities.

The breeding of Thoroughbreds in this country has become a tremendous business. There is hardly a section of the country where some breeding is not done though certain parts, namely the middle South and the West, are the most suitable and produce the best colts. The prices run from a few hundred for a yearling that has been disappointing as a track prospect to many thousands for an established race horse. All Thoroughbreds are registered with the American Jockey Club. All are considered to have the same birthday, January First. For a list of the most famous American Thoroughbreds see page 103. See also *RACE HORSE*.

THOROUGHPIN

A thoroughpin is a puffy little swelling at the side of the hock. As a rule it does not cause lameness and may be ignored.

THROAT

The throat or throttle of the horse, or juncture of head and neck, should be clean cut and not too angular. The horse whose neck is "set on like a hammer head" is never as flexible as one with a good throttle. Any enlargement of the glands at the throat should be looked on with suspicion as such horses usually have bad wind.

THROAT LATCH
See *SADDLE and BRIDLE, parts of.*

THROTTLE
See *THROAT*.

THROW (to throw tongue)
See *HUNTING TERMS*.

THRUSH

This is an infection of the frog. It is quite common but fortunately readily cured. The cause is not definitely established; horses turned out to grass will sometimes get bad cases of thrush while those kept in dirty stables will often not. Generally speaking, the horse that has his feet properly cared for and whose stall is kept clean will rarely develop thrush.

The symptoms of thrush are extreme lameness, usually very sudden, tenderness around the frog, a watery or thick discharge from the frog, and a very repulsive odor at that point. The simplest cure is to pack the frog with finely ground blue stone (copper sulphate or blue vitriol) which can be bought from the druggist or hardware man. The powder should be kept in place with a bit of cotton and, if the infection is caught early the horse will go sound in a day or two. If the condition is neglected, the whole sole is affected and may be eaten entirely away in which case the horse will probably have to be shot. Be particularly careful to keep an eye on the sound feet of a horse that is lame on one foot for some time due to other injuries. He will tend to keep the injured leg off the ground, resting all his weight on the others and so preventing the circulation of air. Thrush develops very readily in such cases and as the horse is already lame it is sometimes not noticed.

THRUSTER
See *HUNTING TERMS*.

TIE ROPES

Tie ropes, sometimes called halter shanks, should be five or six feet long, of good rope with a clip at one end. They will have to be renewed at intervals as they eventually twist and wear out. The horse that chews his rope will have to be fastened with a chain.

TIMIDITY

In Horses

Timidity is one of the fundamental characteristics of the horse and is one of the factors which makes it possible for man to train him. But extreme timidity is not desirable for it tends to make the animal unreliable and unmanageable. Foals, even those of high-spirited temperaments, soon lose their natural timidity if handled gently and frequently from birth. On the other hand, rough treatment will make a horse forever timid and often dangerous. Excitable horses easily become hysterical and, when so, are completely unreliable. The sensitive horse which, on shying, suddenly feels the heels of his inexperienced rider dig into his sides becomes a runaway and he is just as apt to run directly in front of a car or into a blank wall as not. The horse that has been hit over the head will always be head-shy even though he may receive good treatment from then on.

There is another cause for timidity in horses, namely, poor eyesight. All horses are nearsighted but some are exceptionally so. This means that they do not see an object until they are right on top of it, then, if it is unusual or if it moves suddenly the horse will be terrified. Some horses are what is known as "wall-eyed." In such cases one eye is sound and the other is either nearsighted or it magnifies. If your horse is very head-shy on one side and not at all on the other, you may suspect him of being wall-eyed. There is nothing to be done about such horses and under good hands they are safe but the rider should be on the constant lookout for objects that may startle them. See also *FEAR*.

In the Rider

Horses are no longer common, therefore young children do not accept them as part of everyday living. Just because you tell your child that his pony is gentle and will not hurt him does not prove it to the child. He must learn by *successful experience* that this is so. In older pupils timidity is also often present. This is largely from the feeling of insecurity due to lack of balance. A person in the saddle for the first time is often as tense as someone who tries to walk a narrow plank over a gully. This person will relax in due time especially if taken very slowly and made to do the flexing exercises and to ride without stirrups at slow gaits. It goes without saying that both for the timid child and for the tense adult the mount should be as quiet and well mannered an animal as it is possible to obtain. See also *TEACHING*.

TIN CUP RECORDS

Before the standardization of conditions for trotting records which occurred with the advent of the bicycle-tired sulky and the establishment of the Trotting Association, it was the practice of dealers to offer a small trophy or cup and run a horse under very advantageous conditions, establishing a record and thus raising his value. Such contests, which reached the number of two thousand in the year 1892, were known as "tin cup records."

TOE

Of the Horse

The prehistoric horse had three soft toes behind and four in front. As he ran he came to use only the center toe and finally he ran on the very tip of the center toe. The toe nail became the wall. The other toes gradually receded through lack of use. One does not think of the hoof as a toe, but that is what it is, the knee joint corresponding to our wrist and the hock to the ankle. See Figure 52.

The way a horse carries his toes is important. The horse that toes out is liable to speedy cutting and brushing. The horse that toes in is usually a stumbler.

Toeing-in may also indicate a tendency to navicular trouble.

Of the Rider

Twenty-five years ago riders were taught to keep the toes parallel to the horse's body. The tendency now is to carry the toe at about the angle one does when walking. A toe turned too far out means that the rider is contacting the saddle and horse with the back of his calves instead of the inside of his leg and knee. Toes turned too far in call for a muscular stiffness which is unnecessary and fatiguing. The toe should not be pushed down, it should be higher than the heel at all times, nor should the foot be pushed home in the stirrups. This gives a stiff and inflexible ankle as well as forming a hazard should rider be thrown. See *FEET*.

TONICS

If a horse's coat seems dull and the animal has a poor appetite and appears lethargic the veterinary may prescribe a conditioning powder or a liquid tonic. The former will probably contain saltpetre for the kidneys, ferrous sulphate for the blood, and possibly a vermifuge. A good stimulant to the appetite is small doses of arsenic put up under the name of "Fowler's Solution." Such conditioning powders and tonics can be very well worth trying and should by all means be used. Vitamin compounds for horses are also on the market, some are in powder form and others are put up in molasses. Molasses itself is a beneficial tonic.

TOP LINE

The prospective buyer always looks at the "top line" of a horse with a critical eye. The angle of withers and croup, the set of tail, the length of back, will tell him much as to the breeding and substance of the horse. See also *PRO-FILE*.

TOUCH-AND-OUT

This is a jumping competition in which the horse is given the gate as soon as he touches a hurdle. The horse that clears the most hurdles before touching, wins. Slip fillets are usually used in these contests. See also *HORSE SHOW CLASSES*.

TOUCHES

It is sometimes difficult to distinguish between an actual touch and the sound caused by dirt or stones hitting the obstacle. Slip fillets, little strips of light wood placed on top of the topmost bar of the hurdle will settle the matter for if the strip fillet does not fall the horse is not considered to have touched. Touches usually do not count in hunter classes though they may be taken into consideration in event of a tie but they do count in jumping classes. For the scoring of such jumping faults see *JUMPING FAULTS, Scoring of*.

T.R.A.

The Thoroughbred Racing Association, known as the T.R.A. was formed in 1942 for the purpose of promoting the common business interest in racing, to maintain and promote public interest in Thoroughbred racing in the United States, to prepare and distribute information concerning racing and to generally co-ordinate and enforce the rules of racing throughout the United States.

Since its formation the T.R.A. has surveyed the insurance set up for jockeys and exercise boys and recommended an increase of allowance for hospitalization. This recommendation has been put into effect at its member tracks. It has taken a stand against off-course wagering.

It has surveyed and made a study of the problem of claiming races which has resulted in a considerable reduction in the proportion of claiming.

By means of setting up relief days at race tracks throughout the country the T.R.A., in three years, netted $16,000,000 for various war agencies and charities. This was done by scheduling a procedure for the tracks which was satisfactory to the Bureau of Internal Revenue.

In October, 1944, the T.R.A. sponsored the first national conference of racing's publicity men.

It also sponsors a radio program consisting of dramatizations of famous races. In order to encourage advancement in turf reporting the T.R.A. offered a collateral award for turf stories accepted by the Dutton Anthology of Sports Stories.

The T.R.A. Service Bureau issues weekly news and radio bulletins. It has published a number of booklets as well as the book from which these statistics are taken, namely, *THOROUGHBRED RACING AND BREEDING*.

All of the major tracks are members of the T.R.A. and the formation of this association cannot help but have a wide and beneficial effect upon the breeding, training and racing of Thoroughbreds.

The offices of the T.R.A. are at 200 East 42nd Street, New York.

TRAINERS

See Appendix.

TRAINING

The word "training" to describe the education of a colt is more satisfactory than the customary "breaking" though the latter is more often used. For steps in training see *COLTS, Breaking and Training of.*

TRANDEM

To drive trandem is to drive three horses one in front of the other. This was a sporting fad for a while but is really only useful in draft teams.

TRANSPORTATION

Horses may be transported either by vans or trailers or by railroad. The first two methods are becoming more and more popular as the van can be brought right to the stable door. Transporting by railroad can be either by express or by freight. Special "horse pullmans" may be obtained with built-in stalls. Even large horses are sometimes shipped in

crates by express and this method is both inexpensive and safe for small or medium sized ponies. Horses from the West are often shipped in by car load in an ordinary freight car. This is the cheapest method for a number of horses that are to be moved a long distance. See also *VANNING*.

TRAVEL ON TWO PATHS

See *TWO-TRACK; SIDESTEP; PAS DE COTÉ; SIDE GALLOP; TRAVERSAL*.

TRAVELLER

See *FAMOUS HORSES*.

TRAVERS

The *travers,* or *haunches-in,* is a movement whose purpose, like the *renvers* and the *shoulder-in,* is to improve the horse's lateral flexion. In the *travers* the hindquarters of the horse are pushed just sufficiently off the track that his outside hind foot travels in line with his inside front foot and his inside front foot forms a path of its own to the inside of the other three feet. As in the other above-mentioned figures the horse's spine must be bent in a smooth curve from poll to dock. For diagram and methods of obtaining this figure see *RIDING, The Advanced Rider*.

TRAVERSAL (Two-track)

This is a *dressage* movement often asked for in competitions. In it the horse moves on a diagonal line with his spine parallel to the long wall of the arena. He crosses both his front and back legs, and if the head is bent at all it must be in the direction of the movement. It may be executed at all gaits. See *RIDING, The Advanced Rider; DRESSAGE; THE COLT, Training of.*

TREASURE HUNTS

Treasure hunts on horseback are great sport. The clues should be widely enough distributed so that the riders can cover plenty of territory without bunching up. Hunt clubs and riding stables which want to engender interest may well run series of treasure hunts or paper chases.

TREE (saddle)

The saddle tree gives the saddle its shape. It is customary among horsemen to speak of the "tree" not only meaning the actual tree but the whole shape of the saddle.

TRIPLE-BAR CLASSES

These are jumping competitions in which three bars of ascending heights are set up with some little distance between each. The horse is required to take all three at a leap. In event of a tie either the distance between the bars may be increased or the height may be raised. Women are not allowed to compete in triple-bar classes. See also *HORSE SHOW CLASSES.*

TRIPLE CROWN

Race horses which win the Kentucky Derby, the Preakness and the Belmont are said to win the Triple Crown. The English Triple Crown comprises the Derby (at Epsom Downs), the Ascot Gold Cup and the Oaks.

TROTTERS

Many European countries breed and race Trotting Horses. Of these Russia is outstanding, having originated a famous breed known as the *Orloff Trotter.* See *RUSSIAN HORSES.*

In the United States we have a breed of trotting horses descended from Messenger, an English Thoroughbred. The most famous family of trotters of this line is the Hambletonian, all of which go back to Rysdyk's Hambletonian. There have been other famous trotting families, such as the Morgans, the Clays and the Black Hawks, but these have given way to the Hambletonians.

The trotter is distinguished by his powerful haunches with their pistonlike action. He has rather a longer barrel than the Thoroughbred. He does not hold his head high as do the Saddlers. His mane is clipped over the poll and kept thinned and shortened. His tail is allowed to hang long. In disposition the trotter is amiable and not nearly as inclined to hysteria as his hot blooded cousin, the Thoroughbred. He makes a good Saddler though it is sometimes difficult to teach him a slow canter. Trotters are known as "standard breds." See also *HAMBLETONIAN; HARNESS RACING; HARNESS; STANDARD BRED; FAMOUS RACE HORSES.*

TROTTING RECORDS

See *RECORDS AND STATISTICS—HARNESS RACING* (appendix).

TUCKED UP

A horse which is built like a greyhound is said to be "tucked up." This is not a desirable characteristic and such a horse is subject to intestinal troubles and rarely has much stamina.

TURF

The race course is sometimes spoken of as "the turf."

TURKISH, TURKOMAN or TOOKMAN

These horses are closely related to the Arabian, the Byerly Turk being one of the foundation sires imported into England. They are said to be descended from the Nisaean horses of Media and the Parthian horses. They are larger and less docile than the Arabian. The predominating color is gray. Rustum's horse, *RAKHSH,* is thought to have been of this breeding.

TURNING

The horse should never be asked to turn on the use of the reins alone. The weight and legs should also be brought into play. Just how the aids are used will depend on what kind of turn the horse is asked to make. The leading or direct rein or the indirect rein together with the outside leg will cause the horse to turn while moving and follow the track of his forelegs with his hindquarters. A different use of reins and legs will turn the horse in place, with forehand around croup or vice versa. See *PIVOTS; REINS; AIDS; RIDING; THE COLT, Training of.*

TURNING OUT TO GRASS

At the end of the season the horse will benefit by being turned out for a few weeks. If the flies are bad he must be protected with a fly sheet, sprayed with a fly repellent or he may be kept in a screened stable in the daytime and turned out at night. If there are no rocks he may have his shoes removed or he may be shod with tips. If the grass is not very luxuriant he may have to have supplementary feedings of hay or grain. When he is brought in it must be remembered that he will have to be conditioned before being hunted, or he will suffer injury to limb, tendon or wind.

TUSHES

The teeth which appear in male horses during the fourth year and are situated on the bars about an inch behind the corner teeth are known as "tushes." They are rarely present in mares though they do sometimes occur. They are of no apparent importance and will probably some day disappear.

TWISTED GUT

This ailment is very serious and fairly common. The animal shows signs of intense pain and cannot bear any weight. The hindquarters sway. The horse wants to roll and nips continually at his flanks. Enemas, hot blankets applied over the loins, and colic medicines may help. The veterinarian should be sent for at once.

TWITCH

The twitch is an instrument used to subdue a restless horse. It consists of a short stick of wood to one end of which is attached a loop of soft cord. The horse's upper lip is inserted in the cord and the stick is twisted until the lip is pinched. This distracts the horse's attention. A twitch is often used with a horse

that refuses to allow itself to be clipped or shod or which must receive medical treatment or surgery. It is far more humane than any other form of restraint and cannot do the horse any harm. The twitch must only be left in place a short time or the lip will become numb and the horse will forget the pinch and be as restless as before. Make sure that the end of the stick is rounded and that the cord is soft and not hard.

TWO-TRACK

Literally, to *two-track* is to make two tracks, one generally being made with the fore feet and one with the hind. This applies to such movements as the "side-step," in which the horse moves directly sideways, as well as to the *traversal,* in which the horse moves on a line from one corner of the hall to the corner diagonally opposite it. However, in so doing, he keeps his spine parallel to the long wall of the hall and crosses both his front and his back feet, thus traveling forward and to the side and leaving two parallel tracks. It is this movement, the *traversal,* which is generally referred to in speaking of the *two-track.* For correct execution of the *two-track* or *traversal,* see *RIDING, The Advanced Rider (traversal).*

TYING THE HORSE

There are various methods of tying the horse depending on the situation. A horse is usually tied in his stall by means of a halter shank attached to a ring. If he has a tendency of getting his foot over his tie rope this may be remedied by running the shank through the ring and attaching a weight to the end. The weight keeps the rope always short yet permits the horse to pull the shank to its length when he desires.

Horses to be given medicine may best be controlled by a loop around the nose behind the incisors. This should not be a slip knot. The best form of knot to use here is to tie a regular knot in the end of the rope, then measure the circumference of the horse's upper jaw and tie the first part of another knot here. Put the rope around the jaw and nose running it through the mouth and behind the incisors, slip the first knot through the second and tighten the latter. Now throw the other end of the shank, which should be ten or twenty feet long, over a beam above the animal's head. His head can then be kept in an elevated position while the medicine is poured down his throat.

As a general rule horses should not be tied by the bridle reins but, if this must be done, select a branch over the animal's head that swings freely. Tie the reins in such a fashion that they cannot slide off and be sure that the horse cannot get his head down to the ground.

U

UNIFORMS (for hunt and show ring)
See *APPOINTMENTS, Hunting; DRESS; HABITS.*

UNITED STATES TROTTING ASSOCIATION

All harness racing, which includes both pacing and trotting, comes under the guidance and supervision of the United States Trotting Association. This association was organized in 1938 and 1939 and welded all the Standardbred racing interests under one roof. Its present address is 750 Michigan Avenue, Columbus 15, Ohio.

Its officials in 1962 are, Walter J. Michael, *President;* Don R. Milier, *Executive Vice-President;* Eugene J. Hayes, *Chairman of the Board of Directors.* A total of 7,353 foals were registered in 1961.

Qualifications for registration, printed by kind permission of the Association, are as follows:

Standardbreds, regardless of gait, can be registered "Standard" if purebred or "Non-Standard" if crossbred. In the former classification, all progeny of established bloodlines are covered as are also all horses registered through their bona fide accomplishment on the track. Speed at either gait renders them eligible to "Standard" registration, if they have a sufficient basis of "Standard" breeding.

A Non-Standard horse is the trotter or pacer, whose bloodlines are not clear or whose proof of ancestry has been lost.

In each and every case of requested registration, both for the Standard or Non-Standard, all applicants must provide a true statement of breeding, which is checked in detail by the U.S.T.A. registration department for accuracy and authenticity. The applicant must also provide the Association with accepted mating certificates which are further proof of mating by given sires and dams at exact dates.

Ohio has ranked as leading state in the registration of foals for the past few years with Illinois second and New York third. Pennsylvania, Indiana, Kentucky, Michigan, California, Iowa and Delaware complete the top ten.

A total of 7,353 foals were registered by the U.S.T.A. in 1961 mainly from this country, but also from Canadian breeding farms. See also *HARNESS RACING; RECORDS AND STATISTICS—HARNESS RACING* (appendix).

URTICARIA (nettlerash)

This is a skin condition caused by stings, bites or errors in diet. It is noncontagious and if from diet is more apt to occur in young animals than in older. Bumps varying from the size of a pea to that of a quarter appear under the skin. These sometimes disappear without breaking open, or they may open and form a dry scab which later flakes off. Nettlerash comes on very suddenly, somewhat like hives in humans. Its most frequent cause is too much heatening food for the condition of the animal. Horses brought in from grass and put on a large grain diet, especially corn, will often develop it. A good dose of Epsome salts or Glauber salts in a bran mash and a change in diet will generally relieve the condition. If the lumps are due to stings treat with cooling lotions, soda, etc.

V

VANNING

All horses should be trained to enter a van readily and ride quietly. If the horse is afraid to enter the van try leading a quieter and more experienced animal in first and he will probably follow. Some horses go in readily if they are first allowed to sniff the gangway and then, while they are standing there, if a helper lifts and places their front feet on it. If all else fails the following method will succeed: Lead the animal up to the gangway. Now attach a long rope to one side of the gangway or to the van body, carry the rope behind the horse just above the hocks. Two men on the free end will now be able to force the horse into the van by pulling on the rope and taking up the slack as the horse moves forward.

Sometimes two ropes are used, one end of each being attached to the van on each side of the gangway. A man holds the free end of each rope and when the horse has been brought up to the gangway the men change places, crossing the ropes just above the hocks. They then pull the horse into the van as described above. Still another method is to use ladders, jump standards and rails or jump wings to build a corridor extending out from the gangway and of the same width as the latter. As the horse is led along this corridor two helpers, holding the ends of an ordinary jump rail, follow and, if the horse tries to stop, bring the rail quietly against his upper legs and push him on. It is surprising how many horses, on seeing the approaching rail, walk quietly into the van.

Of course all this trouble is easily avoided if the horse is taught to follow wherever he is led as a weanling.

Once in the van the horse should be cross-tied. Some vans are constructed to carry the horses crossways. In others stalls are built at the front and back with an aisle between. The flooring should be of matting so that the horses do not slip. It is a wise precaution to bandage the tails and to put heavy layers of cotton wool held in place by bandages on the legs to prevent injury. If more than one horse is being vanned it may be well to muzzle any that show nipping tendencies. A hay bag hung where he can reach it will often quiet a restless animal on a long journey.

Horses stand vanning surprisingly well but the driver must be experienced. Any sharp turns or sudden stops or starts will cause the horses to lose their balance completely and perhaps injure themselves permanently.

VAQUERO

The vaquero is the Argentine cowboy. He is a ready and dextrous rider though he may be a bit rough with his mount.

VARMINT

This is a hunting term for a fox.

VAULTING

Vaulting on and off horses is a fine gymnastic exercise. The Cossacks and the American Indians are noted for their ability at this. Though every rider may not be active enough to vault on a moving horse, all riders should learn to vault off at all gaits to teach them to fall properly. Try to land facing the direction in which the horse is moving with the feet together, the knees slightly bent and the weight even on the balls on both feet. See also *MONKEY DRILL; MOUNT (v.); MOUNTED GYMNASTICS.*

VEHICLES

When driving was the only means of wheeled transportation the variety of vehicles to be seen was enormous. As there is no longer the interest in this sport it seems unnecessary to go into this subject too deeply. However, the question often comes up as to the most appropriate vehicle to purchase for show or country use, especially for the pony for one still finds interest in pony driving.

Vehicles may be roughly classified as those with two wheels and those with four. Each division has its advantages and its disadvantages. For breaking colts, for driving skittish horses and for the inexperienced, the two-wheeled vehicle or cart is by far the best. This type can be easily turned in a small space. The governess or basket cart and the breaking cart are built so low to the ground that it is virtually impossible to upset them. The Hempstead and Mineola carts are somewhat higher but are still pretty safe. Some of these carts come with special fittings for sleigh runners which increases their usefulness. The breaking type of cart has metal guards on the shafts which make breeching unnecessary. These are discussed more fully in this text under *CARTS*. The governess cart, though safe, is extremely heavy, especially when overloaded, as happens all too frequently. Only a heavy, draft type of animal should be used in this kind of cart. The dogcart and the cocking-cart are not suitable for any except experienced drivers and well-broken horses as they tip over extremely readily. They are sporting vehicles, however, and for the person who craves excitement there is nothing which will satisfy that craving to such an extent as to hitch a pair of partly broken colts tandem to one of these high carts. Mr. David Gray, in his "Gallops" gives us a very graphic description of what happens in such a case.

The disadvantage which the two-wheeled vehicle has in contrast to the four-wheeled is its rough, bobbing motion. In these vehicles the shafts are in one piece with the body, hence as the horse trots the whole body of the vehicle bobs.

In the four-wheeled vehicles we may again classify as to those which are "cut-unders" and those which are not. The cut-under is so made that the front wheels, in turning, slide under the body, hence there is much less danger of overturning. The four-wheeled vehicle is unquestionably far more comfortable than the cart. For Ladies classes in the shows the Phaeton is usually required. For Light Harness (trotting horse) classes the road wagon or the bike (racing sulky) is required.

Hackney ponies and other Heavy Harness horses are shown in special show wagons with bicycle wheels. Fine Harness horses (saddle type) are shown to four-wheeled road wagons.

For country use the station wagon is useful with its removable back seat. These come both in horse and pony sizes. The old fashioned standby, the "top buggy" is rarely seen now except in rural districts. This last had the advantage of giving maximum protection in bad weather but was never considered fashionable and the ordinary type without the cut-under is extremely top-heavy.

VENTILATION (in the stable)

Cross ventilation in the stable is extremely important in warm climates. Without it horses will stand and sweat away condition in their stalls. But all windows should be so placed that there is no direct draft on the animals. In the case of double doors for box stalls the upper halves may be safely left open provided the horse is not put away overheated and provided that in cold and windy weather he is sufficiently well blanketed. Doors at either end of the aisle which ordinarily runs behind the straight stalls will provide cross ventilation with no fear of direct drafts. The stable should be so planned that these doors take advantage of the prevailing winds.

VESTS

The riding vest, especially the hunting vest, allows the only display of bright colors permissible if one excepts the brilliant hunting coats. In most hunts the vest is part of the uniform of that organization and is of a specially chosen broadcloth in either a plaid or a plain color with the special hunt buttons. One may also get the "tattersall" patterns in a great variety of color, the yellow or buff with contrasting lines being the most popular.

VETERINARIANS

It is to be regretted that because of the scarcity of horses the modern veterinarian has little chance for field practice and most of his knowledge is that learned in medical schools. Only too often the sign outside the veterinary hospital reads "for small animals." However, many of the laboratories are beginning now to work on veterinary science and are attempting to interest the veterinarians in their new discoveries. We find the sulfa drugs in universal use, and special vitamin compounds are being put out for horses and cows, etc. The experienced owner can get along without the veterinarian except in emergencies. As a matter of fact, horses are far less subject to ills than dogs and cats, though more liable to injury, and in a well-organized stable the veterinarian's bill can be kept to a minimum.

VICES

Many are the vices which horses acquire and they can nearly always be traced back to bad handling. The young colt is like the young child. His habits have yet to be formed and whether the habits he forms are good ones or bad ones depends largely on his training. Once formed, a vice is difficult to cure and only too often the animal will indulge his humors only with the inexperienced rider. Consequently, when the expert gets on him with the intention of curing him once and for all of his evil ways the erstwhile evildoer becomes the most obedient of angels and the trainer has no opportunity to instill discipline.

Vices may be classified as follows: *Stable vices; vices indulged in when the rider is not mounted; and vices to which the horse resorts as a means of defense against the rider.*

The following are the most common stable vices; *Kicking* either at another horse or at a passer-by. This vice may well be very dangerous, it is also rather difficult to cure without making the horse even more nervous. The ordinary remedy is to attach a small ball, by means of an elastic, to the horse's fetlock or back cannon. The elastic should be of such length that the ball hangs free of the ground. Now when the horse kicks the ball will fly out and hit the animal on the foot. The advantage of this method over that of punishing the horse by slapping or whipping him is that the punishment is simultaneous with the crime and also that it is inevitable.

Biting. The vice of biting is very common in male colts (especially before gelding), in young stallions and ridgelings. Colts that are brought up in pairs have a chance to take out their instincts of biting and nipping on each other and do not often develop this vice. Stallions often continue to give trouble in this respect until they are mature. Generally speaking, consistent alertness and punishment in the form of a sharp cuff across the nose will cure the average young horse. An oldster that has been allowed to get away with it and the ridgeling are sometimes almost incurable, although they will learn to respect someone they know. Always watch the ears of a known biter and as soon as you see them go back speak sharply to him and let him know that you are prepared to punish if he misbehaves. Do not, however, allow anyone to give the punishment before the horse has misbehaved; to do so will lead to other and even more undesirable vices.

Crowding is another very common stable vice and fortunately is very readily cured. Horses with this habit will wait until the person gets into the stall and then will try and crowd him against the partition of the stall. The remedy is to enter the stall carrying a pointed stick longer than the width of the body. Carry this stick in front of you and enter the stall facing towards the front. As the horse crowds brace one end of the stick against the stall partition and let the horse come against the pointed end. As a rule one lesson is sufficient to teach him manners.

Cribbing and *windsucking* are stable vices which render the horse technically unsound. There is a good deal of disagreement among authorities as to exactly what causes these habits. Some feel that it is purely nervous, some that it is a question of indigestion and the horse is trying to expel gas. Some believe that it may be caused by a foal being taken from its mother too soon. As many horses develop this habit after maturity one feels that the latter cause is not *always* to be blamed. It is seldom that the cribber or windsucker can be cured. The best that one can do is to prevent the habit and this can be done by means of a cribbing strap. A broad strap is put on so that it encircles the horse's neck at the throat. It is tightened to such an extent that the horse cannot distend the muscles at the throttle which he must distend if he is to suck wind or crib. It will be found that this does not interfere with his eating or drinking and of course it must not be put on so tightly that it cuts off his wind.

Backing suddenly out of the stall may be cured by having a chain behind the horse and letting him come up against it once or twice. Then undo the chain and back him out a step at a time, bringing him into the stall again and repeating the lesson until he is willing to come out quietly.

Tearing the stable blanket. This is an annoying habit. The horse deliberately tears the blanket with his teeth. Nervous high-strung horses will often develop this vice when not given enough work. A special "cradle" may be bought which will prevent it but these are expensive and entirely unnecessary. Instead, use a short, stout stick or piece of two-by-four. This should be of such length that it may be attached at one end to the side

ring of the halter and at the other end to the surcingle of the blanket. It will now be found that though the horse is at liberty to raise and lower his head he cannot bend his neck sideways and so cannot reach his blanket to tear it.

Weaving is a nervous disease in which the horse waves his head back and forth and sways continually in his stall. A similar vice is that in which the horse walks around and around his stall. Sometimes these habits have become so ingrained as to be virtually nervous "tics" and so incurable. Their disadvantage is that such a horse will rarely stay in condition. Putting the horse in a stall where he can look out of a window at passing traffic will sometimes help, and keeping him in a paddock as much as possible may also work.

Restlessness while being tacked up might be termed a stable vice. In the question of the horse that throws his head up until it is impossible to reach it one may try the advice given in this volume under *BRIDLING THE HEAD-SHY HORSE*. Many horses will throw their heads up if the person tacking them is short but will try no such defense with a taller person. It may become necessary to back such a horse into a stall and then stand on a box to bridle him. Rewards just don't seem to work in these cases. The horse that kicks at you as you tighten the girth has probably at one time or another been cinched up too tight or been used when he had a girth sore. Stand well forward by the shoulder, speak sharply or slap the horse as he kicks and only tighten the girth slightly at first. Then, when the rider is mounted, it can be drawn a little tighter. The general tendency among the inexperienced is to make the girth much too tight; with a horse with good withers, shoulders and ribs the saddle will stay in place with no girth at all and it is foolish to punish the horse by tightening the girth to such an extent that it is uncomfortable.

Some horses will kick or bite as soon as they see a person approaching with the tack. Such horses should never be tacked up in the stall. They must be led out in the halter, cross-tied and approached from the front.

The horse that continually wheels to present his rear to a person entering the box stall is very dangerous. He should not be left loose but should be tied with his head to the entrance to the stall. Some horses will let you enter peaceably enough if you only carry grooming tools or feed but will let fly if you bring a bridle or saddle with you. With such horses get your hands on the halter and turn the horse around before you bring in the tack.

Many of the vices here mentioned vanish when the horse is sufficiently well exercised and not fed too much. With some horses weather has a great deal to do with their dispositions, the first hint of frost bringing on the bad habits and the coming of summer doing away with them.

In the class of vices when the rider is dismounted we have that of *charging in the pasture*. The horse will wait until the person trying to catch him comes near and then will rush at him, teeth bared. The best remedy is to carry a stout stick and catch the animal across the nose once or twice. It takes nerve but is very effective and will cure the vice once and for all though it will not teach him to come up to you readily. See also *HORSE, handling of in Pasture*.

Restlessness while being mounted may range from the negative defense of backing away, pivoting the hindquarters or bolting forward as soon as the rider has one foot in the stirrup to kicking the unwary in the small of the back if he is foolish enough to mount from the rear. The cure for all this type of restlessness is to carry a carrot or an apple. If the horse is very restless have another person hold him while you mount. The minute you are in the saddle reach down and give him the tidbit. Now dismount and repeat the performance again and again until the horse learns to expect the reward and will stand quietly in anticipa-

tion. I have cured some of the most difficult cases by this method in only a half an hour.

Pulling back while being led is an annoying habit. With such a horse always have the reins pulled forward over the head, carry the end in your left hand with the right hand on them six inches below the bit. Be on the lookout and when the horse pulls back suddenly stay with him. Correct him with a sharp word and, if necessary, turn him around once or twice before leading him forward. If he still persists an assistant will have to come up from behind and give him a sharp whack over the rump. Carry carrots or apples with you and by constantly coaxing the horse to follow you he may often be cured of this habit but force must be used when he displays deliberate force against you.

Refusing to move forward when being led is easily prevented if one remembers that a horse thinks of only one thing at a time. If the horse plants his front feet, throws up his head and braces his neck, don't waste your time trying to pull him forward for he is stronger than you. Instead, turn him sharply first to one side for a step or two and then to the other. He will follow readily enough.

Vices Under the Saddle

Rearing is one of the vices to which some horses resort while being ridden if they do not want to be held back or if they do not want to leave their companions or go in a certain direction. It is a vice generally acquired while being ridden by a person with heavy hands and poor legs. In rearing the rider's purpose must be to make the horse move forward. He should lean well forward himself, loosen the reins and apply his legs as strongly as possible. If the horse is known to be a rearer the rider should be prepared and the instant he feels the animal collecting himself he should bring his crop down hard on the rump. Another method is to turn the animal with a very short rein and keep him turning until he is a little dizzy. If the horse is rearing from pure vice a good rider can sometimes deliberately pull him over backwards, at the same time getting out of the way himself. I have also found the following method extremely successful in correcting the vice of rearing in the horse that is not rearing from fright. Such horses usually give a little warning before they go up, and nearly all display this vice only in certain situations, such as when being asked to leave a group of horses or to leave the stable. The rider, knowing this, is prepared, and the instant the horse shows signs of being about to rear the rider leans forward and slips his right bridle rein under the sole of his right foot. He then pulls up on the rein; this brings the horse's head around to the rider's right toe. In this position he is off balance and cannot possibly go up. As soon as he has the horse thus under control the rider uses his opposite leg strongly, causing the horse to turn around and around. All this time he keeps his weight well forward. After a few moments the rider lets the rein slip out from under his foot, uses both legs strongly and pushes the horse forward, repeating the procedure at once whenever the horse asks for it. Even the most confirmed rearer will quit after one or two lessons of this sort, though he may go back to his old habits under a weak rider. Horses with such vices as rearing and bolting should never be ridden by any except competent riders and in their hands will usually give up when they find that their little tricks do not work. *Whirling* is often combined with rearing. If the horse whirls do not try and pull him back but keep him going around until he completes the circle and is once more facing in the direction you want him to take.

Bolting and running away are acquired vices. Once the horse has found that he can get away from the rider and dash for the stable he will try it again and again. Such a horse should be punished by being yanked back suddenly in a heavy bit before he has a chance to get started. If the animal gets out of hand and has a hard mouth and inflexible neck he may best be stopped by being turned sharply in a short circle. Pulling straight back does not work with a runaway, the horse is stronger physically than the man. Sudden sharp jerks are more effective but the best method is to pull his head around for the horse that is not looking straight ahead cannot go very fast. It is not hard to stay on a runaway horse and most accidents occur through the rider becoming petrified, throwing away his reins, digging in his heels and so inciting the horse to further speed. See also *REINS, Use of, the pulley rein.*

Refusing to leave the stable alone or leave his companions is a vice often resorted to by the horse who finds himself mounted by the weak or inexperienced rider. Turning him from one side to the other with vigorous use of the correct leg will often take him out. "Rolling him up" or turning him in short circles is the old German method. The good rider rarely has serious trouble with such a horse, being able to apply his whip at the psychological moment and, at the same time, retaining his seat if the horse jumps suddenly forward under punishment. It is useless for the tyro to attempt to ride such a horse for he simply has not the necessary skill.

Jibbing or jogging, i.e., taking little dancing steps and fighting the restraint of the bit instead of walking quietly comes from being ridden in too severe a bit with too heavy a hand. The horse must be induced to relax and lower his head. Training him to two-track or side-step will sometimes cure him as it distracts his attention. More work and less grain is also a cure if the trouble is simply lack of exercise.

Bucking may be either playfulness or vice. In the former case, after he has flung his heels to the sky a few times the horse will settle down and go quietly enough, but if he succeeds in putting off his rider the playfulness may develop into a real vice. If this happens the horse must be ridden only by competent riders who must be prepared to urge him forward at the first sign of trouble.

Shying is a difficult vice to combat coming, as it does, from fear. A firm use of the aids, particularly of the legs, is the best cure. The rider should develop the habit of being constantly on the alert for frightening objects and should try and keep the horse moving past such an object, meanwhile talking quietly to him. The most important factor to remember is that the more frightened the horse becomes the more quiet and calm should be the rider.

Stall courage and agoraphobia are readily developed in high-strung horses that are overfed and underworked. Cut down on the feed. Increase the exercise and turn such animals out into the paddock as much of the time as is possible. If it becomes necessary to have them ridden by inadequate riders some of the playfulness may be taken out of them by saddling and bridling the horse, running up the stirrups and putting the reins behind them and then turning him into the riding hall. The trainer stands in the middle and keeps the horse moving, allowing him to kick and buck as much as he likes but not permitting him to roll. After fifteen minutes the trainer should mount and ride the horse at a steady trot on a loose rein. If he goes quietly he may then be cantered. When he will keep the canter with the reins dangling he is ready for the beginner, but until then he is unsafe.

Refusing and shying out at jumps. The horse that refuses or shies out consistently while being jumped has been spoiled by too much jumping or by being asked to negotiate obstacles which are too high for his ability or degree of training. Such a horse must be reschooled from the beginning. The horse that refuses in the hunt field should be pulled out of line and the field should be allowed to all go over the jump. The reluctant horse will then usually follow rather than be left alone. Give a refusing horse a very short run so that he does not have too much time to think.

With the horse that shies out one must approach the jump from the side to which he has shied, only straightening him out just in time to take the obstacle. Thus if he has shied out to the left start from the left, head for the extreme right-hand end of the obstacle and, one length from the jump, straighten him out.

Eating in the bit. This is a common habit of ponies. Knowing that the child is not as strong as he the pony will often stop and duck his head suddenly for the grass along the roadside. The average young child will be unable to pull him up again though if he will remember to kick as well as pull he will manage very well. There is no cure but the habit can be prevented by fitting the pony with a muzzle put over the bit. A calf muzzle is about the right size and it may be attached by means of a strap running behind the ears. Riders who should know better often allow their horses to graze while they sit on them. This is a slovenly habit and a dangerous one as the horse's belly may inflate slightly and cause a girth sore.

Kicking or biting at a companion. Many horses go well alone but are jealous of another horse either riding beside them or passing them. This habit is readily broken by the competent horseman who will apply his whip sharply the instant the horse shows any inclination towards causing trouble. The horse that kicks should be swung towards his intended victim as he cannot kick him with his tail turned away. The biter should be pulled back and turned away but sharp and instant punishment will soon teach manners to the bad tempered horse.

Boring. The habit of boring, i.e., lowering the head, bending the neck until the chin is almost touching the chest and, having attained this position, using it as a defense against answering the demands of the bit, is common with mutton-shouldered, thick-necked horses. This is an exceedingly disagreeable habit. Lightening the forehand by means of suppling exercises and by work in the dumb jockey are in order. The rider of a borer must not use direct pulling to steady the horse but must use vibrations of the bit, constant give and take and pronounced use of the legs. Borers readily develops into runaways under inexpert hands.

VILLAIN

This is again one of the many names for our friend the fox.

VIXEN

The female fox is the vixen.

VOICE

The Huntsman uses his voice constantly both to cheer and to rate hounds. The experienced member of the field can judge from the combination of the voice and the horn just about what hounds are doing even though he cannot see them. The actual words used are often indistinguishable but the tone of voice together with the sequence of the notes emitted paint a clear picture of just what is going on. See also *HUNTING CALLS.*

Use of the voice in riding. The voice is one of the aids but it should not be used incorrectly. The thoughtless rider who "clucks" at his horse when riding in company tells the horse of his companion to increase his gait as well as his own. As the other horse may already be going too fast or be excitable this can cause trouble. But the voice can be used soothingly to give the timid horse confidence; together with a pat of approbation it can be employed to tell the horse that he has done well, and a sharp tone will often be sufficient correction for the animal which is about to misbehave. In general horses like to be talked to and the restless colt will often settle down if the rider will talk quietly to him and reassure him. Furthermore, the use of the voice in this way builds up both sympathy and understanding between horse and rider.

W

WAGONS

Four-wheeled vehicles used for racing harness horses or showing road-horses are known as wagons.

WALER

The Australian range horse is known as the "Waler." The name is derived from the fact that most of these horses were bred in New South Wales. Many were exported to India for use as polo ponies. The Waler somewhat resembles our cow pony and is sturdy and self-sustaining.

WALK

The walk is a four-beat gait with little elevation. It should be flat-footed and the cadence should be even. The running walk is one of the so called "slow gaits" desired in the Saddler and Tennessee Walking Horse. It too is a four-beat gait but it is not flat-footed and is much quicker. Every horse should be taught to walk out quickly and without excitement. Speed at the walk usually indicates speed at the gallop. The horse that jogs and jigs may be helped by being trained to two-track. He should be induced to lower his head and relax at the poll and jaw. This habit is frequently brought on by too strong collection.

WALKING HORSE

See *PLANTATION WALKER, HORSE SHOW CLASSES, Saddle Horse Division; TENNESSEE WALKING HORSE ASSOCIATION.*

WALKING RACE

Beginners will enjoy this competition. The horses are lined up and at the command race at a walk to the finish line, any horse breaking is eliminated.

WALK-TROT HORSE

This is a horse show term meaning a

Saddle horse that walks, trots and canters only. It is used to distinguish the three-gaiter from the five-gaiter.

WALL

The horny covering of the foot is known as the wall.

WALLS

Stone walls are common in many parts of the country. Provided there are no loose stones on the take-off or landing they make excellent obstacles as a horse will rarely risk hitting them. However, because horses do make mistakes, it is a wise precaution to have a rider (rail) laid across the top of a section that is often jumped. This also serves as an indication that the landing is clear. The horseman who is riding cross-country for the first time where the walls are not paneled should always examine a wall before he jumps it. Double walls and filled walls, which, decked with poison ivy, may appear of normal width sometimes turn out to be as wide as ten or twelve feet. And granite ledges do not make good landings.

WALTZING

The waltz, as executed by the high school horse is very pretty. Analyzed, it consists of a pivot around croup followed by a pivot around forehand. The owner of the Saddler who wishes to train his horse should first teach him the pivots, later combining them and himself giving the signals in time to the music.

WAR CHARIOT

The war chariot of the Greeks is interesting in that it demonstrates that in those days the fact that a horse could push more than it could pull was unknown. The Greek horse actually pulled the chariot, and it took two or three horses to pull one light chariot and driver. With modern harness the horse leans against the collar and *pushes*.

WAR HORSES

See *CAVALRY*.

WARBLES

These are hard lumps under the skin and are caused by the warble fly which has laid its eggs there. The egg hatches into a maggot which must be ejected. Warbles which are on a part of the horse's body which is not under the saddle may be left alone but warbles which are under pressure will have to be treated with hot fomentations, antiphlogistene, etc. After the maggot emerges the cavity should be syringed out with a mild disinfectant.

'WARE WIRE
See *HUNTING TERMS*.

WARTS

Warts are quite common in horses and may grow to an enormous size. Some types may be treated by tying a silk thread tightly around them at the base. The lack of circulation will cause the wart to drop off. Others may be dissolved with a caustic such as nitrate of silver.

WATER FOUNTAINS

Automatic water fountains are most useful for the stable. They save an enormous amount of work and insure the horse getting all the water he wants at all times. The type used for cattle is very satisfactory. It consists of a small bowl with a paddle. The horse pushes on the paddle with his nose when reaching for the water at the bottom of the bowl, as he pushes the paddle down more water comes in. Horses learn to use these very readily though some are afraid at first. Horses with small noses will sometimes get the water by reaching in at the side. In this case an additional bar may be added to the paddle. Some horses develop amusing habits in regard to the water fountains. Having a dislike of drinking while the water is splashing in, they will press the paddle with their chins, then, when the bowl has filled, lift the paddle up and drink the water.

The only disadvantage to water fountains is that in unheated stables in cold climates it is difficult to keep them from freezing. It is now possible to get an electric cable which, wrapped around the pipe or tied to it vertically, will keep the water from freezing without overheating it. These coils were first devised for use in greenhouses to keep the soil warm. Later they were adapted to use on outdoor water pipes and in gutters to keep ice from forming. They come in various sizes and lengths and may be equipped with thermostats so that they can turn themselves off and on automatically according to the climatic conditions. However, since it is difficult to carry the wire all the way over the plunger which controls the water supply, for safety's sake it is best to buy the type of water fountain which has a washer at this point; thus the washer will expand instead of the whole head breaking.

WATERING

When the horse gets his water is most important. That he should get all he wants goes without saying. In hot weather a horse will drink up to fifteen or twenty gallons a day. In cold weather he will sometimes want only one or two. But whatever he wants he should have.

There are two things to be remembered in watering horses. The first that the horse should not be given large quantities of water just after he has finished a full meal of grain. To do so invites colic. The grain remains in the horse's stomach for some little time after eating. The introduction of water, which passes right through into the kidneys, tends to cause the grain to swell and also brings the risk of whole grains of oats being washed into the intestinal tract before they have been sufficiently digested. This will cause gas which may bring on flatulent colic and, through pressure on the heart, cause death.

The horse that always has water in front of him will not be so thirsty after eating that he will fill himself up with water, hence he may be allowed his water and his grain ration together. But if a horse is brought in from a long ride on a hot day and, having been cooled

out, is turned into his stall where his water awaits him, he should not receive his grain ration until he has had time to drink all he wants.

The horse that is overheated and lathery should not be allowed to drink all he wants and then stand. This invites laminitis or founder. The horse that is hot may be watered and then worked or walked. It is perfectly permissible to water a horse while out on a trail ride provided the horse is kept moving. Don't let a horse fill himself up with water and then gallop immediately either, let him walk or jog slowly for a few minutes.

The horse that is brought in to the stable in a lather, suffering from thirst, should not be kept thirsty. He should be given a few mouthfuls of water to relieve his thirst, then walked a few moments and given more. See *WATERING OUT; STABLE ROUTINE; HORSE, Care of.*

WATERING OUT

This is a racing expression. When the horses are brought in off the track, particularly the harness horses which may have trotted as much as fifteen miles during the afternoon, they are covered with sweat and thoroughly blown. The trainer throws a cooler over his racer, gives him a few mouthfuls of water to relieve his thirst and then walks him. After five minutes or so he gives him another mouthful of water and continues walking. This is continued until the horse has had all the water he wants. The procedure sometimes takes as much as an hour and a half or two hours before the horse is considered "watered out."

WEANING

See *COLTS, Breaking and Training of.*

WEAVING

See *VICES.*

WEIGHTS OF HORSES

The ordinary saddle horse, polo pony

or cavalry mount, averaging fifteen-two in height will normally weigh around a thousand pounds. The hunter usually runs from twelve to fourteen hundred. Draft breeds may go as high as twenty-three hundred though the average is about nineteen hundred. After sixteen hands the muscular strength of the horse when used for jumping or carrying weight does not increase in proportion to his weight so the very large horse has to bear more of a burden for his size than does the smaller animal. See also *SIZE OF HORSES; BURDEN OF HORSES; ENDURANCE.*

WELSH MOUNTAIN PONY SOCIETY OF AMERICA

Unionville, Pa. Mr. Sidney S. Swett, *Secretary.*

WELSH PONY

The Welsh is probably the most popular as well as the most numerous of the various pony types. As a children's hack or hunter it is to be infinitely preferred above the English type Shetland. The breed is very old having been in existence in England and localized in Wales since early Saxon times. In 1825 a Thoroughbred stallion was turned loose in the drove of pony mares and the effect of the hot blood is very evident in the modern Welsh pony for he has the delicate head, dainty limbs and the fine coat of the Thoroughbred. The Welsh is in truth a miniature horse and is most outstanding for his jumping abilities.

The average size for the Welsh is twelve two and such a pony often negotiates jumps of four feet and four feet six inches both in the hunt field and in the show ring. In disposition the Welsh are docile but with spirit. They have none of the stubborn qualities of the Shetland nor the nervousness of the Hackney. The stud book is kept by the Welsh Pony and Cob Society at Lafayette, Indiana.

WESTERN CHUNK

This is a type of small draft horse found in the West. It is obtained by crossing the heavier draft breeds with a lighter breed. The result is a chunky, heavily muscled horse which is strong enough for most farm purposes and active enough to be used for slow saddle work and for driving.

WESTERN HORSE

See *COW PONY; MUSTANG; STOCK HORSE.*

WESTERN PLEASURE HORSE CONTESTS

These contests are for the well-mannered, smooth-gaited Western-trained horse that is not a cow pony or ranch horse but which can provide many hours of pleasure to its rider. Judged on manners, gaits, agility and willingness.

WESTERN RIDERS

The cowboy is an expert horseman. He spends his life in the saddle and his livelihood depends upon his ability. The Eastern imitation who gets most of his ideas from the movies is to be deplored. He knows nothing about either the art of equitation or the horse. The dude who goes West for a summer, learns a little and then tries to apply what he has learned to his riding in the East forgetting that horses, country and tack all differ.

The genuine cowboy looks down on the Easterner as an amateur while he himself is a professional. The horse is rapidly being replaced by mechanical equipment as far as being an instrument of war goes. He remains in sport and it will be many years before a substitute for the cow pony is found. The jeep will undoubtedly take over some of the cow pony's duties. But the jeep cannot live off the land and it cannot assist in roping a steer. As long as there are duties for the cow pony the Western rider will continue as an important figure in our industry. But it should be remembered that his riding and his horse and equipment are governed by his duties. The person who wishes to become an accomplished horseman, i.e., one that can be at home in the saddle, on every type of well trained horse, can demand a maximum of obedience from his mount with a minimum of effort on his part, and who can take a green colt and turn out a finished Saddler, hunter or polo pony, should not take the cowboy and his methods as an example to be emulated.

WESTERN RIDING (competitions for)

These are conducted over a prescribed course to test the all-around disposition and ability of the ranch horse. He must perform the usual ranch chores over trails, give a quiet, comfortable, pleasant ride in open country, through and over obstacles.

WESTERN SADDLES
See *SADDLES, Stock.*

WESTERN TERMS

The cowboy of the West has developed a terminology which is highly descriptive and often completely unintelligible to the "dude." Many of his words are derived from the Spanish. The word "bronc" or "bronco" meaning "wild horse" is an example. Others are simply common horse terms spelled phonetically and used in a slightly different way, "critter" to mean a calf is one such term. Often the cowboy converts an adjective or a noun into a verb. "High tailing it across the plains" to describe a herd of running horses comes under this category. The list below is by no means complete but contains most of the most common and frequently used words in the cowboy vocabulary.

Arroyo, a dried-up stream bed.

Bat wings. Leather "chaps" or chaparos worn by cowboys in the desert countries where protection from underbrush is needed but not warmth.

Broke horse. A horse that has been ridden enough so that he is fairly manageable.

Broomtail. A small wild, runty horse not considered worth bothering with.

Bronc, broncho, bronk. This term is from the Spanish meaning "wild." Originally is meant the wild horses which inhabited the western plains. It is used now to denote a horse that is inclined to wildness or meanness, in a derogatory sense. In the East the term is used to describe any horse shipped in from the West.

Buckeroo. A hard riding cowboy who spends most of his time breaking broncs. Also used to denote a rodeo rider.

Bucking Strap. This is a leather strap applied around the flanks of a horse to pinch and irritate him in order to cause him to buck in a riding contest.

Build a loop. Before a lassoo can be used the cowboy must "build a loop," that is, whirl it around him to form the loop which is to be thrown over the victim. It may be a very small loop or it may be large enough to rope five running horses at once such as is done in the rodeos and circuses.

Bull dogging. This is a steer wrestling contest always part of every rodeo. The cowboy springs from a horse to the neck of the steer and, by twisting his horns, brings him to the ground. See *RODEO* (main headings).

Butte. A conspicuous, isolated mountain or large hill with precipitous sides.

Cavvy. A herd of riding horses used by cowboys in their work.

Cavvy wrango. A cowboy who goes out and brings in the "cavvy" each day before the other cowboys are up.

Cayuse. An Indian pony.

Center Fire Rig. Some stock saddles have two girths or cinchas. Others have only one which is midway between cantle and pommel. The latter are known as "center fire rigs."

Chaparos, chaps, shaps. These are the seatless trousers which the cowboy wears over his "levis" or blue jeans to protect his legs from brush and the pinching of the stirrup leathers. In cold countries they are usually covered with fur, generally sheep or goat. They may also be made of horsehide with the hair left on. In desert countries they are of plain leather and are known as "bat wings."

The cowboy's "chaps" are among the most distinguishing articles of his clothing. Many are highly ornamented with silver and leather work.

Chuck wagon. The wagon which carries the "grub" or food. The chuck wagon, driven by the cook, accompanies the cowboys when their work is too far from the home ranch to allow them to come back and forth for meals.

Chute (shute). The high boarded enclosure in which the horses and steers are herded at the rodeo. One by one they are put in the forward section of the enclosure and, in case of the wild horses, the cowboy drops down on his bucking mount in the chute, the front gate is opened and the animal plunges into the arena. Chutes are also used in herding cattle for dipping.

Cinch, cincha. The western type girth which has no buckles but is fastened by means of two rings to the cinch straps.

Cowboy, cowpunch, cowpoke. A man who makes his living riding herd on cattle.

Cow pony. A pony or horse broken for use in cattle herding. The well trained cow pony often demonstrates a remarkable degree of sagacity which is comparable to the intelligence of the Arabian horse. Also called stock horse.

Critter. Originally a calf. Now often used to denote any cattle.

Cutting grounds. Grounds in which specified animals are "cut out" or separated from the herd for some purpose such as branding.

Cut out. To separate some specified animal or animals from the rest of the herd.

Cutting pony. A cowpony trained for use in separating cattle or horses.

Dab, dab a line. To throw a loop skillfully over a horse's or steer's head.

Dogie. Originally a motherless calf but now often used to denote any forlorn looking, scrubby cattle.

Dude. A tenderfoot or newcomer to the West.

Dude Ranch. A ranch which caters to dudes, making its money by entertaining

Easterners who want to live a ranch life.

Dust a horse, fan a horse. When a cowboy rides in competition on a bucking bronc he "dusts" or "fans" him with his hat to demonstrate his skill and make the horse buck harder.

Ganted up. Gaunt looking from starvation.

Granger. A man from a civilized part of the country, from the custom of farmers being members of "granges." The cowboy will speak of wanting to get into wilder country to get away from the "grangers."

Grub line rider. The professional grub line rider or cowboy who makes his way from place to place working for a short time for his food is usually a bum. He will never settle down and is generally no good. However many cowboys are temporary "grub line riders" in between jobs.

Grub staked. Prospectors are sometimes "grub staked" or provided with food in return for a share of the minerals should they be lucky enough to locate a mine. Herders or cattle owners may also be "grub staked" until the time comes to cash in on their animals.

Hackamore. The Western type of breaking bridle which controls the horse by pressure on the nose. The word is from the Spanish "jaquima." See *Hackamore, Jaquima* (main headings).

Hazing. To herd a horse or a herd along by irritating or scaring it with shouts, pistol shots, etc.

Hightail. To run across country. From the habit the horse has of raising his tail very high when he is excited or running fast.

Hombra, hombre. From the Spanish meaning "man."

Hundred and eleven. The "111" which the cowboy tries to scratch on the hide of the bucking bronco in the rodeo.

Iron. The branding iron. Also used to denote the brand.

Joshua (Yucca). A type of cactus found in the desert countries.

Kayack. A leather pack bag.

Lariat, from the Spanish *la reata,* the

rope. A lasso of throwing rope. The lariat is usually made of hemp, leather or horsehair. It is attached to the pommel of the saddle at one end and has a running noose in the other.

Latigos, the straps which fasten the cinch of the stock saddle.

Loco. Crazy.

Loco weed. A poisonous weed which causes insanity in cattle and horses.

Lope. The uncollected, easy gallop of the Western cowpony.

Malpai. Rough country.

Maverick. An unbranded calf.

Mustang. The original wild horse of the Western plains which was descended from Spanish horses introduced into this country by Cortez and others.

Nester. A homesteader, a man who seldom leaves the home ranch.

Orejana. An unbranded animal.

Ornery. Ill tempered, "cussed." Hard to control.

Outlaw. A horse that is vicious and unridable.

Paint pony. A spotted or parti-colored horse or cowpony.

Piñon, piñion. A type of pine.

Phizog. Face.

Pinto. A spotted horse, from the Spanish meaning "paint."

Posse. A group of men, usually sheriff's men with legal authority.

Ranahan. A good rider.

Reata. Spanish for rope, a lariat.

Reef, to reef a horse. To slide the legs back and forth along the horse's side in a bucking contest in order to make him buck harder.

Remuda. A collection of "broken" horses in a corral from which the ponies to be used that day are chosen. A cavvy.

Rep. A representative sent by a ranch at round-up time to claim any animals belonging to his ranch.

Rodeo. The rodeo originated in the days of the unfenced ranges in the '70's. After the round-up in which cowboys from many ranches came together to claim their cattle and to be paid off, they usually held informal contests in riding, roping, bull dozing and ballad singing.

Later formal rodeos were organized with money prizes. The custom has spread East and the Rodeo held at Madison Square Garden each year attracts riders from many states.

Round up. In unfenced territories and even in fenced territories of large acreage it is necessary, each spring, to round up or collect the cattle and horses for purposes of branding, treating for lice, worms, etc., and segregating those to be fattened for the markets. The round up is the theme of many a song and story. It is at round-up time that the cowboy and his pony come into their own for no mechanical device has been found to take their places.

Savvy, to understand.

Shute. See *Chute.*

Snorty, excited, snorting (in reference to horses).

Snubbing post. The snubbing post in the corral is used for controlling unbroken horses and steers. The cowboy, on foot, first ropes the animal and then runs the rope around the snubbing post to hold him.

Soogan. Bed or bed roll.

Spooky, spooked up. Excited, in reference to horses.

Squatter's right. To take a squatter's right is to be thrown.

Stray. An animal that has wandered into a herd from another district.

String. The group of ponies assigned to an individual cowboy for his use. Some cowboys own their own "strings" and take them with them from job to job.

Sudadero. The broad piece of leather attached to the stirrup strap on a stock saddle which protects the rider's legs from the stirrup leathers and from the sweat.

Sunfish. The motion of the bucking horse in which he twists and turns from side to side.

Vaquero, Mexican for cowboy.

Wrangle. To herd horses or cattle.

Wrango. A cowboy who rounds up the horses to be used by the other men.

Wrango horse. A cow pony used by the wrango.

WEYMOUTH BRIDLE

The Weymouth bridle consists of a bit and bridoon. It is the bridle most usually used for the finished Saddle horse.

WHEEL AT THE GALLOP

When the horse, being at the gallop, executes a short turn, forehand around croup, he is said to wheel. If the horse is so united and the collection so close that one back leg remains stationary he has executed a wheel pirouette.

WHIP

The whip is used in training, not as a severe punishment but to keep the horse's attention, to indicate what is desired of him and prevent his setting up defenses. It may be used as a punishment where the offense is deliberate from vice and not from ignorance or fear. Such a case is that in which one horse kicks or bites at another. The long longeing whip is necessary for that stage of the horse's training, for the trainer, not being mounted, has no means of exciting the horse to action except by his voice and a light laying of the whip on flanks or quarters. The little child riding a phlegmatic pony, who has not enough strength in his legs to obtain obedience from his mount may carry a switch, but the acomplished rider who knows his aids and who wears blunt spurs does not need one except, as stated, to punish a deliberate disobedience.

WHIRLING

See *VICES, under the Saddle.*

WILD HORSES

There are still herds of wild horses in the West. These are descendants of the mustangs which, in turn, descended from the Spanish horses imported by Cortez. Lack of selection in breeding has made most of them inferior, undersized animals with little quality. Their one value is that of being able to live off the land. Occasionally one runs across a good specimen but very often they are so poor that they are slaughtered for meat in order to preserve the pasture for more valuable animals.

WILD HORSES (primeval)

The only survival of the early Wild Horse that is to be found today is the *Przevalski* so called because its skin and skull were first discovered in 1881 by Col. N. M. Przevalski. In 1902 Carl Hagenback, a menagerie owner of Hamburg, sent expeditions into Mongolia to collect living specimens, as it was now known that the breed had survived. They are the most untamable creatures alive, and it was found impossible to capture any adults. However, 32 foals were captured and there are several pure-bred Wild Horses today in different parts of England. These ponies have also had an influence on the Mongolian ponies as they interbreed with them on the steppes. The Przevalski horses were yellowish and are native to the steppes. A similar wild horse in the plains of Northern Europe and Mongolia, the *Tarpan,* more grayish in color and slightly more refined in type, disappeared completely. However, a German zoologist, Professor Lutz Heck, noticed that occasional foals exactly similar to the Tarpans in color and type were being produced in Poland. He started experimental breeding, using the Polish Konik mares and the Przevalski stallions, and has succeeded in reproducing the Tarpan.

WIND

The horse's wind is as important as his legs and eyes. In buying the horse his wind should be carefully tested. It should also be remembered that horses over sixteen hands are much more apt to develop weaknesses of wind than smaller animals. A severe case of shipping fever or strangles which leaves the glands of the throat thickened may permanently impair the wind. Heaves, which is the most common and serious disease of the respiratory system, can be brought on by overwork and bad feeding. Broken wind, which is a thickened condition of the membranes, sometimes yields to surgery though not always. See also *SOUNDNESS, Tests for; HEAVES*.

WIND GALLS

Wind galls or puffs are little rubbery enlargements on the pasterns. They are of no account and rarely cause lameness.

WIND SUCKING

See *VICES*.

WINDOWS (in the stable)

The windows in the stable should be set high to prevent drafts blowing directly on the animals and to insure that he does not stand with the light directly in his eyes. All windows should be screened. Windows which are hinged at the bottom and push out from the top are the most satisfactory. See also *VENTILATION; STABLE; LIGHT*.

WINDPIPE

The horse's windpipe which runs along the base of his neck should be well defined. A narrow, constricted windpipe means less intake of oxygen and consequently poorer staying power.

WINKERS

Winkers or blinders are generally used on harness horses to prevent the animal from seeing something coming up from behind. They should not be set so close that they impair his vision to the front, nor should they flop. Special types of winkers attached to hoods are used on race horses which show fear of the proximity of other horses or of the rail.

WIRE CUTTERS

The wire cutter is an important tool around the stable. One of the Whippers-In also usually carries a pair of wire cutters with him in the hunt field.

WISPING

Some grooms "wisp" a horse, that is, rub him down with a wisp of straw when he returns from work.

WOLF TEETH

These are little supernumerary teeth about the size of a child's first teeth which sometimes appear in front of the molars on the bars. They interfere with the action of the bit and are said to impair the optic nerve and so should be removed as soon as discovered.

WORK

The horse's heaven is to be given enough work to keep him built up muscularly and yet never to be overtaxed. Generally speaking, every horse should have two hours of work a day unless he is being used several days a week for polo or hunting. Steady work is the cure for many vices. The man or woman who cannot give this amount of time to his hobby should not keep a horse. The horse that is worked enough and regularly but not overworked will give as many as twenty or more years active service to his master and at the end of that time will be as sound as ever except for the natural evidences of old age. The horse's physical and mental constitution is the guide by which one judges the amount of work necessary for each animal. Children's ponies, especially, should be kept well exercised or they will shortly become unmanageable.

But no horse should be taxed beyond his strength. If he is very young or has been turned out for a month or more at pasture his muscles and wind must be built up slowly before he is asked to undertake any really strenuous work. Otherwise he will develop defects and weaknesses which may well be incurable. See *ENDURANCE; BURDEN*.

WORKING COW HORSE
(competitions)

These tests combine reining, roping and other ordinary work of the useful cow horse.

WORMS

Worms are nearly always to be expected, especially in horses in poor condition. It is impossible, due to the cycle of development, to eliminate them entirely but they can be kept under control. A teaspoonful of ferrous sulphate given in the feed once a day for a week in the spring is a good tonic and is mildly effective on worms. For a stronger vermifuge one should get professional advice.

FIGURE 144.
IMPORTED WITEZ II, POLISH ARABIAN CHAMPION STALLION.

WRESTLING

Wrestling on horseback is a sport which active boys enjoy. Mounted bareback, each pair brings their horses together and stand. At a given signal each wrestler tries to pull or push his opponent off his horse. It goes without saying that only very quiet animals may be used for this sport.

X

XENOPHON

Xenophon wrote the earliest preserved book on the care and training of horses. Many of his words of advice are still followed. He had a clear understanding of the general nature of horses and was one of the few early writers who advised gentleness. Particularly discerning is his suggestion that the colt be led by the groom through the market place and elsewhere in order that he might become accustomed to strange sights and so not be afraid.

Y

YEARLING

From his first to his second birthday the colt is known as a yearling. Thoroughbreds are all considered to have been foaled on January first so the Thoroughbred yearling is such from one January to the next regardless of his actual age. See *AGE*.

YEARLING SALES

The yearling sales offer the experienced horseman the opportunity of buying highly bred colts at often quite reasonable prices. The colt with very desirable blood-lines, good size and conformation will bring a lot of money but the colt whose sires and dams are not yet proven may well go for little. As certain animals bring low prices so too do those with the popular pedigrees sometimes bring sums amounting to many thousands of dollars. The most famous sales of Thoroughbred yearlings are held annually at Saratoga, N. Y. during the month of August. To these sales are sent the most promising future race horses bred in all parts of the country.

YOUNG ENTRY

Young hounds being introduced to hunting via the cubbing season are known as "young entry." The same term may be applied to children who are making their debut at the covert side.

Z

ZEBRA

It was first thought that the Zebra and the horse descended from the same common ancestor but authorities now believe this to be untrue. The absence of hind chestnuts on the Zebra and the difference in the type of front chestnuts show that if there was a common ancestor it was so far back in the mists of time as to be untraceable.

ZERAPE

This is the Mexican saddle blanket. It is highly decorative and very picturesque.

Appendix

RECORDS AND STATISTICS

AMERICAN QUARTER HORSE

Registration by States as of January, 1961

(The following compilation does not include horses registered in the National Quarter Horse Association which was merged in 1949 with the American Quarter Horse Association)

	Horses		Horses
Alabama	512	Mexico	766
Alaska	3	Michigan	1,739
Arabia	1	Minnesota	1,171
Arizona	5,243	Mississippi	434
Arkansas	1,897	Missouri	2,592
Bolivia	2	Montana	5,627
Brazil	8	Nebraska	5,617
California	16,229	Nevada	1,401
Canada	920	New Hampshire	12
Central America	23	New Jersey	273
Chile	1	New Mexico	7,446
China	8	New York	923
Colorado	10,444	North Carolina	108
Costa Rica	3	North Dakota	1,455
Colombia	26	Ohio	1,325
Connecticut	133	Oklahoma	12,916
Cuba	340	Oregon	3,776
Delaware	37	Pennsylvania	787
Dominican Republic	10	Philippines	18
Equador	2	Rhode Island	8
Florida	1,294	South Carolina	89
Georgia	174	South Dakota	2,918
Guatemala	9	Tennessee	503
Hawaii	18	Texas	42,368
Idaho	3,013	Thailand	3
Illinois	2,894	Utah	2,320
Indiana	1,547	Venezuela	41
Iowa	2,301	Vermont	32
Israel	1	Virginia	128
Kansas	6,496	Washington	2,815
Kentucky	151	Washington, D.C.	24
Louisiana	3,740	West Virginia	60
Maine	2	Wisconsin	940
Maryland	40	Wyoming	3,404
Massachusetts	78		

Racing

Quarter Horse races are held Annually in the following States: California, Idaho, Colorado, Florida, New Mexico, Arizona, Nebraska, Oregon.

Quarter Horse World Records

220 yards	12.1 (seconds)
250 yards	13.4
300 yards	15.5
330 yards	16.9
350 yards	17.5
400 yards	19.9
441 yards	21.7

Top Money-Winning Quarter Horse

Tonto Bars Hank, P-102, 793. In 1960 his total winnings were 93,862.98. Bred by Wayne Rossen, trained by Pat Simpson; races under the colors of C. G. and Milo Whitcomb.

World Champion Quarter Running Horse

Vandy's Flash, P-50, 134. Holds the world champion record in both the 350- and the 440-yard races.

Champions in other types of Quarter Horse competitions under sponsorship of the National Cutting Horse Association, as of 1960

Rondo Bill, P-74,611—Honor Roll and Champion Roping Horse.

Poco Lena, P-30,475—World Champion Cutting Horse.

Anadorno Peppy, P-42,638—Honor Roll Barrel Racing Horse.

Miss Jazebel, P-88,275—Honor Roll Halter Horse.

Letitia, P-35,191—Honor Roll Western Pleasure Horse.

Short Spark, P-58,466—Honor Roll Reining Horse.

Abney's Ginger, P-44,304—Honor Roll Western Riding Horse.

FLAT RACING

The following tables and statistics are taken directly from the 1962 edition of *The American Racing Manual,* published by Triangle Publications, Inc., 525 West 52nd Street, New York, N.Y., and printed here with their kind permission.

Scale of Weights for Age

Distance	Age	Jan.	Feb.	Mar.	Apr.	May	June	July	Aug.	Sept.	Oct.	Nov.	Dec.
Half Mile	Two years	x	x	x	x	x	x	x	105	108	111	114	114
	Three years	117	117	119	119	121	123	125	126	127	128	129	129
	Four Years	130	130	130	130	130	130	130	130	130	130	130	130
	Five years & Up	130	130	130	130	130	130	130	130	130	130	130	130
Six Furlongs	Two years	x	x	x	x	x	x	x	102	105	108	111	111
	Three years	114	114	117	117	119	121	123	125	126	127	128	128
	Four Years	129	129	130	130	130	130	130	130	130	130	130	130
	Five years & Up	130	130	130	130	130	130	130	130	130	130	130	130
One Mile	Two years	x	x	x	x	x	x	x	x	96	99	102	102
	Three years	107	107	111	111	113	115	117	119	121	122	123	123
	Four Years	127	127	128	128	127	126	126	126	126	126	126	126
	Five years & Up	128	128	128	128	127	126	126	126	126	126	126	126
One and a Quarter Miles	Two years	x	x	x	x	x	x	x	x	x	x	x	x
	Three years	101	101	107	107	111	113	116	118	120	121	122	122
	Four Years	125	125	127	127	127	126	126	126	126	126	126	126
	Five years & Up	127	127	127	127	127	126	126	126	126	126	126	126
One and a Half Miles	Two years	x	x	x	x	x	x	x	x	x	x	x	x
	Three years	98	98	104	104	108	111	114	117	119	121	122	122
	Four Years	124	124	126	126	126	126	126	126	126	126	126	126
	Five years & Up	126	126	126	126	126	126	126	126	126	126	126	126
Two Miles	Three years	96	96	102	102	106	109	112	114	117	119	120	120
	Four years	124	124	126	126	126	126	126	125	125	124	124	124
	Five years & Up	126	126	126	126	126	126	126	125	125	124	124	124

Fastest Races at One Mile

The world's record for one mile was set by Swaps at Hollywood Park on June 9, 1956, when he was timed in 1:33⅕ while winning the Argonaut Handicap. He had 128 pounds up. Fractions were :22⅖, :45⅕, 1:08⅘, 1:20⅘ and 1:33⅕.

Swaps' record was equaled by Intentionally, June 27, 1959, at Washington Park when he won the Warren Wright Memorial. With 121 pounds up his fractions were :21⅘, :43⅖, 1:07⅗, 1:20 and 1:33⅕.

The second fastest time for a mile also was set by Swaps on September 2, 1956, at Washington Park with 130 pounds up. Round Table equaled that time on June 13, 1959, also at Washington Park.

In 1961 the best time for the mile distance was made by Mrs. M. H. Hunter's Bluescope, whose 1:33⅘ created a track record at Arlington Park. The Helioscope colt won the eleventh running of the Warren Wright Memorial. He carried 118 pounds, won by a length, and beat out Crozier, Editorialist and other representative three-year-olds.

Complete list of miles run in 1:33⅕ to 1:34⅗:

Year	Horse	Age	Wt.	Track	Date	Time
1956	Swaps	4	128	Hollywood Park	June 9	1:33⅕
1959	Intentionally	3	121	Washington Park	June 27	1:33⅕
1956	Swaps	4	130	Washington Park	September 2	1:33⅖
1959	Round Table	5	130	Washington Park	June 13	1:33⅖
1950	Citation	5	128	Golden Gate Fields	June 3	1:33⅗
1960	Bald Eagle	5	128	Aqueduct	May 30	1:33⅗
1951	Bernwood	3	116	Washington Park	August 4	1:33⅘
1957	Terrang	4	117	Hollywood Park	June 8	1:33⅘
1959	Gleeman	4	122	Washington Park	June 2	1:33⅘
1961	Bluescope	3	118	Washington Park	August 26	1:33⅘
1949	Coaltown	4	130	Washington Park	August 20	1:34
1952	Sub Fleet	3	123	Washington Park	August 27	1:34
1955	Jet Action	4	120	Washington Park	September 5	1:34
1958	Clem	4	110	Arlington Park	September 1	1:34
1959	Honeys Gem	5	115	Washington Park	June 20	1:34
1961	Mail Order	5	114	Aqueduct	April 1	1:34
1961	Equifun	5	110	Washington Park	June 3	1:34
1949	Johns Joy	3	122	Washington Park	August 22	1:34⅕
1960	Kelso	3	117	Aqueduct	July 16	1:34⅕
1960	T. V. Lark	3	116	Arlington Park	September 5	1:34⅕
1961	Free Copy	4	111	Hollywood Park	June 24	1:34⅕
1961	Jolly Jester	3	113	Hollywood Park	June 30	1:34⅕
1961	Colfax Maid	3	119	Arlington Park	August 15	1:34⅕
1932	Equipoise	4	128	Arlington Park	June 30	1:34⅖
1948	Prevaricator	5	118	Golden Gate Fields	October 2	1:34⅖
1949	Cutty Hunk	5	111	Washington Park	August 26	1:34⅖
1949	Bewitch	4	125	Washington Park	August 31	1:34⅖

Year	Horse	Age	Wt.	Track	Date	Time
1950	Curandero	4	110	Washington Park	August 19	1:34⅖
1954	Pet Bully	6	119	Washington Park	September 6	1:34⅖
1955	Quality Quest	4	115	Longacres	August 28	1:34⅖
1956	Ben A. Jones	3	119	Washington Park	August 4	1:34⅖
1957	Round Table	3	122	Hollywood Park	May 30	1:34⅖
1959	Resolved	5	105	Washington Park	June 23	1:34⅖
1960	Top Charger	4	110	Washington Park	June 11	1:34⅖
1960	Intentionally	4	126	Arlington Park	June 16	1:34⅖
1961	Four-and-Twenty	3	126	Hollywood Park	May 30	1:34⅖
1961	Mucho Mucho	4	120	Hollywood Park	July 21	1:34⅖
1961	Mucho Mucho	4	114	Del Mar	August 25	1:34⅖
1950	Curandero	4	118	Arlington Park	July 11	1:34⅗
1951	Curandero	5	115	Washington Park	September 3	1:34⅗
1951	Pension Plan	4	120	Golden Gate Fields	November 3	1:34⅗
1953	High Scud	4	109	Washington Park	August 24	1:34⅗
1957	Nahodah	4	118	Monmouth Park	June 19	1:34⅗

Annual Champions in Various Divisions

Year	Two-Year-Old Colt or Gelding	Two-Year-old Filly	Best Two-Year-Old Colt or Gelding	Three-Year-Old Colt or Gelding	Three-Year-Old Filly	Best Three-Year-Old	Handicap Horse	Handicap Mare	Grass Horse	Steeplechaser	Best of Year
1961	Crimson Satan	Cicada	Crimson Satan	Carry Back	Bowl of Flowers	Carry Back	Kelso	Airmans Guide	T. V. Lark	Peal	KELSO
1960	Hail to Reason	Bowl of Flowers	Hail to Reason	Kelso	Berlo	Kelso	Bald Eagle	Royal Native		Benguala	KELSO
1959	Warfare	My Dear Girl	Warfare	Sword Dancer	Royal Native	Sword Dancer	Sword Dancer	Tempted	Round Table	Ancestor	SWORD DANCER
1958	First Landing	Quill	First Landing	Tim Tam	Idun	Tim Tam	Round Table	Bornastar	Round Table	Neji	ROUND TABLE
1957	Nadir	Idun	Idun	Bold Ruler	Bayou	Bold Ruler	Dedicate	Pucker Up	Round Table	Neji	BOLD RULER
1956	Barbizon	Leallah	Barbizon	Needles	Doubledogdare	Needles	Swaps	Blue Sparkler	Career Boy	Shipboard	SWAPS
1955	Needles	Doubledogdare	Needles	Nashua	Misty Morn	Nashua	High Gun	Misty Morn	St. Vincent	Neji	NASHUA
1954	Nashua	High Voltage	Nashua	High Gun	Parlo	High Gun	Native Dancer	Parlo	Stan	King Commander	NATIVE DANCER
1953	Porterhouse	Evening Out	Porterhouse	Native Dancer	Grecian Queen	Native Dancer	Tom Fool	Sickle's Image	Iceberg II.	The Mast	TOM FOOL
1952	Native Dancer	Sweep Patootie	Native Dancer	One Count	Real Delight	One Count	Crafty Admiral	Real Delight		Jam	ONE COUNT
1951	Tom Fool	Rose Jet	Tom Fool	Counterpoint	Kiss Me Kate	Counterpoint	Hill Prince	Bed o' Roses		Oedipus	COUNTERPOINT
1950	Battlefield	Aunt Jinny	Battlefield	Hill Prince	Next Move	Hill Prince	Noor	Two Lea		Oedipus	HILL PRINCE
1949	Hill Prince	Bed o' Roses	Hill Prince	Capot	Two Lea Wistful	Capot	Coaltown	Bewitch		Trough Hill	CAPOT
1948	Blue Peter	Myrtle Charm	Blue Peter	Citation	Miss Request	Citation	Citation	Conniver		American Way	CITATION
1947	Citation	Bewitch	Citation	Phalanx	But Why Not	Phalanx	Armed	But Why Not		War Battle	ARMED
1946	Double Jay	First Flight	First Flight	Assault	Bridal Flower	Assault	Armed	Gallorette		Elkridge	ASSAULT
1945	Star Pilot	Beaugay	Beaugay	Busher	Fighting Step	Busher	Busher	Stymie		Mercator	BUSHER
1944	Pavot	Busher	Pavot	By Jimminy	Twilight Tear	Twilight Tear	Market Wise Devil Diver	Twilight Tear	Mar-Kell	Rouge Dragon	TWILIGHT TEAR
1943	Platter	Durazna	Platter	Count Fleet	Stefanita	Count Fleet				Brother Jones	COUNT FLEET
1942	Count Fleet	Askmenow	Count Fleet	Alsab	Vagrancy	Alsab	Whirlaway	Vagrancy		Elkridge	WHIRLAWAY
1941	Alsab	Petrify	Alsab	Whirlaway	Painted Veil	Whirlaway	Mioland	Fairy Chant		Speculate	WHIRLAWAY

World's leading money-winning horses

Horse	Sts.	1st	2nd	3rd	Amt. Won	Horse	Sts.	1st	2nd	3rd	Amt. Won
Round Table	66	43	8	5	$1,749,869	Fervent	43	17	8	4	347,135
Nashua	30	22	4	1	1,288,565	Capot	28	12	4	7	345,260
Citation	45	32	10	2	1,085,760	Imbros	36	15	7	7	340,550
Swoon's Son	51	30	10	3	970,605	†How Now	81	26	12	9	339,587
Stymie	131	35	33	28	918,485	Equipoise	51	29	10	4	338,610
†Carry Back	37	14	5	7	851,648	Hill Gail	32	11	5	3	335,625
Swaps	25	19	2	2	848,900	Challedon	44	20	7	6	334,660
Sword Dancer	39	15	7	4	829,610	Busher	21	15	3	1	334,035
†T. V. Lark	55	17	8	6	828,479	Fabius	65	18	9	12	331,384
Armed	81	41	20	10	817,475	†Tempted	45	18	4	9	330,760
†Find	110	22	27	27	803,615	Correlation	46	9	4	5	330,009
Native Dancer	22	21	1	0	785,240	†Restless Wind	20	9	4	1	328,723
First Landing	37	19	9	2	779,577	†Hail to Reason	18	9	2	2	328,434
Bold Ruler	33	23	4	2	764,204	Gallant Fox	17	11	3	2	328,165
Bally Ache	31	16	9	4	758,522	Searching	89	25	14	16	327,381
†Kelso	21	16	3	0	722,255	Vulcan's Forge	50	9	11	6	324,240
Bald Eagle	23	9	5	3	676,442	Dotted Line	67	11	9	5	324,159
Assault	42	18	6	7	675,470	†Manassa Mauler	50	13	10	3	323,996
Social Outcast	58	18	9	6	668,300	Paper Tiger	114	19	24	19	323,782
Hillsdale	41	23	6	4	646,935	Grecian Queen	53	12	8	8	323,575
Bardstown	31	18	7	1	628,752	Sailor	21	12	3	1	321,075
Needles	21	11	3	3	600,355	†Tudor Era	75	23	12	14	477,386
Terrang	66	15	9	12	599,285	Battlefield	44	22	14	2	474,727
†Intentionally	31	16	7	2	589,721	Tim Tam	14	10	1	2	467,475
Mark-Ye-Well	40	14	2	4	581,910	Bewitch	55	20	10	11	462,605
Oil Capitol	80	19	10	9	580,756	Vertex	25	17	3	1	453,424
Determine	44	18	7	9	573,360	Jewel's Reward	22	7	5	2	448,592
Tom Fool	30	21	7	1	570,165	Gallorette	72	21	20	13	445,535
Whirlaway	60	32	15	9	561,161	Alerted	104	20	22	18	440,485
On Trust	88	23	19	13	554,125	Seabiscuit	89	33	15	13	437,730
Rejected	47	11	10	2	549,500	Fisherman	45	13	12	4	436,050
†Tompion	39	11	11	6	545,173	Moonrush	88	18	15	9	434,780
Summer Tan	28	11	12	2	542,796	Nadir	32	11	7	8	434,316
†Promised Land	77	21	10	16	541,707	Traffic Judge	44	13	11	3	432,450
Hasty Road	28	14	5	3	541,402	Mister Gus	46	10	12	4	427,300
Ponder	41	14	7	4	541,275	Joe Jones	175	34	40	32	423,567
Clem	47	12	8	13	535,681	†Royal Native	49	18	13	3	422,769
Dedicate	43	12	9	5	533,200	Hill Prince	30	17	5	4	422,140
†Eddie Schmidt	101	20	10	18	526,292	Amerigo	42	12	12	6	419,171
Porterhouse	70	19	8	12	519,460	Helioscope	25	16	3	2	418,275
Gallant Man	26	14	4	1	510,355	Coaltown	39	23	6	3	415,675
Bobby Brocato	88	21	16	14	504,510	†Warfare	16	7	2	4	414,445
Crafty Admiral	39	18	6	4	499,200	Sickle's Image	73	27	13	16	413,275
High Gun	24	11	5	4	486,025	Phalanx	41	13	7	10	409,235
†Talent Show	90	14	14	19	483,593	Sea O Erin	85	19	12	10	407,309
Queen Hopeful	65	18	17	12	365,044	Iron Liege	33	11	9	5	404,169
High Voltage	45	13	5	7	362,240	First Fiddle	95	23	24	20	398,610
Royal Governor	135	28	15	18	360,900	Next Move	46	17	11	3	398,550
†Venetian Way	20	7	4	3	359,422	†Bowl of Flowers	16	10	3	3	398,504
†Crozier	21	5	8	3	359,438	Idun	30	17	4	4	392,490
Solidarity	52	11	18	10	357,435	†On-and-On	58	12	11	10	390,718
Noor	18	8	5	3	356,940	Honeymoon	78	20	14	9	387,760
†Bagdad	34	9	7	6	353,422	To Market	36	12	4	3	387,325
Dunce	39	9	10	9	351,545	†Tick Tock	93	20	24	16	386,951
Alsab	51	25	11	5	350,015	†Quill	26	14	4	2	386,041

Horse	Sts.	1st	2nd	3rd	Amt. Won
My Request	52	22	7	9	385,495
Your Host	23	13	5	2	384,795
†Cicada	16	11	2	3	384,676
Bed o' Roses	46	18	8	6	383,925
Better Self	50	16	7	6	383,925
†Tomy Lee	17	10	3	1	382,117
Sun Beau	74	33	12	10	376,744
Pavot	32	14	6	2	373,365
Donor	71	20	11	6	367,560
Pet Bully	47	23	4	6	365,702
Olympia	41	15	12	4	365,632
Oh Johnny	76	18	6	17	317,483
Intent	21	8	4	6	317,775
Errard King	18	10	2	2	317,575
Shut Out	40	16	6	4	317,507
Smoke Screen	102	13	20	13	316,555
Admiral Vee	114	24	11	17	315,795
†Airmans Guide	20	13	2	2	315,673
†Silver Spoon	27	13	3	4	313,930
Zev	43	23	8	5	313,639
†Whodunit	65	14	11	7	313,275

Horse	Sts.	1st	2nd	3rd	Amt. Won
Greek Ship	54	17	9	7	312,050
Third Brother	69	9	13	12	310,787
†Better Bee	89	20	8	14	310,739
Polynesian	58	27	10	10	310,410
†Seaneen	66	15	12	8	309,800
†Globemaster	21	8	7	2	309,731
Two Lea	26	15	6	3	309,250
Parlo	34	8	6	3	309,240
Jet Action	40	11	3	3	308,225
One Hitter	88	18	14	16	306,775
Endine	45	10	6	7	306,547
Wise Margin	105	20	19	24	305,980
Faultless	46	13	5	6	304,945
Pucker Up	32	16	8	4	304,585
†Indian Maid	66	24	15	10	303,457
†Crimson Satan	13	7	2	2	302,300
Mate	75	20	14	19	301,810
†Alhambra	80	23	6	17	301,464
†Dotted Swiss	25	9	5	3	300,550

†Raced in 1961.

FIGURE 145. KELSO. BRED BY MRS. R. C. DUPONT. OWNED BY BOHEMIA STABLE. TRAINED BY C. H. HANFORD. *COURTESY OF TRIANGLE PUBLICATIONS.*

Stallion record from 1860 to 1961.

Year	Name	Performers	Races won	Amount	Year	Name	Performers	Races won	Amount
1860	Revenue	10	46	$ 49,450	1911	Star Shoot	36	103	53,895
1861	Lexington	13	27	22,425	1912	Star Shoot	44	126	79,973
1862	Lexington	5	14	9,700	1913	Broomstick	21	114	76,009
1863	Lexington	10	25	14,235	1914	Broomstick	31	90	99,043
1864	Lexington	13	38	28,440	1915	Broomstick	47	108	94,387
1865	Lexington	31	87	58,750	1916	Star Shoot	87	218	138,163
1866	Lexington	34	112	92,725	1917	Star Shoot	81	167	131,674
1867	Lexington	33	86	54,030	1918	Sweep	33	69	139,057
1868	Lexington	33	92	68,340	1919	Star Shoot	55	108	197,233
1869	Lexington	36	81	56,375	1920	Fair Play	27	72	269,102
1870	Lexington	35	82	129,360	1921	Celt	52	124	206,167
1871	Lexington	40	102	109,095	1922	McGee	57	125	222,491
1872	Lexington	28	82	71,915	1923	The Finn	16	31	285,759
1873	Lexington	23	71	71,565	1924	Fair Play	45	84	296,204
1874	Lexington	23	70	51,889	1925	Sweep	65	185	237,564
1875	Leamington	18	32	64,518	1926	Man o' War	26	49	408,137
1876	Lexington	12	34	90,570	1927	Fair Play	38	77	361,518
1877	Leamington	21	49	41,170	1928	High Time	55	109	307,631
1878	Lexington	16	36	50,198	1929	Chicle	41	88	289,123
1879	Leamington	24	56	70,837	1930	Sir Gallahad III	16	49	422,200
1880	Bonnie Scotland	35	137	135,700	1931	St. Germans	15	47	315,585
1881	Leamington	23	67	139,219	1932	Chatterton	47	93	210,040
1882	Bonnie Scotland	36	169	103,475	1933	Sir Gallahad III	49	78	136,428
1883	Billet	17	48	89,998	1934	Sir Gallahad III	55	92	180,165
1884	Glenelg	32	108	69,862	1935	Chance Play	38	88	191,465
1885	Virgil	24	56	73,235	1936	Sickle	48	128	209,800
1886	Glenelg	34	136	113,638	1937	The Porter	45	104	292,262
1887	Glenelg	33	120	120,031	1938	Sickle	43	107	327,822
1888	Glenelg	33	134	130,746	1939	Challenger II	42	99	316,281
1889	Rayon d'Or	27	101	175,877	1940	Sir Gallahad III	63	102	305,610
1890	St. Blaise	27	105	185,005	1941	Blenheim II	30	64	378,981
1891	Longfellow	52	143	189,334	1942	Equipoise	36	82	437,141
1892	Iroquois	34	145	183,026	1943	Bull Dog	75	172	372,706
1893	Himyar	27	138	249,502	1944	Chance Play	71	150	431,100
1894	Sir Modred	36	137	134,318	1945	War Admiral	26	59	591,352
1895	Hanover	40	133	106,908	1946	Mahmoud	47	101	638,025
1896	Hanover	42	157	86,853	1947	Bull Lea	61	128	1,259,718
1897	Hanover	54	159	122,374	1948	Bull Lea	63	147	1,334,027
1898	Hanover	43	124	118,590	1949	Bull Lea	73	165	991,842
1899	Albert	19	64	95,975	1950	Heliopolis	77	167	852,292
1900	Kingston	33	110	116,368	1951	Count Fleet	64	124	1,160,847
1901	Sir Dixon	24	94	165,682	1952	Bull Lea	65	136	1,630,655
1902	Hastings	29	63	113,865	1953	Bull Lea	56	107	1,155,846
1903	Ben Strome	24	91	106,965	1954	Heliopolis	76	148	1,406,638
1904	Meddler	21	55	222,555	1955	Nasrullah	40	69	1,433,660
1905	Hamburg	30	60	153,160	1956	Nasrullah	50	106	1,462,413
1906	Meddler	21	54	151,243	1957	Princequillo	75	147	1,698,427
1907	Commando	12	34	270,345	1958	Princequillo	65	110	1,394,540
1908	Hastings	36	93	154,061	1959	Nasrullah	69	141	1,434,543
1909	Ben Brush	19	67	75,143	1960	Nasrullah	64	122	1,419,683
1910	Kingston	13	41	85,220	1961	Ambiorix	73	148	936,976

Leading American breeders, 1918-1961, in races won by horses bred by them

Year	Breeder	Races Won	Year	Breeder	Races Won
1918	John E. Madden	213	1940	Arthur B. Hancock	302
1919	John E. Madden	311	1941	Willis Sharpe Kilmer	256
1920	John E. Madden	313	1942	Arthur B. Hancock	333
1921	John E. Madden	424	1943	Arthur B. Hancock	346
1922	John E. Madden	366	1944	Arthur B. Hancock	322
1923	John E. Madden	419	1945	Mereworth Farm	307
1924	John E. Madden	318	1946	Arthur B. Hancock	350
1925	John E. Madden	383	1947	Mereworth Farm	358
1926	John E. Madden	368	1948	Mereworth Farm	330
1927	John E. Madden	362	1949	Mereworth Farm	347
1928	Himyar Stud	331	1950	Mereworth Farm	313
1929	Himyar Stud	335	1951	Mereworth Farm	299
1930	Audley Farm	318	1952	Mereworth Farm	270
1931	Audley Farm	359	1953	Mereworth Farm	246
1932	Himyar Stud	267	1954	Calumet Farm	201
1933	H. Payne and C. V. Whitney	282	1955	Henry H. Knight	223
1934	H. Payne and C. V. Whitney	310	1956	Henry H. Knight	293
1935	Arthur B. Hancock	292	1957	Henry H. Knight	284
1936	Arthur B. Hancock	314	1958	Henry H. Knight	260
1937	Arthur B. Hancock	279	1959	King Ranch	227
1938	Arthur B. Hancock	300	1960	E. P. Taylor	267
1939	Willis Sharpe Kilmer	269	1961	E. P. Taylor	265

Leading American breeders, from 1922 to 1961, inclusive, in money won

Year	Breeder	1st	2nd	3rd	Amt. Won
1922	John E. Madden	366	377	338	$ 568,785
1923	John E. Madden	419	366	323	623,630
1924	Harry Payne Whitney	272	201	235	482,865
1925	John E. Madden	383	374	376	535,790
1926	Harry Payne Whitney	351	322	308	715,158
1927	Harry Payne Whitney	271	306	234	718,144
1928	Harry Payne Whitney	234	291	269	514,832
1929	Harry Payne Whitney	278	284	234	825,374
1930	Harry Payne Whitney	294	295	281	698,280
1931	Harry Payne Whitney	264	241	244	582,970
1932	Harry Payne Whitney Estate	244	236	217	560,803
1933	Harry Payne and Cornelius V. Whitney	282	276	320	342,866
1934	Harry Payne and Cornelius V. Whitney	310	295	287	320,955
1935	Arthur B. Hancock	392	245	252	359,218
1936	Arthur B. Hancock	310	271	265	362,762
1937	Arthur B. Hancock	279	279	223	416,558
1938	Cornelius V. and Harry Payne Whitney	154	170	169	374,049
1939	Arthur B. Hancock	242	240	261	345,503
1940	Joseph E. Widener	184	161	153	317,961
1941	Warren Wright (Calumet Farm)	124	127	110	528,211
1942	Mrs. Payne Whitney (Greentree Stable)	175	161	163	536,173
1943	Arthur B. Hancock	346	330	315	619,049
1944	Warren Wright (Calumet Farm)	253	227	231	990,612
1945	E. E. Dale Shaffer (Coldstream Stud)	227	147	142	791,477
1946	Mereworth Farm	341	352	344	962,677
1947	Warren Wright (Calumet Farm)	266	207	168	1,807,432
1948	Warren Wright (Calumet Farm)	227	189	160	1,559,850

Year	Breeder	1st	2nd	3rd	Amt. Won
1949	Warren Wright (Calumet Farm)	270	206	209	1,515,181
1950	Warren Wright (Calumet Farm)	243	219	231	1,090,286
1951	Warren Wright (Calumet Farm)	260	180	217	1,198,107
1952	Mrs. Gene Markey (Calumet Farm)	256	217	209	2,060,590
1953	Mrs. Gene Markey (Calumet Farm)	236	168	169	1,573,803
1954	Mrs. Gene Markey (Calumet Farm)	201	145	176	1,139,609
1955	Mrs. Gene Markey (Calumet Farm)	203	175	148	999,737
1956	Mrs. Gene Markey (Calumet Farm)	208	156	163	1,528,727
1957	Mrs. Gene Markey (Calumet Farm)	178	157	124	7,469,473
1958	Claiborne Farm (A. B. Hancock Sr. and A. B. Hancock Jr.)	146	128	133	1,414,355
1959	Claiborne Farm (A. B. Hancock Jr.)	147	144	138	1,322,595
1960	Cornelius V. Whitney	108	106	92	1,193,181
1961	Mrs. Gene Markey (Calumet Farm)	156	120	144	1,078,894

The 30 leading money-winning owners of 1961

Owner	1st	2nd	3rd	Won	Owner	1st	2nd	3rd	Won
Calumet Farm	62	52	40	$759,856	Jacnot Stable	31	35	24	$372,858
Ellsworth, R. C.	67	61	37	648,026	Rice, Ada, L.	31	34	45	358,160
Hooper, F. W.	45	59	48	623,715	Crimson King Farm	27	21	17	353,205
Meadow Stable	22	10	18	600,079	Elmendorf	44	39	36	352,194
Whitney, C. V.	50	53	48	583,213	Jolley, Mrs. M.	15	5	0	341,385
Dorchester Farm Stable	14	2	8	579,464	Winchell, V. H., Jr.	19	20	16	333,212
Van Berg, M. H.	192	193	144	556,732	Sasso, L. P.	17	16	18	318,005
W. H. Bishop Stable, Inc.	152	172	154	496,552	Brown, J. Graham	36	37	31	312,535
Widener, G. D.	38	36	21	493,968	Darby Dan Farm	33	17	24	303,606
Harbor View Farm	65	49	39	488,837	Windfields Farm	56	59	46	278,704
Kerr Stable	32	25	30	472,075	Rand, Adele L.	14	8	5	277,779
Phipps, O.	28	19	17	440,370	Brookmeade Stable	18	22	21	272,488
Bohemia Stable	9	4	3	435,035	Cain Hoy Stable	24	21	16	266,568
Alberta Ranch, Ltd.	17	14	9	411,625	Llangollen Farm	37	30	28	254,855
Grissom, T. A.	149	99	96	387,274	Grant, H. A.	9	4	3	246,466

Leading trainers of 1961 according to winners saddled follow:

Trainer	Number of Wins	Amount Won	Trainer	Number of Wins	Amount Won
Wright, V. R.	178	$442,650	Bond, B. P.	79	$274,565
Bishop, W. H.	152	499,492	Millerick, M. E.	76	263,100
Merrill, F. H. Jr.	133	309,472	Colcord, F.	75	110,743
Maxwell, P.	116	114,001	Davis, D., Jr.	74	223,855
Murray, R. B.	112	126,870	Foley, D.	74	78,846
Hazelton, R.	110	152,930	Jacobs, H.	74	436,364
Winick, A. N.	105	503,894	Cornell, R.	73	204,358
Carroll, D. W.	103	437,866	Johnson, P. G.	72	281,942
Jones, F. W.	102	423,552	Clayton, C. L.	71	117,704
Irwin, R. L.	93	250,694	Martin, F.	71	357,707
Threewitt, N.	91	393,437	Landers, D.	66	253,460
Stevens, H. K.	87	124,263	Forrest, H.	65	212,119
Branch, W. D.	85	111,872	Neloy, E. A.	64	530,002
Campos, A.	83	102,995	Bond, J. B.	63	266,351
Passero, J.	81	196,559	Meyer, J. C.	63	122,167

Leading trainers of 1961 in terms of earnings:

Trainer	Number of Wins	Amount Won	Trainer	Number of Wins	Amount Won
Jones, H. A.	62	$759,856	Hanford, C.	9	$435,035
Fitzsimmons, J.	54	679,711	Kelly, T. J.	31	434,809
Hayes, J. H.	22	600,079	Parke, B.	48	428,310
Price, J. A.	17	587,514	Jones, F. W.	102	423,552
Tenney, M. A.	40	562,785	Ippolito, S.	34	413,053
Neloy, E. A.	64	530,002	Mulholland, W. F.	28	405,179
Winick, A. N.	105	503,894	Threewitt, N.	91	393,437
Nazworthy, J. I.	34	503,630	Martin, F.	71	357,707
Bishop, W. H.	152	499,492	Jolley, L.	18	357,000
Wheeler, R. L.	49	472,755	Potter, G.	23	346,350
Parke, C. R.	23	451,723	Waller, T. M.	25	334,549
Yowell, E.	56	445,889	Conway, J. P.	33	334,407
Wright, V. R.	178	442,650	Merrill, F. H. Jr.	133	309,472
Carroll, D. W.	103	437,866	Bowles, C. F.	39	294,862
Jacobs, H.	74	436,364	Parker, P. A.	10	290,652

Leading Jockey, 1931 to 1961

Year	Jockey	Mts.	1st	2d	3d	Unp.	P.C.	Amt. Won
1931	Kurtsinger, C.	519	93	82	79	265	.18	$ 392,095
1932	Workman, R.	378	87	48	55	188	.23	385,070
1933	Jones, R.	471	63	57	70	281	.13	226,285
1934	Wright, W. D.	919	174	154	114	477	.19	287,185
1935	Coucci, S.	749	141	125	103	380	.19	319,760
1936	Wright, W. D.	670	100	102	73	395	.15	264,000
1937	Kurtsinger, C.	765	120	94	106	445	.16	384,202
1938	Wall, N.	658	97	94	82	385	.15	385,161
1939	James, B.	904	191	165	105	443	.21	353,333
1940	Arcaro, E.	783	132	143	112	396	.17	343,661
1941	Meade, D.	1,164	210	185	158	611	.18	398,627
1942	Arcaro, E.	687	123	97	89	378	.18	481,949
1943	Longden, J.	871	173	140	121	437	.20	573,276
1944	Atkinson, T.	1,539	287	231	213	808	.19	899,101
1945	Longden, J.	778	180	112	100	386	.23	981,977
1946	Atkinson, T.	1,377	233	213	173	758	.17	1,036,825
1947	Dodson, D.	647	141	100	75	331	.22	1,429,949
1948	Arcaro, E.	726	188	108	98	332	.26	1,686,230
1949	Brooks, S.	906	209	172	110	415	.23	1,316,817
1950	Arcaro, E.	888	195	153	144	396	.22	1,410,160
1951	Shoemaker, W.	1,161	257	197	161	546	.22	1,329,890
1952	Arcaro, E.	807	188	122	109	388	.23	1,859,591
1953	Shoemaker, W.	1,683	485	302	210	686	.29	1,784,187
1954	Shoemaker, W.	1,251	380	221	142	508	.30	1,876,760
1955	Arcaro, E.	820	158	126	108	428	.19	1,864,796
1956	Hartack, W.	1,387	347	252	184	604	.25	2,343,955
1957	Hartack, W.	1,238	341	208	178	511	.28	3,060,501
1958	Shoemaker, W.	1,133	300	185	137	511	.26	2,961,693
1959	Shoemaker, W.	1,285	347	230	159	549	.27	2,843,133
1960	Shoemaker, W.	1,227	274	196	158	599	.22	2,123,961
1961	Shoemaker, W.	1,256	304	186	175	591	.24	2,690,819

Pedigree and record of Kelso
(Bred by Mrs. R. C. duPont, Owned by Bohemia Stable. Trained by C. H. Hanford.)

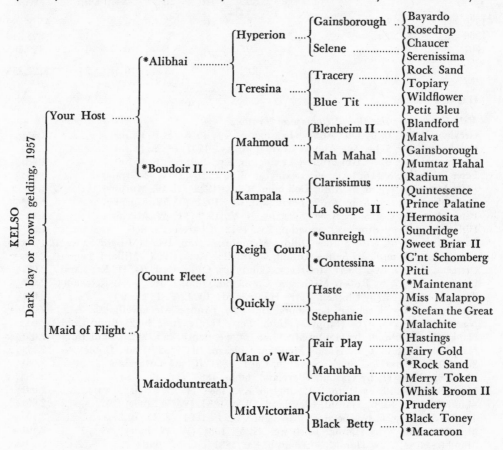

KELSO
Dark bay or brown gelding, 1957

Your Host	*Alibhai	Hyperion	Gainsborough	Bayardo
				Rosedrop
			Selene	Chaucer
				Serenissima
		Teresina	Tracery	Rock Sand
				Topiary
			Blue Tit	Wildflower
				Petit Bleu
	*Boudoir II	Mahmoud	Blenheim II	Blandford
				Malva
			Mah Mahal	Gainsborough
				Mumtaz Hahal
		Kampala	Clarissimus	Radium
				Quintessence
			La Soupe II	Prince Palatine
				Hermosita
Maid of Flight	Count Fleet	Reigh Count	*Sunreigh	Sundridge
				Sweet Briar II
			*Contessina	C'nt Schomberg
				Pitti
		Quickly	Haste	*Maintenant
				Miss Malaprop
			Stephanie	*Stefan the Great
				Malachite
	Maidoduntreath	Man o' War	Fair Play	Hastings
				Fairy Gold
			Mahubah	*Rock Sand
				Merry Token
		MidVictorian	Victorian	Whisk Broom II
				Prudery
			Black Betty	Black Toney
				*Macaroon

Racing Record, 1961

Date	Track	Race	Dist.	Wt.	Fin.	Time	Odds.	Value
May 19	Aqueduct	Cunningham Park Purse	7/8	124	$1^{1\frac{1}{2}}$	1:24 ft	1-3	$ 6,500
May 30	Aqueduct	Metropolitan Handicap	1	130	1^{nk}	1:35 3/5 ft	1-1	74,100
Jun 17	Belmont Park	Whitney Stakes	1 1/8	130	2^{5}†	1:48 ft	2-5	36,400
July 4	Aqueduct	Suburban Handicap	1 1/4	133	1^{5}	2:02 ft	3-5	72,735
July 22	Aqueduct	Brooklyn Handicap	1 1/4	136	$1^{1\frac{1}{4}}$	2:01 3/5 ft	1-2	73,320
Sept 4	Arlington Park	Washington Park Handicap	1	132	$4^{5\frac{3}{4}}$	1:34 3/5 gd	2-3	7,500
Sept 30	Belmont Park	Woodward Stakes	1 1/4	126	1^{8}	2:00 ft	1-2	71,240
Oct 21	Aqueduct	Jockey Club Gold Cup	2	124	1^{5}	3:35 4/5 ft	1-10	68,770
Nov 11	Laurel Race Course	Washington, D.C., International	1 1/2 tc	126	$2^{\frac{3}{4}}$	2:26 1/5 fm	2-5	15,000

† Placed first through disqualification.

Recapitulation

Year	Age	Sts.	1st	2d	3d	Unp.	Won
1959	2	3	1	2	0	0	$ 3,380
1960	3	9	8	0	0	1	293,310
1961	4	9	7	1	0	1	425,565
Totals (3)		21	16	3	0	2	$722,255

HARNESS RACING

Mile Records by the World Champion Trotters

Greyhound, g g, 6, by Guy Abbey; Lexington, Ky., 1938 (S. F. Palin) 1.55¼
Greyhound, g g, 5 by Guy Abbey; Lexington, Ky., 1937 (S. F. Palin) 1.56
Greyhound, g g, 5, by Guy Abbey; Lexington, Ky., 1937 (S. F. Palin) 1.56¾
Peter Manning, b g, 6, by Azoff; Lexington, Ky., 1922 (T. W. Murphy) 1.56¾
Peter Manning, b g, 6, by Azoff; Columbus, Ohio, 1922 (T. W. Murphy) 1.57
Peter Manning, b g, 5, by Azoff; Lexington, Ky., 1921 (T. W. Murphy) 1.57¾
Peter Manning, b g, 5, by Azoff; Syracuse, N. Y., 1921 (T. W. Murphy) 1.58
Uhlan, bl g, 8, by Bingen; Lexington, Ky., 1912 (Charles Tanner) 1.58
Lou Dillon, ch m, 5, by Sidney Dillon; Memphis, Tenn., 1903 (Millard Sanders) 1.58½
Lou Dillon, ch m, 5, by Sidney Dillon; Readville, Mass., 1903 (Millard Sanders) 2.00
Cresceus, ch h, 7, by Robert McGregor; Columbus, Ohio, 1901 (G. H. Ketcham) .. 2.02¼
Cresceus, ch h, 7, by Robert McGregor. Cleveland, Ohio, 1901 (G. H. Ketcham) .. 2.02¾
The Abbot, b g, 7, by Chimes; Terre Haute, Ind., 1900 (E. F. Geers) 2.03¼
Alix, b m, 6, by Patronage; Galesburg, Ill., 1894 (Andres McDowell) 2.03¾
Nancy Hanks, b m, 6, by Happy Medium; Terre Haute, Ind., 1892 (Budd Doble) 2.04
Nancy Hanks, b m, 6, by Happy Medium; Independence, Ia., 1892 (Budd Doble) 2.05¼
Nancy Hanks, b m, 6, by Happy Medium; Chicago, Ill., 1892 (Budd Doble) 2.07¼
Sunol, b m, 5, by Electioneer; Stockton, Calif., 1891 (Charles Marvin) 2.08¼
Maud S., ch m, 11, by Harold; Cleveland, Ohio, 1885 (W. W. Bair) 2.08¾
Maud S., ch m, 10, by Harold; Lexington, Ky., 1884 (W. W. Bair) 2.09¼
Maud S., ch m, 10, by Harold; Cleveland, Ohio, 1884 (W. W. Bair) 2.09¾
Jay-Eye-See, bl g, 6, by Dictator; Providence, R. I., 1884 (E. D. Bither) 2.10
Maud S., ch m, 7, by Harold; Rochester, N. Y., 1881 (W. W. Bair) 2.10¼
Maud S., ch m, 7, by Harold; Pittsburgh, Pa., 1881 (W. W. Bair) 2.10½
Maud, S., ch m, 6, by Harold; Chicago, Ill, 1880 (W. W. Bair) 2.10¾
St. Julien, b g, 11, by Volunteer; Hartford, Conn., 1880 (Orrin Hickok) 2.11¼
St. Julien, b g, 11, by Volunteer; Rochester, N. Y., 1880 (Orrin Hickok) 2.11¾
Maud S., ch m, 6, by Harold; Rochester, N. Y., 1880 (W. W. Bair) 2.11¾
St. Julien, b g, 10, by Volunteer; Oakland, Calif., 1879 (Orrin Hickok) 2.12¾
Rarus, b g, 11, by Conklin's Abdallah; Cleveland, Ohio, 1878 (John Splan) 2.13¼
Rarus, b g, 11, by Conklin's Abdallah; Cleveland, Ohio, 1878 (John Splan) 2.14
Goldsmith Maid, b m, 17, by Abdallah; Boston, Mass., 1874 (Budd Doble) 2.14
Goldsmith Maid, b m, 17, by Abdallah; Rochester, N. Y., 1874 (Budd Doble) 2.14¾
Goldsmith Maid, b m, 17, by Abdallah; Buffalo, N. Y., 1874 (Budd Doble) 2.15½
Goldsmith Maid, b m, 17, by Abdallah; East Saginaw, Mich., 1874 (Budd Doble) 2.16
Goldsmith Maid, b m, 17, by Abdallah; East Saginaw, Mich., 1874 (Budd Doble) 2.16½
Occident, br g, 10, by Doc; Sacramento; Calif., 1873 (George Tennant) 2.16¾
Goldsmith Maid, b m, 15, by Abdallah; Boston, Mass., 1872 (Budd Doble) 2.16¾
Goldsmith Maid, b m, 14, by Abdallah; Milwaukee, Wis., 1871 (Budd Doble) 2.17
Dexter, br g, 9, by Hambletonian; Buffalo, N. Y., 1867 (Budd Doble) 2.17¼
Dexter, br g, 9, by Hambletonian; Boston, Mass., 1867 (Budd Doble) 2.19
Flora Temple, b m, 14, by Bogus Hunter; Kalamazoo, Mich., 1859 (J. D. McMann) 2.19¾
Flora Temple, b m, 14, by Bogus Hunter; Cincinnati, Ohio, 1859 (J. D. McMann) 2.21½
Flora Temple, b m, 14, by Bogus Hunter; Centerville, N. Y., 1859 (J. D. McMann) 2.22
Flora Temple, b m, 14, by Bogus Hunter; Centerville, N. Y., 1859 (J. D. McMann) 2.23½
Flora Temple, b m, 14, by Bogus Hunter; Union Course, N.Y., 1856 (H. Woodruff) 2.24½

Flora Temple, b m, 8, by Bogus Hunter; Utica, N. Y., 1853 (Hiram Woodruff) 2.27
Tacony, ro g, 9, by Sportsman; Union Course, N. Y., 1853 (W. Woodruff) 2.27
Highland Maid, b m, 6, by Saltram; Centerville, N. Y., 1853 (F. J. Nodine) 2.27
Pelham, b g, 12, breeding unknown; Centerville, N. Y., 1849 (Wm. Wheelan) 2.28
Lady Suffolk, g m, 12, by Engineer II; Hoboken, N. J., 1845 (David Bryan) 2.29½

Mile Records by the World Champion Pacers

Adios Butler, b h, 4, by Adios; Lexington, Ky., 1960 (Paige West) 1.54⅗
Adios Harry, br h, 4, by Adios; Vernon, N. Y., 1955 (Luther Lyons) 1.55
Billy Direct, b h, 4, by Napoleon Direct, Lexington, Ky., 1938 (Vic Fleming) 1.55
Dan Patch, br h, 9, by Joe Patchen; Lexington, Ky., 1905 (H. C. Hersey) *1.55¼
Dan Patch, br h, 8, by Joe Patchen; Memphis, Tenn., 1904 (H. C. Hersey) 1.56
Dan Patch, br h, 7, by Joe Patchen; Memphis, Tenn., 1903 (M. E. McHenry) 1.56¼
Dan Patch, br h, 7, by Joe Patchen; Brighton Beach, N. Y., 1903 (M. E. McHenry) 1.59
Star Pointer, b h, 8, by Brown Hal; Readville, Mass., 1897 (D. McClary) 1.59¼
John R. Gentry, b h, 7, by Ashland Wilkes; Glen Falls, N.Y., 1896 (W. J. Andrews) 2.00½
John R. Gentry, b h, 7, by Ashland Wilkes; Glen Falls, N.Y., 1896 (W. J. Andrews) 2.01½
Robert J., b g, 6, by Hartford; Terre Haute, Ind., 1894 (E. F. Geers) 2.01½
Robert J., b g, 6, by Hartford; Indianapolis, Ind., 1894 (E. F. Geers) 2.02½
Robert J., b g, 6, by Hartford; Fort Wayne, Ind., 1894 (E. F. Geers) 2.03¾
Flying Jib, b g, 8, by Algona; Chicago, Ill., 1893 (John Kelly) 2.04
Mascot, b g, 7, by Deceive; Terre Haute, Ind., 1892 (W. J. Andrews) 2.04
Hal Pointer, b g, 8, by Tom Hal; Chicago, Ill., 1892 (E. F. Geers) 2.05¼
Direct, b h, 6, by Director; Independence, Iowa, 1891 (George Starr) 2.06
Johnston, b g, 7, by Joe Bassett; Chicago, Ill, 1884 (John Splan) 2.06¼
Johnston, b g, 6, by Joe Bassett; Chicago, Ill., 1883 (Peter V. Johnston) 2.10
Johnston, b g, 6, by Joe Bassett; Chicago, Ill., 1883 (Peter V. Johnston) 2.11¾
Little Brown Jug, br g, 6, by Tom Hal; Hartford, Conn., 1881 (W. H. McCarthy) 2.11¾
Sleepy Tom, ch g, 11, by Tom Rolfe; Chicago, Ill., 1879 (S. C. Phillips) 2.12¼
Sleepy Tom, ch g, 11, by Tom Rolfe, Columbus, Ohio, 1879 (S. C. Phillips) 2.14½
Rowdy Boy, bl g, 10, by Bull Pup; East Saginaw, Mich., 1879 (C. W. Forth) 2.15
Sweetzer, g g, 10, by Tom Crowder; Oakland, Calif., 1878 (A. M. Wilson) 2.15
Yankee Sam, dn g, age and pedigree unknown; Uhrichsville, O., 1869 (T. Elwood) 2.16½
Pocahontas, ch m, 8, by Iron's Cadmus; Union Course, N.Y., 1855 (J. D. McMann) 2.17½
Pet, ro g, age and pedigree unknown; Union Course, N. Y., 1852 (Unknown) 2.18½
Pet, ro g, age and pedigree unknown; Union Course, N.Y., 1851 (Jas. Whelpley) 2.21¼
Dan Miller, ch g, age and pedgr. unknown; Centerville, N.Y., 1849 (J. Whelpley) 2.23
Unknown, ch g, age and pedigree unknown; Beacon Course, N.J., 1884 (Unkn.) 2.23
Aggie Down, b m, age and pedigree unknown; Beacon Course, N.J., 1884 (Unkn.) 2.29
* With Windshield.

Top Ten Money Winning Trotters

Horse	Record	Sex	Sire	Years Raced	Money Won
Su Mac Lad	2:00h	b g	Potomac Lad	1955-61	$455,499
Darn Safe	1:59	br g	Darnley	1955-61	450,427
Trader Horn	2:00	br h	Worthy Boy	1956-60	370,802
Lord Steward	3, 2:02	b g	Darnley	1949-58	338,831
Pronto Don	1:59⅗	ch g	Donald Truax	1947-55	332,363
Scott Frost	1:58⅗	b h	Hoot Mon	1954-57	310,685
Galophone	1:58⅕	br h	Bill Gallon	1954-57	286,807
Silver Song	1:58⅗	b h	Peter Song	1957-61	264,863
Proximity	1:59⅗	b m	Protector	1944-50	252,929
Tie Silk	3, 2:00⅖	br h	Rodney	1958-61	248,745

Top Ten Money Winning Pacers

Horse	Record	Sex	Sire	Years Raced	Money Won
Bye Bye Byrd	T-1:56$\frac{1}{5}$	b h	Poplar Byrd	1957-61	$554,257
Adios Butler	T-1:54$\frac{3}{5}$	br h	Adios	1958-61	509,844
Widower Creed	1:56$\frac{4}{5}$	bl h	Jimmy Creed	1955-60	401,056
Speedy Pick	1:58$\frac{4}{5}$h	b g	Attorney	1956-61	365,265
Belle Acton	3, 1:58$\frac{3}{5}$	b m	The Widower	1955-59	353,063
Adios Harry	1:55	br h	Adios	1953-58	345,433
Diamond Hal	1:57$\frac{2}{5}$	b h	Hal Dale	1953-58	334,971
Good Time	1:57$\frac{4}{5}$	b h	Hal Dale	1948-52	318,792
O'Brien Hanover	1:59$\frac{2}{5}$	b h	Tar Heel	1957-61	286,276
Duane Hanover	1:58	b h	Knight Dream	1954-59	280,228

Top Ten Drivers, Single Year (Only best year for individual driver listed)

Dashes Won

1. Robert G. Farrington (1961) 201
2. Harry W. Burright (1961) 183
3. William R. Haughton (1958) 176
4. William D. Gilmour (1959) 165
5. Stanley F. Dancer (1956) 163
6. Delmer M. Insko (1960) 156
7. John E. Wilcutts (1961) 139
8. Levi B. Harner (1952) 129
9. Louis A. Rapone (1959) 129
10. Clint Hodgins, Howard Beissinger, George Reed, George Sholty 128

Money Won

1. William R. Haughton (1958) $816,659
2. Stanley F. Dancer (1961) 674,723
3. Clint Hodgins (1959) 609,285
4. Delvin G. Miller (1960) 567,282
5. Joseph C. O'Brien (1959) 489,404
6. John F. Simpson (1957) 483,164
7. George F. Sholty (1961) 477,841
8. Edward Cobb (1960) 396,190
9. Hugh A. Bell (1960) 382,172
10. James W. Arthur (1961) 371,393

Growth of the Sport

Year	Handle	Raceway Attendance*	State's Share	Purses	Horses Racing	Colts Registered	USTA Members	Track Members
1940				$ 1,857,591.65	4,988	3,329		463
1941				2,080,288.49	5,146	1,823		435
1942				1,641,365.93	4,556	2,014		330
1943				1,313,028.87	3,773	1,695		301
1944	$ 26,569,202	918,378	$ 1,212,418	2,634,977.58	5,029	1,923	3,871	575
1945	48,919,994	1,383,966	2,223,865	3,445,906.13	5,679	2,117	5,531	485
1946	111,569,313	3,017,800	5,049,215	6,290,600.00	7,757	2,418	5,918	598
1947	134,066,712	3,871,485	6,187,389	7,528,870.98	8,563	3,247	7,352	625
1948	193,781,327	5,494,636	9,174,678	9,805,079.05	9,323	3,460	7,353	612
1949	209,377,545	6,793,607	11,973,870	11,303,247.75	9,798	4,140	8,636	593
1950	242,835,529	7,037,540	13,885,384	11,527,711.94	10,281	4,386	8,411	546
1951	303,986,301	7,719,922	16,605,388	13,119,753.57	11,187	4,879	8,731	518
1952	362,662,754	8,539,117	20,231,251	16,052,772.91	11,927	3,871	9,776	501
1953	443,637,912	10,021,578	25,824,182	18,832,740.79	13,194	4,885	10,669	503
1954	444,845,200	10,147,255	31,767,467	18,961,265.17	13,997	4,496	11,352	497
1955	476,728,009	10,241,101	34,342,535	20,626,774.10	14,548	4,512	11,754	489
1956	534,857,847	10,484,133	38,048,028	21,862,611.30	14,622	4,660	12,267	482
1957	614,920,402	11,807,547	42,694,237.39	24,249,842.69	15,212	4,700	12,680	467
1958	712,872,993	12,769,494	48,256,905.05	27,572,830.48	15,906	5,485	13,481	454
1959	776,487,454	14,128,702	53,100,866.91	29,748,582.31	16,666	5,517	15,122	462
1960	819,152,619	15,009,569	56,069,914.42	31,581,922.54	17,702	6,794	15,593	454
1961	857,587,384	15,719,479	58,490,816.54	32,635,694.33	18,694	7,353	17,272*	431**

* Does not include an estimated 9,000,000 attendance at fairs and non-wagering tracks.

* Plus 14 contract members.

Steeplechase and hunt, 1961

Leading Money Winner and Owner, 1961

G. H. Bostwick	Total winnings 1961 $86,767	Total winnings $999,858
	No. of races won 11	
Harry A. Love	Total winnings 1961, $73,137	
	No. of races won 4	
Allison Stern	Total winning 1961, $65,192	
	No. of races won 10	

Leading Money-Winning Horses, 1961
Peal—Trainer H. A. Love; total winnings 1961, $73,137
Naval Treaty—Owner Allison Stern; total winnings 1961, $45,452.
Barnaby's Bluff—Owner-Trainer, G. H. Bostwick; total winnings 1961, $38,925

Leading Trainers, 1961

	No. races won
Sidney Watters, Jr.	36
D. M. Smithwick	30
W. Burling Cocks	19

Leading Steeplechase Riders (Professional), 1961

Jockey	1st	2nd	3rd	No. mounts
J. L. Aitcheson, Jr.	37	28	25	155
A. P. Smithwick	26	30	36	163
Thomas Walsh	21	18	16	135

Note: Above records refer to winnings over jumps only.

Amateur Rider Table, 1961

Jockey	1st	2nd	3rd	No. mounts
Alan H. Duftan	4	3	4	21
William H. Turner, Jr.	3	6	2	22
Michael Wettach	3	2	4	13

World's Leading Money-Winning Steeplechaser
Neji, Ch. gelding, born 1950, by *Hunter's Moon* out of *Accra*
Owner, Mrs. Ogden Phipps
Breeder, Mrs. Marion duPont Scott

Total Starts	1st	2nd	3rd	Gross Earnings
49	17	11	9	$274,047

All the above statistics concerning Steeplechasing and Hunt Racing are quoted from the 1961 edition of *Steeplechasing in America* with the kind permission of the National Steeplechase and Hunt Association. Those interested may obtain complete records, as shown in this book, by writing to the Association.

STEEPLECHASE AND HUNT ASSOCIATIONS
National Steeplechase and Hunt Association, 300 Park Ave., New York 22, New York

Officers
S. Bryce Wing, *President*
Stephen C. Clark Jr., *Vice-President*
A. C. Bostworth, *Treasurer and Secretary*
John E. Cooper, *Executive Secretary*
Olive R. Keeley, *Assistant Secretary*

Stewards

A. C. Bostwick	Amory L. Haskell	F. S. Von Stade
G. H. Bostwick	John M. Schiff	Newell J. Ward, Jr.
Stephen C. Clark	John M. Sullivan	S. Bryce Wing

Racing Secretary and Handicapper, John E. Cooper
Association Stewards
Aqueduct, Belmont Park and Saratoga, John E. Cooper
Delaware Park, Joseph E. Flanagan

UNITED HUNTS RACING ASSOCIATION, 300 Park Ave, New York 22, New York

Officers
Amory L. Haskell, *President*
Fred F. Alexandre, *Vice-President*
T. H. McKoy, Jr., *Secretary-Treasurer*
W. Helen Eden, *Assistant Secretary*

Executive Committee
Amory Haskell, *Chairman*   Mrs. Ogden Phipps
Fred F. Alexandre   T. H. McKoy, Jr.
Alvin Untermeyer

Directors
Fred F. Alexandre   Mrs. June M. McKnight
Russel M. Arundel   Thomas M. McKoy, Jr.
George H. Bostwick   Mrs. Ogden Phipps
F. Eugene Dixon, Jr.   Randolph D. Rouse
Amory L. Haskell   Alvin Untermeyer
Charles I. Heekin   S. Bryce Wing
Associate Directors
Mrs. A. C. Randolph   Mrs. John R. H. Thouron
Mrs. Dodge Sloane   Mrs. Cortright Wetherill
Mrs. Marion duPont Scott

Field Director, Chris Wood, Jr.

MIDWEST HUNT RACE ASSOCIATION, 4 West 4th St., Cincinnati 2, Ohio

Officers
Carl G. Berger, *President*
E. S. Bonnie, *Vice-President*
Louis M. Prince, *Secretary-Treasurer*

HORSE SHOWS

Listed below are horse shows held in 1961, first published in *The Chronicle of the Horse* (March 23, 1962). All of the shows offered hunter, jumper, pony or hunter equitation classes.

1. Aiken. Aiken, S. C.
2. Alberta Light Horse Ass'n. Calgary, Alta., Can.
3. American Royal. Kansas City, Mo.
4. Amherst Hack & Dressage. Vancouver, B. C., Can.
5. Angelica Creek. Vienna, Va.
6. Angelica Creek. Vienna, Va.
7. Annapolis Elks Club. Annapolis, Md.
8. Arizona Horse Lovers Club. Phoenix, Ariz.
9. Arlington Lions Club. Arlington, Vt.
10. Atlanta Junior. Atlanta, Ga.
11. Avon Springs Downs. Avon, N. Y.
12. Barrington. Barrington, Ill.
13. Bath County. Hot Springs, Va.
14. Bath Saddle Club. Hornell, N. Y.

15. Battle Creek Hunt. Stoney Lake, Mich.
16. Bedford. Bedford, N. Y.
17. Bedford County. Bedford, Va.
18. Bennett College. Millbrook, N. Y.
19. Bennett College. Millbrook, N. Y.
20. Bennett-Skidmore. Millbrook, N. Y.
21. Bent Creek. Ashville, N. C.
22. Bergen County. Paramus, N. J.
23. Berkshire, Litchfield, Conn.
24. Bethesda Hospital. Delray Beach, Fla.
25. Bit & Spur Riding Club. Chevy Chase, Md.
26. Blackberry Hill. Germantown, Tenn.
27. Black Mountain. Black Mountain, N.C.
28. Bladensburg Riding Club. College Park, Md.
29. Blandford Fair. Blandford, Mass.

30. Bloomfield Hunter Trials. Bloomfield Hills, Mich.
31. Bloomfield Junior Olympics. Bloomfield Hills, Mich.
32. Blowing Rock. Blowing Rock, N. C.
33. Blue Grass Riding Club. Lexington, Ky.
34. Blue Meadow Farm Jr. Westport, Conn.
35. Blue Ridge Hunt. Millwood, Va.
36. Blue Ridge Hunt Junior. Boyce, Va.
37. Bonnie Brook. Furlong, Pa.
38. Boulder Brook. Scarsdale, N. Y.
39. Boulder Brook. Scarsdale, N. Y.
40. Boulder Brook. Scarsdale, N. Y.
41. Boumi Temple. Owings Mills, Md.
42. Boys' Home Benefit. Norfolk, Va.
43. Brampton. Brampton, Ont., Can.
44. Branchwater Hunt Club Hunter Trials. Maylene, Ala.
45. Brandywine Valley. Kennett Square, Pa.
46. Brattleboro. Brattleboro, Vt.
47. Brentwood Camp Jr. Angelica, N. Y.
48. Briarcliff-Bennett College, Scarborough, N. Y.
49. Briarwood Farm. Raleigh, N. C.
50. Bridlespur. St. Louis, Mo.
51 Bridlespur Hunt Hunter Trials. New Melle, Mo.
52. Broadacres Farm. Sudbury, Mass.
53. Brookville Junior. Brookville, L. I., N. Y.
54. Brookville Junior. Brookville, N. Y.
55. Brush Hills. Milton, Mass.
56. Buckwheat Festival. Kingwood, W. Va.
57. Buffalo International. Buffalo, N. Y.
58. Buffalo Saddle & Bridle Club. Buffalo, N. Y.
59. Bull Run Hunt Junior. Manassas, Va.
60. Cabell-Huntington Hospital. Huntington, W. Va.
61. Caledon Fair. Caledon, Ont., Can.
62. Calgary Spring. Calgary, Alta. Can.
63. California State Horsemen's Ass'n. Stockton, Calif.
64. Camargo Hunt Hunter Trials. Indian Hill Village, O.
65. Camden. Camden, S. C.
66. Camp Greystone. Tuxedo, N. C.
67. Canadian National Exhibition. Toronto, Can.
68. Casanova Hunt Spring. Casanova. Va.
69. Castle Park. Castle Park, Mich.
70. Cedarholm. Canton, Mass.
71. Center Farm Saddle Club. Ft. Mitchell, Ky.

72. Central Ontario. Kitchener, Ont., Can.
73. Chagrin Valley Hunt. Gates Mills, O.
74. Chagrin Valley Hunt Jr. Gates Mills, Ohio.
75. Chagrin Valley Trails & Riding Club. Chagrin Falls, O.
76. Channel City. Santa Barbara, Calif.
77. Chapel Hill. Chapel Hill, Tenn.
78. Charles Town. Charles Town, W. Va.
79. Chatham County. Pittsboro, N. C.
80. Cherry Lane. Tallman, N. Y.
81. Chestnut Ridge Hunt. Smithfield, Pa.
82. Children's Services. Farmington, Conn.
83. Clarksdale. Clarksdale, Miss.
84. Clearbrook Junior Jumpers. Seattle, Wash.
85. Colorado Springs Jr. League. Colorado Springs, Colo.
86. Columbus. Columbus, Ohio.
87. Columbus Jaycee. Columbus, Mont.
88. Cooper Hospital. Delaware Township, N. J.
89. Country Lanes Schooling. Jericho, N.Y.
90. Cowichan District Riding Club. Duncan, V.I., B.C., Can.
91. Crippled Children's Benefit. Albuquerque, N. M.
92. C. W. Post College, Brookville, N. Y.
93. Dana Hall Interschool. Wellesley, Mass.
94. Dayton. Dayton, Ohio.
95. Dedham, Dedham, Mass.
96. Deep Run Hunt Club. Manakin, Va.
97. Deep Run Hunt Jr. Manakin, Va.
98. Delaware County. Newtown Square, Pa.
99. Devon. Devon, Pa.
100. Donelson. Donelson, Tenn.
101. Dorchester Farm Stables. Kirtland, O.
102. Dunham Woods. Wayne, Ill.
103. Dutchess County Fair. Rhinebeck, N. Y.
104. Dutchess County P.H.A. Millbrook, N. Y.
105. Eastern States. West Springfield, Mass.
106. Easton Junior. Easton, Conn.
107. Edgepark Stables. Houston, Texas.
108. Edgewood Farm. Evans, Ga.
109. Edmonton Spring. Edmonton, Alta., Can.
110. El Conquistador Saddle Club. Tucson, Ariz.
111. El Paso Riding & Driving Club. El Paso, Texas.
112. Emma Willard. Troy, N. Y.
113. Equitation Lodge Junior. Bayport, N. Y.
114. Erie County Fair. Hamburg, N. Y.
115. Essex Junction Lions Club. Essex Junction, Vt.
116. Fairfax Hunt. Sunset Hills, Va.

117. Fairfield Co. Hounds Hunter Trials. Southport, Conn.
118. Fairfield County Hunt Jr. Westport, Conn.
119. Fairfield County Hunt Pony. Westport, Conn.
120. Fairview Akers Farms. West Medway, Mass.
121. Falls Church Jaycees. Burke, Va.
122. Far Hills Jr. Horse & Pony. Far Hill, N. Y.
123. Farmington Hunt Club. Charlottesville, Va.
124. Farmington Hunt Club. Charlottesville, Va.
125. Fayetteville. Fayetteville, N. C.
126. Fayetteville Lions Club. Fayetteville, N. Y.
127. February Junior Schooling. Huntington, N. Y.
128. Fenimore School Junior. Cooperstown, N. Y.
129. First City Troop. Valley Forge, Pa.
130. Flintridge-La Canada Guild. Pasadena, Calif.
131. Florissant Valley. St. Louis, Mo.
132. Fort Lewis. Fort Lewis, Wash.
133. Fortunato Riding Club. Jericho, N. Y.
134. 4-H State Championship. Flemington, N. J.
135. Fox Den Jr. & Pony. Potomac, Md.
136. Foxhall Village. Lancaster, N. Y.
137. Fox Hill Farms. Pleasantville, N. Y.
138. Fox Hill Stables Jr. Lake Grove, N. Y.
139. Fredericksburg Fair. Fredericksburg, Va.
140. Fredericksburg Horse & Pony. Fredericksburg, Va.
141. Friendly Horsemen's Club. Denver, Pa.
142. Friendly Schooling. Chester Springs, Pa.
143. Fuzzydele. Glen Moore, Pa.
144. Gadsden. Nogales, Ariz.
145. Garrison. Garrison, N. Y.
146. Genesee Valley Breeders Ass'n. Avon, N. Y.
147. Germantown Charity. Germantown, Tenn.
148. Germantown Hunter-Jumper. Germantown, Tenn.
149. Gill School. New Vernon, N. J.
150. Girl Scout Benefit. Burke, Va.
151. Glastonbury Junior. Glastonbury, Conn.
152. Glen Head. Muttontown, N. Y.
153. Glen Head Junior. Huntington, N. Y.
154. Glenmore Hunt Club. Staunton, Va.
155. Golden's Bridge. North Salem, N. Y.
156. Golden's Bridge Colt Young Hunter & Pony. North Salem, N. Y.

157. Goodlettesville. Goodlettesville, Tenn.
158. Grand National. San Francisco, Calif.
159. Grand Rapids Charity. Grand Rapids, Mich.
160. Great Barrington. Great Barrington, Mass.
161. Greater Cincinnati. Cincinnati, Ohio.
162. Greater Falls Church. Burke, Va.
163. Great Western Fair. Los Angeles, Calif.
164. Green Bay. Green Bay, Wisc.
165. Greene Co. Waynesburg, Pa.
166. Green Meadow Farm. Oyster Bay, N. Y.
167. Greenville. Greenville, S. C.
168. Greenwich. Greenwich, Conn.
169. Grier School. Tyrone, Pa.
170. Grosse Pointe Hunt. Grosse Pointe Woods, Mich.
171. Grosse Pointe Hunt. Grosse Pointe, Mich.
172. Grosse Pointe Hunt. Grosse Pointe Mich.
173. Grosse Pointe Hunt. Grosse Pointe Woods, Mich.
174. Groton Hunt. Groton, Mass.
175. Groton Hunt. Groton, Mass.
176. Groton Hunt Junior. Groton, Mass.
177. Hamilton Hunt. Caledonia, Ont., Can.
178. Hamilton Hunt Hunter Trials. Caledonia, Ont., Can.
179. Harford Horse & Pony. Havre de Grace, Md.
180. Harford Horse & Pony Club. Havre de Grace, Md.
181. Harrisburg. Harrisburg, Pa.
182. Hawaii State Fair. Honolulu, Hawaii.
183. Helping Hand. Old Westbury, N. Y.
184. Henry County. Martinsville, Va.
185. Hickory. Hickory, Pa.
186. High Hopes Benefit. Wynantskill, N. Y.
187. Highland. Portland, Ore.
188. High Ridge Stables. Montvale, N. J.
189. High View Farm Jr. Pittsford, N. Y.
190. Hillsboro. Franklin, Tenn.
191. Holiday Show. Huntington, N. Y.
192. Holland Tulip Time. Holland, Mich.
193. Hollins College. Hollins, Va.
194. Hollows School. Huntington, N. Y.
195. Hood College, Frederick, Md.
196. Horse Sense Riding Tournament. Nashville, Tenn.
197. Horseshoe Acres. Raleigh, N. C.
198. Horseshoe Acres Jr. Hunter Trials. Raleigh, N. C.
199. Horses of Houston Jr. Houston, Texas.
200. Howard County Fair. West Friendship, Md.
201. Howard County Hunt. Glenelg, Md.

202. Huntington. Huntington, N. Y.
203. Huron River Stables. Ann Arbor, Mich.
204. Huron River Stables. Ann Arbor, Mich.
205. Huron River Stables. Ann Arbor, Mich.
206. Huron River Stables Jr. Ann Arbor, Mich.
207. Immanuel Horse & Pony. Glencoe, Md.
208. Imperial. Winter Haven, Fla.
209. Interior Provincial. Armstrong, B. C., Can.
210. Iron Bridge Hunt. Laurel, Md.
211. James Madison - Thoreau Schools. Vienna, Va.
212. James River Hunt. Hampton, Va.
213. James River Hunt. Hampton, Va.
214. January Schooling. Huntington, N. Y.
215. June Fete. Huntingdon Valley, Pa.
216. Junior Beaufort Hunt. Harrisburg, Pa.
217. Jr. Equestrian Federation. Sacramento, Calif.
218. Jr. Equitation School Hunter. Vienna, Va.
219. Junior Essex Troop. West Orange, N. J.
220. Junior Olympics. Huntington, N. Y.
221. Kalamazoo. Kalamazoo, Mich.
222. Kempsville. Norfork, Va.
223. Kent County Horse & Pony. Chestertown, Md.
224. Keswick. Keswick, Va.
225. Kimberton. Ludwig's Corner, Pa.
226. Lake Erie College. Painesville, Ohio.
227. Lake Forest. Lake Forest, Ill.
228. Lake Mohawk Junior. Sparta, N. J.
229. Lake Oswego Hunt Show & Hunter Trials. Lake Oswego, Ore.
230. Lake Washington Saddle Club. Kirkland, Wash.
231. Lancaster. Lancaster, Pa.
232. Lance & Bridle Jr. Ashland, Va.
233. Larger Cross Roads. Far Hills, N. J.
234. L.B. & Conn. Horsemen. Middletown, Conn.
235. Lebanon. Lebanon, Tenn.
236. Lewis M. Allen Riding Club. Berryville, Va.
237. Lexington Junior League. Lexington, Ky.
238. Limestone Creek Hunter Trials. Cazenovia, N. Y.
239. Lincroft. Lincroft, N. J.
240. Linden Hall. Lititz, Pa.
241. Linden Hall Invitational. Lititz, Pa.
242. Linville-Edom Ruritan. Harrisonburg, Va.
243. Litchfield. Litchfield, Conn.
244. Little Acres Riding Club. Perryman, Md.
245. Little Acres–Stony Forest. Aberdeen, Md.
246. Little Plains Junior. Huntington, N. Y.
247. Little Plains Junior. Greenlawn, N. Y.
248. Londonderry Fair. Londonderry, N. H.
249. Lone Oak Riding & Hunt Club. Concord, N. C.
250. Long Acres Farm. Aiken, S. C.
251. Long Island PHA Junior. St. James, N. Y.
252. Los Altos Hunt. Woodside, Calif.
253. Loudoun Hunt. Leesburg, Va.
254. Loudoun Pony & Junior. Middleburg, Va.
255. Ludwig's Corner Hunt Club. Ludwig's Corner, Pa.
256. Madison. Madison, Tenn.
257. Manchester-Bedford. Bedford, N. H.
258. Manitoba Provincial Exhibition. Brandon, Mani., Can.
259. Manlius Bridle Pals. Fayetteville, N. Y.
260. Maple Ridge Equitation Centre. Haney, B.C., Can.
261. March Schooling. Huntington, N. Y.
262. Marlynn Farms Schooling. Bayside, Va.
263. Maryland Pony Breeders' Yearling Show. Timonium, Md.
264. Maryland P.H.A. Schooling.
265. Maryland P.H.A. Monkton, Md.
266. Maryland Pony Show. Timonium, Md.
267. Meadowbrook Jr. Horse Club. Meadowbrook, Pa.
268. Mecklenburg Hounds, Charlotte, N. C.
269. Mecklenburg Hounds Hunter Trials. Charlotte, N. C.
270. Melfort Fair. Melfort, Sask., Can.
271. Mendon. Pittsford, N. Y.
272. Mercer Hospital. Trenton, N. J.
273. Metamora Hunt. Oxford, Mich.
274. Metamora Hunt Young Entry. Metamora, Mich.
275. Metamora Schooling. Metamora, Mich.
276. Miami Charity. Miami, Fla.
277. Midas Show Stable. Orangeburg, N. Y.
278. Middlebury Hunt Hunter Trials. Middlebury, Conn.
279. Middlesex County. New Brunswick, N. J
280. Middleton Light Horse Show & Combined Event. (Combined Event). Middleton, N.S., Canada.
281. Middletown Rotary. Middletown, N. Y.
282. Mid-South Final. Pinehurst, N. C.
283. Mill Creek Hunt Hunter Trials. Wadsworth, Ill.
284. Millwood. Framingham Center, Mass.

285. Millwood Hunt. Framingham Center, Mass.
286. Milwaukee Hunt Final. Milwaukee, Wisc.
287. Milwaukee Hunt Junior. Milwaukee, Wisc.
288. Monmouth County. Oceanport, N. J.
289. Monterey National. Monterey, Calif.
290. Montpelier. Montpelier, Vt.
291. Moore County Hounds Hunter Trials. Southern Pines, N. C.
292. Moorestown. Moorestown, N. J.
293. Moundsville Lions Club. Moundsville, W. Va.
294. Mt. Airy Lions Horse & Pony. Mt. Airy, Md.
295 Nanticoke. Seaford, Del.
296. Nashville Jr. Riding Club. Nashville, Tenn.
297. National. New York, N. Y.
298. National Welsh Pony Show. Canfield, Ohio.
299. National Western. Denver, Colo.
300. Netherwood Acres Junior. Hyde Park, N. Y.
301. New Canaan Mounted Troop. New Canaan, Conn.
302. New Canaan Mounted Troop. New Canaan, Conn.
303. Newfields Youth Athletic Assn. Newfields, N. H.
304. New Hope. New Hope, Penna.
305. New Jersey P.H.A. Junior. Morristown, N. J.
306. New Jersey State Fair. Trenton, N. J.
307. New London Benefit. New London, N. H.
308. New Mexico State Fair. Albuquerque, N. M.
309. New Orleans Charity. New Orleans, La.
310. Newport. Portsmouth, R. I.
311. New York State Breeders. Syracuse, N. Y.
312. New York State Fair. Syracuse, N. Y.
313. N-H Riding Club. Durham, N. H.
314. North Carolina State Championship. Raleigh, N. C.
315. Northern Westchester P.H.A. Tilly Foster, N. Y.
316. North Middleboro Flying Club. North Middleboro, Mass.
317. North Shore. Stony Brook, N. Y.
318. North Shore Club of Equitation. Laurel Hollow, L.I., N. Y.
319. North Wind Farm. Burtonsville, Md.
320. Novato. Novato, Calif.

321. Oak Brook. Hinsdale, Ill.
322. Oak Hill Stables. Fredericksburg, Va.
323. Ogden Farms. Closter, N. J.
324. Ohio State Fair. Columbus, Ohio.
325. Oklahoma Hunter-Jumper. Oklahoma City, Okla.
326. Old Chatham Hunt. Old Chatham, N. Y.
327. Oldham County. Louisville, Ky.
328. Old Pueblo. Tucson, Ariz.
329. Onondaga Horseman's Ass'n. Fayetteville, N. Y.
330. Orange Co. Sheriff's Posse. Orlando, Fla.
331. Ottawa Valley Hunt. Aylmer, P.Q., Can.
332. Ould Newbury. Newbury, Mass.
333. Ox Ridge. Darien, Conn.
334. Ox Ridge Hunt Junior. Darien, Conn.
334-A. Pacific International. Portland, Ore.
335. Pacific National Exhibition. Vancouver, B.C., Can.
336. Parish Stables. Houston, Texas.
337. Pebble Beach. Pebble Beach, Calif.
338. Pebble Beach. Pebble Beach, Calif.
339. Pecos Valley Horsemen. Roswell, N. Mex.
340. Pecos Valley Jr. Championship. Roswell, N. M.
341. Pelham Bridge Stables. Pelham Bay Park, N. Y.
342. Pelham Bridge Stables. Pelham Bay Park, N.. Y.
343. Pelham Bridge Stables. Pelham Bridge, N. Y.
344. Pennsylvania National. Harrisburg, Pa.
345. Philomont. Philomont, Va.
346. Phoenix Hall Farm Jr. International. Cedar Valley, Ont., Can.
347. Phoenixville Area Jr. Phoenixville, Pa.
348. Pickering Hunt Hunter Trials. Chester Springs, Pa.
349. Pine Brae Club. Blawenburg, N. J.
350. Pinellas County Fair.
351. Riding Club. Buckingham, Pa.
352. Pin Oak Stables Charity. Houston, Texas.
353. Piping Rock. Locust Valley, N. Y.
354. Pittsford. Pittsford, N. Y.
355. Plains District Post. Broadway, Va.
356. Plymouth State Fair. Plymouth, N. H.
357. Pompano Beach. Pompano Beach, Fla.
358. Pony Patrol. Kirtland, Ohio.
359. Portland Meadows. Portland, Ore.
360. Prince Albert Fair. Prince Albert, Sask., Can.

361. Princess Anne Rotary. Princess Anne, Md.
362. Quentin. Quentin, Pa.
363. Quentin Riding Club. Quentin, Pa.
364. Ram Tap. Fresno, Calif.
365. Ravenhill Academy. Philadelphia, Pa.
366. Red Raider Camp Winter Championships. Novelty, Ohio.
367. Red River. Winnipeg, Man., Can.
369. Regina Winter Fair. Regina. Sask., Canada.
370. Rice Farms. Huntington, N. Y.
371. Rice Farms Jr. Huntington, N. Y.
372. Rideaway Farm Schooling. Weston, Conn.
373. Rio Grande. Albuquerque, N. Mex.
374. River Farms. Avon, Conn.
375. Rockbridge Hunt. Lexington, Va.
376. Rock Creek–Kentucky Home School. Louisville, Ky.
377. Rock Spring. West Orange, N. J.
378. Rolling Rock Hunt. Ligonier, Pa.
379. Rombout. Rhinebeck, N. Y.
380. Rose Tree Hunter Trials & Colt Show. Media, Pa.
381. Rose Tree Pony Show. Media, Pa.
382. Royal Oak. Northbrook, Ill.
383. Royal Winter Fair. Toronto, Can.
384. Rush Hospital. Malvern, Pa.
385. Sacramento Horsemen's Assn'. No. Highlands, Calif.
386. Sacramento Horsemen's Ass'n Greenies. No. Highlands, Calif.
387. Sacramento Horsemen's Assn. Jr. North Highlands, Calif.
388. Sacramento Riding Club. North Highlands, Calif.
389. Sacramento Valley Gymkhana Club. North Highlands, Calif.
390. St. Catharines. St. Catharines, Ont., Can.
391. St. James School of Horsemanship. Hauppauge, N. Y.
392. St. John's Church. New Vernon, N. J.
393. St. Jude's. Wynantskill, N. Y.
394. St. Paul's Parish. Haymarket, Va.
395. St. Stephen's Schooling. Catlett, Va.
396. Sands Point. Port Washington, N. Y.
397. Santa Barbara County Fair. Santa Maria, Calif.
398. Santa Barbara Co. Riding Club Jr. Santa Barbara, Calif.
399. Santa Barbara National. Santa Barbara. Calif.
400. Santa Barbara National Jr. Santa Barbara, Calif.
401. Saratoga Springs. Saratoga Springs, N. Y.

402. Saskatoon. Saskatoon, Sask., Can.
403. Saskatoon Exhibition. Saskatoon, Sask., Can.
404. Secor Farms. White Plains, N. Y.
405. Secor Farms. White Plains, N. Y.
406. Secor Farms. White Plains, N. Y.
407. Sedgefield. Greensboro, N. C.
408. Sedgefield Hunt Hunter Trials. Greensboro, N. C.
409. 1747 Farm. Weston, Mass.
410. Sewickley Hunt. Sewickley, Pa.
411. Shakerag Hounds Hunter Trial. Ocee, Ga.
412. Skidmore-Bennett. Saratoga Springs, N. Y.
413. Skyline Farm Junior. Valley Forge, Pa.
414. Sleepy Hollow. Scarborough, N. Y.
415. Sleepy Hollow. Scarborough, N. Y.
416. Sleepy Hollow Country Club. Scarborough-on-Hudson, N. Y.
417. Smith College. Northampton, Mass.
418. Smith College. Northampton, Mass.
419. Smithtown. Smithtown, N. Y.
420. Smithtown Hunt Hunter Trials. Stony Brook, N. Y.
421. Southampton. Southampton, N. Y.
422. Southampton Jr. Southampton, N. Y.
423. Southern California. Del Mar, Calif.
424. Southern Michigan P.H.A. Metamora, Mich.
425. Southern Seminary. Buena Vista, Va.
426. South Miami. South Miami, Fla.
427. Springbrook Driving & Riding Club. Rhinebeck, N. Y.
428. Spring Valley. New Vernon, N. J.
429. Staunton River. Altavista, Va.
430. Sterling School. Dover, Pa.
431. Stone Ridge Jr. Potomac, Md.
432. Stowe Riding & Driving Club. Stowe, Vt.
433. Sugartown. Newtown Square, Pa.
434. Sunnyfield Farm. Bedford, N. Y.
435. Sunnyfield Farm. Bedford, N. Y.
436. Sussex County, Branchville, N. J.
437. Sussex County 4-H. Newton, N. J.
438. Sutton. Sutton, Ont., Can.
439. Sweet Briar Spring. Sweet Briar, Va.
440. Syracuse P.H.A. Syracuse, N. Y.
441. Talbot Co. Combined School Show. St. Michaels, Md.
442. Talbot County Children's Combined Show. Easton, Md.
443. Talbot County Horse & Pony. Easton, Md.
444. Tampa. Tampa, Fla.
445. Tatum Chamber of Commerce. Tatum, N. M.
446. The Country Meet. Ambler, Pa.

447. The Riding Club, Inc. Indian Hill, Ohio.
448. Thornhill Junior. Thornhill, Ont., Can.
449. Tidewater Horse & Pony. Norfolk, Va.
450. Timber Trails Riding Club. Sherman, Conn.
451. Toronto. Willowdale, Ont., Can.
453. Tracefield Hunter Trials. Franklin, Tenn.
454. Trout Valley. Cary, Ill.
455. Troy Lions Club. Clums Corners, N. Y.
456. Truro Church. Fairfax, Va.
457. Tryon & Hound. Tryon, N. C.
458. Tryon Hounds Colt Show. Landrum, S. C.
459. Tulsa Charity. Tulsa, Okla.
460. Twenty Mile Farm Hunt. Grapevine, Texas.
461. Twin Benefit. Woodinville, Wash.
462. Twin Brooks. Linglestown, Pa.
463. Twin Brooks. Linglestown, Pa.
464. Tyrell Park Charity. Beaumont, Texas.
465. Tyrrell Park Junior Riders. Beaumont, Texas.
466. Union Hose Fire Co. Annville, Pa.
467. University League Spring. Charlottesville, Va.
468. Upland. Unionville, Pa.
469. Upper Darby. Newtown Square, Pa.
470. Upperville Colt & Horse Show. Upperville, Va.
471. U.S.E.T. Benefit. Avon, Ohio.
472. U.S.E.T. Benefit. Denver, Colo.
473. Valley Forge Farm Hunter Trials. Valley Forge, Pa.
474. Valley Hunt Club. Lewis Run, Pa.
475. Valley Hunt Club Jr. Lewis Run, Pa.
476. Valley Inter-School. Waynesboro, Va.
477. Vassar. Poughkeepsie, N. Y.
478. Vassar Collegiate. Poughkeepsie, N. Y.
479. Vermilion Fair. Vermilion, Alta., Can.
480. Vestavia Jr. Birmingham, Ala.
481. Victoria Riding Academy Jr. Victoria, B.C., Can.
482. Victory Lee. Concord, Mass.
483. Virginia State. Richmond, Va.
484. Warrenton. Warrenton, Va.
485. Warrenton Hunt Hunter Trials. Warrenton, Va.
486. Warrenton Pony Show. Warrenton, Va.
487. Warrington Horse & Pony. Warrington, Pa.
488. Washington Bridle Trails. Washington, D. C.
489. Washington Bridle Trails Jr. Chevy Chase, Md.
490. Washington International. Washington, D. C.
491. Washington-Lee. Merrifield, Va.
492. Washington Lions Club. Washington, Pa.
493. Washington State Hunter-Jumper. Seattle, Wash.
494. Washington State Hunter-Jumper. Seattle, Wash.
495. Washington State USET Benefit. Kirkland. Wash.
496. Watchung Hunter. Summit, N. J.
497. Watchung Riding & Driving Club. Union County Park, Summit, N. J.
498. Waterloo Hunt. Grass Lake, Mich.
499. Waverly Farms Schooling. Ojus, Fla.
500. Waynesville. Waynesville, N. C.
501. Wayzata Country Club. Wayzata, Minn.
502. Western New York P.H.A. Avon, N. Y.
503. Western Pa. P.H.A. Sewickley, Pa.
504. Western Run 4-H. Timonium, Md.
505. West Jersey Hospital. Camden, N. J.
506. Westmoreland Hunt. Greensburg, Pa.
507. West Virginia State Championship. Charleston, W. Va.
508. West Virginia State Fair. Lewisburg-Ronceverte, W. Va.
509. Whitelands Hunter. Exton, Pa.
510. Williamsport Charity. Williamsport, Pa.
511. Windward Stable. Long Grove, Ill.
512. Winnipeg Jr. Horsemen. Winnipeg, Mani, Can.
513. Winston-Salem. Winston-Salem, N. C.
514. Wisconsin State Fair. Milwaukee, Wisc.
515. Wissahickon Valley. Philadelphia, Pa.
516. Woodbrook Hunt Club. Tacoma, Wash.
517. Woodhill. Wayzata, Minn.
518. Woodland Riding Club. West Orange, N. J.
519. Woodstock. South Woodstock, Vt.
520. Wyomissing Riding Club. Wyomissing, Pa.

ANNUAL ROSTER OF THE ORGANIZED HUNTS OF AMERICA, 1962-1963
The following list was supplied by the Masters of Foxhounds Association of America and is reprinted here from *The Chronicle of the Horse* (September 21, 1962.)

Aiken Hounds. Box 317, Aiken, South Carolina.

Arapahoe Hunt. Route 1, Box 62, Littleton, Colorado.

Battle Creek Hunt. Riverside Drive, Battle Creek, Michigan.

Beaufort Hunt. R.D. 1, Harrisburg. Pennsylvania.

Bloomfield Open Hunt. Bloomfield Hills, Oakland County, Michigan.

Blue Ridge Hunt. Millwood, Clarke County, Virginia.

Branchwater Hunt. Fox Valley Farm, Route 1, Maylene, Alabama.

Brandywine Hounds. R.D. No. 5, West Chester, Pennsylvania.

Bridlespur Hunt. Defiance, St. Charles County, Missouri.

Bull Run Hunt. Manassas, Virginia.

Camargo Hunt. 628 Dixie Terminal Building, Cincinnati 2, Ohio.

Camden Hunt. Camden, South Carolina.

Casanova Hunt. Casanova, Virginia.

Chagrin Valley Hunt. Gates Mills, Ohio.

Chestnut Ridge Hunt. New Geneva, Pennsylvania.

Deep Run Hunt. Richmond, Virginia.

Eagle Farms Hunt. R.F.D. 1, Chester Springs, Pennsylvania.

Eglinton Hunt. R. R. 1, Don Mills, Ontario, Canada.

Elkridge-Harford Hunt. Monkton, Maryland.

Essex Fox Hounds. Peapack, New Jersey.

Fairfax Hunt, The. Sunset Hills, Virginia.

Fairfield County Hounds. Westport, Connecticut.

Farmington Hunt. R.F.D. No. 2, Charlottesville, Virginia.

Foxcatcher Hounds. Fair Hill (P.O., Elkton), Cecil County, Maryland.

Fox River Valley Hunt. 357 Donlea Road, Barrington, Illinois.

Genesee Valley Hunt. The "Homestead," Box 5, Geneseo, New York.

Glenmore Hunt. Staunton, Virginia.

Golden's Bridge Hounds. North Salem, New York.

Goshen Hunt. Box 222, Olney, Maryland.

Green Spring Valley Hounds. Glyndon, Maryland.

Groton Hunt. Box 107, Pepperell, Massachusetts.

Hamilton Hunt. 848 Main Street East, Hamilton, Ontario, Canada.

Harts Run Hunt. R. D. 5, Gibsonia, Pennsylvania.

Hillboro Hounds. Brentwood, (P.O. 3312 West End Avenue, Nashville 5,) Tennessee.

Howard County Hunt, The. Ellicott City, Maryland.

Mr. Hubbard's Kent County Hounds. Chestertown, Maryland.

Huntingdon Valley Hunt. Doylestown, Pennsylvania.

Iroquois Hunt. Lexington, Kentucky.

Mr. Jeffords' Hounds. Andrews Bridge, Christiana, Pennsylvania.

Keswick Hunt. Keswick, Albemarle County, Virginia.

Lake of Two Mountains Hunt, The. Como, Vaudreuil County, Quebec, Canada.

Lauray Hunt. Bath, Ohio.

Limestone Creek Hunt. Troop "K" Road, Manlius, New York.

Litchfield County Hounds. Litchfield, Connecticut.

London Hunt. P. O. Box 2094, London, Ontario, Canada.

Longreen Fox Hounds. Germantown, Tennessee.

Long Lake Hounds. 1385 E. County Road, E., White Bear Lake, Minnesota.

Los Altos Hunt. Woodside, California.

Loudoun Hunt. Leesburg, Virginia.

Marlborough Hunt. Upper Marlboro, Maryland.

Meadow Brook Hounds. Glen Head, Long Island New York.

Mecklenburg Hounds. Route 1, Box 314, Matthews, North Carolina.

Metamora Hunt. 5614 Barber Road, Metamora, Lapeer County, Michigan.

Miami Valley Hunt. Highview Terrace, Bellbrook, Ohio.

Middleburg Hunt. Middleburg, Loudoun County, Virginia.

Middlebury Hunt. Middlebury, (P.O. 711, Pearl Lake Road, Waterbury), Connecticut.

Midland Fox Hounds, The. P.O. Box 1360, Columbus, Georgia.

Millbrook Hunt. Millbrook, Dutchess County, New York.

Mill Creek Hunt. Wadsworth, Illinois. (P.O. Address: Box 510, Lake Forest, Illinois).

Millwood Hunt. Edmands Road, Framingham, Massachusetts.

Mission Valley Hunt. Bunting Farm, Route 1, Stillwell, Kansas.

Monmouth County Hunt. Box 588, Red Bank, New Jersey.

Montpelier Hunt. Montpelier Station, Virginia.

Montreal Hunt. P.O. Box 58, St. Andrews East, P. Q. Canada.

Moore County Hounds. Southern Pines, Moore County, North Carolina.

Myopia Hunt. South Hamilton, Massachusetts.

Norfolk Hunt. Dover, (P.O. c/o Mr. Neil Morse, 294 Washington St., Boston 9) Massachusetts.

Oak Brook Hounds. R.D. 2, Hinsdale, Illinois.

Oak Grove Hunt. Box 39, Germantown, Tennessee.

Old Chatham Hunt. Old Chatham, New York.

Old Dominion Hounds. Orlean, Virginia.

Orange County Hunt. The Plains, Fauquier County, Virginia.

Ottawa Valley Hunt. 341 3rd Avenue, Ottawa 1, Ontario, Canada.

Pickering Hunt. R.D. 2, Phoenixville, Pennsylvania.

Piedmont Fox Hounds. Upperville Fauquier County, Virginia.

Potomac Hunt, The. 12200 Glen Road, Rockville, Maryland.

Radnor Hunt. White Horse (P.O. Malvern), Chester County, Pennsylvania.

Rappahannock Hunt. Sperryville, Virginia.

Redland Hunt. Clover Hill, Brookeville, Maryland.

Rockbridge Hunt. Box 1156, Lexington, Virginia.

Rocky Fork-Headley Hunt. Clarke State Road, Gahanna, Ohio.

Rolling Rock Hunt. Ligonier, Pennsylvania.

Rombout Hunt. Salt Point, New York.

Rose Tree Fox Hunting Club. Media, Pennsylvania.

Sedgefield Hunt. c/o W. C. Boren, III, P.O. Box 9172, Greensboro, North Carolina.

Sewickley Hunt. Sewickley, Pennsylvania.

Shakerag Hounds. 3134 Maple Drive, N.E., Atlanta 5, Georgia.

Smithtown Hunt. Wide Water Farm, Stony Brook, L. I., N. Y.

Spring Valley Hounds. New Vernon, New Jersey.

Mr. Stewart's Cheshire Foxhounds. Unionville, Chester County, Pennsylvania.

Toronto and North York Hunt. Beverley Farm, Aurora, Ontario, Canada.

Traders Point Hunt. R.D. 1, Zionsville, Indiana.

Tryon Hounds. Tryon, North Carolina.

Vicmead Hunt. P.O. Box 3501, Wilmington, Delaware.

Warrenton Hunt. Warrenton, Virginia.

Waterloo Hunt. Katz Road, Route No. 3, Grass Lake, Michigan.

Wayne–Du Page Hunt. Wayne, DuPage County, Illinois.

West Hills Hunt. 11050 Winnetka Boulevard, Chatsworth, California.

Westmoreland Hunt. Greensburg, Pennsylvania.

Whitelands – Perkiomen Valley Hunt. Guthriesville, Pennsylvania.

Wissahickon Hounds. Gwynedd Valley, Pennsylvania.

Woodbrook Hunt. 5818 Orchard Street, S.W., Tacoma 99, Washington.

Bibliography

The following are the source materials used in obtaining the facts in this encyclopedia. In addition to the works of the authors listed I consulted the *Encyclopedia Britannica,* the *Encyclopedia Americana* and special literature sent to me by the various breeder's associations, The Jockey Club, the T. R. A., and the Steeplechase Associations.

THE ORIGIN OF THE HORSE AND SPECIFIC BREEDS

AMERICAN THOROUGHBRED BREEDER'S ASSOCIATION. *The Blood Horse.* A weekly published in Lexington, Ky.

BORDON, SPENCER, *The Arab Horse.* Doubleday, Page and Co., New York, 1906.

BROWN, W. ROBINSON. *The Horse of the Desert.* The Macmillan Co., New York, 1936.

BRUNS, URSULA. *Ponies.* D. Van Nostrand Company, Inc., Princeton N.J.

COLLINS, ROBERT W. *Race Horse Training.* The Blood Horse, Lexington, Ky., 1938.

DINSMORE, WAYNE AND JOHN HENRY. *Our Equine Friends.* Horse and Mule Association, Chicago, 1944.

DISSTON, GENERAL HARRY. *Know About Horses.* Devin-Adair Co., New York, 1961.

DODGE, THEODORE AYRAULT. *Riders of Many Lands.* Houghton, Mifflin and Co., Boston, 1901.

HARRIS, ALBERT W. *The Blood of the Arab.* The Arabian Horse Club of America, Chicago, 1941.

KAYS, D. J. *The Horse: Judging, Breeding, Feeding, Management, Selling.* A. S. Barnes and Co., New York, 1953.

KELLEY, ROBERT. *The Thoroughbred Horse.* The Thoroughbred Racing Associations, New York, 1943.

LINDSLEY, D. C. *Morgan Horses.* C. M. Saxton and Co., New York, 1857.

LUARD, L. D. *The Horse, Its Anatomy and Action.* Countryman Press, New York.

RASWAN, CARL. *Drinkers of the Wind.* The Creative Age Press, New York, 1943.

ROOSEVELT, THEODORE. *Ranch Life and the Hunting Trail.* Century Co., New York, 1897.

STONG, PHIL. *Horses and Americans.* Frederick A. Stokes and Co., New York, 1939.

SUMMERHAYS, R. S. *The Observer's Book of Horses and Ponies.* Frederick Warne & Co., Ltd., London.

TAYLOR, W. G. LANGWORTHY. *The Saddle Horse.* Henry Holt and Co., New York, 1925.

TENNESSEE STATE DEPARTMENT OF AGRICULTURE. *The Horse and His Heritage in Tennessee.* Nashville, 1945.

TREVATHAN, CHARLES E. *The American Thoroughbred.* Macmillan, New York, 1905.

WINDISCH-GRAETZ, MATHILDE. *The Spanish Riding School.* The Countryman Press, New York.

THE HORSE IN SPORT AND WAR

AKERS, DWIGHT. *Drivers Up,* G. P. Putnam's Sons, New York, 1938.

ALDIN, CECIL. *Ratcatcher to Scarlet,* Charles Scribner's Sons, New York.

———, *Scarlet to M.F.H.,* Charles Scribner's Sons, New York, 1933.

AMERICAN HORSE SHOWS ASSOCIATION. *Rule Book, New York,* 1945.

BECKFORD, PETER. *Thoughts upon Hunting.* Cape and Ballou, New York, 1932.

BENT, NEWELL. *American Polo,* Macmillan, New York, 1929.

BERRY, MICHAEL. *Hunting by Ear,* D. W. E. Brock, London, 1937.

BIRKET, LADY. *Hunting Lays and Ways.* McRae Smith, Philadelphia.

BROCK, D. W. E., *The A. B. C. of Foxhunting,* Charles Scribner's Sons, New York, 1936.

CARTER, WM. S. H., *Horses, Saddles and Bridles,* The Baltimore Press, Baltimore.

DISSTON, HARRY. *Equestionaire,* Harper Bros., New York, 1926.

DEVEREUX. W. B., *Polo,* Brooks Bros., New York, 1914.

FREDERICH (and others), *Foxhunting,* The Lonsdale Library, Lippincott, Philadelphia, 1930.

HIGGINSON, E. HENRY, M.F.H., *Try Back,* Huntingdon Press, New York, 1931.

HIGGINSON & CHAMBERLAIN, *Hunting in the United States and Canada,* Derrydale Press, New York, 1928.

JOCKEY CLUB, *Rules of Racing,* Jockey Club, New York, 1943.

KNOTT, O'MALLY, *Gone Away with O'Mally,* Doubleday, Doran & Co., New York, 1944.

LYON, W. E., *In My Opinion,* Constable, London, 1928.

MILLER, LT. COL. E. D., C.B.E., D.S.O., *Modern Polo,* Hurst & Blackett, London.

MILITARY SERVICE PUBLISHING CO., *R.O.T.C. Cavalry Manual, Basic,* Harrisburg, Pa., 1942.

"SCRUTATOR," *Letters on Hunting,* Phillip Hallan & Co., Philadelphia.

THOMAS, JOSEPH B., *Hounds and Hunting Through the Ages,* Windward House, New York, 1928.

THOROUGHBRED RACING ASSOCIATIONS, *Thoroughbred Racing and Breeding,* New York, 1945.

WINN, MATT J., *Down the Stretch,* Smith and Durrell, New York, 1945.

WRENCH, F. A., *Horses in Sport,* Morrow, New York, 1937.

EQUITATION; CARE AND TRAINING OF HORSES

ANDERSON & COLLIER, *Riding and Driving,* Macmillan, New York.

BARRETT, MAJ. L. M., *Practical Jumping,* Country Life Ltd., London, 1930.

BEACH, BELLE, *Riding and Driving for Women,* Charles Scribner's Sons, New York, 1912.

BEUDANT, E., *Horse Training, Outdoor and High School,* Charles Scribner's Sons, New York, 1931.

BROOKE, MAJ. GEN. GEOFFREY, *Horse Sense and Horsemanship,* Charles Scribner's and Sons, New York, 1934.

———. *Horsemen All.* Scribner, New York, 1938.

———. *Way of a Man With a Horse.* Scribner, New York, 1924.

———. *Horse Lovers.* Scribner, New York. 1937.

CHAMBERLIN, LT. COL. HARRY D. *Training Hunters and Jumpers and Hacks.* Derrydale Press, New York, 1937.

———, *Riding and Schooling Horses,* Derrydale Press, New York, 1937.

DE SOUSA, BARON, *Principles of Equitation,* E. P. Dutton and Co., New York, 1922.

———, *Advanced Equitation,* E. P. Dutton and Co., New York.

FAWSETT, WM., *Thoroughbred and Hunter,* Charles Scribner's Sons, New York, 1934.

HAYES, CAPT., *Veterinary Notes for Horse Owners,* Hurst and Brockett, London, 1924.

HANCE, CAPT. J. E., *School for Horse and Rider,* Charles Scribner's Sons, New York, 1932.

"JORROCKS," *The Private Stable,* Little, Brown and Co., Boston, 1899.

LITTAUER, CAPT. V. S., *Jumping the Horse, Riding Forward, More About Riding Forward,* all privately printed in New York, no dates given.

LYON, W. E., *First Aid Hints for the Horse Owner,* Charles Scribner's Sons, New York, 1934.

McTAGGART, COL. M. F., D.S.O., *Mount and Man,* Country Life Ltd., London, 1925.

SANTINI, PIERRO, *The Forward Impulse,* Huntingdon Press, New York, 1936.

SELF, MARGARET CABELL, *Teaching the Young to Ride,* Harper Bros., 1935.

———, *Horses, Their Selection, Care and Handling,* A. S. Barnes and Co., New York, 1943.

———, *Fun on Horseback,* A. S. Barnes and Co., New York, 1944.

WIDMER, JACK, *Practical Horse Breeding and Training,* Charles Scribner's Sons, New York, 1945.

INDEX

(Page numbers in italics indicate illustration)

A

Abdallah, 131
Abrasions, 198
Accidents, 7
  bolting, 39
  cast horse, 58
  falls, 101
  leading horse through narrow door, 7, 91, 218
Across the board, 8
Adios Butler, *142*
Adonis, 106
Age, 8
  average, 8
  how to tell, 8
Aged horse, 8
Agoraphobia, 9, 372
  stall courage, 9, 118, 342, 372
Aids (natural), 9
  between the rider's hands and legs, 34
  collection, 70
  dressage, 93
  leg employment, 9
  punishment, 10
  reins, use of, 9, 295
  reward, 10
  riding, 297
  training the horse, 362
  weight, distribution of, 9
Aids (artificial), 10
Albino horses, 10
  Hirohito's, *11*
  origin, 153
Allen, 103
Allowance race, 10
Alter, 10
Amateur, 10
  classes, 11
  driving fine harness horse, 170
  driving single harness horse, 136, 171
  hunters, 167
  jumpers, 168
  riding five-gaited saddle horse, 169

  riding three-gaited saddle horse, 169
  riding walking horse, 173
Amazonia, 131
Amble, 11
  rompu, 293, 322
American
  Breeding Associations, 46
  breeds, 11, 46
  Hackney Horse Society, 11
  Horse Shows Association, 11
  Quarter Horse Association, 12
  racing manual, 12
  Saddle Horse. *See* Saddle Horse
  Saddle Horse Breeders Association, 13
Anthrax, 13
Antitoxin, 13, 330
Apaloosa, 14
Apocalypse, Four Hosremen of, 13
Apoplexy, 14
Appetite, 15
  loss of, 15, 356
Apples, 110
Appointment classes, 15
Appointments, 15, 92
  coachman, 15
  Corinthian hunters, 167
  four-in-hands with park harness, 15, 136, 171
  gig class, 15, 136, 170
  harness classes, 15, 136, 171
  honorary huntsman, 16
  honorary whipper-in, 16
  hunt teams, 167
  hunting, 16, 190
  lady member, 17
  lady's phaeton, 15
  master, 16
  member, 17
  pairs of roadsters, 170
  personal, 16
  pony classes, 16
  professional huntsman, 16
  professional whipper-in, 16

  servant, 15
  single roadster, 170
  stock horse, 17
  tack, 17, 352
Appuyer, 18, 308, *310*, 364
Aptitudes, 18
  in riders, 18
  natural, in horses, 18
Arab and his horse, 18
Arab Horse Journal, 18
Arabian horse, 18, *19*, *156*, 157
  Associations, 22
  characteristics, 20
  classification, 19
  News, 22
  origin, 19
Arabian saddle, 318
Arms, 23, *150*
Arroyo, 23
Arterxerxes, 104
Arthritis, 23
Artillery gun teams, 174
A.S.P.C.A., 23
Asthma, 23
Auction system of betting, 33
Australian horses, 23
  "walers," 23
Automobiles, 23
Azoturia (Monday morning disease), 24

B

Babbler, 181
Back, 24
  double back, 24
  hogback, 24
  to try back, 24
  to back, 24
Backing, 24
Backing out of stall, 369
Backing race, 24
Bagman, 181
Balance, 24, 54
  balance seat, 25, *26*
  burden of horse, 54
  horse's balance, 24, 54
  rider's balance, 25

Balking, 218, 370, 372
Ballasting, 27
Bandages, 27
  for infections, 197
  for injuries, 197
Bank, 27, 29
Bar bit, 34
Bar shoe, 334
Barb, 29
Barbary pack, 181
Bareback riding, 29
Barn rat, 30, 371
Barranca, 30
Barrel racing, 30
Basketball (mounted), 30
Basket cart. See Carts, 58
Bat wings, 377
Bay horse, 31, 70
Beagle, 181
Bearing reins, 64
Belgian Draft Horse
  Corporation of America, 31
Belgian horse, 31
Belle Beach, 31, 149
Bellfounder, 131
Bending race, 32
Betting systems, 32, 290
  auction system, 33
  bookmaking, 32
  pari-mutuel, 33
  stake holder, 32
Bike, 34
  single roadster shown to,
    170
Billet, 182
Billet straps, 312
Binder, 182
Birth, 52, 71
Birthday, 34
Biting, 368
  at other horses, 372
Bits, 34 35. See also Bridles
  adjustment of, 36
  bridoon, 34
  champing of, 62
  choosing of, 36
  curb, 34
  double ring snaffle, 36
  driving bits, 34
  eating in, 372
  fitting, 36
  Hanoverian pelham, 36
  hunting snaffle, 36
  Kimberwick, 36
  pelham, 34, 35
  riding bits, 34
  snaffle, 35, 35
  twisted snaffle, 36

wire snaffle, 36
Bitting, 36, 78
Bitting rig, 37, 78
Black Beauty, 105
Black Hawk family, 37, 103
Black horse, 70
Black points, 37
Blank, 182
Blanket tearing, 369
Blankets, 37
Bleeder, 38
Blemishes, 38
Blind country, 182
Blind staggers. See Megrims,
  231
Blistering, 38
Blood (blooded), 182
Blood bay, 70
Blood heat, 39
Blood tests, 39
Blue ticked, 182
Body inclination, 192
Bog spavins, 39, 201, 334
Boils, 199, 334
Bolt, 39
Bolt a fox, 182
Bolting, 39, 371
Bone, 39
  side bones, 202, 336
  spavins, 201
Book, 40
Bookmaking, 32
Boots, 40
  for horse, 40
  quarter boot, 284
  shoe boil boot, 334
  for rider, 41
Boring, 372
Bottom, 182
Bowed tendon, 41, 201
Bowing, 41
Box stall, 42
Breaking, 72
Breaking cart, 43
Breast high scent, 182
Breastplate, 43
Breeches, 44
Breeching, 135
Breeders, leading, 392
Breeding, 44
  Associations, 47
  nicks, 44
Breeding classes, 46, 172
  general specifications, 172
  heavy harness ponies, 172
Breeds, 46
  origin of horse, 153
Breeze, 47

Bridle path hacks, local, 166
Bridles, 35. See also Bits
  adjustment, 47
  care, 48
  full bridle, 35
  hackamore, 76
  types and parts, 48
Bridling, 49
  headshy horse, 50, 51
  placing bit, 50
Bridoon bit, 34
Brisket, 51
Broke horse, 377
Broken amble, 51, 293
Broken knees, 51
Broken lines, 51
Bronc, 51, 377
Brood-mares, 52
Broom polo, 53
Broomtail, 53, 377
Brown horse, 70
Bruises, 200
Brush jumps, 146
Brush of fox, 53, 182
Brush racing, 53, 137
Brushes, 53
Brushing, 53
Bucephalus, 103
Buckeroo, 53, 377
Bucking, 371
Bucking strap, 377
Buckling over, 54
Buckskin dun, 71
  black points, 37
Buffalo Bill, 54
Build a loop, 377
Bulldogging, 54, 377
Bullfinch, 54, 182
Bun eating contest, 54
Burden of horse, 54. See
  also Balance
Burning scent, 182
Burns, 200
Burst, 182
Busqué, 55
Butte, 377
Buying the horse, 55
  age, 8
  manners, 228
  soundness, 338
  vices, 368
Bye Day, 56, 182
Byerly Turk, 56, 103

C

Cadence, 56
Calgary Stampede, 56

Camp, 56
Camuse, 20, 57
Canadian pox, 57
Cannon bone, 39, 57
Canter, 57, 103
  false start, 103
  flying change, 117
  gallop depart, 119, 301
  leads, 219
  of walking horse, 173
Cantle, 57, *320*
Canyon pony, 57
Capped elbow (shoe boil)
  58, 334
Capped hock, 58
Capping fee, 58
Capriole, 94
Carriage (of head), 58
Carrots, as food, 110
Cart (two-wheeled vehicle),
  58, 366
  breaking cart, 43
Cast, 58, 182
Cast horse, 58, 101
Cat foot, 183
Catch hold, 182
Catch weights, 59
Cavalletti, 59
Cavalry, 59, *60*
Cavalry schools, 60
Cavesson, 48, 61
Cavvy, 377
Cavvy wrango, 377
Cayuse, 65, 377
Centaur, 61
Center fire rig, 61, 377
Certification, 61
Cesaresco, Count Martinengo,
  62
Challenge, 183
Challenge trophy, 62
Champing the bit, 62
Championship classes, 62
  fine harness, 170
  five-gaited saddle horse,
    169
    junior, 169
  heavy harness horse, 170
  hunter, 63
  jumper, 168
  single roadster, 170
  stock horse, 172
  three-gaited saddle horses,
    169
    pony class, 169
  walking horse, 173
Change foxes, 183
Change of lead, 63, 117, 119

Chaparajos (or "chaps"),
  63, 377
Charger (officer's), 63, 174
Charging, 370
Charles, Charles James, 183
Charlier shoe, 335
Charro, 63
'Chaser, 64
Check, 183
Check pieces, 48
Checkreins (bearing reins),
  64
Cheek strap, 48, *135*
Cheer, 183
Chicken coop, 64
Chinese tag, 352
Chop, 183
Chronicle of the Horse, 64
Chuck wagon, 65, 378
Chute, 65, 378
Cinch (cincha), 378
Circles, 65
Circus horse, 66
Claiming race, 67, 291
Classes. See Horseshow classes
  appointments, 15
Classical seat, 329
Clay family, 67
Claybank dun, 71
Clean limbs, 67
Cleaning, 121, 152
Cleveland Bay, *67, 68*
Cleveland Bay Society of
  America, 68
Clever, 68
Clipping, 152
Close a cast, 182
Close order drill, 68
Clover hay, 110
Clucking, 68
Clydesdale, 68, *69*
Clydesdale Breeders
  Association, 68
Coachman, 15
Coat, 68
Cob, 68
Cocking cart, 58
Cockstail, 183
Coffin bone, 69
Cold blooded horse, 69
Cold line, 183
Colds, 69
Colic, 69
Collected gaits, 24, 69
Collection, 70
Color patterns, 71
Colors of horse, 70

Colt, 71, *73*
  bitting, 36, 78
  bitting rig, 37, 78
  breaking cart, 43
  care, 73
  feeding, 73, 112
  hackamore, 76
  halter-breaking, 75
  hunters, 165
  longe, 76
  mounting, 80
  saddle instruction, 80
  training, 75
  weaning, 74
Combination horses, 81, 169
Combination ticket, 8
Comic bareback jumper
  class, 168
Commercial horsefeed, 110
Conditioning, 81
  feeding, 112
  general care, 152
Conestoga horses, 81
Confidence, 81
Conformation, 82
  hunter championships, 63
  hunter classes, 165
Congestion of lungs, 82
Connemara, 88
Consolation working
  hunters, 168
Constipation, 82
Contracted heels, 82, 113,
  202
Controlling horse, 297
Coolers, 82
Cooling lotions, 82
Copenhagen, 103
Copperbottom, 103
Corinthian classes, 15, 83,
  167
Corkran of Clamstretch, 105
Corn feed, 110
Corns, 202
Coronet, *150*
Coughs, 83
Counter, 183
Counterchange (of hands),
  83
Couples, 83, 183
Courbette, 94
Course, 183
Courtesy, 83
Covert, 85, 183
Covert-hack, 183
Cowboy, cowpunch, cow-
  poke, 85, 378
Cowboy seat, 329

Cowhocked, 85
Cow pony, 85, 378
Cracked heels, 200
Crash, 183
Crest, *150*
Cribbing, 86, 369
Criollo, 86, 157, 277
Critter, 86, 378
Crop, 86
Crop eared, 86
Cropper, 183
Crosstag, 86
Croup, *150*
Crowding, 368
Crown piece, 48
Crupper, 86
Cry, 183
Cub, 183
Cub hunting, 86, 183
    rat-catcher, 188
Cubbing, 86
Curb, 87
Curb chain, 34, 148
Curby hocks, 87
Currant jelly, 184
Curry comb, 121
Cut and come again
    countries, 88, 184
Cut and laid fence, 184
Cuts, 233
Cutting, 88
Cutting grounds, 378
Cutting out, 88, 378
Cutting pony, 88, 378

D

Dab, dab a line, 378
Daily double, 88
Daisy-cutter, 88
Dam, 88
Dandy brush, 121
Darley Arabian, 88, 103
David Harum's balky horse,
    105
Dead heat, 88, *89*
Dealers, 55
Den, 184
Den bark, 184
Den dog, 184
Denmark, 89, 103
Derby, 89
Dew claw, 184
Dewlap, 184
Diagonals, 90
Diamond, 105
Diarrhea in horses, 327
Dictator, 103

Direction, changes of, 90
Diseases, *See* Injuries and
    diseases
Dishing, 90
Dismounting, 90, 297
Distance, 90
    long distance rides, 96
Dock, 91
Docking, 91
Dog, 91
Dogcart, 58
Dog fox, 184
Dog hound, 184
Dogie, 378
Doors in stable, 91
Doping, 91
Double, 184
Double back, 91
Double oxer, 92, 187
Doubling the horn, 184
Draft, 184
Draft horses, 173
Drag, 92, 184
Drag hounds, 184
Drain, 184
Draw, 184
Draw blank, 184
Draw rein, 92
Dress, 15, 92. *See also*
    Appointments
    boots, 40
    breeches, 44
    rat-catcher clothes, 188
    vests, 367
Dressage, 93, 222, 303
Drivers, 398
Driving, 94
    with long reins, 76
Drop fence, 184
Dropped fox, 184
Dropped noseband, 61
Dude, 95, 378
Dude ranch, 95, 378
Dumb jockey, 37, 78
Dun, 70
    black points, 37
    Claybank dun, 71
    mouse, 71
Dust a horse, fan a horse,
    378
Dutch book, 32
Dwelling, 184

E

Ears, 95
Earth, 184
Earth stopper, 185

Earth stopping, 185
Eating in bit, 372
Egg and spoon race, 96
Egyptian horses, early, *154*
Eleuin, 185
Encephalitis, 96
Endurance (of horse), 96
England (development of
    horse in), 97
English hunting seat, 98
English saddle, 316
Enlisted men's jumping
    classes, 174
Enter, 185
Entering a stall, 98
Equestrian, 98
Equestrian classes, 98
Equipment, 98
    appointments, 15
    bits, 34
    blankets, 37
    bridles, 47
    dress, 92
    grooming tools, 121
    saddles, 316
    stable equipment, 341
    tack, 352
    tack room, 352
Equitation, 98
    breaking and training of
        colts, 75
    care and training of
        horses, 411
    classes, 98, 174
        jumping classes, 174
        riding classes, 174
        stock classes, 175
    dressage, 93
    exercises, 299
    jumping, 209
    riding, 297
Equus Agilis, 154
Equus Przewalskii, 154
Equus Robustus, 154
Equus Tarpanus, 154
Ergot, 99
Ethan Allen, 104, 370
Evolution of horse, 154
Ewe-neck, 99
Exercise
    for horse, 99, 350
    for rider, 299, 350
Exmoor pony, 99
Eye (of horse), 99
    ophthalmia, 254
    test for soundness, 357
Eye to hounds, 185

Eyesight (of horse), 100

F

Falls, 101
  cast horse, 58, 101
  horse falling, 101
  injuries, 200
  lameness, 215
  rider falling, 101
False quarter, 202
False start, 103
Famous horses, 103
Famous horses of fiction, 104
Farcy, 107
Fastest races at one mile, 386
Fault (check), 185
Faults in jumping, 107, 212
Fear, 107
  in horse, 107
  in rider, 108
Feathered shoe, 117
Feathering, 185
Feathers, 109
Federation Equestre Internationale, 114, 173, 213
Feed, 109, 111
  apples, 110
  bran, 109
  carrots, 110
  commercial horsefeed, 110
  corn, 110
  fresh forage, 110
  grass, 110
  hay, 110
  Hydroponic Green Feeds, 111
  linseed meal, 110, 222
  mashes, 230
  New Hope, 111
  oats, 109, 253
  salt, 111, 325
Feeding, 112
  laxative diet, 217
  of colts, 73
  overfeeding, 254
  schedule, 112
  watering, 375
Feed mangers, 113
Feel, 113
Feet of horse, 113, *114*
  brittle feet, 202
  injuries, 202
  nail in foot, 199
  pricked sole, 281
  seedy toe, 202
  shoe boil, 334

shoe boil boot, 199, 334
shoeing, 334
shoes, 334
slipper, 337
stone in foot, 347
Feet of rider, 297
Feet on dashboard, 114
F. E. I. rules, 213
Fencing, 114
Fever, 115
Field, 185
Field master, 115
Fighting, 368
Fighting the bit, 115
  bitting, 36, 78
Figure Eight, 115, 301, *302*
Filly, 115
Find, 185
Fine harness horses, 116, 170
Finish, 116
Fiord ponies, 116
Firing (pin-firing), 116
First aid. *See* Injuries and
  disease, treatment
Fistula (fistulous wither), 116
Five-gaited saddle horses, 169
  junior championship or
    stake, 169
  junior stallion, mare,
    gelding, four years old
    or under, 169
  local, 170
  mare or gelding, ridden by
    lady, 170
  ridden by amateur, 169
Fixture, 185
Flashy, 185
Flat racing, 116, 297
Flat ribs, 116
Flax mane, 117
Flewed, 185
Flexing exercises, 75
Flicka, 105
Flighty, 185
Fling, 185
Float (teeth), 117, 355
Flooring (for stalls), 42
Florian, 105
Fly (to fly jumps), 117
Flying change, 94, 117
Foil, 185
Food, *See* Feeding *and* Feed,
  109, 111, 112
Forage, fresh, 110
Forearm, *150*
Forelock, 117
Forging, 117, 334

Formation riding, 117
Forrard, 185
Fort Riley, 60, 118
Fort Riley seat, 118, 328
Forward seat, 118
Foundation sires of Arabian
  horse, 18
Founder, 217
Four Horsemen of
  Apocalypse, 13
Four-in-hand, 15, 136, 171
Fox, 185
Fox trot, 118
Fresh forage, 110
Fresh line, 185
Freshness (in horses), 118
Frog, 113
Front, 119
Full cry, 185
Futurity races, 119, 292

G

Gag snaffle, 36
Gaited horse, 119
Gaits, 119
  collected, 69
  five-gaited saddle horse,
    169
  mixed gaits, 233
  rack, 293, 322
  running walk, 173, 315
  Spanish walk and trot, 338
  square trot, 340
  three-gaited saddle horse,
    169
  walk, 373
Gall sores, 120, 198
Gallop, 119. *See also* Canter
  flying change, 94, 117
  leads, 219
  side-gallop, 308
  wheeling, 380
Gallop departs, 119, 301
  false start, 103
Galloway, 119
Galvayne's groove, 8, 357
Games. *See also* Races
  broom polo, 53
  bun eating contest, 54
  crosstag, 86
  guessing game, 122
  gymkhana, 122
  hat snatching, 145
  hide and go seek, 147
  musical chairs, 249
  musical stalls, 249
  paper chase, 258

polo, 272
prisoner's base, 281
push polo, 282
red rover, 294
sew a button, 330
tag, 352
treasure hunts, 362
wrestling, 382
Ganted up, 378
Garrison finish, 120
Gaskin, *150*
Gelding, 120
fine harness horse, 170
five-gaited saddle horse,
170
gig class harness horse, 171
heavy harness horse, 171
three-gaited saddle horse,
169
walking horse, 173
Gig class, 15, 136, 171
Girth, 120
Girths, 120
adjustment, 120
sores from, 198
Give tongue, 185
Glanders, 120
Gloves, 16, 121
Godolphin barb, 104, 120
Gone away, 185
Gone to ground, 185
Good bone, 39
Good hands, 120, 133
Good hands classes, 121,
159, 174
Good hands horse, 121
Governess cart, 58
Grand championship, 63
Granger, 378
Grass as food, 110
Gravel, 121
Gray horse, 70
Great horse, 127, 154, 333
Grecian horse, early, *155*
Green horse, 121
Green hunter, 121
Green Jaquima class of
stock horse, 173
Gretna Green race, 121
Greyhound, 141, *142*
Griffin, 121, 233
Groom, 121
Group riding, 122. *See also*
Games *and* Races
courtesy, 83
Grub line rider, 378
Grub staked, 378
Guessing game, 122

Gun teams, artillery, 174
Gymkhana, 122. *See also*
Games
Gymnastics (mounted), 122,
125, 238

H

Habit (force of), 126
Habit (riding) 16, 126
Hack
bridlepath, 127
hunter, 127
park hack, 258
pleasure horses, 127
road hack, 258
Hackamore, 76, 126, *127,* 378
Hackney, 127
Hackney Horse Society, 11
Hackney Ponies, 128
Half bred hunters,
registered, 167
Half halt, 129
Half shoe, 334
Half turn, 129, 299
in reverse, 130, 299
Halloo, 186
Halt, 130
camping, 56
Halter breaking, 75
Halter shank, 130
Halters, 130
Halting a group of riders,
130
Hambletonian
Rysdyk's, 130, *131*
society, 132
stake, 132
Hamstring, 132
Hand, 132
Hand up (when mounting),
132
Handicap jumping, 132
Handicaps (in racing), 133
Handkerchief (teaching pony
to pick up), 133
Hands
good hands, 120, 133
heavy hands, 146
light hands, 133
position in riding, 133
Handy hunter, 134, 167
Handy jumpers, 168
Hanover, 60
Hanoverian pelham bit, 36
Hark forward, 186
Harness
care of, 134

first lessons in, 75
fitting of, 134
parts of, *135*
Harness horses, 15, 134, 170
amateur class, 136, 170
championship harness
horse stake, 136, 170
collection of three harness
horses, 136, 171
fine harness, 136, 170
championship or stake,
136, 169
driven by amateur,
136, 170
general specifications,
170
stallion, mare or gelding,
136, 170
four-in-hand, 15, 136, 171
gig class, 15, 136, 171
heavy harness, 136, 170
collection of three, 136,
171
four-in-hand, 15, 136,
171
park drag, 171
road coach, 136, 171
general specifications, 170
marathon, 172
open tandem, 136, 171
pairs, 171
championship or stake,
171
lady's, mares or geldings,
171
limit, 171
maiden, 171
novice, 171
open, 171
over 15 and under 15:2,171
over 15:2, 171
under 15 hands, 171
ponies, 172
single, 171
championship or stake,
171
driven by amateur, 171
driven by owner or
member of immediate
family, 171
gig class, 136, 171
lady's mare or gelding
shown to a phaeton,
136, 171
limit, 136, 171
maiden, 136, 171
novice, 136, 171
open, 136, 171

over 15 and under
15:2, 171
over 15:2, 171
under 15 hands, 171
light harness, 136, 170
general specifications,
170
pair of roadsters, 170
appointments, 170
roadster under saddle,
170
single roadster, 170
appointments, 170
championship or stake,
170
single stallion or gelding
roadster shown to
bike, 170
pony classes, 136, 171
road coach, 136, 171
selection of three harness
horses, 136
stallion in harness, 136
tandem, 136, 171
Harness racing, 136, 396
Hambletonian, 132
records, 396
Harrier, 144
Hat guard, 145
Hat snatching, 145
Hay, 110
Hazing, 378
Head, 145
Head a fox, 186
Headed to death, 186
Headless Horseman of
Sleepy Hollow, 145
Heads up, 186
Heat (in stable), 145
Heats (in racing), 145
Heaves, 111, 146
Heavy hands, 146
Heavy harness division, 146,
170
Heavy harness horse, 146
Heavyweight hunters, 165
Heavyweight stock horse, 173
Hedge (black thorn), 146
Heel, to, 146
Heel, running to, 186
Heels (of horse)
contracted, 82, 113, 202
cracked, 200
Heels (of rider), 146
aids to riding, 9
Height of horse, 147
Hempstead cart, 58
Herod, 56

Hide and go seek, 147
Hidebound, 147
High blowing, 147
Hightail, 378
Hill topper, 186
Hinges (of rider), 147
Hinny, 148
Hipparion, 154
Hiring horses, 148
Hit off the line, 186
Hobbles, 148
Hock, 148
Hogged mane, 149
Hoick, 186
Hold hard, 186
Hold on horse, 149
Hold them forward, 186
Holloa, 186, 205
Hombra, hombre, 378
Honest hound, 186
Honor a line, 186
Honorable scars, 38
Hood, 149
Hoof. See Feet
Hopples, 149
Horse, 149
at work, 159
balance, 24
characteristics, 149
colors, 70
colts, 71
feeding, 112
fiction horses, 104
general care, 152
grooming, 121
handling in pasture, 152
handling in stable, 151
ideal, 191, 261
in art and literature, 157
in sport, 158
in sport and war, 410
in war, 59, 158
leading, 218
money-winning horses,
389
origin and development,
153, 410
perfect, 191, 261
pleasure, 157
points, 150
police, 174, 270
race horses, 103, 104
shoeing, 334
size, 336
trooper's 174
tying, 364
vices, 368
Horseman, 159

inexperienced, 7
Horsemanship, 159, 297
Horsemanship classes, 121,
159, 161, 174
equitation classes, 99, 174
championship equitation
tests, 174
Horseshoes, 160
Horse shows, 161, 401
Horseshow classes, 161
breeding classes, 161, 172
broodmare, 161
draft horse division, 173
equitation classes, 174
fine harness horses, 170
four-year-olds, 161
heavy harness division,
170
hunters, 161, 163
jumpers, 161, 168
light harness division, 170
mare, 161
military classes, 173
polo division, 172
saddle horse division, 169
stallion, 161
stock division, 172
three-year-olds, 161
two-year-olds, 161
walking horse division, 173
yearlings, 161
Horse show judges, 161
Horse show ribbons and
trophies, 162
Hounds, 162
in covert, 178
in open, 179
puppy walking, 282
Hundred and eleven, 378
Hunt teams, 167
Hunter classes, 164
Hunters, 163, 166
amateurs', 167
championship, 63
classification, 164
colts, 165
conformation classes, 63
165
Corinthian, 167
fillies, 165
green, 164
hacks, 165
local, 166
handicap, 165
handy, 164, 167
heavyweight, 164, 165,
166, 167
Irish, 204

ladies', 167
lightweight, 164, 165, 166, 167
limit, 164
local, 167
maiden, 164, 165
middleweight, 164, 165, 166, 167
model, 164, 165
novice, 164, 165
open, 167
pair abreast, 167
pair tandem, 167
qualified, 164
registered half bred, 167
schooling, 163
sporting tandem, 168
suitable to become, 164, 165
sweepstake, 167
teams, 167
three abreast, 167
three tandem, 167
thoroughbred, 165
trials, 168, 175
working, 164, 168
consolation, 168
non-winners, 168
Hunting, 175
appointments, 16
calls, 178
hounds in the open, 179
cap, 179
countries, 179
field master, 115
horn, 181
hounds, 162
Masters of Foxhounds Association of America, 231
pinks, 261
secretary, 330
snaffle, 35
terms, 181
thong, 86, 191
watch, 191
whipper-in, 190
Hunts
Annual Roster of the Organized Hunts of America, 1962-1963, 408
Huntsman, 186, 191
appointments, 16
Hurdles, 191
Hyracotherium, 71

I

Iceland pony, 191
Ideal horse, 191
Ideal rider, 192
In hand, 197
Inbreeding, 186
Incisions, 198
Inclination of body, 192
Inclines, maneuvering, 192
Independence (of rider's seat as opossed to hands), 193
Indian methods of training horses, 194
Indian ponies, 195
Indian riders, 195
Indiana pants, 195
Indirect lighting (in stables), 195
Indirect rein, 295
Indoor riding, 195. See also Games
Indoor riding hall, 195
Infections, 197
Influence, 197
In hand, 197
Injuries and diseases, 197
abrasions, 198
agoraphobia, 9, 372
anthrax, 13
apoplexy, 14
arthritis, 23
asthma, 23
azoturia (Monday morning disease), 24
blemishes, 38
blistering, 38
bog spavin, 39, 201, 334
bowed tendon, 41
brittle feet, 202
broken knees, 51
bruises, 200
Canadian pox, 57
capped hock, 58
colds, 69
constipation, 82
contracted heels, 82, 113, 202
corns, 202
coughs, 83
cracked heels or scratches, 200
curb, 87
diarrhea, 327
falls, 101
false quarter, 202
farcy, 107
fever, 115
firing, 116
fistula, 116
gall sores, 120, 198
glanders, 120
gravel injuries, 121
heaves, 111, 146
hidebound horse, 147
incisions, 198
infections, 197
insanity, 202
joint evil, 207, 251
lacerations, 198
lameness, 217
laminitis, 217
laryngitis, 217
lice, 221
lung congestion, 82
mange, 228
megrims (blind staggers), 231
mouth injuries, 202
mud fever, 200
nail in foot, 199, 250
navicular disease, 251
nosebleed, 252
ophthalmia, 254
pleurisy, 267
pleuro-pneumonia, 268
pneumonia, 269
poll evil, 272
pricked sole, 281
proud flesh, 282
puncture wound, 198
quarter cracks, 284
quarter cuts, 199, 284
quittor, 202, 286
ring bones and side bones, 202
rope burns, 200
saddle sores, 120, 198
sand cracks, 326
scalds, 326
scouring, 327
scratches, 200
seedy toe, 202
shoe boil, 199, 334
shoulder injuries, 201
sit fast, 336
sleeping sickness, 96
sores, 120, 198
spavins, 201, 334
speedy cut, 199, 339
splints, 200, 339
split pastern, 339
sprains and strains, 200
stall courage, 9, 118, 342, 372

stifle sprains, 201
strangles, 347
string halt, 348
sunstroke, 350
swaying, 351
swollen legs, 351
tetanus, 358
thoroughpins, 201, 359
thrush, 359
treatment
    antitoxin, 13, 330
    bandages, 27
    liniment, 222
    poultices, 280
    powders, 280
    pressure bandages, 280
    quarantine, 283
serums, 13, 330
    tonics, 361
twisted gut, 363
urticaria, 365
warbles, 374
warts, 375
weaving, 369
wind-galls, 201, 381
worms, 382
Insanity in horses, 202
Intelligence in horses, 202
Interfering, 117, 203
International Arabian Horse
    Association, 203
Interpret, 204
Irish cart, 58
Irish hunters, 204
Irish martingale, 230
Iroquois, 104
Italian
    forward seat, 329
    influence on horsemanship,
        204
    saddle, 318, 329
    school of horsemanship,
        60, 204

J

Jack hare, 186
Jaquima, 127, 173, 205, 378
Jay, 205
Jennet, 205
Jenny, 205
Jewelry (for riding), 205
Jibbing, 371
Jigging, 205
Jockey, 206
Jockey Club, 206
    officials, 207
Jockey seat, 207, 329

Jockeys, leading, 394
Jog trot, 207
Jogging, 371
Joint evil, 207, 251
Jorrocks, 208
Joshua, 378
Jump, 186
Jumpers, 168, 208
    amateur ladies', 168
    bareback comic class, 168
    championship, 168
    handicap class, 165
    handy, 168
    knock down and out
        class, 168
    limit, 168
    local, 168
    maiden, 168
    military, 173
    novice, 168
    open to all, 168, 253
    pair abreast, 168
    pair tandem, 168
    sweepstake, 168
    team of three abreast, 168
    team of three tandem, 168
    touch and out class, 168
Jumping, 208
    competitions, 212
    equitation classes, 174
    faults, 212
        disobediences, 213
        falling of horse or rider,
            213
        knock-downs, 213
        scoring, 213
        F.E.I. table, 213
        jumpers, 213
        pairs, teams, unicorns
            abreast or tandem, 213
        table, 213
        working hunters, 213
    flying jumps, 117
    learning to jump, 211
    maze jumping, 231
    mental hazard, 232
    privet hedges, 281
    refusing and shying, 294,
        370, 372
    rider rail, 297
    rushing jumps, 315
    scurry contest, 168
    slip fillets, 337, 361
    touch-and-out, 168, 361
    triple bar, 168, 363
Junior five-gaited saddle
    championship or stake, 169
Junior walking horse, three

years old, 173
Justin Morgan, 104, 139, 214,
    234, 336

K

Kayack, 378
Kelso
    pedigree and record of,
        395
Kennel, 186
Kennels, 186
Kent Mare, 131
Kicking, 368
    at other horses, 372
Kill, 186
Knee spavins, 201
Knock down and out class,
    jumping, 168

L

Lacerations, 198
Ladies
    appointments, in harness
        classes, 15
    hunters, 167
    jumpers, 168
    Phaeton, 15
    riding five-gaited saddle
        horse, 170
    riding walking horse, 173
    single harness horse, mare
        or gelding shown to a
        Phaeton, 171
Lair, 186
Lameness, 215
    diagnosis, 216
    prevention, 215
Laminitis (founder) 217
    cause, 217
    symptoms, 217
    treatment, 217
Lampas, 217
Landing, 217
Lariat, 378
Larking, 186, 217
Laryngitis, 217
Latches (for stable), 217
Latigos, 379
Laxatives, 217
Lead rein (use of), 218
Leading
    breeders, 392
    jockeys, 394
    money-winning horses,
        389, 393

money-winning owners, 393
stallions, 391
trainers, 393, 394
Leading the horse, 218
balky horse, 218
by foretop, 218
through narrow door, 218
with rope or strap, 218
Leads, 219
canter, 47, 103
false start, 103
flying change, 117
gallop, 119
gallop departs, 119, 301
Leaping powder, 219
Leather
care and selection, 219
reaching for, 219
Leathers, 219
stirrup, 347
Leg up, 221
Legs
of horse, 219, *220*
of rider, 9, 219
"Lepper," 221
Leucoderma, 221
Leveret, 186
Levrette (cheval levrette), 221
Liberty horses, 66, 221
Lice, 221
Life span of horse, 8
Lifting hounds, 186, 222
Light dressage, 93
Light hands, 133
Light harness horse, 170
Lighting (in stables), 222
Lightweight hunters, 164, 166, 222
Lightweight stock horse, 173
Limit classes, 222
Line, 186, 222
Line breeding, 186
Line hunter, 186
Liniment, 222
Linseed meal, 110, 222
Lipizzan, 222, *223*
Lips, 225
Lithuanian, 106
Liver chestnut, 70
Livery, 187
Local
bridle path hacks, 166
five-gaited saddle horse, 170
five-gaited saddle horse, 170

hunter hacks, **166**
hunters, 167
jumpers, 168
three-gaited ponies, 169
three-gaited saddle horses, 169
walking horse, 173
Loco, 379
Loco weed, 379
Long distance rides, 96
Longe, 76, 225
ploughlines, 268
Loose rein riding, 225
Lope, 225. *See also* Canter
Loss, 187
Lou Dillon, 226
Lung congestion, 82
Lying, 187

M

Maclay Cup, 226
Mahogany bay, 70
Maiden classes, 226
heavy harness horse, 170, 131
hunters, 164, 165
jumpers, 168
Main earth, 187
Making a cast, 226
lifting hounds, 186, 222
Mallender, 226
Malpai, 379
Maltese Cat, 106
Mambrino, 104, 226
Mane, 227
Manege, 228
Maneuvering steep inclines, 192
Mange, 228
Mangers, 113
Manners, 187, 228
Man O'War, 228
Manure, 228
Marathon heavy harness class, 172
Mare, 229
fine harness horse, 170
five-gaited saddle horse, 169
gig class harness horse, 171
heavy harness horse, 171
three-gaited saddle horse, 169
walking horse, 173
Marengo, 104
Màriles, 229
Mark to ground, 187

Martingale, 230
Irish, 230
standing, 343
Mashes, 230
Mask, 187, 230
Massage, 231
Master's appointments, 16
Masters of Foxhounds Association of America, 231
Matchem, 104
Matinees, 141, 231
Maverick, 379
Maze jumping, 231
McClellan saddle, 231, 317
Meadow Brook cart, 58
Meet, 187, 231
Megrims, 231
Mental hazard jumping, 232
Messenger, 104, 131
Messenger's Mambrino, 104, 131
M.F.H. (master of fox hounds), 187, 232
Middle distance, 233
Middleweight hunters, 165, 166, 233
Military horses, 59, 173
artillery gun teams, 174
enlisted men's jumping classes, 174
general specifications, 173
officers' chargers, 174
officers' jumping classes, 173
police mounts, 174
trooper's mounts, 174
Mixed gaits, 233
Mixer, 187
Mob, 187
Model hunter, 164, 165
Molars, 233, 355
Money winners, leading American, 389, 393
Mongolian ponies, 121, 233
Monkey drill, 122, 238
Morgan horse, 234. *See* Justin Morgan
Morgan Horse Club, 236
Mount, 236
hand up, 132
leg up, 221
Mounted drill, 237
close order, 238
commands, 237
definition of terms, 237
general rules, 238
leaders, 237
open order, 238

Mounted gymnastics, 122, *125*, 238
Mounted troops, 248
Mounting of colt, 80
Mouse dun, 70
Mouth injuries, 202
Mouthy, 187
Moving pictures, 248
Mud, 248
Mud fever, 200
Muscles, 248
Music
    in teaching, 249
    of hound, 187
    rides, 249
Musical chairs, 249
Musical stalls, 249
Mustang, 250, 379
Mute, 187

N

Nail in foot, 199, 250
Narragansett Pacer, 250
National Cutting Horse Association, 250
Navel of horse, 251
    joint evil, 207
    treatment at birth, 251
Navicular disease, 251
Neapolitan noseband, 251
Near side, 251
Neck, 251
Neck reining, 252
Neckwear, 16, 252
Nelson, 103
Nester, 379
Nettlerash, 365
Nicks, 44
Night line, 187
Nipping, 372
Noisy, 187
Nose of horse, *150*
    bleeding, 352
Nose of hound, 187
Noseband, *320*
    Neapolitan, 251
Novice, 253
Novice classes, 253
    heavy harness horse, 170, 171
    hunters, 164, 165
    jumpers, 168
    three-gaited saddle horse, 169
    walking horse, 133
Nursing, 52, 73, 253

O

Oats, 109, 253
Occult spavins, 201
Odds-on, 253
Off side, 253
Officer's chargers, 174
Officer's jumping classes, 174
Officer's field saddle, 318
On the bit, 253
One Eye, 131
Open classes
    heavy harness horse, 171
    hunters, 167
    jumpers, 168, 253
    pairs of heavy harness horses, 171
    tandem harness, 171
    three-gaited saddle horse, 169
    three-gaited saddle pony, 169
Opposition, reins of, 107
Opthalmia, 254
Orejana, 379
Origin of horse and specific breeds, 153, 410
Orloff, 316
Ornaments, 254
Ornery, 379
Out-cross, 187
Outlaw, 254, 379
Overfeeding, 254
Override, 187
Overrun, 187
Own, 187
Owners
    driving heavy harness horse, 171
    in betting systems, 33
    leading, 393
Oxer, 92, 187

P

Pace, 254
Pacers, 136, 255, 398
Pack, 187
Pack sense, 187
Pad, 187
Paddling, 255
Paddock, 255
    mud in, 248
Pad-groom, 187
Paint pony, 379
Pair classes, 167, 168, 170, 171, 255
Palomino, 70, 255, *256*

Palomino Horse Breeders Association, 256, 258
Panel, 258
Paper chase, 258
Pari-mutuel, 33
Park hack, 258
Park riders, 258
Parlay, 258
Parrot mouth, 259
Parthenon horses, 259
Pas de côté, 259
Passage des cingles, 259
Passenger, 259
Passing other horses, 83, 259
Pastern, *150*
Pastures, 259
Pate, 187
Pato, 259
Pecking, 259
Pegasus, 104
Pelham bit, 34, 259
Percheron, 173, 259
Perfect horse, 191, 261
Performance, 261
Petizo, 261
Phaeton, 171, 261
Phenacodus Primaevus, 154
Phizog, 379
Piaffe, 261, *262*
Pick-me-up, 261
Pie, 106, 187
Piebald horse, 71
Pierre Oller, 33
Pigeon toes, 261
Pinerolo, 60
Pink, 188
Pink coat, 261
Pinon (pinion), 379
Pinto, 262, 379
Pinto Horse Association, 261
Pirouette, 266
Pivot, 266
Place, 266
Plantation Walker, 173, 266, *268*, 323, 357
Plate, 267
Plater, 267
Plates, 267
Pleurisy, 267
Pleuro-pneumonia, 268
Pneumonia, 269
Point, 188
Point rider, 188
Point-to-point, 188, 269
Pointing, 269
Points of horse, *150*
Pole, 270

Pole bending, 270
Police horse, 270
Policed, 271
Polish Arab, 271
Poll, 271
Poll evil, 116, 272
Polo, 272, *273*
Polo ponies, 172, 276, 277
Pony, 278
  buying, 55
  cowpony, 293
  Criollo, 86, 157, 277
  cutting, 88, 378
  Exmoor, 99
  Fiord, 116
  Griffin, 121, 233
  Hackney, 136, 171
  heavy harness, 172
  Indian, 195
  Irish Cob, 128
  paint, 379
  Petizo, 261
  polo, 172, 276
  Shetland, 331
  three-gaited saddle, 169
  Welsh, 278
Pony classes, 16
Posing, 279
Posse, 379
Post entry, 279
Posting, 279
Potato race, 280
Potatoes, 280
Potterer, 188
Poultices, 280
Powders, 280
Prad, 280
Prepotency, 280
Pressure bandages, 280
Pricked sole, 281
Primitive horse, 153
Prisoner's base 281
Privet hedges (for jumps),
  281
Produce race, 281
Profile, 281
  dished profile, 20
  Roman nose, 315
Proportions of horse, 282
Protest, 282
Proud flesh, 282
Puffs (wind galls), 381
Pulling back while being
  led, 370
Pulse, 282
Puncture wounds, 198
Punishment, 10
Puppy walking, 282

Purchasing horses, 55
Purgatives, 217, 282
Push polo, 282
Puss, 188
Put down, 188
Put to, 188

Q

Quad, 282
Quadrille, 283
Qualified hunter class, 164
Quality, 283
Quarantine, 283
Quarry, 188
Quarter, 283
Quarter boot, 284
Quarter clips, 284
Quarter cracks, 284
Quarter cuts, 284
Quarter horse, 384
  racing, 385
  registration by States, 384
  top money-winner, 385
  world champion, 385
  world records, 385
Quartering, 286
'Quarters, 286
Quinella, 286
Quittor, 202

R

Race horses, 286
  American thoroughbred,
    103
  quarter horse, 384
  standard bred, 343
  thoroughbred, 358, 361
Races. *See also* Games
  backing race, 24
  bending race, 32
  egg and spoon race, 96
  Gretna Green race, 121
  point to point, 188
  potato race, 280
  tacking, 352
  walking, 373
Racing, 287
  betting systems, 32, 290
  claiming race, 67, 291
  dead heat, 88
  flat
    annual champions, 388
  fastest races at one mile,
    386
  records and statistics, 386

scale of weights for age,
    385
  futurity, 119, 292
  growth of the sport, 399
  handicaps, 133
  harness racing, 136, 396
  heats, 145
  Jockey Club, 206
  Quarter horse records, 385
  saddle, *318*
  scratch, 327
  shoes, 335
  steeplechase, 344
  thoroughbred, 358
  T.R.A., 361
Racing and Breeding
  Organizations, 47
Racing bat, 86
Racing colors, 293
Rack, 188, 293, 322
Ranahan, 379
Ranch, dude, 95, 378
Range horse, 293
Rapping pole, 293
Rasper, 188
Rasping, 293
Rassembler, 62
Rat catcher, 188
Rat tailed, 188
Rate, 188
Rations. *See* Feeding
Rearing, 370
Reata, 294, 379
Records and statistics, 384
Recover, 188
Recovery, 294
Red and golden chestnut, 70
Red Pony, 106
Red Rover, 294
Reef (to reef a horse), 379
Refusing horse
  at jumps, 188, 294, 370
  leaving stable, 371
Registered half bred hunters,
  166
Registration of birth, 34
Registry of horses, 294
Reining, 295
Reining back, 295
Reins, 295. *See also* Bridles
  checkreins, 64
  loose rein riding, 225
  neck reining, 252
  types, 295
  uses, 9, 295
Remount, 297
Remuda, 379
Rep, 379

Resting the horse, 297
Restlessness
  while being mounted, 370
  while being tacked, 369
Rewards, 10, 297
Ribs, 297
Ride, 188
Ride, drive and jump classes, 297
Ride in the huntsman's pocket, 188
Ride straight, 188
Rider rail, 297
Riders, 159
  advanced, 303
  ideal, 192
Riding, 297
  aids, 9
  balance, 24, 25
  bareback, 29
  circles, 65
  courtesy, 83
  dressage, 93
  equitation classes, 174
  equitation exercises, 299
  exercises to promote control, 299
  figure of eight, 301
  flying change, 117
  gallop departs, 119, 301
  half turn, 299
  half turn in reverse, 299
  hands, 120, 133, 134, 146
  instructors, 313
  legs of rider, 9, 219
  monkey drill, 122, 238
  seat, 327
  serpentine, 301, 303
  side-stepping, 308, 336
  teaching, 354
  training colts, 75
  two-tracking, 364
Ringer, 313
Ringing fox, ringer, 188
Riot-riotous, 188
Rising scent, 188
Risling (ridgeling), 313
Roach-backed, 188
Road hack, 314
Road harness of four-in-hands, 172
Road-hunter, 188
Roadster, 170, 314
  pairs, 170
    appointments, 170
  single, 170
    appointments, 170

championship or stake, 170
  under saddle, 170
Roan, 71, 314
Rodeo, 379
Roland, 106
Roller, 314
Rolling up, 314
Roman nose, 315
Rope burns, 200
Roping, 315
Rosettes, 48
Rosinante, 106
Round book, 32
Round up, 315, 379
Rounding, 188
Rub rag, 315
Rubber nummahs, 315
Rubber pads, 315
Rubbing down, 315
Rug, 315
Run, 188
Runaways, 39, 371
Running walk, 315
Rushing, 315
Russian horses, 316

S

Saddle, 316
  breaking of colt, 80
  forward seat saddle, 318
  hacking saddle, 318
  history of, 316
  McClellan, 317
  parts of, 320
  racing saddle, 318
  selection and care, 318
  sores, 120, 198
  stock saddle, 317
  types of modern saddle, 316
  vices under, 370
  Western, 316
Saddle bags, 319
Saddle classes, 169
Saddle horses, 169, 319
  five-gaited, 169
  seat, 327
  three-gaited, 169
Saddler, 323
Saddling the horse, 323
Saliva tests, 325
Salt in horse's diet, 111, 325
Sand cracks, 326
Sandshifter, 326
Sandwich case, 326
Sandy bay, 70

Saumur, 60, 326
Savvy, 379
Scalds, 326
Scent, 188
School riding, 326
Schooling, 326
Schools of horsemanship, 326
Scissors, 327
Score, 189
Scoring, 327
Scouring, 327
Scratch, 327
Scratches, 200
Screw, 327
Scurry jumpers, 168, 327
Scut, 189
Seat, 327
  balance, 25, 328
  classical, 329
  cowboy, 329
  English hunting, 328, 329
  Italian forward, 329
  jockey, 207, 329
  saddle-horse, 329
  steeplechase, 329
Second horseman, 189, 330
Secretary, 330
Seedy toe, 202
Selection of horse, 55
Serpentine, 301, 303
Serums, 13, 330
Servant, 15, 330
Set tail, 330
  docking, 91
Settle, 189
Sew a button, 330
Shadbelly, 330
Sheet, 330
Shetland pony, 331
  miniature type, 332
  show type, 333
Shire horse, 333
Shoe boil, 199, 334
Shoe boil boot, 199, 334
Shoeing, 334
Shoes, 334
  bar shoe, 334
  Charlier shoe, 325
  feathered shoe, 117
  half shoe, 334
  racing, 335
  slipper, 337
  three-quarter shoe, 335
  tip, 334
  wedge, 334
Shoulder, 335
  injuries, 201
Show, 335

Showing, 335
Shows. See Horseshow
  classes, 161
Shute, 379
Shying at jumps, 372
Side bones, 202, 336
Side cart, 58
Side-gallop, 308
Side-stepping, 308, 364
Side wheeler, 336
Signals. See Aids
Silks, 336
Silvertail, 131
Single-foot, 336
Sinking fox, 189
Sire, 336
Sit fast, 336
Size of horses, 336
Skewbald horse, 71, 337
Skinner, 337
Skirter, 189
Skull, 337
Sleeping sickness, 96
Sleepy Tom, 103
Sling his tongue, 189
Slip fillets, 337
Slipper, 337
Snaffle, 35, 36, 47, 337
Snorty, excited snorting, 379
Snubbing post, 379
Soft mouth, 189
So-ho, 189
Soogan, 379
Sores, 120, 198
Sorrel, 70, 338
Soundness, 338, 357
Spanish horses, 338
Spanish Riding School of
  Vienna, 222
Spanish walk and trot, 338
Spavins, 201
Speak, 189
Speed of horses, 339
Speedy cut, 199, 339
Splints, 200, 339
Split pastern, 339
Split wall, 326
Spooky (spooked up), 379
Spotty scent, 189
Spout, 189
Sprains, 200
  bandages, 27
  stifle, 201
Sprinter, 339
Spurs, 339
Square dancing (mounted),
  339
Square trot, 340

Squatter's right, 379
Stable, 340. See also Stall
  doors, 91
  equipment, 341
  heat, 145
  indirect lighting, 195
  latches, 217
  lighting, 222
  manners, 341
  routine, 341
  tack room, 352
  ventilation, 367
  vices, 368
  water fountains, 374
Staggers, 231
Stained, 189
Stake and bound fence, 342
Stake classes, 342
Stake holder, 32
Stake horses, 342
Stakes, 342
Stakes race, 342
Staking out a horse, 342
Stale horse, 342
Stale line, 189
Stall, 342
  box stall, 42
  entering, 98
Stall courage, 9, 118, 342,
  372
Stallion, 343
  fine harness horse, 170
  five-gaited saddle horse,
    169
  gig class harness horse,
    170
  leading, 391
  prepotency, 281
  record, 1860-1960, 391
  stud, 348
Standard bred, 343
Standing martingale, 343
Start, 189
Starting the horse, 343
Statistics, 384
Stayer, 343
Staying power, 189
Steady, 189
Steadying (the horse), 343
Stealing sticks, 281
Steeldust, 343
Steeplechase and Hunt
  Association, 400
Steeplechase seat, 329
Steeplechasing and hunt
  races, 400
Steeplechasing and hurdle
  racing, 344

Stern, 189, 346
Stick, 189
Stiff-necked fox, 189
Stifle, 150
  sprains, 201
Stimulants, 346
Stirrup leathers, 219, 347
Stirrups, 347
Stock, 347
Stock horses, 347
  advanced Jaquima class,
    173
  championship or stake, 173
  equitation class, 175
  faults, 173
  general specifications, 172
  green Jaquima class, 173
  heavyweight, 173
  judging rules, 172
  lightweight, 173
  performance rules, 172
  showing, 172
  working, 172
Stock saddle, 317
Stockings, 347
Stomach, 347
Stone in the foot, 347
Stooping to scent, 189
Stop, 189
Stop hounds, 189
Stopping (the horse), 347
Strains, 200
Strangles, 348
Strapped lightning, 347
Strapper, 348
Straw, 348
Stray, 379
Streaming along, 189
Stretching, 56, 348
Strike, 189
Striking, 348
String, 379
String halt, 348
Strong trot, 348
Stub-bred, 189
Stud, 348. See also Stallion
Stud book, 348
Stud fees, 348
Stumbling, 348
Subscriptions, 349
Substance, 391
  quality, 283
Sudadero, 349, 379
Suffolk horse, 349
Sugar, 349
Suitable to become hunters,
  164, 165, 349
Sulky, 349

Sunfishing, 350, 379
Sunstroke, 350
Suppling exercises, 350
Surcingle, 351
Sureness of foot, 351
Swaying, 351
Sweat scraper, 351
Sweating, 351
Sweepstake, 351
    hunter, 167
    jumper, 168
Swellings, 351
Swine-chopped, 189
Swollen legs, 351
Syringes, 351

T

Tack, 352
    appointments, 17
    care of, 352
    room, 352
Tacking race, 352
Tackle, 352
Tag
    Chinese tag, 352
    crosstag, 86
Tag the foxes, 189
Tail, 352
Tail hounds, 190
Tailing, 190
Taking the bit, 253
Tally-ho, 190
Tally-ho coach, 353
Tandem, 353
    open harness class, 171
    sporting, 167
Taste in dress, 353. See also
    Appointments and Dress
Tattersall, 353
Teaching riding, 354
    advanced tests, 355
    beginner's tests, 354
    intermediate tests, 355
Team jumping, 355
Tearing stable blanket, 369
Teeth, 355
Temperature of horse, 357
Tendons, 357
    bowed, 41
Tennessee Walking Horse,
    173, 266, 268, 323, 357
Tennessee Walking Horse
    Breeder's Association, 357
Tests for soundness, 357
Tetanus, 358
Thong, 358
Thoroughbred, 358

American race horses, 103
    hunters, 165
    racing and breeding, 362
Thoroughpins, 201, 359
Three-gaited saddle horses,
    169
    championship, 169
    combination, 169
    gelding, 169
    general specifications, 169
    local, 169
    mare, 169
    novice, 169
    open, 169
    pairs, 169
    park, 169
    ponies, 169
        championship or stake,
        169
        local, 169
        open, 169
        over 13:2 but under
        14:12, 169
        under 11:2, 169
        under 13:2, 169
    ridden by amateur, 169
    road hack, 169
    shown under saddle, 169
    stake, 169
Three-quarter shoe, 335
Throat, 359
Throat latch, 320
Throttle, 359
Throw off, 190
Throw up, 190
Thrown out, 190
Thrush, 359
Thruster, 190
Thunderhead, 106
Tie, 190
Tie ropes, 359
Timber, 190
Timidity
    in horses, 360
    in riders, 360
Tin cup records, 360
Tip shoes, 334
Toe, 360
    of horse, 360
    of rider, 361
Tongue, 190
Tonics, 361
Top line, 361
Tor di Quinto, 60, 193
Touch-and-out, 361
T.R.A., 361
Trainers, 393
Training, 75, 362

Trandem, 362
Transportation, 362, 366
Travel on two paths, 308,
    363, 364
Traveller, 103
Travers, 362
Traversal, 362
Treasure hunts, 362
Treatment of horses. See
    under Injuries and diseases
Tree (saddle), 363
Trials, working hunter, 168
Triple-bar classes, 168, 363
Triple crown, 363
Trojan horse, 106
Trooper's mounts, 174
Trotters, 363. See also
    Harness horses
Trotting records, 396
Tucked up, 363
Turf, 363
Turkish, Turkoman, or
    Tookman, 363
Turning, 266, 363
Turning out to grass, 363
Tushes, 363
Twisted gut, 363
Twisted snaffle, 36
Twitch, 364
Two-track, 364
Tying the horse, 364

U

Uniforms. See Appointments,
    Dress and Habits
United States Trotting
    Association, 365
Urticaria (nettlerash), 365

V

Vanning, 366
Vaquero, 366, 379
Varmint, 366
Vaulting, 366
Vehicles, 361
Ventilation (in stable), 367
Venus and Adonis, 106
Vests, 367
Veterinarians, 372
Vices, 368
    agoraphobia, 9, 372
    backing suddenly out of
        stall, 369
    barn rat, 30
    biting, 368
    bolting, 371

boring, 372
bucking, 371
charging in pasture, 370
cribbing, 369
crowding, 368
eating the bit, 372
jibbing or jogging, 371
kicking, 368
kicking or biting at
    compainon, 368
pulling back while being
    led, 370
rearing, 370
refusing and shying out
    at jumps, 370
refusing to leave stable
    alone or leave com-
    panions, 371
refusing to move forward,
    370
restlessness while being
    mounted, 370
restlessness while being
    tacked up, 369
running away, 371
shying, 372
stall courage, 372
tearing stable blanket, 369
under the saddle, 370
windsucking, 369
View halloo, 190
Viewed away, 190
Villain, 373
Vixen, 190, 373
Voice, 190, 373

W

Wagons, 373
Walers, 23, 373
Walk, 373
Walking horse, 173, 266,
    323, 357
Walking puppies, 282
Walking race, 373
Walk-trot horse, 373
Wall, 374
Walls, 374
Waltzing, 374
War chariot, 374
War horses, 59
Warbles, 374
'Ware hole, 'Ware wire, 190
'Ware hounds, 190
'Ware riot, 190
Warren, 190
Warts, 374
Water fountains, 374
Watering, 375
Watering out, 375
Weaving, 369
Wedge shoes, 334
Weedon, 60
Weights of horses, 375
Welsh Mountain Pony
    Society of America, 376
Welsh pony, 376
Western
    chunk, 376
    horses, 85, 250, 379
    pleasure horse contests,
        376
    riders, 376
    saddle, 316
    terms, 377
Weymouth bridle, 380
Wheel at the gallop, 380
Whelp, 190
Whip, 380
Whipper-in, 190
Whoo-hoop, 190
Wild horses, 380
Wind, 380
    broken wind, 146
Wind-galls, 381
Windows (in stable), 381
Windpipe, 381
Windsucking, 369
Winkers, 381
Wire cutters, 381
Wire snaffle, 36
Wisping 381
Witez II, 271, 382
Wolf teeth, 381
Work, 381
Work a line, 191
Working cow horse, 381
Working hunter class, 164
    consolation, 168
    non-winners, 168
    trials, 168
Worms, 382
Worried, 191
Worry, 191
Wounds, 198. See also
    Injuries
Wrangle, 379
Wrango, 379
Wrango horse, 380
Wrestling, 382

X

Xenophon, 382
Xerxes, 104

Y

Yearling, 383
    sales, 383
Young entry, 191, 383

Z

Zebra, 383
Zerape, 383